Lecture Notes in Computer Science 13229

More information about this series at https://link.springer.com/bookseries/558

Andreas Drechsler · Aurona Gerber ·
Alan Hevner (Eds.)

The Transdisciplinary Reach of Design Science Research

17th International Conference on Design Science Research
in Information Systems and Technology, DESRIST 2022
St Petersburg, FL, USA, June 1–3, 2022
Proceedings

Editors
Andreas Drechsler
Victoria University of Wellington
Wellington, New Zealand

Aurona Gerber
University of Pretoria
Pretoria, South Africa

Alan Hevner
University of South Florida
Tampa, FL, USA

ISSN 0302-9743 ISSN 1611-3349 (electronic)
Lecture Notes in Computer Science
ISBN 978-3-031-06515-6 ISBN 978-3-031-06516-3 (eBook)
https://doi.org/10.1007/978-3-031-06516-3

This Springer imprint is published by the registered company Springer Nature Switzerland AG
The registered company address is: Gewerbestrasse 11, 6330 Cham, Switzerland

Preface

This volume of Springer LNCS (LNCS 13229) contains the revised accepted research papers of DESRIST 2022, the 17th International Conference on Design Science Research in Information Systems and Technology.

We were excited to return to a fully in-person conference after several years of virtual and hybrid conferences. Face-to-face research collaborations and networking with valued colleagues provide essential experiences to enable innovative research progress. The conference was held during June 1–3, 2002, at the gorgeous University of South Florida (USF) St. Petersburg campus. The urban campus combines natural beauty with the appeal of city life. Dubbed "The Sunshine City", St. Petersburg, Florida, is home to some of the country's best beaches and a highly rated quality of life.

The important theme of DESRIST 2022 was "The Transdisciplinary Reach of Design Science Research". Today's world faces many complex challenges (i.e., wicked problems) that offer no easy solutions. Inter-related economic, environmental, social, political, and ethical drivers emphasize the need for a changing research landscape quite different from the disciplinary framing found in current institutional structures and processes. The sundering of disciplinary walls has been widely advocated but rarely achieved in the academic research communities. We seek a new frame of transdisciplinary (TD) research that transcends disciplinary, interdisciplinary, multi-disciplinary, and cross-disciplinary models to truly synthesize research disciplines in search of innovative solutions. At the core of transdisciplinary research there are three key characteristics that stand out in all working descriptions:

- Problem Focus: TD research starts with a real-world wicked problem that impacts real people. This presents a major challenge to capture and represent the complexities of the problem space in order to support both relevant and rigorous solutions. A single discipline does not own the problem.
- Emergent Research Methods: The goals of TD research call for the construction of novel research methods or the novel combination of disciplinary research methods as a process of emergence during investigation of the research problem. An iterative and incremental TD research process supports the selection and fusion of the most appropriate research methods as the research evolves.
- Collaboration: The richness of TD research requires active participation from the full variety of problem stakeholders (researchers, practitioners, clients, managers, and community members) who are impacted by the designed solution. Knowledge, wisdom, and creativity are maximized via a collaborative process in pursuit of balanced and satisfactory solutions.

The appropriateness of Design Science Research (DSR) to serve as an epistemo-logical and methodological foundation for transdisciplinary research can be seen by matching the concepts, methods, and processes of DSR and Action Design Research (ADR) to the key TD characteristics above. The unique mix of creative design to solve relevant problems and rigorous science to grow theory around the intervention and use of the novel solutions provide a compelling frame for transdisciplinary research projects.

The theme of DESRIST 2022 was selected to challenge the DSR community of researchers from many diverse disciplines to engage in more relevant and rigorous transdisciplinary projects. The conference research tracks aimed to move beyond traditional disciplinary siloes. Research papers, panels, workshops, and prototypes in the program demonstrated the transdisciplinary characteristics of problem focus, emergent research methods, and rich collaborations of stakeholders for the solution of complex and wicked problems. DESRIST 2022 provided convincing evidence that DSR makes a difference.

The DESRIST 2022 proceedings contains 37 full research papers organized in ten research tracks. In addition, 15 research-in-progress papers were presented and 10 prototypes were demonstrated at the conference. With slightly more than 100 papers submitted, the acceptance rate for full research papers was less than 37%, and the overall acceptance rate was approximately 50%. The review process was rigorous with every paper receiving at least three substantive reviews from an international Program Committee. A distinguished group of Research Track Chairs managed the review process and supported the author teams to revise their papers to the quality results seen in this proceedings. We send our deepest gratitude to these outstanding Track Chairs and Program Committee reviewers for their hard work and dedication on very aggressive time schedules. Thank you to the authors of all the submitted papers for sharing their exciting Design Science Research projects. We hope the opportunity to participate in DESRIST 2022 will provide a lasting impact on the quality and productivity of your future research.

Thank you to three prominent keynote speakers who addressed the conference with insightful research perspectives. Agnis Stibe, Ben Shneiderman, and Peter Warren Singer challenged the DESRIST community to engage important real-world problems with pragmatic and actionable design innovations. The conference participants also delighted in hearing presentations from the CEO of the Florida Orchestra, Mark Cantrell, and the Co-Director of Innovation Labs at the Salvador Dali Museum in St. Petersburg, Kim Macuare.

We must also acknowledge the enthusiasm and outstanding contributions of the local organizers of DESRIST 2022. The administration, faculty, and staff of the University of South Florida supported the planning, funding, and execution of the conference with their generosity and energy. The warmth and hospitality of the setting provided a rich research environment for the growth of design solutions for transdisciplinary real world problems. Thank you to everyone who contributed to the success of DESRIST 2022.

June 2022

Alan Hevner
Aurona Gerber
Andreas Drechsler

Organization

Conference Chairs

Matthew Mullarkey   University of South Florida, USA
Alta van der Merwe   University of Pretoria, South Africa

Program Chairs

Alan Hevner   University of South Florida, USA
Aurona Gerber   University of Pretoria, South Africa
Andreas Drechsler   Victoria University of Wellington, New Zealand

Doctoral Consortium Chairs

Jeff Parsons   Memorial University, Canada
Anol Bhattacherjee   University of South Florida, USA

Prototype Chairs

Clinton Daniel   University of South Florida, USA
Sidney Fernandes   University of South Florida, USA

Panel and Workshop Chairs

Varol Kayhan   University of South Florida, USA
Onkar Malgonde   University of North Texas, USA

Local Arrangement Coordinator

Sylvia Raymond   University of South Florida, USA

Website Chair

Jason Zipperer   University of South Florida, USA

Industry and Government Chairs

Dennis Edwards   K-Force
Joe Partlow   ReliaQuest
Isaiah Wilson   Joint Special Operations University

General Chairs

Moez Limayem   University of South Florida, USA
Shirley Gregor   Australian National University, Australia
Jan vom Brocke   University of Liechtenstein, Liechtenstein

Track Chairs

Transdisciplinary Research and DSR (Theme Track)

Christine Legner   University of Lausanne, Switzerland
Sandeep Purao   Bentley University, USA
Michael Rosemann   Queensland University of Technology, Australia

Blockchain Information Systems

Kaushik Dutta   University of South Florida, USA
Gary Patterson   University of South Florida, USA
Carson Woo   University of British Columbia, Canada

Intelligent Systems and Human Interaction

Pierre-Majorique Leger   HEC Montreal, Canada
Alexander Maedche   Karlsruhe Institute of Technology, Germany
Barbara Weber   University of St. Gallen, Switzerland

Healthcare Systems and Quality of Life

Reima Suomi   University of Turku, Finland
Monica Chiarini Tremblay   William & Mary, USA
Debra Vander Meer   Florida International University, USA

Innovation and Entrepreneurship

Henrik Berglund   Chalmers University of Technology, Sweden
Christoph Seckler   ESCP Berlin, Germany

Sustainability and Responsible Design

Nigel Melville   University of Michigan, USA
Nicolas Prat   ESSEC Business School, France
Stefan Seidel   University of Liechtenstein, Liechtenstein

Human Safety and Cybersecurity

Mohammadreza (Reza) Ebrahimi   University of South Florida, USA
Mala Kaul   University of Nevada, Reno, USA
H. Raghav Rao   University of Texas at San Antonio, USA

Emerging DSR Methods and Processes

Kieran Conboy   National University of Ireland Galway, Ireland
Hanlie Smuts   University of Pretoria, South Africa
John Venable   Perth University, Australia

Designers and Collaborative DSR

Leona Chandra Kruse   University of Liechtenstein, Liechtenstein
Rob Gleasure   Copenhagen Business School, Denmark
Pascal Le Masson   Mines ParisTech, France

Education and DSR

Asif Gill   University of Technology Sydney, Australia
Lisa Seymour   University of Cape Town, South Africa
Robert Winter   University of St. Gallen, Switzerland

Program Committee

Antragama Ewa Abbas   Delft University of Technology, The Netherlands
Marine Agogue   HEC Montréal, Canada
Frederik Ahlemann   University of Duisburg-Essen, Germany
Stephan Aier   University of St. Gallen, Switzerland
Antti Airola   University of Turku, Finland
Oluwafemi Akanfe   University of Texas at San Antonio, USA
Nagla Alnosayan   Claremont Graduate University, USA
Yehia Alzoubi   American University of the Middle East, Kuwait
Chadi Aoun   Carnegie Mellon University in Qatar, Qatar
Michel Avital   Copenhagen Business School, Denmark
Tamara Babaian   Bentley University, USA
Catherine Ball   Independent Consultant
Richard Baskerville   Georgia State University, USA
Rouzbeh Behnia   University of South Florida, USA
Ivo Benke   Karlsruhe Institute of Technology, Germany
Paras Bhatt   University of Texas at San Antonio, USA
Eva Bittner   University of Hamburg, Germany

Jared Boasen	HEC Montreal, Canada
Lina Bouayad	Florida International University, USA
Marvin Braun	University of Göttingen, Germany
Sophia Braun	ESCP Business School, Germany
Alfred Benedikt Brendel	Technical University of Dresden, Germany
Mirella Cacace	Catholic University of Applied Sciences Freiburg, Germany
Marcel Cahenzli	University of St.Gallen, Switzerland
Gültekin Cakir	Maynooth University, Ireland
Christer Carlsson	Abo Akademi University, Finland
Arturo Castellanos	William & Mary, USA
Alfred Castillo	Florida International University, USA
Dilek Cetindamar	University of Technology Sydney, Australia
Leona Chandra Kruse	University of Liechtenstein, Liechtenstein
Friedrich Chasin	University of Münster, Germany
Samir Chatterjee	Claremont Graduate University, USA
David Coghlan	Trinity College Dublin, Ireland
Ann-Kristin Cordes	University of Münster, Germany
Paul Coughlan	Trinity College Dublin, Ireland
Stefan Cronholm	University of Boras, Sweden
Malshika Dias	University of New South Wales, Australia
Christian Dietzmann	University of St. Gallen, Switzerland
Barbara Dinter	Chemnitz University of Technology, Germany
Brian Donnellan	Maynooth University, Ireland
Philippe Doyon-Poulin	Polytechnique Montréal, Canada
Adela Drozdibob	Queensland University of Technology, Australia
Polina Durneva	Florida International University, USA
Christin Eckerle	Karlsruhe Institute of Technology, Germany
Sven Eckhardt	University of Zurich, Switzerland
Ismail Elnaggar	University of Turku, Finland
Christian Engel	University of St. Gallen, Switzerland
Mahdi Fahmideh	University of Southern Queensland, Australia
Andri Färber	Zurich University of Applied Sciences, Switzerland
Michael Fellmann	University of Rostock, Germany
Chen Feng	University of British Columbia, Okanagan, Canada
Thomas Fischer	Johannes Kepler University Linz, Austria
Guy Gable	Queensland University of Technology, Australia
Kiran Garimella	University of South Florida, USA
Michael Gau	University of Liechtenstein, Liechtenstein

Yuan Li	University of Tennessee, USA
Johan Lilius	Abo Akademi University, Finland
Yong Liu	Aalto University, Finland
Johanna Lorenz	University of Hamburg, Germany
Roman Lukyanenko	HEC Montréal, Canada
Mahed Maddah	Suffolk University, USA
Munir Mandviwalla	Temple University, USA
Sarah Manthey	Karlsruhe Institute of Technology, Germany
Matti Mäntymäki	University of Turku, Finland
Carolin Marx	Hasso Plattner Institute, University of Potsdam, Germany
Hanna Marxen	University of Luxembourg, Luxembourg
Silvia Masiero	University of Oslo, Norway
René Mauer	ESCP Business School, Germany
Tobias Mettler	University of Lausanne, Switzerland
Leonard Michels	Friedrich-Alexander-Universität Erlangen-Nürnberg, Germany
Matti Minkkinen	University of Turku, Finland
Mahdi Mirhoseini	Concordia University, Canada
Stephanie Missonier	Université de Lausanne, Switzerland
Hans Moen	Aalto University, Finland
Frederik Möller	TU Dortmund, Germany
Stefan Morana	Saarland University, Germany
Roland M. Mueller	Berlin School of Economics and Law, Germany
Anik Mukherjee	Indian Institute of Technology, Roorkee, India
Pavankumar Mulgund	SUNY Buffalo, USA
Helena Müller	Technical University of Darmstadt, Germany
Bjoern Niehaves	University of Siegen, Germany
Pascal Nitiema	University of Oklahoma, USA
Jacob Norbjerg	Copenhagen Business School, Denmark
Anna Maria Oberländer	University of Bayreuth, Germany
Jacques Ophoff	Abertay University, UK
Burak Oz	HEC Montreal, Canada
Mario Passalacqua	Polytechnique Montreal, Canada
Teijo Peltomäki	University of Turku, Finland
Erik Perjons	Stockholm University, Sweden
Nargis Pervin	Indian Institute of Technology, Madras, India
Sophie Petzolt	Hasso Plattner Institute, University of Potsdam, Germany
Miloslava Plachkinova	Kennesaw State University, USA
Shweta Premanandan	Uppsala University, Sweden
Jan Pries-Heje	Roskilde University, Denmark

Sandeep Purao	Bentley University, USA
Armel Quentin	Université de Sherbrooke, Canada
Jaziar Radianti	University of Agder, Norway
Sudha Ram	University of Arizona, USA
Florian Rampold	University of Göttingen, Germany
Jan Recker	Universität Hamburg, Germany
Johannes Reichgelt	University of South Florida, USA
Rene Riedl	Johannes Kepler University Linz, Austria
Michael Rosemann	Queensland University of Technology, Australia
Holly Rosser	University of Nebraska Omaha, USA
Matti Rossi	Aalto University, Finland
Marcel Ruoff	Karlsruhe Institute of Technology, Germany
Daniel Rush	Boise State University, USA
Maylis Saigot	Copenhagen Business School, Denmark
Thorsten Schoormann	University of Hildesheim, Germany
Gerhard Schwabe	University of Zurich, Switzerland
Isabelle Seeber	Grenoble Ecole de Management, France
Stefan Seidel	University of Liechtenstein, Liechtenstein
Amin Shoji	Florida International University, USA
Vivek Singh	University of Missouri–St. Louis, USA
Jonas Sjöström	Uppsala University, Sweden
Matthias Söllner	University of Kassel, Germany
Nicola Staub	University of St.Gallen, Switzerland
Veda Storey	Georgia State University, USA
Hemang Subramanian	Florida International University, USA
Sandeep Suntwal	University of Colorado, USA
Mohan Tanniru	Oakland University, USA
Orestis Terzidis	Karlsruhe Institute of Technology, Germany
Frank Teuteberg	Universtät Osnabrück, Germany
Devinder Thapa	University of Agder, Norway
Maxime Thomas	Mines ParisTech, France
Karthikeyan Umapathy	University of North Florida, USA
Chipten Valibhay	Mines ParisTech, France
Judy van Biljon	University of South Africa, South Africa
Alta van der Merwe	University of Pretoria, South Africa
Benjamin van Giffen	University of St.Gallen, Switzerland
John Venable	Curtin University, Australia
Gerit Wagner	HEC Montréal, Canada
Lena Waizenegger	Auckland University of Technology, New Zealand
Sofie Wass	University of Agder, Norway
Lauri Wessel	European New School of Digital Studies, Germany

Contents

Innovation and Entrepreneurship

Sustainability and Responsible Design (Environmental Issues, Human Values and Ethical Design)

Human Safety and Cybersecurity

Emerging DSR Methods and Processes

Transdisciplinary Research and DSR
(Theme Track)

Introduction to the Theme Track: Transdisciplinary Research and DSR

Christine Legner[1], Sandeep Purao[2], and Michael Rosemann[3]

[1] Université de Lausanne
christine.legner@unil.ch
[2] Bentley University, Waltham, MA
spurao@bentley.edu
[3] Queensland University of Technology, Brisbane
m.rosemann@qut.edu.au

Abstract. The problem-driven nature of design science research lends itself naturally to transdisciplinarity as single-discipline viewpoints tend to be inadequate for problems of real-world complexity. The theme track for DESRIST 2022 invited scholars to explore design science research that requires the integration across disciplines. Of the eight papers in the track, five propose new solutions to organizational or societal problems; three consider design science research and information systems as their domain of interest. We identify three pathways that show the promise and challenges for the DSR community, and map these against work related to transdisciplinarity and the role of DSR in the system of disciplines.

Keywords: Transdisciplinary research · Problem-driven research

1 Purpose of the Theme Track

The theme track for DSR 2022 invited DSR scholars to address today's organizational and societal challenges that require integrating theoretical, conceptual and methodological perspectives from multiple disciplines [1]. The goal of this track is to surface the inherently transdisciplinary nature of DSR efforts that focus on relevant problems, use research techniques, and explore relevant kernel theories that naturally cross disciplinary boundaries [2]. In doing so, DSR scholarship can propose and evaluate novel solutions as well as cultivate new theory by combining scholarly rigor with authentic participation from organizations, government agencies, and communities. Such "problem-driven research" with a "transdisciplinary lens" can address concerns of global importance such as pandemic responses, disease prevention, economic development, adequate technology utilization, social inequality, climate change and others. Submissions to the track address a wide range of problems with diverse research approaches and theoretical perspectives. Constructive, articulate and timely inputs from the reviewers provided advice to all authors and ensured required academic quality.

2 Transdisciplinary DSR: The Promise and Challenges

As an introduction to the track, we point out some opportunities and identify challenges based on the methodologies used and contributions made by the research papers in the track. A concise synopsis of papers provides the backdrop for this effort. The papers in the track fall in two clusters. One explores specific problems with a transdisciplinary approach, e.g. human-drone collaboration in emergencies. The other refines or proposes new frames to pursue transdisciplinary efforts, e.g. boundary objects. Across the set of papers, we note a few interesting possibilities that we outline below and which we hope will provide DSR scholars new pathways to pursue research opportunities.

The first pathway deals with identifying and integrating emerging technologies as part of the solution development strategy. Examples of the pathway are seen in those papers in this track that deal with human-drone collaboration, immersive virtual reality, and conversational agents. Although these research efforts remain problem-driven, the use of increasingly sophisticated technology platforms provides the research efforts new frames that point to potential solutions. We note that this pathway parallels the ideas described as 'the stimulus of generative technologies' [1]. This pathway holds much promise for future DSR scholars with the caveat that the selection and use of emerging technologies requires a match with the problems.

The second pathway explores new ways of building on established technology frames to develop solution strategies. Examples of the pathway are seen in work from the authors in this track that deals with digital broker platforms, and trend analysis with sentiment detection. The advantage of this pathway is that research can build upon design efforts in these established technology regimes and focus on innovative applications to new problems. This pathway parallels the ideas expressed as 'exploration of problems at the interface of disciplines' [1]. The challenge for the scholars is to ensure that they can demonstrate a significant advance in the design to make contributions.

The third pathway points out that although transdisciplinarity is core to design science research, the community will need new frames and approaches to incorporate such considerations in their efforts. Examples of this pathway are seen in the work from authors in this track that suggests the use of boundary objects, ontologies, and the design of new platforms to facilitate transdisciplinary research. A parallel to this pathway is seen in the role of design science research community in the system of professions [2]. This pathway holds much promise to encourage the DSR community to engage in transdisciplinary research.

Together, the papers in the track point to the promise and potential for transdisciplinary research in the DSR community, and suggest possibilities that can spawn a new generation of scholarship that emphasizes work across disciplinary boundaries.

References

1. National academy of sciences, national academy of engineering, and institute of medicine Facilitating Interdisciplinary Research. The National Academies Press, Washington (2005). https://doi.org/10.17226/11153
2. Purao, S., et al.: The sciences of design: observations on an emerging field. Commun. AIS. **23** (29) (2008). Also available as Harvard Business School Finance Working Paper No. 09–056

List of Reviewers

Track: Transdisciplinarity and DSR

Adela Drozdibob
Alexander Herwix
Amir Haj-Bolouri
Ann-Kristin Cordes
Anna Maria Oberländer
Carolynne Hultquist
Catherine Ball
Christian Dietzmann
Frank Teuteberg
Frederik Ahlemann
Friedrich Chasin
Guy Gable
Hippolyte Lefebvre
Holly Rosser

Jan Pries-Heje
Jan Recker
Jaziar Radianti
John Venable
Lauri Wessel
Michel Avital
Pavankumar Mulgund
Roman Lukyanenko
Sofie Wass
Stephan Aier
Stephanie Missonier
Sudha Ram
Tamara Babaian

An Information Systems Design Theory for Digital Broker Platforms

Katja Bley[1,2(✉)] [iD], Raoul Hentschel[2], and Ilias Pappas[1,3]

[1] Department of Computer Science, Norwegian University of Science and Technology, Trondheim, Norway
{katja.bley,ilias.pappas}@ntnu.no
[2] Business Information Systems, Esp. IS in Trade and Industry, TU Dresden, Dresden, Germany
raoul.hentschel@tu-dresden.de
[3] Department of Information Systems , University of Agder , Kristiansand, Norway

Abstract. Service platforms are becoming dominant drivers of daily business operations in a digitalized environment. Research focuses on technological and network effects of such platforms, while socio-technical opportunities remain limited. Guidance support in selecting appropriate digital services on a multisided market platform may help companies with low domain knowledge as it increases their benefits by reducing existing barriers in adopting emerging technologies. We adapt the concept of a broker to a digital platform, which instantiates guidance support on multisided markets as core platform element. Further, we abstract the concept of a digital broker platform as an Information Systems (IS) design theory. By providing the necessary components of an IS design theory, we offer the possibility to derive digital broker platform artifacts, which are theoretically and conceptually grounded. We provide design principles for the method artifact and describe their applicability in an exemplary instantiation of the design theory in the domain of cloud computing. Lastly, we present the artifact's mutability as well as its testable propositions.

Keywords: Digital platform · Information Systems Design Theory · Guidance support · Broker · Cloud computing

1 Introduction

The ongoing digital transformation of organizations and processes leads to opportunities but also to challenges for companies [1]. On the one hand, they need to align their IT and business strategy to keep up with emerging technologies to enter new digital markets and to implement digital services in order to stay competitive. On the other hand, they need to identify the most suited service or application, which is able to represent their respective business model; either by digitally supporting their IT infrastructure or by digitally implementing and offering value propositions [1, 2].

The instantiation of multifaceted digital phenomena leads to an increasing complexity when selecting available digital solutions, challenging consumers with the formulation and knowledge about their own requirements and needs. Likewise, vendors and

A. Drechsler et al. (Eds.): DESRIST 2022, LNCS 13229, pp. 5–16, 2022.
https://doi.org/10.1007/978-3-031-06516-3_1

providers of digital applications and services rely on consumers of their products and thus need to provide an adequate description of their products' functionality and features. However due to the lack of a consistent and unified terminology on the demand and supply side, the establishment of an initial contact between digital service provider and consumer remains complex and resource consuming. Even though digital platforms nowadays offer the possibility for both sides to match their potential interests, the selection problem due to missing domain knowledge remains present. However, this issue should not be neglected as especially smaller companies are increasingly forced to deal with emerging technologies like software-as-a-service (SaaS) or infrastructure-as-a-service (IaaS), due to efficiency and data protection issues, as well as the protection of other digital values.

As a solution to this challenging situation, we present a so-called broker platform (BP). It represents a multisided market, which *"bring[s] together (or match[es]) distinct groups, whereas the value for one group increases as the number of participants from the other group increases"* [3]. Such platforms are characterized by a consulting component, enabling users like companies of different classes to distinguish between a variety of provided products and to find the most suited service or application. Thus, on a meta-level, a digital BP can be understood as a solution artifact to the problem class of multisided guidance support. Whereas existing research investigates for instance capabilities for value co-creation and value capture in large platform ecosystems [4], or service network effects on service platforms [5], our research focuses on the causal socio-technical relations of guidance support on digital platforms. Thus, we provide an abstracted description of the development of a multi-sided BP, which can support consumers and providers of digital products in maximizing their benefits by matching both sides' interests.

Our research thereby answers the existing call for research by de Reuver et al. [3] for considering digital platforms from a design science perspective for understanding design practices and making them more dynamic and evolvable over time. Thereby, we extend our previous research focusing on cloud broker platforms [6] by transferring and abstracting the results for the development of digital broker platforms as Information Systems Design Theory (ISDT) according to Gregor and Jones [7]. Thus, it can be understood as a blueprint for future developments of the same artifact type. The remainder of the paper is structured as follows. First, the theoretical background provides an overview of digital BPs and positions our approach in IS theorizing. A conceptual approach of our research is presented in Sect. 3, followed by the description of the components of an ISDT in Sect. 4. The expository instantiation of the ISDT in the domain of cloud computing afterwards can be understood as a first evaluation of the instantiated components and offers an overview of the functionality of a cloud BP. The paper ends with a discussion and summary of the results.

2 Theoretical Background

2.1 Digital Platforms and Brokerage

Digital platforms, and their core concepts, have become subject of research in recent years [3]. They can be defined *technically* as *"software-based external platforms consisting of the extensible codebase of a software-based system that provides core functionality shared by the modules that interoperate with it and the interfaces through which they interoperate."* [8] Since platforms are often part of larger ecosystems [9], which merge interests groups with differing needs like consumer, provider, buyer, seller, or developer, there does also exists a *sociotechnical* consideration of platforms, which also considers associated organizational processes and standards [3]. However, due to the very nature of such platforms as multisided markets, differing interests and asymmetric information between participants arise.

Originating from the domain of finance, brokers have emerged to act as an intermediary, aiming at bridging the interests of both market sides. They operate as human or digital consulting agents to initiate and improve the match between suppliers and customers of financial products. Transferred to a broader scope, brokers perform tasks such as aggregating information concerning goods or fostering and reducing search costs (e.g., searching for products, sellers, or buyers), contract costs (e.g., initiating and carrying out the contract), and adaptation costs (e.g., costs incurred in making changes during the life of a contract) for both parties [10]. Due to their versatile applicability, we adapt the concept of a broker and include its functionality into a digital platform. Especially for novice users (e.g., customers with little to no knowledge or expertise within a domain) a digital broker platform can provide guidance to successfully handle existent information asymmetry between consumers and providers of digital services.

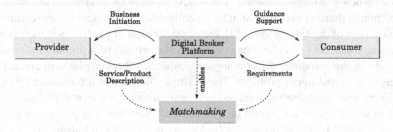

Fig. 1. Conceptual overview of a Digital Broker Platform.

Figure 1 provides an overview of the conceptual functionality of a digital BP. Accordingly, a provider offers a description of their available services or products, which are stored as abstract description within the BP. Likewise, consumers submit their requirements about desired functionalities of digital solutions in abstract descriptions to the BP. By providing an ontology that contains the relevant concepts and represents corresponding constructs within a domain, both the provided and required products are compared and ranked according to their suitability. Thus, a matchmaking of the provider and consumer side is enabled, offering the provider the possibility for a business initiation and to the consumer a solution to the selection problem.

2.2 Design Theory and Theorizing

Design theories (DT) can be regarded as the main artifacts of design science research in the body of knowledge in IS research. Their intention is to explain and prescribe the fundamentals and interdependencies of "the natural world, the social world, and the artificial world of human constructions" [11] as abstracted and generalized phenomena. Thus, when developing a DT, it is necessary for the researcher to explain the ontological positioning towards theory and theorizing. We build our approach on Gregor's [11] conception that a theory "is seen as having an existence separate from the subjective understanding of individual researchers". Following Gregor, we further adopt Habermas' [12] and Popper's [13] three world paradigm. The first (objective) world contains states, processes, and material things typically studied by natural sciences; the second (subjective) world is defined by conscious and unconscious mental states, and the third world consists of man-made entities that objectively exist but are highly abstracted. Accordingly, a DT is assigned to world three as the DT itself exists outside the researcher's mind and belongs to entities like science and theoretical knowledge [11, 13]. The intended goal of our ISDT is a description (method artifact) for the development of a BP by providing relevant components like underlying kernel theories, constructs, and principles of form and function for the BP. Thus, we position our ISDT as *"Theory for Design and Action"* according to Gregor and Jones [7]. Thereby, it aims at enhancing the body of knowledge in IS by providing utility to a group of users, the novelty of the artifact itself, and persuasiveness of claims about its effectiveness [14, 15].

3 Conceptual Approach

The consideration of platform design and development has been subject of research for decades with new platforms constantly being developed in IS and related disciplines [3–5, 16]. Although there exists discussion for an embedding of design science research into the development of digital platforms [3], the consideration of platforms in their function as brokering artifacts is so far missing. Whereas the artifact of a digital platform itself focuses on the instantiation of technological features, a broker platform artifact aims at solving a principal-agent-problem. The desired solution for a consumer (principal) is identifying and choosing the required and best-suited service or application from a software or service provider (agent) on a multisided platform. The process of guidance support is enabled by the concept of a broker, as it provides the abstracted setting of matchmaking and the required infrastructure. Whereas the mere instantiation of a *digital platform* can be regarded as a technical instantiation, the additional component of a *broker* addresses the reduction of information asymmetry that exists between the consumer and provider of digital services. Thus, the artifact of a digital BP combines both, the technical component of IT instantiation and the sociotechnical component of user guidance support and uncertainty reduction. However, since both components rely in their instantiation—and thus usefulness—on each other, their underlying theories and constructs should be regarded from an abstracted perspective. Therefore, we discuss and elaborate the characteristics of a digital BP as *Information Systems Design Theory* according to Gregor and Jones as it *"allows the prescription of guidelines for further artifacts of the same type"* [7]. Thus, we provide the entirety of components relevant for the theoretical and conceptual functionality of a digital BP and thereby offer primarily prescriptive statements about its development process [17].

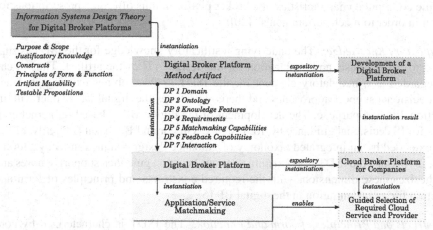

Fig. 2. Conceptual overview of the ISDT for Digital Broker Platforms and its instantiations [17].

Figure 2 offers an overview of our research. The digital BP relies in its instantiation on the BP method artifact which is again an instantiation of the theoretical and conceptual components of the ISDT. Thus, the ISDT combines the necessary components for the BP method and platform artifact and can be regarded as providing a "high level definition of the functioning of an artifact to achieve a design goal and direction toward its construction" [18]. We focus on the construction of such a digital BP by following the derived Design Principles (DPs), enabling us to provide an expository instantiation of the design method, resulting in a digital cloud computing BP.

4   IS Design Theory for Digital Broker Platforms

The anatomy of an ISDT according to [7] consists of eight components out of which six are mandatory: *purpose and scope* (the goal of the Design Theory), *justificatory knowledge* (underlying kernel theories), *constructs* (relevant entities of the theory), *principles of form and function* (the architecture of the artifact), *artifact mutability* (possible changes in the state of the artifact), as well as *testable propositions* (truth statements). Furthermore, we develop an IT broker platform in the domain of cloud computing as *expository instantiation*, thus non-mandatory component of the ISDT.

Purpose and Scope: The goal of the ISDT for digital BPs is to provide a design method for the development of an IT broker platform, which is specifically suited for the guidance of organizations in a multisided market selection process of digital services or applications in a defined domain. We provide design principles [19] and thus offer a methodological description of how to achieve guidance support for a multisided selection problem scenario which is instantiated in a digital platform. However, the ISDT for

BPs does not provide an explanation of the functionality of a service platform as those are depending on the underlying algorithms and technical features. Rather, it describes the methodological conjunction of the concept of guidance (justificatory knowledge) and the conceptual characteristics of a broker platform, thus offering "prescriptions for action in order to reach certain goals" [20].

Justificatory Knowledge: The underlying justificatory knowledge for the ISDT is supposed to "give a basis and explanation for the design" [7] of the artifact. Thus, it can be regarded as a mandatory element for the ISDT as it combines existing guidance and decisional support approaches and thereby provides the digital BP artifact with its functionality and purpose. The development of the digital BP is based on kernel concepts for IS decisional guidance by, for instance, Gregor and Benbasat [21], Silver [22], and extended by an integrated taxonomy of guidance design features in IS by Morana et al. [23]. Thus, the ISDT uses existing relations between guidance support features and synthesizes these dimensions with the required constructs and principles of form and function for an instantiation in the digital BP [6].

Constructs and Principles of Form and Function: The ISDT is characterized by constructs representing necessary components of a digital BP which are used to propose DPs. The entirety of the DPs, with their foundations in the other components of the ISDT can be regarded as digital BP method artifact (see Fig. 2) and the instantiation will lead to an actual digital BP in a pre-defined domain. For their formulation, we followed Chandra et al. [19] and developed action driven and materiality-oriented DPs that prescribe what an artifact should enable users to do and how it should be built in order to do so. Thus, the DPs have a prescriptive character and can be regarded as principles of form and function in the formulation of an ISDT [24]. They were derived from a set of design requirements for guidance systems, which were based on the results of qualitative expert interviews and a systematic literature review [6].

Constructs: Based on the structure of IT service platforms in combination with the underlying knowledge base, we introduce the constructs *domain, ontology, features, requirements, matchmaking capabilities, feedback capabilities,* and *interaction* for the ISDT. Due to their strong interconnectedness, the principles of form and function rely in their existence on the constructs, which is why they are represented in the DPs.

Principles of Form and Function: The construct of domain defines the scope for which the intended artifact of the digital BP is valid. In this context it enables the developer of the BP artifact to derive target group and domain specific requirements which will be valid for the pre-defined domain. A domain refers to an abstraction of the business context to which the method artifact is applied and in which the instantiated BP artifact will be valid afterwards.

DP1: Define a *domain* for the BP to distinguish a field of interest for the artifact and to identify target group specific requirements.

Due to the lack of universal definitions and standards for digital services, a unified terminology is needed to make information readable by machines and humans alike.

Therefore, ontologies as popular solutions can be used to leverage information sharing through a system of vocabularies. Making use of a reasonable ontology is a mandatory prerequisite for all further forms of guidance.

DP2: Provide the BP with an *ontology* that allows the detection of commonalties and differences of digital services to create a common understanding.

To identify possible relevant service features that fulfil consumers' requirements, for instance, storytelling in the form of user stories has become a well-accepted practice of agile software development [25]. In the context of a digital broker platform, this can be accomplished by mapping questions posed about predefined use cases from a platform owner (e.g., I need features A and B to perform C).

DP3: Provide the BP with *features* that allow consumers to find relevant digital services with no/low domain-specific knowledge from multiple sources to enhance knowledge for decision-making.

During the selection process, the consumer decides which requirements should be covered by the given digital service and which should not. However, ambiguity and inconsistency can occur when defining requirements due to missing knowledge or a non-specific formulation of needs. In these cases, a functionality must be added that recognizes the actual requirement.

DP4: Provide the BP with features which allow consumers to elaborate and validate the defined *requirements* to enable adequate matching results.

To provide guidance that is not merely informative, the BP should provide a mechanism for providing service recommendations to consumers. Since every manual review of the automatically identified digital service configurations would mean additional effort for the consumer, a recommendation system is important.

DP5: Provide the BP with *matchmaking capabilities* that allow consumers to get recommendations for digital services to limit the effort required for selection and to improve decision-making.

In addition to the informative guidance from the matchmaking service and the suggestive guidance from the recommendation system, the platform should also provide dynamic and participative guidance. This form of guidance is particularly effective for improving decision quality, as well as improving consumers' learning and decision performance [26]. This means that a feedback method is required, as the system should "learn" from former consumers' input.

DP6: Provide the BP with a *feedback capability* that allows consumers to provide/get knowledge from former selection projects to enhance matchmaking capabilities.

Last, a mechanism is needed to validate the provided guidance via third-party actors (e.g., consultants, integrators). The feedback from other consumers provides additional knowledge about the validity of a proposed solution and can help reduce the uncertainty of consumers using digital services and improve decision quality and performance.

DP7: Provide the BP with features that allow for an *interaction* of consumers with other actors (e.g., consultants, integrators) to have access to expertise and obtain participative guidance.

Artifact Mutability: We distinguish between the method artifact for the development of the BP and its mutability as instantiation. Since the described constructs of the ISDT for digital BPs can be transferred to various IT domains, like software-as-a-service (SaaS) or infrastructure-as-a-service (IaaS), the artifact of a digital BP can change its scope of validity depending on the application domain. Furthermore, the technical aspects of the platform's instantiation rely on the researcher or practitioner, who is instantiating the artifact. However, the mere development process of a digital BP, which is characterized by the design principles or the method artifact, refers to basic components of the ISDT itself and thereby needs to remain stable over time.

Testable Propositions: Testable propositions can be regarded as truth statements about the ISDT. Their intention is to demonstrate that the instantiation of the BP method artifact, which follows the principles of form and function, will result in a BP, which can provide a better solution for the digital service selection problem than existing approaches. Thus, propositions like *"Digital Broker Platforms based on the derived DPs are able to better provide guidance support in IT service selection processes than platforms without a brokerage function"* can be tested and evaluated with hypotheses in a real-world setting. This can be done, for instance, by asking the consumer and provider about perceived benefits. Furthermore, it is possible to investigate the service selection in two groups of companies with the same requirements. One group applies the broker platform and is supported by decisional guidance, whereas the other group runs the selection process without guidance support. Thus, if researchers can verify their testable propositions, the DPs are indirectly evaluated as well, since the instantiated artifact was developed by applying them.

5 Expository Instantiation

As instantiation of the ISDT for digital BPs we present the development of a BP in the domain of cloud computing (CC).

Following **DP1,** we chose the domain of CC, as it is an approach to IT sourcing that enables companies to access a shared pool of managed and scalable IT resources (e.g., networks, servers, storage, applications, and services) that are accessible via the internet on a pay-per-use basis without requiring long-term investments [27]. We further refined the validity of our BP for SaaS services. SaaS services have a high number of potential service configurations and the selection of SaaS services is often made by the business departments directly (i.e., without the involvement of the IT department) [28]. This makes decision support for SaaS services highly useful. For the technical implementation, we created a web application consisting of a graphic user interface (GUI) that allows for interaction with and visualization of the platform among the different stakeholders. Thus, our instantiated cloud broker platform (CBP) will be valid for the problem class of SaaS selection in companies, so-called cloud service consumers (CSC). We further derived specific requirements for the platform design as we intended to develop a CBP for guidance support for the class of small companies. **DP2** was instantiated by providing an ontology-based matchmaking component for the platform. It consisted of two elements. First, the decision components, which can be dynamically added and/or removed by the cloud platform owner. Each decision component can contain further sub-components that can be addressed and enriched with information provided by CSPs, who join the platform. In our prototype, we limited the implementation of a technical component, more precisely, a SaaS catalog with features of cloud storage offerings (e.g., encryption, replication, etc.). Second, the matchmaking component, which generates options determined by CSCs' preferences through a pairwise comparison using previously defined weightings of every available cloud service option. To discover and represent the commonalities of the services and to make automated matchmaking possible, we adapted feature models for service design [29] to create a common SaaS profile.

We then applied **DP3** and provided the CSC with a possibility to use a multi-level input on the CBP's front-end, where the CSC can specify requirements, that the cloud service should satisfy. Since complex technologies can be hidden within the services, this specification is provided as questions about the planned use cases, which in turn reduces complexity and simplifies the handling for novice CSCs. As the correct identification of requirements is essential for the later matchmaking, we followed **DP4** by enabling the system to ask the CSC a minimum number of questions, which can be understood as a prerequisite for the matching process. Afterwards, each requirement can be weighted to identify CSC's priority requirements using rating scales. We then used feature models as a representation mechanism for service properties, considering features to be on the right level of abstraction. To gather initial data, we collected publicly available information (e.g., service descriptions, API documentations, user manuals) from cloud storage providers. To ensure the prerequisites for a later automated processing (i.e., for CSPs to provide information directly), we made the catalog available via web services. Subsequently, the matchmaking can be performed by filtering options and presenting those services, which are most suitable in the form of recommendations (**DP5**). We implemented the matchmaking based on a comparison of a requirement vector on the CSCs' side, and a service vector on the CSPs' side. In other words, the consumer's requirements were normalized and represented as a vector. On the provider side, the (satisfied) features are provided as a service vector to enable a comparison of the two vectors. The matchmaking result is a selection of suitable cloud services ordered and displayed according to the degree of fulfilment. **DP6** were instantiated by providing a possibility for CSCs to submit feedback from completed cloud selection projects to improve matchmaking mechanism. The feedback component is implemented as an AI-based algorithm, learning from successful or non-successful use cases. This information is provided by the CSC who submits their degree of satisfaction with each criterion. Subsequently, the matchmaking can be improved by training the algorithm with the results of successful combinations. Also, qualitative feedback can be submitted via a textual description, allowing the platform owner to modify the matchmaking manually. Finally, the instantiation of **DP7** enables CSCs to engage with third parties such as consultants or integrators to receive expertise. Opening the platform to other parties allows them to offer value-adding services and enables CSCs to receive expertise, build trust, and confidence in potential partners and vendors.

6 Discussion and Conclusion

Our ISDT for digital BP offers the blueprint for a platform artifact which instantiates guidance support by a broker as core element for consumers and providers of digital services and products. Thus, the broker does not only help consumers in their decisional process but also enables providers to be recognized as fulfilling the required needs and provides them with an opportunity for business initiations. Especially novice consumers might feel overwhelmed when it comes to the selection of digital services or products due to missing knowledge in the respective digital domain [6]. Thus, a BP is a suitable tool to reduce uncertainties and help maximize stakeholders' interests. Due to the artifact's mutability, the ISDT offers, on the one hand, stability as it provides with the method artifact and the DPs a clear description and conceptual relations for the development of a digital BP. However, since it can be instantiated in any digital domain and adapted to the contextual requirements, the instantiated BP artifact also provides flexibility, which allows the researcher or practitioner to consider and implement new or emerging components. Therefore, our ISDT can be regarded as a possible answer to the *paradox of change*, which was initially described by Tilson et al. [30] and refers to *"the need for digital platforms to simultaneously remain stable to form a solid foundation for further enrolment, and yet to be sufficiently flexible in order to support seemingly unbounded growth"* [3]. Although the authors initially described this phenomenon in the context of digital infrastructures, we provide, with the described anatomy of the ISDT, the necessary components of stability and change for an adaptation into the context of digital platforms. Existing digital platform research often focuses on the technological instantiation and incorporation of software and thereby focuses on reduced deployment times, minimized long term overheads, as well as reduced upfront implementation [5]. Thus, our approach adds to existing research in the domain of digital platforms by focusing on the principal-agent relationship between the consumer and provider of digital services or products, and which is reduced by the instantiation of guidance support by a broker. Even though information asymmetry relationships were previously investigated in a platform context, they rather focused on the stakeholder groups of platform providers and software or app developers [31, 32] than consumers of such services.

Our research approach provides several contributions to the body of knowledge in IS. First, we provide the conceptual model of a digital BP, which represents a matchmaking platform and offers a solution to the problem of information asymmetry between consumers and providers on digital platforms. Thereby, we offer a stronger sociotechnical perspective on the concept of digital platforms, which will, in its instantiation, be especially helpful for smaller or novice companies that do not have the financial or personnel resources for professional consulting. Second, we abstract this concept of guidance support from a design science research perspective and develop an ISDT for digital BP, which answers the call for research by de Reuver et al. [3]. The formulation of DPs for the conjunction of the consumers and providers digital market side is so far missing in the body of knowledge in IS research.

Thus, as practical contribution of our research, the derived components of the ISDT provide researchers and practitioners the possibility to build guidance support BP artifacts of the same type but in different domains. Thereby, the artifact of a digital BP offers an improvement in the selection process of digital services and products for companies of different sizes and sectors as well as for the respective providers.

Like every research project, our approach has limitations. The description of the ISDT components is highly theoretical, which is why our presented development approach lacks practical depth. However, this is explained by the high level of abstraction in theory components, which is needed for the formulation of a method artifact, and which can be applied in various domains. Furthermore, even though the developed DPs are based on an extensive literature review in the field of decisional guidance support, the complex domain of digital transformation requires an ongoing adaption to new and emerging phenomena. Thus, the knowledge base for the ISDT can be considered as constantly evolving and should therefore be subject to ongoing research in IS.

References

1. Wessel, L., Baiyere, A., Ologeanu-Taddei, R., Cha, J., Jensen, T.B.: Unpacking the difference between digital transformation and it-enabled organizational transformation. J. Assoc. Inf. Syst. **22**, 102–129 (2021)
2. Barrett, M., Davidson, E., Prabhu, J., Vargo, S.L.: Service innovation in the digital age: key contributions and future directions. MISQ. **39**, 135–154 (2015)
3. de Reuver, M., Sørensen, C., Basole, R.C.: The digital platform: a research agenda. J. Inf. Technol. **33**, 124–135 (2018)
4. Schreieck, M., Wiesche, M., Krcmar, H.: Capabilities for value co-creation and value capture in emergent platform ecosystems: a longitudinal case study of SAP's cloud platform. J. Inf. Technol. **36**, 365–390 (2021)
5. Janiesch, C., Rosenkranz, C., Scholten, U.: An information systems design theory for service network effects. J. Assoc. Inf. Syst. **21**, 1402–1460
6. Hentschel, R.: Developing design principles for a cloud broker platform for SMEs. In: 2020 IEEE 22nd Conference on Business Informatics, p. 10 (2020)
7. Gregor, S., Jones, D.: The anatomy of a design theory. J. Assoc. Inf. Syst. **8**, 312–335 (2007)
8. Ghazawneh, A., Henfridsson, O.: A paradigmatic analysis of digital application marketplaces. J. Inf. Technol. **30**, 198–208 (2015)
9. Burkhalter, M., Betz, C., Auge-Dickhut, S., Jung, R.: Orchestrating value co-creation in business ecosystems. In: Wendt, K. (ed.) Theories of Change: Change Leadership Tools, Models and Applications for Investing in Sustainable Development Sustainable Finance, pp. 257–291. Springer, Cham (2021). https://doi.org/10.1007/978-3-030-52275-9_16
10. Wigand, R.T.: Whatever happened to disintermediation? Electron. Mark. **30**(1), 39–47 (2020). https://doi.org/10.1007/s12525-019-00389-0
11. Gregor, S.: The nature of theory in information systems of theory in information systems. MIS Q. **30**, 611–642 (2006)
12. Habermas, J.: The Theory of Communicative Action, Volume 1: Reason and the Rationalization of Society. Heinemann, London, UK (1984)
13. Popper, K.R.: Unended Quest. An Intellectual Autobiography. Open Court, La Salle (1985)
14. March, S.T., Smith, G.F.: Design and natural science research on information technology. Decis. Support Syst. **15**, 251–266 (1995)

15. Hevner, A., March, S.T., Park, J., Ram, S.: Design science in information systems research. MIS Q. **28**, 75–105 (2004)
16. Tiwana, A., Konsynski, B., Bush, A.A.: Research commentary—platform evolution: coevolution of platform architecture, governance, and environmental dynamics. Inf. Syst. Res. **21**, 675–687 (2010)
17. Bley, K.: An information systems design theory for maturity models in complex domains. In: PACIS 2021 Proceeding, p. 45 (2021)
18. Kuechler, W., Vaishnavi, V.: A framework for theory development in design science research: multiple perspectives. J. Assoc. Inf. Syst. **13**, 395–423 (2012)
19. Chandra, L., Seidel, S., Gregor, S.: Prescriptive knowledge in IS research: conceptualizing design principles in terms of materiality, action, and boundary conditions. In: 2015 48th Hawaii International Conference on System Sciences (HICSS), pp. 4039–4048 (2015)
20. Goldkuhl, G.: Design theories in information systems – a need for multi-grounding. JITTA. **6**, 59–72 (2004)
21. Gregor, S., Benbasat, I.: Explanations from intelligent systems: theoretical foundations and implications for practice. MIS Q. **23**, 497–530 (1999)
22. Silver, M.S.: Decisional guidance for computer-based decision support. MIS Q. **15**, 105 (1991)
23. Morana, S., Schacht, S., Scherp, A., Maedche, A.: A review of the nature and effects of guidance design features. Decis. Support Syst. **97**, 31–42 (2017)
24. Gregor, S., Kruse, L., Seidel, S.: The anatomy of a design principle. J. Assoc. Inform. Syst. **21**, 1622–1652 (2020). https://doi.org/10.17705/1jais.00649
25. Rising, L., Janoff, N.S.: The Scrum software development process for small teams. IEEE Softw. **17**, 26–32 (2000)
26. Parikh, M., Fazlollahi, B., Verma, S.: The effectiveness of decisional guidance: an empirical evaluation. Decis. Sci. **32**, 303–332 (2001)
27. Yang, H., Tate, M.: A Descriptive Literature Review and Classification of Cloud Computing Research. Communications of the Association for Information Systems, p. 31 (2012)
28. Winkler, T., Goebel, C., Benlian, A., Bidault, F., Günther, O.: The impact of software as a service on IS authority: a contingency perspective. In: Proceedings of the International Conference on Information Systems. ICIS (2011)
29. Wittern, E., Zirpins, C.: On the use of feature models for service design: the case of value representation. In: Cezon, M., Wolfsthal, Y. (eds.) ServiceWave 2010. LNCS, vol. 6569, pp. 110–118. Springer, Heidelberg (2011). https://doi.org/10.1007/978-3-642-22760-8_12
30. Tilson, D., Lyytinen, K., Sørensen, C.: Digital infrastructures: the missing IS research agenda. Inf. Syst. Res. **21**, 748–759 (2010)
31. Ghazawneh, A., Henfridsson, O.: Balancing platform control and external contribution in third-party development: the boundary resources model: control and contribution in third-party development. Inf. Syst. J. **23**, 173–192 (2013)
32. Eaton, B., Elaluf-Calderwood, S., Sørensen, C., Yoo, Y.: Distributed tuning of boundary resources: the case of Apple's iOS service system. Manag. Inf. Syst. Q. **39**, 217–244 (2015)

Morphological Analysis for Design Science Research: The Case of Human-Drone Collaboration in Emergencies

Mateusz Dolata$^{(\boxtimes)}$ [iD] and Kiram Ben Aleya

Department of Informatics, University of Zurich, Zurich, Switzerland
dolata@ifi.uzh.ch

Abstract. Drones are becoming pervasive in private and professional settings. The engineering of human-drone collaboration poses unique challenges. Specifically, drones' distinctive capabilities yield a vast design space. Yet, the relevant guidance is scattered across literature such that an overview of various design dimensions is missing. This paper synthesizes adequate research and provides an overview of essential design dimensions in the form of a morphological box (MB) to support designers of drones for emergencies. Using this MB, practitioners and researchers become aware of design decisions they will have to make when designing drones or collaboration between drones and humans. It prevents fragmented or partial perspectives on drones design and provides a basis for structured, holistic design explorations. Using the case of drones, we discuss the potential of morphological analysis for design science research (DSR). New types of sociotechnical systems involve a vast, multidimensional design space, and singular studies frequently address domain or discipline-specific subsections of this space. We claim that morphological analysis supports a systematic exploration of the design space across disciplinary boundaries and might contribute towards a more transparent and traceable design of DSR artifacts.

Keywords: Morphological analysis · Morphological box · Drones · Unmanned aerial vehicles · Multi-copters · Emergency · Literature review · Sociotechnical systems

1 Introduction

The use of drones, both privately and in a professional setting, is steadily increasing. Human-piloted drones are used widely in crises and have proven to benefit emergency response scenarios. However, human-piloted drones also have considerable disadvantages in emergencies. They can easily lead to an information overload and a high workload for the pilots [2]. Recent advances and new autonomous features have enabled drones to function without human interference. Yet, the design of effective human-drone collaboration patterns poses further challenges to researchers and designers.

A drone, a multi-copter, or an unmanned aerial vehicle (UAV) is an aircraft designed to operate without an onboard pilot, and it does not carry passengers. A drone can

© Springer Nature Switzerland AG 2022
A. Drechsler et al. (Eds.): DESRIST 2022, LNCS 13229, pp. 17–29, 2022.
https://doi.org/10.1007/978-3-031-06516-3_2

be autonomous (controlled by an onboard computer) or wholly or partially remotely controlled by a human or an on-ground computer [60]. Especially autonomous drones, using contemporary AI, can take over monotonous, tedious, or challenging tasks from humans allowing them to focus on other tasks. Their broad applicability and autonomy make them adequate for application in emergencies like natural disasters. However, drones are restricted by the cognitive capabilities of the AI and physical limitations like their maximal payload or battery life. Thus, they can be most effectively applied when collaborating with humans [2].

Designing for human-drone collaboration is particularly challenging. Drones might possess the ability to act autonomously: from autonomously deciding on the trajectory of flight up to planning their actions [2]. However, drones' capabilities and limitations differ significantly from those of humans. They can reach positions previously unreachable to a human quickly while using its sensors (navigation systems, altimeters). Therefore, humans might struggle to make sense of the drone's actions or 'put themselves in the shoes' of a drone [21]. Collaboration without mutual understanding and shared meanings causes problems, primarily under time pressure [62]. Collective sensemaking and mutual understanding are particularly important in emergencies – high-risk organizations carefully engineer protocols and procedures for it [61, 62]. Accordingly, designing for human-drone collaboration in emergency situations goes beyond simply creating the technology: it requires a holistic and sociotechnical approach.

However, existing literature lacks a comprehensive perspective on interactions and collaborations between humans and drones. The emerging discourse focuses mainly on the technical aspects of the drones or, to a much lesser extent, the user interfaces for interacting with drones [2]. A structured overview of various dimensions in the design space is missing. Designers find themselves overwhelmed by the complexity and variety of decisions they need to take when engineering collaboration between humans and drones for emergency response. Instead of exploring the design space systematically, they might implicitly default on dominant patterns (e.g., use of singular drone equipped with multiple sensors leading to a heavy payload) rather than on alternatives (e.g., use of several cooperating drones each carrying a single sensor). This paper makes the first step towards a systematic overview of the relevant design dimensions addressed in different disciplines like computer science (CS), emergency management, or the law. The practitioners receive an overview of the relevant design aspects to be considered.

To identify those dimensions, the study employs morphological analysis (MA) based on recent articles from various disciplines. Whereas MA, leading to establishing the so-called morphological boxes or taxonomies, is frequently used in information systems (IS) research [15, 63], reflection on its usage for designing systems is only in its infancy [41]. To our best knowledge, MA's potentials and procedures for the DSR have not yet been studied. Using the case of human-drone collaboration, we propose and employ the morphological analysis for sociotechnical systems (MASS). We discuss how MASS taxonomies inform IS design while adhering to high rigor standards. We argue why a systematic description of a transdisciplinary design space forms an individual contribution and suggest how it might be used for bridging the creative gap in design.

Overall, the study has two contributions towards IS. First, it offers a nascent overview of the design space for human-drone collaboration based on transdisciplinary literature analysis. This taxonomy can benefit developers and design researchers involved in this growing application area. Second, it discusses the potential of using morphological analysis in DSR. It contributes towards the toolset associated with DSR.

2 Background

Consider crisis situations such as an avalanche: A drone or a team of drones could autonomously scan the area for survivors (e.g., using thermal imaging) and notify rescue units. It could provide exact geographic coordinates and pilot the units to the emergency scene. On-site, drones could quickly transport material between rescue units, collect information about the operation from above, providing specific, selected cues to the coordinator (e.g., detected rapid movements below the snow), or inform uninvolved individuals to stay off the scene. Completion of those tasks depends on successful collaboration with human stakeholders or other drones. However, a human-drone assemblage is a complex sociotechnical system. One way of dealing with this complexity is by decomposing it into its singular dimensions. It allows for finding a suitable configuration across the dimensions. In the following, we first summarize the discourse on human-drone collaboration and then propose a sociotechnical perspective.

2.1 Human-Drone Collaboration

Human-drone collaboration can be subsumed under the larger discourse on human-autonomy teaming [9, 40, 45] and machines as teammates [53, 54]. The articles follow mostly a conceptual approach and provide guidance regarding the design and work with autonomous team members. They yield frameworks referring to transparency, communication, authority, or situational awareness. Yet, they frequently assume a general notion of an agent [9, 45] or explicitly refer to conversational agents mimicking human abilities and communication [23, 53, 63]. This discourse induced major interest in the IS field. Yet, ambivalence towards differences between classes of digital agents (DA) has drawbacks. It abstracts from the dependency of successful collaboration on the ability to put oneself in the DA's place. Successful teams embrace empathizing and taking each other's perspectives as a core way to establish a common sense [24, 37, 62]. Some agents might be easier to empathize with than others. The more distinct an agent is from a human, the more difficult it gets to make assumptions about its behavior [21, 49]. It is essential in the case of drones that provide capabilities unavailable and sometimes hardly imaginable for humans. Consequently, the collaboration between humans and drones requires a specific approach different from, e.g., designing collaboration with conversational agents or agents without physical representation and capabilities.

However, most of the research on drones happens outside of IS. Accordingly, available meta-studies in CS focus on, for instance, architectural issues [14], path planning and navigation [38, 64], or control mechanisms [6]. Law studies review research on regulatory aspects [57]. Studies in other disciplines summarize application scenarios in specific domains like agriculture [18] or traffic management [32]. There are also recent reviews addressing the application of drones in crisis and emergency situations [28, 46,

56]. However, they focus on bibliometric analysis, description of envisioned or implemented uses of drones for specific tasks, and technical challenges. They do not attend to the agency of drones or the collaboration between humans and drones, framing drones as passive tools at humans' disposal. The studies point a designer to relevant literature, but they provide little support for designing human-drone collaboration.

2.2 A Sociotechnical View of Human-Drone Collaboration

The IS community has not yet established its own approach towards human-drone collaboration. Individual conference papers discuss the domain-specific application of drones in transportation [51, 59] and healthcare [33, 52]. They concentrate on the advantages and disadvantages of specific drone applications or elaborate on operations and business models in a defined context. A sociotechnical view on human-drone collaboration remains absent despite the sociotechnical perspective being considered the core axis of IS research [50]. We argue that given the tight interdependency between drones and human agents in most application areas, framing it as a sociotechnical system provides a sound foundation to analyze and engineer drones' applications.

The notion of sociotechnical systems has influenced IS research and practice for decades [19, 22, 50]. The workings of a sociotechnical system involve interaction between humans and technology. Individuals, collectives, and their relations framed by hierarchies, cultures, rituals, practices, or economies form the *social component* [36]. The technology, including human-made hardware, software, data, and techniques associated with them, forms the *technical component* [36, 50]. The social and technical components enter reciprocal, iterative, and complex *mutual interactions* in the process of joint optimization [50]. If successful, the interactions between the social and technical components impact the *context* by achieving instrumental objectives like work efficiency or profitability and humanistic objectives like wellbeing or job satisfaction [50]. The interactions between social and technical components are frequently complex and subject to mutual adaptations, such that one cannot predict the working of the whole sociotechnical system based on the performance of its single components [62]. We claim that this complexity increases when the technical component relies on non-deterministic autonomous technologies using artificial intelligence (AI): the relation between technical and social components can stabilize faster if the output of the technical component is predictable, allowing humans to establish mental models of its working. It gets harder if the technical component relies on probabilities, like in the case of agentic or (semi-) autonomous drones. Overall, human-drone collaboration can be framed as a complex sociotechnical system that requires a holistic, multidisciplinary approach.

MA helps deal with complex systems by identifying multiple dimensions of their working and explicating various combinations of their characteristics rather than dissecting them into individual components [48]. Originally proposed to investigate the complete set of relationships in non-quantifiable problem complexes, MA quickly became applied for the artifacts' development. IS applies MA to explicate technical dimensions of classes of systems [63], classify technological phenomena [44], or frame field results [16]. Only recently, the community started reflecting on the use of MA in design processes and IS research [41]. Yet, this reflection focuses on MA for designing technical artifacts rather than sociotechnical assemblages. We aim to explore design dimensions of a complex sociotechnical system at the example of human-drone collaboration. We, thus, ask the following research question: *What design dimensions describe the state-of-the-art collaboration between humans and drones in emergency situations?* We employ a multidisciplinary literature review, MA, and the structure of a sociotechnical system to systematize those dimensions and their characteristics.

3 Methodology

This section describes the process we applied to characterize the sociotechnical system' human-drone collaboration' as an object of engineering and design. Simultaneously, it systematically describes an MA-based method to explore the design space of a sociotechnical system systematically and rigorously regarding past research. First, we provide an abstract view of this method. Then, we describe the instantiation of this method for the study employed to answer the research question.

3.1 Morphological Analysis for Sociotechnical Systems (MASS)

MA was conceived as a method for discovery, invention, research, and construction with a specific focus on complex real-world phenomena and problems [65, 66]. It shall support the systematic exploration of a problem and relationships associated with this problem without defaulting on pre-assumptions or biases [65]. It is applicable to complex problem fields that are non-quantifiable, contain non-resolvable uncertainties, cannot be causally modeled or simulated, and require a judgment [48]. MA proposes a set of techniques, including the *morphological box* (MB) [66] also referred to as (morphological) taxonomy [35, 41, 43]. This technique particularly fits the goal of investigating a total set of configurations contained in a problem complex or the design space [47]. 'In the process, we build up a problem laboratory where we can generate alternative solutions depending on different hypothesized conditions. In a sense, we build a non-quantified input-output model, in which we can define independent and dependent variables, test certain conditions against others, and hypothesize relationships' [48].

The technique we propose sources at *the method of the MB* defined by Zwicky [66], *the MA-based process of collective creativity* by Ritchey [47, 48], and *steps for standalone descriptive literature reviews* by Templier and Paré [58]. Table 1 lists and describes the steps while referring to the individual methodological guidelines.

3.2 Applying MASS to Human-Drone Collaboration

We aimed to identify the relevant design dimensions and their values for human-drone collaboration without selecting specific configurations. Accordingly, we followed steps 1 to 8 from Table 1. In the following, we attend to each step as we employed it:

1. As illustrated in the introduction, collaboration between drones and humans is not explored enough to allow for quantified or causal statements. Designing for this collaboration requires judgments concerning design directions under uncertainty.

Table 1. MASS procedure. Steps 1 to 8 (green) deal with generating a MB. Steps 9 to 13 (blue)instruct how to employ the box to explore the design space.

Steps of the MASS procedure	Explanation and source of the guideline
1 Check **entry conditions**: - design space is non-quantifiable - contains uncertainties - cannot be causally modeled - requires a judgment	MA is dedicated to dealing with a 'mess', wicked problems which are complex, ill-defined, ambiguous, unstable. The goal of MA is to transfer the mess into dimensioned and structured problems to enable systematic exploration of the issue and the definition of a solution [48].
2 **Formulate a design problem** you want to address. A problem describes the gap between the status quo and the desired state. It might be concrete, provided by a project or case (e.g., a specific organizational issue), or abstract, based on literature or a vision of a system (e.g., exploration of capabilities needed to achieve X).	Zwicky [66] requires 'the problem which is to be solved must be exactly formulated.' The guidance for transparent literature review is more specific: 'define topic, formulate research question' for the literature review [58]. The defined problem should involve designing a sociotechnical system as one of the possible solutions.
3 Identify **potential and partial solutions** to the problem from the existing literature: a. run a systematic, traceable search in established databases using keywords or a set of seed articles b. if adequate, apply backward and forward search c. screen the articles based on inclusion and exclusion criteria, assess the quality and relevance of the articles	There exist multiple guidelines for conducting a transparent and traceable literature review. We rely on Templier and **Paré's** [52] indications for a descriptive review for their comprehensive treatment of this topic. Since MA aims to structure and describe a problem/design space, we refrain from suggesting higher-level reviews like critical reviews, meta-analyses, or realist reviews.
4 **Extract dimensions** of the solutions thematized in the literature. These include manipulated variables or differences in various designs, aspects presented as a challenge, or discussion of further developments. No need to collapse synonymous dimensions from various papers.	The MB method requires identifying parameters that might enter into the solution of the given problem [66]. Those are the primary parameters of the problem complex [48]. This overlaps with the **step'** extract data from studies' in the literature review [58].
5 For each dimension, define **a spectrum of potential values** based on the analyzed literature. Those values represent alternative solutions to singular issues related to each dimension. At this stage, there is no need to collapse dimensions or their values if they occur in several papers. Keep them all separate.	The MA requires that the taxonomy contains all of the solutions that might be given to a problem [66]. Various values in various dimensions represent those. All values in a dimension should be of the same type. They might be scales, nominals, idea packages, binary combinations, social or technical scenarios, etc. [48]
6 **Reduce and systematize** the morphological taxonomy: a. unify synonymous & overlapping dimensions, apply the union operation on dimensions when applicable b. collapse synonymous values within a dimension	A collective creative approach towards MA suggests a cross-consistency assessment which requires preprocessing of the values to repair vague concepts, synonymous meanings, or sources of confusion [48].
7 **Assure completeness** by checking finishing conditions: - each dimension's value appears in at least one paper - no new dimensions/values are added with new papers - dimensions and values do not repeat/are unique - every known dimension and value is in the box	MA requires a comprehensive coverage of the problem space [66]. We suggest using completion conditions proposed by Nickerson et al. [43] for taxonomy building. If a condition is not met, steps 3 to 6 should be repeated.
8 Use the sociotechnical perspective to **structure the identified dimensions**: context, social component, technical component, mutual interactions, and objectives. This step structures the MB and indicates unexplored gaps with potential innovative solutions.	None of the used guidance explicitly proposes this step. Yet, it might be helpful to employ some theoretical framing for conducting a literature review [58]. We claim that sociotechnical system framework is adequate for structuring most of the design spaces in IS discipline.
Steps 1–8 yield a MB **synthesizing and reproducing the literature** coverage of the design space. Steps 9–13 use the box in a generative manner to **create new configurations** of a sociotechnical system.	
9 (optional) **Complement the MB** with: a. missing values in obviously incomplete dimensions (e.g., range-based dimension missing a middle range) b. dimensions specific for **one's** problem, project context, or the sociotechnical framing (see step 8).	Creative MA approaches [48] recommend workshops as a primary way to identify relevant dimensions. We identified them from the literature. Yet, literature might be incomplete. Systematically filling the gaps might yield innovations that outperform earlier systems.
10 **Find contradictions**, i.e., values that cannot co-exist or are incompatible within a single configuration. Document the contradictions or mark them directly in the MB. A cross-consistency matrix might be appropriate for larger MB.	Cross-consistency assessment reduces the set of possible solutions to those free of internal contradictions between values in different dimensions. A matrix with cells standing for each unique relationship between two values is proposed as an approach [47].
11 **Select relevant input values** that need to remain stable in one's design or exploration. They are a starting point for identifying dimensions and values configurations compatible with potential predefined conditions.	This allows for exploring the design space in a generative manner, i.e., yielding individual solutions and their configurations [47, 48]. Those configurations are combinations of single values from different dimensions.
12 **Evaluate all potential, non-contradictory configurations** compatible with **one's** input condition according to criteria relevant for **one's** project. Use results from the literature to identify which configurations were used in practice and how they performed.	Zwicky [66] suggests analyzing and evaluating solutions from the MB against purposes to be achieved. Evaluating key results and conclusions is also core for a descriptive literature review [58]. Yet not all possible configurations were studied before.
13 Informed by the literature, available resources, and project context, **identify design configurations to be explored further** (e.g., implemented and evaluated). This process might lead to discovering previously unattended dimensions or values for future research.	MA suggests selecting and implementing promising solutions [66]. An additional MA study might be necessary for problems occurring during implementation and application. Using results from literature might support the selection of best solutions and prevent repetitions [58].

2. The hypothetical design problem we address is the development of effective and adequate human-drone collaboration patterns for use in emergencies. We need to identify relevant design dimensions and their potential values to do so.

3a. We run a systematic search with two queries: *autonomous* AND *drone* AND *emergency* and *autonomous* AND *drone* AND *disaster* in titles and abstracts included in Elsevier Scopus since 2010. We selected 50 best-cited items for each query.

3b. We added 20 other items in the set based on the forward and backward search.

3c. We applied a set of selection criteria to retain articles which: (i) discuss a specific human-drone collaboration possibility, (ii) feature a semi or fully autonomous drone involved in the collaboration, (iii) feature an emergency application scenario except for policing and military contexts. Overall, we identified 53 relevant articles. The MA used all those papers, yet we refer to 20 exemplary papers that covered the design space to the most significant extent for presenting the results.

4., 5., 6. We extracted dimensions and values from the considered papers and then grouped by similarity. We collapsed synonymous dimensions and values, reducing the number of dimensions from 115 to 19. No dimensions were excluded. We introduced self-explanatory naming when appropriate.

7. We controlled the finishing conditions. Specifically, we assured that the taxonomy applies to all emergency situations presented in the source literature.

8. Finally, we grouped the dimensions in line with a sociotechnical system's structure.

4 Results

Table 2 presents the output of applying the above procedure to the design of human-drone collaboration for emergencies. Values and dimensions come solely from the literature study, such that the MB reflects previously studied aspects. Based on it, one could identify new configurations, see steps 9 to 13 from the procedure (cf. Table 1).

The analysis of the MB leads to several observations. First, the social components is barely covered in the literature. The only aspect considered for the social component is the skillset of the drone's operator. The analyzed papers barely attend to the social and organizational setting in which the collaboration happens and how internal developments within those components reflect the usage of drones. Second, studies do not explicitly, empirically attend to the humanistic or instrumental objectives, e.g., like proportionality or fairness of drone's use. Instead, they rely on the implicit assumption that emergencies are about saving human life, health, and possession in a most effective manner. Accordingly, drones are presented as means to enhance the effectiveness of the recovery missions. Consequently, the instrumental and humanistic objectives do not occur in the MB at all. Third, mutual interactions are studied by various structural aspects (number and type of agents, direction of communication). Variation in terms of mechanisms applied for distribution of roles or responsibilities and exchange of information, intentions, or desires were barely touched upon in the literature. However, the literature deals with the context and elaborates on the specifics of individual emergencies and technical requirements to enable an effective use of drones in those situations. The coverage reflects domains dealing with the topic: CS and emergency management.

Table 2. MB showing dimensions and characteristics relevant to designing collaborations between humans and drones with adequate sources.

	Dimensions	Values							Example Sources
Context	Emergency event	fire	drowning	avalanche	nuclear	chemical	multiple	unspecific	[1, 3–5, 7, 8, 11–13, 20, 30, 31, 34, 39, 42, 55]
	Drones' main task	search & rescue		surveillance		delivery		communication	
	Intervention time	pre-event		during event		post-event		independent	
	Operation duration	short (< 1h)		middle (< 12h)		long (> 12h)		unspecified	[10, 31, 42]
	Operation location	indoor			outdoor			flexible	[4, 7, 30, 42]
Social	Operator's skillset	trained				untrained			[1, 4, 5, 8, 31]
Mutual interactions	Number of drones	single drone				multiple drones			[1, 2, 7, 13, 42]
	Interaction agents	humans and drones				a team of drones			[7, 8, 10, 12, 55]
	Communication direction (general)	human → drone		drone → human		drone → drone		omnidirectional	[17, 26]
	Communication with humans	unidirectional				bidirectional			[4, 8, 39, 55]
	Information transfer	collect information			provide information			exchange information	[1, 2, 11, 17, 26]
	Structure (humans:drones)	many:one		one:one		one:many		many:many	[1–3, 7, 8, 13, 31, 34, 55]
Technical component	Autonomy	semi-autonomous		fully autonomous			mixed mode		[2, 5, 13]
	Availability	off the shelf				specialized			[4, 30, 55]
	Flight range	short		middle		long		free	[3, 4, 10, 31]
	Payload	none		light		middle		heavy	[10, 12, 39]
	Battery runtime	short			middle			long	[3, 4, 30]
	Overall cost	low			medium			high	[3, 10, 13, 31, 34]
	Decision process	distributed				onboard decision system			[4, 7, 30, 31]

Overall, the MB provides insights into the focus of the existing literature. It points to research potentials. Additionally, it could be used for exploring the design space by generating new configurations of values and exploring their applicability. For instance, one could set on the case of an avalanche (as described in Sect. 2) and identify which configurations of human-drone collaboration were employed in this context or whether other possibilities might be more successful given previous evidence from other emergency events. This can inform design research projects in IS.

5 Discussion

The generated taxonomy and the proposed method have implications for DSR and IS. In the following, we, first, attend to the potentials of DSR for designing human-drone collaboration. Then, we discuss the proposed procedure as a transdisciplinary approach.

5.1 Design Science Research for Human-Drone Collaboration

Human-drone collaboration is a research area demanding attention because of the proliferation of the technology and the potential of drones in emergencies. Its specifics results from drones' physical abilities and limitations, which might be hard to imagine for humans, making the collaboration with drones harder than with other digital agents. The analysis shows that the nature and mechanics of human-drone collaboration have not been researched much. We see two ways to fill this gap.

First, IS should revisit its own and adjacent discourses on human-machine teaming [9, 40, 45, 53, 54] to examine the applicability of the generic guidance for collaboration involving drones. We claim that some design principles developed for, e.g., conversational agents concerning transparency or explainability, can be adapted to drones, whereas those on, e.g., verbal conduct might be omitted or abstracted [23, 53, 63].

An exciting line of research might reflect the need to support mutual sensemaking of each other between humans and drones [21, 24, 37, 49, 62]. Humans can only hardly put themselves in a drone's 'shoes', thus making coordination of activities harder. Also, the current generation of drones lacks an understanding of human behavior, probably following the assumption that encountering humans up in the air is unlikely (as opposed to streets where self-driving cars frequently interact with uninvolved individuals). Designing ways to bridge this divide might be specifically crucial for the use of drones.

Second, technical researchers and designers developing drones should pair up with HCI or IS experts to include social and organizational aspects of drones' application. It is necessary to go beyond the technical focus [6, 32, 38, 46, 56, 64] and investigate the social characteristics of the application domains. Accordingly, the conducted literature review offers only a partial answer to the research question (*What design dimensions describe the state-of-the-art collaboration between humans and drones in emergency situations?*); the social dimensions yet need to be specified in a creative step of the MASS procedure. We invite the community to apply the MB to classify real projects.

5.2 MASS in Design Science Research

The sociotechnical perspective forms the axis of IS research [19, 22, 36, 50]. DSR is a paradigm for engineering and exploring the application of technological artifacts in social and organizational contexts [29]. What emerges from DSR projects are sociotechnical systems designed to support humanistic and instrumental objectives. DSR has positioned literature review as a relevant source for definitions of problems and theoretical underpinnings of the solutions [29]. However, design space exploration has been frequently seen as subject to creative and abductive processes [25, 27]. Recent considerations on MA suggest its use for generating design principles, i.e., prescriptive design knowledge [41], or taxonomizing design research outputs [35, 43]. The original purpose of MA is to explore possible relationships in a complex system [48, 65, 66] and multidimensional space [15]. This potential of MA fades away in IS despite its potential for understanding the transdisciplinary nature of design endeavors.

This paper outlines a technique that combines MA [47] and the MB technique [66] with a systematic literature study [58]. This technique helps (1) get a systematic overview of research addressing a related problem, (2) identify design decisions they will have to make during development, (3) select the most promising design ideas for each dimension based on past research, (4) spot untouched or underestimated aspects which might be the ultimate gamechanger for the overall performance. The sociotechnical framing calls researchers' attention to all equally important components. The procedure helps approach the creative gap systematically across disciplinary lines.

6 Conclusion

This article attends to human-drone collaboration in emergencies according to the proposed MASS technique. It indicates the need to explore the social aspects of this collaboration and to explicate the objectives of applying drones in emergency situations. This insight offers new areas of multidisciplinary inquiry for design and IS researchers, e.g., about multimodal platforms or swarming risks. It also informs practitioners on what relevant aspects have been addressed in the literature for the development of real-world applications. Additionally, the described literature-supported procedure can be replicated to explore design space for solving other complex, sociotechnical problems studied across disciplines. The proposed MB can be strengthened by considering a broader literature basis and real-world, industry applications to avoid publication bias.

References

1. Agrawal, A., et al.: Model-driven requirements for humans-on-the-loop multi-uav missions. In: Proc. Model-Driven Requirements Engineering (MoDRE), pp. 1–10. IEEE (2020)
2. Agrawal, A., et al.: The next generation of human-drone partnerships: co-designing an emergency response system. In: Proc. ACM Conf. on Human Factors in Computing Systems, pp. 1–13. ACM, Honolulu HI USA (2020)
3. Albanese, A., et al.: SARDO: an automated search-and-rescue drone-based solution for victims localization. ArXiv Prepr. ArXiv200305819 (2020)
4. Alex, C., Vijaychandra, A.: Autonomous cloud based drone system for disaster response and mitigation. In: Proc. Intl. Conf. Robotics and Automation for Humanitarian Applications
5. Allen, R., Mazumder, M.: Toward an autonomous aerial survey and planning system for humanitarian aid and disaster response. In: Proc. Aerospace Conf., pp. 1–11. IEEE (2020)
6. Amin, R., et al.: A review of quadrotor UAV: control methodologies and performance evaluation. Int. J. Autom. Control. **10**(2), 87–103 (2016)
7. Apvrille, L., et al.: Autonomous drones for assisting rescue services within the context of natural disasters. In: Proc. URSI General Assembly and Sci. Symp., pp. 1–4. IEEE (2014)
8. Ardiansyah, M.F., et al.: EagleEYE: aerial edge-enabled disaster relief response system. In: Proc. European Conf. Networks and Communications (EuCNC), pp. 321–325. IEEE (2020)
9. Baird, A., Maruping, L.M.: The next generation of research on IS use: a theoretical framework of delegation to and from agentic IS artifacts. MIS Q. **45**(1), 315–341 (2021)
10. Ballous, K.A., et al.: Medical kit: emergency drone. In: Unmanned Systems Technology XXII, p. 114250V. International Society for Optics and Photonics (2020)
11. Baumgärtner, L., et al.: Emergency communication in challenged environments via unmanned ground and aerial vehicles. In: Proc. Global Humanitarian Tech. Conf. IEEE (2017)
12. Brunelli, D., et al.: DRAGoN: drone for radiation detection of gammas and neutrons. In: Proc. IEEE SENSORS Conf., pp. 1–4. IEEE (2020)
13. Busnel, Y., et al.: Self-organized disaster management system by distributed deployment of connected UAVs. In: Proc. Intl. Conf. ICT for Disaster Mgmt., pp. 1–8. IEEE (2019)
14. Campion, M., et al.: UAV swarm communication and control architectures: a review. J. Unmanned Veh. Syst. (2018)

15. Card, S.K., et al.: A morphological analysis of the design space of input devices. ACM Trans. Inf. Syst. **9**(2), 99–122 (1991)
16. Ciriello, R.F., Richter, A.: Scenario-based design theorizing. Bus. Inf. Syst. Eng. **61**(1), 31–50 (2018). https://doi.org/10.1007/s12599-018-0572-y
17. Cleland-Huang, J., et al.: Requirements-driven configuration of emergency response missions with small aerial vehicles. In: Proc. Conf. Systems and Software Product Line (2020)
18. Daponte, P., et al.: A review on the use of drones for precision agriculture. IOP Conf. Ser. Earth Environ. Sci. **275**(1), 012022 (2019)
19. Davison, R.M., Tarafdar, M.: Shifting baselines in information systems research threaten our future relevance. Inf. Syst. J. **28**(4), 587–591 (2018)
20. Dayananda, K.R., et al.: An interconnected architecture for an emergency medical response unmanned aerial system. In: Proc. Digital Avionics Syst. Conf., pp. 1–6. IEEE (2017)
21. Dennett, D.C.: The Intentional Stance. MIT press (1989)
22. Dolata, M., et al.: A sociotechnical view of algorithmic fairness. Inf. Syst. J. early view (2021)
23. Dolata, M., et al.: When a computer speaks institutional talk: exploring challenges and potentials of virtual assistants in face-to-face advisory services. In: Proc. Hawaii Intl. Conf. Syst. Sci. (2019)
24. Dolata, M., Schwabe, G.: Call for action: designing for harmony in creative teams. In: Tremblay, M.C., VanderMeer, D., Rothenberger, M., Gupta, A., Yoon, V. (eds.) DESRIST 2014. LNCS, vol. 8463, pp. 273–288. Springer, Cham (2014). https://doi.org/10.1007/978-3-319-06701-8_18
25. Dolata, M., Schwabe, G.: Design thinking in IS research projects. In: Brenner, W., Uebernickel, F. (eds.) Design Thinking for Innovation, pp. 67–83. Springer, Cham (2016). https://doi.org/10.1007/978-3-319-26100-3_5
26. Doran, H.D., et al.: Conceptual design of human-drone communication in collaborative environments. In: Proc. Intl. Conf. Dependable Syst. and Networks Workshops (DSN-W), pp. 118–121. IEEE (2020)
27. Fischer, C., Gregor, S.: Forms of reasoning in the design science research process. In: Jain, H., Sinha, A.P., Vitharana, P. (eds.) DESRIST 2011. LNCS, vol. 6629, pp. 17–31. Springer, Heidelberg (2011). https://doi.org/10.1007/978-3-642-20633-7_2
28. Garnica-Peña, R.J., Alcántara-Ayala, I.: The use of UAVs for landslide disaster risk research and disaster risk management: a literature review. J. Mt. Sci. **18**(2), 482–498 (2021). https://doi.org/10.1007/s11629-020-6467-7
29. Hevner, A.R., et al.: Design science in information systems research. MIS Q. **28**, 1 (2004)
30. Hummel, K.A., et al.: A distributed architecture for human-drone teaming: timing challenges and interaction opportunities. Sensors **19**(6), 1379 (2019)
31. Iob, P., et al.: Avalanche rescue with autonomous drones. In: Intl. Workshop on Metrology for AeroSpace, pp. 319–324. IEEE (2020)
32. Khan, M.A., et al.: UAV-based traffic analysis: a universal guiding framework based on literature survey. Transp. Res. Procedia. **22**, 541–550 (2017)
33. Krey, M.: Drones: application and business models in Swiss hospitals. In: Proc. Hawaii Intl. Conf. Syst. Sci. (2018)
34. Krishna, S.L., et al.: Autonomous human detection system mounted on a drone. In: Proc. Intl. Conf. Wireless Comm. Signal Processing and Networking, pp. 335–338. IEEE (2019)
35. Kundisch, D., et al.: An update for taxonomy designers. Bus. Inf. Syst. Eng. (2021)
36. Lee, A.S., et al.: Going back to basics in design science: from the information technology artifact to the information systems artifact. Inf. Syst. J. **25**(1), 5–21 (2015)
37. Leifer, L.J., Steinert, M.: Dancing with ambiguity: causality behavior, design thinking, and triple-loop-learning. In: Gassmann, O., Schweitzer, F. (eds.) Management of the Fuzzy Front End of Innovation, pp. 141–158. Springer (2014)

38. Lu, Y., et al.: A survey on vision-based UAV navigation. Geo-Spat. Inf. Sci. **21**, 1 (2018)
39. Marconi, L., et al.: The SHERPA project: smart collaboration between humans and ground-aerial robots for improving rescuing activities in alpine environments. In: Proc. Intl. Symposium on Safety, Security, and Rescure Robotics, pp. 1–4. IEEE (2012)
40. McNeese, N.J., et al.: Teaming With a synthetic teammate: insights into human-autonomy teaming. Hum. Factors J. Hum. Factors Ergon. Soc. **60**(2), 262–273 (2018)
41. Möller, F., et al.: Design of goal-oriented artifacts from morphological taxonomies: progression from descriptive to prescriptive design knowledge. In: Proc. Intl. Conf. Wirtschaftsinformatik (2021)
42. Narang, M., et al.: A cyber physical buses-and-drones mobile edge infrastructure for large scale disaster emergency communications. In: Proc. Intl. Conf. Distributed Computing Systems Workshops, pp. 53–60. IEEE (2017)
43. Nickerson, R.C., et al.: A method for taxonomy development and its application in information systems. Eur. J. Inf. Syst. **22**(3), 336–359 (2013)
44. Oliveira, L., et al.: To token or not to token: tools for understanding blockchain tokens. In: Proc. Intl. Conf. Information Systems (2018)
45. O'Neill, T., et al.: Human–autonomy teaming: a review and analysis of the empirical literature. Hum. Factors J. Hum. Factors Ergon. Soc. 001872082096086 (2020)
46. Pulsiri, N., Vatananan-Thesenvitz, R.: Drones in emergency medical services: a systematic literature review with bibliometric analysis. Int. J. Innov. Technol. Manag. **18**(4), 2097001 (2021)
47. Ritchey, T.: General morphological analysis. In: Proc. Conf. Operational Analysis (1998)
48. Ritchey, T.: Modelling complex socio-technical systems using morphological analysis. Adapt. Address Swed. Parliam. IT Comm. Stockh. (2002)
49. Rozendaal, M.C., et al.: Objects with intent: designing everyday things as collaborative partners. ACM Trans. Comput.-Hum. Interact. **26**(4), 26:1–26:33 (2019)
50. Sarker, S., et al.: The sociotechnical axis of cohesion for the IS discipline: its historical legacy and its continued relevance. MIS Q. **43**(3), 695–719 (2019)
51. Schaarschmidt, M., et al.: Last mile drone delivery services: adoption barriers before and during the COVID-19 pandemic. In: Proc. Intl. Conf. Information Systems. (2021)
52. Scott, J., Scott, C.: Drone delivery models for healthcare. In: Proc. Hawaii Intl. Conf. Syst. Sci. (2017)
53. Seeber, I., et al.: Collaborating with technology-based autonomous agents: issues and research opportunities. Internet Res. **30**(1), 1–18 (2020)
54. Seeber, I., et al.: Machines as teammates: a research agenda on AI in team collaboration. Inf. Manage. **57**(2), 103174 (2020)
55. Shaikhanov, Z., et al.: Autonomous drone networks for sensing, localizing and approaching RF targets. In: Proc. Vehicular Networking Conf., pp. 1–8. IEEE (2020)
56. Stampa, M., Sutorma, A., Jahn, U., Thiem, J., Wolff, C., Röhrig, C.: Maturity levels of public safety applications using unmanned aerial systems: a review. J. Intell. Rob. Syst. **103**(1), 1–16 (2021). https://doi.org/10.1007/s10846-021-01462-7
57. Stöcker, C., et al.: Review of the current state of UAV regulations. Remote Sens. **9**(5), 459 (2017)
58. Templier, M., Paré, G.: Transparency in literature reviews: an assessment of reporting practices across review types and genres in top IS journals. Eur. J. Inf. Syst. **27**, 5 (2018)
59. Thangavelu, S., et al.: Commercial drones: peeping tom or precision operator? a governance, risk and compliance framework for a secure drone eco-system. In: Proc. Americas Conf. Information Systems (2020)
60. Um, J.-S.: Drones as Cyber-Physical Systems: Concepts and Applications for the Fourth Industrial Revolution. Springer, Singapore (2019)

61. Weick, K.E.: The collapse of sensemaking in organizations: the Mann Gulch disaster. Adm. Sci. Q. **38**(4), 628–652 (1993)
62. Weick, K.E., Sutcliffe, K.M.: Managing the Unexpected: Sustained Performance in a Complex World. John Wiley & Sons Inc, Hoboken, New Jersey (2015)
63. Wellnhammer, N., et al.: Studying with the help of digital tutors: design aspects of conv. agents that influence the learning process. In: Proc. Hawaii Intl. Conf. Syst. Sci. (2020)
64. Yang, L., et al.: A literature review of UAV 3D path planning. In: Proceeding of the 11th World Congress on Intelligent Control and Automation, pp. 2376–2381 (2014)
65. Zwicky, F.: Discovery, Invention, Research Through the Morphological Approach. Macmillan, New York (1969)
66. Zwicky, F.: The morphological approach to discovery, invention, research and construction. In: Zwicky, F., Wilson, A.G. (eds.) New Methods of Thought and Procedure, pp. 273–297. Springer, Berlin, Heidelberg (1967)

A Personalized Conversational Agent to Treat Depression in Youth and Young Adults – A Transdisciplinary Design Science Research Project

Florian Onur Kuhlmeier[1,2]([⊠]), Ulrich Gnewuch[2], Stefan Lüttke[1], Eva-Lotta Brakemeier[1], and Alexander Mädche[2]

[1] Department of Psychology, University of Greifswald, Greifswald, Germany
{stefan.luettke,eva-lotta.brakemeier}@uni-greifswald.de

[2] Institute of Information Systems and Marketing, Karlsruhe Institute of Technology, Karlsruhe, Germany

{florian.kuhlmeier,ulrich.gnewuch,alexander.maedche}@kit.edu

Abstract. Depression is a large-scale and consequential problem in youth and young adults. Conversational agents (CAs) can contribute to addressing current barriers to seeking treatment, such as long waiting lists, and reduce the high dropout rates reported for other digital health interventions. However, existing CAs have not considered differences between youth and adults and are primarily designed based on a 'one-size-fits-all' approach that neglects individual symptoms and preferences. Therefore, we propose a theory-driven design for personalized CAs to treat depression in youth and young adults. Based on interviews with patients (i.e., people diagnosed with depression), we derive two design principles to personalize the character of the CA and its therapeutic content. These principles are instantiated in prototypes and evaluated in interviews with experts experienced in delivering psychotherapy and potential nondiagnosed users. Personalization was perceived as crucial for treatment success, and autonomy and transparency emerged as important themes for personalization. We contribute by providing design principles for personalized CAs for mental health that extend previous CA research in the context of mental health.

Keywords: Conversational agent · Mental health · Personalization · Transdisciplinary research

1 Introduction

Depression is one of the most common mental disorders in adolescence and early adulthood. Approximately 5.6% of young people worldwide are affected by depression [1]. The individual and social consequences are enormous. Affected individuals are more likely to exhibit physical impairment and substance abuse, have poorer academic results, and have an elevated risk of suicide [2–4]. Furthermore, depression causes high health

A. Drechsler et al. (Eds.): DESRIST 2022, LNCS 13229, pp. 30–41, 2022.
https://doi.org/10.1007/978-3-031-06516-3_3

economic costs [3]. Psychotherapy, delivered by human therapists, is an effective treatment and often the first choice to mitigate the individual and social consequences associated with depression [5, 6]. However, treatment resources are scarce: On average, people seeking help have to wait almost five months to start psychotherapy treatment [7]. In addition, young people experience two additional barriers when seeking treatment: First, they are significantly less likely to use professional support [8] due to feelings of shame, insecurity, and a greater desire to solve problems themselves [8]. Second, weekly in-person sessions with an adult therapist may not match the technology-driven lifestyle of youth and young adults. Although digital health interventions (DHI) are available and effective, studies have shown high dropout rates [5, 9]. Using a conversational agent (CA) may have great potential to tackle this problem. CAs are software systems that mimic human conversational behavior [10]. In contrast to other DHI, CAs can not only realize (1) the specific effects of therapy [11] by delivering therapeutic content, such as providing information on depression and working through exercises but also (2) the common factors of therapy [11], such as the alliance between patient and therapist, because CAs offer an interactive, conversational format that mimics human-delivered therapy [12–14]. By adding the realization of common factors, CAs seem thus promising to increase engagement and reduce dropout rates to match human-delivered therapy and ultimately improve treatment success. CAs in the context of mental health, such as the highly cited [13, 14] and successful commercial apps Woebot (woebothealth.com) and Wysa (wysa.io), provide self-guided therapy based on the principles of cognitive behavioral therapy (CBT), interpersonal therapy (IPT), or dialectical therapy and have shown promising effectiveness in reducing symptoms of depression [13, 14]. Moreover, users of mental health CAs report experiencing relationship building [15] and feelings of social support [16], which supports the argument that mental health CAs can also realize common factors of therapy and may thus be better suited than other DHI to treat mental health problems. Although preliminary evidence shows promising potential for CAs to reduce depressive symptoms, there are several limitations. First, the majority were tested in pilot studies with a focus on adults. However, youth differ from adults in terms of cognitive and emotional development, social relationships, and problem behavior [17]. In addition, neither the development nor the evaluation included participants diagnosed with clinical depression. Thus, the development and evaluation of CAs for youth (13–17 years) and young adults (18–25 years) must consider these aspects. Second, existing CAs are designed primarily based on a 'one-size-fits-all' approach that neglects individual symptoms and preferences [18]. This is particularly important for youth and young adults because they are used to personalizing the content and appearance of digital applications according to their own needs and preferences. Therefore, it is necessary to consider how CAs can be designed in a way that allows for personalization.

Against this backdrop, our research focuses on the question of how to design a personalized CA to treat depression in youth and young adults. To address this research question, we are conducting a comprehensive transdisciplinary design science research (DSR) project [19, 20]. In the first cycle, we first conducted interviews with youth suffering from depression to gain an in-depth understanding of the problem, their needs, and preferences. Based on the interviews, CBT and IPT, and theories of personalization [18, 21], we derived two initial design principles (DPs) for personalized CAs to treat depression. Next, we instantiated these two initial design principles in four prototypes, which were evaluated in interviews with five experts and five potential users. Our results suggest that personalizing character and content is crucial to designing effective CAs to treat depression. In addition, transparency and agency are the most important aspects to consider when implementing personalization.

2   Related Work

2.1   Conversational Agents for Mental Health

The use of CAs to provide self-help psychotherapy interventions has been explored in several studies [22]. For example, a 2-week use of Woebot, a CA developed based on the theoretical foundations of CBT to work on depression-typical, dysfunctional thoughts or behaviors of depression, significantly reduced symptoms of depression [13]. Symptom reduction was also shown after using Wysa [14]. Recent reviews of mental health CAs reported high user satisfaction, sufficient effectiveness, and safety to conduct research with clinical populations [22]. In summary, CAs seem more suitable than other DHI, as users have reported experiencing social support [16] and a stronger working alliance [15].

2.2   Personalization

In the context of information technology, personalization has been defined as a 'process that changes the functionality, interface, information access, and content, or distinctiveness of a system to increase its relevance to an individual or a category of individuals [12, p. 183]. Users appreciate personalization features because they can improve ease of use, efficiency, and provide users with a feeling of being in control [23]. Our work draws on the frameworks of personalization approaches of Fan and Poole [21] and Kocaballi et al. [18]. Depending on the specific field of research and discipline, personalization is often used synonymously with adaptation, customization, and tailoring [21]. We decided to use the term personalization because it is commonly used in the medical and health literature [17]. Fan and Poole [21] conceptualize personalization along three dimensions: (1) what is personalized, i.e. the elements of the system that are being changed, (2) for whom is the personalization, i.e., the target: individual vs. group, and (3) who is in control of personalization, i.e. the user or the system. Within dimension (3), the authors differentiate between implicit (i.e., executed by the system) and explicit personalization (i.e., executed by the user), Kocaballi et al. [18] extended Fan and Poole's framework with (4) the purpose of personalization. Table 1 below illustrates the dimensions of personalization that serve as the basis for our proposed design.

In their review of personalization features in health CAs, Kocaballi et al. [18] pointed out that several CAs implemented personalization, such as tailoring content or interaction styles to individuals. However, they also identified a lack of investigating personalization within a theoretically grounded and evidence-based framework [18]. In our work, we mainly focus on the dimensions of purpose, elements, and agency.

Table 1. Dimensions of personalization (based on [18, 21])

Dimension	Question	Values (examples)
Purpose	What is the purpose of personalization?	Increased user motivation
Elements	What is personalized?	Content Functionality
Target	To whom is personalized?	Single-User vs. Group of Users
Agency	Who is in control of personalization?	System: implicit/adaptive User: explicit/adaptable Mixed initiative

3 Methodology

Our research project follows DSR approach [19] to solve an important real-world problem and design a personalized conversational agent to treat depression in youth and young adults. We chose this research approach because it allows iterative design [19, 25] and the participation of users and experts in the design and evaluation phases [19]. We conduct a transdisciplinary project due to (1) the focus on a complex problem, (2) the inclusion of an interdisciplinary team consisting of researchers from information systems, clinical psychology, and psychotherapists, and (3) involving societal actors (i.e., patients) as process participants [20]. A transdisciplinary approach is particularly important given that poorly designed mental health interventions can have fatal consequences. The DSR project is based on the well-established approach suggested by Kuechler and Vaishnavi [25] and divided into three design cycles to incrementally improve the functionality and impact of our artifact. In this paper, we report the results of the first design cycle, which focused on understanding the problem space (i.e., treating depression in youth and young adults using CAs) and exploring personalization to improve treatment success (Table 2).

Table 2. Overview of our DSR approach

DSR Project Phases	1. Design Cycle	2. Design Cycle	3. Design Cycle
Awareness of Problem	Interviews with patients	Analysis of Initial Evaluation	Analysis of prior evaluations
Suggestion	Formulation of the initial design principles	Refinement of DPs	Refinement of DPs
Development	Implementation of first prototype	Implementation of a fully functional prototype	Implementation of final software artifact
Evaluation	Interviews with experts and potential users (N=10)	Online experiment with potential users.	Field experiment with patients
Conclusion	Reflection of initial design and evaluation results	Reflection of fully functional prototype and evaluation results	Formulation of nascent design theory

In the problem awareness phase, we reviewed the literature on mental health CAs in clinical psychology and conducted interviews with 15 youth diagnosed with depression, which we analyzed by first creating a coding scheme and then deriving higher-order themes. In the suggestion phase, we drew upon frameworks of personalization approaches [18, 21] as well as CBT and IPT to propose two design principles on how to personalize mental health CAs for the treatment of depression. Subsequently, we instantiated design principles in four different prototypes of text-based mental health CAs (i.e., chatbots) developed with Figma (figma.com) and Botsociety (botsociety.io). These prototypes were evaluated in interviews with five experts, experienced in clinical psychology and psychotherapy, and five potential users. For the evaluation, we selected the technical risk and efficacy strategy [26] due to the sensitive context of depression: We decided to first evaluate the proposed DPs with a group of experts and potential users to get feedback and improve our design before evaluating a fully functional prototype in a more naturalistic setting.

As shown in Table 1, we plan two more design cycles. We will first use the open-source conversational AI framework Rasa to develop a fully functional prototype. Subsequently, we will refine the DPs and improve the prototype based on studies in an online and naturalistic setting.

4   Design Science Research Project

4.1   Problem Awareness

To improve our understanding of the problem space, we first conducted interviews with youth diagnosed with depression. We recruited 15 participants between 14 and 17 years of age, all female, through local clinical psychologists and psychiatrists. The previous experience of the participants with psychotherapy varied. In line with the literature [7], all participants previously struggled to find professional treatment due to long waiting lists. Some participants were frustrated by the lack of interventions to bridge the waiting time. One participant stated: *'[I] signed up for this study, because there were no other forms of treatment when I was on a waiting list. So, [I] wanted to help creating one'*. Another participant expressed her dissatisfaction with a self-help book she had tried. Adding to the literature [8], multiple participants reported feelings of insecurity, stigma, and the desire to solve their problems on their own as barriers to seeking treatment. The participants also identified several advantages of CAs compared to face-to-face psychotherapy. For example, participants mentioned that CAs would be neutral, non-judgmental, and anonymous, which facilitates sharing sensitive information. In addition, they appreciated that they could rely on CAs being continuously available and not limited to a single therapy session per week. In summary, there is evidence that CAs can address some of the issues raised in the introduction, particularly bridging waiting times.

Regarding the design, the participants expressed a wide variety of needs and preferences, revealing the importance of personalization. Some participants desired CAs to be like a friend, that uses similar language. Yet, others wanted the CA to resemble a human therapist due to the distant, professional relationship, which facilitates conversations about sensitive topics. Another frequently mentioned topic was the usage of emojis. While some participants wanted the mental health CA to include emojis (and gifs) in its

messages, others stated that this would look unprofessional and counteract the serious-
ness of depression. While some preferred to access the CA through instant messaging
apps such as WhatsApp, others suggested a standalone app. For a standalone app, the
design preferences ranged from a very colorful appearance to a 'professional' black-
grey-white appearance, which was associated with professionalism. Yet, current mental
health CAs do not accommodate the wide-ranging needs and preferences mentioned by
our participants [18]. In addition, our participants explicitly requested personalization
features regarding the character and the content: '*I would like to choose a name, change
the avatar and select the topics I want to work on*'. One participant wanted the CA to automatically adapt to her therapeutic needs and language style. Taken together, our findings
suggest that a 'one-size-fits-all' approach to designing CAs to treat depression may not
be able to reach its full potential. Although our interviews revealed potential advantages
of CAs compared to human therapists and other interventions, they also emphasized the
crucial role of personalization to improve the user experience and subsequently improve
therapy outcomes.

4.2 Suggestion

From the interviews, we obtained substantial evidence for the importance of personalization. However, personalization is complex due to its elusive and multifaceted nature and
the variety of definitions assigned to it by scholars from different fields (e.g., information systems, health, computer science). To guide our design, we, therefore, drew upon
established frameworks of personalization [18, 21] that were introduced in Sect. 2.1.
According to these frameworks, the fundamental dimension of personalization is the
element of personalization (i.e. what is being personalized). In the context of CAs, these
elements primarily include the CA's character (i.e., gender, age, social role etc.) and
the content (i.e., the content of the messages, knowledge base, etc.) [27]. In the interviews, 8 out of 15 participants expressed the desire to personalize the name, gender, and
social role of a CA, suggesting that personalizing the character should represent a major
design principle (DP). Therefore, we propose DP1: *To improve treatment outcomes for
depressed youth and young adults, provide the conversational agent with the capability
to personalize its character to match user needs and preferences because a personalized character helps users to form a stronger relationship with the CA*. The second key
element of personalization is the CA's (therapeutic) content. According to the health
literature, personalized content improves the use [28] and the perceived helpfulness of
DHI [29]. Thus, we propose DP2: *To improve treatment outcomes for depressed youth
and young adults, provide the conversational agent with the capability to personalize
the therapeutic content to match user needs and preferences because personalized content increases the relevance and efficiency of the CA*. As introduced above, the second
dimension of personalization is agency (i.e., who controls the personalization). As our
participants expressed their interest in both adaptable CAs, in which they are in control
of personalization, and adaptive CAs, in which CAs control personalization, we integrate
adaptable, adaptive, and mixed-initiative personalization into our DPs. By instantiating
prototypes that demonstrate all these approaches, we aimed to evaluate and prioritize
these approaches and then refine the DPs accordingly.

4.3 Development

To instantiate our initial DPs, we developed four prototypes. As the participants' preferences varied substantially, we aimed to explore different elements and degrees of agency of personalization in our prototypes. Based on the evaluation results, we aim to find the most important features and refine the DPs accordingly. The first two prototypes instantiated the personalization of the CA's character (DP1). The first prototype provided the user with the opportunity to personalize the name, gender, typing speed, avatar, and social role. These characteristics were selected based on our findings from the interviews with patients. The second prototype showcased the possibility for the CA to automatically adapt to the users' use of emojis, since the use of emojis emerged as a polarizing element during the interviews (Fig. 1).

Fig. 1. DP1 – Personalization of character: prototypes 1 (left) and 2 (center and right).

The other two prototypes instantiated the personalization of the content (DP2). In CBT and IPT, content comes in the form of modules (e.g., behavioral activation, sleep hygiene). We instantiated two prototypes that reflect the personalization of these modules in different ways. Prototype three contained the task to respond to items from a depression scale and the relevant modules were selected based on their responses. For instance, the module on sleep improvement is only integrated if a user reports sleep problems. Prototype four instantiated a more flexible version of the second design principle. Here, instead of personalizing the content once in the beginning, a matching module is suggested when users report specific issues on a particular day. For example, CADY suggests the module sleep hygiene if users report sleep problems during daily check-in (Fig. 2).

Fig. 2. DP2 – Personalization of content: prototypes 3 (left) and 4 (center and right).

4.4 Evaluation

To evaluate our prototypes, we conducted interviews with five independent experts with experience in delivering psychotherapy (3 female, $M_{age} = 29$) and five potential users (3 female, $M_{age} = 24$). By including experts, our objective was to understand whether our proposed design is consistent with established principles of psychotherapy. We decided to recruit non-diagnosed individuals as potential users to first ensure the safety of the prototypes before including young people diagnosed with depression. In each interview, we first explained the concept of CAs and introduced our research project. Subsequently, we explained the DPs and demonstrated their instantiations. During the presentation and afterwards, participants were asked to evaluate the prototypes and to provide ideas for further personalization. The interviews lasted 40 min on average. All interviews were recorded and transcribed. To analyze the feedback from the participants, we used a bottom-up approach to synthesize the interviews into higher-order themes.

5   Results and Discussion

All participants appreciated the personalization of the CA to suit their own needs and preferences (or those of their clients), providing evidence of the utility of both DPs. Moreover, all participants emphasized personalization as a crucial feature for the success of mental health CAs. In terms of DP1 and prototype 1, every participant supported the idea of personalizing the agent's name, gender, and avatar as a mechanism for relationship building. Especially gender was identified as an important characteristic for users to feel safe and comfortable in case they've had negative experiences regarding one gender in the past. Using a robot or an animal avatar was suggested as an additional gender-neutral and nonhuman version to satisfy users who prefer to talk with a robot instead of a human. The participants also suggested adding age as a variable to choose from. Instead of personalizing each aspect separately, multiple participants suggested combining variations of gender, avatar, age, and social role into 3–4 different characters, from which users can choose. They argued that presenting a few characters instead of each characteristic separately would decrease the variables to choose from, which could otherwise be overwhelming and result in annoyance or dropout. In addition, participants suggested comprehensive information (e.g., brief introductory videos) about each character, so users can imagine what interacting with them would feel like. In terms of the specific social role, participants expressed interest in a non-human, agender robot, an older therapist-like role and a younger coach-like role. Most experts advised against implementing a friend-like role (like in prototype 1) as they feared that the lack of a professional relationship could endanger the therapeutic process. Therefore, they suggested that one should be able to choose between professional roles that encompass different personality traits: *'For example, I would suggest that social roles differ between warm, understanding, empathic versus rather cool, rational, direct.'* Regarding prototype 2, experts and users generally valued the idea of providing the CA with the agency to adapt to their use of emojis and language more generally, as experts explained that adapting to the clients' language resembles therapist-client relationship building in the context of psychotherapy. In addition, potential users indicated that they regularly adapt the emoji and language use to their friends and that this could improve the human-chatbot relationship. However, some participants were concerned with implementing the feature before it had reached sufficient accuracy. They stated that an insufficient automated adaptation would be worse than a non-adaptive system. Participants also requested the feature to turn off the automated adaption and information on how the CA adapts to them. Instead of automatically regulating emoji and language usage, one participant suggested integrating different language styles and emoji use into the different characters to give users control and counter potential technical limitations.

In terms of DP2, experts and potential users perceived the personalization of the therapeutic content, i.e. the purpose of the personalization, to be crucial for the success of a CA to treat depression and more important than DP1. Regarding prototype 3, experts and potential users liked the idea of personalizing content at the beginning based on responses to a depression scale: *'I think it is important that the agent asks about the symptoms of depression. And it's also important that it's highly structured because most of the time it's very, very difficult for my clients to verbalize their issues'*. One expert suggested an extension of prototype 3: *'In addition to the depression scale, it should be possible for a user to openly state the most pressing issue. If users feel that the agent listens and prioritizes this issue, it will increase their motivation, which is crucial for the treatment success.'*

When evaluating prototypes 3 and 4, a trade-off between flexible personalization and a structured plan emerged. On the one hand, experts and potential users emphasized the need for autonomy, i.e., the ability to flexibly choose or change a module instead of a fixed schedule, and its potential to increase motivation and engagement. On the other hand, experts emphasized the importance of a plan with compulsory modules and a fixed sequence. The fixed sequence was deemed important because some modules can be tiring and difficult but play a crucial role in achieving treatment success and therefore need to be completed. Experts mentioned that a structured plan also provides users with certainty and transparency, which makes CAs more reliable and the treatment goals more visible. However, an inflexible plan, which does not sufficiently integrate individual needs and preferences, could reduce motivation, user engagement, and thus lead to dropout. Consequently, the challenge is a compromise between personalizing therapeutic content flexibly and maintaining a structured program, which one expert summarized: '*Some content should be fixed, but users should still feel that they can decide for themselves. But not only depending on the momentary mood. If users only choose based on the momentary mood, then there will probably not be much change. You will have to build some feature that makes sure users are also doing the exercises and consume the information no matter what their mood is like.*' A possible solution emerged from combining prototypes 3 and 4: Experts suggested keeping the personalization of the therapy modules in the beginning based on psychometric data and presenting these results as a personalized structured program while being able to deviate when a specific issue (like sleep problems or low energy) arises. However, when deviating, it should be explicitly framed as a deviation from the personalized structured treatment plan. In prototype 4, the CA suggested a module because it recognized sleep problems in the users' text messages during daily check-in. Although participants appreciated that the CA was able to handle an acute problem, experts reiterated that young people often cannot verbally express their problems. Therefore, one expert suggested personalizing the daily check-in: '*Maybe it is helpful to ask 'how are you today' in different ways because there are people who just never know an answer to this question. You could work with something like a thermometer or emojis. So, the agent could first ask 'I would like to know how you are doing, in what way do you want to tell me today?'* and then the user can select a thermometer, choose an emotion from a list, or select to write a text message.'

Based on feedback from our participants, we identified several opportunities to improve the prototypes. While both DPs received positive feedback, the feedback also revealed that the automatic personalization of the character may be less promising than initially expected. Combining this feedback with the technical challenges of making the CA's character adaptive, we have decided to no longer pursue automatic adaptation. Regarding DP1, we will focus on user-controlled personalization of the mental health CA's character and regarding DP2, we will implement explicit personalization and mixed-initiative. This refinement and the suggested improvements for the prototypes serve as the entry point into the second cycle. In general, participants discussed two themes the most: (1) autonomy, i.e., giving user control over personalization features, and (2) transparency, i.e., being transparent about what is being personalized and how it is done.

6 Conclusion

This paper presents insights from our ongoing transdisciplinary DSR project to design a personalized CA to treat depression in youth. Based on interviews with our target group, we corroborated the need to integrate personalization features into the design process. We proposed two DPs to guide the design of a personalized CA and instantiated the DPs in four prototypes. We evaluated the prototypes in interviews with experts and potential users. Overall, the feedback was positive, and the importance of personalization was confirmed. However, participants also expressed concerns about automated personalization performed by a CA since they were sceptical of the technical feasibility and emphasized the loss of control. In general, autonomy and transparency emerged as important themes guiding the design of personalization efforts. Finally, our participants gave valuable feedback for (1) refining and extending the proposed personalization features and (2) suggesting additional personalization features (e.g. personalized reminders), which we will incorporate into our next DSR cycle. In summary, our results show that personalized mental health CAs are a promising approach to accommodate users' symptoms and preferences. However, to comprehensively evaluate the impact of personalization, more research is needed that compares CAs with and without personalization features. Although our research follows established guidelines for conducting DSR [19, 25], we need to highlight some limitations. First, the samples for the problem awareness and the evaluation interviews were relatively small. In addition, the evaluation interviews included only nondiagnosed individuals. Consequently, for the results to be more comprehensive and generalizable, larger sample sizes are necessary. Second, we used an interactive prototype and brief prototype videos to demonstrate our proposed design. Although we argue that this approach is appropriate for a first DSR cycle, further research based on a fully functional prototype is crucial. Therefore, in our second DSR cycle, we will implement the most important personalization features in a fully functional prototype. Evaluating our DPs again in the second DSR cycle will also contribute to further refining and validating our DPs, which is a crucial next step. With our research presented in this article, we contribute valuable design knowledge that serves as a starting point for future research on the design of personalized mental health CAs.

References

1. Jane Costello, E., Erkanli, A., Angold, A.: Is there an epidemic of child or adolescent depression? J. Child Psychol. Psychiatry 47, 1263–1271 (2006)
2. Ellsäßer, G.: Unfälle, Gewalt, Selbstverletzung bei Kindern und Jugendlichen 2017. Ergebnisse der amtlichen Statistik zum Verletzungsgeschehen 2014. Fachbericht. (2017)
3. Greiner, W., Batram, M., Witte, J.: Kinder- und Jugendreport 2019. Gesundheitsversorgung von Kindern und Jugendlichen in Deutschland. Schwerpunkt: Ängste und Depressionen bei Schulkindern, in Beiträge zur Gesundheitsökonomie und Versorgungsforschung. Bielefeld und Hamburg (2019)
4. Thapar, A., Collishaw, S., Pine, D.S., Thapar, A.K.: Depression in adolescence. Lancet 379, 1056–1067 (2012)
5. Oud, M., et al.: Effectiveness of CBT for children and adolescents with depression: a systematic review and meta-regression analysis. Eur. Psychiatry J. Assoc. Eur. Psychiatr. 57, 33–45 (2019)
6. Cuijpers, P., Noma, H., Karyotaki, E., Vinkers, C.H., Cipriani, A., Furukawa, T.A.: A network meta-analysis of the effects of psychotherapies, pharmacotherapies and their combination in the treatment of adult depression. World Psychiatry 19, 92–107 (2020)
7. Bundespsychotherapeutenkammer: Ein Jahr nach der Reform der Psychotherapie-Richtlinie (2018)
8. Gulliver, A., Griffiths, K.M., Christensen, H.: Perceived barriers and facilitators to mental health help-seeking in young people: a systematic review. BMC Psychiatry 10, 113 (2010)
9. Leech, T., Dorstyn, D., Taylor, A., Li, W.: Mental health apps for adolescents and young adults: a systematic review of randomised controlled trials. Child. Youth Serv. Rev. 127, 106073 (2021)
10. Dale, R.: The return of the chatbots. Nat. Lang. Eng. 22, 811–817 (2016)

11. Cuijpers, P., Reijnders, M., Huibers, M.J.H.: The role of common factors in psychotherapy outcomes. Annu. Rev. Clin. Psychol. **15**, 207–231 (2019)
12. Ahmad, R., Siemon, D., Gnewuch, U., Robra-Bissantz, S.: Designing personality-adaptive conversational agents for mental health care. Inf. Syst. Front. (2022)
13. Fitzpatrick, K.K., Darcy, A., Vierhile, M.: Delivering cognitive behavior therapy to young adults with symptoms of depression and anxiety using a fully automated conversational agent (Woebot): a randomized controlled trial. JMIR Ment. Health. **4**, e19 (2017)
14. Inkster, B., Sarda, S., Subramanian, V.: An empathy-driven, conversational artificial intelligence agent (Wysa) for digital mental well-being: real-world data evaluation mixed-methods study. JMIR MHealth UHealth. **6**, e12106 (2018)
15. Darcy, A., Daniels, J., Salinger, D., Wicks, P., Robinson, A.: Evidence of human-level bonds established with a digital conversational agent: cross-sectional retrospective observational study. JMIR Form. Res. **5**, e27868 (2021)
16. Brandtzaeg, P., Skjuve, M., Dysthe, K., Følstad, A.: When the social becomes non-human: young people's perception of social support in chatbots social support in chatbots. Presented at the April 3 (2021)
17. Lohaus, A. ed: Entwicklungspsychologie des Jugendalters. Springer-Verlag, Berlin Heidelberg (2018)
18. Kocaballi, A.B., et al.: The personalization of conversational agents in health care: systematic review. J. Med. Internet Res. **21**, e15360 (2019)
19. Bichler, M.: Design science in information systems research. Wirtschaftsinformatik **48**(2), 133–135 (2006). https://doi.org/10.1007/s11576-006-0028-8
20. Lawrence, M.G., Williams, S., Nanz, P., Renn, O.: Characteristics, potentials, and challenges of transdisciplinary research. One Earth. **5**, 44–61 (2022)
21. Fan, H., Poole, M.S.: What is personalization? Perspectives on the design and implementation of personalization in information systems. J. Organ. Comput. Electron. Commer. **16**, 179–202 (2006)
22. Vaidyam, A.N., Linggonegoro, D., Torous, J.: Changes to the psychiatric chatbot landscape: a systematic review of conversational agents in serious mental illness: Changements du paysage psychiatrique des chatbots: une revue systématique des agents conversationnels dans la maladie mentale sérieuse. Can. J. Psychiatry. 0706743720966429 (2020)
23. Blom, J.o, Monk, A.F.: Theory of personalization of appearance: why users personalize their PCs and mobile phones. human–computer interact. 18, 193–228 (2003)
24. Huibers, M.J.H., Lorenzo-Luaces, L., Cuijpers, P., Kazantzis, N.: On the road to personalized psychotherapy: a research agenda based on cognitive behavior therapy for depression. Front. Psychiatry. 11 (2021)
25. Kuechler, B., Vaishnavi, V.: On theory development in design science research: anatomy of a research project. Eur. J. Inf. Syst. **17**, 489–504 (2008)
26. Venable, J., Pries-Heje, J., Baskerville, R.: FEDS: a framework for evaluation in design science research. Eur. J. Inf. Syst. **25**, 77–89 (2016)
27. Diederich, S., Brendel, A., Morana, S., Kolbe, L.: On the design of and interaction with conversational agents: an organizing and assessing review of human-computer interaction research. J. Assoc. Inf. Syst. **23**, 96–138 (2022)
28. Radomski, A.D., et al.: Design and delivery features that may improve the use of internet-based cognitive behavioral therapy for children and adolescents with anxiety: a realist literature synthesis with a persuasive systems design perspective. J. Med. Internet Res. **21**, e11128 (2019)
29. Garrido, S., et al.: Young people's response to six smartphone apps for anxiety and depression: focus group study. JMIR Ment. Health. **6**, e14385 (2019)

Design Principles for Boundary Spanning in Transdisciplinary Design Science Research

Frederik Möller[1,2(✉)], Leona Chandra Kruse[3], Thorsten Schoormann[4], and Boris Otto[1,2]

[1] TU Dortmund University, Dortmund, Germany
{Frederik.Moeller,Boris.Otto}@tu-dortmund.de
[2] Fraunhofer ISST, Dortmund, Germany
[3] University of Liechtenstein, Vaduz, Liechtenstein
Leona.ChandraKruse@uni.li
[4] University of Hildesheim, Hildesheim, Germany
thorsten.schoormann@uni-hildesheim.de

Abstract. Design principles capture prescriptive design knowledge to guide design science researchers and design professionals in their design works. In the context of a transdisciplinary team, design principles can also be a powerful vehicle to bridge knowledge barriers and facilitate collaboration among team members with different backgrounds and expertise. These heterogeneous actors use design principles as a boundary object which helps to mediate their diverse perspectives. The paper draws from boundary object theory to explore the goals and the mechanisms of boundary spanning through 'design principles-in-use' and 'design principles-in-formulation'. We discuss the applicability of our findings using a case of formulation and application of design principles for data spaces in a transdisciplinary research consortium. Our results add the layers of transdisciplinary collaboration to the ongoing discourse on design principles and design knowledge accumulation and evolution.

Keywords: Design principles · Boundary objects · Transdisciplinary DSR

1 Introduction

Since the importance of transdisciplinary research has gained momentum, numerous projects face the key challenge of integrating knowledge and experiences from diverse actors across disciplinary boundaries [1]. Consider, for example, the case of designing international data spaces that aim at creating sovereign digital environments for data exchanges. While the design of such spaces knowledge from different domains, such as Computer Science, Law, Ethics, and Business Administration, needs to be integrated, the actual space deployment demands coordinating diverse actors from academics to policymakers (e.g., [2, 3]). To overcome those hurdles, transdisciplinary teams need to manage their knowledge boundaries appropriately [4].

As the process of codifying knowledge and experiences in a language shared by a team can help to find consensus, facilitate discourse, and foster the exchange of mutual

© Springer Nature Switzerland AG 2022
A. Drechsler et al. (Eds.): DESRIST 2022, LNCS 13229, pp. 42–54, 2022.
https://doi.org/10.1007/978-3-031-06516-3_4

learning [5], we argue that this is a promising approach to particularly leverage trans-disciplinary design science research (DSR). In such DSR settings, diverse stakehold-ers need to synthesize the knowledge that they have gathered throughout a project to promote a shared understanding and to inform future DSR projects addressing similar problems. The resulting design-relevant knowledge is commonly captured in the form of design principles [6], which help researchers to transcend a single success story by using the knowledge at a different time and in different application scenarios as well as practitioners to get formalized findings [7–9]. Given the aforementioned challenges of transdisciplinarity, we see the potential of design principles to become an interface between different actors, contexts, and domains. For examining this potential, we asked:

- *RQ: How to support transdisciplinary research with design principles?*

In attempting to answer this, we draw from boundary object theory. Doing this, we explore the goals and the mechanisms of boundary spanning through *design principles-in-use* (i.e., applying produced design principles in new settings) and *design principles-in-formulation* (i.e., the process of jointly creating a shared language). Boundary objects mediate between different users by facilitating a stable core to enable consensus but still allow for interpretative flexibility in local application [10]. Design principles as a prod-uct do share these characteristics. This perspective is not new since Romme et al. [11] have already pointed to *design rules* and *construction principles* as boundary objects. Similarly, Gurzick and Lutters [12] positioned *design guidelines* at the border between theory and practice and as a bridge between practitioners and researchers. We contribute to this perspective by taking into account the practices involved in spanning the knowl-edge boundaries with design principles. Following this, we suggest both formulating and using design principles are boundary-spanning activities. By building on the notions of boundary object and boundary spanning, we aim to extend the functionality and applica-bility of design principles. Our results add the layers of transdisciplinary collaboration to the ongoing discourse on design principles as well as design knowledge accumula-tion and evolution. These perspectives contribute to the practical implication of DSR: Considering design principles as a boundary object can help to blur or even span the boundaries between DSR and design practice.

The paper is structured as follows. Section 2 briefly describes the idea of boundary object and boundary spanning as well as the *modus operandi* of *design principles-in-use* and *design principles-in-formulation*. In Sect. 3, we conceptualize design principles as an object that supports boundary spanning. Section 4 demonstrates our conceptualization using the case of design principles for data spaces. Section 5 highlights contributions and limitations as well as outlines avenues for further research.

2 Research Background

2.1 Boundary Object and Boundary Spanning

Boundary objects are interfacing agents that mediate between actors from different backgrounds, which are, according to Star and Griesemer, "(…) both plastic enough to adapt to local needs and the constraints of the several parties employing them, yet robust enough to maintain a common identity across sites" [10 p. 393]. They are useful in case they allow for a spectrum of conceptual density and interpretative flexibility; they are 'weakly structured' when used by many and 'strongly structured' when employed in the local application context [13 p. 393]. The application programming interface (API) and integrated development environment (IDE) are two prominent examples of boundary objects, both serving as an interface for third-party developers [14]. These objects enable third-party developers to interact with each other (e.g., through forums) and contribute new applications using a standardized technological infrastructure [15].

Boundary objects help to blur and even extend the boundaries between members of transdisciplinary teams or between teams in a consortium. A mechanism referred to as boundary spanning [16]. Boundary spanning can be done by using or creating boundary objects: "*As the amount of novelty increases, the organizational capability necessary for successful knowledge integration shifts from one of efficiently using (exploitation) current boundary objects to one of effectively creating (exploration) boundary objects.*" [17 p. 1192]. Our paper relies on Carlile's [4, 18] view on the roles of boundary objects in managing knowledge across boundaries (see Table 1).

Table 1. Fundamental characteristics of boundary objects (adapted from [18]).

Boundary	Characteristic	Selected definition
Syntactic	Shared language	"[A] boundary object establishes a shared syntax or language for individuals to represent their knowledge." [18 p. 451]
Semantic	Codification of knowledge	"An effective boundary object at a semantic boundary provides a concrete means for individuals to specify and learn about their differences and dependencies across a given boundary" [18 p. 452]
Pragmatic	Dynamic use	"At a pragmatic boundary an effective boundary object facilitates a process where individuals can jointly transform their knowledge" [18 p. 452]

2.2 Design Principles-in-Use and Design Principles-in-Formulation

Design principles capture "knowledge about creating other instances of artifacts that belong to the same class" [21 p. 39] and thereby guide designers to create an artifact successfully [19]. Although there is a variety of approaches to develop design principles [20], for this paper, we make a distinction between two main activities, namely *design principles-in-use* and *design principles-in-formulation*. Referring to in-use, as design principles are so-called meta-artifacts, designers need to contextualize them when solving a specific problem [22]. Because of the heterogeneity of instance scenarios, the varying degrees of condensed knowledge, and the claim of generic applicability, design principles instantiation requires interpretation [23, 24]. In contrast, the formulation of design principles involves abstraction from a specific problem to a more general class of problems [22] and matching them to a class of artifacts [20, 25, 26]. Figure 1 visualizes the continuing life-cycle of design principles [22].

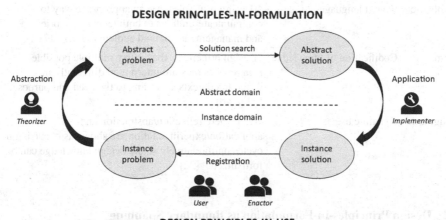

DESIGN PRINCIPLES-IN-FORMULATION

DESIGN PRINCIPLES-IN-USE

Fig. 1. Conceptualization of 'design principles-in-use' (instance domain) and 'design principles-in-formulation' (abstract domain) adapted from Gregor et al. [22] and Lee et al. [27].

3   Design Principles for Boundary Spanning

In this section, we begin our arguments by conceptualizing design principles as a boundary object with supporting literature statements. Then we propose viewing formulating and using design principles as boundary spanning activities. In so doing, we provide two visualizations of both activities in the context of transdisciplinary DSR.

3.1   Design Principles as a Boundary Object

Design principles codify knowledge about a solution class to a particular problem class for which reason it can be translated or adapted to other similar design contexts. In the field of Organization Science and Organization Design, design principles have long been considered a boundary object between the research and the practice of organization design (e.g. [11, 28]). The boundaries can be bridged by the use of design principles as a shared language and conceptual framework to bring together scholars and practitioners to action [11]. Boundary objects require a spectrum of interpretative flexibility to implement different application scenarios. Design principles, per se, address a class of artifacts, which subsequently require contextualization once used in a particular instance and must be tailored to the local requirements of their application [23]. They enable designers to codify their knowledge as a shared understanding (i.e., shared language) and transcend a single instance's boundaries [29]. Table 2 maps statements from the literature on design principles to the characteristics of a boundary object.

Table 2. Design principles as a boundary object.

Boundary	Characteristic	Supporting literature statement(s)
Syntactic	Shared language	"[Design principles] are an appropriate way to communicate findings to both technology-oriented and management-oriented audiences (…)." [7]
Semantic	Codification of knowledge	"Design principles, thus, carry multiple possible meanings as they are interpreted differently in different contexts according to the need and purpose." [23 p. 40]
Pragmatic	Dynamic use	"(…) where reflection/abstraction and application/experimentation are shown as occurring in cycles until relatively stable design knowledge can be formalized." [22]

3.2 Design Principles-in-Formulation as Boundary Spanning

Based on Fig. 1, we can infer the following about what happens when a transdisciplinary team formulates design principles: Team members generalize from their design projects in order to generate abstracted design principles. When abstracting, each team member moves from her/his specific scope and responsibilities in the project. They communicate the insights (either grounded in theory or from project experience) in a language understandable to all team members with different expertise and knowledge domains. Hence, they align their collaboration using this shared language.

Formulating design principles can assist the team in overcoming knowledge barriers between design team members with different backgrounds (see Fig. 2). By integrating viewpoints from numerous disciplines and stakeholders into a shared set of design principles, the boundaries are blurred or even spanned. Accordingly, the process of formulating those principles should allow for participation and collaboration.

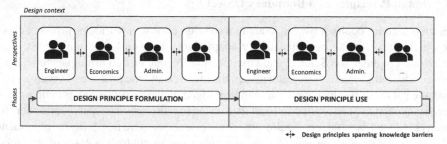

Fig. 2. Formulating design principles as boundary spanning.

3.3 Design Principles-in-Use as Boundary Spanning

From Fig. 1 we can also draw the following insights about the act of using design principles: Team members apply design principles to the shared context of their specific project. Each member adds her/his specific expertise and perspective to the application at hand. Then they consolidate their ideas into a shared project blueprint.

Using design principles can assist in overcoming certain knowledge barriers. The design context is the sum of all relevant elements referring to the design of an artifact, its environment, actors, as well as relevant parts of the problem and solution space [30]. Team members can build upon a shared understanding of how to design an artifact and apply (interpret) this to the individual situation based on their knowledge (see Fig. 3). While the 'in-use' activities of applying known solutions might be classified as *routine design* [36], 'in-formulation' can result in improvements or completely new solutions.

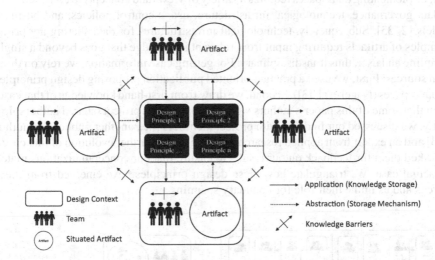

Fig. 3. Using design principles as boundary spanning.

Concerning the interplay of application and abstraction, we see the *application* as the contextualization of design knowledge to develop a situated artifact. On the other hand, *abstraction* is the mechanism that feeds knowledge back to the design principles to append learnings gathered from each situated artifact. Formulating design principles involves a sort of *storage mechanism* which accumulates design knowledge through abstraction and codification of situated design knowledge [31]. Using design principles, in contrast, is about applying and specifying the knowledge to the design context. In doing so, team members draw on design principles from a sort of *knowledge storage* [12]. The codification process requires condensing design knowledge into a new form which is stored permanently so that others can use it at different times and place [32].

The *knowledge storage* of design principles in boundary spanning plays a different role across the syntactic, semantic, and pragmatic levels of the knowledge boundaries [4]. When spanning syntactic boundaries, the transdisciplinary team can treat the knowledge storage as a repository [18, 33]. Teams can retrieve the knowledge and use it directly in their projects without any changes. When spanning semantic boundaries, the knowledge storage is treated as a method [18, 33]. When using this, team members need to translate their domain-specific insights to contribute to a joint understanding. Finally, pragmatic boundaries are spanned by treating the knowledge storage as a map [18, 33] or a blueprint. Here, teams need not only translate the blueprint but also transform it (adding, changing the knowledge) to be applicable in their context.

4 Illustration: The Use Case of Data Spaces

Our illustrative use case for using design principles as boundary objects is concerned with mediating large consortia dealing with the design of data spaces. Data spaces are complex artifacts enabling data sharing in a data ecosystem facing multiple challenges [34]. Implementing data spaces requires a variety of views and concepts to consider, such as data governance, technological infrastructure, usage control policies, and business models [2, 35]. Subsequently, technological infrastructures for data sharing are prime examples of artifacts requiring input from relevant knowledge that goes beyond a single discipline and user, thus transdisciplinary. For getting case information, we rely on three main sources: First, we used a practice-oriented publication proposing design principles for data spaces (Nagel et al. [3]). Second, we draw from first-hand knowledge of that case, given that some of this paper's authors worked close to that project (shared authorship). Lastly, we discussed our findings with project members (i.e., another publication author of [3] and an expert from applied research working on the further evolution of that case). We asked them for feedback on our results to ensure that our conceptualizations match the actual case. We triangulate how these design principles have emerged from these sources and examine their role for boundary spanning.

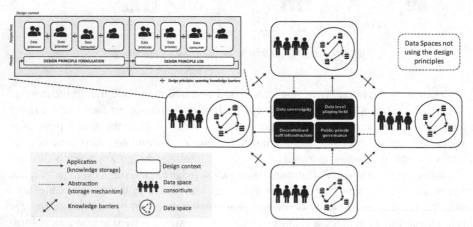

Fig. 4. Formulating and using design principles in designing data spaces.

4.1 Case Description

The case reports on four design principles to guide the implementation of data spaces [3]: *Data Sovereignty, Data Level Playing Field, Decentralized Soft Infrastructure*, and *Public-Private Governance*. The design principles govern an ecosystem (a federation) of data spaces that have heterogeneous properties. They differ in the data they share, the domains they address, or the number of participants participating in them. The users of the design principles are data space consortia that can consist of public institutions, private companies, and/or applied research institutes in different roles and perspectives. For example, the stakeholders can take on perspectives, such as data consumers, data providers, or data producers, each with a distinct set of requirements, goals, and intentions for participation in a data space [2, 3]. The case's design principles were derived from a large consortium that organizes various European data spaces consortia to enable federalization and interoperability. Subsequently, the initiative is highly complex, encompasses many actors, and requires high alignment. Against this background, the design principles were formulated to facilitate a common denominator between these data spaces and pose a set of minimal guidelines and a shared understanding. Given that these cases are practice-relevant and tend to focus on instantiating available knowledge, they can most likely be characterized as *routine design* [36].

4.2 Formulating and Using Design Principles for Boundary Spanning

The case is an illustrative, practice-oriented example of how formulating and using design principles supports boundary spanning (see Fig. 4). The design principles were formulated in workshops, group discussions, and meetings between stakeholders of different data space consortia and their respective perspectives. Formulating them helped to bridge knowledge barriers between perspectives in one data space and bridge knowledge gaps between entire data space consortia. The principles represent a *shared language*, a shared set of guidelines for designing data spaces that must be customized for local use. For instance, some data spaces are tailored to distinct domains (but do not have to be), such as manufacturing, mobility, healthcare, or agriculture, that usually encompass localized terminology and data understanding [3]. Consider, for instance, the design principle 'Data Level Playing Field' (see Table 3): The generic design principle prescribes that data spaces must be organized fairly. That means no monopolistic position should dominate the ecosystem. In specific scenarios, the playing field is different for participants. There are other 'rules' in the field of healthcare (e.g., anonymization and pseudonymization of data) as opposed to supply chains that are organized across different tiers (*semantic knowledge barrier*). As another example, imagine instantiation of the design principle 'Data Sovereignty', which can vary in the degree of implementation. A decisive factor can be the exchanged data: personal data has unique requirements that other data may not have.

In their role as a shared language, the design principles enable the transdisciplinary *codification of knowledge* at an agreed level of abstraction; in such a way that all consortia and disciplines they represent can be mapped to. In detail, the consortia consist of two levels of transdisciplinary boundary spanning. First, each data space has multiple roles, such as the data provider, data consumer, and data orchestrator, that have

Table 3. Example of the design principle *Data Level Playing Field* [3].

Design principle for 'Data Level Playing Field': "Implies that new entrants face no insurmountable barriers to entry because of monopolistic situations (…)"			
Domain instantiation			
Manufacturing	Agri-food	Healthcare	Energy
Collaboration between OEMs logistics service providers on supply chain tiers. Access, data sovereignty, control	The level playing field between users, farmers, small businesses, and Agri-food companies in general	Fair practices and necessary regulation for the use of health data (research and innovation)	The level playing field for shared data to provide better equipment and value-added services

individual requirements. Second, the teams mainly consisted of people from different backgrounds (e.g., IT), projects (e.g., national or domain-specific), and institutions (e.g., companies, applied research, or public institutions). Using these design principles helped the consortium to better align its efforts through a shared consensus. Hence, the design principles bridge that *syntactic barrier* through accumulating, aggregating, and abstracting domain-specific knowledge about designing data spaces to actionable statements for all data spaces that "are accepted by all participants" [3 p. 8].

Finally, the design principles are not set in stone but are iteratively developed over time in different dimensions (e.g., validity, wording) from user feedback (*dynamic use*), enabling designers to contribute new insights and cross *pragmatic boundaries*.

Table 4 summarizes the boundary spanning and how the design principles can be used to cross knowledge boundaries (e.g., [37]).

Table 4. Spanning the boundaries with design principles for data spaces.

Boundary	Design principles-in-formulation	Design principles-in-use
Syntactic	The consortium aims for a formulation that is generic enough to foster consensus but leaves every design consortium the means to apply it	The design principles bridge knowledge barriers between design consortiums and/or perspectives in a design consortium. Team members retrieve the knowledge and use it in their design
	Using design principles to transmit knowledge between data spaces	

(*continued*)

Table 4. (*continued*)

Boundary	Design principles-in-formulation	Design principles-in-use
Semantic	When formulating the principles, the consortium addresses the requirements of hyper-dynamic and heterogeneous data spaces. The members consider multiple scenarios and codify the knowledge	The design principles enable consortia to agree on a common denominator with different focuses. Team members translate the principles into their domain-specific language first. Then they translate them back to the multi-consortium language
	Using design principles as a translating agent between data spaces	
Pragmatic	The consortium can collect knowledge on data space design principles over time and iterations	Team members add to the knowledge, change, and subtract parts of it, making it applicable in their design
	Using design principles to codify new knowledge iteratively	

5   Contributions, Limitations, and Outlook

This paper reports on an unexplored view on design principles as boundary objects. In doing so, we contribute to research on DSR since we broaden the scope of using design principles and open up new paths to explore the concepts and their utility more in-depth. We show by two visualizations how design principles support transdisciplinary design teams and thereby distinguish between two main activities for *'design principles-in-use'* and *'design principles-in-formulation.'* From a theoretical viewpoint, we contribute to recent research that emphasizes the need to specify abstraction levels of design principles [24]. Since our case shows that the design principles should be very abstract to enable participation and collaboration among diverse teams and actors, other stakeholders might demand more specific knowledge that can be implemented more easily. So, exploring the trade-offs between abstractedness and operationalizability seems to be relevant for the future. In terms of practical contributions, we illustrate the promising potential of how design principles can bridge knowledge barriers between heterogeneous teams and even consortia through. With our work, we aim at creating awareness of the potential of design principles to overcome knowledge barriers within those project environments. Practitioners can build upon the presented use case and its results to get impulses for the organization of their next design projects.

Naturally, our work has **limitations**. Our paper is conceptual and mirrors our deductive findings and reasoning against one case used as an illustrative example. The case we report on is highly complex and organizes an artifact that can be described as extreme. It is not a software tool implemented in one company. The artifact itself – the data space – is a complex entity including many actors, perspectives, and components (e.g., business model, technical infrastructure, or ecosystems). Subsequently, our case shows very well how design principles work in this scenario as a boundary object, yet, more research on this case and more cases are required to triangulate our findings.

Our work opens up multiple avenues for **further research**. For one, we did not analyze the case in terms of how the design principles are used (e.g., through using the components of Gregor et al. [22]) but only focused on their role as boundary objects and boundary spanning. Second, given that the design principles for data spaces are still evolving, their analysis in a longitudinal study would be a unique opportunity to enrich design principle research on multiple levels, such as their evolving role as boundary objects, how they are used in practice over time, or what elements of design principles crystallize over time and what elements change, i.e., the dynamics. In our paper, we used the Data Space case as an illustrative example. Further analysis with deeper characteristics of boundary objects [37] is a possibility to gain additional insights.

References

1. Jahn, T., Bergmann, M., Keil, F.: Transdisciplinarity: between mainstreaming and marginalization. Ecol. Econ. **79**, 1–10 (2012)
2. Otto, B., Jarke, M.: Designing a multi-sided data platform: findings from the international data spaces case. Electron. Mark. **29**(4), 561–580 (2019)
3. Nagel, L., et al.: Design principles for data spaces – position paper (2021)
4. Carlile, P.R.: Transferring, translating, and transforming: an integrative framework for managing knowledge across boundaries. Organ. Sci. **15**, 555–568 (2004)
5. Scholz, R., Steiner, G.: The real type and ideal type of transdisciplinary processes: part I – theoretical foundations. Sustainability Sci. (Invited & In review) **10**, 527–544 (2015)
6. Möller, F., Schoormann, T., Otto, B.: 'Caution - principle under construction' - a visual inquiry tool for developing design principles. In: Chandra Kruse L., Seidel S., Hausvik G.I. (eds.) The Next Wave of Sociotechnical Design. DESRIST 2021. Lecture Notes in Computer Science, vol. 12807, pp 223–235. Springer, Cham (2021)
7. Seidel, S., Chandra Kruse, L., Székely, N., Gau, M., Stieger, D.: Design principles for sensemaking support systems in environmental sustainability transformations. Eur. J. Inf. Syst. **27**, 221–247 (2017)
8. Heinrich, P., Schwabe, G.: Communicating nascent design theories on innovative information systems through multi-grounded design principles. In: Tremblay, M.C., VanderMeer, D., Rothenberger, M., Gupta, A., Yoon, V. (eds.) DESRIST 2014. LNCS, vol. 8463, pp. 148–163. Springer, Cham (2014). https://doi.org/10.1007/978-3-319-06701-8_10
9. Chandra Kruse, L., Seidel, S.: Tensions in design principle formulation and reuse. In: Proceedings of the 12th International Conference on Design Science Research in Information Systems and Technology (2017)
10. Star, S.L., Griesemer, J.R.: Institutional ecology, translations' and boundary objects: amateurs and professionals in Berkeley's Museum of Vertebrate Zoology, 1907–39. Soc. Stud. Sci. **19**, 387–420 (1989)
11. Romme, A., Endenburg, G.: Construction principles and design rules in the case of circular design. Organ. Sci. **17**, 287–297 (2006)
12. Gurzick, D., Lutters, W.: Towards a design theory for online communities. In: Proceedings of the 4th International Joint Conference on Autonomous Agents and Multiagent Systems (2005)
13. Star, S.L.: This is not a boundary object: reflections on the origin of a concept. Sci. Technol. Human Values **35**, 601–617 (2010)
14. Ghazawneh, A., Henfridsson, O.: Balancing platform control and external contribution in third-party development: the boundary resources model. Inf. Syst. J. **23**, 173–192 (2013)

15. Bianco, V.D., Myllärniemi, V., Komssi, M., Raatikainen, M.: The role of platform boundary resources in software ecosystems: a case study. In: 2014 IEEE/IFIP Conference on Software Architecture, pp. 11–20 (2014)
16. Levina, N., Vaast, E.: The Emergence of boundary spanning competence in practice: implications for implementation and use of information systems. MIS Quart. **29**, 335–363 (2005)
17. Carlile, P.R., Rebentisch, E.S.: Into the black box: the knowledge transformation cycle. Manage. Sci. **49**, 1180–1195 (2003). https://doi.org/10.1287/mnsc.49.9.1180.16564
18. Carlile, P.R.: A pragmatic view of knowledge and boundaries: boundary objects in new product development. Organ. Sci. **13**, 442–455 (2002)
19. Chandra Kruse, L., Seidel, S., Gregor, S.: Prescriptive knowledge in is research: conceptualizing design principles in terms of materiality, action, and boundary conditions. In: Proceedings of the 48th Hawaii International Conference on System Sciences (2015)
20. Möller, F., Guggenberger, T.M., Otto, B.: Towards a method for design principle development in information systems. In: Hofmann, S., Müller, O., Rossi, M. (eds.) DESRIST 2020. LNCS, vol. 12388, pp. 208–220. Springer, Cham (2020). https://doi.org/10.1007/978-3-030-64823-7_20
21. Sein, M.K., Henfridsson, O., Purao, S., Rossi, M., Lindgren, R.: Action design research. MIS Quart.: Manag. Inform. Syst. **35**, 37–56 (2011)
22. Gregor, S., Chandra Kruse, L., Seidel, S.: The anatomy of a design principle. J. Assoc. Inf. Syst. **21**, 1622–1652 (2020)
23. Chandra Kruse, L., Seidel, S., Purao, S.: Making use of design principles. In: Proceedings of the 11th International Conference on Design Science Research in Information Systems and Technology, pp. 37–51 (2016)
24. Wache, H., Möller, F., Schoormann, T., Strobel, G., Petrik, D.: Exploring the abstraction levels of design principles: the case of Chatbots. In: Proceedings of the 17th International Conference on Wirtschaftsinformatik, pp. 1–16 (2022)
25. Markus, M.L., Majchrzak, A., Gasser, L.: A design theory for systems that support emergent knowledge processes. MIS Quart. **26**, 179–212 (2002)
26. Walls, J.G., G.J., Widmeyer, R.G., El Sawy, O.A.: Building an information system design theory for vigilant EIS. Inform. Syst. Res. **3**, 36–59 (1992)
27. Lee, J.S., Pries-Heje, J., Baskerville, R.: Theorizing in design science research. In: Jain, H., Sinha, A.P., Vitharana, P. (eds.) DESRIST 2011. LNCS, vol. 6629, pp. 1–16. Springer, Heidelberg (2011). https://doi.org/10.1007/978-3-642-20633-7_1
28. Romme, A.G.L., Damen, I.C.M.: Toward science-based design in organization development: codifying the process. J. Appl. Behav. Sci. **43**, 108–121 (2007)
29. Romme, G.: Making a difference: organization as design. Organ. Sci. **14**, 558–573 (2003)
30. Herwix, A., Zur Heiden, P.: Context in design science research: taxonomy and framework. In: Proceedings of the 55th Hawaii International Conference on System Sciences (2021)
31. Vom Brocke, J., Winter, R., Hevner, A., Maedche, A.: Accumulation and evolution of design knowledge in design science research - a journey through time and space. J. Assoc. Inf. Syst. **21**, 520–544 (2020)
32. Cohendet, P., Meyer-Krahmer, F.: The theoretical and policy implications of knowledge codification. Res. Policy **30**, 1563–1591 (2001)
33. Gasson, S.: A genealogical study of boundary-spanning IS design. Eur. J. Inf. Syst. **15**, 26–41 (2006)
34. Gelhaar, J., Otto, B.: Challenges in the emergence of data ecosystems. In: Proceedings of the 24th Pacific Asia Conference on Information Systems (2020)
35. Zrenner, J., Möller, F.O., Jung, C., Eitel, A., Otto, B.: Usage control architecture options for data sovereignty in business ecosystems. J. Enterp. Inf. Manag. **32**, 477–495 (2019)

36. Gregor, S., Hevner, A.R.: Positioning and presenting design science research for maximum impact. MIS Quart.: Manag. Inform. Syst. **37**, 337–355 (2013)
37. Abraham, R., Aier, S., Winter, R.: Crossing the line: overcoming knowledge boundaries in enterprise transformation. Bus. Inf. Syst. Eng. **57**(1), 3–13 (2015)

Toward an Information Systems Ontology

Roland M. Mueller[1]([⊠]), Sebastian Huettemann[1], Kai R. Larsen[2], Sen Yan[2],
and Abram Handler[2]

[1] Berlin School of Economics and Law, Badensche Straße 52, 10825 Berlin, Germany
{roland.mueller,sebastian.huettemann}@hwr-berlin.de
[2] University of Colorado, Boulder, CO 80309, USA
{kai.larsen,sen.yan,abram.handler}@colorado.edu

Abstract. We introduce the Information Systems Ontology (ISO), a new ontology
for the Information Systems (IS) discipline designed to enable automated knowledge synthesis and meta-analysis of research findings in IS. We constructed ISO in
a methodical manner, following known best practices for ontology construction.
We also conducted a series of ontology refinement steps in which we compared
and extended ISO by extracting and examining both overlapping and missing key
phrases from scientific articles and existing classification schemas. To evaluate
ISO, we extracted author-defined keywords from more than 7,000 articles of the
senior scholars' basket of journals and measured terminological coverage. In one
experiment, we found that our ontology included 3.6 times more author-defined
keywords than an established classification schema for IS. In the future, we plan
to use ISO to automatically annotate important IS terms and concepts in IS articles
to help synthesize and analyze knowledge in IS.

Keywords: Ontology · Taxonomy · Information systems research · Information
systems · Knowledge synthesis · Meta-analysis

1 Introduction

A large world-wide community of scholars devotes time, energy and resources to building new knowledge of Information Systems (IS). But because the community stores
and disseminates this information in unstructured free-text documents, it is difficult to
systematically and comprehensively examine the body of new and existing knowledge
in the IS field. For instance, faced with a corpus of leading journals in IS, researchers and
practitioners would have to painstakingly analyze each document in the corpus to answer
questions about which new machine learning methods have recently been adapted for IS
research or which research methods the IS field has historically used to study IT service
management.

Storing knowledge in unstructured documents also presents additional problems.
Researchers only loosely familiar with a given topic area (e.g., *deep learning*), may not
know the complex array of named entities and sub-entities in a document collection
(e.g., *long short-term memory*). Moreover, when researchers, reviewers and editors are

© Springer Nature Switzerland AG 2022
A. Drechsler et al. (Eds.): DESRIST 2022, LNCS 13229, pp. 55–67, 2022.
https://doi.org/10.1007/978-3-031-06516-3_5

no longer able to keep track of past contributions, it becomes harder to integrate new findings into a growing body of knowledge.

One possible approach to tracking and synthesizing the growing unstructured IS literature is automatically analyzing keywords in scientific articles, using a taxonomy or ontology to group keywords in a hierarchical and semantically meaningful manner. However, the most recent keyword classification schema in IS [4] was updated in 1993 and consequently doesn't contain current topics and technologies, such as *design thinking, model-driven development, cryptocurrency,* or *MapReduce.*

Therefore, in this work we propose the Information Systems Ontology (ISO) which aims to cover the broad IS field by organizing its topics, technologies, methodologies, and theories. We designed ISO based on known best practices from Arp et al. [2], motivated by the possibility of supporting new views and tools for understanding, systematizing, and exploring IS. While developing ISO, we performed an extensive series of refinement steps where we added terminology from automatically extracted scientific key phrases and existing classification schemas. Through this process, we created a comprehensive IS ontology with more than 2,700 entities and 380,000 synonyms. An entity represents a concept such as *design science* that could have multiple synonyms such as *design science research* or *design science method.* To evaluate ISO, we identified the most frequently used author-defined keywords in IS articles in eight top journals in IS [1] and found that our ontology includes 3.6 more author-defined keywords than a well-established classification schema for IS [4]. In the future, we plan to use ISO to build multiple systems for reviewing literature, researching topics and integrating knowledge from the IS field.

2   Taxonomies and Ontologies in IS and CS

The academic community has proposed a number of taxonomies and ontologies, as shown in Table 1. In IS, the classification schema of Barki et al. [4, 5] may be the most well-known taxonomy. Although it established an ontological foundation for IS, it was released almost 30 years ago. More recently, Gregg et al., Nickerson et al. and Springer et al. [13, 23, 29] developed taxonomies for e-commerce, mobile applications, and digital platforms. But they focused on sub-areas of IS, not on the discipline as a whole. Fteimi and Lehner [11] proposed a classification schema to support an integrated overview of Knowledge Management publications.

In Computer Science (CS), the ACM Computing Classification System [33] was created manually and may be the most widely used classification schema. It contains about 2,000 categories and its most recent version was released in 2012. The latest version (3.3) of the Computer Science Ontology (CSO) [27] was released in 2020 and is an example of an ontology that is created automatically via an algorithm.

There are differences between IS-specific and CS-specific classification schemas. CS-specific schemas, for instance, tend to contain more technical terms than IS-specific schemas, such as *packet processing, routing problems, signal encoding* or *combinatorial algorithm.* However, there are many overlaps as well, for instance regarding technologies such as *deep learning,* conceptual methods such as *dynamic programming* or analysis methods such as *natural language processing*. Because of the many overlaps, we compared our ontology to the most recent classification schemas in both IS and CS, namely Barki et al., the CSO and the ACM Classification System, in Sect. 5 of this paper.

Table 1. Related classification schemas and ontologies

Name	Author	Year	Domain	Approach	Evaluation method
Keyword classification schema for IS	Barki et al. [4, 5]	1993	IS	Manual	User feedback
Taxonomy generation for text segments	Cuang and Chien [8]	2005	IS	Automatic	User feedback
Taxonomy for personal health systems	Beranek et al. [6]	2006	IS (Health System)	Manual	–
Taxonomy for complaints about EBay sellers	Gregg et al. [13]	2008	IS (E-commerce)	Manual	–
Taxonomy of mobile applications	Nickerson et al. [23]	2009	IS (Mobile applications)	Manual	Expert assessment
AcademIS	Triperina et al. [30]	2013	General	Manual	Case study
Scholarly ontology	Pertsas and Constantopo-ulos [25]	2017	General	Manual	User feedback & expert assessment
CSO	Salatino et al. [27]	2018	CS	Automatic	Automatic
SemSur	Fathalla et al. [10]	2018	General	Manual	Questionnaire & expert assessment
Taxonomy to gamify information systems	Schöbel et al. [28]	2018	IS (Gamification)	Manual	Case study
Knowledge management classification scheme	Fteimi and Lehner [11]	2018	Knowledge management	Manual	Expert assessment
Taxonomy in business analytics	Ko and Gillani [17]	2020	IS (BA)	Hybrid	Expert assessment
Taxonomy of digital platform pricing	Springer and Petrik [29]	2021	IS (Digital platform pricing)	Manual	Expert assessment

3   Ontology Development

We developed ISO using known best practices [2]. The development proceeded in a series of steps. We began by developing a top-level hierarchy and defining inclusion and exclusion criteria for entities and their synonyms in the ontology.

We use the word **entity** to refer to a term in our ontology, e.g., *artificial intelligence*. Each entity can have additional **synonyms**, e.g., *AI*. Entities can be added below other entities to create a hierarchy, resulting in different hierarchy **levels**. We use the term **candidate entity** or **candidate** to refer to terms that might be added to the ontology during refinement.

After that, we reviewed terminology from standard textbooks and IS articles in order to identify entity candidates. We also developed a program that used wild card patterns to identify additional entities in IS articles. Further refinement steps included the automated extraction of scientific key terminology from IS articles and a comparison with an existing classification schema in IS.

3.1   Development and Population of a Top-Level Structure

We followed a series of steps for designing a domain ontology, defined by Arp et al. [2]. In order to identify entities for the two top levels of the ontology, two authors with a combined experience of more than 20 years in IS analyzed IS-specific as well as general social science taxonomies, thesauri and ontologies [12, 18, 31] and standard textbooks [7, 14, 20–22, 24, 26, 32]. From these resources, the researchers created a list of entity candidates and considered each individual candidate for possible inclusion in the top-level structure. The researchers selected candidates which were abstract and closely related to IS, so that the ontology could answer how research is conducted in the IS discipline. For instance, we consider *data analysis method* to be an abstract entity and *multimodal sentiment analysis* to be a specific entity. For reasons of feasibility, we decided to limit the scope to IS-related terminology and excluded terms that represent business terminology without a close relation to IS, e.g. *marketing, management*. The resulting top-level structure consists of three entities on the first and fourteen entities on the second hierarchy level as illustrated in Fig. 1.

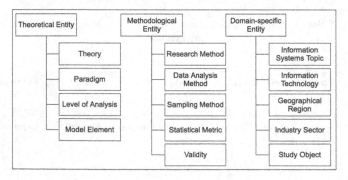

Fig. 1. Ontology top-level structure

3.2   Development and Population of Lower Hierarchy Levels

For the addition of entities into lower hierarchy levels of the ontology, we defined several inclusion and exclusion criteria as illustrated in Table 2.

Table 2. Inclusion and exclusion criteria

Criteria	Description
Inclusion	- the term must be abstract - the term must be used in many different papers - if the term is an acronym, it is only added if it is introduced with parentheses, i.e., *Information Systems (IS)*. Otherwise, it is ambiguous
Exclusion	- terms that are construct names - terms that are measurement items (questions) from surveys - terms that represent business administration concepts, e.g. sales, marketing - terms found in diagrams and tables - terms that are ambiguous or unspecific, e.g. least squares, management system, value chain, business strategy, critical success, total number

To define and populate the ontological hierarchy, the same two researchers as in Sect. 3.1 performed several ideation sessions in order to collect and discuss terminology from standard textbooks. After that, they grouped and included entity candidates in an iterative process to further develop the hierarchy. Table 3 details which sources were used to determine entities for lower hierarchy levels.

3.3   Refinement with IS Articles

To refine the ontology, the researchers created a corpus of articles in IS. This corpus consisted of 7,304 scientific articles from the senior scholars' basket of journals, published between 1989 and September 2021. This *basket* of journals represents the top eight journals in IS [1]. The researchers manually analyzed a sample of this corpus consisting of roughly 150 articles for missing entities and potential synonyms. During enhancement, one researcher informally picked the relevant sections from a paper and added possible entity candidates to a list. In a second step, this list was compared with existing entities in the ontology and missing entities were added.

3.4   Refinement with Wild Card Patterns

In order to identify additional entity candidates, the researchers developed an automated procedure using wild card-patterns for analyzing text. These patterns used part-of-speech (POS) tags to identify common multi-word sequences or phrases in IS articles; researchers have long used POS tags to identify scientific terminology [15]. For example, to identify additional entity candidates related to the entity *theory*, we searched IS articles using the pattern "theory of $ADJ? $NOUN|PROPN +" to detect word sequences

Table 3. Top-level entities with examples and sources

Level 1 entity	Level 2 entity	Examples	Source
Theoretical entity	Theory	Information systems theory, social sciences theory, management theory, economic theory	[19, 22]
	Research paradigm	Realism, pragmatism, positivism	[7, 32]
	Level of analysis	Macro level, meso level, micro level	[32]
	Model element	Construct, variable	[7, 26]
Methodological entity	Research method	Conceptual methods, e.g., design science, simulation; Data collection methods, e.g., case study, experimental design	[14, 18, 24, 26]
	Data analysis method	Triangulation, synthesis, machine learning or descriptive statistics	[12, 21]
	Sampling method	Purposive sampling, critical case sampling, cross validation and bootstrap sampling	[32]
	Statistical metric	Goodness of fit, standard deviation, mean squared error	[12, 21, 32]
	Validity	Diagnostic validity, construct validity, design validity	[32]
Domain specific entity	Information systems topic	Knowledge management, business process management, gamification, information systems strategy	[20]
	Information systems technology	Internet technology, social media or mobile systems, semantic web, ubiquitous computing	[20]

(*continued*)

Table 3. (*continued*)

Level 1 entity	Level 2 entity	Examples	Source
	Geographic names	Europe, Western Europe, United Kingdom, England, London	[31]
	Economic sector	Manufacturing industry, chemical industry, pharmaceutical industry	[31]
	Study object	Company types or participants, e.g., startup, small and mid-size enterprise, individual participant, group participant, organizational participant	[31, 32]

starting with *theory of* followed by zero or one adjectives and one or more nouns or proper nouns (e.g., *Theory of organizational creativity*). We developed multiple patterns to identify additional entity candidates. The researchers analyzed pattern matches in the corpus of IS papers (defined in Sect. 3.3) according to the inclusion and exclusion criteria.

3.5 Refinement with Extracted Scientific Key Terminology

We compared and refined our ontology with automatically extracted scientific key terminology from IS papers to test and improve the terminological coverage of our ontology. Therefore, we identified the most frequent scientific terms from articles in our corpus consisting of 7,304 scientific articles from the senior scholars' basket of journals, published between 1989 and 2021 and compared those terms against the entities in our ontology. If an extracted term was missing in the ontology, two researchers discussed the term as a potential entity candidate and decided whether to include it or not, based on the criteria in Table 2.

To extract terms, we used the combo basic term extraction algorithm [3] from PyATE, a term extraction library in Python [16]. This algorithm identified key terms from natural language text related to their frequency. Applying the algorithm to all full text articles in our corpus resulted in a list of 32,517 terms. We ranked the terms based on the number of articles where a term was among the top 10 extracted terms. The term *information systems* was for instance among the top 10 terms in 2,487 papers, followed by the term *information technology* in 1,371 papers.

We only reviewed terms that were among the top 10 terms in at least 10 articles. This resulted in a new list of 600 entity candidates where 384 of them were not included in our ontology. Two authors performed a review and discussed all of these 384 entity candidates: 123 entities were added to the ontology, 213 were excluded and 48 were regarded as subjects for possible future inclusion.

Terms starting with *information* or *data* are common in IS. Out of the 32,517 terms, we therefore reviewed another 1,199 entity candidates starting with such terms. 1,026 candidates didn't meet the inclusion criteria, 52 were marked for possible future inclusion and 121 entities were added to the ontology.

3.6   Refinement with IS Classification Schema

In 1988, MIS Quarterly published an IS classification schema by Barki et al. [5] that was updated by Barki et al. in 1993 [4]. The updated version contained around 1,300 keywords. We refined our ontology by comparing it to this updated classification schema.

We extracted the terminology from the classification schema of Barki et al. into a digital format and automatically searched for matching entities in our ontology. Out of the 1,300 terms, 228 were already included which also means that the classification schema of Barki et al. didn't contain 2,524 entities (382,873 including synonyms) that were contained in our ontology. For instance, Barki et al. didn't include terms such as *knowledge management, open source, human centered design* or *usability.*

For terms in the classification schema of Barki et al. that were not in our ontology, one senior and one junior researcher independently performed a review on whether those should be added. The inter-annotator agreement [9] for these 1,072 terms resulted in a Cohen's Kappa value of 0.56 which is regarded as moderate agreement. The kappa value may reflect the difference in research experience or ambiguity in some terms. The two researchers discussed all terms where the evaluation indicated disagreement (n = 231) and decided whether those should be added to the ontology. As a final result, the researchers added 336 entities and additional synonyms.

We analyzed a random sample of terms that were contained in the classification schema of Barki et al., but not in our ontology and found that most of these terms didn't meet our inclusion criteria. Table 4 provides an overview with examples.

Table 4. Terminology from Barki et al. that is not in ISO

Exclusion category	In Barki et al., not in ISO (n = 736)
Unspecificity	Data structure, graphic design, information, measurement
Ambiguity	Accessibility, homes, output, piracy
Different focus	Accounting, human resources, management level

As demonstrated by Table 7, the differences between ISO and the classification schema of Barki et al. seem to stem from the lack of specificity, the ambiguity or simply terms from Barki et al. that were not sufficiently focused on IS to meet the inclusion criteria for ISO.

4   The Information Systems Ontology

In total, ISO contains a total of 2,752 entities and 383,101 synonyms. The tree is organized with three top-level entities, named methodological entity, theoretical entity and domain-specific entity. These three entities provide a logical grouping of fourteen core entities on the second hierarchy level that we believe are central to describe scholarly papers in IS. Table 5 provides an overview of these entities including three metrics to get an impression of the ontology contents: *count of levels* stands for the maximum number of hierarchical levels below a top-level entity, *count of entities* stands for the total count of entities below a top-level entity and *count of synonyms* stands for the count of included synonyms (each entity can have many different synonyms).

We enhanced the list of entities in our ontology with various synonym-, prefix- or suffix-lists (where prefix and suffix mean the first or the last word in a multi-term word) that are directly encoded within the ontology. For instance, for the entities *design science methods* and *case study methods*, we apply the same synonym-list to automatically generate additional terms by exchanging the last word. This results in terms such as *design science technique* or *design science methodology* and *case study technique* or *case study methodology*.

Table 5. Ontology overview

Ontology top-level entities	Count of levels	Count of entities	Count of synonyms
Theoretical entity	**10**	**321**	**2,758**
Level of analysis	7	14	44
Model	6	35	1,278
Research paradigm	6	14	326
Theory	9	258	1,110
Methodological entity	**11**	**841**	**85,715**
Research method	9	290	63,020
Data analysis method	10	411	3,779
Validity	6	27	16,874
Sampling	8	28	172
Statistical metric	7	85	1,870
Domain specific entity	**11**	**1,590**	**294,628**
Information systems topic	10	392	19,031
Information systems technology	9	488	36,124
Study object	8	24	235,750
Economic sector	10	338	2,849
Geographical names	10	348	874
		2,752	**383,101**

5 Evaluation and Discussion

In IS journals, authors often provide keywords that help define the contents of an article. The assumption is that author-defined keywords are relevant to IS. To evaluate our ontology, we extracted all author-defined keywords from the articles in our corpus (defined in Sect. 3.3), resulting in a list of 13,987 unique terms. In order to evaluate how well our ontology is suited to detect relevant IS terminology, we counted how many of the extracted author-defined keywords are contained as entities in ISO. For this search, we specified that an author-defined keyword was included in our ontology, if the exact string matched an entity or one of its synonyms. We performed the same search for keyword-matches in the classification schema of Barki et al. [4], the CSO [27] and the ACM classification schema [33].

We performed two tests: first, we counted matches among all extracted keywords and second, we examined the 1,000 most frequently used keywords. Frequency is defined as the number of papers which contain a keyword at least once. Table 6 shows the results.

Table 6. Comparison with author-defined keywords

	Matches (all 13,987 keywords)		Matches (top 1,000 keywords)	
Ontology	#	%	#	%
ISO	1,830	13.1%	456	45.6%
Barki et al.	384	2.7%	129	12.9%
CSO	726	5.2%	170	17.0%
ACM	239	1.7%	75	7.5%

ISO includes 4.8 times more author-defined keywords than Barki et al. (i.e. 1,830/384), 2.5 times more than CSO (i.e. 1,830/726) and 7.7 times more than ACM (i.e. 1,830/239) for all keywords. ISO also includes 3.6 times more author-defined keywords among the top 1,000 most frequent keywords in IS articles than Barki et al. (i.e. 456/129), 2.7 times more than CSO (i.e. 456/170) and 6.1 times more than ACM (i.e. 456/75). These results suggest that ISO may be more appropriate for automatic tagging of IS articles than either alternative ontology or classification schema.

To gain further insight, we sampled keywords that were not captured by our ontology and found that most of these keywords didn't meet our inclusion criteria. Table 7 provides an overview with examples.

We developed ISO as an extensive ontology for the IS discipline aiming to automatically identify entities in scientific articles. ISO includes more relevant terminology than current classification schemas for the task of keyword detection in IS articles and covered 45.6% of the top 1,000 most used keywords.

During development, we focused on integrating as much appropriate terminology as possible and evaluated ISO based on its coverage of domain specific terminology. As our aim is to develop ISO as a keyword-detection tool, we focused on coverage as the main indicator for performance in this article.

Table 7. Examples of unspecific and ambiguous keywords

Exclusion criteria	In author-defined keywords, not in ISO
Unspecificity	Adoption, performance, culture, motivation, satisfaction, escalation, addiction
Ambiguity	Ethics, information, decision making, autonomy, success, web

In the future, more refinement will be necessary to increase the terminological coverage. We further plan to integrate the socio-technical perspective by adding more general business terminology. Ideally, a semi-automated approach can be developed for this task, similar to the approach of CSO where the ontology is automatically generated through the use of an algorithm. In addition to evaluating the coverage, an evaluation of the hierarchical structure of ISO through expert interviews could be a future refinement step.

6 Conclusion

This work introduces the Information Systems Ontology (ISO), a new hierarchical schema for IS research. ISO is motivated by a need to systematize and organize an ever-growing body of IS knowledge stored in unstructured documents. As described throughout this work, we developed ISO because we found that existing scientific classification schemas were either poorly suited to IS or did not cover the many important technological and methodological developments introduced to the IS field in recent decades. To create ISO, we followed known best practices for ontology development and performed a series of extensive ontology refinement steps to improve our schema's coverage of concepts in IS. In our final evaluation, we found that ISO included 3.6 times more author-defined keywords than the established ontology for IS. In the future, we plan to use ISO to identify similarities and relationships among IS articles and to support knowledge synthesis and meta-analysis in the IS field.

References

1. AIS: Senior scholars' basket of journals. https://aisnet.org/page/SeniorScholarBasket. Accessed 15 Nov 2021
2. Arp, R., Smith, B., Spear, A.D.: Building Ontologies with Basic Formal Ontology. MIT Press, Cambridge, MA (2015)
3. Astrakhantsev, N.: ATR4S: toolkit with state-of-the-art automatic terms recognition methods in scala. Lang. Res. Eval. **52**(3), 853–872 (2016)
4. Barki, H., Rivard, S., Talbot, J.: A keyword classification scheme for is research literature: an update. MIS Quart. **17**(2), 209–226 (1993)
5. Barki, H., Rivard, S., Talbot, J.: An information systems keyword classification scheme. MIS Quart. **12**(2), 299 (1988)
6. Beranek, D., Horan, T.: Toward an empirical user taxonomy for personal health records systems. In: AMCIS 2006 Proceedings (2006)

7. Bhattacherjee, A.: Social Science Research: Principles, Methods, and Practices. Global Text Projct, Textbooks Collection, Tampa, Florida (2012)
8. Chuang, S.-L., Chien, L.-F.: Taxonomy generation for text segments: a practical web-based approach. ACM Trans. Inform. Syst. **23**(4), 363–396 (2005)
9. Cohen, J.: A coefficient of agreement for nominal scales. Educ. Psychol. Measur. **20**(1), 37–46 (1960)
10. Fathalla, S., Vahdati, S., Auer, S., Lange, C.: SemSur: a core ontology for the semantic representation of research findings. Procedia Comput. Sci. **137**, 151–162 (2018). https://doi.org/10.1016/j.procs.2018.09.015
11. Fteimi, N., Lehner, F.: Analysing and classifying knowledge management publications – a proposed classification scheme. J. Knowl. Manag. **22**(7), 1527–1554 (2018)
12. Gonzalez-Beltran, A., Rocca-Serra, P.: Statistics ontology - NCBO BioPortal. https://bioportal.bioontology.org/ontologies/STATO. Accessed 28 Jan 2022
13. Gregg, D.G., Scott, J.E.: A typology of complaints about eBay sellers. Commun. ACM **51**(4), 69–74 (2008)
14. Hevner, A.R., Chatterjee, S.: Design Research in Information Systems: Theory and Practice. Springer, New York, London (2010)
15. Justeson, J.S., Katz, S.M.: Technical terminology: some linguistic properties and an algorithm for identification in text. Nat. Lang. Eng. **1**(1), 9–27 (1995). https://doi.org/10.1017/S135132490000048
16. Kevin Lu: PyATE documentation homepage. https://kevin-lu.tech/pyate/index.html. Accessed 17 Nov 2021
17. Ko, A., Gillani, S.: A Research review and taxonomy development for decision support and business analytics using semantic text mining. Int. J. Inf. Technol. Decis. Mak. **19**(01), 97–126 (2020)
18. Kupfer, A.: Research methods in the information systems discipline: a literature analysis of conference papers. In: Proceedings of the Twenty-fourth Americas Conference on Information Systems (AMCIS) (2018)
19. Larsen, K.R., Eargle, D.: Theories used in IS research Wiki. https://is.theorizeit.org. Accessed 25 Nov 2021
20. Laudon, K.C., Laudon, J.P.: Management Information Systems: Managing the Digital Firm. Pearson, Hoboken, NJ (2020)
21. Mertens, W., Pugliese, A., Recker, J.: Quantitative Data Analysis: A Companion for Accounting and Information Systems Research. Springer International Publishing, Switzerland (2018)
22. Miles, J.A.: Management and Organization Theory: A Jossey-Bass Reader. Jossey-Bass, San Francisco, CA (2012)
23. Nickerson, R., Muntermann, J., Varshney, U., Isaac, H.: Taxonomy development in information systems: developing a taxonomy of mobile applications. In: HAL, Working Papers (2009)
24. Oates, B.J.: Researching Information Systems and Computing. SAGE Publications, London (2006)
25. Pertsas, V., Constantopoulos, P.: Scholarly ontology: modelling scholarly practices. Int. J. Digit. Libr. **18**(3), 173–190 (2017). https://doi.org/10.1007/s00799-016-0169-3
26. Recker, J.: Scientific Research in Information Systems. Springer, Berlin, Heidelberg (2013)
27. Salatino, A.A., Thanapalasingam, T., Mannocci, A., Osborne, F., Motta, E.: The computer science ontology: a large-scale taxonomy of research areas. In: Vrandečić, D., et al. (eds.) ISWC 2018. LNCS, vol. 11137, pp. 187–205. Springer, Cham (2018). https://doi.org/10.1007/978-3-030-00668-6_12

28. Schöbel, S., Janson, A.: Is it All About Having Fun? - Developing a taxonomy to Gamify information systems. Presented at the European Conference on Information Systems (ECIS) June 24 (2018)

29. Springer, V., Petrik, D.: Towards a taxonomy of impact factors for digital platform pricing. In: Gregory, P., Kruchten, P. (eds.) XP 2021. LNBIP, vol. 426, pp. 115–124. Springer, Cham (2021). https://doi.org/10.1007/978-3-030-88583-0_11

30. Triperina, E., Sgouropoulou, C., Tsolakidis, A.: AcademIS: an ontology for representing academic activity and collaborations within HEIs. In: Proceedings of the 17th Panhellenic Conference on Informatics, pp. 264–271. Association for Computing Machinery, New York, NY, USA (2013)

31. ZBW - Leibniz information centre for economics: STW thesaurus for economics. https://zbw. eu/stw/version/9.12/about.en.html. Accessed 25 Nov 2021

32. Zedeck, S.: APA Dictionary of Statistics and Research Methods. American Psychological Association, Washington (2014)

33. ACM: Digital library: communications of the ACM. https://dl.acm.org/doi/fullHtml/https:// doi.org/10.1145/2366316.2366320. Accessed 31 Jan 2022

Supporting Product Development by a Trend Analysis Tool Applying Aspect-Based Sentiment Detection

Janik Wörner[(⊠)] [iD], Daniel Konadl [iD], Isabel Schmid [iD], and Susanne Leist [iD]

University of Regensburg, Regensburg, Germany
{Janik.Woerner,Daniel.Konadl,Isabel.Schmid,Susanne.Leist}@ur.de

Abstract. Incorporating product trends into innovation processes is imperative for companies to meet customers' expectations and to stay competitive in fiercely opposing markets. Currently, aspect-based sentiment analysis has proven an effective approach for investigating and tracking towards products and corresponding features from social media. However, existing trend analysis tools on the market that offer aspect-based sentiment analysis capabilities, do not meet the requirements regarding the use case Product Development. Therefore, based on these requirements, we implemented an artifact by following the design science research. We applied our tool to real-world social media data (37,638 Yelp reviews) from one major fast-food restaurant in the US, and thereby demonstrated that our tool is capable of identifying remarkable and fine-grained product trends.

Keywords: Trend analysis tool · Aspect-based sentiment · Product development

1 Motivation

Social media such as Yelp or Twitter have evolved rapidly over the last years. These platforms have become increasingly important for interaction in both private and business contexts [1, 2]. As social media is a channel for the exchange of user-generated content and unfiltered voices about products, services and the company in general, social media data contain the so-called "Voice of the Customer" (VoC). Thus, the VoC provides deep insights into customers' current expectations. To meet customers' expectations, marketing representatives need to identify and continuously track trending topics regarding product and service features and incorporate the VoC into product innovation processes. For example, identified product features and correspondingly mentioned opinions may indicate shortcomings (e.g., low battery capacity of a smartphone) and which improvements to be made to meet customers' requirements (e.g., [3]). One possibility to identify these shortcomings in an automated way from social media texts is to conduct aspect-based sentiment analysis [4].

The potential of aspect-based sentiment analysis for tracking fine-grained trends over time has already been recognized in practice and in theory (e.g., [3, 5–9]). This has led to the emergence of trend analysis tools that include aspect-based sentiment analysis

© Springer Nature Switzerland AG 2022
A. Drechsler et al. (Eds.): DESRIST 2022, LNCS 13229, pp. 68–80, 2022.
https://doi.org/10.1007/978-3-031-06516-3_6

functionalities. However, trend analysis tools available on the market have remarkable drawbacks as they do not cover the comprehensive requirements that are deemed essential within the extant literature for the use case Product Development (e.g., [3, 5–9]).

With this work at hand, we make practical as well as theoretical contributions. We address drawbacks of existing software tools by suggesting a comprehensive artifact for automated trend analysis that allows marketing representatives to conduct aspect-based sentiment analysis. To meet several use case-specific requirements, we focus especially on the combination of different data analysis methods regarding the particular requirements, leading to a constructive trend analysis. By this, we aim to propose an automated solution for identifying ideas as the basis of (incremental) product innovation. Summing up, the research at hand is guided by the following research question:

What could an aspect-based sentiment analysis tool that supports trend analysis for Product Development purposes look like, and which requirements should such a tool meet?

The remainder of this paper is structured as follows: In the next section, we provide conceptual basics and related work. Following on this, we turn to the Design Requirements (DRs) and Design Principles (DPs) for implementing our tool, and to the short-comings of trend analysis tools on the market. Next, we show the research methodology. After a description of the tool's design and development as well as its demonstration, the paper concludes with a discussion and its contributions to theory and practice.

2   Foundations and Related Work

2.1   Conceptual Background

Social media serves as an important interface between companies and customers. In content communities, users can evaluate products by disseminating their opinions in form of online customer reviews (OCR). In doing so, customers not only rate products as a whole but express their opinions and attitudes towards different features of the rated items (e.g., service quality in a Yelp restaurant review). In this way, OCR not only help customers to make informed decisions but are also beneficial for driving innovations of products within companies. As OCR include customers' experiences and expectations of product features [10], unfiltered and in real-time [11], they can serve as a valuable resource for product innovations. Thus, OCR can be harnessed to identify ideas, to either develop new value propositions (i.e., disruptive innovation) or to improve the performance of existing products (i.e., incremental innovation) [12, 13].

To identify ideas for product improvements as well as product development and therefore to drive incremental product innovations, marketing representatives can conduct aspect-based sentiment analysis. The first step of an aspect-based sentiment analysis deals with extracting aspects from OCR. For this purpose, unsupervised as well as super-vised techniques can be applied. Topic modeling techniques (e.g., LDA [14]) suggest a possibility to identify aspects without prior knowledge (i.e., unsupervised) [14]. Compared to that, supervised techniques (e.g., artificial neural networks) need first to be trained on training data (e.g., ontologies) to extract the proper aspects (cf. [4]). Subsequently, the expressed tonalities can be identified for each of the aspects [4] by means of automated sentiment analysis techniques [4, 15]. Therefore, aspect-based sentiment analysis offers benefits in terms of Product Development. For marketing representatives that lack the ability to implement aspect-based sentiment analysis themselves, trend analysis tools on the market offer this functionality in a ready-to-use way. However, these tools show remarkable drawbacks as they do not cover the comprehensive requirements that are deemed essential within the extant literature for the use case of Product Development.

2.2 Design Requirements and Available Tools on the Market

In a first step, we have comprehensively searched and consolidated literature (cf. [16]) to identify DRs of a trend analysis tool that applies aspect-based sentiment analysis for Product Development purposes. Based on the attention and importance received, we could derive several DRs (DR1)-(DR10) (see Fig. 2) from the extant literature.

Concerning the identification of product features, the tool (DR1) should be capable of extracting the aspects autonomously from social media posts (e.g., [6–8, 17]). However, if marketing representatives have already knowledge documented about a domain problem (e.g., domain ontologies or product trees), the tool (DR2) should provide the option to include this prior knowledge into the automated identification of aspects (cf. [6, 7, 17, 18]). Beyond that, customers' self-reported opinions of product features play an important role for Product Development. Marketing representatives aim to retain the features that evoke positive perceptions, while features evoking negative perceptions need to be improved. Thus, (DR3) determining the polarity as well as the intensity of the opinions expressed about respective aspects is mandatory [3, 6, 8, 19, 20]. Subsequently, the product features can be adapted so that customers' requirements are met (e.g., increasing smartphone screen size). However, adapting features may influence perceptions of the features customers currently appreciate (e.g., high battery capacity of the smartphone). Therefore, to support informed improvement decisions, the tool (DR4) needs to identify the dependencies between product features [7, 9, 17]. Furthermore, to be successful and competitive in a targeted market, marketing representatives must decide which product features to propose in which way to meet customers' expectations within geographical markets. Product trends do also converge over time as they are dynamic developments and not solely static points in time. It is therefore essential that the tool (DR5) can flexibly match aspect-sentiment relations to different geographical (e.g., continents, countries, federal states) and temporal (e.g., days of a week, phases of a day) parameters [3, 5, 17–20]. The huge volume of available social media posts requires the incorporated techniques (DR6) to deal with vast amounts of textual data [8, 9, 18–20]. As past developments of trends are essential for assessing the current state of trending topics, the tool (DR7) needs to allow the user to consider historical data [3, 17–19]. To support Product Development in prioritizing product improvement decisions, the tool (DR8) needs to output aggregated sentiment values for the identified aspects [3, 6, 8, 19, 20] and (DR9) illustrate the frequency of the identified aspects [3, 8, 20, 21]. To immediately identify the most important aspect-sentiment relations, the tool (DR10) should provide means to rank the results in either descending or ascending order [3, 21].

In the second step, we searched the market for available trend analysis tools. We took an up-close look at the most popular tools (e.g., Brandwatch, Meltwater, Symanto) that offer trend analysis by means of aspect-based sentiments. We thoroughly analyzed the functionalities by installing and applying demo versions of these tools. The analysis process offered within the demo versions and the provided diagrams and charts that are offered to illustrate the results enabled us to apply the DRs to the existing tools, and to assess them both conceptually and visually. Based on our observations, we could conclude that there is no software tool that meets all the specific requirements for the use case Product Development, as we could derive them from extant literature. While we could agree that existing tools are able to meet most of the requirements, there are nevertheless remarkable drawbacks regarding DR1, DR2 and DR5. To confirm these observations, we subsequently turned to sales representatives from these companies. As it turned out, there are trend analysis tools that indeed provide pre-defined possibilities to contextualize the identified aspect-sentiment relations (e.g., time within a day or continents). However, the ability to flexibly match further temporal (e.g., phases of a day) and geographical parameters (e.g., countries or federal states) to aspect-sentiment relations is missing. Nonetheless, perceptions of product features may differ across countries or federal states and trends are temporal developments (e.g., days of a week, phases of a day). As reaching out to the sales representatives also could confirm, existing trend analysis tools that apply aspect-based sentiment analysis extract aspects, either with or without incorporating prior knowledge. Literature unveils the need for a comprehensive trend analysis tool that meets all the requirements for the use case Product Development. With this research, we aim to close this gap.

3   Research Procedure

In order to systematically develop an artifact for the automated trend analysis in marketing, we followed the Design Science (DS) approach [22, 23] and aligned our research activities with the DS procedure as proposed by [23] (see Fig. 1).

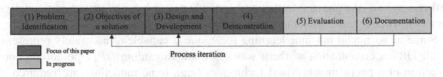

Fig. 1. Design science research (DSR) procedure

As a first step, (1) corresponding problems and drawbacks of previously existing approaches regarding the automated trend analysis using aspect-based sentiment analysis were identified (see Sects. 1 and 2.2). Hence, the revised tools supporting trend analysis by aspect-based sentiment detection do not meet the requirements that are indispensable to the successful application. Consequently, our (2) objective is to address drawbacks of existing software tools by suggesting a comprehensive artifact for automated trend analysis that allows marketing representatives to conduct aspect-based sentiment analysis (see Sects. 2.2 and 4). The third step of our DS process model contains the (3) design and development (see Sect. 4) of an artifact. To fill the gaps identified within phase (1), we focus on the design of the technical realization of the tool by combining different machine learning techniques, following our derived DPs. Thus, our approach was established to support the trend analysis and to eliminate the existing disadvantages. By (4) demonstrating our artifact (see Sect. 5.1), we highlight the application of our tool on 37,638 Yelp reviews [24]. Thus, we showed the implementation of the requirements identified in literature. In Step 5 the usefulness, applicability and usability of the tool are to be analyzed in a larger field study. Finally, the tool will be further enhanced before it is provided to marketing departments of large companies (6).

4 Design and Development

First, the composition of Meta Requirements (MRs) that describe *"what the system is for"* ([26], p. 325) is based on the purpose and scope of the tool that was discussed in the motivation. Thus, we define the solution objectives based on the investigations´ problems and present them in Fig. 2. Besides the MRs, the Design Principles (DPs) are synthesized in a next step. DPs are defined as prescriptive statements that show how to do something to achieve a goal [27]. These DPs are deduced from the design requirements (DRs) that are further influenced by prior theories and current research literature [25]. Gregor and Jones (2007) state that this foundation in form of theories disclose "an explanation of why an artifact is constructed as it is and why it works" (p. 328). Thus, these DR offer guidance by designing the artifact and advise the DPs [26]. So, we derived the DRs from prior research literature to develop supportive DPs a priori to any instantiation of our artifact. These principles refer to at least one requirement and serve as an abstract "blueprint" of our artifact [26, 27]. By establishing these design principles, we made sure that they follow the value grounding (reference to the requirement) and the explanatory grounding (design principles are based on the current literature) [27, 28]. The DPs we derived fall into the category of "action and materiality-oriented design principles", describing what an artifact should enable users to do and how the artifact should be built to do so [28]. The development of the DPs follows the guidelines of [28] and [27]. Furthermore, we take one step further and append another layer by including the design features respectively the implementation of the DPs [28].

Since no particular machine learning technique is capable of accurately representing all DRs, a combination of them was essential. Regarding *DP1*, the autonomous extraction of aspects, unsupervised techniques (e.g., topic modeling) are required to enable an explorative analysis without prior domain knowledge. However, as stated by [29] the potential of totally unsupervised techniques is stymied by their purely unsupervised nature. Thus, semi-supervised techniques have arisen, facilitating an effective way to guide the analysis specific to a user by manipulating the analysis process even without structured prior domain knowledge [30]. Therefore, to take advantages of semi-supervised techniques while maintaining the flexibility of unsupervised ones, the known semi-supervised topic modeling technique GuidedLDA found application as it achieves convincing analysis results [30]. Besides the explorative analysis, the artifact must provide the ability to incorporate prior domain knowledge (*DP2*). Thus, the artifact provides a supervised aspect extraction using deep learning. Specifically, it applies a convolutional neural network (CNN) as proposed by [31], using two types of pre-trained embeddings for the aspect extraction: a general-purpose embedding and a domain specific embedding, containing domain related information used by the CNN

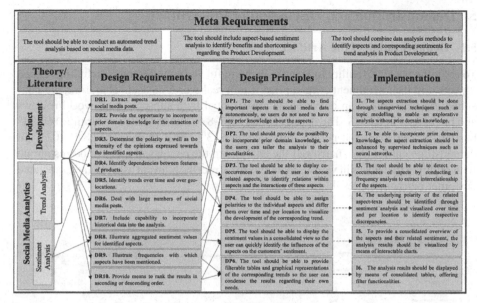

Fig. 2. Design of the artifact

to learn the domain specific peculiarities. Hence, the analysis can easily be adapted and tailored by changing the underlying domain embedding, resulting in a highly generic and customizable artifact. With respect to *DP3*, the artifact must depict co-occurrences of the related aspects to detect their interrelationship. As probabilistic topic modeling techniques such as GuidedLDA infer the resulting topics based on various probabilistic distributions, depicting the relations of the underlying topic words (and thus the resulting aspects) [32], the identification of their interrelationships is met through the nature of topic modeling itself. Considering the CNN, the artifact depicts the co-occurrences of the aspects by conducting a frequency analysis. Here, sub-aspects are identified for each extracted (main-)aspect by analyzing their respective occurrence in the context of the related main-aspect, resulting in an n-dimensional occurrence-tree. To determine the tonality of each aspect (*DP4*), the "Valence Aware Dictionary for sEntiment Reasoning" (VADER) [33] technique (a lexicon and rule-based sentiment analysis technique specifically attuned to sentiments expressed in social media) has been implemented. To further consolidate and visualize (*DP5*) the underlying aspects' sentiment as well as its evolution over time, corresponding line-charts are implemented using the python library matplotlib [34]. Finally, to ensure an adequate illustration of the analysis results (*DP6*), the extracted aspects, the corresponding sentiment values and their means, but also specific references to the extracted aspects are displayed using filterable tables and lists as demonstrated in the following section.

5   Demonstration and Discussion of the Artifact

5.1   Demonstration of the Artifact

To examine the tool's ability to identify meaningful and sound trends (including related aspects and their sentiment), we applied it to a real-world dataset. Therefore, we consulted the academic Yelp dataset [24], represented by a subset of real-world reviews and businesses in the US. The dataset comprises ~8.6 million OCR concerning 160,585 businesses and spans the period from October 13th, 2004 to January 28th, 2021. To demonstrate our tool, we narrowed the analysis to the reviews of a fast-food restaurant with multiple franchises in various locations to extract the relevant aspects and associated customer perceptions, resulting in 37,638 reviews.

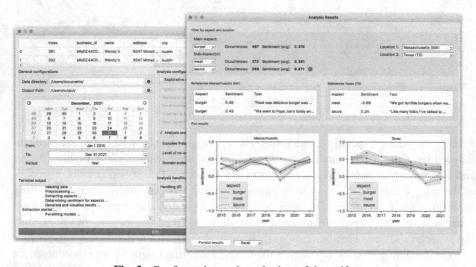

Fig. 3. Configuration and result view of the artifact

Figure 3 represents the tool's configuration view (left) and results view (right). By the configuration view, the underlying analysis can be customized to the one's own needs. For the purposes of our demonstration, the analysis was conducted using data spanning the years 2015 to 2021, prior domain knowledge to extract the aspects and all sentiment levels (*positive, neutral, negative*). The domain knowledge used was extracted from the renowned dataset of the 2016 SemEval task [35]. By using this word embedding tailored to the use case of restaurant reviews, the CNN is trained in the domain of the food and restaurant industry. The level of co-occurrences has been set to two, resulting in a two-dimensional occurrence-tree. The result view represents the sentiments of the extracted aspects with respect to the years, resulting in the monitoring of their evolution based on their customer perceptions.

Table 1 presents a detailed excerpt of the resulting Excel file, containing the elicited sentiment values per aspect and year. Here, both locations refer to the same aspects (main-aspect: burger; sub-aspects: meat, sauce), facilitating a comparison of temporal

Table 1. Analysis results - sentiments per year and location

Aspect	Location	Sentiment per Year						
		2015	2016	2017	2018	2019	2020	2021
Burger	*MA*	0.373	0.214	0.435	0.381	0.131	0.353	0.459
	TX	0.413	0.40	0.378	0.419	0.312	0.216	0.222
Meat	*MA*	0.515	0.447	0.421	0.521	−0.109	0.291	0.422
	TX	0.495	0.682	0.55	0.514	0.433	0.348	0.283
Sauce	*MA*	0.241	0.382	0.509	0.524	0.503	0.427	0.414
	TX	0.582	0.588	0.39	0.416	0.212	−0.186	0.12

and location-based discrepancies, thus enabling conclusions about different customer perceptions. In Massachusetts (MA), the main-aspect *burger* exhibits slight oscillation across the years but generally remains stable (see Fig. 3, Table 1). The worst average customer perception occurs in 2019 and is represented by a slightly positive sentiment score of 0.131. Furthermore, the two sub-aspects *meat* and *sauce* differ strongly in their course in 2019. Here, the course of *meat* collapses drastically (−0.109), while the course of *sauce* remains nearly constant (0.503) compared to the previous year, leading to the assumption that the negative reflections of *meat* may influence the main-aspect *burger*. Moreover, this assumption is supported by the development of the respective aspects. Here it becomes apparent that the significant improvement of the *meat* also potentially causes an improvement of the *burger*, supporting the conclusion that our tool can identify meaningful and sound trends based on the corresponding aspects and customer perceptions. Moreover, our tool has revealed discrepancies across the respective locations, as the perception of *sauce* overall has remained quite constant in MA but consistently decreases in Texas (TX) (see Fig. 3, Table 1).

Generally, the development of our tool was based on the DPs (see Fig. 2). Accordingly, all expectations posed were technically realized. In addition, several trends and their evolution could be identified by applying our tool to a real-world dataset, validating its functionality. To subsequently evaluate its practical applicability by identifying meaningful and sound trends, an evaluation will be conducted in future work.

5.2   Discussion of the Demonstration

The implementation of the DPs enabled us to design and develop a tool which has provided interesting results. As we establish the opportunity to extract the aspects in either a supervised or an unsupervised way (*DP1, DP2*), we can identify in the first instance aspects and/or product features which are discussed in the OCR. This allows us to identify those aspects which are most important from the customer's point of view and, above all, which must be considered in Product Development [3, 8, 20, 21]. Figure 4 shows that the most frequently named aspects are *burger, meat* and *sauce* (497, 372 and 268 occurrences). In the case of Product Development, the restaurant can start screening these aspects as they are particularly important for the customers. The extraction of aspects is possible on the one hand via a CNN including word embedding, providing the restaurant to incorporate prior domain knowledge (*DP2*) such as aspects about food, drinks, and processes in the restaurant. So, the extraction of the aspects is tailored precisely to the company. But, on the other hand, if a restaurant wants to extract aspects without exerting any influence, the tool can also identify them autonomously.

Moreover, the demonstration of the artifact has also shown that the customers have spoken differently about the three aspects. Here, our results show that users spoke about *sauce* more positively (0.471) over the years than about the aspects *burger* (0.376) and *meat* (0.391). Thus, numerous opportunities for improving products can be identified, and certain features can be given greater importance [5, 19]. Figure 4 shows that for MA the values of the individual aspects can change considerably: While in 2015–2018 the sentiment values of *meat* range between 0.40 and 0.52, in 2019 it slipped down into the negative range with −0.12. Simultaneously, the sentiment value of *burger* has fallen too. In this context, it is therefore possible that the negative sentiment about the *meat* had also influenced the customers' opinion about *burger*. If a company did not have this fine-grained information gained through the aspect-based sentiment analysis and wanted to adjust the product in 2019 based on the negative reviews, they potentially would have changed product features which were actually rated positively. In TX, considering these aspects is inevitable as the results show that *sauce* needs to be changed so the customers' opinions about it and thus of the whole burger can be improved again. Already existing trend analysis tools often include sentiment analysis to show the general tonality about the company or the product over time – without considering that different aspects influence the product's evaluation. However, this leads to a distortion of the results and the benefit for companies is no longer a given.

Furthermore, including geolocations and therefore considering location-based discrepancies can also create significant benefits. To be competitive in a targeted market, companies need to know which features should be designed in which way to meet the local customers' expectations [17, 36]. This becomes particularly evident when comparing MA and TX (see Fig. 4). While in MA the *burger* exhibits a positively connotated trend over the years, the sentiment over time in TX shows worse values. Especially in 2020 and 2021, the sentiment of the *burger* differs immensely (MA: 0.35, 0.45; TX: 0.28, 0.22). In both locations, there are different reasons for the burger's better (MA) or worse (TX) rating. While in TX the *sauce* must be adjusted to the taste of the people, this is not necessary in MA due to the steady positive values. Without including geolocations and also sentiment values, these discrepancies would not have been revealed, which clearly is a benefit in comparison to other existing tools.

6   Conclusion, Contribution and Outlook

Assessing and identifying people's opinions about a particular aspect and its future impact (thus a social media trend), is difficult, especially given the vast amount of social media data. Thus, techniques for analyzing textual social media data, e.g., aspect-based sentiment analysis, topic modeling and neural networks, have gained in importance, as companies need to be aware of customers' expectations regarding products. However, prior literature and existing tools do not include external parameters and do not cover specific requirements crucial in the field of Product Development (see Sect. 2.2). However, the early identification of new and auspicious ideas and trends means a competitive advantage for companies [19]. Thus, we provide a comprehensive tool by combining several machine learning techniques and transfer them in a highly responsive and platform-independent GUI. By demonstrating our tool on 37,638 Yelp OCR we have shown that considering all identified requirements is necessary to analyze trends.

Besides creating value for practitioners, theoretical contributions in the research area of IS are also provided. To acknowledge the importance of different DSR perspectives, we have related our DSR contribution to the category "design artifacts" according to [37], including both: the demonstration of the artifacts practical benefit and design theory contributions [38]. Therefore, by providing a tool for automated trend analysis that can identify aspects that are discussed within social media, we enable companies to gain deep insights into customers' current opinions and future expectations to tailor their products. Hence, to meet these customers' needs, a company has to identify and continuously track product features by incorporating the VoC into internal Product Development processes. Thus, as tracking evolving and changing customer requirements is imperative to meet customers' wishes [36, 39], companies can respond to them quickly and with minimal effort. Compared to existing trend analysis tools, our tool meets all the specific requirements set out within the literature regarding Product Development. In particular, our tool can flexibly match different temporal and geographical parameters to identify aspect-sentiment relations and it provides users the possibility to extract the aspects either with or without prior domain knowledge. Thus, customer perceptions for specific periods or geolocations can be displayed to track fine-grained variabilities. On the one hand, this makes it possible to visualize influences affecting the sentiment. On the other hand, downward trends can be counteracted and upward trends can be strengthened. Hence, this combined with the integration of geolocations can especially support large companies with multiple branches in their efforts to easily perceive location-specific sentiment changes and explicitly react to them. As we have combined different techniques and designed our tool modularly, companies can adapt the analysis to their specific needs. A further contribution is that the tool can be supportive in identifying the aspects of the products to be changed to meet the customer's expectations (remove existing aspects, others need to be enhanced) with the realization of (*DP4*)–(*DP6*). In summary, companies can benefit from our comprehensive and modular artifact by analyzing large amounts of data in a way best suited to their circumstances, aiming to analyze trends regarding their aspect-based sentiment values.

Besides our technical contribution (i.e., the artifact), we achieved prescriptive theoretical contributions as a further outcome of our DSR project. Therefore, we formulated and proposed DPs based on the DRs derived from current research literature. By applying them an implicit empirical grounding of the DPs was achieved. Our DPs capture design-related knowledge and can therefore support the development of further IS (design) theories and new artifacts. For designing further (trend analysis) tools in related areas, our DPs can be applied as we have formulated them in a prescriptive and abstract manner by generally describing what the artifact should enable users to do and how it should be built. Furthermore, the formulation of DPs allows us to abstract away from individual settings and DRs, and rather align with generalizing prescriptive knowledge whereby they contribute to "nascent design theory" [38, 40]. For example, by DP4, the importance of including time, geolocation and/or further external parameters (e.g., customers' characteristics) in a trend analysis tool is highlighted. As these external parameters have a direct impact on the customers' sentiment and therefore on the analysis results (cf. [41]), the alignment to them will lead to a more targeted trend analysis tool. Thus, for researchers that intend to design such a tool, we suggest considering the influences that are evoked by external factors. So, with the compilation of the DPs, we made a first step towards contributing to nascent design theory. To take a next step towards a more mature design theory, we intend to verify our DPs by further evaluating our tool. Therefore, we will first evaluate our tool in a formative and artificial environment (i.e., a laboratory experiment). Here, participants will use it to identify relevant aspects and associated customer perceptions. Subsequently, they will complete a questionnaire to indicate their perceptions of the analysis quality and tool usability. This allows us to identify difficulties and improve our tool (whereby our DPs can be confirmed or adapted) before conducting a more elaborate evaluation in a more natural setting. This second evaluation will be a field study with a large restaurant chain that plans to integrate a tool to support its marketing departments.

However, there are also some limitations to this research: Although we included a large set of investigations, we could identify probably even more requirements the tool should meet in further literature.

References

1. Kaplan, A.M., Haenlein, M.: Users of the world, unite! The challenges and opportunities of Social Media. Bus. Horiz. **53**(1), 59–68 (2010)
2. Kim, Y.K., Lee, D., Lee, J., Lee, J.-H., Straub, D.W.: Influential users in social network services: the contingent value of connecting user status and brokerage. ACM SIGMIS: The Database Adv. Inform. Syst. **49**(1), 13–32 (2018)
3. Tuarob, S., Tucker, C.S.: Quantifying product favorability and extracting notable product features using large scale social media data. J. Comput. Inf. Sci. Eng. **15**(3), 031003 (2015)
4. Schouten, K., Frasincar, F.: Survey on aspect-level sentiment analysis. IEEE Trans. Knowl. Data Eng. **28**(3), 813–830 (2015)
5. Tucker, C.S., Kim, H.: Predicting emerging product design trend by mining publicly available customer review data. In: 18th International Conference on Engineering Design (2011)
6. Mirtalaie, M.A., Hussain, O.K., Chang, E., Hussain, F.K.: Sentiment analysis of specific product's features using product tree for application in new product development. In: Barolli, L., Woungang, I., Hussain, O.K. (eds.) INCoS 2017. LNDECT, vol. 8, pp. 82–95. Springer, Cham (2018). https://doi.org/10.1007/978-3-319-65636-6_8
7. Mirtalaie, M.A., Hussain, O.K., Chang, E., Hussain, F.K.: Extracting sentiment knowledge from pros/cons product reviews: discovering features along with the polarity strength of their associated opinions. Expert Syst. Appl. **114**, 267–288 (2018)
8. Mirtalaie, M., Hussain, O.: Sentiment aggregation of targeted features by capturing their dependencies: making sense from customer reviews. Int. J. Inform. Manag. **53**, 102097 (2020)
9. Vo, A.-D., Nguyen, Q.-P., Ock, C.-Y.: Opinion–aspect relations in cognizing customer feelings via reviews. IEEE Access **6**, 5415–5426 (2018)
10. Hicks, A., Comp, S., Horovitz, J., Hovarter, M., Miki, M., Bevan, J.L.: Why people use Yelp.com: an exploration of uses and gratifications. Comput. Human Behav. **28**(6), 2274–2279 (2012)

11. Yan, Z., Xing, M., Zhang, D., Ma, B., Wang, T.: A context-dependent sentiment analysis of online product reviews based on dependency relationships. In: 35th ICIS (2014)

12. Ye, H.J., Kankanhalli, A.: User service innovation on mobile phone platforms: investigating impacts of lead userness, toolkit support, and design autonomy. MIS Quart. **42**(1), 165–188 (2018)

13. Axtell, C.M., Holman, D.J., Unsworth, K.L., Wall, T.D., Waterson, P.E., Harrington, E.: Shopfloor innovation: facilitating the suggestion and implementation of ideas. J. Occup. Organ. Psychol. **73**(3), 265–285 (2000)

14. Blei, D.M., Ng, A.Y., Jordan, M.: Latent dirichlet allocation. J. Mach. Learn. Res. **3**, 993–1022 (2003)

15. Liu, B.: Sentiment analysis and opinion mining. In: Synthesis Lectures on Human Language Technologies, vol. 5, 1st edn. Morgan & Claypool Publisher (2012)

16. Vom Brocke, J., Simons, A., Riemer, K., Niehaves, B., Plattfaut, R., Cleven, A.: Standing on the shoulders of giants. Commun. Assoc. Inform. Syst. **37**(1), 205–224 (2015)

17. Han, Y., Moghaddam, M.: Analysis of sentiment expressions for user-centered design. Expert Syst. Appl. **171**, 114604 (2021)

18. Cheng, L.-C., Chen, K., Lee, M.-C., Li, K.-M.: User-defined SWOT analysis – a change mining perspective on user-generated content. Inform. Process. Manag. **58**(5), 102613 (2021)

19. Jeong, B., Yoon, J., Lee, J.-M.: Social media mining for product planning: a product opportunity mining approach based on topic modeling and sentiment analysis. Int. J. Inform. Manag. **48**, 280–290 (2019)

20. Zhang, J., Zhang, A., Liu, D., Bian, Y.: Customer preferences extraction for air purifiers based on fine-grained sentiment analysis of online reviews. Knowledge-Based Syst. **228**, 107259 (2021)

21. Yu, J., Zha, Z.-J., Wang, M., Chua, T.-S.: Aspect ranking: identifying important product aspects from online consumer reviews. In: 49th Annual Meeting of the ACL, pp. 1496–1505 (2011)

22. Hevner, M., Park, R.: Design science in information systems research. MIS Quart. **28**(1), 75–105 (2004)

23. Peffers, K., Tuunanen, T., Rothenberger, M.A., Chatterjee, S.: A design science research methodology for information systems research. J. Manag. Inform. Syst. **24**, 45–77 (2007)

24. Yelp open dataset (2021). https://www.yelp.com/dataset, Accessed on 15 Dec 2021

25. Purao, S., Kruse, L.C., Maedche, A.: The origins of design principles: where do... they all come from? In: Hofmann, S., Müller, O., Rossi, M. (eds.) DESRIST 2020. LNCS, vol. 12388, pp. 183–194. Springer, Cham (2020). https://doi.org/10.1007/978-3-030-64823-7_17

26. Jones, D., Gregor, S.: The anatomy of a design theory. J. Assoc. Inform. Syst. **8**(5), 312–335 (2007)

27. Heinrich, P., Schwabe, G.: Communicating nascent design theories on innovative information systems through multi-grounded design principles. In: Tremblay, M.C., VanderMeer, D., Rothenberger, M., Gupta, A., Yoon, V. (eds.) DESRIST 2014. LNCS, vol. 8463, pp. 148–163. Springer, Cham (2014). https://doi.org/10.1007/978-3-319-06701-8_10

28. Möller, F., Guggenberger, T.M., Otto, B.: Towards a method for design principle development in information systems. In: Hofmann, S., Müller, O., Rossi, M. (eds.) DESRIST 2020. LNCS, vol. 12388, pp. 208–220. Springer, Cham (2020). https://doi.org/10.1007/978-3-030-64823-7_20

29. Chang, J., Gerrish, S., Wang, C., Boyd-Graber, J.L., Blei, D.M.: Reading tea leaves: How humans interpret topic models. In: Bengio, Y., Schuurmans, D., Lafferty, J., Williams, C., Culotta, A. (eds.) Advances in neural information processing systems, pp. 288–296. Curran Associates, Inc. (2009)

30. Jagarlamudi, J., Daumé III, H., Udupa, R.: Incorporating lexical priors into topic models. In: 13th Conference of the European Chapter of the ACL, pp. 204–213 (2012)

31. Xu, H., Liu, B., Shu, L., Philip, S.: Double embeddings and CNN-based sequence labeling for aspect extraction. In: 56th Annual Meeting of the ACL, pp. 592–598 (2018)
32. Crain, S.P., Zhou, K., Yang, S.-H., Zha, H.: Dimensionality reduction and topic modeling: From latent semantic indexing to latent dirichlet allocation and beyond. In: Aggarwal, C.C., Zhai, C.X. (eds.) Mining Text Data, pp. 129–161. Springer US, Boston, MA (2012). https://doi.org/10.1007/978-1-4614-3223-4_5
33. Hutto, C., Gilbert, E.: Vader: A parsimonious rule-based model for sentiment analysis of social media text. In: International AAAI Conference on Web and Social Media (2014)
34. Hunter, J.: Matplotlib: a 2D graphics environment. Comput. Sci. Eng **9**(3), 90–95 (2007)
35. Pontiki, M., et al.: Semeval-2016 task 5: aspect based sentiment analysis. In: International Workshop on Semantic Evaluation, pp. 19–30 (2016)
36. Lozano, M.G., Schreiber, J., Brynielsson, J.: Tracking geographical locations using a geo-aware topic model for analyzing social media data. Decis. Support Syst. **99**, 18–29 (2017)
37. Baskerville, R., Baiyere, A., Gergor, S., Hevner, A., Rossi, M.: Design science research contributions: finding a balance between artifact and theory. J. Assoc. Inform. Syst. **19**(5), 358–376 (2018)
38. Gregor, S., Hevner, A.R.: Positioning and presenting design science research for maximum impact. MIS Quart. **37**(2), 337–355 (2013)
39. Hong, L., Ahmed, A., Gurumurthy, S., Smola, A.J., Tsioutsiouliklis, K.: Discovering geographical topics in the twitter stream. In: 21st International Conference on WWW, pp. 769–778 (2012)
40. Gregor, S., Kruse, L., Seidel, S.: Research perspectives: the anatomy of a design principle. J. Assoc. Inform. Syst. **21**, 1622–1652 (2020)
41. Konadl, D., Wörner, J., Leist, S.: Identifying sentiment influences provoked by context factors–results from a data analytics procedure performed on tweets. In: 54th HICSS (2021)

Blockchain Information Systems

Introduction to Blockchain Information Systems Track

Kaushik Dutta[1], Gary Patterson[1], and Carson Woo[2]

[1] University of South Florida
duttak@usf.edu
pattersg@usf.edu
[2] University of British Columbia
carson.woo@sauder.ubc.ca

Abstract. Blockchain technology is widely considered as a solution to many of today's challenging information systems applications that require trust without a third party. This technology is new because of its emergent behavior of combining several existing technologies. However, when combining technologies, this increases the complexity of blockchain applications. As a result, research needs to progress by: isolating various blockchain components into different artifacts and then combining them for use together; or studying use cases to analyze blockchain's applicability in various settings. This track incorporates research papers in both of these directions.

Keywords: Blockchain · Abstraction · Complexity · Artifact · Application · Use case studies

Although blockchain technology has been in existence for some time, it remains a promising technology to address ongoing, complex problems, in today's world. This is due, in part, to its emergent characteristics that result from combining existing technologies, such as hashing, smart contracts, and private and public keys. In some application areas, such as supply chain management or health care, it can be difficult, if not impossible, to find a trusted third party upon which all stakeholders agree. For example, in countries where the government is the sole sponsor of healthcare, the government plays the role of a trusted third party. In this situation, blockchain would not be the only technological solution that would be useful for health care applications. In countries where health care has different, influential stakeholders, such as insurance companies or pharmacies, then blockchain might be the only solution for dealing effectively with the different players who are involved and their dominant interests.

Despite the promise of applying blockchain to solve previously unresolved problems, its complexity and emergent behaviors are challenging to understand and analyze. To better predict the emergent behaviors and manage the complexity, different parts of blockchain development needs to be isolated, managed, and controlled. This is where research in design science research can help. For example, abstraction can be used to design artifacts that can hide details and operate as expected in blockchain applications.

An example of abstraction mechanism is the entity-relationship (ER) model [1]. Before the ER model was invented, the design of a database involved addressing issues related to the different types of data storage (e.g., hierarchical database versus relational database), the management of empty storage spaces, and the need for new storage spaces so that data could be retrieved and processed quickly. The ER model is, in essence, an abstraction that hides implementation details so users and analysts can quickly consider information needs, without being concerned that the outcome will be insufficient for implementing a database. The equivalent of an ER model would be very useful for developing blockchain applications and provide artifacts to improve its operations.

Today blockchain technology is where relational database was in 1970s. The basic framework of the technology is well understood. However, how to effectively use this technology for business and social causes is still unclear. The use of blockchain requires further enhancement on the underlying technology and the innovative use of the platform. The research in design needs to encompass both. Just recently USA's first real estate transaction on blockchain-based technology happened in Tampa Bay. A house was tokenized in the form of NFT (non-fungible token) and then the ownership was transferred immediately through a blockchain platform [2]. Thus, having a blockchain specific track in DESRIST 2022 in Tampa Bay goes along with the spirit of the region in becoming a leader in blockchain based platform.

Without the equivalent of a higher-level abstraction mechanism to generally support blockchain development, research in blockchain mainly proceeds in two ways, which is reflected in the papers in this track. First, if there is a clear artifact that can be isolated and improved (e.g., random number generator), it can be explored. Second, if there is an application that requires the use of blockchain (e.g., healthcare), it provides a way to experiment with blockchain independent of abstractions. The results of such research effort can lead to the development of a needed higher-level model from which blockchain progression can be made and evaluated. This track provides an interesting set of papers that can progress blockchain in design science research.

References

1. Chen, P.P.-S.: The entity-relationship model-toward a unified view of data. ACM Trans. Database Syst. **1**(1), 9–36 (1976)
2. https://therealdeal.com/miami/2022/02/19/tampa-area-home-billed-as-first-in-us-to-be-sold-as-an-nft/

Transient Random Number Seeds
in Permissionless Blockchain Systems

Riaan Bezuidenhout(✉) ⓘ, Wynand Nel ⓘ, and Jacques Maritz ⓘ

University of the Free State, Bloemfontein, South Africa
{BezuidenhoutR,NelW,MaritzJM}@ufs.ac.za

Abstract. Permissionless blockchain systems are highly dependent on probabilistic decision models, for example, the block addition process. If it were possible
to use blockchain systems as pseudo-random number generators, they could be
used to select, for example, new block proposers. The first step in this process is to
embed random number seeds in the blockchain for use in pseudo-random number
generation. This paper proposes transient random number seeds (TRNS), which
produce random number seeds as part of each transaction. TRNS, belonging to
each recipient in a transaction and are confidential, tamper-resistant, unpredictable,
collision-resistant, and publicly verifiable. TRNS enable recipients to produce
pseudo-random numbers to participate in any process where the blockchain system depends on random selection. The TRNS protocol is highly scalable with
constant computational complexity and space complexity linear in the number of
transactions per block.

Keywords: Block addition · Permissionless blockchain · Random number
generator · Transient random number seed

1 Introduction

Many blockchain operations require a source of publicly verifiable random numbers. This
is particularly true of blockchain consensus algorithms in permissionless blockchain
systems, where the goal is to select the party that has the right to add a new block
to the blockchain at random [1]. The most famous blockchain consensus algorithm is
proof-of-work (PoW) which is represented in more than 80% of cryptocurrencies when
measured by market capitalisation [2]. PoW has, however, also gained notoriety through
its high electricity demand, particularly in its use by Bitcoin [3]. This weakness of PoW
means that researchers are constantly searching for alternative ways to select new block
proposers for blockchain systems.

In addition to attempts to improve the power consumption of PoW, like non-linear
proof-of-work [4], alternative consensus algorithms, like proof-of-stake (PoS), delegated proof-of-stake (DPoS) and proof-of-importance, exhibit the possibility for the
consensus mechanism to be skewed in the direction of a minority of stakeholders
in the blockchain network [5–7]. Proof-of-elapsed time, proof-of-luck, and proof-of-
responsibility depends on input from a centralised authority, which is at odds with the

© Springer Nature Switzerland AG 2022
A. Drechsler et al. (Eds.): DESRIST 2022, LNCS 13229, pp. 85–96, 2022.
https://doi.org/10.1007/978-3-031-06516-3_7

decentralised idea of blockchain systems [8–10]. Attempts have been made to exchange electricity use for an alternative resource, for example, PoW with a cuckoo hash function (random access memory), proof-of-space (data storage capacity), and proof-of-burn (blockchain tokens) [11–13].

Whatever the strategy, all consensus algorithms reduce to the same fundamental idea expressed by Glaser [1]. They attempt to make the block addition process random by selecting the block proposer randomly. It makes sense then to seek ways in which permissionless blockchain systems themselves can act as pseudo-random number generators, which in turn can be used to select block proposers. Pseudo-random number generators are, however, deterministic and depend solely on seed values. Each seed value results in the same pseudo-random number when used as input in the same pseudo-random number generator [14]. If it were possible then to assign random number seeds to stakeholders in the blockchain, these seeds could be used by these stakeholders to produce pseudo-random numbers, which in turn could serve to select block proposers at random from among the stakeholders. Specifically, these seeds must be embedded in the blockchain data structure, be tamper-resistant and publicly verifiable. Tamper-resistant refers to tampering by a would-be block proposer, as well as anyone who may want to assist or hinder that would-be proposer. Public verifiability is required because, in the absence of a central authority, the data in a permissionless blockchain system must constantly be scrutinised by all stakeholders in the system.

We propose a confidential, tamper-resistant, unpredictable, collision-resistant, publicly verifiable, and scalable protocol to embed transient random number seeds (TRNS) in blockchain transactions. Each recipient in a transaction receives a random number seed that remains usable by the recipient until the transaction output is spent (the asset is transferred), in which case the new recipient receives a random number seed. Each random number seed is transient because it lives only while the recipient holds the asset. This has two advantages. First, it is customary for stakeholders to maintain a database of unspent transactions and consequently live random number seeds, as it is more efficient for checking the validity of transactions than traversing the blockchain. Second, only current asset holders can participate in the block proposition process. The TRNS protocol adds low computational and space complexity to the blockchain system.

The rest of the paper is organised into four parts, Sects. 2, 3, 4 and 5. Sections 2 and 3 summarise the most important recent work on publically verifiable number generation and then gives the reader an overview of the relevant blockchain topics and cryptographic concepts referenced throughout the rest of the text. Section 4 describes the TRNS protocol, and the paper concludes with Sect. 5.

2 Related Work

Publicly verifiable random numbers, also referred to as beacons or random beacons, have been widely studied [15]. Andrychowicz and Dziembowski [16] used the properties of cryptographic hash functions in peer-to-peer PoW blockchain systems to produce an unpredictable public beacon. It differs from TRNS protocol by providing a single beacon to all parties. PoW algorithms complete in non-deterministic polynomial time and do not scale well.

Scrape uses a distributed ledger and publicly verifiable secret sharing to produce a single random beacon among a set of participants [17]. Scrape does not scale well as it exhibits cubic computational complexity [18].

RandHound [19] provides individualised, publicly verifiable random numbers to participating stakeholders, using a commit/reveal scheme, publicly verifiable secret sharing [17] and threshold signatures [20]. RandHerd [19] extends RandHound, producing a stream of publicly verifiable, non-individualised random numbers. Both exhibit quadratic computational complexity.

HydRand [21] functions in permissioned environments, employs publicly verifiable secret sharing [17] and random leader selection to produce a stream of publicly verifiable random beacons. The protocol has quadratic computational complexity.

Dfinity is a blockchain consensus protocol that uses a built-in pseudo-random number generator as a basis for selecting new block proposers [22]. It uses distributed key generation and Boneh-Lynn-Shacham threshold signatures [23] to produce a random beacon. Participants may freely join or depart from the network, but it requires that all participants are identified for each epoch (a fixed number of consecutive block additions). A special opening block is used at the beginning of each epoch where participants register their intention to join or depart. The distributed key generation protocol at the beginning of each epoch has quadratic computational complexity [24], but the repeated signing process for generating random numbers during the rest of the epoch is linear [22].

Randao uses the Ethereum blockchain to produce a publicly verifiable random beacon [25]. During each round, stakeholders share the hash values of locally produced seeds on the blockchain. Once all seed hashes are registered, participants reveal their seeds, which are combined to produce a random value. Randao has linear computational complexity but is vulnerable to look-ahead attacks.

Ginar lets individual participants request a random number in cooperation with a set of disintermediated participants on a blockchain system [15]. Each participant uses a verifiable random function [26] to determine their eligibility threshold, and eligible participants then encrypt a secret value with the requester's public key. The encrypted secret is stored on a blockchain, and the requester can decrypt the sum of the encrypted secrets using the homomorphic property of Elgamal encryption. The decrypted sum is the requester's random number. Ginar is linear in computational complexity [15].

Single Secret Leader Election (SSLE) enables the selection of a random block proposer (leader) in a blockchain system [27]. SSLE uses threshold fully homomorphic encryption [28] to hide the leader's identity until it reveals itself. This obfuscation protects the leader against a denial-of-service attack by a malicious party. SSLE relies on public randomness beacons, which the designer of the final SSLE implementation must decide. SSLE consists of two phases. First, participants must register to participate during the setup phase and second, repeated election rounds are held until there is a change in participants [27]. The authors did not report the computational complexity, but most of the computational load is required for registering the participants during the setup phase, presumably with quadratic complexity. The initial computational investment is then amortised over many election rounds.

3 Preliminaries

Before embarking on a description of the proposed approach, it is necessary to clarify some terminology for simplifying the discussions. Blockchain transactions refer to the transfer of an electronic asset or collection of assets between a sender or group of senders (in a cryptocurrency sense, the payor, or payors) and a recipient or group of recipients (payee or payees). We assume a single sender and a single receiver per transaction to simplify the explanation, but the method can easily be applied to the more complex case. Verifiers are stakeholders that may wish to verify the validity of data on the blockchain but are not necessarily a party to any transaction. A simplified, generalised blockchain transaction is shown in Fig. 1.

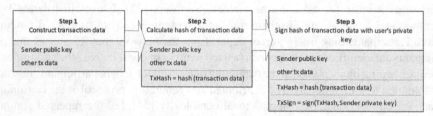

Fig. 1. The generalised blockchain construction process

In essence, a blockchain transaction consists of three steps. In this study, a transaction is treated in its most general sense. Step 1 constructs the transaction data. The sender public key denotes the blockchain address of the party initiating the transaction (the sender). In practice, it may be that a transaction contains multiple addresses belonging to the sender, and the address may obfuscate the public key, but this is irrelevant for illustration purposes. Step 2 calculates the hash of the transaction data (TxHash) and appends it to the existing data. TxHash serves as a unique identifier for the transaction. In Step 3, the sender signs TxHash with its private key and appends it to the data. This allows verification that the transaction was created by the rightful owner of the public key and that the transaction data has not been tampered with.

It is assumed that parties to a transaction (sender or recipient) have access to suitable *local* cryptographic services for public-key cryptography, cryptographic hash functions and cryptographic quality pseudo-random number generation. This is a reasonable assumption as many programming languages supply these services, for example, C# [29]. Table 1 gives a synopsis of the essential public-key cryptography services [30].

Table 1. Essential services of public-key cryptography

Service	Description
Key generation	Creates a private and public key-pair (Private key, Public key) for use in the other four functions and provide protocols to exchanging keys between parties
Encryption	Encrypted message = encrypt (Plain-text message with public key)
Decryption	Plain-text message = decrypt (Encrypted message with private key)
Message signature	Signature = sign (Plain-text message with private key)
Signature verification	Verification = verify (Plain-text message, signature with public key)

4 Proposed Approach

This paper proposes a method for embedding TRNS with each new transaction. It functions on the principle that the recipient of a transaction receives a random number seed enabling it to participate in blockchain processes that are based on probabilistic decision models. Once the owner of a TRNS transfers its assets to a new owner, its TRNS expires, and the recipient from the transaction receives a TRNS. This ensures that only active asset holders on the blockchain can participate in decision processes designed to use TRNS. Each TRNS has five important properties:

- Each TRNS is *confidential*. This means that it is only known to the owner of the TRNS until such time that it is used.
- The seed is *tamper-resistant* and *unpredictable* because no party can manipulate it in a meaningful way. This includes the owner of the TRNS.
- The TRNS is made *collision-resistant* using cryptographic hash functions.
- Once a TRNS is used by its owner, it is *publically verifiable*.
- Embedding TRNS into blockchain transactions is *scalable* and does not add significant space and computational complexity to the blockchain system.

Embedding a TRNS into a blockchain transaction is part of the transaction construction process and requires specific actions by the recipient and the sender. The TRNS protocol governs these actions, and the responsibilities of the participating parties are described in Sects. 4.1, 4.2, 4.3 and 4.4.

4.1 TRNS Recipient Protocol

When a transaction is initiated on a blockchain system, the recipient must generate a set of payment details that specify the destination of the transfer. While the specification for this destination information may differ between different blockchain implementations, it can, for the sake of simplicity, be thought of as the public key from a public-private key pair. This will throughout be referred to as the destination key-pair. The TRNS recipient protocol requires two additional data items (Fig. 2).

Fig. 2. TRNS recipient protocol

First, the recipient creates a second public-private key pair – the participation key-pair. We assume a single party recipient to simplify the explanation, but for multi-party recipients, a distributed key generation protocol can be used as in [24]. Second, the recipient constructs a secret by calculating the hash of a locally generated pseudo-random number. Third, the recipient signs the secret with its participation private key. Finally, the recipient sends the destination public key, participation public key and signature of the secret to the sender. The reason the recipient does not use its destination public key to also sign its secret is to preserve the best practice to use a key-pair only once for signing. Once the sender has the destination data, it uses the TRNS sender protocol to add the seed fields (participation public-key and secret signature) to the transaction it creates. The TRNS transaction construction protocol adds constant computational complexity to the recipient and constant space complexity to the destination data.

4.2 TRNS Sender Protocol

The sender follows the generic blockchain transaction construction process and, in addition to the normal transaction data, appends the receiver's participation public-key and secret signature (Steps 1 and 2 in Fig. 3).

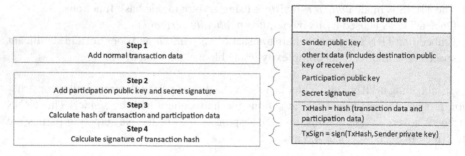

Fig. 3. TRNS sender protocol

After adding all the transaction data, the sender follows the usual signing procedure by first calculating the hash of the transaction data and then signing it with its sender private key (Steps 3 and 4 in Fig. 3). The TRNS sender protocol adds constant space complexity to each transaction. In terms of each new block created by a block proposer, the space complexity is linear in the number of transactions.

4.3 TRNS Retrieval Protocol

The receiver can retrieve its TRNS as soon as its transaction is confirmed on the blockchain. This is done by calculating the hash of Merkle root and recipient secret (Fig. 4).

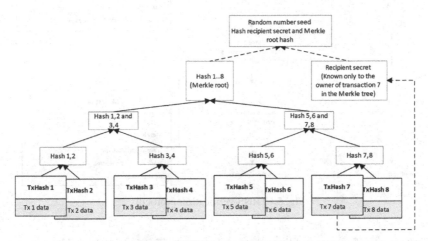

Fig. 4. TRNS retrieval protocol

The TRNS becomes stable when the block in which the transaction is recorded becomes persistent, so it makes sense that a TRNS may only be used by the recipient from that point onward. Note that the recipient secret and its TRNS are only known to the recipient. The TRNS and accompanying receiver secret need only be made public by the recipient once it is used in a decision process. By making the receiver secret public, any party can verify the validity of the receiver's TRNS. The TRNS retrieval protocol can be executed in constant time by the receiver.

The authors note that the random number seed has two weaknesses. First, a recipient and a block proposer may collude to manipulate the random number seed, and second, the seed remains fixed (the same) for all future operations for which it may be used. Both concerns can be mitigated through seed hardening. For example, when the recipient chooses to use its seed to engage in a blockchain process, say, attempt to become a leader in a block selection process, the protocol may prescribe that the seed be used in combination with the previous block hash of the newly proposed block to compute the final pseud-random number.

4.4 TRNS Verification Protocol

A verifier requires only the receiver secret to verify the receiver's TRNS. The Bitcoin PoW consensus algorithm requires the successful miner to publish its nonce on the blockchain. A similar approach can be followed with the receiver's secret by requiring that the receiver publishes its receiver secret and TRNS on the blockchain when it is used. The steps in the TRNS verification protocol are shown in Fig. 5.

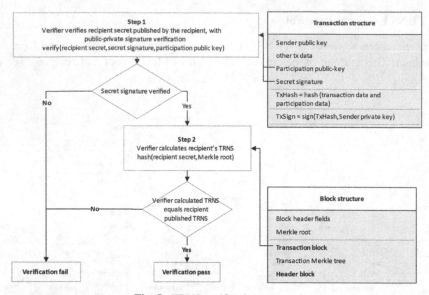

Fig. 5. TRNS verification protocol

First, the verifier uses public-private signature verification to check if the signature of the recipient secret recorded in the transaction is that of the secret made public by the receiver. Second, the recipient recalculates the TRNS by hashing the recipient secret and the Merkle root of the block where the transaction was recorded and checking it against the TRNS used by the recipient. TRNS verification is linear in the number of transactions per block.

4.5 Using the TRNS for Consensus

Research is currently underway to design a consensus protocol using the TRNS. A simplified example where a new block proposer is selected by way of a lottery can be illustrated as follows. First, candidate proposers from the pool of recipients with unspent transactions, each generate a lottery ticket (Ticket) from their TRNS. Second, each proposer constructs a new transaction block and publishes the ticket information and the secret from which the TRNS was derived in the block header. Finally, the network follows the consensus rule of accepting the block with the largest ticket as the next valid block to extend the blockchain.

Since each recipient constructs its secret locally, the network cannot control how each owner produces it. In practice, the Rivest method for producing a pseudo-random number from a hash function should be sufficient for honest participants, as hash functions are a good source of pseudo-randomness [31]. Recipients who follow an insecure method for producing the owner seed, for example, by hashing a predictable value, compromise the confidentiality of their TRNS, but it has no impact on the seeds of other honest owners. Once the transaction containing the TRNS is stable on the blockchain, the recipient can retrieve it using the TRNS retrieval protocol.

Candidate proposers generate the lottery ticket at the time it constructs a new candidate block. The Ticket for proposer i, T_i is the hash of $TRNS_i$ and the hash of the preceding block (H_{n-1}).

$$T_i = hash(TRNS_i, H_{n-1}) \tag{1}$$

Each candidate proposer records its secret and Ticket by adding the fields to the proposed block's header. Each node in the blockchain network evaluates each candidate block to ascertain the validity of the secret, TRNS, and Ticket. The valid candidate block with the largest Ticket is chosen as the new block. Since the Ticket is tied to the previous block hash, each new block round will produce a new ticket for each recipient. The consensus algorithm can be adapted to place restrictions on the age of each TRNS, for example, the TRNS may need to be buried by a minimum number of blocks or must be used within a certain number of block rounds. The layout of a candidate block is shown in Fig. 6.

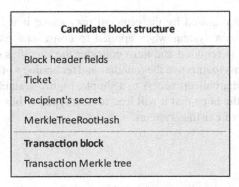

Fig. 6. Candidate block structure

5 Conclusion

The TRNS protocol is a method for embedding random number seeds into blockchain transactions. These random number seeds are transient, meaning that they are valid only if the transaction is unspent. Designers of blockchain systems may, of course, impose additional constraints on each random number seed, for example, by requiring that the seed must mature before being used (be buried under a fixed number of new blocks in the blockchain), expire after a fixed number of blocks even if the transaction remains unspent, or be used only once.

Each TRNS is confidential, tamper-resistant, unpredictable, collision-resistant, and publicly verifiable. These properties open avenues for blockchain designs where probabilistic decision making is required. Uses include the selection of new block proposers, especially in blockchain systems where it is impossible to weigh the value of digital assets directly, as is the case with PoS or DPoS systems. Other uses may include input values in smart contracts, inputs that determine a random ordering of blockchain processes, inputs for distributed applications (for example, gaming), or new types of blockchain applications such as publicly verifiable distributed random number generation. The TRNS protocol is highly scalable, as is summarised in Table 2.

Table 2. Summary of TRNS computation and space complexity

TRNS protocol	Computational complexity	Space complexity
Receiver	$O(1)$	$O(1)$
Sender	n/a	Transaction: $O(1)$ Block: $O(n)$, n = transactions/block
Retrieval	$O(1)$	n/a
Verification	$O(n)$, n = transactions/block	n/a

The low overheads required by the protocol may make it vulnerable to low-cost attacks on the blockchain system when applied to consensus protocols, but further research in this regard is required and must consider the specifics of each application. The TRNS protocol aims to improve the foundational technology of blockchain systems by allowing blockchain architects access to a simple, highly scalable source of random number generation in the hope that it will lead to new types of blockchain systems and improve the efficiency of existing systems.

References

1. Glaser, F.: Pervasive decentralisation of digital infrastructures: a framework for blockchain-enabled system and use case analysis. In: Proceedings of the 50th Hawaii International Conference on System Sciences (2017)
2. Binance Capital Mgmt: CoinMarketCap. https://coinmarketcap.com/
3. De Vries, A.: Bitcoin's growing energy problem. Joule. **2**, 801–805 (2018). https://doi.org/10.1016/j.joule.2018.04.016
4. Bezuidenhout, R., Nel, W., Burger, A.: Nonlinear proof-of-work: improving the energy efficiency of bitcoin mining. J. Constr. Proj. Manag. Innov. **10**(1), 20–32 (2020). https://doi.org/10.36615/jcpmi.v10i1.351
5. Bentov, I., Gabizon, A., Mizrahi, A.: Cryptocurrencies without proof of work. In: 2016 Financial Cryptography and Data Security Conference (2016)
6. NEM: Proof-of-importance. https://nemplatform.com/wp-content/uploads/2020/05/NEM_techRef.pdf. Last accessed 12 Nov 2019
7. BitShares Blockchain Foundation: Delegated Proof-of-Stake Consensus. https://bitshares.org/technology/delegated-proof-of-stake-consensus/. Last accessed 11 Aug 2019
8. Hasib, A.: 101 Blockchains. https://101blockchains.com/consensus-algorithms-blockchain/#6. Last accessed 12 Nov 2019
9. Milutinovic, M., He, W., Wu, H., Kanwal, M.: Proof of luck: an efficient blockchain consensus protocol. IACR Cryptol. ePrint Arch. 2017 (2016)

10. Coinspace.com: Electroneum's Revolutionary Proof of Responsibility Blockchain is Now Live. https://coinspace.com/news/altcoin-news/electroneums-revolutionary-proof-responsibility-blockchain-now-live
11. Tromp, J.: Cuckoo Cycle: A memory bound graph-theoretic proof-of-work. https://eprint.iacr.org/2014/059.pdf. Last accessed 14 Nov 2019
12. P4Titan: Slimcoin: A peer-to-peer crypto-currency with proof-of-burn (2014)
13. Dziembowski, S., Faust, S., Kolmogorov, V., Pietrzak, K.: Proofs of space. In: CRYPTO: International Cryptology Conference (2015). https://doi.org/10.1007/978-3-662-48000-7_29
14. Schindler, W.: Random number generators for cryptographic applications. In: Koç, Ç.K. (ed.) Cryptographic Engineering, pp. 5–23. Springer US, Boston, MA (2009). https://doi.org/10.1007/978-0-387-71817-0_2
15. Nguyen Van, T., et al.: Scalable distributed random number generation based on homomorphic encryption. In: 2019 IEEE International Conference on Blockchain, pp. 572–579. Atlanta (2019). https://doi.org/10.1109/Blockchain.2019.00083
16. Andrychowicz, M., Dziembowski, S.: Distributed cryptography based on the proofs of work. IACR Cryptol. ePrint Arch. **2014**, 796 (2014)
17. Schoenmakers, B.: A simple publicly verifiable secret sharing scheme and its application to electronic voting. In: Annual International Cryptology Conference, pp. 148–164. Springer (1999). https://doi.org/10.1007/3-540-48405-1_10
18. Cascudo, I., David, B.: SCRAPE: scalable randomness attested by public entities. In: International Conference on Applied Cryptography and Network Security, pp. 537–556 (2017). https://doi.org/10.1007/978-3-319-61204-1_27
19. Syta, E., et al.: Scalable bias-resistant distributed randomness. In: 2017 IEEE Symposium on Security and Privacy, pp. 444–460 (2017). https://doi.org/10.1109/SP.2017.45
20. Stinson, D., Strobl, R.: Provably secure distributed schnorr signatures and a (t, n) threshold scheme for implicit certificates. In: Proceedings of the 6th Australasian Conference on Information Security and Privacy, pp. 417–434 (2001). https://doi.org/10.1007/3-540-47719-5_33
21. Schindler, P., Judmayer, A., Stifter, N., Weippl, E.: HydRand: practical continuous distributed randomness. IACR Cryptol. ePrint Arch. **2018**, 319 (2018)
22. Hanke, T., Movahedi, M., Williams, D.: DFINITY technology overview series, consensus system. ArXiv. abs/1805.0 (2018)
23. Boneh, D., Lynn, B., Shacham, H.: Short signatures from the weil pairing. In: Boyd, C. (ed.) Advances in Cryptology — ASIACRYPT 2001, pp. 514–532. Springer, Berlin Heidelberg, Berlin, Heidelberg (2001)
24. Gennaro, R., Jarecki, S., Krawczyk, H., Rabin, T.: Secure distributed key generation for discrete-log based cryptosystems. In: Proceedings of the 17th international conference on Theory and application of cryptographic techniques, pp. 925–963 (2005). https://doi.org/10.1007/3-540-48910-X_21
25. Alturki, M., Roşu, G.: Statistical model checking of RANDAO's resilience to pre-computed reveal strategies. In: Goos, G. and Hartmanis, J. (eds.) Formal Methods. FM 2019 International Workshops, pp. 337–349. Springer (2020). https://doi.org/10.1007/978-3-030-54994-7_25
26. Dodis, Y., Yampolskiy, A.: A verifiable random function with short proofs and keys. In: Proceedings of the 8th International Conference on Theory and Practice in Public Key Cryptography, pp. 416–431 (1970). https://doi.org/10.1007/978-3-540-30580-4_28
27. Boneh, D., Eskandarian, S., Hanzlik, L., Greco, N.: Single secret leader election. In: AFT '20: 2nd ACM Conference on Advances in Financial Technologies, pp. 12–24 (2020). https://doi.org/10.1145/3419614.3423258
28. Bonehy, D., et al.: Threshold cryptosystems from threshold fully homomorphic encryption. Adv. Cryptol. – CRYPTO 2018. CRYPTO 2018. Lect. Notes Comput. Sci. 10991 (2018). https://doi.org/10.1007/978-3-319-96884-1_19

29. Microsoft: Cryptographic Services. https://docs.microsoft.com/en-us/dotnet/standard/security/cryptographic-services
30. Paar, C., Petzl, J.: Understanding Cryptography. Springer, Heidelberg (2010). https://doi.org/10.1007/978-3-642-04101-3
31. Stark, P.B., Ottoboni, K.: Random Sampling: Practice Makes Imperfect. arXiv.org (2018)

Blockchain-Enabled Secure and Smart Healthcare System

Debendranath Das[1](✉) [iD], Amudhan Muthaiah[2] [iD], and Sushmita Ruj[3] [iD]

[1] Indian Statistical Institute, Kolkata, India
debendra_r@isical.ac.in
[2] IBM India Pvt. Ltd., Bengaluru, India
[3] UNSW, Sydney, Australia
sushmita.ruj@unsw.edu.au

Abstract. Technology has developed over the years, making our lives easier. The healthcare sector has benefited from the advancement in technology, leading to an increase in the average life expectancy of human beings. However, there are several problems with the way the sector functions. There is a lack of transparency in the healthcare system, which results in inherent trust problems between patients and hospitals. There is no guarantee of getting the proper treatment from the hospital for the fee charged. Blockchain integrated with the smart contract is a well-known disruptive technology that builds trust by providing transparency to the system. In this paper, we propose a blockchain-enabled *Secure and Smart HealthCare System*. Fairness of the two entities, patient and hospital, involved in the system are guaranteed if they behave honestly. Privacy and security of patients' medical data are ensured as well. We have implemented the prototype in the Ethereum platform and Ropsten test network and have included the analysis as well.

Keywords: Blockchain · Healthcare · Data security · Privacy · Fairness

1 Introduction

IoT devices in the healthcare sector generate massive amounts of patients' medical data. This digital data is a part of EHRs (Electronic Health Records), typically stored in databases. Owing to the personal nature of EHRs, they must not be made available publicly. Failure to do so can have grave implications on the patient's life - such as discrimination by an employer based on medical history or failure to get insurance. Further, tampering of medical data has the potential to jeopardize a person's life. A third party might also use such sensitive data to inflict harm or sell it to other parties.

Each entity involved in providing medical service to the patient must be made accountable for their action. Unethical behavior on the part of medical professionals includes hospitals overcharging patients or providing inadequate medical service. According to a survey conducted by *Jan Arogya Abhiyan* and

A. Drechsler et al. (Eds.): DESRIST 2022, LNCS 13229, pp. 97–109, 2022.
https://doi.org/10.1007/978-3-031-06516-3_8

Corona Ekal Mahila Punarvasan Samiti in September 2021, 75% of the patients admitted for COVID-19 were overcharged. This happened despite the government capping the treatment expenses of COVID patients.

Patients may put false accusations on doctors and hospitals of mistreating them. Relying on a third party for resolving a dispute is not a good solution. Further, rules and regulations imposed by the country on medical treatment can be easily bypassed. Keeping all these problems in mind, we inferred that blockchain-based solutions would perfectly fit in this case.

The proposed patient-centric healthcare system ensures privacy, security of patients' medical data and fairness of the entities involved. If a patient has given consent to a party, the latter can access the medical data. An access control matrix stored in blockchain disallows any sort of malicious intervention. The digital footprint of the medical data is stored in the blockchain to provide integrity and immutability, while digital signature ensures accountability. The hospital authority cannot extort any arbitrary amount from a patient by providing unfair treatment or denying treatment. In that case, our system will penalize the hospital authority. On the other hand, if a patient claims that s/he has received an invalid medical report or denies receiving treatment, the logic encoded in the smart contract prevents such behavior by penalizing the patient.

1.1   Objective

We intend to propose a *patient-centric hospital management system* which realizes the following objectives:

- *Fairness*: An honest party will never lose money even if the rest of the parties are malicious and try to cheat and claim money without providing the desired service or data.
- *Privacy*: Any party cannot view a patient's data until and unless it gets consent from the patient.
- *Data Security*: Data of a patient stands protected and cannot be tampered.

1.2   Our Contribution

We briefly discuss the salient features of our proposed patient-centric healthcare system that bring novelty to the design:

- We propose a *Secure and Smart Healthcare System* which coordinates the interaction between patient and hospital while the patient is getting treated;
- The proposed system ensures that no one has access to the patient's data stored in the medical database until the patient grants permission. Any external agent without access cannot tamper with the data. Any malicious behavior can be detected using the digital fingerprint of the data recorded in the blockchain.
- A patient cannot be overcharged for seeking treatment from a hospital. Simultaneously, a hospital has to start the treatment within a specified period. If they fail to do so, the patient can withdraw any deposit made.

- A patient can either keep the data with himself or store it in a medical database, which is assumed to be semi-trusted. The database owner checks the validity of the data provided by the patient before storing it in the database to prevent the storage of any spurious data.
- We have implemented the prototype in the Ethereum platform and Ropsten test network and have evaluated the performance. Code for the protocol is available on pCloud[§].

1.3 Organization

The rest of the paper is structured as follows - we have discussed the state-of-the-art in Sect. 2. Section 3 briefly discusses the basic building blocks. In Sect. 4, the system model and high-level view of our construction are presented. In Sect. 5, we have addressed our security claims. Section 6 shows the results of our proposed system and also discusses the outcome. Finally, we have concluded the paper in Sect. 7.

2   Related Work

We discuss the state-of-the-art blockchain solution for the healthcare system. Although state-of-the-art tries to enhance the security of the healthcare system using blockchain framework, these have certain drawbacks. Xiao et al. [9] has proposed a blockchain architecture model to store and enable different parties to view EHRs. However, this blockchain model is prone to a single point of failure. Xia et al. [8] had proposed a cloud-based blockchain platform for sharing files with untrustworthy parties seeking access to medical files. However, the solution is not scalable and suffers from key management problems. Jiang et al. [4] designed a medical data exchange system using blockchain by developing off-chain and on-chain verification for the security of the system's storage. Their work has addressed the problem of scalability. However, the solution does not guarantee the fairness of the entities involved.

The data preservation system in work proposed by Li et al. [5] basically contains two programs - the data access program and the blockchain interaction program. Zhang et al. [12] proposed PSN-based healthcare by designing two protocols for authentication and sharing of healthcare data. The drawback of these two systems is that it lacks a data access control policy. Additionally, [12] does not provide a protocol for sharing of EHR.

A *healthcare data gateway* was proposed by Yup et al. [11]. It is a blockchain approach to healthcare intelligence to address users' privacy by proposing a data access control for privacy. Liang et al. [6] proposed a mobile-based healthcare record sharing system using blockchain. They designed a secure user-centric approach to provide access control and privacy using a channel formation scheme. Zhang and Poslad [13] proposed an access control policy for electronic medical records with finer granular access. Yang and Li [10] proposed architecture for securing EHR based on distributed ledger technology. However, these works lack any formal algorithm or proper implementation, and the authors have not evaluated system performance.

Fan et al. [2] proposed an improved consensus mechanism to get enhanced security and privacy of medical data. Sun et al. [7] designed a distributed attribute-based signature scheme for medical systems based on blockchain and proposed a blockchain-based record sharing protocol. Gorenflo et al. [3] proposed a performance optimization for the Hyperledger blockchain framework. However, this work requires high storage, high power and computation cost.

Our model has addressed most of the existing problems by proposing a decentralized, distributed healthcare system using a permission-less blockchain framework. It also ensures the privacy of patients' medical data (using Access Control Policy), data security, and fairness of various entities involved in the system.

3   Preliminaries

In this section, we discuss the building blocks and other proposed methodologies that we have used in our system.

3.1   Basic Cryptographic Primitives

- **Encryption Scheme:** Encryption Scheme serves the purpose of privacy or confidentiality of the messages exchanged between a sender and recipient. We have used two types of encryption - *Private Key Encryption* or *Symmetric Key Encryption (SKE)* and *Public Key Encryption* or *Asymmetric Key Encryption (ASKE)*.
- **Digital Signature Scheme:** Digital Signature (DS) serves the purpose of user authentication in the system. On obtaining the DS of an entity, any recipient can verify if the message originated from the intended sender or not.
- **Hash Function:** A Hash function ensures data integrity in the system. It can be defined as $h : \{0,1\}^* \rightarrow \{0,1\}^k$ that maps messages of arbitrary length to a fixed size message digest of length k. An ideal hash function must satisfy the following three properties: *One Way or Pre-image Resistant, Second Pre-image Resistant* and *Collision Resistant*.
- **Merkle Tree:** Merkle Trees are binary trees, which are used to prove the membership of data belonging to a set. The leaf node comprises the data present in the set, and the output of a leaf node is the hash of the data. For every non-leaf node, the output is the hash of the concatenated children node's outputs. The output of the root node is referred to as the *Merkle Root* (acronym as MR).

3.2   Other Building Blocks

- **Blockchain:** A Blockchain (BC) is an immutable, decentralized, and verifiable ledger that is duplicated and distributed across a P2P network. Tampering data stored in the BC is impossible (or can be done with negligible probability), which is the foundation of data immutability. The cryptographic hash function assures data security. Miners mine a block by solving a difficult mathematical puzzle. The solution provided is called proof-of-work. Mining secures the bitcoin system. Parties achieve a network-wide consensus without a central authority.

– **Smart Contract:** Smart Contracts (SC) are self-executing contracts, where the terms of an agreement between parties are encoded using a programming language (e.g., solidity). The smart contract also helps to build trust in the system by eliminating the role of intermediaries or middle man.

4   High-Level View of the System

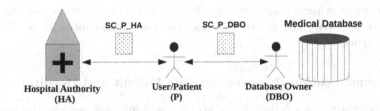

Fig. 1. Healthcare system model

4.1   System Model

The major actors or parties involved in our proposed system, as shown in Fig. 1, are as follows -

1. **Patient (P)/User**
2. **Hospital Authority (HA)**
3. **Database Owner (DBO)**

In our system, we have the following smart contracts. The protocol suite is written in the form of functions inside the smart contracts.

– Smart Contract between Patient and Hospital Authority : **SC_P_HA**
– Smart Contract between Patient and Database Owner : **SC_P_DBO**

We have one additional smart contract, **SC_Registration**, where the entities of the systems can register themselves before participating in the protocol. Thus, we have three smart contracts to build up the entire system. In the following subsections, we will discuss how these different actors interact in the system. Before that, let us state the assumptions taken.

4.2   Assumptions

a) In our system, every single party has a unique ID. A smart contract generates these IDs at the time of registration in the system. One unique ID corresponds to a particular *PublicKey*. Every party must register first to be a part of the system.

b) Medical Data Repository Owner or simply the Database Owner (DBO) is considered semi-trusted in our system. DBO can have open access to the stored data as the data is stored in plain-text form. However, this assumption can be removed by adding the scope of handling encrypted data in the database, and the model can be changed accordingly. The DBO's activity log is maintained in the blockchain. In case DBO misbehaves, then it can be questioned and penalized accordingly. Patients can also keep their records to their private storage locally or appeal to the DBO to remove their records in case of privacy concerns.

c) Database Owner (DBO) must satisfy certain prerequisite conditions to be a part of the system and appeal to the government expressing their interest. The conditions or criteria may vary for different Governments of various countries. If all the necessary criteria are satisfied, the government introduces DBO into the system.

4.3   Communication Protocol Between Patient and Hospital

When a patient visits a hospital, the hospital will initially analyze the patient's problems. After preliminary scanning, the hospital generates an estimated cost of the treatment. Hospitals and patients need to lock this amount in the smart contract (SC_P_HA).

Access Control: For accessing the patient's medical records from the medical repository, the hospital authority asks the patient to grant proper access permission. The hospital can read the patient's medical history if permission is granted. The patient can revoke access permission, if needed, at any instant. Information related to this access control is stored in the blockchain.

Locking of Hospital Treatment Cost: The patient locks the estimated cost in the smart contract. Then the hospital must start the treatment within a fixed time window and register the treatment's timestamp in the blockchain. If the hospital fails to do so, the patient can unlock their money.

Storing Patient's Record after Treatment: The hospital generates the patient's medical files - reports, prescriptions etc. However, these files are not transferred to the patient immediately because of security reasons, which are addressed in Sect. 5. With the help of some cryptographic computations and fair exchange protocol, as shown in Fig. 2, the hospital sends the medical files to the patient. The hospital stores the following crucial attributes as the metadata in the blockchain - MR of the file chunks M_1, MR of the encrypted file M_2, the signature of the hospital on MR of the file, and signature of the hospital on H(Patient ID $\|$ Date of Report $\|$ MR of Encrypted File). MRs M_1 and M_2 are used for verification by the protocol on behalf of the patient and other associated entities like DBO. The signature on the MR makes the hospital accountable for its encrypted file. The signature on the hash of the patient's attributes and the hash of the encrypted

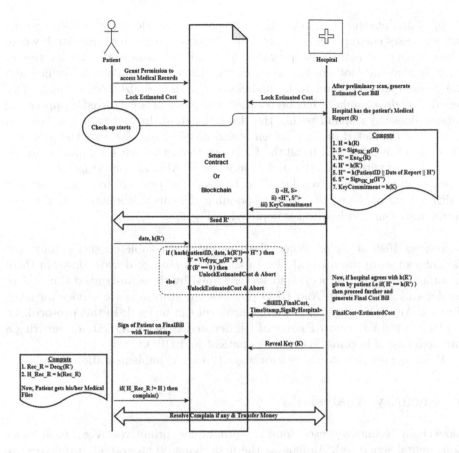

Fig. 2. Interaction between Patient and Hospital

file adds much more accountability, giving the patient the chance to complain if the hospital misbehaved.

Upon receiving these file attributes offline, the patient verifies and gives consent. If the attributes match, the patient invokes a function to give consent and sign on the file. If the patient finds a mismatch in the file attributes, s/he can withdraw the locked amount.

Hospital Bill Settlement: Meanwhile, the hospital provides the final medical bill to the patient. We assume that the final bill amount is not greater than the estimated cost. The patient has two options: give consent or raise a dispute for being overcharged. The hospital and patient agree on the price through offline communication. Furthermore, this pathway involves two additional transactions by the parties before agreeing to the revised final bill.

Receiving the patient's consent on the final bill, the hospital sends the decryption key to the patient. Suppose the MR of the decrypted file does not match the one in the contract. In that case, the patient raises a complaint by providing a

Proof of Misbehavior [1]. In that case, the patient provides the positions and the two witnesses corresponding to both file chunk and encrypted file chunk where a mismatch occurred. It also provides intermediate nodes in the Merkle tree as proof so that the root can be reconstructed. Once the complaint is verified and the counterparty is found to be malicious, s/he is penalized accordingly. Vice versa, if a false complaint has been raised, the party gets penalized. Suppose the patient does not respond within the timeout period. In that case, the hospital withdraws the locked money (patient's and hospital's) and aborts the protocol. There is a timeline check in all the functions to ensure that each process in the protocol runs within the allocated time window. Also, at each stage of the protocol, both parties are given functions to abort the protocol to avoid indefinite waiting if one of the parties stops responding. The above communication model between patient and hospital is depicted in Fig. 2.

Uploading Medical Data: When the treatment is completed successfully, the patient can store the medical files in their local storage devices or store them in some medical repository/cloud server owned by the semi-trusted third-party vendor (a.k.a. as DBO). And DBO provides the storage space service for some charges. Any two-party fair exchange protocol can be used; In this protocol, we implement the **Fairswap Protocol** [1], denoted as **SC_P_DBO**, for ensuring a fair exchange of information between patient and DBO.

Readers may refer to[1] for major algorithms and implementation details.

5   Security Analysis

Blockchain technology uses some cryptographic primitives (e.g., hash function, digital signature). As long as the underlying cryptographic primitives are secured, the blockchain is secure, and so is our system. Assuming that the blockchain is secure, the money locked in the blockchain is protected, and hence the payment involved in the system is also safe. We claim that our system takes care of essential security aspects and provides fairness to the parties involved in the system. Detailed proof of our claims is provided in[2].

5.1   Fairness

We discuss the fairness of each party, i.e., Patient and Hospital Authority. Even if one of the parties acts malicious and tries to cheat, the malicious party gets penalized and the money is used to compensate the honest party.

Proposition 1. *(Patient's Fairness) The honest patient must not lose money or gets mistreated, no matter if the other party (i.e. hospital) is behaving maliciously, under the assumption that the owner of Medical Data Repository is semi-trusted and the underlying blockchain is secure.*

---

[1] http://u.pc.cd/lJx.
[2] http://u.pc.cd/g5X.

Proposition 2. *(Hospital's Fairness) An honest hospital authority will get its money for all the services provided to the patient, despite the patient's misbehavior (say, the patient tries to take services from the hospital without paying the bill amount and then leave), under the assumption that the underlying blockchain is secure.*

5.2 Privacy

A patient's medical data is sensitive information. If a person's health record is available publicly, s/he may face embarrassment and might be subjected to discrimination in daily life. Hence, it must be ensured that access to patient data is provided only with the patient's consent.

Proposition 3. *(Patient's Privacy) In our proposed system, none of the entities can access a patient's data unless granted permission. At the same time, personally identifiable attributes of the patient remain hidden from public view.*

6 Result and Discussion

Implementation Setup: We have implemented the Healthcare Management System on Ethereum test networks in a system having Intel(R) Core(TM) i7-6700HQ running Linux Mint 18.04 19.1 (Tessa), a 64-bit operating system using 16.00GiB of RAM. We have used the Ropsten test network and an infura endpoint. Source code is provided on pCloud[3].

The two main factors that determine the feasibility of any blockchain model are cost of implementation and time taken. Since each Ethereum transaction requires computational resources to execute, each transaction requires a fee. Gas refers to the fee required to conduct a transaction on Ethereum successfully, and the miners get the fees. Gas price denotes the current price for a single unit of gas. Gas price is given in Gwei, where 1 Gwei is equal to 10^{-9} ETH. Gas cost is given by multiplying the gas price with the gas required for a transaction.

Table 1. Deployment addresses of smart contracts

Smart Contract	Address
SC_Registration	0x5a818296705cC24Feec4CfEAF1DfdaE056fEf037
SC_P_HA_1	0x9528dA5753ae928Eb1e0284C7b1771e2FC17a766
SC_P_HA_2	0x7b88e153aC1b2BCA865CD58E1082f50Ed69f4c3c
SC_P_DBO	0xC062E1eF5EdB815bcF5B93C6BaD497ABCA407f31

Table 2. Deployment cost of smart contracts

Smart Contract	Deployment Cost(Ether)
SC_Registration	0.0353157
SC_P_HA_1	0.0994202
SC_P_HA_2	0.0583187
SC_P_DBO	0.04783231

Table 1 specifies the addresses of the deployed contracts. The contract deployment is a one-time occurrence. The transaction cost and the time taken for each

---

[3] http://u.pc.cd/Od0.

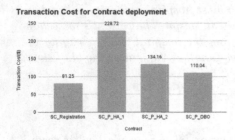

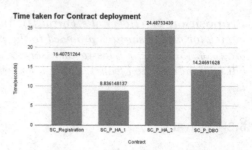

Fig. 3. Transaction cost for contract deployment

Fig. 4. Time taken for contract deployment

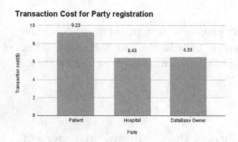

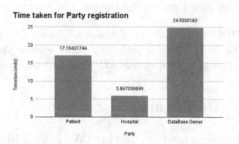

Fig. 5. Transaction cost for party registration

Fig. 6. Time taken for party registration

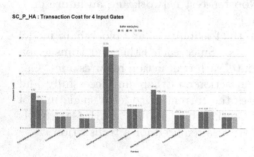

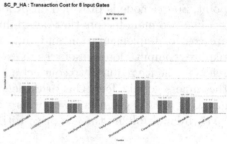

Fig. 7. SC_P_HA transaction cost for 4 input gates

Fig. 8. SC_P_HA transaction cost for 8 input gates

contract deployment have been depicted in Fig. 3 and Fig. 4 respectively. The gas price was 18.9 Gwei, and the ether cost was 2300.54 dollars at the time of deployment. Depending upon the size of the contracts, the deployment cost varies (Table 2). These are one-time costs. So, once deployed, we can get the benefits throughout the usage of this protocol.

The smart contracts for patients and hospitals (SC_P_HA_1 & SC_P_HA_2) have been split into two parts, citing the limited gas limit for blocks in Ethereum.

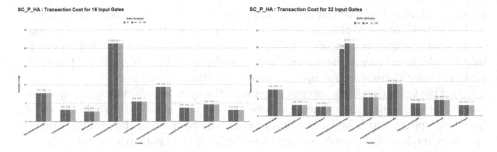

Fig. 9. SC_P_HA transaction cost for 16 input gates

Fig. 10. SC_P_HA transaction cost for 32 input gates

The high gas for the collective patient and hospital contracts reflects the slightly higher steps involved in the protocol.

The transaction costs and time taken associated with the entities' registration process, depicted in Fig. 5 and Fig. 6 respectively, are similar in scale for different parties except for the patients, which are slightly higher due to the few more variables involved in the registration for patients.

The transaction cost for certain functions involved in the protocol depends on the size of the files. The file size may vary depending upon the treatment and the corresponding result produced. The base file is constructed indifferently for subsequent usage in the protocol. The file is divided into numbers of chunks. The number and size of the chunks are the varying parameters, referred to as the number of input gates and the buffer size of the gate, respectively.

We have shown the cost associated with various functions call for the contracts SC_P_HA (Fig. 7, 8, 9, 10) with varying number of input gates and the buffer size. The number of input gates varies in the range of 4, 8, 16, 32 and the buffer sizes used are 32, 64, and 128. The file size can be derived by multiplying the number of input gates and the buffer size. So, a file having 4 input gates and a buffer size of 32 would have a file size of 128 bytes.

We find from the graphs of SC_P_HA (Fig. 7, 8, 9, 10) that they follow a similar kind of trend with varying numbers of input gates. The transaction cost for different functions hardly varies while keeping the number of input gates constant and varying the buffer size. The graphs show that some functions require a higher cost due to their heavy functionalities. It is viable as the utilities of the functions outweigh the cost.

7   Conclusion

In this paper, we have proposed a novel *Secure and Smart Healthcare System* where every involved party's fairness is preserved without trusting each other. Electronic Health Records (EHRs) are tamper-proof and free from unauthorized access in our healthcare system enabled by blockchain technology. Our system also ensures that the patient's privacy does not get compromised. We proposed, prototyped, and deployed our healthcare system, which works fine in the private and Ropsten test networks. Experimental result shows the satisfactory outcome of various performance metrics. Our protocol demonstrates blockchain's capability and importance in healthcare sector and proves that it could be the next revolutionary technology to replace current healthcare systems.

As a part of future work, we will generalize the system considering the involvement of the Medical Insurance Company. The aim should be to build trust between a policy buyer and an insurance company by making the processes (such as policy buying, claim verification and settlement, etc.) transparent through the blockchain framework. Also, We will propose an approach whereby the research community will get the data for the purpose of analysis without compromising on patients' privacy.

References

1. Dziembowski, S., Eckey, L., Faust, S.: Fairswap: how to fairly exchange digital goods. In: Proceedings of the 2018 ACM SIGSAC Conference on Computer and Communications Security, pp. 967–984 (2018)
2. Fan, K., Wang, S., Ren, Y., Li, H., Yang, Y.: Medblock: efficient and secure medical data sharing via blockchain. J. Med. Syst. **42**(8), 1–11 (2018)
3. Gorenflo, C., Lee, S., Golab, L., Keshav, S.: Fastfabric: scaling hyperledger fabric to 20 000 transactions per second. Int. J. Netw. Manag. **30**(5), e2099 (2020)
4. Jiang, S., Cao, J., Wu, H., Yang, Y., Ma, M., He, J.: Blochie: a blockchain-based platform for healthcare information exchange. In: 2018 IEEE International Conference on Smart Computing (smartcomp), pp. 49–56. IEEE (2018)
5. Li, H., Zhu, L., Shen, M., Gao, F., Tao, X., Liu, S.: Blockchain-based data preservation system for medical data. J. Med. Syst. **42**(8), 1–13, e2099 (2018). https://doi.org/10.1007/s10916-018-0997-3
6. Liang, X., Zhao, J., Shetty, S., Liu, J., Li, D.: Integrating blockchain for data sharing and collaboration in mobile healthcare applications. In: 2017 IEEE 28th Annual International Symposium on Personal, Indoor, and Mobile Radio Communications (PIMRC), pp. 1–5. IEEE (2017)
7. Sun, Y., Zhang, R., Wang, X., Gao, K., Liu, L.: A decentralizing attribute-based signature for healthcare blockchain. In: 2018 27th International Conference on Computer Communication and Networks (ICCCN), pp. 1–9. IEEE (2018)
8. Xia, Q., Sifah, E., Asamoah, K., Gao, J., Du, X., Guizani, M.: Medshare: trust-less medical data sharing among cloud service providers via blockchain. IEEE Access **5**, 14757–14767 (2017). https://doi.org/10.1109/ACCESS.2017.2730843
9. Xiao, Y., Liu, Y., Wu, Y., Li, T., Xian, X., Jiang, W.: Healthchain: a blockchain for electronic health records (preprint). J. Med. Internet Res. **23** (2019). https://doi.org/10.2196/13556
10. Yang, G., Li, C.: A design of blockchain-based architecture for the security of electronic health record (ehr) systems. In: 2018 IEEE International Conference on Cloud Computing Technology and Science (CloudCom), pp. 261–265. IEEE (2018)
11. Yue, X., Wang, H., Jin, D., Li, M., Jiang, W.: Healthcare data gateways: found healthcare intelligence on blockchain with novel privacy risk control. J. Med. Syst. **40**(10), 1–8 (2016)

12. Zhang, J., Xue, N., Huang, X.: A secure system for pervasive social network-based healthcare. IEEE Access **4**, 9239–9250 (2016)
13. Zhang, X., Poslad, S.: Blockchain support for flexible queries with granular access control to electronic medical records (EMR). In: 2018 IEEE International Conference on Communications (ICC), pp. 1–6. IEEE (2018)

Intelligent Systems and Human Interaction

Intelligent Systems and Human Interaction Track

Pierre-Majorique Leger[1], Alex Maedche[2], and Barbara Weber[3]

[1] HEC Montreal
pierre-majorique.leger@hec.ca
[2] Karlsruhe Institute of Technology
alexander.maedche@kit.edu
[3] St. Gallen University
barbara.weber@unisg.ch

Abstract. Intelligent systems leveraging Artificial Intelligence (AI) technologies are ubiquitous in our daily life. To exploit the full potential of intelligent systems, it is important to follow a human-centered AI perspective. The interdisciplinary research area of Human-Computer Interaction (HCI) in general is concerned with the design, evaluation and implementation of interactive computing systems for human use and with the study of major phenomena surrounding them. This track specifically aims to provide a platform for discussing the latest advances in design science research at the intersection of intelligent systems and HCI.

Keywords: Intelligent systems · Human-computer interaction

Artificial intelligence (AI) technologies such as machine learning, computer vision, or natural language processing enable machines to sense, comprehend, act, and learn. Intelligent systems based on AI technologies are ubiquitous today. We use intelligent systems daily as part of our mobile phones or consumer electronics such as smart speakers or TVs. They are embedded in our cars providing safety and mobility services, as in the form of adaptive cruise control or navigation systems. We encounter intelligent systems as consumers on the Internet supporting individualized online shopping and media consumption experiences or in the form of chatbots in customer service. Finally, intelligent systems are also becoming more and more part of our workplace. For example, they support us in the form of digital assistants in carrying out tasks and making decisions. Besides augmentation of work, robotic process automation assistants even take over routine tasks from us. With the growing number of connected sensors, more data will be generated that will create opportunities to design even more powerful intelligent systems, e.g., in the form of user-adaptive systems using bio-signals captured by wearables or eye trackers.

However, from a human user's point of view we often just do not understand what intelligent systems expect from us. Or alternatively said, today's intelligent systems do not understand what we humans expect from them. Thus, the ubiquity of intelligent systems does not necessarily make our lives easier. In a world increasingly permeated by intelligent systems, understanding and designing human interaction with intelligent systems considering instrumental and humanistic outcomes becomes absolutely essential. The interdisciplinary research area of Human-Computer Interaction (HCI) in general is concerned with the design, evaluation and implementation of interactive computing systems for human use and with the study of major phenomena surrounding them. The HCI field recently pushed the notion of human-centered AI (HCAI) emphasizing the importance of human aspects in AI technology in a sense that it better serves human needs, and is more reliable, safe, and trustworthy.

We argue that there is a need to connect the two fields of intelligent systems and HCI more tightly as well as combine it with the design science research (DSR) paradigm. Despite rapid technological progresses, the potential of intelligent systems to solve fundamental societal problems is not sufficiently exploited. Even worse, intelligent systems create new problems, such as biases, invasion of privacy, lack of transparency and trust, loss of control and autonomy, and loss of authority. To exploit the full potential of intelligent systems it is fundamental to deeply understand the actual problems and challenges of humans and subsequently find appropriate solutions for these problems. DSR aims to generate design knowledge about the design of information systems (IS) artifacts. Design knowledge is about means-end relationships between problem and solution spaces and can appear in the form of innovative artifacts for real-world problems as well as design principles and theories. DSR provides solid methodological foundations as well as means to generate and accumulate design knowledge for providing intelligent systems that solve real-world problems of humans and society.

With this DESRIST 2022 track we aim to provide a platform for discussing the latest advances in DSR at the intersection of intelligent systems and HCI. Designing human-centric intelligent systems that matter requires the interdisciplinary collaboration of scholars from different disciplines, e.g., economics and management, information systems, psychology, and computer science. Furthermore, beyond interdisciplinarity we consider the three characteristics of transdisciplinary (TD) research i) problem focus, ii) emergent research methods, and ii) collaboration as central for successfully designing human-centric intelligent systems. First, we believe that specifically in the context of intelligent systems the problem focus needs to be strengthened. Today, intelligent systems are often designed from either a technology or a provider perspective. Where the technology perspective emphasizes technological opportunities, the provider perspective just implements a business model. However, to provide relevant solutions that positively impact the lives of people, it is fundamental to get a deep understanding of the problem. By nature, problems do not belong to individual disciplines, so close collaboration is needed here. Second, DSR provides solid methodological foundations and guidance for delivering impactful design knowledge. However, designing human-centric intelligent systems places very high methodological demands. It requires novel methods or combinations of research methods from different disciplines. For example, to enable participation of citizens in the design, it may be fruitful to follow a digital citizen science paradigm. Furthermore, value-sensitive design can support in considering the values of all affected stakeholders systematically in the design process. Third, we are strongly convinced that in the design process of human-centric intelligent systems active participation of all relevant stakeholders impacted by the designed solution should be pursued. Managing this collaborative process in a DSR project is challenging and may require dedicated methods, techniques, and tools.

Can Artificial Intelligence Help Used-Car Dealers Survive in a Data-Driven Used-Car Market?

Sven Eckhardt[1]([✉]) [ID], Kilian Sprenkamp[1] [ID], Liudmila Zavolokina[2] [ID], Ingrid Bauer[1] [ID], and Gerhard Schwabe[1] [ID]

[1] University of Zurich, Binzmuehlestrasse 14, 8050 Zurich, Switzerland
{eckhardt,sprenkamp,bauer,schwabe}@ifi.uzh.ch
[2] University of Zurich, Raemistrasse 69, 8001 Zurich, Switzerland
liudmila.zavolokina@dsi.uzh.ch

Abstract. The used-car market is notoriously untrustworthy and shady. Certified data has been shown to help mitigate the information asymmetry, one of the major factors to an untrustworthy market. In recent times, more and more used-car dealers have had problems surviving in this competitive data-driven market. In this study, we conduct 12 interviews with used-car dealers and several meetings and workshops with employees and executives from the AMAG Group, one of the largest automotive companies in Switzerland. This creates insight into current problems for used-car dealers and how artificial intelligence can help. The problems can be abstracted to the problem of high transaction cost and its subcategories. In reducing transaction costs by utilizing artificial intelligence, new secondary problems arise. People need to trust the certificate, the analytics, and the predictions. Additionally, the data and analytics need to be transparent and understandable, and privacy concerns must be addressed. The implications of this study are manifold. First, we define the problems for used-car dealers on the used-car market and introduce artificial intelligence approaches to the current data-driven used-car market. Afterward, we stress that artificial intelligence needs to follow a human-centered perspective and be designed for trust.

Keywords: Used-car market · Transaction costs · Trust · Artificial intelligence

1 Introduction

The used-car market has been historically described as untrustworthy. The primary reason for that is the information asymmetry between seller and buyer. The seller has complete information about the car, and the buyer needs to rely on the seller to provide the truth about the car. For example, as estimated by the European Parliament, up to 50% of cars traded across borders within the EU have manipulated odometers [1]. Trading a used car is a challenge for buyers and sellers alike.

When the seller is a professional dealer, ways to mitigate the information asymmetry include, for example, guarantees or online reviews [2]. Furthermore, previous research

© Springer Nature Switzerland AG 2022
A. Drechsler et al. (Eds.): DESRIST 2022, LNCS 13229, pp. 115–127, 2022.
https://doi.org/10.1007/978-3-031-06516-3_9

has shown that certificates, that store data on the blockchain, can mitigate the information asymmetries between seller and buyer by providing trusted and certified data. These certificates help the private individual when buying a car from used-car dealers.

However, it is unclear how these certificates can help used-car dealers survive in the highly competitive and more and more data-driven used-car market. Especially in recent times, fueled by the COVID-19-pandemic and chip shortage, fewer and fewer cars are available on the used car market [3]. Therefore, helping used-car dealers survive and gain a competitive edge in the used-car market is relevant as ever. However, first, the problems used-car dealers face in the used-car market need to be analyzed.

If we utilize existing certificates and blockchain technology, we can ensure our data is trusted and certified, giving it some quality. One can easily think of deploying artificial intelligence (AI) to generate insights and increase the general information on the state of a used car. Nonetheless, AI is known to introduce socio-technical problems, especially in mistrust and intransparency of systems. Therefore, it would be assumed that introducing AI in used-car trading would be without problems. This motivates us to formulate the following research question:

RQ *Can artificial intelligence help used-car dealers survive in a data-driven used-car market?*

To answer this question, we collaborate with the AMAG Group, one of the largest automotive companies in Switzerland. Recently, the AMAG Group has had an ever-increasing problem with the used-car dealers, which have a hard time surviving on the competitive market. Therefore, by analyzing the issues for the AMAG Group and deriving early design objectives and design requirements, we postulate how trusted, and certified data in combination with AI can help the used-car dealers survive in a data-driven used-car market being transformed by certified data.

The study is structured as follows. In the subsequent chapter, the background and related work are introduced. In Sect. 3, we lay down the methodology for this study, and in Sect. 4, we define the problems. The defined solution objectives and design requirements are laid down in Sect. 5. Section 6 introduces the new, secondary problems that arise from our design requirements. We end the paper with a discussion in Sect. 7 and an outlook in Sect. 8.

2 Background and Related Work

The trade volume on the used-car market is negatively correlated with the transaction costs [4]. Thus, a dealer's margin decreases with rising transaction costs. Some economists describe the transaction costs as proportional to the sale price [4] or as the difference between retail and wholesale price [5]. These definitions are relatively easy to calculate but cannot catch the complex nature of transaction costs. Another definition of transaction costs describes transaction costs as *"resource losses incurred due to imperfect information"* [6] (based on [7]), which need to be considered on a case-to-case basis. It is also considered for seller and buyer equally.

Further, the used-car market is a prime example of a market with asymmetric information [8]. The critical problem of asymmetric information is that buyers and sellers do not have the same information about a good or service, resulting in different quality and price perceptions. Often these trades are disadvantageous for one party. Examples of methods to overcome asymmetric information include guarantees, certificates issued by experts, and third-party assessment [8]. A first indicator for the effect of mitigating information asymmetries are markets that have regulations in place. One example is the housing market, where mandatory energy performance certificates increase transparency and reduce information asymmetry, which directly affects the housing price [9, 10]. Another example is the food market, where it has been shown that nutrition labels can impact consumer behavior and health [11, 12]. However, while buying a car is often associated with significant investment for the private individual, the used-car market finds less attention from the regulatory body. Therefore, the problem of information asymmetry is still prevailing. One recent approach to mitigate the information asymmetry in the used-car market is the inclusion of blockchain to store trusted data. An example of such an approach is the so-called cardossier [13]. The cardossier platform leads to increased data quality [14], new business models [15], and increased market transparency [16]. It ultimately moves more used car business from the garage to online platforms [17]. Used-car dealers may use the certified data of the cardossier platform (1) to apply advanced analytics to evaluate the car state and value, (2) to buy used cars on online platforms, and (3) to offer advanced warranties [18]. With new technology like the cardossier, the used-car market more and more becomes data-driven. But it remains open what precisely the problems of used-car dealers are and how potential solutions can be designed and implemented to help them survive in this market.

In this paper, we utilize the data-richness and look at applying advanced analytics, i.e., AI. In this study, we consider machine learning and deep learning as major approaches to achieve AI, which is in line with [19]. A method on the border of AI is Robotic Process Automation (RPA) [20], where we use technology to automate tasks. RPA can use AI to make decisions; however, it follows a simple logic most of the time. On the other hand, Software Agents [21] are AI as they act autonomously and use machine learning and deep learning methods. In marketplaces, like a used-car marketplace, AI has been shown to help mitigate information asymmetry and make the marketplace more efficient [22]. Further, AI also has the potential to solve additional problems in the used-car market that have not yet been addressed. Price prediction models have successfully been applied in the used-car market [23]. Additionally, the topic of predictive maintenance also impacts the used-car market [24, 25]. However, the advantages of AI come at a cost. Modern AI, especially neural networks, has shown to be an intransparent black box [26] that people have difficulty understanding [27]. However, explainability is one of the major concerns in human-centered AI to achieve trustworthy AI [28, 29]. While a continuous effort is to introduce transparency in the used-car market, we are not aware of explainable and transparent AI applications deployed up to now.

3   Methodology

This study is a part of a larger project and reports on the outcomes of the first steps of the Design Science Research (DSR) cycle, i.e., Problem Definition, Solution Objectives, and Design [30]. In this project, we collaborate with the AMAG Group, one of the largest automotive companies in Switzerland, which has a high two-digit number of associated and independent used-car dealers. In cooperation with its used-car dealers, the AMAG Group aims to solve several problems in the used-car market. Our study aims to analyze the problems the AMAG Group and its used-car dealers have. This analysis helps us derive the objectives and design requirements for a potential AI-based solution for the used-car market.

Fig. 1. Phases in this study and the data source used in each phase

There are several sources of empirical data in our study. We interviewed several experts in the used-car market and conducted workshops and meetings with employees from the AMAG Group. As shown in Fig. 1, first, we define the primary problems using information gathered through workshops, meetings, and interviews. Then, we derive the solution objectives and design requirements. These design requirements entailed new, secondary problems, which also must be considered in the problem identification.

We conducted 12 interviews (abbreviated as I1-I12) with used-car dealers. We included participants that are currently or formerly working as used-car dealers in the AMAG Group and have several years of experience. Further, we excluded former used-car dealers who no longer work in the AMAG Group or are not closely linked to the used-car dealers in their current position. This ensures that all participants have a close relation to the used-car market. On average, the participants have 20.1 years of experience in the automobile industry and 8.6 years in the used-car market. These interviews were transcribed using an intelligent verbatim transcription and analyzed using qualitative coding [31] in MAXQDA software. The interviews were conducted in German and translated into English. Used-car dealers are optimal interview partners for this case, as they can take on a double-role: they buy and sell cars, thus, knowing the requirements for both sides. The workshops and meetings were conducted with several employees from the AMAG Group. The initial goal of these was to derive the current problems the used-car dealers have. After the problems were analyzed, we derived potential solutions for the problems. For the workshops and meetings, we have comprehensive documentation in the form of meeting notes, (digital) whiteboards, and other similar records. With this documentation, we can reconstruct the statement about the current problems and the solution ideas, which motivate the design requirements in this study. This approach provided us with an in-depth view of the problems faced by the AMAG Group and ensured an extensive problem identification.

4   Problem Definition

This section introduces the AMAG Group's primary problems in the emerging data-driven used-car market. The situation for the AMAG Group is that its used-car dealers cannot buy enough cars from private sellers and thus cannot take part in the used-car trade. Further, they cannot generate revenue for the car dealer. Additionally, the automotive company cannot conduct enough cross-selling, like selling new cars or warranties on used cars. Based on the data, we identified the following primary problem areas:

(A) *Finding sellers willing to sell their cars*: To buy cars, the used-car dealers need to find sellers that are willing to sell their cars. Without that, no used cars can be purchased. The executives in the workshops and meetings stated that the used-car dealers do not get enough cars to participate in the used-car market fully. Additionally, the used-car dealers state, for example, that they *"get many vehicles from the new car departments"* (I5). This statement shows that the used-car dealers rely on the AMAG Group to give them the cars they sell and cannot find enough sellers themselves.

(B) *Quality management and car maintenance*: Used-car dealers need to ensure the quality of the car they buy. But even lengthy inspections cannot always detect malicious fraud (like a manipulated odometer) or hidden defects. Nonetheless, the used-car dealers must ensure the quality of the used cars they buy and then sell again. Further, cars need to be maintained to be sold later. If the car breaks shortly after being bought, the costs will significantly exceed the profit from this trade. As one interviewee stated, the needed steps are as follows: *"you look at the car, make an assessment of the vehicle, the service team makes a test, looks at the car, are there damages, are there defects, document that, make a dossier."* (I10). This process involves several people and a lot of time and effort simply for assessing the car and its future potential.

(C) *Market monitoring*: Used-car dealers need to constantly monitor the market to get insight into current market prices and subsequently adequate prices for the cars to buy and sell. This is mainly done individually by the used-car dealers and is based on existing tools or websites. When asked about how to monitor the market, one interviewee stated that they are using several tools, they start with *"Eurotax [and] Auto-Data"*, but more importantly, the *"market gives the price [which are] internet-platforms [like] Autolina or Autoscout"* (I4). This highlights how many systems and tools are consulted to monitor the market and set the price of a used car.

(D) *Reputation management and providing trust*: There are many used-car dealers, and some of them act shady. To participate in the used-car trade, the used-car dealers need to be perceived as trustworthy and of high reputation. This reputation management, while being crucial, is sometimes hard to achieve. Nearly all interviewees stated that having AMAG's brand associated increases their reputation compared to other used-car dealers. Further, the brand, for example, is *"associated with trust"* (I10). However, reputation management is an active and ongoing effort.

The above-introduced problems can be generalized to one abstract problem: the problem of high transaction costs on both sides of the trade. Transaction costs can be categorized into three categories with five different types of transaction costs [6]. This categorization and the concrete transaction costs in the used-car market are shown in Table 1. Table 1 also includes an indicator of whether the transaction cost is relevant for the used-car dealer or the seller in this setting. Several transaction costs need to be considered in our study. Problem *(A)* can directly be mapped on search cost. Used-car dealer needs to spend resources to find potential sellers (e.g., online advertisement), and the seller needs to spend resources finding a used-car dealer willing to buy the car. Additionally, high bargaining and decision costs for the seller decrease the willingness to sell the car. The problem *(B)* can be mapped on information cost for the used-car dealer. The used-car dealer needs to spend resources to figure out the complete information about the quality of the car and possible future issues with the car. The problem *(C)* can be mapped to the bargaining and decision costs of the used-car dealer. The used-car dealer needs to spend resources to figure out an adequate price for the car, communicate the price, and convince the potential seller that the price is adequate. At the same time, these costs also occur for the seller, who, albeit not as thorough as the used-car dealer, needs to conduct similar market monitoring to find the desired price. The problem *(D)* can be mapped on the police/enforcement cost of the seller. The seller must spend resources to determine whether the used-car dealer is trustworthy and will adhere to its part of the trade, i.e., the agreed-on price. All in all, this introduces five problems in the present case: *(1) high search cost for used-car dealer and seller, (2) high information cost for the used-car dealer, (3) high bargaining cost for used-car dealer and seller, (4) high decision cost for used-car dealer and seller,* and *(5) high policing/ enforcement cost for the seller.*

Table 1. Transaction costs and indication if they occur for the used-car dealer or the seller

Transaction cost	Definition (based on [6])	Used-car dealer	Seller
Search cost	Imperfect information about the existence and location of trading opportunities	✓	✓
Information cost	Imperfect information about the quality or other characteristics of items available	✓	
Bargaining cost	Resources spent in finding out the desire of economic agents to participate in trading at certain prices and condition	✓	✓
Decision cost	Resources spent in determining whether the terms of the trade are mutually agreed	✓	✓
Policing/enforcement cost	Lack of knowledge as to whether one (or both) of the parties involved in the agreement will violate his part of the bargain		✓

5   Solution Objectives and Design Requirements

Based on the five problems introduced in the previous chapter, we defined solution objectives and proposed design requirements based on the meetings, workshops, and interviews. The solution objectives are introduced and summarized in Table 2, together with the design requirements. To solve problem *(1)*, we need to increase the information about possible trading opportunities. This leads us to the solution objective of *(i) Provide better access to potential market partners for used-car dealer and seller*, which will help reduce the search cost. Next, to solve problem *(2)*, we need to focus on the used-car dealer and increase the information about the quality of the car. Thus, we introduce solution objective *(ii) give the used-car dealer faster access to the full information about the car*, including predictions about the future life cycle. Additionally, to address problem *(3)*, we need to reduce the resources spent in the actual bargaining. This is mainly the time needed for bargaining for the used-car dealer. For the seller, this is the time and the cognitive effort for the bargaining. Private individuals do not like to bargain, which is also cost for the seller. Therefore, we introduce solution objective *(iii) reduce the need for bargaining for both market participants*. Furthermore, to solve problem *(4)*, we need to reduce the effort to decide if the bargaining outcome is desirable for both parties. This again increases the cognitive effort of the seller. At the same time, it is also important for the used-car dealer to be sure if the outcome is desirable. Therefore, we introduce solution objective *(iv) simplify the final decision for both market participants*. Finally, to solve problem *(5)*, we need to increase the seller's knowledge that the used-car dealer will hold up to its end of the trade, i.e., will hand over the agreed-on amount of money. Therefore, we introduce solution objective *(v) ensure the compliance of the used-car dealer for the trade*. The solution objectives are also summarized in Table 2, together with the design requirements introduced in the subsequent chapter.

Based on the problems and the solution objectives, five design requirements were derived in internal workshops. First, a digital app (implemented as a web app) should be provided where a seller can automatically get assigned to a potential buyer. This platform can be supported by AI by providing a suitable buyer–seller pairing and solving the resource allocation problem. Second, as stated by an executive of the car dealer, an *"awesome"* certificate should be defined based on certified and trusted data, containing the essential data about the cars, including predictions about the car life cycle. These predictions should utilize AI to predict the car's future life cycle. The most common use case for that is predictive maintenance. Third, an adequate price for the specific car at hand should automatically be calculated and shown to the seller and used-car dealer. AI approaches have successfully been applied for price prediction models, e.g., regression models based on historical data. If the market participants rely on this predicted price, this greatly reduces the bargaining cost. Another option that would at least reduce the bargaining cost for one side is software agents that take over the bargaining. Fourth, the car's market price should be shown, making the profit margin of the used-car dealer more transparent. Currently, used-car dealers can scrape the internet for the current market price by searching on marketplaces like Autolina or AutoScout. However, this task takes up time, which increases the decision cost. By directly showing the price, the

Table 2. Problems, solution objectives, design requirements in the present setting

Problem	Solution objective	Design requirement
(1) High search cost for dealer and seller	(i) Provide better access to potential market partners	(a) Provide an application where sellers directly get allocated a potential buyer
"We don't find enough seller of used cars" (paraphrased, internal workshop with executives)		
(2) High information cost for dealer	(ii) Give the used-car dealer faster access to the full information about the car	(b) Provide trusted and certified car data and prediction about the car's life cycle
"The added value (of the certificate) is, I can trade in faster or better because I have the confidence in the car, I can offer the customer more for the car than the others" (I12) *"If you can prove the service history well, that also creates trust. That would certainly be good." (I5)* *"[If] a seller has a certificate [...] that would take away great fears or create great security." (I2)* *"Because the driving data alone don't mean anything to me, an analysis of this data would be useful" (I2)*		
(3) High bargaining cost for dealer and seller	(iii) Reduce the need for bargaining for both market participants	(c) Suggest an adequate automatically calculated price for the specific car at hand based on the data
"If everything is defined [it leaves no room for the] bargain leeway of the used-car dealer" (I1) *"Analyses [...] is of course an advantage, because we don't know all the markets either" (I7)*		
(4) High decision cost for used-car dealer and seller	(iv) Simplify the final decision for both market participants	(d) Show the market price to simplify the decision process
"[For deciding prices] I am mainly oriented to the market; I am interested in the market" (I9) *"I orient myself very strongly, also in pricing [at the car market] (I8)*		
(5) High policing/enforcement cost for seller	(v) Ensure the compliance of the used-car dealer for the trade	(e) Incorporate independent organizations and components into the system
"[A car] is the second highest investment you make [...] I think that's where trust is very important." (I12) *"If [the customer] has confidence [they even] pay a few francs more for the vehicle." (I11)* *"[the car dealer's brand is] associated with trust" (I10)*		

decision cost is reduced. This task can be optimized, for example, by Robotic Process Automation. This can also be solved more sophisticatedly by AI that can learn the importance of different online marketplaces based on various factors to filter the actual market price. Finally, independent organizations or components should be integrated to generate more trustworthiness and reputation. This could be done by other AI solutions, like machine learning-based ratings of car dealerships or simple solutions like manual ratings of said dealerships.

6 Secondary Problems

During the interviews, it became apparent that the proposed design requirements lead to new problems. These problems arise from solving the initial problems. Therefore, it is also inevitable to consider these problems. These secondary problems are summarized in Table 3 and explained in the following. Overall, we derived four secondary problems from the interviews. First, there is the problem of *trust in self-issued certificate.* Since the certificate is issued by the AMAG Group itself and supports their used-car dealers, this might come across as untrustworthy. The AMAG Group could have the incentive to manipulate the certificate to generate more profit. Here an independent instance needs to be introduced to create more trust in the certificate. The quote underlines this: *"The certificate needs to be independent and [...] created by an independent institution"* (I12). Second, there is the problem of *trust in analytics.* Many participants still do not trust analytics. Some have problems with analyzing the driver behavior (I1). Some other interviewee states that price predictions could be daunting for the seller (I5). This is especially the case as stating exactly that factors that decrease the price might lead the seller to think that the price is too low—but it is just the regular price. Finally, one problem with the trust in analytics is that some interviewees do not trust the performance of the predictions (I9). That means that price predictions need to be very accurate to outperform the expert user and thus gain trust. As the used-car dealers are experts in their field, they rely on their knowledge rather than analytics and predictions. Third, there is the problem of *interpretability of data and analytics.* Interviewee (I11) stated that data is hard to interpret, leading to intransparency. This is especially true if too much data is present (I1)—too much detail might lose the user (I8). Further, the uninformed user might have additional questions that arise through analyses and predictions, which

Table 3. Secondary problems identified with the interviews

Problems	Description
Trust in self-issued certificate	People tend to have a lower trust in the certificate if it is self-issued and would prefer a certificate of an independent vendor (I12)
Trust in analytics	Some have problems, if the driving behavior is analyzed (I1) and think that price predictions and analyses could be daunting (I5). Further, some do not rely on analytics, since they are unsure of its quality and rather rely on their own assessment (I9)
Interpretability of data and analytics	The analytics is described as intransparent and the data as hard to interpret (I11) and additional question may arise because of these analyses and predictions (I6). Further, there is too much information (I1), and too much detail that may lose the customer (I8)
Data privacy concerns	Many people have data privacy concerns and are unsure what data should be included in the first place (I1, I3, I5, I7, I8, I12)

might confuse them more than help (I6). Fourth, there is the problem of *data privacy concerns*. Many of our participants have privacy concerns (I1, I3, I5, I7, I8, I12). They are unsure which kind of data should be stored and how they should be allowed to have access to the data. They especially do not like the idea of tracking granular data or including personal information.

7 Discussion

This paper addressed the following research question: *Can Artificial Intelligence help used-car dealers survive in a data-driven used-car market?* To answer it, we first analyzed the primary problems of used-car dealers, derived the solution objectives, and design requirements for an AI-based solution. By introducing AI in the data-driven used-car market that builds on trusted and certified data, new, secondary problems arise that need to be considered. The overall contribution of this paper can broadly be divided into two parts: (1) the problem analysis and design requirements for AI to increase the value and performance in the used-car market, contributing to the discourse on data-driven used-car markets; (2) the discussion on human-centered AI, contributing to its practical usage and challenges when using AI.

First, our design requirements leverage AI to simplify tasks, like the active comparing of market price as needed for *(C) Market Monitoring*, and with this, reduce transaction costs. However, the final trade still must be done by the used-car dealer, i.e., AI does not replace the used-car dealer but instead supports them. Nonetheless, many design requirements have the potential to reduce the tasks of used-car dealers to a minimum. Additionally, our design requirements can mitigate information asymmetry, e.g., by transparently showing the market price, or utilizing price prediction models, like [23], to give both parties the same information. At the same time, a reduced information asymmetry further reduces the transaction costs since, for example, the need for bargaining and the cost to gather information about the car is reduced. By reducing the transaction costs, the used-car dealers can be helped to survive in the market. More so, the potential to increase sales in the new car market is increased. Therefore, not only used-car dealers but also new-car dealers will be interested in the presented design requirements. We point out potential solutions to reduce the high transaction costs. These solutions build on concepts like a cardossier [13]. We propose solutions that leverage AI (e.g., prediction models [23], or predictive maintenance [24]). This can further accelerate the current shift of responsibilities in maintenance from service workers to data-driven approaches, as introduced in [25]. However, such approaches depend on good data quality. A cardossier has been shown to increase the data quality [14] and, thus, is a good foundation for well-built AI models. This AI then can be used to extend the online platforms introduced in [17] with the new functionalities.

Second, even though, in theory, AI solutions seem to reduce transaction costs instantly, we still need to consider the secondary problems that come with an AI solution. In this specific case, the problems that come with the introduction of AI are the trust and the interpretability of the system, trust in the certificate, and data privacy concerns. Thus, our results confirm the current developments in AI research that focuses on explainable AI [27, 29]. However, our results achieve more. We also point out the need for trust in AI. Trust is the central topic in the secondary problems. That means for the context we studied, i.e., the used-car market, more design for trust is needed. Given our results, explainable AI and FATE AI are good candidates to design for trust; however, that alone is not enough. This is also in line with the concept of human-centered AI. With this, we also contribute to the general discussion of AI. We highlight that while AI methods, like price prediction models [23] or predictive maintenance [24], in theory, are capable of reducing information asymmetries and transaction costs. However, in practice, new problems arise that prevent the direct implementation of these methods. Solutions to the secondary problems must be human-centered. They could include strategies like validating the quality and completeness of the certificate and data by an independent authority or instance, creating transparency by deploying state-of-the-art explainable AI and ensuring data privacy. This also raises the question of if AI is always necessary. Some tasks do not need to incorporate sophisticated AI solutions, but the simpler logic-based rule could work equally well. RPA [20] could be used to solve tedious tasks without the need for AI. In software development, a common rule is to keep things as simple as possible. This should also hold for AI development. Additionally, several technological implementation and economic challenges will occur. We do not have any indication if people are willing to pay for such a system, and thus, the question of pricing remains unanswered. Additionally, practical problems arise when such a system is implemented. We need to ensure data sources with high data quality for AI models to perform well.

All in all, to answer the RQ on whether *Artificial Intelligence can help used-car dealers survive in a data-driven used-car market*, the answer to that is yes, potentially. Our design requirements are a substantial step towards a holistic solution. However, all solutions entail additional problems that need to be considered for the development.

8   Conclusion

To conclude, we showed how AI could be used to potentially solve the major problems of used-car dealers in the used-car market. However, new, secondary problems arise with these potential solutions that need to be addressed. These secondary problems are not easy to solve as they require unique properties to remain human-centered, like transparent and explainable AI. AI can only bring added value to the used-car dealers and *help used-car dealers survive in a data-driven used-car market*.

This study comes with some limitations. One limitation is the focus on used-car dealers as interview partners. While we argue that used-car dealers can take on both roles, sellers, and buyers, there still is a difference in experience between dealers and private individuals. This might lead to different requirements. Further, the design was evaluated with project partners on the level of the design requirements. The next step would be to design the solution based on these requirements and test it in experimental settings and the field. Additionally, we only follow one automotive company, the AMAG Group, with several used-car dealers. While still trying to be as general as possible, we cannot rule out that other automotive companies might have different or additional problems. The findings can also be different for other cultural or business contexts. Overall, it will be interesting to investigate the secondary problems and find further solutions for them for future research. Lastly, the system can be developed for practical use. Nonetheless, this study is a fitting starting point for future research.

Acknowledgements. We thank Alex Scheitlin for assisting with the data collection and conducting the interviews as part of his master's thesis. Further, we thank the AMAG Group for their close collaboration during the duration of this study.

References

1. European Parliament: Odometer Manipulation in Motor Vehicles in the EU: European Added Value Assessment. Publications Office, LU (2018)
2. Park, S., Nicolau, J.L.: Asymmetric effects of online consumer reviews. Ann. Tour. Res. **50**, 67–83 (2015)
3. KPMG: Used car prices could crash – will they? https://advisory.kpmg.us/articles/2021/used-car-prices-could-crash.html. Last accessed 07 Feb 2022
4. Gavazza, A., Lizzeri, A., Roketskiy, N.: A Quantitative analysis of the used-car market. Am. Econ. Rev. **104**, 3668–3700 (2014)
5. Porter, R.H., Sattler, P.: Patterns of Trade in the Market for Used Durables: Theory and Evidence. National Bureau of Economic Research, Inc. (1999)
6. Dahlman, C.J.: The problem of externality. J. Law Econ. **22**, 141–162 (1979)
7. Coase, R.H.: The nature of the firm. Economica **4**, 386–405 (1937)
8. Akerlof, G.A.: The market for "lemons": quality uncertainty and the market mechanism. Q. J. Econ. **84**, 488–500 (1970)
9. Brounen, D., Kok, N.: On the economics of energy labels in the housing market. J. Environ. Econ. Manage. **62**, 166–179 (2011)
10. Frondel, M., Gerster, A., Vance, C.: The power of mandatory quality disclosure: evidence from the German housing market. J. Assoc. Environ. Resour. Econ. **7**, 181–208 (2020)
11. Kolodinsky, J.: Persistence of health labeling information asymmetry in the United States: historical perspectives and twenty-first century realities. J. Macromarketing **32**, 193–207 (2012)
12. Mathios, A.D.: The impact of mandatory disclosure laws on product choices: an analysis of the salad dressing market. J. Law Econ. **43**, 651–678 (2000)
13. Zavolokina, L., Ziolkowski, R., Bauer, I., Schwabe, G.: Management, governance and value creation in a blockchain consortium. MIS Q. Exec. **19**, 1–17 (2020)
14. Zavolokina, L., Spychiger, F., Tessone, C.J., Schwabe, G.: Incentivizing data quality in blockchains for inter-organizational networks – learning from the digital car dossier. In: ICIS 2018 Proceedings (2018)
15. Bauer, I., Zavolokina, L., Leisibach, F., Schwabe, G.: Value creation from a decentralized car ledger. Front. Blockchain **2** (2020)
16. Bauer, I., Zavolokina, L., Schwabe, G.: Is there a market for trusted car data? Electron. Mark. **30**, 211–225 (2020)
17. Zavolokina, L., Schlegel, M., Schwabe, G.: How can we reduce information asymmetries and enhance trust in 'The Market for Lemons'? Inf. Syst. E-Bus. Manage. **19**, 883–908 (2021)
18. Baumann, J., Zavolokina, L., Schwabe, G.: Dealers of Peaches and Lemons: How Can Used Car Dealers Use Trusted Car Data to create value? (2021)
19. Goodfellow, I., Bengio, Y., Courville, A.: Deep Learning. MIT Press (2016)
20. van der Aalst, W.M.P., Bichler, M., Heinzl, A.: Robotic process automation. Bus. Inf. Syst. Eng. **60**, 269–272 (2018)
21. Nwana, H.S.: Software agents: an overview. Knowl. Eng. Rev. **11**, 205–244 (1996)
22. Marwala, T., Hurwitz, E.: Artificial Intelligence and Asymmetric Information Theory. arXiv: 1510.02867 [cs] (2015)

23. Gegic, E., Isakovic, B., Keco, D., Masetic, Z., Kevric, J.: Car price prediction using machine learning techniques. TEM J. **8**, 113 (2019)
24. Oberländer, A.M., Röglinger, M., Rosemann, M., Kees, A.: Conceptualizing business-to-thing interactions – a sociomaterial perspective on the internet of things. Eur. J. Inf. Syst. **27**, 486–502 (2018)
25. Poor, P., Ženíšek, D., Basl, J.: Historical overview of maintenance management strategies: development from breakdown maintenance to predictive maintenance in accordance with four industrial revolutions (2019)
26. Touretzky, D.S., Pomerleau, D.A.: What's hidden in the hidden layers. Byte. **14**, 227–233 (1989)
27. Adadi, A., Berrada, M.: Peeking inside the black-box: a survey on explainable artificial intelligence (XAI). IEEE Access. **6**, 52138–52160 (2018)
28. Thiebes, S., Lins, S., Sunyaev, A.: Trustworthy artificial intelligence. Electron. Mark. **31** (2020)
29. Shin, D.: User perceptions of algorithmic decisions in the personalized AI system: perceptual evaluation of fairness, accountability, transparency, and explainability. J. Broadcast. Electron. Media **64**, 541–565 (2020)
30. Peffers, K., Tuunanen, T., Rothenberger, M.A., Chatterjee, S.: A design science research methodology for information systems research. J. Manag. Inf. Syst. **24**, 45–77 (2007)
31. Saldaña, J.: The Coding Manual for Qualitative Researchers. SAGE, Los Angeles (2013)

Assessing the Reusability of Design Principles in the Realm of Conversational Agents

Edona Elshan[1]([⊠]) [iD], Christian Engel[1] [iD], Philipp Ebel[1], and Dominik Siemon[2] [iD]

[1] University of St. Gallen, 9000 St. Gallen, Switzerland
{edona.elshan,christian.engel,philipp.ebel}@unisg.ch
[2] LUT University, 53850 Lappeenranta, Finland
dominik.siemon@lut.fi

Abstract. Conversational Agents (CAs) provide the means to foster user experience design through seizing their interaction capability, knowledgeability, and human-like behavior. To support practice and academia in designing CAs, IS researchers have been creating design knowledge in the form of design principles (DPs) guided by the Design Science paradigm. However, scientific literature in this vein is dispersed and lacks an axis of cohesion and transferability to sustained practice usage. This raises the question of reusability of design principles in the realm of CAs. Therefore, in this study, we conduct a Systematic Literature Review to retrieve and assess design principles of existing design science papers dealing with CAs with regard to their reusability. Our findings indicate that the Design Science community, in our case in the domain of CAs, seems to face challenges in creating reusable design principles. We discuss this observation and provide avenues on how to move forward.

Keywords: Conversational Agents · Design Science · Design principles · Reusability assessment

1 Introduction

Conversational agents (CAs) are up-and-coming, fostering individualized interactions between users and companies due to their innovative properties, such as the various possibilities to interact, their knowledgeability, and their human-like behaviour. With the rise of end-user-oriented CAs, the access to these novel applications has been democratized. CAs can be regarded as software agents that are designed to aid users in performing various activities by interacting with users via natural language [1, 2]. These CAs are gradually evolving to become the dominant mode of delivering user experiences designed by miscellaneous service providers [3]. However, designing CAs in a manner that leads to high levels of user satisfaction still poses a challenging task for user experience designers due to the novelty of this class of systems and the ambiguity of design outcomes.

To counteract this, research has started to elaborate on corresponding design knowledge seizing Design Science Research (DSR) as a guiding paradigm to structure CA-oriented design endeavors [4]. Due to its suitability for constructing socio-technical

The original version of this chapter was revised: an error in spelling of a co-author name was corrected. The correction to this chapter is available at
https://doi.org/10.1007/978-3-031-06516-3_37

artifacts, DSR has become widely used in the field of Information Systems [5]. The notion of design science is described as a process of originating novel artifacts in Information Systems. Thereby, a particular problem set is addressed and further assessed regarding the usefulness of addressing that specific set of problems in multiple steps. Outstanding DSR artifacts may result in impact through novelty and generalized theories of design, enabling practical application to real-world problems. Thus, DSR offers the opportunity of providing guidance to both practitioners and researchers within the development process and to ensure that the developed CA is serving its intended purpose.

However, the scientific literature is dispersed into different thematic axes and research areas [6, 7]. Furthermore, the scientific and practical knowledge about CAs has also grown in a dispersed manner, given a shortage of integrative perspectives to support CA development and design processes [8, 9]. This leads to challenges in the field of DSR, as emphasized by Iivari et al. [10, 11], as well as Cronholm and Goebel [12]. The authors stress the necessity for Design Science researchers to not neglect reusability of design principles (DPs), as design DPs "found applicable by practitioners and not useful in practice" pose a mismatch with the basic idea of DSR. Taking action on the raised concerns, Iivari et al. [11] recently presented a proposal for assessing existing DPs of DSR papers by systematically evaluating the extent of their reusability based on different criteria. This provides a suitable framework for appraising any DPs with respect to their reusability.

Against this backdrop, we aim to address the mentioned shortage of integrative perspectives on CA development and design processes; we assess DPs of existing research papers dealing with CAs by actively evaluating their reusability for practitioners. Thus, we formulated the following research question (RQ) that we aim to address in this paper, performing a two-step analysis.

RQ: To what extent are existing DPs in the realm of CAs reusable by other researchers and chatbot designers?

By answering this research question, we intend to contribute on the one hand to the DSR community by evaluating the usability of DSR artifacts in a specific context, on the other hand, we intend to contribute to the research field of CAs by shedding light on the reusability of DPs for academia as well as practice. We hope to foster and contribute to the ongoing discussion in the field of design science. Overall, this work shall present the first evaluation of DPs in a specific research area and should highlight opportunities for improvement and action for the future creation of prescriptive Design knowledge in IS. The remainder of this paper is structured as follows. First, we provide a brief overview of the current research on CAs and introduce our conceptual notion of DPs. In the next step, we describe the method regarding the systematic literature review as well as the reusability framework proposed by Iivari et al. [11]. Subsequently, we present our descriptive findings and insights into the current state of CA literature within design science research. Furthermore, we present our results regarding the reusability of prescriptive design knowledge, i.e., DPs. Based on this, we discuss our results, lay out the imminent limitations of our analysis, and provide areas for future research on advancing both the field of CAs and DSR. Finally, we close this paper with implications for practice and academia and some concluding remarks.

2   Conceptual Background

2.1   Conversational Agents

AI-based CAs assist users by interacting with them using natural language [13]. CAs can respond to user input, adapt their responses, and build up a dialogue with them, similar to human–human interaction. CAs are distinguished from other intelligent system entities by their interaction and intelligence capabilities [13]. Mainstream conversational intelligent systems follow strict behavioral patterns. Those agents could only match user inputs against stored patterns [1]. However, CAs can now process compound natural language and thus respond to more complex user requests [14]. They can also adapt their responses to the user's workflows, knowledge state, and dialogue routines. CAs are thought to improve quality in various personal and professional tasks. They are expected to increase worker productivity by adapting to their tasks and routines [15]. They are intended to improve user comfort and well-being in private settings.

Considering the widespread of CAs, the industry anticipates high user adoption [16]. However, the opposite has proven to be true [17]. The high level of contextualization required to provide a flawless user experience makes designing a new CA a difficult task. However, design elements are the distinctive technical, conceptual, and knowledge features that frame a CA [18]. Even though a large body of research, mostly in the IS domain, investigated the design of CAs in various contexts, there are no general CA design guidelines, only high-level suggestions and domain-specific advice. As a result, many CAs confuse, frustrate, and even annoy users [19]. Thus, an integrated analysis aggregating design science insight on the diversity of CA design knowledge could help us better understand CA design and identify future research needs. Moreover, despite the rapid yet segregated growth of practical and scientific knowledge in this area, we are unaware of any review or evaluation that focuses on CAs design knowledge. Thus, we address the lack of an integrative perspective by systematically analyzing the DS literature on CAs to identify design knowledge, assess reusability, and identify research needs.

2.2   DPs as Generalizable Design Knowledge

Hevner et al. [20] consider DSR as a proactive paradigm when it comes to IT as DSR enables entities to address relevant problem sets in IT through the conception and assessment of novel artifacts. Therefore, when it comes to technology, DSR appears to be more hands-on and agile as this kind of research is in the continuous process of new artifact creation and utility assessment of corresponding addressed problems. Baskerville et al. [21] show that DSR requires the creation of artifacts and the formulation of their design. Thereby, DSR artifacts show a considerable impact on the dimensions of theory as well as practice. DSR is widely seen as an opportunity to respond to calls for academics to commit themselves to work that has a greater resonance outside the scientific community [22].

Taking up on this, scholars have been exploring the codification of knowledge in the field of DSR (e.g., [23]). The purpose of creating design knowledge in DSR projects is homogenous in its overarching goal of creating utility but heterogeneous in how this is realized in as many different configurations as possible for creating and evaluating design knowledge in IS exist [24]. Taking this into consideration, Sturm and Sunyaev [25] observed that most knowledge is used by practitioners for designing artifacts, i.e., CAs. A form of representation of design knowledge can be found in DPs. Following Gregor and Hevner [5], DPs can be described as "generalized knowledge contribution in DSR". Moreover, DPs are comparable to Gregor and Jones [26] component of Level 3. The idea for the term of DP was shaped by the research of Gregor and Hevner [5] and Sein et al. [27]. It is noteworthy that Gregor and Hevner [5] have a slightly different perspective on DPs than Sein et al. [27]. While Sein et al. [27] are of the opinion that DPs should be theory-ingrained as a part of an action design research approach, Gregor and Hevner [5] argue that DPs emerge from DSR efforts.

Early on, Sein et al. [27] argued that DPs are how prescriptive knowledge should be expressed within design science research. Nevertheless, it should not be neglected that, in addition to DPs, other forms of presentation can be used to record design knowledge. Thus, design knowledge can also appear in patterns or requirements (e.g., [28]). Nevertheless, within the DSR community, it is widely shared that DPs are seen as the right way to formalize DSR efforts and abstract the research findings to allow knowledge accumulation within the community [29]. This accumulation of knowledge is reflected in how DPs describe how other instances belonging to the same class of systems can be created and designed [27]. According to Chandra et al. [30], design principles have two audiences. On the one hand, they add to a corpus of knowledge [31] regarding the design of various types of IT artifacts [32, 33]. On the other hand, they are also meant to provide practitioners with meaningful insights that can be used to develop new versions of related artifacts.

Recently, Purao et al. [23] discussed that it is naive to assume that practitioners simply take the DPs designed by scholarly researchers and apply them in their context. Other researchers have already addressed the underlying problem, namely that DPs reported in research articles currently find little application in practice (e.g., [11, 22]). Gregor et al. [22] assume that one of the main factors causing this is the formulation of DPs. Their study notes that there are many discrepancies and inconsistencies in the literature when it is a matter of how DPs should be formulated. In this context, they propose a formulation scheme that should help researchers to formulate DPs better. This awareness of the issue is also being shared through research by others. Lukyanenko and Jeffrey [34] conclude that design knowledge should be formulated in "clear, accessible and unambiguous language". In connection with the use of language to describe the design knowledge, Gregor et al. [22] note that hardly any attention is currently paid to the "people's aspect" within DPs. These perceptions are also common to the framework's authors for reusability evaluation. Iivari et al. [11] claim that DPs should make explicit who the target community is, which should reuse this prescriptive form of knowledge.

3 Research Approach

3.1 Paper Selection Process

Our procedure for this paper contains two main steps: gathering and analyzing relevant literature, which is conducted as follows. First, to evaluate existing DSR research papers on CAs using the suggested proposal by Iivari et al. [11], we reviewed current work in design science research, particularly on CAs. To identify relevant literature as the basis for the systematic analysis, we conducted a systematic literature review (SLR) following Webster and Watson [35] and vom Brocke et al. [36]. The overall scope of the conducted SLR can be defined along the dimensions of process, source, coverage, and techniques of the SLR [36]. We used a comprehensive set of techniques to establish our data set and thereby the basis for the reusability evaluation (i.e., keyword search, backward search, and forward search).

Selection of Search String. To identify a wide range of literature on CAs, the search string is chosen to be rather broad. Based on recent literature reviews (e.g., [6, 7]), we identified different keywords researchers used to describe CAs. This resulted in the following search string:

> *"conversational agent" OR "chatbot" OR "chat bot" OR "interactive agent" OR "talkbot" OR "virtual assistant" OR "artificial intelligence assistant" OR "smart personal assistant" AND "design science"*

Selection of Databases. For the literature search process in the first phase, we needed to identify relevant papers for our research paper to test the reusability of DPs. Research in the context of CAs has recently gained a lot of attention; therefore, we have chosen to conduct our literature review database-based. To ensure a high quality of the papers we analyze and evaluate, we relied on highly-ranked databases [37]. We conducted our search mainly using the following databases: AIS Electronic Library, IEEE Xplore Digital Library, ScienceDirect, ProQuest, and EBSCOhost. Eventually, we conducted a final search query using Google Scholar.

Selection of Papers. By searching in the title, abstract, and keywords of the papers, the database-based search reveals 1032 hits. The identified papers are analyzed based on their abstracts in an initial screening process. We only included papers that referred to any type of CAs and presented any kind of design knowledge (DPs, guidelines, or design decisions). This first screening resulted in a set of 350 papers. In a subsequent step, we excluded paper that did not conduct design science research, did not report their design knowledge as well as papers that did not present design knowledge in our chosen context of CAs. Finally, the forward and backward search was carried out. Through screening the references and applying forward as well as backward searches using GoogleScholar, 21 articles were added to the set. Thus, resulting in the final number of 86 papers. After reviewing the search hits, reading through their abstract, and conducting a full-text search, we reached a total of 35 research papers that we can analyze regarding the reusability of their DPs subsequently. We excluded many of the articles since they did not formulate DPs but instead reported the design knowledge differently.

3.2 Paper Analysis

In the next step, we proceeded with our analysis of the selected research papers referring to the proposal for minimum reusability evaluation of DPs by Iivari et al. [11]. We thoroughly read this paper to understand the rationales of the proposal for evaluating DPs according to their reusability and the suggested procedure. In this context, we used the framework for reusability evaluation to analyze our selected set of academic literature thoroughly and comprehensively. Therefore, we carefully read the selection of DSR papers on CAs once again, screening for DPs, elements, or artifacts and depicting them in a structured spreadsheet. Subsequently, we evaluated every single DP, element or artifact suggested in science by assessing them concerning the specific criteria, accessibility, importance, novelty and insightfulness, actability and guidance, and effectiveness suggested by the authors. Based on the applicability check of IS research from Rosemann and Vessey [38], Iivari et al. [11] propose a reusability evaluation for DPs as artifcats of DSR. It is important to note that the criteria do not have measurable scales or classifications; they merely indicate whether the criterion is applicable. Therefore, we decided to rate each of the DPs on a 5-point-Liker scale and assess whether their reusability would be low or high.

Furthermore, the framework requires that particular order of the criteria is followed, and therefore, the reusability framework cannot be called "flat" [10]. In this sense, the DPs are not considered reusable if one of the criteria is answered with no. We briefly discuss the individual criteria and describe their content in the following.

The first criterion is accessibility, intended to determine whether the DP has been formulated in such a manner that a member of the target community can grasp it with ease and without much effort [10]. Roseman and Vessey [38] also state that accessible representation is a representation that has adapted tonc, style structure, and semantics to the target audience. If this is not the case, practitioners may not understand the DPs or their consequences, and they may not find acceptance and application outside the scientific literature. A possible workaround to enhance comprehensibility and usability is for researchers to formulate a practitioner-oriented version of their DPs [11]. Although this suggestion seems to be reasonable, it stands in contradiction to the actual purpose of DSR [5]. The authors argue that the importance is assessed in terms of the severity and relevance of the real problems they ultimately propose to overcome [11]. In a similar vein, importance is interpreted by Roseman and Vessey [38]. Namely, research is to be classified as being of importance if it "meets the needs of practice by addressing a real-world problem in a timely manner, and in such a way that it can act as the starting point for providing an eventual solution" (p. 3). Having a look at the novelty and insightfulness criterion, it is evident that the novelty is typically assessed by fellow researchers solely and seldom by practitioners [11]. Thereby, the authors propose that practitioners should evaluate whether they perceive that the DPs have any kind of impact in a real-world context and do not only display knowledge that they already know (confirmatory). An extension of the novelty evaluation to include practitioners seems to make sense to the extent that research sometimes lags behind practice. Consequently, it is possible that something that is described as "new and innovative" in research may not be innovative in practice. This phenomenon was observed, for example, in the development of digital maturity assessment models and can currently be observed with artificial intelligence maturity assessment models that were developed instead by consulting firms rather than scholars. The fourth criterion considers the actability and guidance of DPs. In the understanding of the authors' reusability framework, actability refers to the assumption that the DPs "can be acted and carried out in practice, i.e., under the control of the practitioners in question" [11].

Further, they suggest that DPs shall be "realistic to be carried out". It is important to note that Chandra Kruse et al. [29] have highlighted that tacit knowledge is compromised within DPs. In addition, they argue that no set of DPs is adequate to design the proposed instance without further guidance. Iivari et al. [11] take up this point and add that through appropriate guidance, this problem shall be addressed without being too restrictive. Lastly, the framework proposes to assess the effectiveness of the DPs. The authors refer "to effects or consequences of reusing the DPs in the adopting unit" (p. 12), even though DPs might have effects at different levels as well. Having these criteria in mind, we were challenged to change perspectives and neutrally evaluate the DPs from a practitioner's point of view and assess whether the criteria are fulfilled or not. To facilitate the evaluation process, we bore in mind the presented example by Iivari et al. [11] and continuously referred to the more detailed elaboration of the defined criteria to be able to evaluate to what extent the design artifacts fulfill the criteria for reusability.

4   Results

We organized the findings into two sections. The first section examines descriptive statistics based on the meta-data of found literature. The second section examines the reusability of the proposed DPs in the context of CAs.

In total, we have analyzed 35 publications in the context of conversational agents that apply Design Science methodologies in order to generate design knowledge. The youngest paper is from 2021, and the oldest paper from 2005. Although at that time, the concept of DPs had not yet been introduced to the DSR, it was possible to identify approaches of guidelines in the paper which go in the direction of DPs. Therefore, this paper was kept in the dataset. Most papers have been published within the last three years, which supports our initial assumption that CAs indeed represent an emerging research area in DSR. This argument is underpinned by the fact that most papers are from conference proceedings, which gives testament to the relative youth of the field. In addition to distribution along the timeline also a distribution along application domains is visible within our results. It appears that there exists no application domain, that appears not suitable for design science research. This is evident from the many different contexts and application areas in which CAs are used. Further, it is noteworthy that a multitude of investigated studies is conducted in the HCI discipline, while publications in IS conferences and outlets are only recently picking up. Next, we provide more specific insights concerning the reusability of DPs in the context of CAs. In this sense, the following table summarizes the results along with the criteria of the reusability evaluation framework. Due to space limitations, the table includes only five papers. However, the analysis and evaluation of the whole data set identified 35 papers suggesting DPs in any context of CAs as their contribution to research and practice. It is also worth noting that the sample of papers selected in the following table is drawn entirely at random. In addition, we do not claim the actual quality of the papers but only examine their DPs.

The results of Table 1 indicate that almost all papers, with Lechler et al. [39] as an exception, somehow evaluated their DPs. The authors of the four papers demonstrated how the principles were implemented in a first mockup [40] or showed how the DPs were translated into design decisions and then implemented in prototypes [41] or even executed in the real world [42]. Other evaluation methods used were, for example, user experience evaluations [43], qualitative experiments [44], focus group discussion [45], or interviews [46].

Table 1. Evaluation of DPs of expository papers.

		Wambsganss et al. [40]	Winkler and Roos [41]	Meier et al. [47]	Lechler et al. [39]	Gnewuch et al. [48]
Design princples		6 DPs for CA for course evaluations	11 DPs for CA for online educational context	4 DPs for CAs in health awareness context	6 DPs for CAs for feedback exchange	4 DPs for CAs in customer service
Evaluation method		Online questionnaire	Focus group discussion	Experiment	N/A	Field study for prototype
	Accessibility	Mostly	Most of the times not clear	Sometimes not clear what is addressed	Formulation quite abstract	Mainly accessible
	Importance	Overall addresses a real-world problem, DP not	DP, not referring to a significant real- world problem	Overall important real-world problem, DPs not referring this	Address mostly an important real-world problem	Most of the DP address a real-world problem
	Novelty and Insightfulness	DPs are somehow insightful, not novel	DPs might be insightful, yet not very novel	DPs are insightful for the context, but not very novel	Some DPs are insightful, yet not all of them novel	Novel, regard to state of research at that time
	Actability and Guidance	Rather high actability and guidance	Most probably actable and can be carried out in practice	Most probably actable and can be carried out in practice	Actability relatively moderate	Guidance within DPs appropriate
	Effectiveness	Positive, online survey with students	Positive, experiment	Positive,: questionnaire	Not sure if positive	Might affect adopting unit positively
Final evaluation		Moderate reusability	Rather low reusability	Moderate reusability	Rather low reusability	Moderate reusability

Although there are many different approaches to how DPs have been evaluated, they are rarely evaluated with the help of the target community, which should use the DPs one day. Instead, most of the evaluations are conducted with the end-user, although many focus on the artifact that the DP is reflected in rather than the DP itself. For example, Wambsganss et al. [40] formulated six DPs, which they shaped by applying the DSR approach of Hevner [49]. The DPs were composed of literature research and interviews with end-users. Thus, requirements for a CA were derived from the interviews. However, a look at these requirements shows that not all of them are aimed at concrete aspects of design. To evaluate the DP, the authors of this paper have created a mockup of a CA. For the design of this CA, they first transferred the DPs into a set of 12 design features. Unfortunately, the reader is not told how this step is done. Therefore, it is difficult to understand if the DPs could have been converted into other design features. Although design features are then used for the mockup, the authors describe the goal of the evaluation as follows: "The evaluation serves to verify if the DPs are of value to the lecturers and students and to identify change requests and additional DPs. This would lead one to conclude that the DPs were evaluated with the later designer of the artifact (the lecturer), but later in the process, it is explained that the evaluation was done with the help of 28 students. In their next step, they tested the CA in a real-world setting with 12 students and one lecturer. However, even this evaluation did not directly aim to evaluate the DP. In this "proof-of-usefulness" evaluation, the authors tested the CA they designed against a conventional survey tool.

In their study, Winkler et al. [41] proposed a set of 11 principles for the design of a CA as a learning tutor. For the evaluation of their DPs, they conducted a proof-of-concept evaluation in the form of a focus group discussion. With this, they aimed to check the validity of the requirements as well as the translation into DPs. Similar to the evaluation conducted by Wambsganss et al. [40] also, these authors did not involve real practitioners in their evaluation but rather students as end-users of the designed artifact. This issue can also be observed in other papers.

Interestingly Meier et al. [47] discuss critical findings regarding their DPs after their evaluation with end-users and experts. However, in their key findings, only the user's perception and usefulness are addressed. No further indications of the applicability of the DPs are given. However, this conflicts with the intended goal of their DPs, which the authors of this paper state as: "the presented DPs contribute to the information systems discipline by providing important guidance in designing successful CAs for practical challenges [...]".

We think that, especially with regard to the comprehensibility of the DPs, it would be useful to have this tested by a potential user (e.g., CA designer) of the DPs. Further, our analysis reveals that most of the DPs are not accessible without further explanations. More specific, many of the DPs contain very specific terms, which are not understandable for inexperienced potential users. Tavanapour et al. [50], for instance, describe in their paper that the CA should resemble a social actor. However, they do not elaborate on what a social actor is or what it looks like. As a result, it is not clear how this DP should be instantiated. This may ultimately lead to the DPs not being applied for this very particular reason. Regarding the importance, it can be stated that most of the papers contain a problem that is important for the real world or the question came from a real-world problem. We think that this is since in many DSR studies requirements are also derived from the practitioners or users and therefore are incorporated into the DPs. However, it must be pointed out that on the level of the DPs, the real-world problem does not always have priority. Here the question arises, whether it is sufficient that the set of DPs and their instance address a real-world problem or whether each individual DP should represent this circumstance.

With regards to the criterion of novelty and insightfulness, it must be noted that this is a difficult-to-evaluate criterion. An assessment of the novelty of the DPs presupposes that the reader is well versed in the field of CAs as well as in the specific context. Nevertheless, we have tried to evaluate whether the papers are novel or not through the seniority of the papers and their proposed DPs. However, this criterion cannot be verified merely by a temporal comparison, such as whether a DP formulated in 2021 takes up a new aspect compared to the previous DPs. In order to be able to carry out a comprehensive evaluation of novelty and insightfulness, the respective context must also be considered. It may be that certain DPs have a new meaning in the context of CAs, but this design knowledge has already been applied to other instances of artifacts. The question now is whether the transfer to a new class of systems is sufficiently innovative and new, or whether more than this "incremental" innovation is needed. Altogether, the results shown here based on these five research contributions can be transferred to the entire data set. However, there is hardly a single paper in the entire data set that presents flawless DPs. This is problematic from several points of view. First of all, this could mean that research, such as the development of taxonomies based on these DPs, also contains design elements that are not understandable to practitioners. In a subsequent logical step, the question arises of whom these DPs should be formulated. Our analysis has shown that the DPs are usually not formulated in an understandable way for practitioners.

Nevertheless, not only practitioners fall back on these DPs. It seems to be a bit worrying that other researchers are not able to transfer these DPs to their context. Consequently, it would be possible that research could lapse into creating DPs for each specific use case.

5   Discussion and Concluding Remarks

Our goal was to address the shortage of integrative perspectives on CA development and design processes. Thus, we assessed DPs of existing research papers dealing with CAs by evaluating their reusability using the framework proposed by Iivari et al. [11]. This shall contribute to research and practice in a three-fold manner. First, reviewing the reusability of DPs in the field of CAs, led to the insight that in DSR, the community is still faced with a low level of reusability of DPs. To assess reusability for practice, we left our scientific perspective and viewed DPs through a practice lens. Our analysis reveals that in many cases, the evaluation of the first criterion, i.e., accessibility, led to negative assessment as the DPs were not formulated in a way facilitating to be easily understood by non-academic readers. This finding is also in line with prior insights [22, 23], which have already noted that the formulation of DPs needs to be rethought to facilitate sustainable use in practice. Consequently, we encourage future research to position and formulate DPs guided by the notion established by Gregor et al.[22]. This bears the potential to foster transparency and clarity when communicating and conveying design knowledge. We also anticipate that this will provide more guidance when instantiating respective DPs into concrete artifacts.

Regarding transferability of design knowledge, the majority of analyzed papers faced challenges in using DPs to bridge the gap between conceptual scientific knowledge and its deployment in practice. In this sense, we also think that other approaches are needed to evaluate DPs in the context of design efforts. In many research papers, the DPs were not evaluated according to their usefulness and usability of the designed artifacts, although, in many research papers, this was the intended purpose of the evaluation. By using the reusability evaluation framework in a specific context, we show its applicability in another domain of IS research. This indicates a certain level of generalizability of the framework, which raises the question of whether the reusability evaluation framework could benefit the review process of research articles to account for the utility of the developed Design Science artifacts. Therefore, future research opportunities could be building up on Ivari et al. [11] by further detailing the single analysis steps to reach higher levels of intersubjectivity and comparability between individual evaluations. A next step could be formulating concrete questions that need to be answered in the individual criteria and thus to move in the direction of a standardized assessment. We believe that this be very useful for a review process. The DP formulation scheme [22] offers a promising foundation for enhancing comparability when assessing the reusability of DPs. This could be facilitated by combining and integrating both approaches in a structured method. However, also the framework for reusability must also be studied critically. While numerous criteria are available, evaluating DPs using these criteria is not always straightforward and leaves a great deal of space for interpretation.

Additionally, it should be noted that a DP is only reusable if it meets all requirements; if one of the criteria, for example, novelty or insightfulness, is not met, the DP is classified as not reusable. We would like to emphasize that it is feasible for a DP to be reusable even if the novelty value is not exceptionally high. As a result, a weighting of the criteria or a revision to the minimal standards for designating a DP as reusable should be explored in the future.

However, our paper does not come without limitations. First, the scope of this SLR cannot claim to be exhaustive. However, we intended to reach a representative coverage of Design Science literature in the domain of CAs by applying a rigorous research method for searching and analyzing the papers. Second, the indicated reusability and by this the assessment along the criteria of accessibility, importance, novelty and insightfulness, actability and guidance, and effectiveness of the DPs are based on our interpretation of the reported design knowledge in the studies. Thus, a certain residual level of subjectivity remains as this process involves individual human judgement. However, by assessing the DPs independently, we aimed to mitigate this issue. Future studies could also ask CAs designers independently to assess the DPs to prevent subjectivity.

References

1. McTear, M., Callejas, Z., Griol, D.: Conversational interfaces: devices, wearables, virtual agents, and robots. In: The Conversational Interface, pp. 283–308. Springer, Cham (2016). https://doi.org/10.1007/978-3-319-32967-3_13
2. Pfeuffer, N., Benlian, A., Gimpel, H., Hinz, O.: Anthropomorphic information systems. Bus. Inf. Syst. Eng. **61**, 523–533 (2019)
3. McLean, G., Osei-Frimpong, K.: Hey alexa… examine the variables influencing the use of artificial intelligent in-home voice assistants. Comput. Hum. Behav. **99**, 28–37 (2019)
4. Feine, J., Gnewuch, U., Morana, S., Maedche, A.: A taxonomy of social cues for conversational agents. Int. J. Hum. Comput. Stud. **132**, 138–161 (2019)

5. Gregor, S., Hevner, A.R.: Positioning and presenting design science research for maximum impact. MIS Quarterly **37**(2), 337–355 (2013). https://doi.org/10.25300/MISQ/2013/37.2.01
6. Diederich, S., Brendel, A.B., Morana, S., Kolbe, L.: On the design of and interaction with conversational agents: an organizing and assessing review of human-computer interaction research. J. Assoc. Inf. Syst. **23**(1), 96–138 (2022). https://doi.org/10.17705/1jais.00724
7. Elshan, E., Zierau, N., Engel, C., Janson, A., Leimeister, J.M.: Understanding the design elements affecting user acceptance of intelligent agents: past, present and future. Inf. Syst. Front. (2022). https://doi.org/10.1007/s10796-021-10230-9
8. Brandtzaeg, P.B., Følstad, A.: Why people use chatbots. In: International Conference on Internet Science, pp. 377–392. Springer (2017)
9. Jain, M., Kumar, P., Kota, R., Patel, S.N.: Evaluating and informing the design of chatbots. In: Proceedings of the 2018 Designing Interactive Systems Conference, pp. 895–906 (2018)
10. Iivari, J., Hansen, M.R.P., Haj-Bolouri, A.: A Framework for light reusability evaluation of design principles in design science research. In: 13th International Conference on Design Science Research and Information Systems and Technology: Designing for a Digital and Globalized World (2018)
11. Iivari, J., Hansen, M.R.P., Haj-Bolouri, A.: A proposal for minimum reusability evaluation of design principles. Eur. J. Inf. Syst. **0**, 1–18. https://doi.org/10.1080/0960085X.2020.1793697
12. Cronholm, S., Göbel, H.: Guidelines supporting the formulation of design principles. In: Australasian Conference on Information Systems 2018. University of Technology, Sydney (2018). https://doi.org/10.5130/acis2018.ak
13. Maedche, A., et al.: Advanced user assistance systems. Bus. Inf. Syst. Eng. **58**, 367–370 (2016). https://doi.org/10.1007/s12599-016-0444-2
14. Knote, R., Janson, A., Söllner, M., Leimeister, J.M.: Value co-creation in smart services: a functional affordances perspective on smart personal assistants. SSRN Electron. J. (2020). https://doi.org/10.2139/ssrn.3923706
15. Jalaliniya, S., Pederson, T.: Designing wearable personal assistants for surgeons: An egocentric approach. IEEE Pervasive Comput. **14**, 22–31 (2015)
16. Nordheim, C.B., Følstad, A., Bjørkli, C.A.: An initial model of trust in chatbots for customer service—findings from a questionnaire study. Interact. Comput. **31**, 317–335 (2019)
17. Zierau, N., Elshan, E., Visini, C., Janson, A.: A review of the empirical literature on conversational agents and future research directions (2020)
18. Janssen, A., Passlcik, D., Rodrıguez Cardona, D.: Virtual assistance in any context – a taxonomy of design elements for. business and information systems engineering 62 (2020)
19. Chakrabarti, C., Luger, G.F.: Artificial conversations for customer service chatter bots: architecture, algorithms, and evaluation metrics. Expert Syst. Appl. **42**, 6878–6897 (2015)
20. Hevner, A., Prat, N., Comyn-Wattiau, I., Akoka, J.: A pragmatic approach for identifying and managing design science research goals and evaluation criteria (2018)
21. Baskerville, R., et al.: Design science research contributions: finding a balance between artifact and theory. J. Assoc. Inf. Syst. **19**, 3 (2018)
22. Gregor, S., Kruse, L., Seidel, S.: Research perspectives: the anatomy of a design principle. J. Assoc. Inf. Syst. **21**, 1622–1652 (2020). https://doi.org/10.17705/1jais.00649
23. Purao, S., Kruse, L.C., Maedche, A.: The origins of design principles: where do... they all come from? In: Hofmann, S., Müller, O., Rossi, M. (eds.) Designing for Digital Transformation. Co-Creating Services with Citizens and Industry: 15th International Conference on Design Science Research in Information Systems and Technology, DESRIST 2020, Kristiansand, Norway, December 2–4, 2020, Proceedings, pp. 183–194. Springer International Publishing, Cham (2020). https://doi.org/10.1007/978-3-030-64823-7_17
24. Engel, C., Leicht, N., Ebel, P.: The imprint of design science in information systems research: an empirical analysis of the AIS senior scholars' basket (2019)

25. Sturm, B., Sunyaev, A.: A Good Beginning makes a good ending: incipient sources of knowledge in design science research (2019)
26. Jones, D., Gregor, S.: The anatomy of a design theory. J. Assoc. Inf. Syst. **8**(5), 312–335 (2007). https://doi.org/10.17705/1jais.00129
27. Sein, M.K., et al.: Action design research. MIS Quarterly, 37–56 (2011)
28. Knote, R., et al.: From requirement to design patterns for ubiquitous computing applications. In: Proceedings of the 21st European Conference on Pattern Languages of Programs, pp. 1–11 (2016)
29. Kruse, L.C., Seidel, S., Purao, S.: Making use of design principles. In: International Conference on Design Science Research in Information System and Technology, pp. 37–51. Springer (2016)
30. Chandra Kruse, L., Purao, S., Seidel. S.: How designers use design principles: design behaviors and application modes. J. Assoc. Inf. Syst. (Forthcoming.)
31. Wieringa, R.: Design science as nested problem solving, pp. 1–12 (2009)
32. Baskerville, R., Pries-Heje, J.: Explanatory design theory. Bus. Inf. Syst. Eng. **2**, 271–282 (2010). https://doi.org/10.1007/s12599-010-0118-4
33. Fischer, C., Winter, R., Wortmann, F.: Design theory. Bus. Inf. Syst. Eng. **2**, 387–390 (2010)
34. Lukyanenko, R., Parsons, J.: Research perspectives: design theory indeterminacy: what is it, how can it be reduced, and why did the polar bear drown? J. Assoc. Inf. Syst. **21**(5), 1343–1369 (2020). https://doi.org/10.17705/1jais.00639
35. Webster, J., Watson, R.T.: Analyzing the past to prepare for the future: writing a literature review. MIS Quarterly, xiii–xxiii (2002)
36. Vom Brocke, J., et al.: Standing on the shoulders of giants: challenges and recommendations of literature search in information systems research. CAIS **37**, 9 (2015)
37. Levy, Y., Ellis, T.J.: A systems approach to conduct an effective literature review in support of information systems research. Informing Science: The International Journal of an Emerging Transdiscipline **9**, 181–212 (2006). https://doi.org/10.28945/479
38. Rosemann, M., Vessey, I.: Toward improving the relevance of information systems research to practice: the role of applicability checks. Mis Quarterly, 1–22 (2008)
39. Lechler, R., Stöckli, E., Rietsche, R., Uebernickel, F.: Looking beneath the tip of the iceberg: the two-sided nature of chatbots and their roles for digital feedback exchange (2019)
40. Wambsganss, T., et al.: Designing a conversational agent as a formative course evaluation tool. In: WI2020 Zentrale Tracks, pp. 1234–1249. GITO Verlag (2020). https://doi.org/10.30844/wi_2020_k7-wambsganss
41. Winkler, R., Roos, J.: Bringing AI into the classroom: designing smart personal assistants as learning tutors (2019)
42. Gnewuch, U., Morana, S., Heckmann, C., Maedche, A.: Designing conversational agents for energy feedback. In: Chatterjee, S., Dutta, K., Sundarraj, R.P. (eds.) Designing for a Digital and Globalized World, pp. 18–33. Springer International Publishing, Cham (2018). https://doi.org/10.1007/978-3-319-91800-6_2
43. Chen, Z., Lu, Y., Nieminen, M.P., Lucero, A.: Creating a Chatbot for and with migrants: chatbot personality drives co-design activities. In: Proceedings of the 2020 ACM Designing Interactive Systems Conference, pp. 219–230 (2020)
44. Ahmad, R., Siemon, D., Fernau, D., Robra-Bissantz, S.: Introducing "Raffi": a personality adaptive conversational agent. In: PACIS, pp. 28 (2020)
45. Elshan, E., Ebel, P.: Let's team up: designing conversational agents as teammates (2020)
46. Strohmann, T., et al.: Virtual moderation assistance: creating design guidelines for virtual assistants supporting creative workshops. In: PACIS, pp. 80 (2018)
47. Meier, P., et al.: FeelFit-design and evaluation of a conversational agent to enhance health awareness. In: ICIS (2019)

48. Gnewuch, U., Morana, S., Maedche, A.: Towards designing cooperative and social conversational agents for customer service (2017)
49. Hevner, A.R.: A three cycle view of design science research. Scand. J. Inf. Syst. **19**, 4 (2007)
50. Tavanapour, N., Poser, M., Bittner, E.A.C.: Supporting the idea generation process in citizen participation – toward an interactive system with a conversational agent as facilitator. **18** (2019)

Let's Team Up with AI! Toward a Hybrid Intelligence System for Online Customer Service

Mathis Poser$^{(\boxtimes)}$ (iD), Christina Wiethof (iD), Debayan Banerjee (iD),
Varun Shankar Subramanian (iD), Richard Paucar (iD), and Eva A. C. Bittner (iD)

Universität Hamburg, Hamburg, Germany
{mathis.poser,christina.wiethof,debayan.banerjee,
eva.bittner}@uni-hamburg.de, varunshankar55@gmail.com,
rfpaucar@gmail.com

Abstract. Customers desire convenient, fast, and personalized service encounters. Hence, service companies deploy self-service technology for online customer service. However, as solutions based on Artificial Intelligence cannot reliably answer the full range of requests and the demands on service employees (SEs) in live chat interaction are high, Hybrid Intelligence Systems (HIS) provide great potential to overcome current pitfalls by combining the complementary strengths of artificial and human intelligence. To ensure optimal performance of this socio-technical ensemble, human-centered design approaches are needed to realize real-time augmentation of decision-making in chat-based service encounters. Following a Design Science Research approach, we generate theory-based design principles (DPs) and implement them in a web-based HIS prototype. We contribute to Hybrid Intelligence research with results showing that the DPs enable task mastery and decision efficiency and provide avenues for future research.

Keywords: Hybrid Intelligence System · Real-time decision · Customer service

1 Introduction

Striving for operational efficiency, companies across various industries deploy automation technology enabled by Artificial Intelligence (AI) to process the ever-increasing number of requests in customer service [1, 2]. This development is expected to culminate by 2025 with 95% of all customer encounters being processed by AI [3]. Thereby, companies can increase their availability to customers, especially via online customer service (OCS) channels [4]. However, so far, full automation of online service interactions is not feasible, as narrow AI is not capable of handling all types of customer requests. Hence, strategies are needed to process the full range of customer requests while avoiding overload of service employees (SEs). In this context, research and practice postulate augmentation approaches relying on close collaboration between humans and AI to execute tasks [1, 5]. For real-time service encounters in OCS, the combination of AI's capabilities to rapidly process textual input and provide suitable decision suggestions [6] with SEs' ability to understand semantically complex content and handle unforeseen situations, can lead to effective customer request handling with increased

© Springer Nature Switzerland AG 2022
A. Drechsler et al. (Eds.): DESRIST 2022, LNCS 13229, pp. 142–153, 2022.
https://doi.org/10.1007/978-3-031-06516-3_11

decision-making efficiency. This augmentation approach can serve to meet customers' growing demand for personalized service encounters via text-based channels [7, 8]. In addition, real-time decision augmentation, e.g., displaying suitable information, can help SEs to rapidly process requests with increasing variability in content [9, 10].

In organizational contexts, the focal concept for augmentation strategies is Hybrid Intelligence (HI), which proposes the integration of the complementary strengths of humans and AI in a Hybrid Intelligence System (HIS) for joint task execution involving hybrid decision-making and hybrid learning [11]. To leverage associated potentials of a HIS, human–computer interaction (HCI) needs to be designed concerning suitable input and output formats while meeting human needs for task mastery [12, 13]. However, so far, socio-technical approaches to design the collaboration between AI and humans for hybrid decision-making are under-researched [14, 15]. Thus, human-centered design approaches for AI are needed for the decision-making augmentation of text-based, real-time service encounters in HIS enabling optimized task performance and hybrid learning [12]. To address these knowledge gaps, we adopt the Self-Determination Theory (SDT) to select suitable psychological constructs, ensuring the fulfillment of SEs' needs. Accordingly, we pursue the following research question: *How should a HIS be designed in a human-centered way to augment real-time decision-making for online customer service encounters?* The goal is to enable augmentation in a HIS to sustain SEs' task mastery, efficient decision-making in service encounters and simultaneously meet the requirements for hybrid learning. With this study, we present the second cycle of a larger design science research (DSR) project with the following structure. First, we present the conceptual background. Second, we outline the research approach by describing the cycles and steps of the DSR project. Third, the derived meta-requirements (MRs) and design principles (DPs) are presented and the instantiation illustrated. Last, we present evaluation results followed by a discussion and conclusion.

2 Conceptual Background

OCS constitutes a pervasive form to deliver intangible services mediated via technology [2]. To meet customer needs, service is directed toward people or objects [16]. This service is knowledge-intensive, as SEs need to handle an increasing plethora of diverse content from explicit (e.g., data) to meta-knowledge (e.g., advice) to make multiple decisions during request processing [9]. In OCS, AI can enable flexibility in the external (frontstage) and support in the internal (backend) environment to deliver service [17]. However, the automation of frontstage encounters reduces the success-generating characteristics of social presence and personalization [8, 18]. To overcome this tendency, AI-enabled agents are designed in a human-like fashion to handle repetitive, simple requests via natural language interaction [19]. Nevertheless, these AI solutions have yet to create satisfactory customer experiences for complex, emotional requests. To achieve improved organizational and individual outcomes, the competencies of AI and SEs are increasingly integrated [6, 20]. In this context, the concept of HI is adopted to combine the complementary strengths of AI and humans [11] involving augmentation and hybrid learning leading to better results than each of the entities could reach alone [21]. For service encounters, [2] propose the augmentation of SEs invisibly to the customer during real-time interaction, to leverage advantageous conditions for service co-creation with high synchrony of communication as well as personal support [8, 22]. For this augmentation scenario, high demands in the form of instant knowledge retrieval for dynamic decision situations and emotion work should be met [9, 23]. Therefore, AI and SE can take over different roles: AI can provide analytical insights into the customers' requests (e.g., solution proposal) and the SE contributes intuition by contextualizing this information and leading an empathic interaction with a customer [4].

To ensure the success of HIS, conditions for a high degree of SEs' task mastery should be established during customer interaction. Thus, according to the Self-Determination Theory (SDT), augmentation should fulfill human desires for **autonomy**, **competence**, and **relatedness** [24]. SEs should experience the feeling of control over their behavior and make decisions independent of external conditions, as **autonomy** promotes the intensity of post-adoption usage behavior, engagement, and satisfaction with information systems (IS) [25, 26]. In addition, SEs should be able to actively interact with the environment to achieve desired results. By experiencing this **competence** using IS, SEs' self-efficacy could be elevated and decision efficiency increased [27]. Moreover, building a relationship (**relatedness**) with IS due to their social characteristics could influence SEs' perceived usefulness of and intention to reuse the technology [28, 29]. As the consideration of human psychological demands for the design of HIS is scarce, we utilize SDT to select suitable theories that help to meet the three basic needs of SEs in OCS. To promote SEs' autonomy and competence in dynamic customer interactions with a variety of interdependent decisions [9], we adopt the Dynamic Decision Theory (DDT) to support decision-making strategies [30]. Regarding Cognitive Load Theory (CLT) [31, 32], we integrate insights on the nature of information presentation, as decision suggestions should be designed considering their load on SEs' working memory due to intrinsic, extraneous, and germane factors. Following Advice Response Theory (ART) [33], the characteristics of advice have an impact on perceived quality. Therefore, to influence competence, the aspects of efficacy, and feasibility, and absence of limitations are considered for decision suggestions. To establish relatedness in a HIS, we consider Social Response Theory (SRT) [34], which states that the use of social cues in IS has relationship-enhancing effects.

3   Research Approach

To establish a human-centered design of HIS for organizational augmentation endeavors, we conduct a multicyclic DSR project. By adopting the interior mode of DSR, we (1) define and evaluate prescriptive design knowledge to "construct a HCI artifact for a given problem space" [35, p. 4] and (2) present a designed HIS artifact [36]. To ensure research rigor, we structure our project by applying the process model of [37] (see Fig. 1). In two design cycles, we incrementally identify MRs as goal and boundary descriptions of an artifact and derive DPs providing prescriptive statements [38–40]. To ensure validity in addressing the identified problem, we iteratively instantiate and evaluate the design of our HIS artifact in an organization that specializes in selling traineeships and projects abroad to customers. To address this real-world use case, the HIS is supposed to augment the processing of customer questions and identification of their interests (where, when, what) and the recommendation of suitable projects. To do so, in the first cycle [41], we derived theory- and practice-based MRs to define initial DPs for reciprocal augmentation through hybrid collaborative learning. This mutual learning scenario improves the performance of AI by SE experts as well as expands novice SEs' knowledge by AI. As a proof-of-concept, the tentative DPs were implemented in a web-based prototype with a user interface (UI). By conducting a wizard-of-oz study, the instantiated design and expected learning effects for novice SEs could be demonstrated. In the second cycle, covered in this paper, the design is extended and integrated with aspects for real-time decision-making augmentation to fully address the problem of this DSR project. In **(1) Awareness of Problem** (see Sects. 1 and 2), we reassessed and elaborated on the problem relevance and need for a solution that integrates hybrid learning and real-time decision augmentation. For **(2) Suggestion**, MRs for real-time augmentation for decision-making are derived based on kernel theories (see Sect. 4.1) [36]. In **(3) Development**, DPs and matching design features (DFs) are determined to construct a full-featured AI-based HIS prototype (see Sect. 4.2) as an expository instantiation. For **(4) Evaluation** (see Sect. 5), following the risk and efficacy strategy [42], the prototype is implemented to conduct an online field study with 18 SEs (ten male, eight female) from the described organization. The study follows a standardized procedure: (1) the setting and prototype are presented; (2) participants use the artifact to counsel a customer while sharing their screen; (3) a semi-structured interview is conducted. As the customers are simulated by the research team, the evaluation is semi-naturalistic. By using three prepared customer profiles with scripts comprising question-and-answer variations, originality of interactions is ensured. To evaluate the designed artifact in terms of its applicability, feasibility, and effect on users, a multi-method approach is applied. The qualitative interview is structured with questions about demographic data, decision-making, trust in and satisfaction with the prototype, and changed task characteristics. In addition, quantitative measures of usage behavior were obtained from screen recordings (e.g., frequency of used functionalities). To analyze the rich data, a qualitative content analysis of the interview transcripts according to [43] is conducted, and descriptive statistical methods are applied for the assessment of the quantitative usage data.

DSR Research Cycle	Cycle one: Hybrid collaborative learning	Cycle two: Real-time AI-based decision-making augmentation
(1) Awareness of Problem	Integrate human and artificial intelligence in online customer service	Refinement and extension of problem relevance
(2) Suggestion	Derivation of MRs for hybrid collaborative learning	Derivation of MRs based on kernel theories for real-time decision-making augmentation
(3) Development	Definition of DPs and instantiation in web-based prototype	Extension of DPs and instantiation in full-featured web-based artifact
(4) Evaluation	Artificial evaluation (wizard-of-oz) of design with mixed-method approach	Semi naturalistic evaluation of design with mixed-method approach
(5) Conclusion	Codification of design knowledge as contribution to body of knowledge [currently under review]	Report, embed and contribute design knowledge about artifact's construction and effects

Fig. 1. DSR approach based on [37] with research activities.

4 Design and Development

4.1 Theory-Derived Meta Requirements

Autonomy and Competence. Following DDT [30], SEs apply strategies to make inter-dependent and real-time decisions in response to dynamic customer interactions [44]. Under time pressure, individuals make decisions by comparing information of options based on assigned values to identify an alternative with the greatest utility [45, 46]. There-fore, multiple suggestions should be proposed (*MR1*), presented in sequence allowing SEs to view alternating combinations (*MR2*) with relevant utility information (*MR3*). To promote comparability, suggestions should be displayed in descending order with respect to utility (*MR4*). The AI settings should be adjustable (*MR5*) to sustain auton-omy. Besides facilitating decision-making strategies, the nature of information presen-tation has to be considered, as it affects SEs' processing ability [47, 48]. According to CLT, dynamic decision-making induces a high intrinsic cognitive load in SEs due to the necessity of monitoring the changing customer demands to make punctual decisions [49]. As this task occupies a significant portion of SEs' capacity, a low load of presented information (extraneous cognitive load) is required [32, 45]. By presenting information in a concentrated format, SEs' information comprehension can be improved [50, 51]. Hence, a limited number of suggestions should be displayed (*MR6*) according to the pace of the changing environment (*MR7*) and their effortless utilization facilitated (*MR8*) to avoid cognitive overload. In addition, characteristics of presented information impact decision-making [48]. Following ART, SEs' high rating of advice quality facilitates their decision-making, whereas discrepancies in expected and provided advice quality impede decision support [52]. To establish efficacy, the applicability and effectiveness of advice to solve a problem have to be present [48]. The quality of advice can also be enhanced by its distinctive workability (feasibility) and presentation of limited risks after its enact-ment (absence of limitation) [52]. Followingly, insights on the effectiveness should be provided by revealing the context-specificity of suggestions (*MR9*). The applicability and workability should be established by presenting explanatory information for sugges-tions (*MR10*). Reliability of suggestions should be provided to demonstrate the absence of limitations (*MR11*).

Relatedness. Advice-related decisions are also influenced by relational aspects such as respecting the autonomy of the decision-maker [53]. SRT postulates that social attributes promote a sense of social presence in users and have a positive effect on the intention to reuse, enjoyment of using, and self-efficacy in use [28, 29, 54]. Consequently, the appearance of and interaction with the AI should elicit a sense of social presence by mimicking human sociability (*MR12*) to promote the establishment of a relationship.

4.2 Design Principles, Design Features, and Instantiation

We present eleven DPs of the type form and function from two design cycles (see Fig. 2) [55]. In the **first cycle**, seven DPs were identified for hybrid collaborative learning, which combines the augmentation of both human intelligence through AI and AI through human

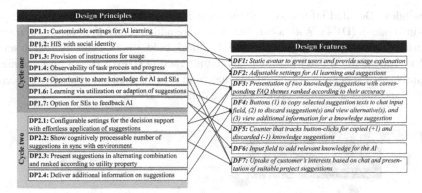

Fig. 2. DPs of cycles one and two with DFs

intelligence [11, 56]. To enable this, the HIS should include customizable settings so that SEs can individually determine whether the AI learns from them (**DP1.1**). Furthermore, the AI should be equipped with a social identity so that SEs perceive it as a collaboration partner (**DP1.2**). As instructional support, the HIS UI should include explanations of how the AI works to increase SEs' understanding of how to use it (**DP1.3**). For hybrid learning, the process and progress of the task should be observable (**DP1.4**) and an opportunity for AI and SE to share knowledge for decisions should be provided (**DP1.5**). To allow AI learning, an option for SEs to use or adapt AI suggestions (**DP1.6**) and the possibility to feedback the AI should be provided (**DP1.7**). In the **second cycle**, four additional DPs were generated to allow real-time decision-making augmentation. Thus, the HIS should provide configurable AI settings and the possibility to easily use suggestions to increase SEs' task mastery (**DP2.1**: *MR5,8*). A manageable number of context-specific suggestions in sync with the dynamic interaction should be displayed to augment SEs' decision-making (**DP2.2**: *MR1,6,7*). To support SEs' strategies for decision making, suggestions should be shown in sequence according to their utility and allow the display of alternating combinations upon request (**DP2.3**: *MR2,3,4,11*). Additional information about suggestions should be viewable so that SEs can verify their applicability (**DP2.4**: *MR9,10,11,12*).

Based on DFs, we instantiated these DPs in a web-based HIS prototype comprising frontend and backend (see Fig. 3). The web based frontend was designed with Bootstrap and ReactJS to, inter alia, greet users with an avatar that presents a brief usage explanation (**DF1**). In addition, setting options for AI support and learning behavior are provided (**DF2**). The integrated chat window is based on the open-source framework Rocket. Chat. The backend generates a ranked list of FAQ suggestions based on chat interactions using Dense Passage Retrieval (DPR) technology [57]. The DPR model was pre-trained on the Google Natural Questions dataset by Facebook and further fine-tuned with conversational data from test runs. In the frontend, two FAQ items - including theme and accuracy in percent - with the highest agreement are displayed (**DF3**). The discard-buttons can be used to sequentially display four additional FAQ suggestions with decreasing accuracy. The copy-to-chat buttons insert FAQ text into the input field of the chat window. Detailed information about a respective FAQ can be viewed via the get-more-info button (**DF4**). With a counter, points are added (copy-to-chat) or subtracted (discard), if buttons are clicked (**DF5**). A feedback field allows entering search terms to select and submit a FAQ that matches the interaction (**DF6**). Based on customers' chat messages, exact keyword-based text matching is performed to automatically record interests and suggest suitable projects from a database (**DF7**).

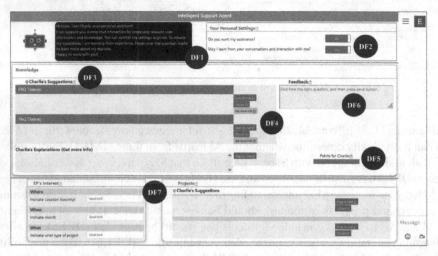

Fig. 3. Screenshot of web-based HIS prototype with DFs

5   Evaluation

To evaluate the augmentation with the HIS prototype and its influence on the work task, we conducted interviews with 18 SEs after usage. Additionally, we inspected their usage behavior via screen recordings to supplement the qualitative results. Overall, SEs indicated that they would continue to use the prototype and highlighted that it is particularly helpful for SEs who do not have much experience in counseling customers.

DF1. The feeling of relatedness did not emerge consistently, as some SEs perceived the prototype as a tool and others as a co-customer manager ("*he definitely was co-customer manager because he gave me all the prompts to answer questions*" (SE13)).
DF2. The analysis of screen recordings revealed that all SEs approved of support by the prototype and 12 consented that their data can be used for AI learning via the settings.
DF3. During customer interactions, SEs sent on average 16 (*SD*: 5; *Median*: 14) messages during the customer interaction. 17 SEs used the FAQ answer suggestions via the copy-to-chat-button at least three times. On average, SEs edited two (*SD*: 2; *Median*: 2) of the suggested responses in the input field before sending them. The analysis of interview transcripts revealed that SEs were satisfied with the support provided by the prototype, as the provided suggestions appeared promptly, and the interaction was intuitive due to the functionalities and layout of the interface. Regarding customer interaction, SEs

felt supported in their decision-making by provided suggestions, as the information allowed them to reassure themselves: *"it is a good thing to know what is going on and what could I answer, what are possibilities and what should I focus on. Also finding out the main point of the question of this customer"* (SE5). The decision- making was further supported by the trustworthiness of suggestions (e.g., SE17: *"in 80% of the times it was the right answer, so for me that is trustworthy"*). Their correctness was reported to be verifiable *"[...] when I pressed the get more information button, I could see what exactly was meant"* (SE4). Moreover, *"suggestions gave more time to think and then go into detail"* (SE3). However, some SEs experienced delays or hesitation when suggestions did not match the interaction: *"[...] that made the speed of me answering the question a little bit slower because I had to look for the answers myself"* (SE13). Also, proposals should be adjusted in wording and capitalized to simplify their use. Regarding customer interactions, SEs reported that they were able to autonomously manage them with provided suggestions (e.g., *"If I wanted to bring the conversation in another direction, I would have done it - so it was not forced"* (SE11)) and make independent decisions without feeling constrained (the prototype *"[...] is presented in a way that it was clear that I can work with him, but I don't have to"* (SE15)). In addition, the prototype assisted them to achieve their goals in counseling the customer: e.g., *"I was able to control the interaction. And I think the counseling was actually better because of Charlie's help because he explained things way more detailed than I would have done"* (SE15). However, SEs reported that the personal touch is reduced due to the provided wording in suggestions. **DF4.** Overall, an average of six (*SD*: 2.5; *Median*: 7) suggestions were used, whereby the detailed version via get-more-info button (*Mean*: 3.7; *SD*: 2.6; *Median*: 4.5) was used more frequently than the short version (*Mean*: 2.6; *SD*: 2.4; *Median*: 2). To receive alternative FAQ answer suggestions, the discard-button was clicked on average 15 times (*SD*: 10.8; *Median*: 15). The display of two suggestions and the option for additional explanatory information via the get-more-info-button were perceived as helpful *"so that you can think in which direction you might go"* (SE1). SEs experienced relief through displayed suggestions and the majority saved time making decisions, especially by using the copy-to-chat-button: *"[...] I just had to copy them, which affected the speed"* (SE14). **DF5 & DF6.** 16 SEs utilized the feedback function on average four times, while nine people successfully provided feedback. However, SEs expressed the need for an adaptation of the feedback function, as it was unclear. **DF7.** Concerning the recommendation of projects, the pressure to recall knowledge or search in parallel to the customer interaction was reduced as relevant information was presented. Thereby, it *"[...] took out the uncomfortable part of working with such a consultation, which is looking up stuff"* (SE16).

6   Discussion and Conclusion

Our multi-cycle DSR project contributes to HI research [11, 21] by taking a human-centered perspective to design HIS [12, 13] for text-based, real-time service encounters [2] in OCS for mutual augmentation [15]. Particularly, we examine hybrid decision-making and hybrid learning. While we cover the enablement of hybrid learning in the first cycle, we extend this initial design in the second cycle to sustain hybrid real-time decision-making. To address our research question, we derived four additional DPs by considering relevant theories to define requirements that satisfy SEs' need for autonomy, competence, and relatedness. Based on the evaluation, the instantiated DPs successfully supported SEs' autonomy and task mastery in conducting customer interactions allowing efficient and independent decision-making. The SEs' feeling of control is supported by the analysis of screen recordings which showed that all SEs used the configurable settings to approve augmentation by the prototype (DP2.1). However, the evaluation revealed a high reliance of the SEs on the suggestions (DP2.2) partly leading to uncertainty and delays. Although SEs could conduct the service encounter without AI augmentation, they rather clicked the discard-button several times instead of formulating a new answer. In contrast, one SE only read and verified the suggestions and formulated new answers based on the provided content indicating a high level of SEs' autonomy. The need for competence could be addressed by supporting SEs' achievement of counseling goals via suggestions. In this regard, DP2.2 and DP2.3 successfully supported the dynamic decision situation by showing relevant information. Furthermore, the analysis of SEs' usage behavior demonstrates an intuitive application of suggestions by using the copy-to chat button in effortless ways (DP2.1). With this, DP2.1 is the main contributor to experienced relief, time savings, and efficiency. Moreover, SEs particularly recognized the usefulness of the get-more-info button (DP2.4), which is supported by the screen recording results that showed SEs' preference for the detailed version of suggestions. Regarding the need for relatedness, the evaluation did not show consistent results, as some SEs perceived the prototype as a tool and others as a co-customer manager.

All in all, we provide relevant and promising results demonstrating a potential solution to integrate hybrid learning and real-time decision augmentation within a HIS. We thereby make a two-fold contribution. First, following [38], we present a nascent design theory with utility character by delivering a possible solution for the identified problem and demonstrating improvements in the application field [36]. This contribution has epistemological implications, as we present DPs about user activity and an artifact that links prescriptive knowledge about design and action with explanatory knowledge about effects [40, 55, 58]. Second, we present a designed entity by demonstrating a full-featured AI-based artifact, which represents one possible instantiation of our design [36, 40]. Besides the promising results, there are, however, a few limitations to consider. First, we conducted one semi-naturalistic evaluation episode with simulated customers without a pre-evaluation of the instantiated DPs. Second, we limited the implementation and application of our DPs to only one organization. Thus, future research should implement and evaluate our DPs in various naturalistic environments. In doing so, factors should be examined causing different usage behavior and decision-making effects. For instance, while copy-to-chat might increase efficiency, it might also decrease human attention and learning. Especially when trying to educate novice employees with such a tool, proper usage of the suggestions needs to be ensured. In addition, SEs' decisions should be investigated in terms of quality due to influences of heuristics or biased AI. At last, as the feedback function was not clear to several SEs, we call for future research on how to ensure valuable and continuous feedback toward the AI.

Acknowledgements. The research was financed with funding provided by the German Federal Ministry of Education and Research and the European Social Fund under the "Future of work" program (INSTANT, 02L18A111).

References

1. Gupta, A.: 4 Key Tech Trends in Customer Service to Watch. https://www.gartner.com/smarterwithgartner/4-key-tech-trends-in-customer-service-to-watch (2021)
2. de Keyser, A., Köcher, S., Alkire, L., Verbeeck, C., Kandampully, J.: Frontline service technology infusion: conceptual archetypes and future research directions. JOSM **30**, 156–183 (2019)
3. Servion: What Makes Emerging Technologies the Future of Customer Experience?. https://servion.com/blog/what-emerging-technologies-future-customer-experience/. (2018)
4. Huang, M.-H., Rust, R.T.: Artificial Intelligence in Service. J. Ser. Res. **21**, 155–172 (2018)
5. Wilson, H.J., Daugherty, P.R.: Collaborative intelligence: humans and AI are joining forces. Havard Bus. Rev. **96**, 115–123 (2018)
6. Graef, R., Klier, M., Kluge, K., Zolitschka, J.F.: Human-machine collaboration in online customer service – a long-term feedback-based approach. Electron Markets **31**, 319–341 (2021)
7. Mero, J.: The effects of two-way communication and chat service usage on consumer attitudes in the e-commerce retailing sector. Electron Markets **28**, 205–217 (2018)
8. Verhagen, T., van Nes, J., Feldberg, F., van Dolen, W.: Virtual customer service agents: using social presence and personalization to shape online service encounters. J Comput-Mediat Comm **19**, 529–545 (2014)
9. Cheung, C.F., Lee, W.B., Wang, W.M., Chu, K.F., To, S.: A multi-perspective knowledge-based system for customer service management. Expert Sys. Appl. **24**, 457–470 (2003)
10. Ulfert, A.-S., Antoni, C.H., Ellwart, T.: The role of agent autonomy in using decision support systems at work. Comp. Hum. Behav. **126**, 106987 (2022)
11. Dellermann, D., Ebel, P., Söllner, M., Leimeister, J.M.: Hybrid intelligence. Bus. Inf. Syst. Eng. **61**, 637–643 (2019)
12. Xu, W.: Toward Human-centered AI: A Perspective from Human-computer Interaction. Interactions **26**, 42–46 (2019)
13. Ebel, P., Söllner, M., Leimeister, J.M., Crowston, K., de Vreede, G.-J.: Hybrid intelligence in business networks. Electron Markets **31**, 313–318 (2021)
14. Shneiderman, B.: Human-centered artificial intelligence: three fresh ideas. THCI **12**, 109–124 (2020)
15. Benbya, H., Pachidi, S., Jarvenpaa, S.L.: Artificial intelligence in organizations: implications for information systems research. J. Ass. Inf. Sys. **22**, 1–25 (2021)
16. Froehle, C.M.: Service personnel, technology, and their interaction in influencing customer satisfaction. Decision Sci. **37**, 5–38 (2006)
17. Bock, D.E., Wolter, J.S., Ferrell, O.C.: Artificial intelligence: disrupting what we know about services. JSM **34**, 317–334 (2020)
18. Ameen, N., Tarhini, A., Reppel, A., Anand, A.: Customer experiences in the age of artificial intelligence. Comp. Hum. Behav. **114**, 106548 (2021)
19. Zierau, N., Elshan, E., Visini, C., Janson, A.: A review of the empirical literature on conversational agents and future research directions. In: 41st International Conference on Information Systems (ICIS). virtual conference (2020)
20. Raisch, S., Krakowski, S.: Artificial intelligence and management: the automation-augmentation paradox. AMR (2020)

21. Dellermann, D., Calma, A., Lipusch, N., Weber, T., Weigel, S., Ebel, P.: The future of human-AI collaboration: a taxonomy of design knowledge for hybrid intelligence systems. In: 52nd Hawaii International Conference on System Sciences (2019)
22. Kahai, S.S., Cooper, R.B.: Exploring the core concepts of media richness theory: the impact of cue multiplicity and feedback immediacy on decision quality. J. Manage. Inf. Sys. **20**, 263–299 (2003)
23. Ishii, K., Markman, K.M.: Online customer service and emotional labor: an exploratory study. Comp. Hum. Behav. **62**, 658–665 (2016)
24. Deci, E.L., Ryan, R.M.: Self-determination theory: a macrotheory of human motivation, development, and health. Canadian Psychol./Psychologie canadienne **49**, 182–185 (2008)
25. Ahuja, M., Thatcher, J.B.: Moving beyond intentions and toward the theory of trying: effects of work environment and gender on post-adoption information technology use. MIS Q. **29**, 427–459 (2005)
26. Ozkara, B.Y., Ozmen, M., Kim, J.W.: Exploring the relationship between information satisfaction and flow in the context of consumers' online search. Comp. Hum. Behav. **63**, 844–859 (2016)
27. Hung, S.-Y., Liang, T.-P.: Effect of computer self-efficacy on the use of executive support systems. Ind. Manage. Data Sys. **101**, 227–237 (2001)
28. Hassanein, K., Head, M.: The impact of infusing social presence in the web interface: an investigation across product types. Int. J. Elec. Comm. **10**, 31–55 (2005)
29. Pavlou, P.A., Liang, H., Xue, Y.: Understanding and mitigating uncertainty in online exchange relationships: a principal-agent perspective. MIS Q. **31**, 105–136 (2007)
30. Edwards, W.: Dynamic decision theory and probabilistic information processings. hfes **4**, 59–74 (1962)
31. Sweller, J.: Cognitive load during problem solving: effects on learning. Cognitive Science **12**, 257–285 (1988)
32. Brünken, R., Plass, J.L., Leutner, D.: Direct measurement of cognitive load in multimedia learning. Edu. Psychol. **38**, 53–61 (2003)
33. MacGeorge, E.L., Feng, B., Guntzviller, L.M.: Advice: expanding the communication paradigm. Ann. Int. Comm. Ass. **40**, 213–243 (2016)
34. Nass, C., Moon, Y.: Machines and Mindlessness: Social Responses to Computers **56**, 81–103 (2000)
35. Adam, M.T.P., Gregor, S., Hevner, A., Morana, S.: Design science research modes in human-computer interaction projects. THCI **13**, 1–11 (2021)
36. Baskerville, R., Baiyere, A., Gergor, S., Hevner, A., Rossi, M.: Design science research contributions: finding a balance between artifact and theory. JAIS **19**, 358–376 (2018)
37. Kuechler, W., Vaishnavi, V.: A framework for theory development in design science research: multiple perspectives. JAIS **13**, 395–423 (2012)
38. Gregor, S., Hevner, A.: Positioning and presenting design science research for maximum impact. MIS Q. **37**, 337–355 (2013)
39. Gregor, S., Jones, D.: The anatomy of a design theory. JAIS **8**, 312–335 (2007)
40. vom Brocke, J., Winter, R., Hevner, A., Maedche, A.: Accumulation and evolution of design knowledge in design science research: a journey through time and space. JAIS **21**, 520–544 (2020)
41. Wiethof, C., Bittner, E.: Toward a hybrid intelligence system in customer service: collaborative learning of human and AI. In: 30th European Conference on Information Systems (ECIS), under review. Timisoara, Romania (2022)
42. Venable, J., Pries-Heje, J., Baskerville, R.: FEDS: a framework for evaluation in design science research. Euro. J. Inf. Sys. **25**, 77–89 (2016)
43. Mayring, P.: Qualitative Content Analysis: Theoretical Foundation. Basic Procedures and Software Solution (2014)

44. Gonzalez, C.: Decision support for real-time, dynamic decision-making tasks. Org. Behav. Hum. Deci. Proc. **96**, 142–154 (2005)
45. Johnson, E.J., Payne, J.W.: Effort and accuracy in choice. Management Sci. **31**, 395–414 (1985)
46. Cook, G.J.: An empirical investigation of information search strategies with implications for decision support system design. Decision Sci. **24**, 683–698 (1993)
47. Paas, F., Renkl, A., Sweller, J.: Cognitive load theory: instructional implications of the interaction between information structures and cognitive architecture. Instructional Sci. **32**, 1–8 (2004)
48. Guntzviller, L.M., Liao, D., Pulido, M.D., Butkowski, C.P., Campbell, A.D.: Extending advice response theory to the advisor: similarities, differences, and partner-effects in advisor and recipient advice evaluations. Comm. Monogra. **87**, 114–135 (2020)
49. Lerch, F.J., Harter, D.E.: Cognitive support for real-time dynamic decision making. Inf. Sys. Res. **12**, 63–82 (2001)
50. Hong, W., Thong, J.Y.L., Tam, K.Y.: The effects of information format and shopping task on consumers' online shopping behavior: a cognitive fit perspective. J. Manage. Inf. Sys. **21**, 149–184 (2004)
51. Eick, S.G.: Graphically displaying text. J. Comp. Graph. Stat. **3**, 127–142 (1994)
52. MacGeorge, E.L., van Swol, L.M.: Advice across Disciplines and Contexts. In: MacGeorge, E.L., van Swol, L.M. (eds.) The Oxford Handbook of Advice, pp. 3–20. Oxford University Press, New York (2018)
53. Feng, B., MacGeorge, E.L.: The influences of message and source factors on advice outcomes. Comm. Res. **37**, 553–575 (2010)
54. Fortin, D.R., Dholakia, R.R.: Interactivity and vividness effects on social presence and involvement with a web-based advertisement. J. Bus. Res. **58**, 387–396 (2005)
55. Gregor, S., Kruse, L., Seidel, S.: Research perspectives: the anatomy of a design principle. JAIS **21**, 1622–1652 (2020)
56. Wiethof, C., Bittner, E.: Hybrid intelligence - combining the human in the loop with the computer in the loop: a systematic literature review. In: 42nd International Conference on Information Systems. Austin (2021)
57. Karpukhin, V., et al.: Dense Passage Retrieval for Open-Domain Question Answering (2020)
58. Gregor: The nature of theory in information systems. MISQ **30**, 611–642 (2006)

Gamified Expert Annotation Systems: Meta-Requirements and Tentative Design

Simon Warsinsky[1]([⊠]) [iD], Manuel Schmidt-Kraepelin[1] [iD], Scott Thiebes[1] [iD],
Martin Wagner[2] [iD], and Ali Sunyaev[1] [iD]

[1] Karlsruhe Institute of Technology, Kaiserstr. 89, 76133 Karlsruhe, Germany
{Simon.Warsinsky,Manuel.Schmidt-Kraepelin,Scott.Thiebes,
sunyaev}@kit.edu
[2] Department of General, Visceral and Transplantation Surgery, Heidelberg University Hospital,
Im Neuenheimer Feld 420, 69120 Heidelberg, Germany
Martin.Wagner@med.uni-heidelberg.de

Abstract. Poorly annotated data is a common problem for data-intensive applications like supervised machine learning. In domains like healthcare, annotation tasks require specific domain knowledge and are thus often done manually by experts, which is error-prone, time-intensive, and tedious. In this study, we investigate gamification as a means to foster annotation quality through annotators' increased motivation and engagement. To this end, we conducted a literature review of 70 studies as well as a series of 16 workshops with a team of six experts in medical image annotation. We derive a set of seven meta-requirements (MRs) that represent the desired instrumental and experiential outcomes of gamified expert annotation systems (e.g., high-quality annotations, a sense of challenge) as well as a tentative design that can address the derived MRs. Our results help to understand the inner workings of gamification in the context of expert annotation and lay important groundwork for designing gamified expert annotation systems that can successfully motivate annotators and increase annotation quality.

Keywords: Gamification · Annotation · Expert annotation · Annotation quality

1 Introduction

Data-intensive applications like machine learning (ML) increasingly require large quantities of annotated data (i.e., relevant metadata has to be added to raw data) [1]. Poorly annotated training data may decrease the predictive performance of ML models [1], endanger their instrumental purpose (e.g., adequate camera control in surgeries [2]), or lead to negative consequences for organizations such as wasted human efforts or revenue losses [3]. To ensure adequate annotation quality, annotation tasks in some domains require a specific set of skills or domain knowledge and are thus mainly done by experts. Medical image annotation, for example, is mainly done by medical professionals with pertinent knowledge about human anatomy [4]. Other examples include the annotation

---

M. Wagner and A. Sunyaev—These authors contributed equally.

© Springer Nature Switzerland AG 2022
A. Drechsler et al. (Eds.): DESRIST 2022, LNCS 13229, pp. 154–166, 2022.
https://doi.org/10.1007/978-3-031-06516-3_12

of legal documents [5] or fisheries acoustics echograms [6]. Manual annotation is error-prone [1], as well as time-intensive, monotonous, and exhausting [6, 7]. Thus, it is often difficult for annotators to stay motivated and engaged with the task, which is however an important determinant of annotation quality [8, 9]. One approach that has shown potential to motivate and engage information system (IS) users in various areas (e.g., health interventions [10]) is gamification, which is the process of transforming a system into one which affords more gameful experiences [11]. Here, we look at gamification as a means to motivate expert annotators and support annotation quality.

While gamification holds great motivational potential, the design of successful gamified expert annotation systems (GEAS) is difficult. In general, gamified IS have to produce both instrumental as well as experiential outcomes, a design goal that Liu et al. [12] characterize as *meaningful engagement*. While identifying desired instrumental outcomes is usually straightforward [12], the desired experiential outcomes are often less clear, as they require an understanding of the psychological mechanisms behind gamification and are highly-dependent on a system's users [13, 14]. Thus, identifying desired experiential outcomes is an important first step in the design of any gamified IS [12, 14]. However, for GEAS, these outcomes remain unclear. While some studies have given insights into important experiential outcomes of gamified annotation systems (e.g., autonomy [15] or system immersion [16]), that research almost exclusively focuses on non-expert annotators. We argue that those findings are not readily transferable to expert annotators, as experts fundamentally differ from non-experts in the way they process information in their domain of expertise [17]. For example, in an X-ray image, a layman would require considerable cognitive effort to grasp depicted anatomical structures, whereas an experienced radiologist can simply draw on their expertise to swiftly and precisely recognize anatomical structures and pathologies [4]. Yet, we are only aware of few studies that investigate GEAS, and those that do focus largely on instrumental outcomes (e.g., high-quality annotations [18]) or on annotators' motivation [19], thus neglecting crucial experiential outcomes like affective-cognitive factors [13, 14]. Given this apparent lack of knowledge on the desired experiential outcomes of GEAS and how to design for them, we ask: *What instrumental and experiential outcomes make up meaningful engagement in gamified expert annotation systems?*

To answer our research question, we follow a problem-centered design science research (DSR) approach, where we conduct a systematic literature review as well as a series of 16 workshops with six experts in medical image annotation. By doing so, we formalize the desired experiential and instrumental outcomes of GEAS as meta-requirements (MRs) for GEAS. To further our understanding of the MRs, we also derive a tentative GEAS design as an inspiration for how to address them. The contributions of our study are best exemplified by construing design knowledge as a means-end relationship between problem and solution space [20]. First, our MRs advance an understanding of the problem space in that they represent intended outcomes of GEAS [20] and thus mark out the purpose and scope of a GEAS [21]. Second, we contribute to a better theoretical understanding of gamification by providing insights into its inner workings in this particular individual and situational context (i.e., expert annotation) [14]. Lastly, our tentative design provides a step toward the solution space and can serve as an inspiration for the design of successful GEAS in practice.

2 Foundations: Gamification of Expert Annotation Tasks

Gamification describes the intentional process of transforming a system so that it affords more gameful experiences [11]. Despite an overall optimistic stance toward the benefits of gamification [13], research also recognizes that successful gamification design is difficult. Designers of gamified IS have to identify instrumental as well as experiential system outcomes and delicately balance them to achieve meaningful engagement [12]. Additionally, the effects of gamification are subject to contextual factors such as the application context or system users [13, 14]. Accordingly, to design successful GEAS, we need an understanding of the experiences that gamification has to evoke in this particular application context (i.e., expert annotation). In annotation systems, these experiences can represent an important source of motivation [8, 22], whereby increased motivation of annotators is linked to increased engagement with the annotation task [7] and ultimately increased annotation quality [9]. Extant research highlights gamification's potential to improve annotators' performance and motivation [9, 23] and thus contribute to important instrumental system outcomes (e.g., annotation quantity [18] or accuracy [22]), but struggles to explain the causal mechanisms behind these effects [9]. Some studies give hints toward important experiential outcomes of gamified annotation systems, like autonomy [15] or system immersion [16]. However, most of this research focuses on non-experts [8, 23] or does not discern between expert and non-expert annotators in light of the provided experience [24]. As we argued earlier, these findings do not easily translate to expert annotators due to their unique characteristics (e.g., difference in cognitive abilities [17]) and the context-sensitivity of gamification with regard to system users [13]. Those few studies that investigate GEAS either operate on a conceptual level [25, 26] or focus on annotation quality and motivation as outcomes [18, 19]. Hence, research has not been able to tease out the specific experiential outcomes that contribute to meaningful engagement in GEAS [12].

3 Research Design

Our study adapts the DSR paradigm. In DSR, design knowledge should describe a means-end relationship between the problem and the solution space [20]. Here, we focus mostly on intended outcomes (i.e., goals) of GEAS, which are considered the key conceptual entity in the problem space [20]. We also propose a tentative design to progress toward the solution space, but also to help us re-interpret our understanding of the problem space [20, 27]. As our research context, we chose the medical image annotation domain, for two reasons. First, the current rise of ML models in healthcare (e.g., to assist in surgeries [2]) has led to a surge in demand for high-quality annotated medical images as training data. Second, meaningfully interpreting medical images (e.g., CT scans) usually requires knowledge only possessed by medical professionals, which makes it a prime example for a domain where expert annotation is the norm [4].

Our overall approach is guided by the first half of the build-evaluation pattern proposed by Sonnenberg et al. [27] where a continuous evaluation approach is applied to ensure the usefulness of design decisions ex ante (i.e., before artifact instantiation). Accordingly, our approach includes two design activities (*Identify Problem, Design*) and two corresponding evaluation activities [27], as shown in Fig. 1. We first consulted extant literature to derive MRs that represent the desired outcomes of GEAS (Phase 1). We then conducted a series of 16 workshops (online, average duration 35 min) with six experts in medical image annotation to evaluate and refine the MRs (workshops 1–8, Phase 2), build a tentative design that can address the MRs (workshops 9–12, Phase 3) and evaluate and refine the design (workshops 13–16, Phase 4). Our participants were all medical students which were research assistants at a research group with a focus on artificial intelligence and cognitive robotics in surgery, where their main task was the semantic segmentation of objects in interoperative images from laparoscopic surgery videos (e.g., instruments, organs). As such, they represented the perspective of prospective users of GEAS for whom a GEAS experience should ultimately be designed for. Participants remained the same throughout all 16 workshops.

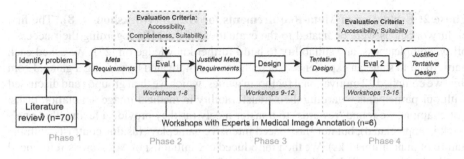

Fig. 1. Overall research approach

Phase 1: Deriving Meta-Requirements for GEAS (Literature Review). As there exists little research on GEAS, we started our literature review with a broad database search for studies on gamification in annotation tasks (Set 1), studies on annotators' motivation and engagement with medical image annotation tasks (Set 2), and studies on gamification to increase data quality (Set 3). For an overview of the data collection process, refer to Fig. 2. We removed duplicates and studies that were not peer-reviewed or not written in English. Then, we screened the abstracts of all remaining papers, and, depending on the literature set, excluded papers not about manual data annotation (Sets 1 and 2), papers not about gamification (Sets 1 and 3), papers not about data quality (Set 3), and, after converging the sets, papers not investigating the quality of data from a manual annotation process. We engaged with 70 papers, on which we conducted a manual concept-centric analysis informed by Webster & Watson [28]. We read the full text of each paper and coded for relevant concepts to compile a concept matrix of the analyzed literature [28], which aside from some meta-information about the featured annotation tasks (e.g., what data is annotated and how) mostly centered on featured instrumental and experiential system outcomes. We synthesized these outcomes, tried to identify more abstract topics, and iteratively discussed their suitability as MRs based on how they are targeted by gamification elements and how they contribute to meaningful engagement. This approach yielded us an initial set of five MRs for GEAS.

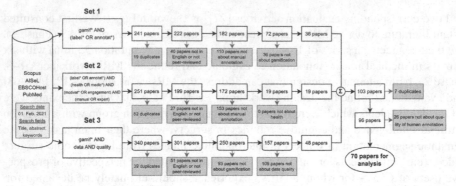

Fig. 2. Literature review: data collection process

Phase 2: Evaluation of Meta-Requirements for GEAS (Workshops 1–8). The first eight workshops were dedicated to the evaluation of the MRs regarding their accessibility, completeness, and suitability to build further knowledge on [27]. We asked each participant to share an experience where they were motivated by playing a game. From this, we compiled 42 motivational factors in games, which we then grouped and discussed with our participants regarding their transferability to medical image annotation tasks. For example, we found 'rewards' to transfer nicely (as they provide a feeling that one's work is appreciated), but not 'fast-paced intensive gameplay' (as this contrasts with the nature of annotation tasks). We then introduced our initial list of MRs, cross-referenced them with the compiled motivational factors from games and, after some refinement, arrived at a set of seven MRs for GEAS (cf. Sect. 4).

Phase 3: Building of Tentative Design (Workshops 9–12). To build the tentative design, we followed the pattern of *expand then contract* [29] in workshops 9–12. We asked each participant to share which gamification design features they would want to have in a GEAS and prioritize them regarding their perceived importance. From this, we compiled 63 design features (most of which were features that had previously emerged from the workshop discussion or were inspired from games), which we consequently grouped and discussed in the whole group regarding their relation to the MRs as well as priority compared to other features. Based on our insights up until this point, we created mockup designs that represented the design decisions we deemed suitable to satisfy the MRs (i.e., contribute to the outcomes represented by the MRs).

Phase 4: Evaluation of Tentative Design (Workshops 13–16). Lastly, in workshops 13–16, we evaluated the mockup designs regarding their accessibility and their suitability to address the MRs [27]. We presented them to our participants and elicited open-ended feedback through focus questions (e.g., 'what do you like/dislike about the mock-ups?') [29]. We discussed concerns or conflicting views on features and iteratively refined the design. For example, our participants remarked that the initial mock-ups were too text heavy. Hence, we opted for icon-based solutions where applicable. Our final design consisted of 24 gamification features in five categories (cf. Sect. 5).

4   Meta-Requirements for Gamified Expert Annotation Systems

MR1 – Annotation Quality: A GEAS must support high-quality annotations. The ultimate goal of annotation is to produce high-quality annotations that can add substantial value to the annotated raw data [1]. What constitutes good data quality is subjective and context-dependent [3]. Thus, data quality is usually considered to be multidimensional [30]. To this end, our reviewed literature and our annotators seemed to align their understanding of annotation quality mostly with the dimensions of *accuracy* (i.e., the conformity of a recorded value with the actual value [30]) and *consistency* (i.e., the degree of adherence to defined syntactic and semantic rules [30]). Our annotators as well as literature largely represented the attitude that gamifying an annotation system entails dangers to annotation quality [e.g., 31]. Accordingly, we highlight that when gamifying an expert annotation system, its utilitarian purpose should be uphold [8], and consolidate annotation quality as the key instrumental outcome of GEAS.

MR2 – Comprehensibility: A GEAS must be comprehensible. A GEAS should be comprehensible for two reasons. The first reason is to avoid a cognitive overload, which can result in adverse effects for both motivation [31] and annotation quality [32]. According to cognitive load theory, all novel information first has to be processed by a limited working memory, whose utilization is described as cognitive load [17]. Annotation tasks intrinsically have a high cognitive load [7], which gamification elements can further increase by being complex stimuli [32], by inducing a multi-task scenario [31] or by choice overload [15]. Second, comprehensibility is important for the acceptance of a GEAS. Medical experts generally exhibit low acceptance of new tools, when they are perceived as distracting or complicated and effort-increasing [33]. Our annotators described a scenario where they had to use a new annotation tool that ultimately substantially increased the annotation effort for them. They described this experience as irritating and infuriating, which in turn decreased their motivation to annotate and their acceptance of the new tool. To avoid such issues, literature recommends the design of easy-to-use interfaces that do not complicate the annotation process [34]. As gamification elements can distract from the main annotation task or affect the ease to use a system [26], we argue that these considerations translate to GEAS.

MR3 – Challenge: A GEAS must provide a sense of challenge. For experts, annotation tasks may be cognitively taxing, but usually not difficult per se [24]. According to flow theory, when a high level of challenge and high level of skill get harmoniously blended, individuals enter a state of flow [35] which is associated with more willingness to spend time and effort in annotation tasks [16]. However, expert annotators usually have a level of skill that far outreaches the difficulty of an annotation task. They are thus susceptible to drifting into a state of boredom, which can cause the motivational effects of gamification to quickly wear off [22]. One intuitive solution to boredom is to increase the task difficulty [25], for example by having users annotate more difficult data instances [22, 24]. To this end, our annotators cautioned us that increasing difficulty can be demotivating if it involves introducing 'weird tools'. Thus, it is important to recognize that challenge captures the idea of difficulty, particularly as it relates to a sense of accomplishment [35], and not to overcoming increased functional complexity.

MR4 – Self-efficacy: A GEAS must evoke self-efficacy beliefs. Our annotators exhibited a strong desire to know about their current progress during annotation, an attitude also reported in our reviewed literature [15, 36]. While showing annotators their progress can indeed have positive effects [8, 26], it can also be demotivating when large numbers of annotations seem unachievable [36]. The moderator in play here is self-efficacy (i.e., an individual's perception of how well they can execute courses of action required to deal with prospective situations [37]). In line with self-efficacy theory, it can be essential to always make annotators perceive their own performance as satisfactory, irrespective of their actual performance or skill level [9]. Concerning this matter, experts may be subject to the Dunning-Kruger effect, which describes a phenomenon where high-performing individuals, like expert annotators, underestimate their own proficiencies and thus have low self-efficacy beliefs [38]. To assess their self-efficacy, annotators generally rely on their confidence in the perceived quality of past annotation [38]. But, it is often hard for annotators to assess the quality of their own work, either because it is not made available to them [36] or because there is no ground truth to compare provided annotations to [34]. This may exacerbate the Dunning-Kruger effect, thus consolidating self-efficacy as a MR for GEAS.

MR5 – Social Experience: A GEAS must make its users experience meaningful social relationships. As annotation tasks are usually done in teams, social mechanisms like peer recognition [16, 26] or competition [24] play a key role for annotator motivation as well as annotation quality [16]. But not all social interaction is motivating for annotators. Competition for example may cause annotators to work harder [22], but may demotivate them if it is unwanted [8]. This resembles the tenet of self-determination theory (SDT) that a key part of motivation is the experience of social relationships that are meaningful (i.e., relatedness [39]). For experts, this may even more so be the case, as they are usually highly specialized in an area (e.g., radiology [33]) and thus can have difficulties to find peers that are on the same level as them. In line with this, our annotators were averse to the thought of 'winning against other annotators', as they feared it may drive animosity into the team and thus damage feelings of relatedness.

MR6 – Purpose: A GEAS must instill a sense of purpose. Ideally, annotation would be done by dedicated experts that have an inherent interest in the annotation task [18]. However, annotators usually do not benefit from the annotated data [26]. This may give rise to a situation akin to the principal-agent problem from economics, where the interests of annotation task giver and annotators interests and thus their preferred courses of action differ [40]. While the task provider (i.e., principal) is interested in meticulously annotated data, the annotators (i.e., agents) may be interested in other things like getting paid [22] or exerting as little effort as necessary [33]. We argue that in GEAS, this should be tackled by providing annotators with a sense of purpose. Literature suggests that giving actions a meaning can motivate annotators (particularly altruistic ones) [8], and a more meaningful framing may lead to higher annotation quality [9]. A discussion with our annotators exemplified this: they remarked that they would not want to annotate if they knew that their annotations would be destroyed immediately after creation, even if they would be paid. Yet, they could imagine annotating for no pay if the annotation contributed to 'something great' like saving people's lives.

MR7 – Autonomy: A GEAS must satisfy its users' need for autonomy.
Annotation systems often have to control annotators' behavior in specific ways to ensure annotation quality [34] and are thus usually not autonomy-supporting. However, our reviewed literature recognizes autonomy as an important moderator of gamification's effect on annotators' motivation [15], and recommends to avoid inducing pressure to use a gamified annotation system [8]. According to causality orientation theory, annotators may differ in the extent they perceive feedback as informational or controlling [9]. Feedback perceived as informational may result in better annotations [9], whereas feedback perceived as controlling can undermine autonomy and thus motivation [34]. Concerning this matter, our annotators remarked that experts, due to the competences in their field, often exhibit a certain pride with their work and thus do not appreciate being forced to behave in a certain way. This suggests that experts' lean more toward perceiving gamification as controlling, thus emphasizing the importance of autonomy.

5   A Tentative Design for a Gamified Expert Annotation System

Our tentative design includes those design features (DFs) that we think are suitable to address MR1 to MR7. An example mockup design can be seen in Fig. 3. To support comprehensibility (MR2), we visually sectioned off most gamification elements to the sidebar so they would not interfere with the actual annotation process (cf. MR1).

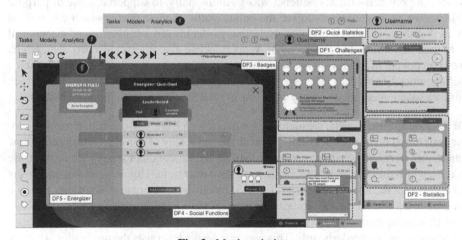

Fig. 3. Mockup design

DF1 – Challenges and Reward Shop. The first feature in our design are daily challenges that involve goals to encourage careful and accurate annotation (e.g., "annotate 10 images with at least 90% of pixels annotated") and can thus serve as an interest alignment mechanic to tackle the principal-agent problem in annotation (cf. MR6). Completing a challenge yields virtual currency, which can be spent in a reward shop (not shown in Fig. 3) to gain cosmetic rewards that allow annotators to express themselves and thus foster autonomy (MR7).

DF2 – Progress and Statistics. To support self-efficacy (MR4), our design includes progress indicators and statistics about the annotation process that show annotators that their actions lead to certain outcomes. Only an easy-to-grasp progress bar and a small selection of statistics—which annotators can customize themselves to support autonomy (MR7)—are visible at all times. More extensive statistics are available on demand. This way, our design regulates the cognitive load of annotators, and ensures that statistics are not distracting from annotation, which supports comprehensibility (MR2).

DF3 – Badges. We include two kinds of badges in our design. First, permanent badges, which are available at any point in time and mostly represent long-term, effort-based tasks (e.g., "annotate one image daily for three months"). These contribute to a sense of purpose (MR6) by providing annotators with meaningful long-term goals. Second, we include seasonal badges, which are available only during specific time frames (i.e., *seasons*) and mostly represent short-term, performance-based tasks (e.g., "annotate 300 liver images in the current season"). The dichotomy of badges ensures that all annotators, regardless of skill level, always have a challenging, yet achievable goal to work toward, which mitigates boredom and fosters a sense of challenge (MR3).

DF4 – Social Functions. Our design includes several social functions to address annotators' desire for meaningful social relationships (MR5). Annotators can showcase obtained badges in their profile to demonstrate outcomes of their actions to their peers, which supports self-efficacy beliefs (MR4). Additionally, to support a sense of purpose (MR6), we allow annotators to see the online status of their peers, which can remind them that they are part of a greater team that works toward a bigger, more meaningful goal than they can individually reach. Annotators can also interact via text chat, which they can opt out of, if they do not want to socially engage or do not want to be distracted during annotation (MR2). Thereby, we allow annotators to stay self-determined, which ensures social interactions to stay meaningful (MR5) and fosters autonomy (MR7).

DF5 – Energizers. Lastly, we include energizers, which are self-contained purely hedonic activities (i.e., minigames) that can break the monotony of annotation tasks and allow annotators to reset their cognitive load (MR2). Annotators can trigger these by using tokens, which they accumulate a maximum of two over time. This ensures that energizers do not disrupt the annotation flow (cf. MR3) by allowing annotators to trigger them on their own volition (cf. MR7). Annotators cannot start a session with an energizer, as this goes against their purpose as a mental break. Annotators may compare their performance in the energizers on leaderboards. This way, our design leverages the motivational effects of competition as a form of social interaction (MR5), without jeopardizing annotation quality (MR1) through annotation performance-based competition.

6 Discussion and Conclusion

Overall, the findings of our study help to better understand the problems associated with the design of successful GEAS. Our MRs demonstrate that expert annotation is a complex context for gamification, where the gameful experience has to be carefully carved based on the unique characteristics of experts while not neglecting annotation quality. From a DSR perspective, our findings emphasize the importance of putting adequate effort into the exploration of the problem space to ensure the usefulness of prospective artifacts [20, 27]. They also highlight the inevitable intertwinement of the problem and solution space in DSR projects, as we found that our efforts toward a solution also allowed us to reflect and reinterpret the underlying problems [20]. We think our MRs help to understand the purpose and scope of GEAS and thus serve as an important baseline to a design theory for GEAS [21]. Our findings also highlight the important role of behavioral theories as descriptive justificatory knowledge [21]. By drawing on theories from various domains, we think that we were able to increase our understanding of the underlying design problems and substantially strengthen our MRs.

From a gamification perspective, our results reaffirm that expert annotators require a different experience than non-expert annotators, and thus demonstrate the context-sensitivity of gamification regarding system users [13, 14]. One interesting point was that although our annotators generally liked the idea of adapting the developed GEAS design in their daily work, they also said they would feel uncomfortable to present it to medical professionals. While this discomfort may stem from the healthcare background of our annotators (as health topics are sensitive and deserve a serious and professional tone), it may also be generally related to experts as the users of gamified IS. As Lowry et al. [41] suggest, many assume that gamification is about games, and that professionals do not deal with games, but rather "stick with austere, tried-and-true, business-like topics free from any trace of play" [41]. We think that designers of gamified IS should be mindful of this attitude, as it may complicate the already sometimes difficult job to demonstrate the benefits of gamification to stakeholders [42].

As a limitation of our study, we acknowledge that including only six participants from the same organizations in our workshops may have limited our ability to triangulate data (i.e., collect different perspectives). Future research may find it beneficial to increase the sample size or collect data from multiple organizations. Another limitation of our study is the lack of an artifact instantiation. While we tried to ensure the usefulness of our artifacts through ex ante evaluations, we acknowledge that vast design knowledge can emerge from instantiating an artifact in practice [20, 27]. Thus, a logical next step for future research would be to instantiate real-world artifacts of GEAS and put our results to the test in the instance domain. Future research may also find it beneficial to formulate GEAS design principles that can serve as prescriptive knowledge that is neither too broad nor too lengthy to be actionable for designers [43].

To conclude, in this study, we explored gamification as an innovative approach to increase the motivation and engagement of expert annotators and increase annotation quality. Following a problem-centered DSR approach, we derived seven MRs that represent those experiential and instrumental outcomes that we think make up meaningful engagement in GEAS. We also derived a tentative design that showcases how the derived MRs could be addressed. Overall, our study helps to understand the inner workings of gamification in the context of expert annotation and thus lays important groundwork for future research on GEAS as well as the design of successful GEAS in practice.

Acknowledgements. We thank Benjamin Müller, Tornike Davitashvili, Marie Raddatz, Rayan Younis, Philipp Petrynowski and Jonathan Chen for participating in our workshops as expert annotators.

The present contribution is supported by the Helmholtz Association under the joint research school "HIDSS4Health – Helmholtz Information and Data Science School for Health."

References

1. Sheng, V.S., Provost, F., Ipeirotis, P.: Get another label? improving data quality and data mining using multiple, noisy labelers In: SIGKDD 2008. ACM, New York, USA (2008)
2. Wagner, M., et al.: A learning robot for cognitive camera control in minimally invasive surgery. Surg. Endosc. **35**(9), 5365–5374 (2021). https://doi.org/10.1007/s00464-021-08509-8
3. Gudivada, V., Apon, A., Ding, J.: Data quality considerations for big data and machine learning: going beyond data cleaning and transformations. Int. J. Adv. Soft. **10**(1), 1–20 (2017)
4. Litjens, G., et al.: A survey on deep learning in medical image analysis. Med. Image Anal. **42**, 60–88 (2017)
5. Nazarenko, A., Levy, F., Wyner, A.: An annotation language for semantic search of legal sources. In: 11th International Conference on Language Resources and Evaluation (2018)
6. Sarr, J., et al.: Complex data labeling with deep learning methods: lessons from fisheries acoustics. ISA Trans. **109**, 113–125 (2021)
7. Viana, P., Pinto, J.P.: A collaborative approach for semantic time-based video annotation using gamification. Hum. Cent. Comput. Inf. Sci., 7(1) (2017)
8. Alaghbari, S., et al.: Achiever or explorer? gamifying the creation process of training data for machine learning In: Mensch und Computer 2020. ACM, New York, USA (2020)
9. Mekler, E.D., Brühlmann, F., Tuch, A.N., Opwis, K.: Towards understanding the effects of individual gamification elements on intrinsic motivation and performance. Comput. Hum. Behav. **71**, 525–534 (2017)
10. Warsinsky, S., et al.: Conceptual ambiguity surrounding gamification and serious games in health care: literature review and development of game-based intervention reporting guidelines (GAMING). J. Med. Internet. Res. **23**(9), e30390 (2021)
11. Hamari, J.: Gamification In: The Blackwell Encyclopedia of Sociology, pp. 1–3. John Wiley & Sons, Ltd, New York, USA (2019)
12. Liu, D., Santhanam, R., Webster, J.: Toward meaningful engagement: a framework for design and research of gamified information systems. MIS Q **41**(4) (2017)
13. Koivisto, J., Hamari, J.: The rise of motivational information systems: a review of gamification research. Int. J. Inf. Manage. **45**, 191–210 (2019)
14. Nacke, L.E., Deterding, S.: The maturing of gamification research. Comput. Hum. Behav. **71**, 450–454 (2017)
15. Lessel, P., Altmeyer, M., Schmeer, L.V., Krüger, A.: "Enable or disable gamification?": analyzing the impact of choice in a gamified image tagging task. In: 2019 CHI Conference on Human Factors in Computing Systems. ACM, New York, USA (2019)
16. Chen, C.-M., Li, M.-C., Chen, T.-C.: A web-based collaborative reading annotation system with gamification mechanisms to improve reading performance. Comput. Educ. 144 (2020)
17. Sweller, J., van Merriënboer, J.J.G., Paas, F.: Cognitive architecture and instructional design: 20 years later. Educ Psychol Rev **31**(2), 261–292 (2019)
18. Ivanjko, T.: Crowdsourcing image descriptions using gamification: a comparison between game-generated labels and professional descriptors. In: MIPRO 2019. IEEE (2019)

19. Lee, J., Yi, J.H., Kim, S.: Cultural heritage design element labeling system with gamification. IEEE Access **8**, 127700–127708 (2020)
20. Maedche, A., Gregor, S., Morana, S., Feine, J.: Conceptualization of the Problem Space in Design Science Research. In: Tulu, B., Djamasbi, S., Leroy, G. (eds.) DESRIST 2019. LNCS, vol. 11491, pp. 18–31. Springer, Cham (2019). https://doi.org/10.1007/978-3-030-19504-5_2
21. Jones, D., Gregor, S.: The anatomy of a design theory. J. Assoc. Inf. **8**(5) (2007)
22. Eickhoff, C., Harris, C.G., Vries, A.P. de Srinivasan, P.: Quality through flow and immersion. In: ACM SIGIR 2012. ACM Press, New York, USA (2012)
23. Jauer, M.-L., Spicher, N., Deserno, T.M.: Gamification concept for acquisition of medical image segmentation via crowdsourcing. In: Proc. SPIE, Medical Imaging 2021 (2021)
24. Dumitrache, A., et al.: "Dr. Detective": combining gamification techniques and crowdsourcing to create a gold standard in medical text. In: CrowdSem 2013: 1st International Workshop on Crowdsourcing the Semantic Web (2013)
25. Balducci, F., Buono, P.: Building a qualified annotation dataset for skin lesion analysis trough gamification In: AVI '18. ACM, New York, USA (2018)
26. Cao, H.-A., Wijaya, T.K., Aberer, K., Nunes, N.: A collaborative framework for annotating energy datasets. In: 2015 IEEE International Conference on Big Data. IEEE (2015)
27. Sonnenberg, C., vom Brocke, J.: Evaluations in the Science of the Artificial – Reconsidering the Build-Evaluate Pattern in Design Science Research. In: Peffers, K., Rothenberger, M., Kuechler, B. (eds.) DESRIST 2012. LNCS, vol. 7286, pp. 381–397. Springer, Heidelberg (2012). https://doi.org/10.1007/978-3-642-29863-9_28
28. Webster, J., Watson, R.T.: Analyzing the past to prepare for the future: writing a literature review. MIS Q **26**(2), xiii–xxiii (2002)
29. Gottesdiener, E.: Requirements by collaboration: workshops for defining needs. Addison-Wesley Professional (2002)
30. Batini, C., Cappiello, C., Francalanci, C., Maurino, A.: Methodologies for data quality assessment and improvement. ACM Comput. Surv. **41**(3), 1–52 (2009)
31. Ogawa, H., Nishikawa, H., Tokunaga, T., Yokono, H.: Gamification platform for collecting task-oriented dialogue data. In: LREC 2020. ELRA, Marseille, France (2020)
32. Lumsden, J., et al.: The effects of gamelike features and test location on cognitive test performance and participant enjoyment. PeerJ **4**, e2184 (2016)
33. Hofmann, P., Oesterle, S., Rust, P., Urbach, N.: Machine learning approaches along the radiology value chain–Rethinking value propositions. In: ECIS 2019 (2019)
34. Öhman, E.S., Kajava, K.S.A.: Sentimentator: gamifying fine-grained sentiment annotation. In: Digital Humanities in the Nordic Countries 2018 (2018)
35. Csikszentmihalyi, M.: Flow and the psychology of discovery and invention. HarperPerennial, New York, pp. 39 (1997)
36. Plappert, M., Mandery, C., Asfour, T.: The KIT Motion-Language Dataset. Big data **4**(4), 236–252 (2016)
37. Bandura, A.: Self-efficacy: toward a unifying theory of behavioral change. Psychol. Rev. **84**(2), 191–215 (1977)
38. Schaekermann, M., Cai, C.J., Huang, A.E., Sayres, R.: Expert discussions improve comprehension of difficult cases in medical image assessment In: 2020 CHI Conference on Human Factors in Computing Systems. ACM, New York, USA (2020)
39. Ryan, R.M., Deci, E.L.: Self-determination theory and the facilitation of intrinsic motivation, social development, and well-being. Am. Psychol. **55**(1), 68 (2000)
40. Eisenhardt, K.M.: Agency theory: an assessment and review. AMR **14**(1), 57–74 (1989)
41. Lowry, P.B., Petter, S., Leimeister, J.M.: Desperately seeking the artefacts and the foundations of native theory in gamification research: why information systems researchers can play a legitimate role in this discourse and how they can better contribute. Eur. J. Inf. Sys. **29**(6), 609–620 (2020)

42. Warsinsky, S., Schmidt-Kraepelin, M., Thiebes, S., Sunyaev, A.: Are gamification projects different? an exploratory study on software project risks for gamified health behavior change support systems. In: HICSS 2021. IEEE, New York, USA (2021)
43. Sturm, B., Sunyaev, A.: Design principles for systematic search systems: a holistic synthesis of a rigorous multi-cycle design science research journey. Bus. Inf. Syst. Eng. **61**(1), 91–111 (2018). https://doi.org/10.1007/s12599-018-0569-6

Healthcare Systems and Quality of Life

Introduction to the Healthcare Systems and Quality of Life Track

Reima Suomi⬤, Monica Chiarini Tremblay⬤,
and Debra VanderMeer⬤

[1] University of Turku
reima.suomi@utu.fi
[2] William and Mary University
monica.tremblay@mason.wm.edu
[3] Florida International University
vanderd@fiu.edu

Abstract. Healthcare is a relatively mature industry field that still has wicked problems. Design science research can help identify non-optimal processes and work practices and suggest redesign and digitalization efforts. Elegant technical solutions to these problems require that design science researchers collaborate with transdisciplinary teams. This track for DESRIST 2022 encourages scholars to submit multidisciplinary submissions with novel solutions to health and social well-being problems on the individual, group, organization, population, country, and world level. The papers in the track include the application of artificial intelligence, the creation of mobile apps for issues such as depression and blood do- nation, and submissions on contemporary topics such as COVID-19 and refugee problems. We identify three subjects that require more research from the DSR community: cost-effective solutions, knowledge management, and long-term evaluations.

Keywords: Healthcare · Quality of life

1 Purpose of the Theme Track

Healthcare is afflicted with many wicked problems, with the current Covid-19 as a concrete contemporary example. Elegant technical solutions to these problems require that technical professionals collaborate with multidisciplinary teams consisting of government officials, policymakers, healthcare providers, and mental health specialists. The most critical but often ignored stakeholder and actor is the patient. There are often complicated relationships between medical providers, IT, and administrative personnel in healthcare organizational settings. These all are further divided into powerful sub-groups. A feasible solution in one environment seldom works in others, and organizational boundaries are rarely respected. In such scenarios, wide-reaching integrative solutions are required. Our call for papers encouraged transdisciplinary submissions with novel solutions to health and social well-being problems on the individual, group, organization, popula- tion, country, and world level. Ideally, proposed artifacts are generalizable across multiple environments, with documented positive impact.

2 Design Science Research for Healthcare Systems and Quality of Life

The submissions to our track included the application of artificial intelligence in the healthcare and well-being field. The received submissions indicate that artificial intelligence is a hot topic. On the other hand, many trendy topics from a few years ago, such as big data or process re-engineering, gained less attention. Most research in the field seems to assess issues from the clinical and health point of view, with topics such as system integration, application portfolios, and IT governance lying in the background. At the very end, we might see the famous metaphor of the archipelago of disintegrated IT solutions, a real risk we as a research community must also take into attention.

Managing the immense amount of data and information on health and well-being demands constant research attention. Problems vary from the basic elements of getting analog information into digital ones to comprehensive solutions in knowledge management. Again, knowledge management was not present in our research topics. In between, we saw efforts to systematize and more effectively exploit available data, but usually in the context of some limited clinical or social problem.

Submissions included the creation of mobile apps for issues such as depression and blood donation. Finally, we saw submissions on contemporary topics such as COVID-19 and refugee problems. It is encouraging to see steps to understand health and well-being as a relatively broad topic area, reaching beyond classical physical health. We hope that the research community will extend its activity in this field, as health and societal problems often have a multidimensional and complex set of issues behind them.

Healthcare is a relatively mature industry field. It is rather easy to identify current processes and work practices established and widely used but not optimal and suggest redesign and digitalization efforts; a reasonable basis for using research methods such as design science. Short-term successes are easy to document, such as more effective use of resources or faster throughput of shorter turnaround times. The long-term effects of different health aspects take more time to mature, especially at the population level, so evaluation and assessment of research findings should be carefully done, remembering the long time needed for a final evaluation.

A somewhat neglected topic in the field is that of costs: economics and business models. We could build a perfect healthcare environment, including excellent processes supported by outstanding information system solutions. The remaining problem is the affordability of these solutions. Admitting that clinical systems are at the core of medical activity, we should simultaneously encourage more research into administrative and other background systems in the healthcare and social fields.

Healthcare is heavily regulated and includes a lot of normative guidance from various parties on how things must be done. The field calls for multi-professional cooperation and integration. Our submissions show that good results are achieved in collaboration among medical, IT, and other professionals. Understanding this complex and heavily regulated domain area remains a challenge for IT researchers. IT solutions are often a mystery for many medical and social science professionals. Constant articulation work between these groups is needed.

Reviewers

Antti Airola	University of Turku
Lina Bouayad	Florida International University
Marvin Braun	University of Göttingen
Alfred Benedikt Brendel	Technical University of Dresden
Mirella Cacace	Catholic University of Applied Sciences Frieburg
Christer Carlsson	Åbo Akademi University
Arturo Castellanos	William & Mary
Alfred Castillo	Florida International University
Polina Durneva	Florida International University
Ismail Elnaggar	University of Turku
Andri Färber	Zurich University of Applied Sciences
Haoqiang Jiang	Northern Kentucky University
Johan Lilius	Åbo Akademi University
Yong Liu	Aalto University
Mahed Maddah	Suffolk University
Matti Mäntymäki	University of Turku
Silvia Masiero	University of Oslo
Matti Minkkinen	University of Turku
Hans Moen	Aalto University
Stefan Morana	Saarland University
Helena Müller	Technical University of Darmstadt
Roland M. Mueller	Berlin School of Economics and Law
Anik Mukherjee	Indian Institute of Technology Roorkee
Teijo Peltomäki	University of Turku
Florian Rampold	University of Göttingen
Gerhard Schwabe	University of Zurich
Vivek Singh	University of Missouri–St. Louis
Amin Shoji	Florida International University
Veda Storey	Georgia State University
Hemang Subramanian	Florida International University
Devinder Thapa	University of Agder
Karthikeyan Umapathy	University of North Florida
Nilmini Wickramasinghe	Swinburne University of Technology

Guiding Refugees Through European Bureaucracy: Designing a Trustworthy Mobile App for Document Management

Alexandre Amard[✉][iD], Alexandra Hoess[✉][iD], Tamara Roth[✉][iD],
Gilbert Fridgen[✉][iD], and Alexander Rieger[✉][iD]

Interdisciplinary Centre for Security, Reliability and Trust,
University of Luxembourg, Luxembourg, Luxembourg
{alexandre.amard,alexandra.hoess,tamara.roth,gilbert.fridgen,
alexander.rieger}@uni.lu

Abstract. After being granted asylum in European countries, refugees
need to go through a multitude of administrative processes before they
can participate in society. However, these processes are often challenging, as refugees struggle to understand them, lack instructions for managing paperwork, and do not possess the required language skills. Prior
research emphasizes the role of information and communication technologies to simplify and enable refugee-friendly administrative processes.
However, recent research and existing applications mainly focus on information retrieval and do not offer assistance for understanding official letters, completing administrative forms, and managing corresponding documents. Furthermore, refugees are often reluctant to use existing applications as they do not trust their host country's governments and public
authorities. In this research, we aim to address this functional and trust
gap. We follow a design science research approach to develop a design for
a refugee-centric and trustworthy mobile application that assists refugees
along administrative processes. In doing so, we identify three design principles that may guide the development of such applications for refugees.

Keywords: Refugees · Trust · Document management

1 Introduction

Global conflicts, human rights violations, and social injustice regularly force
enormous numbers of refugees out of their home countries towards Europe [33].
After being granted asylum in their European host countries, refugees typically
have a hard time participating in and integrating into society [1,2]. They must
go through a series of administrative processes to gain official identity documents, which justify their status and access to public and private services [1]
that they would otherwise have difficulties obtaining [18]. However, these processes are often hard to complete for refugees due to language barriers, missing

---

The original version of this chapter was previously published non-open access. A correction to this chapter is available at https://doi.org/10.1007/978-3-031-06516-3_38

A. Drechsler et al. (Eds.): DESRIST 2022, LNCS 13229, pp. 171–182, 2022.
https://doi.org/10.1007/978-3-031-06516-3_13

instructions, or a lack of understanding of their required contributions [2]. Furthermore, refugees frequently struggle to manage the quantity and diversity of official documents that they receive throughout these processes.

Prior research emphasizes the potential of information and communication technology (ICT) to make such processes more refugee-friendly and lower the barriers to social inclusion [2,18,24]. Research particularly focuses on web and mobile applications that enable refugees to retrieve important information related to administrative processes, healthcare, living, and the local community in simplified language and with an intuitive design [1,29]. While these applications may be helpful for understanding the structure of administrative processes, they currently do not provide support with document management, which ranges from distinguishing and understanding official letters to completing administrative forms and managing corresponding certificates. Consequently, most refugees still depend on the help of refugee assistants to complete administrative processes, which limits refugee's agency, i.e., "people's capacity to act, either individually or collectiv" [13] and perceived self-efficacy [1]. More importantly, refugees often do not trust their host country's public authorities because of negative experiences in their home-, transit- or even host countries [14]. Some refugees are also hesitant to use ICT provided by public authorities, as they fear surveillance and disclosure of personal information that had been used for persecution in their past [8,18,28]. As such, trust is a prerequisite to the refugees' adoption of ICT provided by their host countries.

Adequate ICT solutions need to consider these concerns in their design. They need to give refugees more agency in handling their documents and should foster trust in their host countries' governments [2,8,21]. Acknowledging AbuJarour et al.'s [1] call for research on the design of trustworthy ICT to facilitate administrative processes, this research investigates the following research question: *How to design a user-centric and trustworthy mobile application that assists refugees in administrative processes?*

To answer this research question, we follow a Design Science Research (DSR) approach [26] and develop a design for a mobile application that assists refugees along administrative processes. In doing so, we build upon literature on ICT for refugees as well as institution-based trust. Our design is informed by nine ex-ante interviews with government officials and fourteen ex-post interviews with refugees and refugee assistants, which helped us ensure relevance and rigor. From our final design, we infer three design principles.

2   Background

2.1   The Role of ICT for Refugees

Following their arrival in European host countries, refugees have to complete many administrative procedures to obtain a residence permit, access healthcare, or have educational credentials recognized [1]. As an initial step, refugees typically complete an asylum procedure, which entitles them to access such basic services. While refugees are often guided throughout the asylum procedure by authorities for migration in Europe, subsequent procedures are not directly tailored to refugees anymore, and thus can be even more challenging [25]. They are often complex and may appear arbitrary for those who are not familiar with the system. Not least as many administrative processes in European countries are still paper-based [1]. In particular, refugees often struggle with understanding paperwork, not only because of language barriers but also due to intricate bureaucratic complexities [2,25]. Refugees are also often missing guidance concerning contributions they have to make themselves and various process steps [2,25].

Integrating ICT into administrative procedures can help refugees navigate integration procedures [1]. Yet, while applications exist that support refugees in accessing important information and identifying themselves, we could not pinpoint solutions that assist refugees along administrative procedures and help them manage official documents. Moreover, we found that many existing applications pay too little attention to accessibility for refugees. This is problematic as refugees may have difficulties using interfaces that do not match their levels of digital literacy or have reading directions that only follow European specifications [29]. As a result, improperly designed ICT may also lead to (digital) exclusion. Thus, further research is required on refugee-centric design [1].

An approach to such refugee-centric design is the integration of increased agency [1,2,29]. For instance, mobile apps for refugees can improve accessibility of vital information concerning areas such as healthcare, public administration, education, or everyday life [29]. Mobile applications can provide digital administrative forms including additional instructions to lower barriers for understanding. Mobile apps can also support refugees with identification and authentication, as currently pursued by the UNHCR [18]. However, when using ICT that process personal data, refugees may also face risks of data abuse, discrimination, and surveillance [8,32]. So-called digital wallet apps, can mitigate privacy-related concerns and even grant independence of public institutions in managing identity-related documents [5]. These apps promise refugees a high degree of self-efficacy, control, and privacy regarding their identity information [5,27].

2.2 Antecedents of Institution-Based Trust

As prior research illustrates, trust and distrust beliefs towards an institution can have a significant impact on the trustee's adoption of digital services and technologies [20]. For our particular research, this effectively means that a successful application for the support of administrative processes and management of official documents has to enhance refugees' institution-based trust and reduce their institution-based distrust.

Trust is commonly associated with "the willingness of a party to be vulnerable to another party's actions based on the expectation that the other party will perform a particular action" [9, p. 3]. Most citizens in Europe trust their governments and public authorities to lawfully and reliably deliver public service.

However, many refugees typically do not have such institution-based trust as they have been persecuted by public authorities in their home countries [9,14].

The formation of such institution-based trust typically depends on three factors: the institution's perceived integrity, the institution's perceived competence for reliable action, and its intention to act in a benevolent manner [21,23]. If a trusting party, such as refugees, believes that an institution will not act with integrity and in a competent and benevolent way, trust will decrease or even be undermined. Such lack of trust may even stimulate the emergence of distrust [21]. Distrust manifests itself when there is a "lack of confidence in the other, a concern that the other may act as to harm one, [...] not [caring] about one's welfare [...]" [10, p. 240]. Like trust, distrust also comprises three dimensions: deceit, incompetence, and malevolence [21,23]. Importantly, a lack of trust does not automatically lead to distrust [23].

3   Research Method

To develop our artifact – a design for a refugee-centric and trustworthy mobile application which we call the "Refugee Wizard" – we adopted a DSR approach [12,26]. In doing so, we followed the proposed DSR process model of Peffers et al. [26]. The process starts with the problem identification. To do so, we conducted nine qualitative and semi-structured ex-ante interviews [30] with government officials that are regularly in touch with refugees. With these interviewees, we discussed problems that refugees typically encounter while dealing with administrative procedures. We identified two main problems: the lack of refugees' agency in managing their official documents and administrative procedures, and weak institutional trust or in some cases even distrust. Thus, our Refugee Wizard intends to support refugees in effectively managing their official documents and mediate trust concerns.

Subsequently, we structured and condensed our insights into *design requirements* – generic requirements that any artifact aiming to solve the underlying problem class should meet – for an application that could assist refugees [7, 22,31]. In addition to the interviews, which ensure the practical relevance of our research, we investigated literature on the role of ICT for refugees and institution-based trust and distrust. This warrants the rigor, validity, and effectiveness of our research [36,37]. Based on the design requirements, we developed and iteratively refined our artifact. We first translated the identified requirements into design features which represent the technical specifications and components of our solution [7,22]. Thereafter, we instantiated the design features into a paper-based prototype of our Refugee Wizard, to help demonstrate our design.

For the demonstration, we presented the paper-based prototype to refugees and refugee assistants and discussed with them the *design features* of our solution. These interviews also served as a basis for the evaluation of our design [34]. Overall, we conducted 14 ex-post interviews with three refugees and eleven refugee assistants – who support refugees along administrative processes on a regular basis – to gain feedback from an end-user perspective. In particular, we discussed the design features and the Refugee Wizard's usability and trust-enhancing qualities, as well as potentials for improvement. The interviewed refugees were selected from B1 German classes and had successfully completed their asylum application. This enabled relatively fluent conversations on the topic without additional translators. Refugee assistants were selected from local non-governmental and church organizations as they had the most contact with refugees throughout and after the asylum process. They were also often familiar with current technical applications for refugees. After each interview, we evaluated the feedback and adapted our design features and paper-based prototype, if necessary. The interviews enabled us to abstract our design into *design principles* that provide explanations for how our design features address the identified design requirements and provide a solution to our underlying problem class [7]. More specifically, the design principles offer generalizable guidelines on how to design applications that assist refugees along administrative processes and generic capabilities that may technically support trust [3,11,22].

4   Design and Development

4.1   Design Requirements

Our ex-ante interviews as well as the literature outlined in Sect. 2 provided us with six design requirements for our Refugee Wizard. More specifically, they highlighted the potential for increased agency of refugees through the use of ICT [19,24]. Most refugees are currently relying on information provided by government officials or refugee assistants without the ability to "fully participate [...] and control their own destinies" [2, p. 406]. This does not only create exclusion from the society of their host countries but also takes a mental toll on refugees who find it "difficult to accept help – from a cultural perspective – as they do not want to appear weak" (Gov 7). Thus, granting refugees *control of documents and information flows* (DR 1) is a cornerstone of a refugee-centric ICT design in order to prevent the development of distrust beliefs towards host governments and supporting organizations [6]. An *increased availability of relevant documents for refugees* (DR 2) helps them navigate unfamiliar government procedures and information environments [6,16]. To date, refugees often do not know "what they have to fill in, why they have to fill it in, and where to put the filled in document" (Gov 1). *Indications of completeness of documents* (DR 3) and an *overview of documents and information flows* (DR 4) may enable refugees to better understand these requirements, the current state of their respective procedure, and for which documents their identity-related information is needed. *Understanding the required documents and processes* (DR 5) also helps refugees to be "much more accepting of administrative processes – regardless of how positive or negative the outcome" (Gov 5). Thus, knowledge and understanding can ensure refugees' trust in the integrity of government agencies and supporting organizations. An *increased efficiency of data exchange for refugees* (DR 6) may also improve the interaction with and perceived competence of government officials and public institutions, and thus the trust they place in them. Indeed, should documents be lost or incomplete, refugees may more easily find the "receipt that shows [that] documents have been complete upon submission" (Gov 5).

4.2 Design Features and Instantiation

Guided by our design requirements, we developed design features that were directly relevant for the design of our refugee-centric and trustworthy mobile application [22]. Overall, we identified eleven design features, which either directly concerned document management or increased agency as well as inclusive or culture-specific adaptations of our Refugee Wizard. As a first step towards more knowledge about governmental procedures in their host country, *explanations of unknown procedures* (DF 1) is an important design feature. That is, information in official documents, which is often hidden behind formal bureaucratic language to conform with formal requirements of government documents [4], is didactically reduced to the essential points. To access this information, official documents can be enhanced with QR-codes. Refugees can scan a QR-code provided on a paper-based document with their Refugee Wizard that *automatically allocates* (DF 2) a digital version of the document into *pre-structured document folders* (DF 3) within the relevant application (Fig. 1). These folders concern key areas in the refugees' journey through the administrative processes of their host country, for instance housing, transportation, or health [1,29]. Since refugees "[often] have no idea of folder structures" (RA 5), the pre-structured folders also help refugees to organise their physical documents in folders. In case of successful submission or presentation, another QR-code provided on the receipt issued by responsible government agencies can mark the respective digital document as completed by changing its color to green. This constitutes the *integration of a checklist* (DF 4) to help refugees assess their progress in a procedure and understand the relevant details. Such checklists could also provide information on the due date of document submissions and the intended recipient of a document.

While this design may already allow for more agency, refugee applications also need to *consider different levels of literacy* (DF 5), i.e., not all refugees can read and write [16,27]. To limit discrimination, refugees can choose between written language and sign language combined with audios as basic settings. In both cases, availability of the refugees' native languages is important. This not only includes translations of all information but also *culturally appropriate presentation of information* (DF 6) - such as where information is being provided - to make the user journey more intuitive. Likewise, automation and a simple interface enable the *consideration of different levels of digital literacy* (DF 7), as many refugees are not familiar with using digital devices [16,35].

Inclusive design also extends to the consideration of the refugees' fears and concerns. More specifically, many refugees fear that the use of apps, such as the Refugee Wizard, would allow for tracking of personal information [6]. To address those fears, features of secure digital wallet apps and decentralized digital identities can be included. Comparable to a physical wallet, secure digital wallets can

Fig. 1. Design of the Refugee Wizard.

enable *privacy by design* (DF 8) thanks to methods such as only storing documents and personal information decentrally on refugees' phones, encryption and access management. These features provide refugees with more control and reduce risks of surveillance and the perceived malevolence of governments [5, 6]. Due to the intuitive folder structure, refugees could also better *control document sharing and disclosure* (DF 9), while the use of QR-codes on documents could include features for *verifying the integrity of documents* (DF 10). Finally, providing an overview of the documents they need and what they are required for, as well as when they have submitted their documents to the competent person or authority, enables additional *transparency over processing of disclosed documents* (DF 11). Thus, at all points in time, refugees are aware of what happens with their documents and how many documents they still need to complete.

5 Evaluation

In the evaluation interviews, we asked refugee assistants (RA) and refugees (R) to what extent they deemed the presented Refugee Wizard as trust-enhancing and what other functions they believed would further increase the perceived trustworthiness of our application. Both groups highlighted the intuitive organization of the pre-structured document folders (DF 3). They again emphasized that refugees have difficulties identifying relevant documents - some would appear with the entire contents of their mailbox including newsletters and adverts - and are unable to put these documents into a coherent order (RA 4, 10/11). They particularly appreciated the possibility to automatically allocate documents to pre-structured folders (DF 2) with the help of a QR-code (DF 10). Such an allocation would prevent them from saving irrelevant documents or discarding relevant ones (R 1 - 3; RA 1, 2, 4 - 6, 8, 10/11), making them feel less vulnerable and more confident in their interaction with public authorities.

Refugee assistants also emphasized that being able to check the completeness of application documents and keep track of submission deadlines (RA 4, 5) during the application were indeed valuable features. With incoming documents often referring to more or less the same procedure, refugees felt that a transparent overview would increase their understanding and agency. In addition to more integration-related sub-folders, we therefore also included the checklist function for application documents (DF 4). Moreover, both refugees and refugee assistants suggested the addition of a status-tracking function in the Refugee Wizard (RA 4 - 6, 10/11). This would increase transparency for refugees throughout their administrative procedures (DF 11), making it more understandable where they are in the procedure and when they could expect a decision (DF 1) (R 2 - 3). Such transparency would foster clarity and positive beliefs. At the same time, refugees voiced concern that using an app with a status-tracing function would reveal information about them that they do not wish to share. Since many refugees are not aware of their host countries' privacy and data protection regulations or the legal obligations of those countries' governments, privacy assurance would either require extensive explaining or a technology-mediated guarantee (RA 2, 4, 6, 7, 10/11). Overall, many refugee assistants and most refugees would prefer technology-mediated guarantees, in which refugees may trust more than in governments, and they thus appreciated the inclusion of intrinsic privacy and control features (DF 8, DF 9). For explanations of documents and procedures, interviewees collectively appreciated the simplification of content as an addition to official documents (DF 1) as well as the consideration of different levels of (digital) literacy (DF 5, DF 7) to increase understanding and the availability of information. As documents must still be filled in manually, refugees suggested reference examples as part of the explanation for each document in their target languages to make it easier for them to fill in the forms (DF 1, DF 6) (R 1 - 3).

6 Discussion

We consolidated the iterations and evaluations of our design with refugee assistants and refugees in a nascent design theory, i.e. in generalizable design principles [3, 11]. We have identified three design principles that provide knowledge on how to design technical applications that help restore institution-based trust [21, 23] and mediate institution-based distrust [15, 20] of refugees (Fig. 2 and 3). We add to theory by proposing that aside from inclusive or culture-sensitive design, document management and increased agency may be trust-enhancing factors. Furthermore, our design principles may provide potential solutions for practitioners who wish to develop applications for refugees that build on the same underlying class of problems.

DP1 – Guided Document Management: When evaluating the refugee assistants' and refugees' feedback, we found that distrust beliefs in governmental agencies [6] based on incomplete documents or repetitive requests can be mediated by having a mobile document management application. This would not only support refugees in allocating official documents to dedicated folders but would

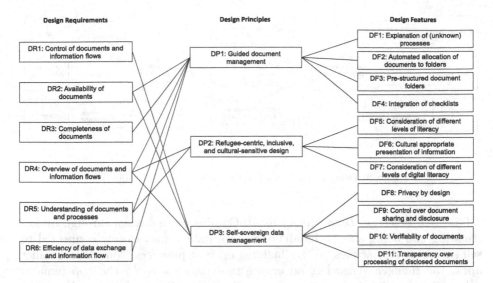

Fig. 2. Overview of design requirements, principles, and features.

also help them understand the purpose and content of such documents, potentially breaking the cycle of distrust. Imparting knowledge of the procedures and requirements in an accessible manner would put refugees in a position of control. With increased control, refugees may not only reduce their distrust beliefs but may be able to better assess bureaucratic requirements and the integrity and competence of governmental procedures, and thereby also build trust [20, 21, 23]. The additional checklist function of our Refugee Wizard further emphasizes the refugees' position of control. Having something that would not only indicate the completeness of a document but also due dates and receiving parties, creates a feeling of safety. This, in turn, increases the institutions' perceived benevolence and competence and thereby positively affect the formation of trust [21, 23].

DP2 – Refugee-Centric, Inclusive and Cultural-Sensitive Design: User-centric design is pivotal in building trust-relations. Newly arriving refugees lack a sense of belonging and agency [17]. In many cases, this sense of alienation and dependency is further emphasized by language barriers and variance in cultural sensitivities. To counteract this trend and bridge the comprehension gap despite the lack of language competencies of many refugees, the Refugee Wizard offers a didactically reduced, personalizable and culturally appropriate design of information presentation [17]. This way, refugees may feel less alienated and more capable to act as they find their needs represented regardless of literacy levels or culture. The same also applies to digital literacy, where automation of key processes, and easy and intuitive icons should prevent less digitally literate refugees from feeling overwhelmed [27]. Overall, positive experiences with the Refugee Wizard and a sense of belonging through culturally appropriate design may foster the belief of benevolence and reduce distrust and fears of malevolence [20, 23].

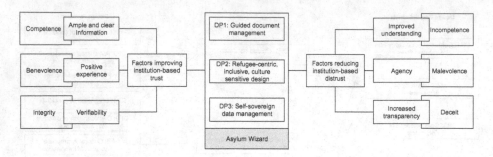

Fig. 3. Design principles for a trust-enhancing design.

DP3 – Self-sovereign Data Management: Gaining more control through understanding and being able to handle one's own data is also closely connected to self-sovereignty principles [8]. By building on best practices from digital wallet apps, the Refugee Wizard could ensure that data stored in the app remains private and in the hands of the refugees [8,27]. Yet, it would also make it possible to share this data with other refugees or trusted refugee assistants in a self-controlled manner to, for instance, provide them with additional samples for filling in documents. Moreover, refugees may share their filled in documents with competent government officials before submission to make sure that the documents are complete. This again may empower refugees and could make them feel more self-sufficient. At the same time, their increased sovereignty may positively reflect on heightened competence beliefs regarding their host country's government and may thus foster institution-based trust [21,23]. Increased transparency through knowledge about processes and having all relevant information available and verified in their app further improves such trust through positive perceptions of the government's integrity and benevolence [20,23].

7   Conclusion

In this study, we discuss how a mobile application that assists refugees in administrative processes can be built in a refugee-centric and trustworthy manner. In a DSR approach based on literature about ICT for refugees and institution-based trust and distrust as well as twenty-three interviews, we infer three design principles from our Refugee Wizard. We find that guided document management and refugee-centric, inclusive, and cultural-sensitive design combined with self-sovereign data management may help to reduce institution-based distrust and enhance trust. Yet, this effect may depend on the availability of privacy-enhancing features which this research only discusses in a limited extent. Future research may extend this work by analyzing in greater details the role of emerging technologies - such as self-sovereign identities and digital wallets - have in enabling trustworthy document management applications. Furthermore, refugees' lack of understanding of the underlying technology to appreciate that governments act in a benevolent manner by providing the app with its proposed features may be detrimental for trust. Overall, our design may help researchers and practitioners to understand the complex interplay of trust and distrust factors in designing trustworthy and user-centric applications for refugees.

Acknowledgments. This research was funded in part, by Luxembourg's Ministry for Digitalization and by the Luxembourg National Research Fund (FNR), PEARL grant reference 13342933/Gilbert Fridgen.

References

1. AbuJarour, S., et al.: ICT-enabled refugee integration: a research agenda. Commun. AIS **44**(1), 874–891 (2019)
2. Andrade, A.D., Doolin, B.: Information and communication technology and the social inclusion of refugees. MIS Q. **40**(2), 405–416 (2016)
3. Baskerville, R., Baiyere, A., Gregor, S., Hevner, A., Rossi, M.: Design science research contributions: finding a balance between artifact and theory. J. Assoc. Inf. Syst. **19**(5), 3 (2018)
4. Bundesamt für Migration und Flüchtlinge: DA-Asyl (2019). https://www.proasyl. de/wp-content/uploads/DA-Asyl_21_02_2019.pdf
5. Bundesamt für Migration und Flüchtlinge: Digitalisierung der Bescheinigungsprozesse im Asylverfahren mittels digitaler Identitäten (2021). https://www. bamf.de/SharedDocs/Anlagen/DE/Digitalisierung/blockchain-whitepaper-2021. pdf?__blob=publicationFile&v=3
6. Carlson, M., Jakli, L., Linos, K.: Rumors and refugees: how government-created information vacuums undermine effective crisis management. Int. Stud. Quart. **62**(3), 671–685 (2018)
7. Chanson, M., Bogner, A., Bilgeri, D., Fleisch, E., Wortmann, F.: Blockchain for the IoT: privacy-preserving protection of sensor data. J. Assoc. Inf. Syst. **20**(9), 1274–1309 (2019)
8. Cheesman, M.: Self-sovereignty for refugees? The contested horizons of digital identity. Geopolitics **27**(1), 134–159 (2022)
9. Cheng, X., Fu, S., de Vreede, G.J.: Determinants of trust in computer-mediated offshore software-outsourcing collaboration. Int. J. Inf. Manage. **57**, 102301 (2021)
10. Govier, T.: Is it a jungle out there? Trust, distrust and the construction of social reality. Dialogue **33**(2), 237–252 (1994)
11. Gregor, S., Hevner, A.R.: Positioning and presenting design science research for maximum impact. MIS Q. **37**, 337–355 (2013)
12. Hevner, A., March, S.T., Park, J., Ram, S., et al.: Design science research in information systems. MIS Q. **28**(1), 75–105 (2004)
13. Hunt, L.: Women asylum seekers and refugees: opportunities, constraints and the role of agency. Soc. Policy Soc. **7**(3), 281–292 (2008)
14. Hynes, T.: The issue of 'trust' or 'mistrust' in research with refugees: choices, caveats and considerations for researchers (2003). https://www.unhcr.org/ research/RESEARCH/3fcb5cee1.pdf
15. Kramer, R.M.: Trust and distrust in organizations: emerging perspectives, enduring questions. Annu. Rev. Psychol. **50**(1), 569–598 (1999)
16. Lloyd, A., Kennan, M.A., Thompson, K.M., Qayyum, A.: Connecting with new information landscapes: information literacy practices of refugees. J. Doc. **69**(1), 121–144 (2013)

17. Lyytinen, E.: Refugees''journeys of trust': creating an analytical framework to examine refugees' exilic journeys with a focus on trust. J. Refug. Stud. **30**(4), 489–510 (2017)
18. Madon, S., Schoemaker, E.: Digital identity as a platform for improving refugee management. Inf. Syst. J. **31**, 929–953 (2021)
19. Majchrzak, A., Markus, M.L., Wareham, J.: Designing for digital transformation: lessons for information systems research from the study of ICT and societal challenges. MIS Q. **40**(2), 267–277 (2016)
20. McKnight, D.H., Choudhury, V.: Distrust and trust in B2C e-commerce: do they differ? In: ICEC 2006, pp. 482–491. Association for Computing Machinery (2006)
21. McKnight, D.H., Lankton, N.K., Nicolaou, A., Price, J.: Distinguishing the effects of B2B information quality, system quality, and service outcome quality on trust and distrust. J. Strateg. Inf. Syst. **26**(2), 118–141 (2017)
22. Meth, H., Mueller, B., Maedche, A.: Designing a requirement mining system. J. Assoc. Inf. Syst. **16**(9), 2 (2015)
23. Moody, G.D., Lowry, P.B., Galletta, D.F.: It's complicated: explaining the relationship between trust, distrust, and ambivalence in online transaction relationships using polynomial regression analysis and response surface analysis. Eur. J. Inf. Syst. **26**(4), 379–413 (2017)
24. Nedelcu, M., Soysüren, I.: Precarious migrants, migration regimes and digital technologies: the empowerment-control nexus. J. Ethnic Migrat. Stud. **48**(8), 1–17 (2020)
25. Pearlman, W.: Culture or bureaucracy? Challenges in Syrian refugees' initial settlement in Germany. Middle East Law Govern. **9**(3), 313–327 (2017)
26. Peffers, K., Tuunanen, T., Rothenberger, M.A., Chatterjee, S.: A design science research methodology for information systems research. J. Manag. Inf. Syst. **24**(3), 45–77 (2007)
27. Rieger, A., Roth, T., Sedlmeir, J., Weigl, L., Fridgen, G.: Not yet another digital identity. Nat. Hum. Behav. 1 (2021)
28. Schoemaker, E., Baslan, D., Pon, B., Dell, N.: Identity at the margins: data justice and refugee experiences with digital identity systems in Lebanon, Jordan, and Uganda. Inf. Technol. Dev. **27**(1), 13–36 (2021)
29. Schreieck, M., Zitzelsberger, J., Siepe, S., Wiesche, M., Krcmar, H.: Supporting refugees in everyday life-intercultural design evaluation of an application for local information. In: PACIS 2017 Proceedings (2017)
30. Schultze, U., Avital, M.: Designing interviews to generate rich data for information systems research. Inf. Organ. **21**(1), 1–16 (2011)
31. Siering, M., Muntermann, J., Grčar, M.: Design principles for robust fraud detection: the case of stock market manipulations. J. Assoc. Inf. Syst. **22**(1), 4 (2021)
32. Taylor, L.: What is data justice? The case for connecting digital rights and freedoms globally. Big Data Soc. **4**(2), 1–14 (2017)
33. UNHCR: UNHCR 2020 Global Report (2021). https://reporting.unhcr.org/download?origin=gtgrpage&file=gr2020/pdf/GR2020_English_Full_lowres.pdf
34. Venable, J., Pries-Heje, J., Baskerville, R.: FEDS: a framework for evaluation in design science research. Eur. J. Inf. Syst. **25**(1), 77–89 (2016)
35. Vollmer, S.: Syrian newcomers and their digital literacy practices. Lang. Issues: ESOL J. **28**(2), 66–72 (2017)
36. Vom Brocke, J., Winter, R., Hevner, A., Maedche, A.: Special issue editorial - accumulation and evolution of design knowledge in design science research: a journey through time and space. J. Assoc. Inf. Syst. **21**(3), 9 (2020)
37. Winter, R.: Design science research in Europe. Eur. J. Inf. Syst. **17**(5), 470–475 (2008)

Just What the Doctor Ordered – Towards Design Principles for NLP-Based Systems in Healthcare

Marvin Braun[1]([⊠]) ⬤, Aycan Aslan[1] ⬤, Till Ole Diesterhöft[1] ⬤, Maike Greve[1] ⬤, Alfred Benedikt Brendel[2] ⬤, and Lutz M. Kolbe[1] ⬤

[1] Georg-August-Universität Göttingen, 37073 Göttingen, Germany
marvin.braun@uni-goettingen.de
[2] Technische Universität Dresden, 01069 Dresden, Germany

Abstract. Patient data is mainly transmitted in the form of unstructured free texts in medical documentation. Natural language processing (NLP)-based systems can help to structure and extract information from these free texts to support the work of healthcare professionals. However, the healthcare sector must meet certain information quality requirements to comply with regulations and provide optimal patient care. Therefore, we argue that a design guideline is needed to tailor NLP-based systems to the unique requirements of clinical processes and to catalyze the practical application of such systems. In this paper, we report the results of a design science research study, focusing on the requirements of NLP-based systems used by healthcare professionals. In doing so, we shed light on the needs of practitioners when working with sophisticated NLP-based systems that extract and analyze text-based information from medical documentation. By providing evaluated, testable propositions and detailed design principles, we support the practical endeavor of such systems.

Keywords: Healthcare · Natural language processing · Design principles

1 Introduction

The digitalization of healthcare services has brought various benefits for health professionals and patients, such as the reduced documentation efforts through the introduction of electronic health records (EHR) [1] or the improvement in disease detection through machine learning (ML) algorithms [2]. In general, the rise of digital information sources such as EHRs increases the volume of available data for patient care and research [3, 4]. Techniques and methods of ML, such as natural language processing (NLP), can be utilized to process this text-based patient information in an automated way. Several studies have shown that this can be utilized in a large variety of healthcare contexts [3, 5]. However, the full potential of NLP in healthcare is still far from being unleashed and practical implementation is still limited [6]. One reason for this is that NLP-based systems need to fulfill the unique requirements of medical care on information quality [7] to be useful for health professionals in daily practice. Information quality can directly influence the medical decision, thus, it needs to be as detailed and accurate as

© Springer Nature Switzerland AG 2022
A. Drechsler et al. (Eds.): DESRIST 2022, LNCS 13229, pp. 183–194, 2022.
https://doi.org/10.1007/978-3-031-06516-3_14

possible [8]. This requirement affects the structure and wording of medical documents. Large parts of EHRs (~70%) still contain free text [9] instead of standardized medical encodings. Free texts allow health professionals to describe the patient's state in more detail [7] and are, therefore, often used to meet the demand of high information quality [9]. Nevertheless, the heterogeneous wordings and structures of documentation are hindering automatic processing [3]. Hence, health professionals often need to transfer the data of patients manually into their health information systems (IS). This process is error-prone and time-consuming [7].

Therefore, the information contained in free text often stays in this unstructured format and hence is not used for further data processing. To relieve the health professionals from this information transferring task, novel NLP-based systems can carry out automated information extraction from free texts. To overcome the limited application of NLP services in healthcare, we identify a demand for a validated and contextualized design guideline that developers can leverage to effectively create NLP-based systems for health professionals (e.g., physicians and nurses) to support clinical processes. Against this background, we aim to answer the following research question:

RQ: How should NLP-based systems be designed to analyze textual medical information and meet the requirements of health professionals?

To address this research question, we follow a design science research (DSR) approach, adapted from the works of Hevner et al. [10, 11]. Our DSR approach is iterative [12], meaning that we refined our design principles through multiple cycles. The paper is structured as follows: The current state of natural language processing in healthcare is described in Sect. 2. Afterward, we present our DSR approach in Sect. 3. Section 4 presents the results of our work, i.e., the design requirements and principles, as well as their evaluation through testable propositions (TP). Last, we discuss our findings and briefly conclude our work in Sect. 5.

2 Natural Language Processing in Healthcare

In healthcare, a rising, aging population and the burden of disease lead to higher expenditures [13] and hence put health service providers under increasing cost pressure [6, 14, 15]. These challenges are emphasized by the global shortage of health professionals [16], which is expected to increase further due to the ongoing COVID-19 pandemic [17], widening the already large gap between demanded and feasible health services. These challenges create the need for innovative solutions [18].

Digitalization, and especially AI, is seen as a part of solving these problems because it has the potential to improve patient care and shorten costs at the same time [19]. AI can achieve this by providing algorithms that efficiently process a large amount of information and overtake tasks that had to be done by humans previously [19]. For instance, it is commonly used for medical decision support (precision medicine), where large amounts of data are used to predict therapy outcomes [4]. These capabilities for decision support are, for example, used in radiology for analyzing images [4] or in cardiology for analyzing free texts [20].

One vital part of the information that needs to be processed in the healthcare domain is text-based information. This type of information is typically processed by NLP, a building block of AI [21]. NLP-based systems can fulfill a wide range of tasks, such as extracting biomedical information from discharge letters, radiology reports, or other health-related documents. The potential benefits of NLP in healthcare have been demonstrated in various for topics around neoplasms, circulatory diseases, digestive and endocrine, nutritional, and mental disorders [3].

However, current research mostly demonstrated the application of sophisticated NLP algorithms (on which we focus in this work) in isolated research environments and not in real practical settings. For instance, most commercial information extraction systems used in patient care still rely on rule-based approaches. In general, rule-based approaches are not flexible and are outperformed by newer, AI-based NLP methods [3]. With the rise of (AI-based) statistical algorithms in NLP, new potentials, but also new challenges for systems occur [3]. Specific problems mentioned are the need for result validation and missing transparency if NLP relies on statistical models because the results are not comprehensible for health professionals. These problems do not exist for rule-based (i.e., hard-coded rules) NLP-based systems [3] because health professionals can comprehend rules in comparison to statistical models. To sum up, NLP is already applied across many different research projects in healthcare. However, to be fully implementable into daily clinical practice. there is still a lack of knowledge on how NLP-based systems should be designed to be supportive for patient care and suitable for usage by health professionals.

3   Research Design

Our study follows a DSR approach based on works Hevner et al. [10, 11] (Fig. 1), similar to [22], and is part of an NLP-based system development project to support patient care-related processes of a German surgery clinic (University Hospital Göttingen).

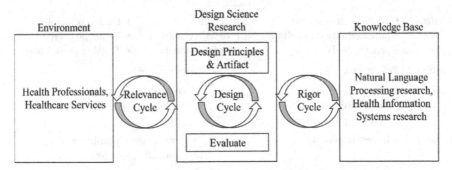

Fig. 1. Configuration of our design science research approach based on [10].

According to health professionals of the clinic, medical documents (e.g., reports or discharge letters) from patients are still transferred manually, which is not only very time-consuming but also error-prone. The objective of the project is the development of a system to automatically process medical documents by extracting pre-defined information such as personal identifiers and relevant medical information (e.g., the primary diagnosis and related symptoms) to reduce the redundant and pressuring workload of medical staff. During a pilot phase, we concluded that sophisticated (ML-based) NLP algorithms are needed to extract the correct information from the very heterogeneous documents. Moreover, we argue that a DSR approach is needed to fully understand and address the practical requirements of health professionals and incorporate these into our solution. Besides instantiating such a system, the project aims to develop a design guideline for dissemination [23] and a blueprint for other clinical use cases.

Our DSR approach follows an iterative process (i.e., two iterations, see Table 1) and considers the contextual environment (i.e., health professionals) to discuss and refine our findings as well as the current knowledge base (i.e., research) (Fig. 1).

Table 1. Design science research process based on [10, 11, 22].

Iteration 1	Relevance Cycle	Rigor Cycle	Design Cycle
Inputs	• Healthcare literature • Health professionals	• Literature review	• Requirements • Health professionals
Methods	• Literature review • Focus groups	• Content analysis	• Prototyping
Steps	• Search and analyze literature • Discuss findings with health professionals	• Analyze publications • Identify challenges of health professionals when operating NLP-based systems • Identify current designs and features of NLP-based systems in healthcare	• Formulate design principles from literature with experts • Create a visual instantiation of the design principles
Results	• NLP-based systems lack usability for health professionals	• Requirements for NLP-based systems of health professionals	• Design principles • Visual prototype • Testable propositions
Iteration 2	Relevance Cycle		Rigor Cycle
Inputs	• Design principles • Visual prototype • Testable propositions		• DSR process • Evaluated design principles, prototype
Methods	• Expert interviews		• Iterative theory building • Publication writing
Steps	• Evaluate the testable propositions • Refine design principles		• Finalize design theory • Summarize DSR process and outputs
Results	• Evaluated design principles and prototype		• Refined design principles • This article

3.1 First Iteration

In the first iteration, we initially identified the underlying problem of NLP-based systems in healthcare, which we described in the introduction. This problem was further discussed with health professionals from our practical cooperation and confirmed (**relevance cycle**).

Next, we conducted a literature review to engage the knowledge base and identified the current state of NLP-based systems in healthcare. We screened recently published literature reviews of NLP in healthcare [3, 24, 25]. Additionally, we screened their referenced literature. To ensure that we did not miss relevant works, we performed a keyword search in the following databases: The Association for Information Systems, PubMed, IEEE, and Web of Science. We chose these databases because they cover different research streams (medicine/health, information systems, and information technology). Our used keywords were: *("health*" OR "medic*" OR "clinic*") AND ("natural language processing" OR "NLP")*. After extensive screening and a forward and backward search, we identified 13 relevant papers for our work. The identified papers either described a use-case of NLP in healthcare and its related usability challenges or specifically focused on one or multiple problems of NLP in healthcare. Our literature review focused on these and excluded studies that solely focused on developing better-performing NLP algorithms for a specific problem. However, most screened studies did not focus on usability for health professionals. The outcome of this cycle is literature-based requirements (**rigor cycle**).

Subsequently, the requirements were discussed with health professionals, and the first suggestions for design principles were made. Additionally, a visual prototype was constructed to evaluate our design principles by TPs according to Gregor et al. [26] (**design cycle**).

3.2 Second Iteration

The second iteration focused on evaluating our findings and preparing these for communication. To verify the design principles and guarantee the visual prototype's usability in our practical cooperation, we conducted seven semi-structured expert interviews with health professionals at the surgery clinic of the University Hospital Göttingen, including physicians, nurses and medical Ph.D. students. We chose this set of interviewees to cover different perspectives on the topic. To verify the elicited requirements, our findings (design principles, visual prototype, and the TPs) were discussed with experts. The interviews were structured as follows. To not bias the interviewees with our visual prototype, they were first asked about their requirements for an information extraction system in the domain of healthcare. Subsequently, we presented the literature-based requirements and design principles and discussed these with the interviewees. Last, the visual prototype was presented, and the interviewees were asked about their first impression and suggestions to improve it further. Moreover, we discussed the derived TPs with the interviewees to confirm the possible impact of the design principles on addressing the derived requirements of health professionals (**relevance cycle**).

Using the findings of the expert interviews, we refined the design principles, summarized our findings (this paper), and prepared them for communication (this submission) (**rigor cycle**). In Sect. 4, we present the **final refined** requirements, design principles, TPs, and the visual prototype.

4 Understanding the Design of NLP-Based Systems in Healthcare

4.1 Meta Requirements and Design Principles

In total, five requirements were derived by conducting the literature review (methodology described in Sect. 3.1). Design principles to address the five meta requirements were developed by discussing them with seven health professionals. In the following, the groups of requirements and matching design principles will be described (Fig. 2).

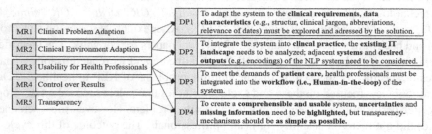

Fig. 2. Matched requirements and design principles.

The first derived meta requirement (**MR1–Clinical Problem Adaption**) refers to the need to adapt NLP solutions to the individual clinical problem it shall support in patient care [7, 27, 28]. Multiple authors described scenarios where their clinical problem had special requirements, e.g., through the uniqueness of the disease it shall capture [27–29]. This has several reasons; first, the high dimensionality of clinical problems that need to be captured by the NLP algorithm, such as the timely detection of symptoms [27] or the high amount of free text for mental health diseases, need to be considered when designing NLP-based systems [29].

Similarly, studies suggest that developers need to be aware of the implementation environment and adapt the NLP-based system accordingly (**MR2–Clinical Environment Adaption**). This requirement has two underlying propositions that need to be considered to fulfill it. First, basic conditions of the implementation environment, such as the institution's infrastructure, system requirements, and data usage agreements, impact the implementation of NLP-based systems [24]. Second, since health data structures are very heterogeneous, even inside single institutions, the heterogeneity of the real-world data needs to be assessed and the NLP-based system needs to be trained on data from a representative dataset [30]. **DP1** is based on the meta-requirements MR1 and MR2 and demands that to adapt the system to the clinical environment and underlying problem, characteristics of the data (e.g., clinical jargon and abbreviations) need to be considered when designing NLP-based systems [25, 31, 32].

The next requirement (**MR3–Usability for Health Professionals**) refers to the ability of the NLP solution to be effectively used by clinical staff to conduct their tasks [6,

25, 32–34] and can be defined as usability of the system. As pointed out by Velupillai et al., there is still a lack of practical evaluations of NLP-based systems because health professionals are often not integrated into the development process [27]. The need to test the developed systems in practice and integrate relevant stakeholders into the development process is emphasized by additional authors [25, 32]. **DP2** is built upon MR2 and MR3 and states that relevant stakeholders must be interviewed to identify adjacent systems and desired outputs (e.g., clinical encodings). DP2 ensures that the NLP solution is integrated into the existing IT landscape of the institution to avoid standalone systems that health professionals cannot use because they do not offer the demanded interfaces to their daily used health IS [25].

The following requirement (**MR4–Control over Results**) states that health professionals demand control over the final results of the NLP-based system [31–34]. Otherwise, they might be reluctant to use AI or feel deprived of their autonomy [24]. **DP3** is derived from MR3 and MR4 and declares that health professionals must be integrated into the workflow of the NLP-based system if it is used for patient care to maintain their control. A human-in-the-loop approach was mentioned several times, where the human makes the final decision if the results are correct [32–34]. This finding is consistent with the contributions of several authors, which state that health professionals demand a high degree of autonomy and control to accept a system [35].

The last requirement, (**MR5–Transparency**), addresses the capability of the NLP-based system to let the health professionals comprehend its working and provide insights into explanations for the results [32, 35]. In general, it is assumed that health professionals highly prefer transparent algorithms over black boxes, despite better results that could be achieved by the latter ones [32]. The last design principle, **DP4**, is derived from MR3 and MR5 and defines that transparency and usability are improved for health experts by highlighting uncertainties of the NLP-based system.

4.2   Evaluation of Findings

In line with the proposed methodology of Gregor and Jones [26], we formulated TPs to evaluate our design principles (Table 2). Gregor and Jones explain that TPs follow the pattern that "if a system or method that follows certain principles is instantiated then it will work, or it will be better in some way than other systems or methods" [26].

Table 2. Testable propositions for evaluation.

Testable proposition	If the system follows the proposed design…
TP1 (DP1)	…it will address the clinical problem more precisely, thereby yielding higher perceived usefulness by health professionals than similar IS
TP2 (DP2)	…it will be integrated into the IT landscape more seamlessly, thereby yielding higher perceived usefulness by health professionals than similar IS

(continued)

Table 2. (*continued*)

Testable proposition	If the system follows the proposed design…
TP3 (DP3)	…it will offer health professionals more control over the system, thereby yielding higher perceived acceptance than similar IS
TP4 (DP4)	…it will offer higher comprehensibility of results for health professionals, thereby yielding higher trust and perceived explainability than similar IS

To validate or reject the TPs, we instantiated the design principles in a visual prototype placed in the domain of (health-related) information extraction. The NLP-based system's purpose was derived from our cooperation project with the University Hospital Göttingen and aimed at extracting relevant patient information, including personal information, diagnosis, treatments, and medication from discharge letters, which is still done manually in a time-intensive and error-prone manner by health experts. The idea was to utilize NLP to encounter the heterogenous wordings and structures with a more flexible approach and partly automatize the process.

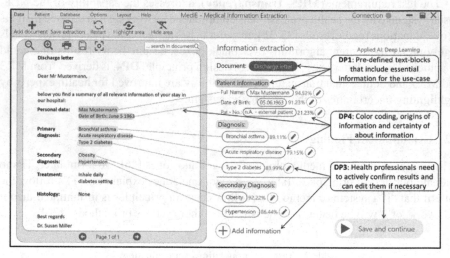

Fig. 3. Visual prototype with design principles.

We incorporated the following design principles into the visual artifact: DP1, DP3 and DP4 (Fig. 3). DP2 was not visually instantiable because it deals with the integration of the system into the environment. The structure of data sources (mainly discharge letters) was screened, and pre-defined text blocks (e.g., patient information and diagnosis) were implemented according to the task to implement DP1 into our visual prototype. DP3 was integrated by involving the health professionals in the workflow. Users can edit and add information. Moreover, they must confirm the correctness of extracted information.

Last, DP4 was included in the visual prototype by two explanation mechanisms. A color-coding scheme and percentages show the algorithm's certainty about the correctness of the information.

With this visual prototype, we aimed to evaluate the TPs, which would either confirm or reject our derived design principles and requirements. Additionally, to interviewing physicians (3), we interviewed Ph.D. students (3) and one study coordinator (1) to leverage varying views of potential adopters (n = 7). Regarding the overall impression of the visual prototype, most interviewees found the design easy to understand and quickly knew how it worked. The general side-to-side layout of the system was positively rated since it allows direct comparison of the original discharge letter with the extracted information.

The first testable proposition, **TP1**, which we visualized through pre-defined categories and information that need to be present (DP1), was confirmed by the health professionals: *"There is certain information that we need. For example, we often use the date of birth to identify the patient."*. The interviewees confirmed that the system would not be perceived as useful if patients cannot be identified. The second testable proposition, **TP2**, was only discussed with the interviewees since we could not visualize it (DP2). However, the interviewees highlighted the need for the system to be interoperable with already implemented systems to be usable in a daily manner. The third testable proposition, **TP3**, which was instantiated by control features (e.g., add and edit buttons) (DP3), was rated positively by the interviewees: *"I can't judge how good the program is. But honestly, in the end, it is about a patient's health, and I would say that you should always be able to control the information again."*. This finding was supported by other interviewees which stated that they would always need to check the information for correctness again. The last testable proposition, **TP4**, which included explainability mechanisms (DP4), was also confirmed by the interviewees. Specifically, the origin indicator and the color-coding were rated positively: *"Basically, I think it would be better if you can understand where the information comes from because that can also be relevant for the clinical course."*. However, the health professionals saw the percentage as somewhat confusing:" *I would leave out the percentages, it suggests that the person may have to interpret the shown number."*. Most experts suggested that color-coding should be sufficient to indicate the correctness of the information. Overall, the evaluation verified our TPs and allowed us to get valuable insights into the perspectives of different health professionals. Moreover, we can confirm the positive effect of applying our design principles in practice.

5   Discussion and Conclusion

Current research often focuses on the fast-advancing technical side of applying NLP to isolated medical problems. However, these technical advances rarely make it into practice or consider any aspects of system implementation [6]. This paper contributes to this research by building a bridge between the technical side of NLP-based systems and the requirements of health professionals in practical use. We provide a comprehensive design guideline for NLP-based systems that acknowledge the specific requirements of health professionals to support the analysis of textual medical information. Following the

DSR contribution levels provided by Gregor and Hevner [23], our work can be classified as a level 2 contribution.

This study is especially targeted at developers and hence provides practical implications. Our design principles address the described practical challenges of NLP in healthcare. By following our design principles, developers will be able to utilize NLP as a technology in healthcare and, thereby, reduce the time health professionals need to spend extracting and analyzing text-based patient information. Nevertheless, the new capabilities of NLP-based systems also put health professionals into a new role of supervising IS. Our design principles address this new role of health professionals through the implementation of active augmentation. This is achieved by explainability and control mechanisms that allow the health professionals to adhere to the demanded information quality. To sum up, by reducing the effort and maintaining the information quality, our design principles aim to ultimately contribute towards improved medical care and enable the implementation of sophisticated NLP algorithms into daily clinical practice.

Regarding the theoretical implications of our study, our research contributes to the following domains: First, this work contributes to the literature on NLP-based systems in healthcare [3, 31]. This domain still lacks design guidelines to address the usability needs of different disciplines when implementing NLP as a technology. Our work emphasizes the need for socio-technical interdisciplinary (IS) research to implement sophisticated NLP algorithms into daily clinical practice. Second, this study contributes to the research area of human-computer interaction in healthcare. In our work, we demonstrate what requirements health professionals have on information and how the interaction can be shaped by single design elements to augment and support the users.

Of course, our study is also subject to limitations. Our findings were validated by experts from only one institution on a qualitative basis, even though they work at different departments and hierarchy levels. Future work could evaluate our validated design guideline by conducting quantitative studies. In our next step, we will develop a usable prototype and test it with health professionals in the field, which should generate further insights into requirements and features demanded by health professionals.

References

1. Mihailescu, M.I., Mihailescu, D., Carlsson, S.A.: Understanding healthcare digitalization: a critical realist approach. In: ICIS (2017)
2. Safdar, S., Zafar, S., Zafar, N., Khan, N.F.: Machine learning based decision support systems (DSS) for heart disease diagnosis: a review. Artif. Intell. Rev. **50**(4), 597–623 (2017). https://doi.org/10.1007/s10462-017-9552-8
3. Wang, Y., et al.: Clinical information extraction applications: A literature review. J. Biomed. Inform. **77**, 34–49 (2018)
4. Davenport, T., Kalakota, R.: The potential for artificial intelligence in healthcare. Futur. Healthc. J. **6**, 94–98 (2019). https://doi.org/10.7861/futurehosp.6-2-94
5. Jiang, F., et al.: Artificial intelligence in healthcare: Past, present and future. Stroke Vasc. Neurol. **2**, 230–243 (2017). https://doi.org/10.1136/svn-2017-000101
6. Panch, T., Mattie, H., Celi, L.A.: The "inconvenient truth" about AI in healthcare. npj Digit. Med. **2**, 77 (2019). https://doi.org/10.1038/s41746-019-0155-4

7. Ford, E., Carroll, J.A., Smith, H.E., Scott, D., Cassell, J.A.: Extracting information from the text of electronic medical records to improve case detection: a systematic review. J. Am. Med. Informatics Assoc. **23**, 1007–1015 (2016)
8. Holzinger, A., Geierhofer, R., Mödritscher, F., Tatzl, R.: Semantic information in medical information systems: utilization of text mining techniques to analyze medical diagnoses. J. Univers. Comput. Sci. **14**, 3781–3795 (2008)
9. Jensen, K., et al.: Analysis of free text in electronic health records for identification of cancer patient trajectories. Sci. Rep. **7**, 46226 (2017). https://doi.org/10.1038/srep46226
10. Hevner, A.: A three cycle view of design science research. Scand. J. Inf. Syst. 19 (2007)
11. Hevner, A., et al.: Design science in information systems research. Manag. Inf. Syst. Q. **28**, 75 (2004)
12. Peffers, K., Tuunanen, T., Rothenberger, M.A., Chatterjee, S.: A design science research methodology for information systems research. J. Manag. Inf. Syst. **24**, 45–77 (2007). https://doi.org/10.2753/MIS0742-1222240302
13. Dieleman, J.L., et al.: Factors associated with increases in us health care spending, 1996–2013. JAMA **318**, 1668 (2017). https://doi.org/10.1001/jama.2017.15927
14. Fernández, E.: Innovation in healthcare: harnessing new technologies. J. Midwest Assoc. Inf. Syst. 107–120 (2017). https://doi.org/10.17705/3jmwa.00034
15. Johansen, F., van den Bosch, S.: The scaling-up of neighbourhood care: from experiment towards a transformative movement in healthcare. Futures **89**, 60–73 (2017). https://doi.org/10.1016/j.futures.2017.04.004
16. World health statistics 2019: monitoring health for the SDGs, sustainable development goals. https://apps.who.int/iris/handle/10665/324835. Accessed 28 Jan 2022
17. Shreffler, J., Huecker, M., Petrey, J.: The impact of COVID-19 on healthcare worker wellness: a scoping review. West. J. Emerg. Med. 21 (2020)
18. Gjestsen, M.T., Wiig, S., Testad, I.: What are the key contextual factors when preparing for successful implementation of assistive living technology in primary elderly care? A case study from Norway. BMJ Open **7**, e015455 (2017)
19. Sunarti, S., Fadzlul Rahman, F., Naufal, M., Risky, M., Febriyanto, K., Masnina, R.: Artificial intelligence in healthcare: opportunities and risk for future. Gac. Sanit. **35**, S67–S70 (2021). https://doi.org/10.1016/j.gaceta.2020.12.019
20. Koleck, T.A., Dreisbach, C., Bourne, P.E., Bakken, S.: Natural language processing of symptoms documented in free-text narratives of electronic health records: a systematic review. J. Am. Med. Informatics Assoc. **26**, 364–379 (2019)
21. Khurana, D., Koli, A., Khatter, K., Singh, S.: Natural Language Processing: State of The Art, Current Trends and Challenges (2017)
22. Brendel, A.B., Brennecke, J.T., Hillmann, B.M., Kolbe, L.M.: The design of a decision support system for computation of carsharing pricing areas and its influence on vehicle distribution. IEEE Trans. Eng. Manag. 1–15 (2020)
23. Gregor, S., Hevner, A.R.: Positioning and presenting design science research for maximum impact. MIS Q. **37**, 337–355 (2013)
24. Fu, S., et al.: Clinical concept extraction: a methodology review. J. Biomed. Inform. **109**, 103526 (2020)
25. Houssein, E.H., Mohamed, R.E., Ali, A.A.: Machine learning techniques for biomedical natural language processing: a comprehensive review. IEEE Access. **9**, 140628–140653 (2021). https://doi.org/10.1109/ACCESS.2021.3119621
26. Jones, D., Gregor, S.: The anatomy of a design theory. J. Assoc. Inf. Syst. **8**, 312–335 (2007). https://doi.org/10.17705/1jais.00129
27. Velupillai, S., et al.: Using clinical natural language processing for health outcomes research: overview and actionable suggestions for future advances. J. Biomed. Inform. **88**, 11–19 (2018)

28. Sterckx, L., et al.: Clinical information extraction for preterm birth risk prediction. J. Biomed. Inform. **110**, 103544 (2020). https://doi.org/10.1016/j.jbi.2020.103544
29. Viani, N., et al.: A natural language processing approach for identifying temporal disease onset information from mental healthcare text. Sci. Rep. **11**, 757 (2021)
30. Fu, J.T., Sholle, E., Krichevsky, S., Scandura, J., Campion, T.R.: Extracting and classifying diagnosis dates from clinical notes: a case study. J. Biomed. Inform. **110**, 103569 (2020). https://doi.org/10.1016/j.jbi.2020.103569
31. Zheng, K., et al.: Ease of adoption of clinical natural language processing software: an evaluation of five systems. J. Biomed. Inform. **58**, S189–S196 (2015)
32. Nehme, F., Feldman, K.: Evolving role and future directions of natural language processing in gastroenterology. Dig. Dis. Sci. **66**(1), 29–40 (2020). https://doi.org/10.1007/s10620-020-06156-y
33. Petitgand, C., Motulsky, A., Denis, J.L., Régis, C.: Investigating the barriers to physician adoption of an artificial intelligence-based decision support system in emergency care: an interpretative qualitative study. Stud. Health Technol. Inform. **270**, 1001–1005 (2020). https://doi.org/10.3233/SHTI200312
34. Wen, A., et al.: Desiderata for delivering NLP to accelerate healthcare AI advancement and a mayo clinic NLP-as-a-service implementation. npj Digit. Med. **2**, 130 (2019). https://doi.org/10.1038/s41746-019-0208-8
35. Liberati, E.G., et al.: What hinders the uptake of computerized decision support systems in hospitals? A qualitative study and framework for implementation. Implement. Sci. **12**, 113 (2017)

A Digitization Pipeline for Mixed-Typed Documents Using Machine Learning and Optical Character Recognition

Tizian Matschak[1]([⊠]) [iD], Florian Rampold[1] [iD], Malte Hellmeier[2] [iD],
Christoph Prinz[1] [iD], and Simon Trang[1] [iD]

[1] University of Goettingen, Wilhelmsplatz 1, 37073 Goettingen, Germany
{tizian.matschak,florian.rampold,christoph.prinz,
strang}@uni-goettingen.de
[2] Fraunhofer ISST, Emil-Figge-Straße 91, 44227 Dortmund, Germany
malte.hellmeier@isst.fraunhofer.de

Abstract. Although digitization is advancing rapidly, a large amount of data processed by companies is in printed format. Technologies such as Optical Character Recognition (OCR) support the transformation of printed text into machine-readable content. However, OCR struggles when data on documents is highly unstructured and includes non-text objects. This, e.g., applies to documents such as medical prescriptions. Leveraging Design Science Research (DSR), we propose a flexible processing pipeline that can deal with character recognition on the one hand and object detection on the other hand. To do so, we derive Design Requirements (DR) in cooperation with a practitioner doing prescription billing in the healthcare domain. We then developed a prototype blueprint that is applicable to similar problem formulations. Overall, we contribute to research and practice in multiple ways. First, we provide evidence for selected OCR methods provided by previous research. Second, we design a machine-learning-based digitization pipeline for printed documents containing both text and non-text objects in the context of medical prescriptions. Third, we derive a nascent design pattern for this type of document digitization. These patterns are the foundation for further research and can support the development of innovative information systems leading to more efficient decision making and thus to economic resource usage.

Keywords: Document image analysis · Optical character recognition ·
Digitization · Machine learning · Preprocessing · Postprocessing

1 Introduction

Modern business is typically driven by computer-based decision making. Data is collected and aggregated along the value-chain and then used as input for, e.g., analysis, simulations, automatization, or predictions. Researchers have already demonstrated that data-driven decision-making can improve the effectiveness of decision-makers [1] and thus can lead to performance improvements [2].

A. Drechsler et al. (Eds.): DESRIST 2022, LNCS 13229, pp. 195–207, 2022.
https://doi.org/10.1007/978-3-031-06516-3_15

However, a significant share of businesses operates with paper-based documents, resulting in the data being unavailable for digitized decision-making algorithms. Especially in processes where plenty of transactions with low individual margins occur, human-based digitization of printed data is not suitable and is an unnecessary waste of resources. A prime example of such a process is the reimbursement of medical prescriptions in health insurances. Although most prescriptions only trigger small reimbursements (< 20 Euro), the total amount of payments performed in 2020 in Germany was 40.9 billion euros [3]. The processing entails verifying whether a patient is a customer of the insurance or whether the pharmacy and the doctor acted according to existing laws and contracts. Human-based processing of all prescriptions is too tedious, resulting in especially small-value prescriptions being not validated systematically, causing damage to the whole healthcare system.

Optical Character Recognition (OCR) is a potential solution since it converts printed text into machine-encoded formats to be analyzable, editable, and searchable [4, 5]. However, modern OCR approaches have in common that they can recognize text in different forms but fail on objects, symbols, or noisy images. Particularly in specialized domains, such as healthcare or legal, symbols, handwritten edits, or other marks on the document pose hurdles for OCR technologies. This is where object recognition comes into play. Object detection can be used to extract additional relevant data from documents where OCR fails. It offers the potential to enrich the available database for decision-makers and computerized approaches. In this context, the problem domain comprises two topics: *OCR* and *object recognition* research.

Current research offers valuable contributions regarding sub-problems of recognizing printed data on documents (e.g., [6, 7]). A significant number of studies have been done on OCR and pre- and postprocessing steps and how to combine these techniques. Object recognition is one of the most prominent subjects in a separate research stream under the artificial intelligent topic. Against this background, we identify the challenge of leveraging past research contributions with our own results in an integrated end-to-end pipeline that allows both recognizing text and non-text objects on documents.

We follow the iterative Design Science Research (DSR) approach by [8] to design a pipeline for digitization in the context of medical prescription documents as a reference process for big-data environments with small transaction margins. Here, we cooperate with a practitioner and domain experts, including IT and pharmacy staff, to capture a full picture of the requirements and test the prototype in the problem domain.

Our research contributes to the discussion of innovative printed data recognition in at least three ways. First, we provide evidence for selected OCR methods provided by previous research and developed additional ones. Second, we designed a machine-learning-based digitization pipeline for printed documents containing both text and non-text objects in the context of medical prescriptions. Third, we derived a nascent design pattern for this type of document digitization. These patterns are the foundation for further research and can support the development of innovative information systems leading to more efficient decision making and thus to economic resource usage.

2 Research Background

As motivated in the introduction, Document Image Analysis (DIA) has been a promising and relevant field of research in recent years. DIA includes various methods to process scanned images of analogous documents to recognize text and graphics and extract valuable information from them [9]. Hence, DIA can be divided into two fields of interest: text recognition and graphics processing. While text recognition aims to identify textual components of document images, graphical processing covers recognition of non-textual elements such as tables, images, and logos [9, 10]. Following our research goal, the underlying research specifically targets textual document processing through OCR as many input formats contain unstructured text elements. OCR requires a multi-staged analysis containing image acquisition, location segmentation, preprocessing, knowledge extraction, and postprocessing of the results [11]. The knowledge extraction process itself is composed of various steps such as segmentation, feature extraction, and classification tasks.

We applied localization segmentation to cut the image into appropriate chunks for the digitization pipeline. Following [10], it is vital to comprehend the physical and logical layout of the document image in advance. The process contributes to the differentiation of segments with text, images, and other graphical content. Therefore, enclosed components need to be separated in a meaningful way for further analysis [12].

Preprocessing ensures that images with noisy quality can be handled and processed efficiently. Depending on the input format, text can be machine-coded or handwritten, which makes it crucial to manipulate document images for high processing quality. In the next step, characters are segmented either implicitly or explicitly to be able to recognize them separately by the OCR engine. In the feature extraction component, relevant information about the textual, geometric, structural, and content-based information is recognized and applied to find features that uniquely identify characters [9, 13]. Once important features are extracted, the classification process ensures that each recognized character is assessed to its corresponding class. Especially the recognition of text segments often utilizes neural networks [14–17]. The knowledge extraction process can be done in two ways. First, existing libraries such as Tesseract can be applied to build on existing trained AI models. Exemplary usage can be found in [18] and [19]. Especially when text is handwritten or highly unstructured, customized approaches in the form of personalized OCR pipelines are used [14, 15, 20]. However, these approaches have the objective of recognizing text exclusively for conventional documents. Medical documents such as prescriptions usually contain handwritten signings, stamps, and symbols. These differ from common characters and require custom handling, which cannot be achieved with standard OCR implementations. We, therefore, aim to make use of AI to build a flexible pipeline that extends existing OCR approaches and contributes to sophisticated DIA.

3 Research Approach

This paper aims to provide an IT artifact as a solution to a real-world business problem. Here, designing such an artifact is complex and calls for creative advances in domains in which existing theory is often insufficient [21]. Therefore, we set up a DSR project by following the IS research framework by [21]. DSR is defined as *"[...] a research activity that invents or builds new, innovative artifacts for solving problems or achieving improvements [...]"* [22] and has been proven to be useful to this type of research in several studies, e.g., [23] and [24].

The iterative process of designing an adequate artifact that contributes to a solution of the research problem is handled by applying the six-step DSR process model by [25]. Here, since the research problem is derived from the operation and related literature, we follow the problem-centered approach starting with step one (see Fig. 1).

The problem statement was formulated in the introduction (step 1). In the second step ("Objectives of a Solution"), we derive requirements (e.g., [26]) based on existing literature, user stories, an analysis of legal requirements. In addition, we conducted expert interviews with employees of a German prescription billing company facing the problem of processing millions of paper-based prescriptions per year. These requirements are prioritized to come to a starting point for an initial prototype. The third step deals with determining the artifact's desired functionality and architecture. This includes selecting suitable frameworks and algorithms as well as designing-related decisions regarding the user interface, amongst others. Based on that, the actual artifactual solution is designed and developed. Subsequently, the efficacy of the developed artifact to solve the problem is demonstrated using documents and their manually digitized content for different types of simulations (step 4).

Afterward, the artifact will be evaluated in a case study by applying it to 1,298 documents, comparing the results to the current approach, and evaluating the results with domain experts of research and practice (step 5). In this case, phases three to five were looped iteratively until the artifact matched the previously defined requirements [8].

Finally, the DSR process concludes with promoting the developed solution and its design patterns in this paper and thus making the insight publicly available and adding our results to the knowledge base of printed data recognition.

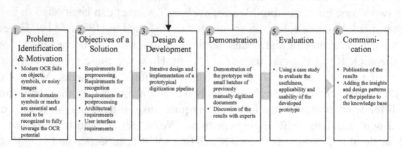

Fig. 1. Adapted research approach following [25]

4 Objectives of a Solution

Following our goal of designing a digitization pipeline for documents that contain both printed text and symbols/objects, we define design requirements (DR) for a corresponding prototype (Fig. 1 – Step 2). Here, as argued by [27], it is crucial for the success of the DSR project to involve those affected by the practical problem that was characterized in the initial problem statement (Fig. 1 – Step 1). To do so, we first interviewed employees of a practitioner to get practical requirements from the end-users firsthand. In this case, the practitioner is a company doing prescription billing focusing on computer-assisted prescription evaluation and fraud detection. Thus, the practitioner has experience with extracting data from a paper-based document and already uses OCR-digitized data as input for further procedures.

Based on these practical requirements, we continued to derive theoretical requirements from related literature and research on the OCR and object detection domain applications. For simplification and emphasis on the business problem, we assume that paper-based documents have been previously scanned, so we have digital images as input to our prototypical pipeline.

In summary, functional and non-functional DR were defined as shown in Table 1. After a prioritization in cooperation with the practitioner, DR1 to DR5 and DR9 to DR13 were planned to be realized in a first iteration of the DSR process (Fig. 1).

Table 1. Design requirements for a prototypical digitization pipeline

Functional Design Requirements	Description	Topic
DR1: Input Robustness	The algorithm handles varying formats of input images to provide a higher utility for the user	Preprocessing
DR2: Quality Harmonization	The approach harmonizes the image quality for improved operation of other algorithms [28–31]	
DR3: Data Localization	Relevant structured data fields are localized and identified. Thus, the algorithm automatically differentiates between structured text and objects/symbols	Data Localization & Segmentation
DR4: Data Segmentation	Data areas are segmented due to their data type (text, no text) [32]	
DR5: Data Labeling	The localized and identified data areas are labeled according to their semantic meaning	

(continued)

Table 1. (*continued*)

Functional Design Requirements	Description	Topic
DR6: Text Recognition	An OCR algorithm digitizes printed text on input images	Recognition
DR7: Object Recognition	The prototype is able to detect and classify objects and transform them into a defined data format	
DR8: Data Validation	Recognized data is validated according to the desired semantical format and logic to evaluate the output quality	Postprocessing
Non-Functional Design Requirements	Description	Topic
DR9: Scalability	The pipeline offers sufficient efficiency to process large image batches in a reasonable amount of time	Performance
DR10: Understandability ad Maintainability	The pipeline is understandable and easily maintainable	Usability
DR11: Modular Expandability to Specialized Use Cases	The pipeline is extendible and offers adaption potentials to specialized use cases due to modularization	Modularization
DR12: Minimal Downtime	The pipeline must be highly reliable and avoid downtimes	Reliability
DR13: Result Accuracy	The pipeline should improve the current business processes. Thus, it should provide a sufficient data quality not to compromise potential efficiency gains	Accuracy

5 Results

As motivated by the research approach, we iteratively build our digitization pipeline based on the introduced DRs. Next, we first describe necessary preprocessing steps to improve the quality of the input documents. The identification of text, objects, and postprocessing steps to further enhance the output are described afterward.

5.1 Preprocessing

In order to improve the output quality of OCR algorithms and pipelines, preprocessing steps are needed, which results in better accuracy [33, 34]. In the context of our use case, color data is not needed to detect font or objects on the document that have to be digitized. Therefore, the process starts with aligning, scaling, and coloring at pixel-data-level to create input robustness (DR1). The information is compressed to an array of lower dimensions, so we can decrease the computation complexity of our digital preprocessing [28]. To do so, we grayscale the digital representation and binarize the cell values (DR2). The resulting data represents the minimum of currently available pixel data. That results in a maximum contrast between background and foreground to detect relevant shapes and fonts. For some algorithms like contour detection that are described later, the colors are inverted to black background pixels and white content pixels to improve the performance.

Furthermore, reducing noisy data is one of the main challenges of the pursued preprocessing. It must deal with error pixels (mostly single or small bunches of pixels without sensible content) and gridlines. To remove error pixels, we implemented a sliding kernel that checks whether the majority of the underlying pixels are the same color. An example is shown on the left side of Fig. 2. The process sometimes leads to a deterioration of the text quality. Therefore, three eroding steps are applied to transform light into thick text strokes in the first iteration. Besides this, a different method for removing gridlines is implemented. By first detecting lines as contours and then filling these contours with the specific background color, disturbing horizontal and vertical lines are removed. The results are illustrated on the right side of Fig. 2.

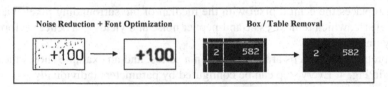

Fig. 2. Removal of noise and lines

We used the pytesseract Python wrapper based on the open-source Tesseract library in our experiments and evaluations with the practitioner for the OCR process. The Tesseract library can recognize multi-line text parts. Our experiment shows that this works well with structured documents like book pages where every line is clearly visible but fails with other more unconstraint types like formulas or freely designed pages. To improve this, we split the document into single one-line part images and disabled Tesseract's multi-line function, which results in more accurate recognition. This is realized by a part segmentation method (DR3&4) based on content areas, as shown on the left of Fig. 3. To do so, we first preprocessed the image with several kernel operations extending the activated pixels using the opencv library. This not only closes minimal gaps between, e.g., characters and thus leads to detecting whole words but also contributes to better image content quality when used sparingly. Consequently, we use this technique also for preprocessing of image parts before OCR or object recognition (see right side of Fig. 3). Subsequently, shapes are detected and compared to other shapes (and their distances) nearby and the overall image to get an idea of whether it is a text row, a single word, or, e.g., a non-text object.

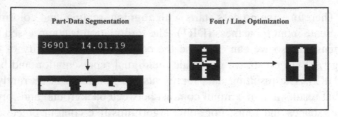

Fig. 3. Part-data segmentation and line optimization

Separating a document into parts results in more opportunities to apply specialized improvement methods to different sections of the document as described in the postprocessing section. Instead of one OCR call, multiple calls are executed, each one for every one-line part image. Moreover, the cropped partial images are first subjected to further preprocessing steps before passing them to the Tesseract OCR engine. After the previously described steps, including the segmentation of the region of interest, an equally sized white border is added around the whole part image, which leads to better detection results because the text is in a more centralized position. Due to the binarization of the image, the edges of the font and other objects have hard edges. They are softened by two blurring steps that result in better OCR results. While average blurring replaces the central pixel with the average of the surrounding pixels based on the kernel size, median blurring replaces the central pixel with the median of the surrounding pixels based on the kernel size, which removes salt-and-pepper noise and yields to a better performance on noisy images [35].

All preprocessing steps are connected in a series, and an example shows the entire pipeline in Fig. 4. Every step can be configured by parameters individually.

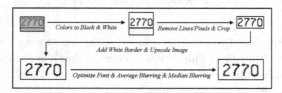

Fig. 4. Entire OCR preprocessing pipeline example

5.2 Recognition

After executing the preprocessing pipeline, image segments are used as input to the actual data recognition. These part images are classified and then processed by their appropriate recognition method (DR5). Thus, printed text (including numbers and characters) is processed by OCR, while our object detection module processes non-text objects. The default Tesseract OCR engine comes with a pre-trained model, which represents a decent compromise of accuracy and runtime. This was used on a first try and was later replaced by the most accurate open-source model, which drastically increases accuracy with an almost imperceptible change in execution time (DR6).

For the detection of non-text objects, self-trained TensorFlow-based RCNNs are used. In our case, the practitioner is interested in recognizing two types of markups within the document (DR7). After evaluating several different RCNN architectures, three hidden dense layers proved to best fit our use case with regard to accuracy and processing. In addition, the RCNN is also enriched by dropout layers to prevent fast overfitting [36]. However, the optimal configuration of this neural network can differ from case to case. Therefore, we also implemented an automatic hyperparameter optimization. Consequently, the user only needs to provide labeled images of the non-text object of interest, and our approach handles cropping out the relevant pixels and training the neural network and optimization of hyperparameters. As a result, our pipeline provides easy adaptability and little effort for users.

5.3 Postprocessing

Postprocessing procedures have been added after the identification and OCR engine steps for further optimization. As mentioned before, the segmentation into part-images allows individual handling for every section. If some parts of the original document are number only fields represented by cropped part-images, a replacement method is added. It uses a simple RegEx pattern to replace letters with their similar-looking number. This transforms, for example, the OCR output "I5Z87" into "15287" (DR8). Similar approaches are implemented for different fields to use the knowledge of the contents of a field or part to postprocess the detected content as much as possible.

5.4 Evaluation

Following the implementation and demonstration of our digitization pipeline, we evaluate our prototype regarding its applicability, usability, and usefulness. To objectively evaluate our application, we used several Key Performance Indicators (KPIs) and expert interviews.

As introduced by DR13, accuracy is a critical KPI, which has to reach a certain threshold to meet our requirements. In our definition, accuracy (subsequently named data accuracy) describes the number of correct data points relative to the total number of recognized data points [37]. In the case of OCR, this means correctly extracted data fields relative to the overall number of processed data fields. Additionally, lead time was also introduced as another relevant OCR KPI (DR9). With reference to [38], we defined lead time as the time difference between the single image workflow started by the user and the finalized associated database entry. The proportion of perfect cases was also added to our KPI set regarding the practitioner and its business context. This is defined as the number of images that have been recognized correctly (with 100% data accuracy) relative to the total number of processed prescription images. The KPI is of high interest for the practitioner since (in theory) perfectly-recognized images must not be reviewed manually again and save limited and costly resources.

We used two different sets of images as input data for the actual evaluation. The first image set (image set 1) consists of 883 images of mixed quality. Thus, our application confronts images with lots of noise, handwritten data, containing grid lines, and good-quality images. The second image set (image set 2) includes 415 images of image set 1 (real subset), which are most comparable to the usual input data our application would face during a productive run at the practitioner's site. We use manually digitized data of all prescription images as a single source of truth for checking the recognition results (Table 2).

Table 2. Evaluation results of image Set 1 and image Set 2

KPI	Image set 1	Image set 2
Data Accuracy	90.69%	94.44%
Lead Time*	≈17 s	≈17 s
Proportion of Perfect Cases	21.76%	33.33%

* The application and the evaluation process ran on a stack of Docker containers having the following hardware resources assigned:16 GB RAM, 2.3 GHz 8-Core Intel Core i9 9th Generation CPU, and three parallel workers.

6 Discussion and Conclusion

The research in this paper aims to implement a feasible prototype to digitize paper-based documents containing text and non-text objects. Followingly, our results will be discussed primarily in the contribution of the research process to theory and practice as stated by [39]. When classifying our research based on the DSR contribution framework by [39], we argue that it can be considered an exaptation mainly since we deal with high solution maturity and a low application domain maturity in our project.

Our developed solution follows design decisions derived from other research and adapts them to our specific problem context. Thereby, an artifact is instantiated that not only solves our explicit requirements but is also scalable and transferable through its modular architecture. It can be applied to other problem domains by using the described design decisions to digitize information of documents having similar characteristics. Thus, the pipeline can be applied on, e.g., the digitization of medical prescriptions of other countries, documents like bank transfer forms that own a certain structure within the documents, and types of data fields that follow specific logics and formats. Therefore, the image preprocessing, data localization, and segmentation modules can be adapted so that the artifact can detect regions of interest on text images in general. Based on that, an OCR engine can transform the located and preprocessed images into text. Followingly, the data validation module is optional whenever a use case requires checking the logic and format of transformed data to evaluate the quality of the transformation. The implemented approaches in preprocessing and data field detection combined with a Machine Learning (ML) model to detect characteristics in the image can be seen as design patterns and contribute to the scientific knowledge base. Because of their striving for generality, they can be applied in different problem contexts.

In addition to the theoretical implications, we were able to derive implications that can be highly useful for practitioners. Next to the theoretical relevance, DSR aims to solve practitioners' real-world problems and thus fulfills practical relevance [21]. In this study, we built a computer-based application that covers a fully-fledged pipeline, starting with image preprocessing and ending with postprocessing recognized data within the healthcare or particularly in the medical prescriptions industry. Our computer-based approach is reusable and can be adapted to similar problems, due to its modularity. Modules dealing with the localization and segmentation of data fields can be adapted to the medium that should be digitized. Thus, the results of this study provide the groundwork for the development of a flexible system that efficiently digitizes documents by reducing time and cost issues since human interaction is limited to a minimum. Furthermore, the data in its digitized form does not only provide the basis for the electronic prescription but also generates a standardized data pool that can be used for further analyses in the healthcare industry. The increased quantity and availability of digitized data can make extensive data analyses possible in the future.

Nevertheless, our research is also subject to limitations. Firstly, the artifact was evaluated particularly within the business context of one practitioner in the healthcare industry. The company provided a limited set of 883 distinct prescriptions our prototype has been evaluated on. Secondly, there are limitations regarding the rigor cycles. In this context, we conducted a several literature reviews that were highly dependent on the chosen search strategy. The limitations are determined by selected search terms and the identified literature. Thirdly, the implemented algorithm mainly covers the processing of images printed in black and white but not in color. The algorithm can read colored input images but fails in recognition due to a lack of input images provided by the practitioner. We are excited to see how research and practice will build on our results and use data to contribute to economical and high-quality healthcare.

References

1. Troisi, O., Maione, G., Grimaldi, M., Moia, F.: Growth hacking: Insights on data-driven decision-making from three firms. Ind. Mark. Manage. **90**, 538–557 (2020)
2. Long, Q.: Data-driven decision making for supply chain networks with agent-based computational experiment. Knowl.-Based Syst. **141**, 55–66 (2018)
3. ABDA, B.D.A.e.V.: Arzneimittel 2020: Weniger Rezepte, aber höhere GKV-Ausgaben im Pandemie-Jahr. (2021)
4. Memon, J., Sami, M., Khan, R.A., Uddin, M.: Handwritten optical character recognition (OCR): a comprehensive systematic literature review (SLR). IEEE Access. **8**, 142642–142668 (2020)
5. Tappert, C.C., Suen, C.Y., Wakahara, T.: The state of the art in online handwriting recognition. IEEE Trans. Pattern Anal. Mach. Intell. **12**, 787–8–8 (1990)
6. Gupta, M.R., Jacobson, N.P., Garcia, E.K.: OCR binarization and image pre-processing for searching historical documents. Pattern Recogn. **40**, 389–397 (2007)
7. Shinde, A.A., Chougule, D.G.: Text pre-processing and text segmentation for OCR. Int. J. Comp. Sci. Eng. Technol. **2**, 810–812 (2012)
8. Hevner, A.R.: A three cycle view of design science research. SJIS. **19**, 87–92 (2007)
9. Akram, S., Dar, M.-U.-D., Quyoum, A.: Document image processing - a review. IJCA. **10**, 35–40 (2010)
10. Javed, M., Nagabhushan, P., Chaudhuri, B.B.: A review on document image analysis techniques directly in the compressed domain. Artif. Intell. Rev. **50**(4), 539–568 (2017). https://doi.org/10.1007/s10462-017-9551-9

11. Singh, S.: Optical Character Recognition Techniques: A Survey. Int. J. Adv. Res. Comp. Eng. Technol. **4**, 6 (2013)
12. Chaudhuri, A., Mandaviya, K., Badelia, P., Ghosh, S.K.: Optical character recognition systems. In: Chaudhuri, A., Mandaviya, K., Badelia, P., and K Ghosh, S. (eds.) Optical Character Recognition Systems for Different Languages with Soft Computing, pp. 9–41. Springer International Publishing, Cham (2017)
13. Islam, N., Islam, Z., Noor, N.: A survey on optical character recognition system. Journal of Information. **10**, 4 (2016)
14. Ning, M.: Id card number identification based on artificial neural network. In: 2016 International Conference on Robots & Intelligent System (ICRIS), pp. 207–212. IEEE, ZhangJiaJie, China (2016)
15. Sakhawat, Z., Ali, S., Hongzhi, L.: Handwritten digits recognition based on deep Learning4j. In: Proceedings of the 2018 International Conference on Artificial Intelligence and Pattern Recognition - AIPR 2018, pp. 21–25. ACM Press, Beijing, China (2018)
16. Trier, F., Afzal, M.Z., Ebbecke, M., Liwicki, M.: Deep convolutional neural networks for image resolution detection. In: Proceedings of the 4th International Workshop on Historical Document Imaging and Processing - HIP2017, pp. 77–82. ACM Press, Kyoto, Japan (2017)
17. Zhai, X., Bensaali, F., Sotudeh, R.: OCR-based neural network for ANPR. In: 2012 IEEE International Conference on Imaging Systems and Techniques Proceedings, pp. 393–397. IEEE, Manchester, United Kingdom (2012)
18. Alday, R.B., Pagayon, R.M.: MediPic: a mobile application for medical prescriptions. In: IISA 2013, pp. 1–4. IEEE, Piraeus, Greece (2013)
19. Carchiolo, V., Longheu, A., Reitano, G., Zagarella, L.: Medical prescription classification: a NLP-based approach. In: Presented at the 2019 Federated Conference on Computer Science and Information Systems September 26 (2019)
20. Tabrizi, S.S., Cavus, N.: A hybrid KNN-SVM model for iranian license plate recognition. Procedia Comp. Sci. **102**, 588–594 (2016)
21. Hevner, A.R., March, S.T., Park, J., Ram, S.: Design science in information systems research. MISQ, 75–105 (2004)
22. Iivari, J., Venable, J.R.: Action research and design science research - seemingly similar but decisively dissimilar. In: ECIS 2009 Proceedings, p. 13 (2009)
23. Hillebrand, K., Johannsen, F.: KlimaKarl – a chatbot to promote employees' climate-friendly behavior in an office setting. In: International Conference on Design Science Research in Information Systems and Technology, pp. 3–15. Springer, Cham (2021)
24. Fruhling, A., Hall, M., Medcalf, S., Yoder, A.: Designing a Real-Time Integrated First Responder Health and Environmental Monitoring Dashboard. In: Hofmann, S., Müller, O., Rossi, M. (eds.) DESRIST 2020. LNCS, vol. 12388, pp. 28–34. Springer, Cham (2020). https://doi.org/10.1007/978-3-030-64823-7_3
25. Peffers, K., Tuunanen, T., Gengler, C.E., Rossi, M., Hui, W.: The design science research process: a model for producing and presenting information systems research. J. Manag. Inf. Syst. **24**, 45–77 (2007)
26. Weigand, H.H.: Value expression in design science research. In: 2019 13th International Conference on Research Challenges in Information Science (RCIS), pp. 1–11. IEEE, Brussels, Belgium (2019)
27. McCarthy, S., Rowan, W., Lynch, L., Fitzgerald, C.: Blended stakeholder participation for responsible information systems research. CAIS. **47**, 716–742 (2020)
28. Gideon, S.J., Kandulna, A., Kujur, A.A., Diana, A., Raimond, K.: Handwritten signature forgery detection using convolutional neural networks. Procedia Comp. Sci. **143**, 978–987 (2018)

29. Tse, J., Jones, C., Curtis, D., Yfantis, E.: An OCR-independent character segmentation using shortest-path in grayscale document images. In: Sixth International Conference on Machine Learning and Applications (ICMLA 2007), pp. 142–147. IEEE, Cincinnati, OH, USA (2007)

30. Gleichman, S., Ophir, B., Geva, A., Marder, M., Barkan, E., Packer, E.: Detection and segmentation of antialiased text in screen images. In: 2011 International Conference on Document Analysis and Recognition, pp. 424–428. IEEE, Beijing, China (2011)

31. Kasar, T., Kumar, J., Ramakrishnan, A.G.: Font and background color independent text binarization. In: Second International Workshop on Camera-based Document Analysis and Recognition, pp. 3–9 (2007)

32. Manikandan, A.V.M., Choudhury, S., Majumder, S.: Text reader for visually impaired people: any reader. In: 2017 IEEE International Conference on Power, Control, Signals and Instrumentation Engineering (ICPCSI), pp. 2389–2393. IEEE, Chennai (2017)

33. Palekar, R.R., Parab, S.U., Parikh, D.P., Kamble, V.N.: Real time license plate detection using openCV and tesseract. In: 2017 International Conference on Communication and Signal Processing (ICCSP), pp. 2111–2115. IEEE, Chennai (2017)

34. Sajjad, K.M.: Automatic License Plate Recognition using Python and OpenCV. Department of Computer Science and Engineering MES College of Engineering, p. 5 (2010)

35. Berk Kaan Kuguoglu: How to use image preprocessing to improve the accuracy of Tesseract. https://bit.ly/3HDmkZY. last accessed 16 July 2020

36. Wager, S., Fithian, W., Wang, S., Liang, P.S.: Altitude training: strong bounds for single-layer dropout. Adv. Neu. Info. Proc. Sys. 1–8 (2014)

37. Jin Huang, Ling, C.X.: Using AUC and accuracy in evaluating learning algorithms. IEEE Trans. Knowl. Data Eng. 17, 299–310 (2005).

38. Tang, O., Grubbström, R.W., Zanoni, S.: Planned lead time determination in a make-to-order remanufacturing system. Int. J. Prod. Econ. 108, 426–435 (2007)

39. Gregor, S., Hevner, A.R.: Positioning and presenting design science research for maximum impact. MISQ. 37, 337–355 (2013)

Fathers with Postpartum Depression: A Problem Space Exploration

Pavankumar Mulgund[1]([✉]), Sandeep Purao[2], and Lavlin Agrawal[1]

[1] University of Buffalo, Buffalo, NY, USA
pmulgund@buffalo.edu
[2] Bentley University, Waltham, MA, USA
spurao@bentley.edu

Abstract. Postpartum depression (PPD) for men is a significant but little-understood public health concern that affects ~14% of men in the US. It has not received adequate attention from society, researchers or health practitioners. This paper describes results from problem space exploration for this concern as the first step in a design science research process. Following the double-diamond model of design thinking, we describe two iterations. The first relies on qualitative analysis of data obtained from a social media platform to extract themes that describe pain points of new fathers. The second uses a participatory design exercise to identify personas and meta-requirements. Member-checking and triangulation efforts following the two iterations validate our findings that provide a rich understanding of this public health concern. A secondary contribution of our work is a demonstration of how design thinking techniques can be used within a design science research process to enhance the relevance cycle. We conclude by pointing to next steps for developing design science solutions in response to the problem.

Keywords: Problem space · Theory of the problem · Postpartum depression among men · Design thinking · Double diamond approach

1 Introduction

Although postpartum depression (PPD) has been traditionally associated with women (Thomas 2010), an increasing body of evidence is starting to point to PPD among new fathers (Kim and Swain 2007). Explanations offered include dramatic shifts in parenting and changes in societal expectations of fathers (Roy 2014). Instead of their traditional role as financial support providers, fathers are increasingly expected to be more actively involved in parenting and childcare, a role that many fathers are underprepared for (Roy 2014). This lack of understanding and skills appears to be a leading cause of greater risk of PPD in many new fathers (Kim and Swain 2007).

Early scholarly work points out that health professionals and family members tend to write off any symptoms (that may point to the incidence of PPD) among new fathers as a normal part of the transition to parenthood. There are, however, adverse consequences

© Springer Nature Switzerland AG 2022
A. Drechsler et al. (Eds.): DESRIST 2022, LNCS 13229, pp. 208–220, 2022.
https://doi.org/10.1007/978-3-031-06516-3_16

of this neglect. Not only does paternal PPD adversely affect the individuals themselves, it can also limit their capacity to provide emotional support to their partners and children (Kim and Swain 2007). Therefore, it is critical to develop technology-based solutions that can address different aspects of the problem and develop greater awareness of this public health concern. Our effort in this project is to use the design science research (DSR) approach to build and evaluate technology artifacts to address (different parts of the) problem (Hevner et al. 2004).

However, as we started the research journey, we realized that we simply did not understand the problem well. Our early explorations with healthcare professionals (partners in this research project) showed that there were several significant differences from other ailments, diseases and public health concerns. Examples included lack of awareness, associated stigma, absence of any preemptive screening and risk assessment services, lack of resources to teach behavior skills, different patient population, new symptoms, lack of acceptance, and several others. With the scale of the problem (af-fecting ~14% of new fathers in the US), we realized that a deeper understanding of the problem space was an important pre-requisite to the design of technological solutions. Contemporary writings about DSR provide few pointers for this important phase of the process beyond describing it as 'awareness of the problem' (Vaishnavi and Kuechler 2012), or suggest actions such as 'performing literature reviews' (Schoormann et al. 2020). For a problem space that is new, not well described, and emerging (such as paternal PPD), we did not consider these approaches as adequate.

This paper, therefore, focuses on exploring the problem space for the challenges faced by new fathers with PPD. We note that our efforts are similar in spirit to the articulation by Majchrzak et al. (2016), who point out the need for "a theory of the problem [that] aims to elucidate a specific organizational or societal challenge to assemble (or illustrate with empirical data) different understandings of how and why a problem occurs". Such exploration of the problem space is particularly relevant for exploring complex multidimensional problems of a substantive nature (such as the incidence of PPD among new fathers). Such problems have several interconnected challenges that may have divergent expectations from different stakeholders, making it difficult to develop on the problem statement (and design effective solutions).

Our goal in this paper is to explore this problem space (PPD in new fathers) in a systematic manner. We do this with specific techniques from design thinking (Brenner 2016) – the double-diamond approach (Gustafsson 2019), and the persona technique (Brangier and Bornet 2011), relying on established practices such as secondary data scraping, thematic analysis of textual data, and inputs from subject-matter experts. Together, these techniques allow us to identify the pain points of new fathers, specific personas, and meta-requirements that can point to solution possibilities. In the remainder of the paper, we first provide a brief background on PPD in new fathers (Sect. 2), describe the research approach (Sect. 3), present the findings of problem space exploration (Sect. 4), and briefly conclude with a discussion of problem space exploration and pointers to next steps (Sect. 5).

2   Background: New Fathers with PPD

Postpartum depression (PPD) is a form of major depressive disorder (MDD) occurring soon after a child's birth. The Diagnostic and Statistical Manual of Mental Disorders, Fifth Edition (DSM-5) defines depression with peripartum onset as a major depressive episode during pregnancy or within four weeks after parturition. PPD among men (the focus on this study) is a significant public health problem affecting approximately 14% of new fathers in the US (Scarff 2019) with the possibility of prevalence much higher in certain at-risk segments such as fathers with lower incomes, young or old age fathers, or fathers with ethnic minority backgrounds. Although not much data exists about fathers in non-traditional settings, such as stay at-home fathers, nonbiological fathers (e.g., stepfathers), or single fathers, scholars speculate that their unique situations may increase the risk for paternal PPD (Eddy et al. 2019). The limited scholarly work conducted over the last decade points to several potential risk factors that can contribute to the development of PPD in men, including a history of depression, marital discord, poverty, maternal depression, and unintended pregnancy (Melrose 2010). Further, the incidence of paternal postpartum depression can be significant where maternal postpartum depression is also present (Melrose 2010). Despite these few studies, and the scale of the problem (potentially affecting ~14% of new fathers in the US), PPD in men has not received adequate attention from researchers, health practitioners and society (Kim and Swain 2007). One factor that contributes to the lack of attention (and possible under-diagnosis of paternal PPD) is the difference in symptomatic manifestation of PPD in men compared to women (Eddy et al. 2019). New fathers with PPD exhibit frustration, annoyance, and anger instead of the telltale signs of maternal PPD such as sadness and listlessness, and new red flags such as emotional withdrawal, focus on work, complaints of pain with no cause, and troublesome behaviors such as extramarital sex, drugs, or gambling (Eddy et al. 2019).

3   Research Approach

We focus on the early stage – problem exploration – within the design science research (DSR) approach (Hevner et al. 2004) where the research team develops awareness of the problem and its nuances (Vaishnavi and Kuechler 2012; Majchrzak et al. 2016). Prior scholarship emphasizes the need to establish problem relevance (Hevner 2007). However, few scholarly reports elaborate this phase of the research process or describe how specific techniques and tools may be used for this purpose. This 'problem of the problem' (Herwix and Haj-Bolouri 2021) is particularly acute for emerging and ill-defined concerns, where appeal to kernel theories and literature review cannot help. On the other hand, work related to design thinking (Brenner 2016) proposes several techniques and guidelines that are squarely aimed at analyzing the problem and generating insights, including any ambiguities and tradeoffs. Examples include adopting a beginner's mindset, ethnographic observation, immersion in the user's context, empathy mapping, and character profiles creation (Brown 2009).

Within the DSR community, there is growing recognition of the importance of problem space exploration in recent years. Purao (2021) proposes several considerations for identifying and articulating design research problems. Maedche et al. (2019) conceptualize the problem space in DSR and clarify the meanings of and relations among terms such as needs, goals, and requirements. Herwix and Haj-Bolouri (2021) develop a problem assessment framework that scholars can use to assess and justify the importance of the research problem. Beyond the DSR community, Majchrzak and colleagues (2016) note the importance of articulating holistic and divergent perspectives about the problem before exploring solutions.

Motivated by these contemporary perspectives, our work focused on exploring the emerging, ill-defined set of concerns broadly outlined as 'postpartum depression among new fathers.' There was one critical difference between how we proposed to use design thinking techniques (Brenner 2016). Instead of relegating these techniques purely towards design (Kelly 2004), we aimed at knowledge generation, similar to a move towards a theory of the problem suggested by Majchrzak et al. (2016). We viewed the design thinking techniques as cognitive and empirical tools to lend tactical support for problem space exploration.

We relied on the double diamond model (DDM) of design thinking (Gustafsson 2019) because of its alignment with the DSR methodology. DDM consists of two divergence-convergence cycles. The first focuses on understanding the perspectives and challenges of the intended users with the objective of 'finding, prioritizing and articulating the right problem'. It corresponds to the relevance cycle of DSR methodology. The second cycle focuses on iteratively designing and evaluating prototypes with the objective of 'developing the right solution' (Gustafsson 2019) and corresponds to the design cycle of the DSR process. Our focus on problem space exploration, therefore, made DDM a suitable choice. Figure 1 maps the double-diamond model to a DSR process, and highlights the scope of our work.

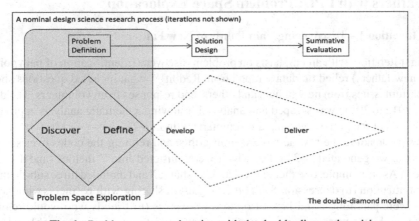

Fig. 1. Problem space exploration with the double-diamond model

Within the problem space exploration phase we conducted two iterations. The first iteration (discover) included data scraping data from a social media platform Reddit™ and analyzing it to discover expressions of pain points from new fathers. Unlike other social media websites (e.g. Facebook or Twitter), Reddit is a social news aggregation and discussion website optimized for community, conversation, and discussion management. It is the 7th most visited website in the US (source: Alexa Internet) with 430 million monthly active users and 30 billion+ monthly views. The subreddit community for new dads with PPD has more than 1800 members. The scraped data included 346 transcripts from 121 individuals seeking help and several hundred others responding to those questions. Each included: the query, response(s) posted, and non-identifiable information about each contributor. We de-identified and cleansed these before moving to qualitative thematic analysis (Fereday and Muir-Cochrane 2006) that included: (a) open coding, (b) refining the codes by examining the tagged fragments, and (c) clustering the codes to identify themes (see Holm and Severinsson 2014).

In the second iteration (definition), we conducted a workshop with subject matter experts (using themes identified in the first iteration as the starting point). The participants included two obstetrics and gynecology nurses, one pediatric nurse, two primary care providers, and one mental health counselor. The inspiration for this workshop were the principles of participatory design (Spinuzzi 2005), which emphasize democracy, mutual learning, tacit knowledge, and collective creativity to acknowledge the central role of potential users in problem understanding and design ideation. During the workshop (which lasted for approximately 2 h), each subject matter expert examined the themes and provided insights into the challenges new fathers face. The workshop produced composite personas (Madsen and Nielson 2010) and mapped pain points for each persona grounded in the themes from the first iteration. Across the two iterations, our efforts lead to exploring the problem space (as part of the larger design science research methodology). Finally, we integrated outcomes from the two iterations to identify meta-requirements from the problem class. We develop these outcomes next.

4   Fathers with PPD: Problem Space Exploration

4.1   Iteration 1 – Discovering Pain Points of New Fathers

The first iteration, with an emphasis on problem discovery (identification of pain points from new fathers) relied on data scraped from Reddit™, what included questions about postpartum issues from new fathers and others, and responses from volunteers. The data (from 2012 to 2021) was scraped and analyzed following a thematic analysis approach. The details of the process applied are summarized in Fig. 2.

By (re-)reading the text across 346 transcripts, and refining the codes over several iterations, we generated 143 codes, which were clustered into 7 themes (and 19 sub-themes). As an example, one theme was labeled "shame," and included three sub-themes: lack of attention (to depression from others), guilt of sharing with partners (who themselves were parenting), and lack of options to express (to friends who would remind that my problems were minor compared to what my wife was going through). Table 1 summarizes the themes and sub-themes (pain points).

Consider the following excerpts. Each illustrates the complex challenges that new fathers face as they battle the feelings of shame (theme 4), deal with panic triggers (theme 5) or engage in self-destructive behaviors (theme 6) and find little support (theme 3).

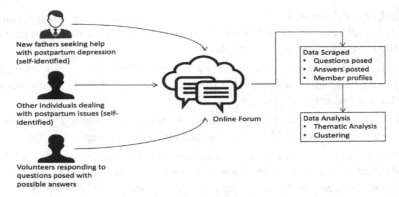

Fig. 2. Data collection and analysis from an online forum

Table 1. Themes and sub-themes (pain points of new fathers)

Theme	Sub-themes
1 Obstacles to self-care	1 Increased time demands
	2 Challenges with sleeping
	3 Challenges with personal grooming
2 Realization of new responsibilities	4 Increased stress
	5 Increased financial pressure
	6 Demands of infant care
3 Lack of support	7 Lack of empathy from friends and family
	8 Feeling of loneliness
	9 Lack of options to express
4 Feelings of shame	10 Lack of attention to depression
	11 Guilt of sharing with partners
	12 Losing a sense of identity
5 Triggers	13 Panic attack
	14 Suicidal thoughts
6 Self-destructive behaviors	15 Substance abuse
	16 Alcoholism
	17 Excessive smoking
7 Changes to home routine	18 Shifting to new role as a parent
	19 Need to attend to new chores at home

"I think one of the reasons why so few men actually will talk about this is because ... I felt really guilty for a while after for not being strong enough." (theme 4, sub-theme: guilt of sharing with partners)

"I finally figured out that it was mostly being caused by my very high anxiety, and it was made worse when I began smoking cigarettes." (theme 5, sub-theme: excessive smoking)

"I had severe depression for our second. At about 2.5 months I was having murder/suicidal thoughts." (theme 6, sub-theme: suicidal thoughts)

"This happened to me when my son was born. I tried talking about this with a good friend of mine ... [who] told me that I needed to shut up and that nothing I was going through could even compare to what my wife must be going through." (theme 3, sub-theme: lack of options to express)

During the analysis cycles, we realized that the themes and sub-themes pointed to concerns that were inherently inter-related. As an example, consider the three sub-themes (e.g. feeling of loneliness) for the theme "lack of support." Excerpts that were coded and mapped to these sub-themes, often had elements of other sub-themes (e.g. guilt of sharing with partners) from the theme "feelings of shame." Although we describe the pain points above as a somewhat ordered table, the greater realization for us was that the lack of attention to PPD among new fathers was tied to the lack of acknowledgement of this public health concern. As we continued our effort (second iteration), we focused on developing an understanding of new fathers as individuals.

4.2   Iteration 2 – Developing Prototypical Personas

The second iteration, to develop a sense of new fathers as individuals (exploring and identifying prototypical personas) relied on a workshop with subject-matter experts (nurses, primary care providers, mental health counselors) who volunteered to participate because of their experiences in dealing with postpartum depression among new fathers. The workshop included a structured discussion, moderated by the lead researcher. A preliminary version of results from the first iteration were used to seed the discussion. The discussion provided insights into the pain points (themes). The participants contributed anecdotes and examples that underscored the importance of several pain points, and the rationale for the incidence of pain points. As an example, the workshop revealed that there were, in fact, few to no resources that new fathers could access (theme: lack of support). Without the acknowledgement of paternal postpartum depression as a concern, new fathers had no descriptors they could use to understand for themselves or express to others what they were going through, which led to guilt (theme: feelings of shame).

Based on the rich anecdotes, the research team constructed prototypical personas (for a holistic understanding of users not only in terms of their pain points, but also their goals and capabilities (Mesgari et al. 2018)). This allowed greater appreciation of the problem scope and ensured that the emphasis shifted (from the researchers) to the potential users of the artifact or the service. The prototypical personas identified (with goals and aspirations, needs, and pain points), were refined via presentations to other health professionals (doctors, nurses and social workers). Table 2 summarizes.

Table 2. Personas discovered

Persona
Peter, Age 21, Young, first-time parent

•   Pain points: Feels lonely, Worried about financing his kid's life
   •   Needs: Support and understanding and friends, Interactions with support group
   •   Goals: Wants to build a financial platform for his kid's life

George, Age 35, Established, first-time parent struggling with substance dependence

•   Pain points: Gets anxious easily, Smokes or uses marijuana to cope with anxiety
   •   Needs: Coping mechanism to deal with anxiety, Support against substance abuse
   •   Goals: Wants to cope with anxiety without getting into substance abuse

Ernesto, Age 28, First-time parent with a struggling spouse

•   Pain points: Overwhelmed with new responsibilities, Depressed spouse
   •   Needs: Interactions with support group, Managing relationship with spouse
   •   Goals: Balancing new work responsibilities with being a father

Amit, Age 42, Established, first-time parent

•   Pain points: Negative feelings and anxiety, Has problems managing sleep and time
   •   Needs: Someone to discuss his problems, Resources to manage time and sleep
   •   Goals: Develop sleep and time management skills

Darius, Age 37, Third-time parent with a history of depression

•   Pain points: Overwhelmed by the responsibility of multiple children, Struggles with loneliness and feelings of shame and guilt
   •   Needs: Friends and social life, Resources to cope with feelings of shame and guilt,
   •   Goals: Looking for quick screening and access to support services

Consider one of the personas above (George, age 35). The structured discussions lead to the following description of his persona.

George has always struggled with depression since grade school and has received treatment and counseling. In his late 20's, things gradually improved, and he got married. He did not report an episode of depression for about seven years. The situation changed dramatically after the baby's arrival. His anxiety is no longer manageable. He has returned to smoking as escape. His wife is not happy about this turn of events. He constantly worries about everything, and his smoking seems to be related to his worrying.

The personas George (described above), Peter (who had an active social life), Ernesto (whose wife also suffers from depression), Amit (who simply needs sleep), and Darius (who tries to manage multiple children) revealed an inter-related and overlapping set of pain points; and helped the research team to appreciate how each may interact with any solutions constructed (with the design science approach). The personas, therefore, served as clues to design ideation (similar to design thinking) as well as problem appreciation (to develop a better understanding of potential users).

4.3 Integrating Across Iterations – Identifying Meta-requirements

A reflective examination of the pain points (iteration 1) and prototypical personas (iteration 2) allowed the research team to gradually transition from (a) a deeper understanding of the problem space to (b) requirements for potential solutions that may be designed in response. This conceptual move required the research team to appreciate the difference between "needs and goals" on one hand, and "requirements" on the other (Maedche et al. 2020), mapped to the ideas of meta-requirements (Walls et al. 1992). As we reflected on and integrated the findings from the two iterations to identify meta-requirements for potential solution(s) for this problem (class), we were able to define the solution space, i.e. possible solutions that can address anxiety disorders among men with the specific case of postpartum depression among new fathers as an instance of this problem class. Table 3 summarizes.

Table 3. Meta-requirements for (potential) solution space

Meta-requirements (elaborated for the problem of PPD among new fathers)

Educating expectant and new fathers about paternal postpartum depression
    Why: Lack of awareness of the condition for new fathers
    How: Education about symptoms, incidence, treatment options, myths
    Potential benefits: Can promote healthy behaviors

Providing self-screening tools for paternal postpartum depression
    Why: Lack of understanding about how the condition can manifest
    How: Preemptive screening (e.g. Edinburgh scale (Cox et al, 1987))
    Potential benefits: Can identify individuals at risk

Offering support and interaction
    Why: Lack of supportive and knowledgeable social connections
    How: Interactive chat, Access to certified professionals as counselors
    Potential benefits: Can answer questions, can help with loneliness

Motivating care-seeking behaviors
    Why: Need for a positive outlook and amplifying a sense of hope
    How: Sharing success stories from others, Gamification, Content framing
    Potential benefits: Better care-seeking can result in faster recovery

Providing resources to deal with specific problems
    Why: Lack of information to address specific problems
    How: Resources for time management, self-care, and others aimed at new fathers
    Potential benefits: New fathers can access specific solution possibilities

Monitoring progress and continued support
    Why: Need for persistence in addressing the condition
    How: Sending reminders and nudges to encourage change
    Potential benefits: Prevent regression, Drive behavioral change

The meta-requirements suggest several possibilities for designing artifacts. These remain on our future agenda following the DSR approach. Here, we describe one last step in problem space exploration, validation of the findings so far.

4.4 Validating the Findings

Our intent was to establish the credibility of our findings as a step towards the design of artifacts following the DSR approach, i.e., we do not claim that the findings represent a comprehensive problem explication. Instead, we articulate (a) pain points, (b) prototypical personas, and (c) meta-requirements towards generating effective design solutions. Our efforts to validate the findings should be seen in this light, following pointers from Maedche et al. (2020) for conceptualizing the problem space. Table 4 summarizes our efforts, similar to qualitative research (e.g. Lincoln and Guba 1985).

Table 4. Validating the findings

Effort	Description	Outcomes
Triangulation	Outcomes from the first iteration (pain points) seeded the discussion in the second iteration	The subject matter experts confirmed the findings and provided rationale
Member-checking	Presentation to five health professionals such as doctors and nurses not involved in the workshop (in iteration 2)	The health professionals confirmed and refined persona descriptions and pain points
Research Presentations	Presentation of initial results from thematic analysis at health IT research conferences (SIG health pre-ICIS workshop)	Positive feedback on methodological rigor for thematic analysis

5 Discussion and Next Steps

In this paper, we have demonstrated a systematic approach to problem space exploration for paternal postpartum depression. Our approach outlines a possible response to an important concern that has received much recent attention (Purao 2021; Herwix and Haj-Bolouri 2021; Maedche et al. 2020). In doing so, we have also demonstrated how the design science research approach can incorporate design thinking techniques that go beyond traditional inputs to problem definition such as literature review and prior theories (see Schoormann et al. 2020), which cannot illuminate the problem space for emerging concerns such as paternal postpartum depression.

Some of our study's findings are in line with other studies exploring mental health illnesses such as depression (Patterson et al. 2022), obsessive-compulsive disorder (Arabatzoudis et al. 2021), and social anxiety disorder (Jarzabek et al. 2018). Similar requirements that can be generalized revolve around the need for information about the condition, self-screening for risk, and encouragement to take the next steps towards seeking care. However, our study extends prior literature by emphasizing the importance of resources needed to manage practical challenges such as finance and time management, and social pressures that result from gendered roles. The study also notes the need for progress tracking and continued support to ensure that fathers with PPD do not acquire and regress to high-risk behaviors such as smoking, binge drinking, or even drugs. Further, our work is unique in that it, through prototypical personas, points to postpartum challenges in young to middle-aged men, a segment of the population that is least likely to admit dealing with PPD due to the stigma associated with such a mental health condition. Our results, therefore, point to the need for new and personalized solutions through specific methods such as gamification, content framing, and shared success stories. Further, our work shows that PPD among men is different from other mental health illnesses due to an appalling lack of awareness and the need for more (online) resources in educating new and expectant fathers, as well as the families and community around them.

The study is not without its limitation. First, although we analyzed a large number of transcripts (346), they were obtained from only one data source. Other sources may provide access to new population segments and yield additional themes. Second, while we attempt to provide as much methodological details as possible, we may not have provided elaborate details on some research considerations due to space constraints. In spite of these, we note that the scale of the problem (14% of new fathers) points to its importance and the need for problem space exploration, and not just appealing to prior theories. Our key contribution to the DSR community is, therefore, illustrating how design thinking techniques can be used in tandem with the DSR approach.

References

American Psychiatric Association: Cautionary statement for forensic use of DSM-5. In: Diagnostic and Atatistical Manual of Mental Disorders, 5th edn. Washington, DC (2013). http://dx.doi.org/10.1176/appi.books.9780890425596

Arabatzoudis, T., Rehm, I.C., Nedeljkovic, M.: A needs analysis for the development of an internet-delivered cognitive-behavioural treatment (iCBT) program for trichotillomania. J. Obsessive-Compuls. Relat. Disord. **31**, 100689 (2021)

Brangier, E., Bornet, C.: Persona: a method to produce representations focused on consumers' needs. In: Human Factors and Ergonomics in Consumer Product Design: Methods and Techniques, pp. 37–61 (2011)

Brenner, W., Uebernickel, F., Abrell, T.: Design thinking as mind-set, process, and toolbox. In: Brenner, W., Uebernickel, F. (eds.) Design Thinking for Innovation, pp. 3–21. Springer, Cham (2016). https://doi.org/10.1007/978-3-319-26100-3_1

Brown, T.: Change by Design: How Design Thinking Transforms Organizations and Inspires Innovation. HarperCollins, New York (2009)

Cox, J.L., Holden, J.M., Sagovsky, R.: Detection of postnatal de-pression: development of the 10-item Edinburgh postnatal depression scale. Br. J. Psychiatry **150**(6), 782–786 (1987)

Eddy, B., Poll, V., Whiting, J., Clevesy, M.: Forgotten fathers: postpartum depression in men. J. Fam. Issues **40**(8), 1001–1017 (2019)

Fereday, J., Muir-Cochrane, E.: Demonstrating rigor using thematic analysis: a hybrid approach of inductive and deductive coding and theme development. Int. J. Qual. Methods **5**(1), 80–92 (2006)

Gregor, S., Hevner, A.R.: Positioning and presenting design science research for maximum impact. MIS Q. 337–355 (2013)

Gustafsson, D.: Analysing the Double diamond design process through research & implementation. G2 Pro gradu, diplomityö. 55 (2019). http://urn.fi/URN:NBN:fi:aalto-201907144349

Herwix, A., Haj-Bolouri, A.: Revisiting the problem of the problem – an ontology and framework for problem assessment In: Is Research. European Conference on Information Systems 2021 Research Papers, p. 154 (2021). https://aisel.aisnet.org/ecis2021_rp/154

Hevner, A.R., March, S.T., Park, J., Ram, S.: Design science in information systems research. MIS Q. 28(1), 75–105 (2004)

Hevner, A.R.: A Three cycle view of design science research. Scand. J. Inf. Syst. 19(2), Article 4 (2007). https://aisel.aisnet.org/sjis/vol19/iss2/412

Holm, A., Severinsson, E.: Surviving depressive ill-health: a qualitative systematic review of older persons' narratives. Nurs. Health Sci. 16(1), 131–140 (2014)

Jarzabek, S., Cheong, K., Lim, Y., Wong, J., Kayanoth, R., Teng, J.: CBT assistant platform: web/mobile co-design solution for cognitive behavioural therapy. J. Hosp. Manag. Health Policy 2, 34 (2018)

Kelly, A.: Design research in education: yes, but is it methodological? J. Learn. Sci. 13(1), 115–128 (2004)

Kim, P., Swain, J.E.: Sad dads: paternal postpartum depression. Psychiatry (Edgmont). 4(2), 35–47 (2007). PMID: 20805898; PMCID: PMC2922346

Kuechler, W., Vaishnavi, V.: A framework for theory development in design science research: multiple perspectives. J. Assoc. Inf. Syst. 13(6), 3 (2012)

Lincoln, Y.S., Guba, E.G.: Naturalistic Inquiry. Sage Publications, Newbury Park (1985)

Madsen, S., Nielsen, L.: Exploring persona-scenarios-using storytelling to identify requirements. IFIP Adv. Inf. Commun. Technol. 57–66 (2010)

Maedche, A., Gregor, S., Morana, S., Feine, J.: Conceptualization of the problem space in design science research. In: Tulu, B., Djamasbi, S., Leroy, G. (eds.) Extending the Boundaries of Design Science Theory and Practice. DESRIST 2019. Lecture Notes in Computer Science, vol. 11491, pp. 18–31. Springer, Cham (2019). https://doi.org/10.1007/978-3-030-19504-5_2

Majchrzak, A., Markus, M.L., Wareham, J.: Designing for digital transformation: Lessons for information systems research from the study of ICT and societal challenges. MIS Q. 40(2), 267–277 (2016)

Melrose, S.: Paternal postpartum depression: how can nurses begin to help? Contemp. Nurse 34(2), 199–210 (2010)

Mesgari, M., Okoli, C., de Guinea, A.O.: Creating rich and representative personas by discovering affordances. IEEE Trans. Softw. Eng. 45(10), 967–983 (2018)

Patterson, V.C., Rossi, M.A., Pencer, A., Wozney, L.: An internet-based cognitive behavioral therapy program for anxiety and depression (tranquility): adaptation co-design and fidelity evaluation study. JMIR Format. Res. 6(2), e33374 (2022)

Ponterotto, J.G.: Brief note on the origins, evolution, and meaning of the qualitative research concept thick description. Qualitat. Rep. 11(3), 538–549 (2006)

Purao, S.: Design science research problems… where do they come from? In: Chandra Kruse, L., Seidel, S., Hausvik, G.I. (eds.) Design Science Research in Information Systems and Technology. LNCS, vol. 12807, pp. 99–111. Springer, Cham (2021). https://doi.org/10.1007/978-3-030-82405-1_12

Roy, C.: Fathering from the long view: framing personal and social change through life course theory. J. Fam. Theory Rev. 6, 319–335 (2014)

Thomas, S.P.: Perinatal depression in men. Issues Ment. Health Nurs. 31(10), 621 (2010). https://doi.org/10.3109/01612840.2010.509988

Scarff, J.R.: Postpartum depression in men. Innov. Clin. Neurosci. 16(5–6), 11–14 (2019)

Schoormann, T., Stadtländer, M., Knackstedt, R. Designing business model development tools for sustainability—a design science study. Electron. Mark. (2021). https://doi.org/10.1007/s12525-021-00466-3

Spinuzzi, C.: The methodology of participatory design. Tech. Commun. Soc. Tech. Commun. **52**(2), 163–174 (2005)

Walls, J.G., Widmeyer, G.R., El Sawy, O.A.: Building an information system design theory for vigilant EIS. Inf. Syst. Res. **3**(1), 36–59 (1992)

A Design Science Approach to Blood Donation Apps

Helena M. Müller⑩ and Melanie Reuter-Oppermann(✉)⑩

TU Darmstadt, Hochschulstr. 1, 64289 Darmstadt, Germany
{mueller,oppermann}@is.tu-darmstadt.de

Abstract. The COVID-19 pandemic has put additional pressure on the healthcare systems worldwide. It also led to a significant shortage of blood products. Delaying surgeries resulted in an increased demand at peak times that aligned with a decrease in blood donations at the same time. While being crucial for many surgeries and also certain types of treatments, blood cannot be produced artificially, but healthcare systems rely on voluntary donations. The relatively short shelf-life of most products makes a close matching of demand and supply necessary. We argue that smartphone applications can help to motivate donors to donate blood when necessary, giving access to all relevant information and services. By applying the design science research methodology, we derived design principles for effective smartphone applications and present a conceptual model in the form of mock-ups. We performed two design cycles and evaluated the design principles and the conceptual model with regular, lapsed, first-time and non-donors from Germany in a focus group discussion.

Keywords: Blood donation · Mobile apps · Design science research

1 Introduction

Due to the COVID-19 pandemic, even countries like Germany experienced a shortage in blood products, especially during the summer months of 2021. Many delayed surgeries were performed leading to a higher as usual demand, while donations decreased with many potential donors being on vacation. The blood donation centres expect another critical shortage once the Omicron wave will be overcome. Blood is a very important resource in all healthcare systems worldwide, crucial for many surgeries and also certain types of treatments. Unfortunately, blood products cannot be produced artificially, but blood must be donated by volunteers. What makes blood logistics and donation management even more challenging is that most blood products have a relatively short shelf-life, so they cannot be easily stored. In order to meet demand from hospitals, sufficient donations are necessary. When donations exceed this demand, they will be wasted, though, which should be avoided. Matching demand and donations as closely as possible is therefore crucial. Unfortunately, due to various influencing factors, there is a high fluctuation of blood donors [25]. For example, young

© Springer Nature Switzerland AG 2022
A. Drechsler et al. (Eds.): DESRIST 2022, LNCS 13229, pp. 221–232, 2022.
https://doi.org/10.1007/978-3-031-06516-3_17

adults between 18 and 25 years in Germany often do not donate blood again after they have donated once [4]. Motivating them to donate again can help to prevent future shortcomings. Therefore, efficient and easy donor management for blood donation centres is important to secure sufficient supply and prevent "over-donation". This means to provide access and information to all groups of donors, regular (rd), lapsed (ld), first-time (fd) and non-donors (nd) [10].

First smartphone applications have been developed in practice to offer access to information for blood donors. So far, no concepts exist for the design of a blood donation app from a user's point of view and theoretical foundations are missing how to design apps that foster a behavioural change and increase the donors' willingness to donate blood to potentially better match donations with demand. By applying the design science research (DSR) methodology, we want to answer the following research question: *How to design smartphone applications to support blood donors and increase their willingness to give blood?*

Section 2 presents existing blood donation apps. In Sect. 3, we discuss relevant theories that we use as a basis for our research approach. Following, we summarise the applied DSR methodology in Sect. 4, present the design principles in Sect. 5 as well as a conceptual model in Sect. 6. The results of the evaluation are presented in Sect. 7. The paper closes with a summary and an outlook on future research in Sect. 8.

2   Existing Blood Donation Apps

In the US, the American National Red Cross provides an app, which can be used to make and manage appointments and find nearby blood donation centres [29]. After making an appointment, the user can apply the app to obtain a so-called "RapidPass" containing all the necessary data. This enables the user to complete the blood donation process more quickly as all data has already been transferred. In addition, the user can overview the donation history including all appointments, locations and vital parameters. The app also allows donors to track the path of their blood donation all the way to the patient, informing about when and where the donation was used for transfusion. For each donation, donors receive digital badges that can be shared with friends.

Some of these functionalities are also provided by the app of the German Red Cross (DRK) [9]. While the app does neither include a "RapidPass" nor an overview of vital parameters or tracking of blood donations, it offers real-time insights when the donor is eligible again and enables reminder services via email. Furthermore, it provides a chat forum where users can exchange information and experiences with other blood donors within Germany.

The German app "Statusplus Blutspende" developed by the start-up Tricode combines all the functions of the two apps mentioned before. Additionally, it even connects hospitals to inform users about their blood values as well as the hospitals' current blood stock to appeal for blood donations, if necessary [28]. This replaces the time-consuming and labour-intensive notification by post and enables a faster response, especially in emergency situations. If there is a need for a specific blood group, individual messages can also be sent to matching donors. So far, the app is used in Kiel and Lübeck. In the future, the app will also include the donor questionnaires to reduce the administrative workload at the donation centres and halving their processing time.

This feature is already available in the app "Mein Blut" of the Austrian Red Cross, which also helps to find appropriate centres and appointments, provides feedback on medical findings and the eligibility to donate again as well as access to information about past donations and the digital donor card [22].

The above mentioned apps represent those with the most functionality. For a detailed overview of blood donation apps, we refer the reader to the review of Ouhbi et al. [24].

3   Behavioural Change Models Regarding Blood Donation

As there is an inextricable linkage between DSR and behavioural research [16], designing socio-technical systems to induce changes in behaviour specifically asks for psychological insights. In the context of blood donation, the theory of planned behaviour (TPB) and its extensions (e.g., [14]) commonly build the basis for the understanding of why people donate blood. Basically, the TPB framework consists of three determinants, i.e., attitude, subjective norm and perceived behavioural control, which are causal for intention, i.e., why people decide to do something. Intention, in turn, determines future behaviour [1]. Regarding the decision-making process for donating blood, attitude refers to the individual's weighing of all positive and negative options towards blood donation, subjective norm to its perception of blood donation being (un)approved by significant others and perceived behavioural control to the individual's judgement of the own easiness or difficulty of donating blood. However, the TPB does not consider past behaviour and the degree of loyalty towards a certain behaviour. That is why it is hard to predict an individual's development and progress in behavioural change [20].

Instead, some researchers [5,11] tested the applicability of the transtheoretical model (TTM) to blood donation behaviour, as this theory mainly focuses on the stages of change and the processes facilitating transitions between these stages [26]. Regarding blood donation, the stage of change characterises how willing an individual is to donate blood. According to the TTM, there are five stages of change: precontemplation (not planning to donate blood, perhaps due to unawareness, lack of knowledge or resistance regarding blood donation), contemplation (thinking about, but not committing oneself to donate blood within half a year, perhaps due to ambivalence regarding the pros and cons or lack of confidence), preparation (after initiating first steps, ready to donate blood within next month), action (actively donating blood for half a year) and maintenance (loyally donating blood for at least half a year). Additionally, the TTM asserts that there are ten processes of change which can be divided into experiential and behavioural transition strategies. The former involve consciousness raising (e.g., recalling given information on blood donation), dramatic relief (e.g., being emotionally touched by the opportunity to save someone's life through own blood donation), environmental re-evaluation (assumption that all of the people in the world would live a better life if every individual, who is eligible, donated blood), self-re-evaluation (e.g., feeling anticipated regret if no blood donation is made despite being eligible) and social liberation (e.g., realising that apart from hospitals there are other places to donate blood). The latter include counter conditioning (e.g., being distracted while donating blood), helping relationships (e.g., donating blood together with a friend), reinforcement management (e.g., having the feeling of a rewarding experience through blood donation), self-liberation (e.g., committing oneself to donate blood), stimulus control (e.g., distributing blood donation stickers at home). The researchers, who tested the applicability of the TTM, demonstrated that the developmental process of a blood donor career starts with the experiential and ends with the behavioural strategies [11].

Even though theoretical frameworks have been efficiently applied to understand blood donor behaviour, when it comes to practice, effective theory-based recruitment and retention interventions are still missing [5]. To the best of our knowledge, only a few researchers [17,27] recently tried to change this through the development and testing of interventions. Klinkenberg et al. [17], who developed and evaluated recruitment interventions for African minorities in Western Europe, even made use of an interplay between the TPB and the TTM, as research demonstrated that there is a relation between the determinants of the TPB and the stages of change of the TTM, i.e., attitude is more relevant in earlier stages like precontemplation and subjective norm as well as perceived behavioural control in the later stages [8]. So far, Sardi et al. [27] have been the first to apply the TTM regarding the development of blood donation apps. However, they mainly dealt with the gamification part in terms of the design of such apps. They used the TTM to ensure that their gamified design suggestions will be useful to all four blood donor types. In this paper, we build upon their innovative work by extending the design suggestions and developing design principles grounded on both theories, TPB and TTM, for the complete app.

4   Design Science Research Project

For addressing the challenge of promoting donors' willingness to give blood, we apply the DSR methodology [16], since we do not only aim to understand issues related to blood donors, but rather to solve them by designing and evaluating an appropriate software artefact in a specific context, i.e., smartphone applications for blood donors in Germany. Moreover, as indicated at the end of Sect. 3, formulating design principles (DPs) grounded on justificatory knowledge for an entire class of blood donation apps has not yet been done in research and thus our study contributes to DSR as well as IS literature. By following the three cycle view of DSR [15], we combine inputs from a blood donation expert and potential end users (relevance) with the existing body of knowledge (rigor) for our DSR project. As shown in Fig. 1, our research project is based on the DSR framework proposed by [18] and is divided into two subsequent design cycles.

Our first design cycle served for the derivation of our DPs and a first evaluation of their theoretical instantiation via fictional blood donation scenarios

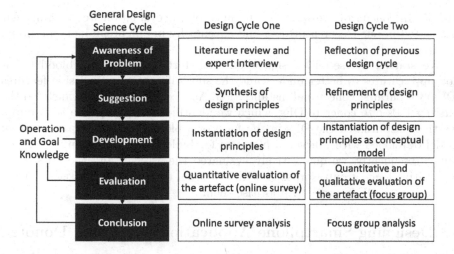

Fig. 1. Design cycles with respective research activities

embedded in an online survey. Our research project started with the conduction of a systematic literature review on blood donation apps and the review of high-quality practical solutions in order to find out which issues faced by potential blood donors need to be and which ones are currently addressed by such apps in an efficient way. In addition, to better understand our user group for derivation of its possible requirements regarding the design of blood donation apps, we also reviewed factors influencing blood donor behaviour grounded on the TPB explained in Sect. 3. Increasing the relevance of our research, we selected an appropriate blood donation expert serving as an interview partner in a semi-structured interview in order to refine and identify requirements that have been and have not been covered by our first set of design requirements (DRs). Building on the results of these research activities, we proposed three DPs for blood donation apps. Subsequently, we theoretically instantiated our DPs via fictional blood donation scenarios shown to potential end users through a survey format. The online survey served for the evaluation of our proposed design and consisted of ten blood donation scenarios representing our identified requirements (e.g., making an appointment for blood donation). For the scenarios, respondents could choose from three alternatives, i.e., website, chatbot and app. In each case they had to decide which one met the presented requirement best. Therefore, we could not only determine if the blood donation app is perceived as useful but even if it is the tool of choice for them. Overall, the survey revealed that in seven out of ten scenarios the app was the most preferred tool. The website was chosen for the remaining three scenarios representing situations that ask for information retrieval. In the future, almost half of the 213 respondents would rather use an app (48.36%) than a website (41.78%) or a chatbot (9.86%). Regarding the demographics of the participants, 55.4% were female and all were between 18 and 68 years old, with the majority (76%) being between 18 and 35. In conclusion, through the findings of our evaluation we generally felt vindicated in our research project and specifically in our preliminary proposed design.

We started the second design cycle with further reading on blood donation app features to better understand the suitability of specific design features (DFs) for our first conceptual instantiation. As a consequence, we translated the existing DPs into concrete DFs, which we identified as appropriate for an app. We then instantiated the DPs in the form of a blood donation app conceptual model developed with Marvel, a platform for building clickable app prototypes [19]. Subsequently, we qualitatively evaluated the artefact and the DPs in an explorative focus group workshop with potential end users and asked for their rating of each DF in order to prioritise them.

5   Designing Smartphone Applications for Blood Donors

Minimising potential barriers such as inconvenience and lack of knowledge as well as fostering motivators, both grounded on the TPB and its extensions, is crucial in order to induce changes in blood donor behaviour [3]. However, most of the studies discussing app design solutions for blood donor mobilisation and management rather take technical issues such as system requirements into consideration than focusing on user-centered design (e.g., [23]). Only Foth et al. [12] as well as Batis and Albarrak [2] not only included perspectives of blood donors but also considered blood donation centres. Even if the research of Batis and Albarrak is closer to a complete app, they both provide a list of design features that other researchers, developers and designers can make use of. Based on their research as well as on those of Sardi et al. [27], the expert interview and the review of existing apps (see Sect. 2), we derived and formulated three DPs for blood donation apps promoting donors' willingness to give blood according to the structure proposed by Chandra et al. [6] and translated them into concrete DFs (Fig. 2).

6   Conceptual Model

For the conceptual instantiation of the proposed DPs, we used the already existing apps mentioned in Sect. 2 for orientation. To the best of our knowledge, we are the first who regard the design of a chatbot-based blood donation app. The survey of Batis and Albarrak among donors revealed that almost 30% of the 383 respondents miss a personal touch when using a blood donation app [2]. Since being perceived as anthropomorphic is one of the main purposes of chatbots, they are appropriate to give the feeling of a human contact [31]. Even though interaction with a chatbot means communicating with a software program emulating human conversation, it feels like talking to another human being while writing text messages in natural language back and forth [7]. We argue that a chatbot as part of a blood donation app offers the opportunity of a follow-up conversation with further questions being answered leading to a deeper engagement

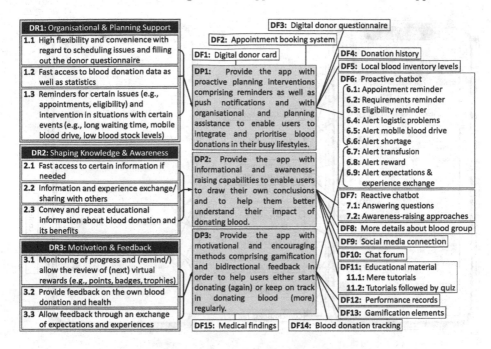

Fig. 2. Derivation of design principles and their mapping to design features

with donors. Moreover, more than half of the survey participants (54.1%) stated that they have concerns about the inability of getting their questions answered promptly. Again, a chatbot counteracts these concerns by its short resolution times and its availability 24 h a day on seven days a week [13].

Since our tailored artefact is not only grounded on the TPB but also on the TTM, when users first register and log into the app, they are asked to answer four questions to determine their initial stage of change [27]. Based on the staging algorithm developed by Burditt et al., the questions comprise the assessment of the eligibility to give blood, the specification of past donations within last year as well as the assessment of the willingness to give blood within the next six months and next month [5]. Similar to the proposal of Sardi et al., if the result depending on the respective answers is "precontemplation", no status is attributed to the user, whereas for the other four stages of change the user's status is symbolised (see example in Fig. 3 on the left in the upper right corner) [27]. According to the determined stage of change, a chatbot can react appropriately with regard to its initiated exchange of expectations and experiences as well as awareness-raising and motivational approaches. Besides the chatbot, by means of a variety of other design features, our blood donation app encourages the user to go through the individual processes of change that positively influence the user's willingness to donate blood. The two snapshots of our conceptual user interfaces in Fig. 3 show which process of change is triggered by which design feature.

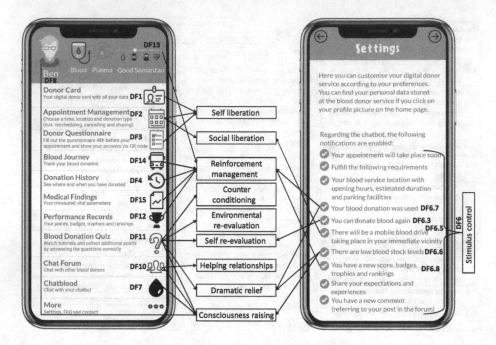

Fig. 3. Mapping of design features to processes of change

7 Evaluation

To receive qualitative feedback on our proposed design, we conducted an exploratory focus group workshop with potential end users of our artefact [30]. In DSR, this evaluation method is common to receive feedback on as well as ideas for further improvement of initial artefacts and designs [21]. Inspired by Morana et al., we performed a strengths, weaknesses, opportunities and threats (SWOT) analysis to get the workshop participants easily involved in interactions and discussions [21]. Overall, we invited eight participants with two representatives of each donor group. Out of the two males and six females, we considered a balanced age mix (from 19 to 60 years) as well as occupational backgrounds (i.e., students of different disciplines as well as employees in different sectors). With this purposeful selection, we wanted to ensure comprehensive feedback from diverse perspectives and investigate if there are differences in terms of age and donor type.

With consent of the participants, the focus group workshop was recorded and conducted via a video-conferencing tool that allowed to share the screen for visualisation of our conceptual model. It lasted a total of two hours and was transcribed afterwards for further analysis. After the model's presentation, we asked the participants to name features that were not covered by our initial design or that seemed unnecessary to them. In their prevailing opinion, features belonging to gamification could be more attractive to younger users. In addition, while the

Table 1. Rating of design features by the focus group participants with respective gender and age in brackets below

	Rank	DF	Mean	nd1 (m, 19)	nd2 (f, 56)	fd1 (m, 27)	fd2 (f, 27)	ld1 (f, 24)	ld2 (f, 60)	rd1 (f, 24)	rd2 (f, 53)
DP1	1	3	4,625	5	4	5	5	4	4	5	5
	2	1	4,125	5	4	3	5	4	3	4	5
	2	4	4,125	5	4	3	4	5	4	3	5
	3	2	3,875	4	4	4	5	5	4	1	4
	4	5	3,750	3	4	5	4	4	3	4	3
	5	6	3,125	4	3	2	3	4	4	3	2
DP2	1	8	4,250	5	3	4	5	4	3	5	5
	2	7.1	3,625	2	4	5	3	5	3	3	4
	3	7.2	2,750	2	2	4	3	3	3	2	3
	4	11.1	2,375	2	4	1	4	2	3	2	1
	5	10	2,125	2	2	3	3	2	3	1	1
	6	9	1,750	1	2	1	2	1	3	1	3
	7	11.2	1,625	2	2	1	2	1	2	2	1
DP3	1	15	4,875	5	4	5	5	5	5	5	5
	2	14	4,375	5	4	4	5	3	4	5	5
	3	6.7	4,250	4	4	4	5	5	4	3	5
	4	6.9	3,375	3	3	4	4	4	3	3	3
	5	13	2,375	1	3	5	3	2	2	2	1
	6	12	2,250	3	2	4	2	1	3	2	1
	6	6.8	2,250	2	2	3	3	2	4	1	1

Table 2. Summary of SWOT results

	Strengths	Weaknesses
DP1:	• Enables to a) easily plan blood donations, b) save time, c) keep an overview, d) remember appointments • Encourages to donate blood spontaneously in the vicinity • Donor card cannot be left behind	• Cognitive overload due to many push notifications • Annoying and ignorable push notifications • High effort to go through long list of activatable settings
DP2:	• Enables to understand the entire donation process chain • Learning effect in combination with fun/pleasant pastime • Experience exchange allays fears and motivates others • Chatbot's ability to quickly answer specific questions	• Cumbersome and often unsatisfactory process of getting questions answered by the chatbot • Quick information overload, unnecessary redundancies & scope for dubious questions and answers in the forum
DP3:	• High transparency • Collaboration and competition among individuals motivate them to frequently donate blood • Chatbot's ability to proactively motivate to donate blood	• Too many push notifications • Disadvantage of certain user groups regarding the ranking/scoring of blood donations (e.g., women are allowed to donate four times vs. men six times per year)
	Opportunities	**Threats**
DP1:	• Calling attention to supply shortages stimulates a feeling of being needed that increases motivation to give blood • Being aware of urgently needed blood donations helps to overcome one's inhibitions to donate blood	• Sensitive data requires strict privacy and data security • Uncertainty about what happens to the personal data • (Unintentional) sensitive information sharing by one click • Short-term appointment cancellation (e.g., alert long wait)
DP2:	• Chatbot allows asking embarrassing questions • Quiz allows integration into everyday life whereby blood donation remains in people's mind • Quiz allows to control knowledge gain	• Dissemination of misinformation in the chat forum • Negative comments/shitstorm • Experience exchange in the forum might unsettle novices • Not being aware of sharing sensitive information
DP3:	• More frequent blood donations through: a) targeted chatbot interventions, b) continuous health checks with possibility for comparison and expansion to recommendations to visit the doctor in case of abnormality	• No direct feedback from the doctor and therefore major uncertainty in case of bad health values or remarkable changes in comparison with health history

younger lapsed donor missed the rating of donation centres regarding criteria like average waiting time or parking facilities, the older one proposed a feedback option on blood values together with suggestions for health improvements (e.g., change of diet).

Next, we explained the three DPs for apps to promote donors' willingness to give blood and demonstrated how each of the DPs was instantiated in our conceptual model. After each demonstration, we asked the participants to evaluate the importance of each DF on a rating scale ranging from 1 (not important) to 5 (very important) via a survey format. The results are presented in Table 1. Each survey was followed by a SWOT analysis of the particular instantiations of the DPs. We asked the participants to write their feedback into four SWOT analysis boxes on a digital whiteboard that we prepared in advance. Afterwards, the moderator read the feedback out loud and discussed it within the group. The results are summarised in Table 2. In general, our participants appreciated the central and direct access to important data and relevant information provided by the app as well as its low complexity. They further stressed that the latter is specifically important to people who might be less skilled in using IT. Regarding the proposed DPs, the focus group acknowledged the importance of all three. DP1 was rated as most important to them, followed by DP3 and DP2. The general discussion showed that the personal (health) benefit is important for most of the participants. Therefore, it is not surprising that DF15 (medical findings) was rated to be most important, followed closely by DF3 (digital donor questionnaire).

At the end of the session, we asked the participants to fill out one last survey asking them if they would personally use the app and why or why not. All participants acknowledged the app's usefulness. For almost all of them, the two features blood donation tracking (DF14) and medical findings on blood levels (DF15) are most important for using a blood donation app. Overall, the feedback of the focus group was promising and we received valuable input for further research and an instantiation of our artefact.

8   Conclusion

In this paper, we addressed the challenge of promoting donors' willingness to give blood by applying the DSR methodology and developed design principles for blood donation apps grounded on two behavioural theories. We instantiated three DPs and a first conceptual model and evaluated them in a focus group workshop with all four groups of donors to investigate the general applicability. As a consequence, we contribute with prescriptive knowledge for designing blood donation apps that increase engagement of regular, lapsed, first-time and non-donors. The main limitation of our work is the focus on the German system.

In future work, we aim to build a functional prototype considering the focus group feedback together with privacy and data security experts. This prototype will then be evaluated in a larger user study with a combination of an online survey and in-depths experiments as well as focus group discussions. We will further investigate and compare the attractiveness of apps and websites. While research shows that rewards can positively affect the willingness to donate, we were surprised that the topic was raised by the focus group, as it contradicts the idea of donation. We therefore want to investigate the actual importance of rewards and potential implications for blood donation in general as well as for the design of blood donation apps. We also want to study how much the design depends on the healthcare system and the cultural context. For example, other cultures may perceive social media or the integrated chat forum as more valuable than German participants do. A current research project allows us to study the applicability and the usefulness of a blood donation app in South Africa. Within this project, we aim to develop solutions that support blood donors as well as blood donation centres. Therefore, apart from blood donors, we also intend to study the design of blood donation apps and chatbots from the perspective of donation centres. As a next step, by conducting expert interviews on site, we want to determine their requirements.

References

1. Ajzen, I.: The theory of planned behavior. Organ. Behav. Hum. Decis. Process. **50**(2), 179–211 (1991)
2. Batis, A., Albarrak, A.: Preferences and features of a blood donation smartphone app: a multicenter mixed-methods study in Riyadh, Saudi Arabia. Comput. Methods Program. Biomed. Update **1**, 100005 (2021)
3. Bednall, T., Bove, L.: Donating blood: a meta-analytic review of self-reported motivators and deterrents. Transfus. Med. Rev. **25**(4), 317–334 (2011)
4. Bundeszentrale für gesundheitliche Aufklaerung: Praevalenz der Blutspende (2018). https://www.blutspenden.de/fileadmin/Blutspende/05_Infothek/03_Studien/11321_9_FINAL_Infoblatt_20Blutspende_180608_Final.pdf. Accessed 06 Feb 2022
5. Burditt, C., Robbins, M., Paiva, A., Velicer, W., Koblin, B., Kessler, D.: Motivation for blood donation among African Americans: developing measures for stage of change, decisional balance, and self-efficacy constructs. J. Behav. Med. **32**(5), 429–442 (2009)
6. Chandra, L., Seidel, S., Gregor, S.: Prescriptive knowledge in IS research: conceptualizing design principles in terms of materiality, action, and boundary conditions. In: 48th Hawaii International Conference on System Sciences, pp. 4039–4048. IEEE (2015)
7. Dale, R.: The return of the chatbots. Nat. Lang. Eng. **22**(5), 811–817 (2016)
8. De Vries, H., Mudde, A., Dijkstra, A., Willemsen, M.: Differential beliefs, perceived social influences, and self-efficacy expectations among smokers in various motivational phases. Prev. Med. **27**(5 Pt 1), 681–689 (1998)
9. DRK-Blutspendedienste: Spenderservice Homepage. https://www.spenderservice.net/. Accessed 06 Feb 2022
10. Ferguson, E.: Predictors of future behaviour: a review of the psychological literature on blood donation. Br. J. Health. Psychol. **1**, 287–308 (1996)
11. Ferguson, E., Chandler, S.: A stage model of blood donor behaviour: assessing volunteer behaviour. J. Health Psychol. **10**(3), 359–372 (2005)

12. Foth, M., Satchell, C., Seeburger, J., Russell-Bennett, R.: Social and mobile interaction design to increase the loyalty rates of young blood donors. In: 6th International Conference on Communities and Technologies, pp. 64–73 (2013)
13. Gnewuch, U., Morana, S., Maedche, A.: Towards designing cooperative and social conversational agents for customer service. In: 38th International Conference on Information Systems, Seoul, pp. 1–13 (2017)
14. Godin, G., et al.: Factors explaining the intention to give blood among the general population. Vox Sang. **89**(3), 140–149 (2005)
15. Hevner, A.: A three cycle view of design science research. Scand. J. Inf. Syst. **19**(2), 87–92 (2007)
16. Hevner, A., March, S., Park, J., Ram, S.: Design science in information systems research. MIS Q. **28**(1), 75–105 (2004)
17. Klinkenberg, E., Huis in't Veld, E., Kort, W., Weert, J., Fransen, M.: Recruiting ethnic minorities of African descent as blood donors through a systematic intervention development. ISBT Sci. Ser. **16**(1), 92–101 (2021)
18. Kuechler, W., Vaishnavi, V.: On theory development in design science research: anatomy of a research project. Eur. J. Inf. Syst. **17**(5), 489–504 (2008)
19. Marvel Homepage. https://marvelapp.com/. Accessed 02 Feb 2022
20. Masser, B., White, K., Hyde, M., Terry, D.: The psychology of blood donation: current research and future directions. Transfus. Med. Rev. **22**(3), 215–233 (2008)
21. Morana, S., Schacht, S., Scherp, A., Maedche, A.: Designing a process guidance system to support user's business process compliance. In: 35th International Conference on Information Systems, Auckland, pp. 1–19 (2014)
22. Oesterreichisches Rotes Kreuz Blutspende-App Homepage. https://www.roteskreuz.at/blutspenden/app-mein-blut. Accessed 06 Feb 2022
23. Ouhbi, S., Fernández-Alemán, J., Idri, A., Toval, A., Pozo, J., Bajta, M.: A reusable requirements catalog for internationalized and sustainable blood donation apps. In: 12th International Conference on Evaluation of Novel Approaches to Software Engineering, pp. 285–292 (2017)
24. Ouhbi, S., Fernández-Alemán, J.L., Toval, A., Idri, A., Pozo, J.R.: Free blood donation mobile applications. J. Med. Syst. **39**(5), 1–20 (2015). https://doi.org/10.1007/s10916-015-0228-0
25. Pirabán, A., Guerrero, W.J., Labadie, N.: Survey on blood supply chain management: models and methods. Comput. Oper. Res. **112**, 104756 (2019)
26. Prochaska, J., DiClemente, C.: Transtheoretical therapy: toward a more integrative model of change. Psychother. Theory Res. Pract. **19**(3), 276–288 (1982)
27. Sardi, L., Kharbouch, M., Rachad, T., Idri, A., de Gea, J.M.C., Fernández-Alemán, J.L.: Blood4Life: a mobile solution to recruit and retain blood donors through gamification and trans-theoretical model. In: Rocha, Á., Adeli, H., Reis, L.P., Costanzo, S. (eds.) WorldCIST'19 2019. AISC, vol. 932, pp. 3–12. Springer, Cham (2019). https://doi.org/10.1007/978-3-030-16187-3_1
28. Schäfer, F.: Studenten der FH Kiel und UKSH veröffentlichen Blutspende-App (2020). https://nachrichten.idw-online.de/2020/06/10/studenten-der-fh-kiel-und-uksh-veroeffentlichen-blutspende-app/. Accessed 06 Feb 2022
29. The American National Red Cross Blood Donor App Homepage. https://www.redcrossblood.org/blood-donor-app.html. Accessed 06 Feb 2022
30. Tremblay, M., Hevner, A., Berndt, D.: Focus groups for artifact refinement and evaluation in design research. Commun. Assoc. Inf. Syst. **26**(27), 599–618 (2010)
31. Verhagen, T., van Nes, J., Feldberg, F., van Dolen, W.: Virtual customer service agents: using social presence and personalization to shape online service encounters. J. Comput.-Mediat. Commun. **19**(3), 529–545 (2014)

Innovation and Entrepreneurship

Introduction to the Innovation and Entrepreneurship Track

Henrik Berglund[1] and Christoph Seckler[2]

[1] Chalmers University of Technology
henrik.berglund@chalmers.se
[2] ESCP Business School
cseckler@escp.eu

Abstract. Entrepreneurship and innovation scholars are attracted by the combination of conceptual fruitfulness, scientific rigor, and practical relevance found in design science research. Suitable topics are important yet unresolved how-to problems in the innovation and entrepreneurship domain such as: 'how to design new ventures', 'how to design innovation ecosystems,' or 'how to design effective entrepreneurship training.' Methodical papers can provide guidance on how to conduct design science research in the innovation and entrepreneurship space.

Keywords: Innovation · Entrepreneurship

1 Introduction

There is growing interest in design theory and design science among entrepreneurship and innovation scholars, who are attracted by the potential to productively combine conceptual fruitfulness, scientific rigor, and practical relevance. These issues are closely related in the sense that particular conceptual frameworks are more or less conducive to sound and managerially relevant research.

Consider the field of entrepreneurship research. Here the so called dual-nexus model has held sway for over 20 years (Shane and Venkataraman 2000; Venkataraman 1997). Building on abstract theories of entrepreneurship as an economic function, entrepreneurship is conceptualized in terms of enterprising individuals who first identify and then exploit lucrative market imperfections. Frustrated with its limitations, the last decade has seen this model come under heavy criticism for being conceptually incoherent (Dimov 2011), empirically intractable (Davidsson 2015), and practically irrelevant (Berglund and Korsgaard 2017). Building on insights from design theory (Sarasvathy 2003), cultural anthropology (Baker and Nelson 2005), and practice theory (Thompson et al. 2020) , there is now a trend to instead conceptualize entrepreneurship in pragmatic terms as a form of artifact centered design, with the artifact in question being the "venture", "business", "startup" etc. (Berglund, Bousfiha and Mansoori 2020).

Closely related to this conceptual shift in focus, scholars increasingly feel attracted to design science research methodology because of its liberal attitude toward disciplinary boundaries. Innovation and entrepreneurship, almost by definition, concern open-ended situations and wicked problems, which are often difficult to understand and solve within any disciplinary framework. Under such conditions, the pursuit of relevant knowledge and useful solutions are often transdisciplinary (Bernstein 2015) with researchers pragmatically using of theories and solution concepts regardless of their origins. Building primarily on insights from Information Systems, there are also efforts underway to develop methodological guidelines for design science research targeting innovative entrepreneurship (Dimov 2016; Seckler, Mauer and Brocke 2022).

The papers in this session reflect this growing interest and emerging entwinement of design theory and design science. We hope that the presentations and discussions will give further energy to this much needed development.

References

1. Baker, T., Nelson, R.E.: Creating something from nothing: resource construction through entrepreneurial bricolage. Adm. Sci. Q. **50**(3), 329–366 (2005)
2. Berglund, H., Bousfiha, M., Mansoori, Y.: Opportunities as artifacts and entrepreneurship as design. Acad. Manage. Rev. **45**(4), 825–846 (2020)
3. Berglund, H., Korsgaard, S.: Opportunities, time, and mechanisms in entrepreneurship: on the practical irrelevance of propensities. Acad. Manage. Rev. **42**(4), 731–734 (2017)
4. Bernstein, J.H.: Transdisciplinarity: a review of its origins, development, and current issues (2015)
5. Davidsson, P.: Entrepreneurial opportunities and the entrepreneurship nexus: a re-conceptualization. J. Bus. Ventur. **30**(5), 674–695 (2015)
6. Dimov, D.: Grappling with the unbearable elusiveness of entrepreneurial opportunities. Entrepreneurship Theor. Pract. **35**(1), 57–81 (2011)
7. Dimov, D.: Toward a design science of entrepreneurship. Adv. Entrepreneurship, Firm Emergence Growth, **18**, 1–31 (2016)
8. Sarasvathy, S.D.: Entrepreneurship as a science of the artificial. J. Econ. Psychol. 24(2), 203–220 (2003)
9. Seckler, C., Mauer, R., Brocke, J. vom: Design science in entrepreneurship: conceptual foundations and guiding principles. J. Bus. Ventur. Des. Forthcoming (2022)
10. Shane, S., Venkataraman, S.: The promise of enterpreneurship as a field of research. Acad. Manage. Rev. **5**(1), 217–226 (2000)
11. Thompson, N.A., Verduijn, K., Gartner, W.B.: Entrepreneurship-as-practice: grounding contemporary theories of practice into entrepreneurship studies. Entrepreneurship Reg. Dev. **32**(3–4), 247–256 (2020)
12. Venkataraman, S.: The distinctive domain of entrepreneurship research. Adv. Entrepreneurship, Firm Emergence Growth **3** (1997)

Reviewers

Developing an Innovation Accounting System for a Professional Service Firm: A Design Science Research Project

Simon David Arsenidis[✉] [iD] and Christoph Seckler[iD]

ESCP Business School, Berlin, Germany
`simon.arsenidis@edu.escp.eu, cseckler@escp.eu`

Abstract. This paper reports on a design science project developing an innovation accounting system for a professional service firm. Innovation accounting is an approach to track the progress of innovation activities. Although the subject of study has a defined product innovation process, there is a lack of measurable information on the outcomes of innovation activities. This implies a blind spot in the effective allocation of resources in innovation activities. In this paper a design science approach is used to bridge the existing concepts on innovation accounting and the needs of user groups. The output of the paper is a conceptual solution design for an innovation accounting system in the context of the product innovation process for a professional service firm. The learnings from the study are transferred into design propositions by using the CIMO-logic. This paper contributes to the body of design knowledge on innovation accounting in professional service firms.

Keywords: Innovation accounting · Professional service firms · Design knowledge · Design principles

1 Introduction

For professional service firms (PSF) it is increasingly important to engage in innovation activities. In general, PSFs can be described as human capital-intensive companies that provide knowledge-intensive services. PSFs are characterized among other things by partnerships, professional knowledge-intensity, mechanisms to ensure the delivery of high-quality expert's output, and a high focus on reputation [1].

Innovation activities comprise activities to identify, develop, implementing, and exploiting digital innovations [2]. Innovation activities help to transform PSFs towards technology-driven companies by exploring new value propositions and digital business models [3]. Under the pressure of rising costs and increasing uncertainty, the creation of new digitalized professional services requires innovation activities that need to be well-structured and outcome-focused [4].

While innovation activities are crucial for PSFs, the question of how they can be measured and managed remains a neglected area. In former times, innovation teams would present a full business plan, including a calculated return on investment and net

© Springer Nature Switzerland AG 2022
A. Drechsler et al. (Eds.): DESRIST 2022, LNCS 13229, pp. 237–248, 2022.
https://doi.org/10.1007/978-3-031-06516-3_18

present value, before starting development. This meant that they would only receive customer feedback once the product was already on the market. Nowadays, companies divide the innovation process into smaller parts and try to gain customer insights right from the beginning to derive evidence-based decisions [5]. The arising question is: how could an innovation accounting system look like to assess the success of digital product innovations developed within a professional service firm.

To tackle this question, we conducted a design science research project [6]. Design science is a scientific approach aiming at developing design knowledge using the scientific method [7]. A design science research project approach can be 'conceptualized as a research strategy, aimed at knowledge that can be used in an instrumental way to design and implement actions, processes or systems to achieve desired outcomes in practice' [8]. We followed van Aken & Berends [6] design science methodology which comprises the following phases: (1) problem definition, (2) diagnosis, (3) solution design, (4) evaluation, (5) learning. The outcome is an innovation accounting system for an end-to-end innovation process in PSFs with a curated holistic set of key performance indicators (KPIs) that considers activity- and outcome-oriented metrics and contrasts them for the different user groups in the PSF.

Overall, this paper contributes to the body of design knowledge and has direct practical implications. First, this study contributes to the body of design knowledge by developing an innovation accounting system for the professional service field. While previous innovation accounting systems were focusing primarily on corporates [e.g., 9, 10], the proposed innovation accounting system accounts for specificities of the PSF sector. Second, based on this project we abstracted more generalizable design principles on innovation accounting in PSFs. While the field of innovation accounting is growing it has not yet considered the perspective of knowledge-intensive services. The derived design propositions will help to close this gap. Third, the developed innovation accounting system had immediate practical implications for the cooperating firm and was implemented to guide the innovation process.

2   Problem Definition and Diagnosis

2.1   Research Question

This study addresses a practical problem of a PSF to develop more general design knowledge. The practical problem can be described as follows:

Shortly after the innovation initiative has been started in the firm, which is the subject of study, the user groups have successfully launched two digital product innovations that went through the firm's defined innovation process. This is an end-to-end process, i.e. spans all development stages from conception and validation of the idea, to the technical implementation and eventual marketing of the new product. The four stages of the firm's process are called Discover, Design, Develop and Deliver.

However, the innovation team perceives a blind spot in the process regarding measurement. They have identified a lack of performance indicators for the digital product innovations across the stages. This could result in the misallocation of resources, e.g. by spending too much time and money on innovation activities. Thus, this leads to the research question: *How could an innovation accounting system look like to assess the success of digital product innovations developed within a professional service firm?*

This paper will explore the research question following Osterwalder's opportunity framework. The framework conceptualizes opportunities as ideas to emerge at the intersection of (a) customer or stakeholder needs, and (b) what can be built [11]. (a): To empirically identify the needs of the key stakeholders within the digital product innovation process, semi-structured interviews with the user groups were conducted. (b): To derive what can be built, the literature on innovation and related literature around innovation and success measurement were reviewed. To derive an answer in accordance with the framework the following sub-questions (SRQ) were investigated:

SRQ1: What are the needs of the user groups in the innovation process? (see Sect. 2.2).
SRQ2: What approaches exist in relation with innovation accounting? (see Sect. 2.3).
SRQ3: What kind of innovation accounting should be designed? (see Sects. 3.1, 3.2).

2.2 What Stakeholders Need: Analysis of Needs of Relevant User Groups

The exploration of stakeholder needs was conducted three sixty-minute semi-structured interviews as well as a ninety-minute workshop in which each user group provided insights about their perception of innovation activities within their department, their role and needs during the process. The user groups involved in the innovation process comprised (a) the management team (senior partner-level) who governs the process and who approves or rejects an innovation to be implemented, (b) the solution owners, i.e. the subject-matter-experts who provide and develop their idea with the support of the innovation team, and (c) the innovation team, which is the intermediary party, that drives innovation activities by guiding the solution owners through the process, evaluating and co-designing the ideas, overseeing the implementation and creating the basis for marketing and sales, as well as for reporting.

The management team's strategic goal is to explore and exploit new business models to generate revenue as well as use cutting-edge technologies to create a digital image to attract talent. The role of the management team is on the one hand to equip the innovation teams with freedom and budget to create innovative business opportunities. On the other hand, they make investment decisions and therefore require objective assessments of the progress and impact of innovation activities.

The solution owners work on innovation ideas alongside their regular professional service projects. They believe that during the next years, services and interaction with clients will change because of the technological progress and they see it as an opportunity to provide ideas that can turn into new business models. During the development of new solutions, their focus is to ensure that the digital solutions meet the high professional standards of the firm. However, they understood the importance of customer-centric design and the importance of validating ideas as early as possible in the process. In addition, they expect that progress tracking should be carried out in each innovation stage and within a reasonable amount of time.

The innovation team is the main user group because of their role to drive the innovation activities, guide the solution owners through the process and report the progress to the management. They provide the resources, tools, and knowledge to realize innovation activities. However, despite the defined innovation process they lack transparency on outcomes in each innovation stage and project. They have a handful of metrics in place, but it does not cover the entire process, which results in an uncertainty about the effectiveness of resource allocation.

At large, the empirical analysis provided insights to derive the stakeholders needs. Throughout all user groups, these needs can be synthesized in design principles which are summarized in the following Table 1:

Table 1. User group's design principles

Design principle 1	Product innovations should contribute to strategic goals.
Design principle 2	Progress should be measurable.
Design principle 3	Progress metrics should cover all development stages.
Design principle 4	Progress metrics should be delimited between development stages.
Design principle 5	Progress metrics should be informative and intuitive for all stakeholders.
Design principle 6	Progress metrics should be consistent for all stakeholders.
Design principle 7	The measurement system should be continuously improved.

2.3 What Can be Built: Existing Innovation Accounting Approaches in Literature

The term innovation accounting was first introduced by Eric Ries in his book "The Lean Startup" and describes a systematic process for startups to track the progress of innovative ideas that face high uncertainty in order to keep them accountable [12]. The concept of innovation accounting has been adopted in the area of innovation management as traditional financial metrics were not suitable and transformative innovation was executed poorly because of using tools and KPIs that are not applicable [13].

A review of literature suggests that three general frameworks on innovation accounting have been proposed. First, Viki et al. [9] provide an innovation accounting framework that takes a holistic view and comprises three types of KPIs: Reporting KPIs are related to activities of the innovation practice. Governance KPIs serve the management for investment decisions. Global KPIs reflect the strategic impact of the innovation activities. Furthermore, the authors suggest measuring activity as well as impact metrics to assess innovation activities, where activity metrics are predominantly used in the early innovation stages and impact metrics in the later stages. Gons & Toma [14] expand the view and add key result indicators to their innovation accounting framework in addition to the KPIs. The result indicators give information about the result of a certain innovation process and provide a broader understanding to the innovation participants.

Second, Osterwalder et al. [10] provide innovation metrics for the exploration of new value propositions. Like Viki et al. and Toma & Gons, they provide a concept that considers different viewpoints of stakeholders in the innovation process. The innovation metrics shall support the innovation teams to de-risk assumptions and reduce uncertainty. In addition, the metrics should make it possible for the management to manage projects in a portfolio view and to provide them with a scorecard that holds information considering the strategic contribution, business opportunity and risks.

Third, Binetti [15] addresses the topic primarily from a finance perspective. He argues that people that provide budget to the innovation teams, need financial metrics to substantiate the investment decisions. With the trinomial tree, the author created an approach to price the options for generated learnings from experiments by the innovation team so that the finance team can value the innovation after each iterative step and can make an investment decision for the next iteration.

The current discussion around the metrics of innovations shows what can be built with the current concepts. The literature agrees that innovation activities should employ accounting measures to achieve the best outcomes when searching for new value propositions and business models. Such metrics should not work against conventional financial metrics but work as additional indicators for a comprehensive innovation evaluation. The metrics to assess the progress and success of innovation activities must start early in the process and should be in line with the respective innovation framework, like lean innovation, business model generation, etc. Finally, innovation accounting provides a fact-based decision-making process for innovations.

3   Solution Design

3.1   Design Requirements

Design requirements are attributes that the artifact being designed must meet, taking into account the expectations of the user groups. There are four design requirement categories: (a) functional requirements, describe core functionalities that drive the performance of the solution; (b) user requirements, which are specifications by the addressed user of the solution; (c) boundary conditions, describe conditions that have to be unconditionally met; (d) design restrictions, which can be described as the solution space that is preferred by the user group [16].

The *functional requirements* are designed by applying the S.M.A.R.T. framework [17]. The innovation accounting system shall contain *specific* metrics that are clearly defined. The metrics must be provably *measured* and provide evidence for the user to make decisions. For each metric a specific *action* must be executed by the user. Each metric in the innovation accounting system must be specified in a way that it is realistic to *reach*. Each metric shall be bounded to a reasonable *time* frame within the innovation process.

The *user requirements* include that the innovation accounting system shall cover the entire innovation process where a sub-set of metrics are specifically defined for each innovation stage. The metrics shall be defined specifically for each relevant stakeholder in the process. Besides the progress tracking of product innovations, the activities and outcomes during the innovation process should be measurable. The metrics must be easy to understand, interpret and use for all stakeholders. Both internal and external perspectives must be considered when determining progress, such as examining feasibility. The measurement system must be fully comprehensive and thus of benefit to all stakeholders during and throughout the process.

The *boundary conditions* comprise that the innovation accounting system needs to consider the existing structures within the company, like innovation process for developing digital products, business procedures, performance systems, or hierarchies.

The *design restriction* is to include only a considerably manageable number of metrics in each innovation stage.

3.2 Object Design

To outline the conditions for a general framework to derive the accounting metrics a systematic determination of the design options of innovation accounting is carried out. For comparing the number of different model proposals, a systematic classification can be established using the morphological box method. The principle of the morphological box is a creative method to structure all potential solutions for a problem [18]. Figure 1 shows the possible combinations and the (darkened) selection of the innovation accounting parameters that represents the outline for the proposed system's design. The selection of metrics follows primarily the idea of Viki et al. [9] especially because of the distinction of the user group's viewpoints and is complemented by specific metrics, that are relevant from the perspective of a PSF. As discovered in the interviews, the strategic goal of the innovation activities is not formalized and therefore the focus of the metrics lies primarily on the progress and activity tracking and not on the strategic impact.

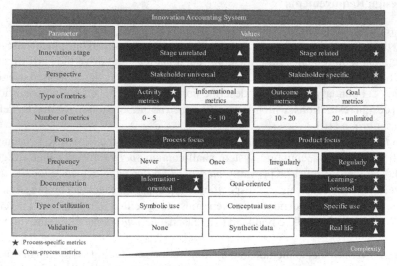

Fig. 1. Morphological box design selection

Solution Design. The designed solution object consists of two parts: (1) process-specific metrics, that is a set of metrics that focus on the progress tracking within each stage of the defined innovation process (marked with a star icon), and (2) cross-process metrics, that is a set of metrics that cut across the innovation process (marked with a triangle icon in Fig. 1).

Process-Specific Metrics. With reference to the requirements described in Sect. 3.1 process-specific metrics are designed alongside the innovation process and should track activities and outcomes in each stage. The progress tracking is relevant for each stakeholder from a different viewpoint and therefore should be defined with respect to each user group. However, to design a rather concise model, not more than five to ten metrics shall be defined per innovation stage that are not product-specific and should be measured in each build-measure-learn iteration. Applying these parameters in the model the complexity of the system is expected to be moderate and manageable (Table 2).

Table 2. Innovation process-specific metrics

User group	Metric type	Innovation stage & metric			
		Discover	*Design*	*Develop*	*Deliver*
Innovation practice	*Activity*	- No. of customer conversations	- No. of user interviews - No. of observations - No. of internal interviews - No. of prototypes built	- No. of milestones - No. of scope changes - No. of defects	- External reach - Internal reach - No. of leads - No. of customer demos - No. of users - Sales split (direct /indirect)
	Outcome	- No. of validated problems	- Time cost per learning - Hypotheses developed	- Development velocity - Sprint burndown - Cumulative flow diagram	- Cost per lead - Growth funnel - Lead conversion rate - Customer lifetime value
Innovation management	*Activity*		- No. of decisions made		
	Outcome		- Risky assumptions identified - Validation velocity - % at problem-solution fit - Strategic fit - Budget spent per stage - Decision time	- % milestones achieved - Budget spent for development	- Return on product development expense - % at product-market-fit - % at scale - Budget spent for campaigning

Cross-Process Metrics. These overarching metrics (marked with a triangle icon in Fig. 1) give insights about the activities throughout the innovation process and provide information to continuously improve the process. The metrics are primarily relevant to the management team to keep track of the innovation activities in general (Table 3).

Table 3. Innovation cross-process metrics

Metric type	Metric
Activity	- No. innovation challenges - No. of discovery workshops - No. of ideas submitted - No. of products per innovation stage - No. of products moving stage
Outcome	- No. validated businesses - Average amount spent per stage - Average amount spent per product

4   Evaluation

At this point in the project, we performed a descriptive evaluation of the artifact. A descriptive evaluation is an informed argument about the artifact's utility [19]. The evaluation of the solution covers a range of criteria which include feasibility, ease of use, operationality, effectiveness and efficiency [20]. Table 4 visualizes the requirement-solution-fit by comparing the requirements with the object design.

Table 4. Requirement-solution-fit

Requirements		Solution fit
Functional requirements	Specific	●
	Measurable	●
	Actionable	●
	Reachable	◓
	Timely	●
User requirements	Innovation stage related	◑
	Role specific	◑
	Process improvement	◑
	Easy to grasp	◕
	Internal and external viewpoint	●
	Comprehensive	◑
Boundary conditions	Company structures	◕
	Innovation process	●
Design restriction	Limited amount of metrics	◕
OVERALL FIT		◕

● Complete fit . . . ◓ Limited fit

Regarding the functional requirements, the reachable attribute shows in the comparison a limited fit to the given solution model. It raises the question if this requirement is of substance in this context. On the one hand, the development happens in iterative steps, where, after each step, knowledge is generated and evidence-based decision making can be applied. Thus, if, for example, the innovation team discovers after the first customer interview that the idea does not solve the customer's problem at all, it could be counterintuitive to spend more time or budget, e.g. on conducting more interviews in order to complete a defined number of interviews which would be required by the system.

The solution model is limited in terms of comprehensiveness. It considers the different viewpoints and activities of the stakeholders. However, it primarily focuses on the execution and governance of innovation activities but covers the strategy perspective only to a limited extend because of information constraints regarding the strategic objectives. As outlined in the literature, the innovation accounting system should integrate the strategic impact of innovation activities as well [9, 10].

With focus on the metrics, it is possible that the stakeholders must introduce new workflows to set the basis for the measurement of certain metrics. Thus, the value of tracking the progress must exceed the effort to introduce new workflows, e.g. agile development workflows like Scrum or Kanban, or technical solutions to track lead generation when marketing the product.

Introducing the innovation accounting system would fundamentally change the conventional approach and would need a shift in the mindset of all stakeholders on the importance of making progress measurable from a very early stage. Tracking the progress from the beginning and thereby creating transparency can lead to skepticism among the participants of the innovation process [21]. This means, that although the innovation accounting system is a tool to create transparency for progress, instead it could be used to judge somebody on the outcomes.

Overall, the solution model addresses the key problem and provides a framework for measuring the progress of digital product innovations in the innovation process. It creates a structured approach towards measuring the success of product innovations and gives insights about the overall innovation activities and through-put. Consequently, the perceived blind spots as of today will be drastically reduced. The user groups gain an early understanding of the product innovation potential and can derive evidence-based decisions in every development stage. As a result, this transparency creates an awareness of the resources used.

5 Learning

By applying the CIMO-logic the learnings from the thesis on the conceptual solution design are synthesized and transferred into design propositions for innovation accounting. The CIMO-logic provides a structured approach to derive the propositions by combining the *context* with specific *intervention* types, which follow certain *mechanisms* and lead to defined *outcomes* [22]. The attributes of the design propositions are summarized in the following illustration (Fig. 2).

This paper developed an innovation accounting system for an end-to-end innovation process in PSFs (C) with a curated holistic set of KPIs that takes into account activity-

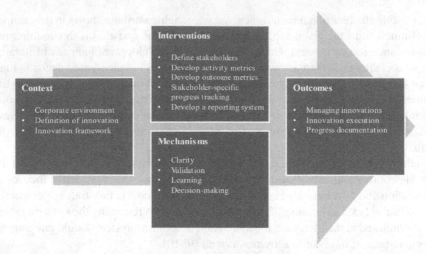

Fig. 2. Design proposition with CIMO-logic

and outcome-oriented metrics and contrasts them for the different user groups in PSFs (I) promoting an evidence-based decision-making (M) to manage innovations efficiently (O).

The existing literature around Viki et al. or Gons & Toma provide holistic performance indicators for innovations in corporations, taking into account a company-wide innovation framework and the different stakeholder perspectives [9, 14]. In contrast, this paper complements the existing literature by proposing an approach that is applicable for the peculiarities of PSFs [1]. The KPIs selected consider on the one hand the importance of decentralized partnership structures, meaning that the innovation accounting system proposed in this paper is applicable for a division of partners who are jointly deciding on funding innovations in the endeavor of new business opportunities. On the other hand, the importance of the connection between the innovation team, that has the expertise to find new business models, and the subject-matter experts, who have the technical expertise that flows into the innovations.

In addition, this paper argues that innovation accounting in such a corporate environment (C) considers introspective learning (I) in addition to extrospective learning, like user tests or any activity that addresses the outside of the company. Introspective learning, i.e. internal interviews, is of importance as it provides evidence about the internal feasibility (M) and to gather evidence on how the innovation performs internally by building a network of supporting actors (O).

As proposed by the literature, innovations should be validated early in the process to de-risk assumptions and reduce uncertainty, e.g. by customer interviews or other external exploration activities [9, 10, 14]. To meet certain characteristics of PSFs, the proposed innovation accounting system adds on to the indicators in the existing literatures by introducing introspective learning to ensure the internal validation and future success of the innovation. Firstly, subject-matter-experts with high professional standards have to validate the quality of the idea to ensure feasibility. Then, customer applicability also needs to be confirmed to reduce the firm's fear of reputational damage. Secondly, as in PSFs, services are sold not by salespeople but by the professional workforce, the internal validation is of importance to gather evidence on acceptance of the innovation and potential network for market distribution.

The design propositions aim to provide a blueprint for actors like the innovation team who confront similar challenges in PSFs. In addition, the design propositions can perhaps also be useful for other industries as well. They point out a comprehensive version of what needs to be done to design and implement an innovation accounting system in a certain context.

6 Conclusion

The designed innovation accounting system for PSFs is a conceptual solution to make each activity and outcome measurable in a defined innovation process. With its implementation the user groups gain relevant information to derive evidence-based decisions. By creating transparency on the outcomes in each innovation stage, the blind spot of the impact of innovation activities is reduced drastically.

The limitation of this work is that the conceptual solution model does only partially include the strategic perspective and has not yet been implemented and tested on its practicability. In addition, the field of innovation accounting is relatively young and thus academic evidence is limited.

To better understand the implications of innovation accounting, future studies could research the impact of measurement systems in innovation processes in a range of PSFs. Furthermore, the proposed solution should be academically refined as well as widely be tested – perhaps in other industries as well.

This paper contributed to the body of design knowledge and has direct practical implications by providing design propositions on the creation of an innovation accounting system in PSFs.

References

1. Von Nordenflycht, A.: What is a professional service firm? Toward a theory and taxonomy of knowledge-intensive firms. Acad. Manag. Rev. **35**(1), 155–174 (2010)
2. Kohli, R., Melville, N.P.: Digital innovation: a review and synthesis. Inf. Syst. J. **29**, 200–223 (2019). https://doi.org/10.1111/isj.12193
3. Prising, J., Weinelt, B.: Digital transformation initiative: professional services industry. World Economic Forum, Cologny/Geneva (2017)
4. Rhodes, J.: How professional services firms can unlock new business value with digital technologies (2018). https://www.digitalistmag.com/digital-economy/2018/11/21/how-professional-services-firms-can-unlock-new-business-value-with-digital-technologies-06194288/. Accessed 18 May 2021
5. Blank, S.: Why the lean start-up changes everything. Harv. Bus. Rev. **91**(5), 63–72 (2013)
6. Van Aken, J.E., Berends, J.J.: Problem Solving in Organizations: A Methodological Handbook for Business Students, 3rd edn. Cambridge University Press, Cambridge (2018). https://doi.org/10.1017/9781108236164
7. Seckler, C., Mauer, R., vom Brocke, J.: Design science in entrepreneurship: conceptual foundations and guiding principles. J. Bus. Ventur. Design (2022). In press

8. Aken, J.E., Berends, J.J., Bij, J.D.: Problem Solving in Organizations: A Methodological Handbook for Business Students, 2nd edn. Cambridge University Press, Cambridge (2016)
9. Viki, T., Toma, D., Gons, E.: The Corporate Startup: How Established Companies Can Develop Successful Innovation Ecosystems. Vakmedianet, Zeist (2017)
10. Osterwalder, A., Pigneur, Y., Smith, A., Etiemble, F.: The Invincible Company. Wiley, Hoboken (2020)
11. Osterwalder, A.: Do you understand what customers want and can you build it? (2018). https://www.strategyzer.com/blog/posts/2018/2/27/do-you-understand-what-custom ers-want-and-can-you-build-it. Accessed 10 Jan 2022
12. Ries, E.: The Lean Startup: How Constant Innovation Creates Radically Successful Businesses. Portfolio Penguin, London (2011)
13. Christensen, C.M., Kaufman, S.P., Shih, W.C.: Innovation killers: how financial tools destroy your capacity to do new things. Harv. Bus. Rev. **86**(1), 98–105 (2008)
14. Gons, E., Toma, D.: Innovation Accounting: A Practical Guide for measuring Your Innovation Ecosystem's Performance. BIS Publishers, Amsterdam (2021)
15. Binetti, D.: Measuring learning in dollars (2015). https://blog.innovation-options.com/innova tion-options-a-framework-for-evaluating-innovation-in-larger-organizations-968bd43f59f6. Accessed 20 Jan 2022
16. Aken, J., Berends, H., Van der Bij, H.: Problem Solving in Organizations: A Methodological Handbook for Business and Management Students, 2nd edn. Cambridge University Press, Cambridge (2012). https://doi.org/10.1017/CBO9781139094351
17. Doran, G.T.: There's a SMART way to write management's goals and objectives. Manage. Rev. **70**(11), 35–36 (1981)
18. Zwicky, F.: The morphological approach to discovery, invention, research and construction. In: Zwicky, F., Wilson, A.G. (eds.) New Methods of Thought and Procedure, pp. 273–297. Springer, Heidelberg (1967). https://doi.org/10.1007/978-3-642-87617-2_14
19. Bichler, M.: Design science in information systems research. Wirtschaftsinformatik **48**(2), 133–135 (2006). https://doi.org/10.1007/s11576-006-0028-8
20. Sonnenberg, C., vom Brocke, J.: Evaluations in the science of the artificial – reconsidering the build-evaluate pattern in design science research. In: Peffers, K., Rothenberger, M., Kuechler, B. (eds.) DESRIST 2012. LNCS, vol. 7286, pp. 381–397. Springer, Heidelberg (2012). https://doi.org/10.1007/978-3-642-29863-9_28
21. Barr, S.: Prove It!: How to Create a High-Performance Culture and Measurable Success. Wiley, Hoboken (2017)
22. Denyer, D., Tranfield, D., Van Aken, J.E.: Developing design propositions through research synthesis. Organ. Stud. **29**(3), 393–413 (2008)

Market of Makers – How to Promote Corporate Entrepreneurship with an Effectuation Intervention

Sophia Marie Braun[✉] and René Mauer

ESCP Business School, Heubnerweg 8-10, 14059 Berlin, Germany
{sbraun,rmauer}@escp.eu

Abstract. Corporate entrepreneurship is a challenge for organizations and their employees, for example because of structural rigidities or inertia. A promising approach of how to spark corporate entrepreneurship lies in effectuation research. Effectuation is a mode of action or decision-making logic that is based on empirical evidence from expert entrepreneurs. Following a Design Science Research (DSR) methodology, we develop and implement an effectuation intervention at a German multinational corporation. The intervention consists of two basic parts: The *Market of Makers*, an event that leads participants through the effectual process, and the *Speedboat Regatta*, a 3-months long project development phase. The intervention successfully generated 23 projects that identified opportunities for process innovation. This study contributes to design knowledge, theory and practice. First, we designed a blueprint for similar effectuation interventions and are able to formulate four design principles, which show how voluntariness, playfulness, and constraints enable effectuation and promote corporate entrepreneurship. Second, we contribute to corporate entrepreneurship theory by showing that effectuation is promising for approaching corporate entrepreneurship's theoretical and empirical problems. Third, we contribute to practice by demonstrating that interventions based on effectuation may shift employees towards leading and engaging with innovative projects.

Keywords: Corporate entrepreneurship · Effectuation · Design science

1 Introduction

Firms are striving to have continuous competitive advantage. In order to achieve and maintain it, streams of literature, such *corporate entrepreneurship*, stress that firms need to engage in transformation, strategic renewal, or corporate venturing [1–3]. Corporate entrepreneurship is concerned with individuals who engage in these behaviors by pursuing opportunities within corporate structures. They are *corporate entrepreneurs*, who engage as enablers for innovation [2]. However, corporate efforts to engage their workforce in entrepreneurial behaviors are seen as challenging [1–3]. For example, corporations usually experience structural inertia, which makes engaging in exploration of

© Springer Nature Switzerland AG 2022
A. Drechsler et al. (Eds.): DESRIST 2022, LNCS 13229, pp. 249–261, 2022.
https://doi.org/10.1007/978-3-031-06516-3_19

new opportunities difficult. Moreover, when individuals within the organization conceptualize new ideas, pushing them toward implementation requires a process that aligns divergent interests across organizational boundaries [3].

In this paper, we study a practical representation of these theoretical and empirical problems. *A.Corp* is a German multinational corporation that mainly operates in industrial manufacturing. 11 months before the start of our intervention, a commercial function has started an innovation initiative, which 450 staff members joined. It offers digital technology trainings. However, these skills were applied seldomly and ideas were not sufficiently converted into real projects. These new skills were only applied by some, and if they were, only in parts, and only within one's immediate team. Cross-functional projects did not emerge. This led to the trainings not having sustainable impact while creating high costs and staff absences, and to frustration among participants. A solution to this problem is valuable, as it has the potential to create new processes, products, or services based on digital technologies that contribute to *A.Corp*'s profitability, as well as to improve motivation among employees. Moreover, a solution may create more robust, cross-functional project teams that drive digital innovation at *A.Corp*, and extend and strengthen intra-organizational networks.

The aim of this paper is to develop an intervention package to foster corporate entrepreneurship, consisting of the *Market of Makers* and the subsequent *Speedboat Regatta*. To do so, we followed a design science research (DSR) approach. We consider DSR as suitable, since we attempt to solve a practical problem by applying theoretical knowledge and by designing a useful artifact [4]. In this way, we contribute to understanding entrepreneurship as a design science [5–7]. Concretely, we follow the DSR methodology by Peffers et al. [8]. We formulated the problem (Activity 1) above. In the following section, we describe the objectives of a solution (Activity 2). We then report how the intervention was designed (Activity 3). We designed the *Market of Makers* based on effectuation, a decision-making logic that was observed with expert entrepreneurs [9, 10]. Effectuation is a promising approach of how to operationalize corporate entrepreneurship. It has been found that effectuation is a valid strategic orientation and may foster practiced creativity, research and development (R&D) output as well as R&D efficiency in corporate contexts [11–13]. Moreover, effectuation can be used to teach entrepreneurship [14]. Afterwards, we show how we applied the *Market of Makers* and hence demonstrate its usefulness at *A.Corp* (Activity 4). Subsequently, we evaluate how well the intervention solved the problem (Activity 5) and are able to show that 64 employees took active part in the intervention, generated 29 new ideas and successfully ran 23 projects over 18 weeks. Communication activities (Activity 6) include disseminating this study.

This study makes important contributions to design knowledge, theory and practice. First, we designed a blueprint that can guide similar corporate entrepreneurship interventions in firms. Moreover, we formulate four design principles. They show how voluntariness, playfulness, and constraints enable corporate entrepreneurship. Second, this paper makes a theoretical contribution to corporate entrepreneurship theory by showing that effectuation [10] is promising for tackling corporate entrepreneurship's theoretical and empirical problems [2, 3]. Moreover, we are able to deduct a question for further effectuation research. Third, this research contributes to practice by demonstrating that interventions based on effectuation may shift employees away from routine behavior towards entrepreneurial behavior that generates innovative, cross-functional projects. Looking forward, we plan to test and refine our intervention with other organizations.

2 Objectives of a Solution

We derive the objectives of a solution based on the corporate entrepreneurship and effectuation literature. We created a list of theoretical prescriptions that included 13 items and five sub-items (the effectuation principles [9]). Interestingly, the items contradict each other regarding access to resources. The corporate entrepreneurship literature sees available resources as an antecedent of entrepreneurial behavior [1, 2]. The effectuation literature highlights that expert entrepreneurs work with their individual resources rather than with an expected return [9, 10].

Following a pattern-matching technique [15], we compared the objectives with data that we collected at *A.Corp*. We organized two meetings with one senior and two middle managers of *A.Corp*. We took notes during these meetings and collected results on a shared digital whiteboard. The middle managers also gave a presentation with their objectives and ideas. Other documents include emails and written collaboration agreements. Moreover, we conducted two semi-structured interviews (30 min each) with the middle managers later in the process, which included questions about their objectives at the beginning. This variety of sources allows data triangulation [15]. If an objective was mentioned at least twice and matched a theoretical prescription, we considered it for our research. In the case of contradicting prescriptions regarding access to resources, our conversations with *A.Corp* managers made clear that they did not intend to spend an additional budget, which is why we formulated the O8 based on the effectuation literature. This process resulted in ten objectives, which are shown in Table 1.

Table 1. Performance objectives

Objective	Description
O1: Internal solution	Find a solution that leads to more innovation and strategic renewal inside the organization [2]
O2: Managerial support	Ensure that managers, especially top-level executives, show their willingness to promote entrepreneurial behavior [1]
O3: Attention	Create a stimulus that triggers the attention of employees and channels it towards non-routine activities [3]
O4: Motivation	Form an experience that is fun and that rewards participants, so that individual and corporate incentives align [1, 2]
O5: Opportunity identification	Invite individuals to identify opportunities [2] based on their interests and skills (i.e. individual means) [9]

(continued)

Table 1. (*continued*)

Objective	Description
O6: Project development	Develop projects that are based on effectual orientation [11, 12] and apply digital technologies
O7: Cross-functional collaboration	Allow random interactions that lead to partnerships between different teams [9, 10]. Ensure that opportunities have a high likelihood to gain *"good currency"* [3]
O8: Resources	Ensure that participants draw on their slack time and resources to shape their projects [9, 10]
O9: Process innovation	Create new processes within a corporation that create a return on investment [2], specifically by digitalizing financial tasks
O10: Culture	Create an organizational (sub-)culture that is supportive, open to transformation, risk-taking and learning from failure [1, 2]

3 Design and Development

Building on the objectives formulated in the previous section, we designed a corporate entrepreneurship intervention based on effectuation that consisted of a kick-off event called *Market of Makers* and subsequent 3-months *Speedboat Regatta*.

Predominantly, effectuation is conceptualized as a set of principles: means orientation (*who I am, what I know, whom I know*), affordable loss orientation (*"predetermines how much loss is affordable and focuses on experimenting with as many strategies as possible with the given limited means"*), strategic alliance orientation (*"emphasizes [...] pre-commitments from stakeholders"*), contingency orientation (*"exploiting contingencies that ar[i]se unexpectedly over time"*), and control orientation (*"to the extent that we control the future, we do not need to predict it"*) [10]. Next to these principles, effectuation is considered as an iteration process (see Fig. 1). This process starts with entrepreneurs assessing their means. Then, entrepreneurs begin doing what they can afford to do, seek

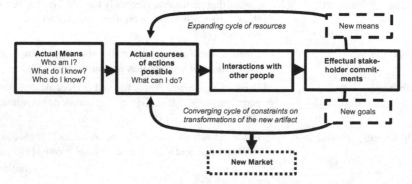

Fig. 1. Effectuation as a process [16]

potential partners, and gain partner commitments. In doing so, they create new means and new goals, which enable them to grow an effectual network over time that eventually may become a new market [16]. The underlying design of our intervention is for participants to go through several iterations of the effectuation process.

Firstly, we designed roles for the intervention (*captains, crew,* and *coaches*) (see Table 2). It is important to note that individuals might have more than one role.

Table 2. Roles

Group	Description
Captains	Launch and control small-scale projects (speedboats) autonomously (*control orientation*), interact with others and find committed crew members (*strategic alliance orientation*)
Crew members	Voluntarily contribute "*effectual stakeholder commitments*" and hence *new means* or *new goals* to speedboat(s)
Coaches	Keep in touch with the captains, support them in the *Captains Club*, and receive guidance from the design scientists

Secondly, we designed an overarching process with multiple elements for the intervention (see Fig. 2), mainly the *Market of Makers* and the *Speedboat Regatta*.

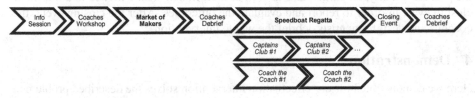

Fig. 2. Intervention process

3.1 Designing the Market of Makers

The intervention process starts with information sessions that are open to employees who are interested in joining the *Market of Makers* or in applying as coach. These sessions should provide basic information about the intervention. Subsequently, 15 coaches should be selected. They are then invited to a first 4-h workshop that explains the background of the *Market of Makers* and introduces effectuation [10].

The *Market of Makers* is a four-hour event, in which the participants are guided through the effectual process [16]. Firstly, on the *Market of Makers*, a minimum of 50 participants are instructed that this event would make them develop, lead and engage with *speedboats*. We defined speedboats as small, autonomous projects or initiatives run by volunteering employees (*control orientation*) that do not require additional budget or time (*affordable loss orientation*). Secondly, the participants should be instructed reflect on their individual, *actual means*. Then, they should develop three ideas for what they could do with these means (*actual courses of actions possible*). Afterwards, they would be sent into randomly assigned breakout rooms (*contingency orientation*) in groups of two for five minutes, in which they should introduce their ideas (*interactions with other people*). Moreover, they should ask for what the other person might want to contribute, and hence collect *effectual stakeholder commitments* that may lead to *new means* or *new goals* (*strategic alliance orientation*). We planned for five of these dialogues. Subsequently, speedboats should be pre-selected and visualized on a digital whiteboard in randomly assigned groups of three. Moreover, the potential speedboat leads (*captains*) should call other employees who they think might be interested in their speedboats even if they are not participating in the *Market of Makers* (*strategic alliance orientation*). The *Market of Makers* results in short pitches of all developed speedboats, which are then sent off by the group, unless someone has a reasoned objection. The *Market of Makers* is afterwards debriefed with the coaches, which includes assigning a coach to each speedboat.

3.2 Designing the Speedboat Regatta

During the 3-months long *Speedboat Regatta*, the captains steer their speedboats autonomously (*control orientation*), but receive guidance from their coach when needed. Moreover, the coaches organize multiple *Captains Club* meetings, in which they facilitate exchange between the captains (*strategic alliance orientation*). The coaches are invited to two two-hour workshops with the design scientists, in which they reflect on the process. Finally, all participants as well as their managers are invited to a four-hour closing event in order to report and evaluate the outcomes. After the closing event, the coaches and design scientists debrief the whole intervention.

4 Demonstration

Here we demonstrate how our effectuation intervention solves the described problem at *A. Corp*, which is the first iteration of our effectuation intervention. *A. Corp* had started an innovation initiative. Seven months after this initiative started, they contacted us design scientists for the first time. The contact intensified and we agreed on conducting an effectuation intervention ten months after the start of the initiative. The final preparations and discussions with *A. Corp* took about a month and the whole intervention spanned five months. During this whole time, we collected data in the form of meeting recordings, meeting and interview notes, documents (emails, presentations, digital whiteboards, tables), and semi-structured interviews with nine captains (3.5 h in total). We now report on the major milestones of the designed intervention process: the *Market of Makers* and coaches workshops and the *Speedboat Regatta* with its closing event and the subsequent coaches debrief. Notably, the intervention was conducted fully online due to the Covid-19 pandemic.

4.1 Applying the Market of Makers

In the coaches workshop that preceded the *Market of Makers*, the coaches reacted positively and were excited. The *Market of Makers* itself was attended by 71 participants.

Finally, 29 speedboats were presented by 25 captains. 28 speedboats were sent off, one was discontinued due to a reasoned objection. Four speedboats did not have committed crew members after the *Market of Makers*, all others had already recruited one to five colleagues as crew (on average 2.3). The debrief workshop with the coaches started with a retrospect. They were positively surprised by the quantity and richness of ideas, the willingness to take action, and the diversity of participants. We then assigned coaches to speedboats. On average, each coach mentored 2.3 speedboats.

4.2 Applying the Speedboat Regatta

The *Speedboat Regatta* went on for 18 weeks. In total, 64 participants were actively involved in speedboats. 31 participants were involved in two or more speedboats (max. seven). The speedboats had an average size of 4.5 members.

In Table 3, we show how the regatta progressed and define the following stages: *In harbor*, and hence before a kick-off meeting, *ready* and hence right after kick-off, *on course* and hence actively working on the project, *in distress* and hence in need of external support, *back in harbor* and hence taking a break as well as *at destination* and hence having completed the project or initiative. 23 speedboats arrived at a destination and were able to present their outcomes at the closing event. Two speedboats remained in harbor the whole time and were hence not kicked off and actively worked on. No captain reported that their speedboat was in distress at any point in time. Two speedboats returned to the harbor for a little while to take a break.

Table 3. *Speedboat Regatta* overview

Week	W0	W3	W6	W9	W11	W14	W16	W18
In harbor	29	9	3	3	2	2	2	2
Ready	0	9	10	4	1	0	0	0
On course	0	9	11	15	20	20	17	0
In distress	0	0	0	0	0	0	0	0
Back in harbor	0	0	1	2	0	0	0	0
At destination	0	0	0	1	2	3	6	23
Total	*29*	*27*	*25*	*25*	*25*	*25*	*25*	*25*

The *Closing Event* was attended by 82 participants and each captain pitched their speedboat. *A.Corp* senior managers gave awards to three that they found particularly novel, collaborative and lean. Finally, *A.Corp* senior managers gave an outlook on how the regatta continues. In our subsequent debrief with the coaches, we collected feedback for the whole intervention process and sharpened the regatta continuation.

5 Evaluation

Our evaluation of the intervention at *A.Corp* are based on quantitative data on the *Speedboat Regatta* as presented above (such as Table 3), documented feedback from all workshops with the coaches, a feedback form filled by *Market of Makers* participants, documentation of *Captains Club* meetings, pitches and impressions shared during the *Closing Event*, as well as interviews with *A.Corp* managers and with nine captains. The interviews followed a semi-structured approach and enquired about the general impression of the *Market of Makers* and the *Speedboat Regatta*, not actively about specific performance objectives. The diversity of data hence allowed for data triangulation [15]. Following a pattern-matching strategy [15], we collected statements and impressions per performance objective as individual data points, counted repetitions, and compared the strongest signals to the objectives set out in Table 2. We show our results in Table 4.

Table 4. Evaluation of performance objectives

Objective	Evaluation
O1: Internal solution	With the *Market of Makers* and *Speedboat Regatta* we designed a purely internal solution that is based on effectuation
O2: Managerial support	The intervention was initiated by senior managers of *A.Corp*. They send out invitation emails, were present at both the *Market of Makers* and the closing event, appreciated the participants publicly and gave rewards (7 data points)
O3: Attention	The *Market of Makers* triggered 64 employees to engage in speedboats. *A.Corp* only provided limited information before, which created positive suspense for some (2 data points), but also frustration, uncertainty and confusion (5 data points)
O4: Motivation	The *Market of Makers* was perceived as having a dynamic, lively and open atmosphere (6 data points) that spurred enthusiasm and creativity (7 data points). The captains and crew were perceived as highly motivated throughout (11 data points)
O5: Opportunity identification	The participants perceived identifying opportunities and generating ideas during *Market of Makers* as easy (3 data points). The number of ideas developed was very high, since *A.Corp* had expected rather 10 than 29 speedboats (3 data points)
O6: Project development	23 speedboats developed during the *Market of Makers* (=79.3%) were based on digital technologies and process innovation. However, a lot of speedboats struggled with maintaining their "speedboat character" and engaged in very detailed discussions (7 data points)

(continued)

Table 4. (*continued*)

Objective	Evaluation
O7: Cross-functional collaboration	The *Market of Makers* allowed participants to meet new people and widen their network (14 data points). The participants highlighted how happy they were with uncomplicated cross-functional exchange during the intervention (15 data points). The speedboats that arrived at a destination on average brought together 3 different corporate functions. Partly, the collaboration between captains and coaches during the *Speedboat Regatta* was perceived as good (6 data points), partly as difficult (3 data points). Some captains did not really feel like they need the coaches (4 data points). The captain/coach relationship was not clear enough (5 data points). The coaches expressed that they turned out to have rather an organizational than a coaching role (6 data points)
O8: Resources	From the beginning, we and *A.Corp* senior managers communicated that there is no additional financial or time budget for the intervention (3 data points). While a lack of a financial budget was not further mentioned by participants, they expressed that finding time for working on their speedboat next to the day-to-day operations is difficult (9 data points)
O9: Process innovation	18 speedboats that arrived at a destination (=78.3%) applied new digital technologies and based new processes on them. Their return on investment cannot be evaluated yet
O10: Culture	The intervention created a sub-culture that is based on voluntary commitments (6 data points), eye-level collaboration (4 data points) and a supportive community (3 data points)

Regarding O1, we conclude that we have successfully designed an internal solution for fostering innovation [2]. The support by top-level executives was excellent, which enabled the intervention to be effective (O2) [1]. For future rounds of the intervention, we will develop a list of managerial best-practices based on the *A.Corp* case, which we will base our conversations with future partner organizations on.

As set out in O3, we created a stimulus that triggers the attention of employees. We successfully had 64 participants engage with non-routine activities [3]. However, for the next iteration of the intervention, we will make sure that extensive information about the intervention are widely available. In O4, we expressed that we want to create a fun, rewarding experience [1, 2]. We conclude that we achieved this objective.

Regarding O5, we conclude that we were very successful in getting individuals to identify opportunities [2] based on their means [9]. Based on this, project development

(O6) based on effectuation [11, 12] was very successful too. Moreover, the vast majority applied digital technologies, which *A.Corp* strived for. In future iterations of the intervention, we will join the *Captains Club* meetings in order to keep working with the captains directly, for example on how to keep their speedboats lean.

With regards to O7, we show that designing the *Market of Makers* with random interactions leads to partnerships between different teams [9, 10]. Having coaches to support creating organizational traction, however, was not sufficiently effective. In future interventions, we will fulfill the coaching role ourselves. Regarding O8, we conclude that participants successfully drew on their slack time and resources.

With regards to O9, we show that our intervention successfully led to speedboats that create new processes within a corporation [2]. By digitalizing financial tasks, they should create a return on investment. Finally, we conclude that the intervention created a voluntary, collaborative and supportive sub-culture [1, 2]. For future interventions, we would like to focus more on the other aspects expressed in O10, namely openness to transformation, risk-taking and learning from failure, for example by delivering specific training elements around these topics.

6   Discussion and Conclusion

Although many organizations try to engage their employees in corporate entrepreneurship, they often suffer from a lack of new initiatives. We designed an intervention called *Market of Makers* and *Speedboat Regatta* based on effectuation [9]. We demonstrated its use at *A.Corp*, a German multinational firm, which led to 29 new project ideas, of which 23 came to a successful endpoint after 18 weeks. 64 employees took active part in these projects. They generated a high number of ideas which led to cross-functional projects based on digital technologies and process innovation. Keeping these projects small and not reverting to corporate practices was perceived as difficult, as well as making time for the projects. The project leads (*captains*) received support from specially trained coaches. However, difficulties regarding the captain/coach relationship and understanding of roles arose. Intra-organizational networks were widened and strengthened, processes innovations were developed, and a sub-culture that is open to transformation emerged.

This design science project is subject to two main limitations. Firstly, certain elements of the problem and the demonstration are specific to *A.Corp*, which means that they are not fully generalizable. Secondly, the intervention has only been applied at *A.Corp*, which is why we are not yet able to assess its usefulness in other settings.

This paper makes important contributions to design knowledge, theory, and practice [17]. First, it contributes to the body of design knowledge on corporate entrepreneurship in the following ways. We designed a blueprint of a corporate entrepreneurship intervention, i.e. the concept of the *Market of Makers* and *Speedboat Regatta*. Specifically, this blueprint contains role descriptions, an intervention process and workshop content. It can be a useful guide for corporate entrepreneurship interventions in other firms. Additionally, we developed a set of four design principles [18]. They explain how and why the implementers of our intervention achieve increased entrepreneurial behavior for managers and employees in large corporations:

1. Employ the principle of voluntariness and allow employees to decide what they do, based on what they are interested in. This raises their control-orientation [10]. Hence, voluntariness boosts individual control, which then motivates employees to act as corporate entrepreneurs.
2. Guide participants through the effectuation process [16] in an interactive event that involves a high degree of playfulness. In this way, employees practice effectuation even though it may be unusual behavior for them. Hence, playfulness sparks deliberate practice which leads employees to engage in corporate entrepreneurship.
3. Do not provide effectual projects and initiatives with a financial/time budget, and force the participants to work under different prerequisites than usual corporate project management. These constraints continuously trigger employees to work with their means base and stick to the effectuation process [10, 16]. Hence, financial and time constraints make employees orient towards their means, which increases corporate entrepreneurship by sparking a new iteration of the effectuation process.
4. Make event participants interact with each other first in small groups. This reduces the number of potential stakeholders significantly. In this way, the barrier of asking others for stakeholder commitments [16] is lowered. Hence, constraining the numbers of participants enables employees to ask for stakeholder commitments, which then lead to contributions to an idea and hence corporate entrepreneurship.

These design principles contribute to corporate entrepreneurship theory by showing how introducing voluntariness and playfulness while imposing constraints makes effectuation in corporate contexts work. This is interesting for corporate entrepreneurship theory, which sees control as an outcome of corporate entrepreneurship [1]. In our study, we show that control-orientation might be an antecedent of it. Second, to our knowledge, the merits of practicing entrepreneurial behaviors have not yet been studied in corporate entrepreneurship literature. Third, corporate entrepreneurship scholars rather see available resources as an antecedent of entrepreneurial behavior and hence not as something that should be denied [1]. In contrast, our study indicates that less may be more. Lastly, corporate entrepreneurship scholars highlight that entrepreneurial behaviors are more successful when they are *"grounded in carefully established, non-imitable, and sophisticated networks"* [1]. Our study shows that in order for such a sophisticated network to come about, it might be helpful to first constrain the number of potential partners. All in all, we make a theoretical contribution to corporate entrepreneurship theory by showing that effectuation [10] is promising in order to solve the theoretical and empirical problems that this literature faces [2, 3].

Moreover, we our design work paves the path towards future confirmatory effectuation research. In this regard, it would be very interesting to apply experimental approaches to capture how successfully an effectuation intervention leads to new ideas and innovative projects in a corporate setting. This would add to a recent experimental study that showed that an entrepreneurship training based on effectuation for small-business owners led to a greater increase of business opportunities identified and pursued [19].

The contribution of this research for practice is that interventions based on effectuation may shift employees from routine behavior to entrepreneurial behavior; increase employee motivation; have the potential to generate a lot of ideas that employees actively turn into innovative, cross-functional projects; may widen and strengthen intra-organizational networks; and may create a sub-culture that is more open to organizational transformation. Looking forward, we plan to design a more general version of this intervention that will then be tested and refined with other organizations.

References

1. Kuratko, D.F., Ireland, R.D., Hornsby, J.S.: Corporate entrepreneurship behavior among managers: a review of theory, research, and practice. In: Advances in Entrepreneurship, Firm Emergence and Growth, pp. 7–45. Emerald (MCB UP), Bingley (2004). https://doi.org/10.1016/S1074-7540(04)07002-3
2. McMullen, J.S., Brownell, K.M., Adams, J.: What makes an entrepreneurship study entrepreneurial? Toward a unified theory of entrepreneurial agency. Entrep. Theory Pract. **45**, 1197–1238 (2021). https://doi.org/10.1177/1042258720922460
3. de Ven, A.H.V., Engleman, R.M.: Central problems in managing corporate innovation and entrepreneurship. In: Advances in Entrepreneurship, Firm Emergence and Growth, pp. 47–72. Emerald (MCB UP), Bingley (2004). https://doi.org/10.1016/S1074-7540(04)07003-5
4. Hevner, M., Park, J., Ram, S.: Design science in information systems research. MIS Q. **28**, 75 (2004). https://doi.org/10.2307/25148625
5. Dimov, D.: Toward a design science of entrepreneurship. In: Katz, J.A., Corbett, A.C. (eds.) Advances in Entrepreneurship, Firm Emergence and Growth, pp. 1–31. Emerald Group Publishing Limited (2016). https://doi.org/10.1108/S1074-754020160000018001
6. Berglund, H., Bousfiha, M., Mansoori, Y.: Opportunities as artifacts and entrepreneurship as design. Acad. Manage. Rev. **45**, 825–846 (2020). https://doi.org/10.5465/amr.2018.0285
7. Zhang, S.X., Van Burg, E.: Advancing entrepreneurship as a design science: developing additional design principles for effectuation. Small Bus. Econ. **55**(3), 607–626 (2019). https://doi.org/10.1007/s11187-019-00217-x
8. Peffers, K., Tuunanen, T., Rothenberger, M.A., Chatterjee, S.: A design science research methodology for information systems research. J. Manag. Inf. Syst. **24**, 45–77 (2007). https://doi.org/10.2753/MIS0742-1222240302
9. Dew, N., Read, S., Sarasvathy, S.D., Wiltbank, R.: Effectual versus predictive logics in entrepreneurial decision-making: differences between experts and novices. J. Bus. Ventur. **24**, 287–309 (2009). https://doi.org/10.1016/j.jbusvent.2008.02.002
10. Sarasvathy, S.D.: Causation and effectuation: toward a theoretical shift from economic inevitability to entrepreneurial contingency. Acad. Manage. Rev. **26**, 243–263 (2001). https://doi.org/10.5465/amr.2001.4378020
11. Werhahn, D., Mauer, R., Flatten, T.C., Brettel, M.: Validating effectual orientation as strategic direction in the corporate context. Eur. Manag. J. **33**, 305–313 (2015). https://doi.org/10.1016/j.emj.2015.03.002
12. Brettel, M., Mauer, R., Engelen, A., Küpper, D.: Corporate effectuation: entrepreneurial action and its impact on R&D project performance. J. Bus. Ventur. **27**, 167–184 (2012). https://doi.org/10.1016/j.jbusvent.2011.01.001
13. Blauth, M., Mauer, R., Brettel, M.: Fostering creativity in new product development through entrepreneurial decision making: fostering creativity in new product development. Creat. Innov. Manag. **23**, 495–509 (2014). https://doi.org/10.1111/caim.12094
14. Sarasvathy, S.D., Venkataraman, S.: Entrepreneurship as method: open questions for an entrepreneurial future. Entrep. Theory Pract. **35**, 113–135 (2011). https://doi.org/10.1111/j.1540-6520.2010.00425.x

15. Yin, R.K.: Case Study Research and Applications: Design and Methods. SAGE, Los Angeles (2018)
16. Sarasvathy, S.D., Dew, N.: New market creation through transformation. J. Evol. Econ. **15**, 533–565 (2005). https://doi.org/10.1007/s00191-005-0264-x
17. Seckler, C., Mauer, R., vom Brocke, J.: Design science in entrepreneurship: conceptual foundations and guiding principles. J. Bus. Ventur. Des. (2022). In press
18. Gregor, S., Kruse, L., Seidel, S.: Research perspectives: the anatomy of a design principle. J. Assoc. Inf. Syst. **21**, 1622–1652 (2020). https://doi.org/10.17705/1jais.00649
19. Zhu, J., Bischoff, K.M., Frese, M., Gielnik, M.M., Handrich, E., Bellstedt, D.: The effectiveness of the effectuation approach on opportunity identification and pursuit: evidence from a randomized controlled field experiment. Acad. Manag. Learn. Educ. **20**, 562–577 (2021). https://doi.org/10.5465/amle.2017.0092

How to Make Smart Collaboration Work in Multidisciplinary Teams

Jolanda Burgers-Pas[1]([✉]) and Christoph Seckler[2]

[1] IG&H, Utrecht, The Netherlands
Jolanda.burgers@igh.com
[2] ESCP Business School, Berlin, Germany
cseckler@escp.eu

Abstract. A key capability to work in multidisciplinary teams is smart collaboration. While previous research has elaborated on starting smart collaboration in firms, less is known about how to move smart collaboration from initial starting projects towards excellent implementation. In this design science project, we address this question and develop design knowledge on how to move smart collaboration from good to great in a firm working with multidisciplinary teams. We outline a situated artifact for the collaborating firm (i.e., The Firm) and infer more general design principles based on this study. This study contributes in three ways. First, it develops a situated artifact for improving smart collaboration in a firm relying on multidisciplinary teams. Second, it develops more general design principles on improving smart collaboration in professional service firms. Third, it provides initial empirical evidence for the quality of the proposed design object.

Keywords: Smart collaboration · Multidisciplinary teams · Innovation · Design knowledge

1 Introduction

Increasingly scholars turn their attention to improve multidisciplinary collaboration. A specific form of multidisciplinary collaboration is known as smart collaboration. Smart collaboration can be defined as the integration of individual, specialized expertise of knowledge workers to deliver high-quality, customized outcomes on complex issues (Gardner 2017). The idea is that smart collaboration helps a team of knowledge professionals to address issues that none could tackle individually. Research has shown that an important reason why clients need to collaborate with partners in their own firm is to make sure they 'bring the full force of the organization to bear the client's issues' (Gardner 2017). Research indicates that smart collaboration is a significant driver of both financial and people-related benefits for firms (Gardner 2017). Four particularly beneficial outcomes of smart collaboration are that firms earn higher margins, inspire greater client loyalty, attract, and retain the best talent, and gain a competitive edge when specialists collaborate across functional boundaries (Gardner 2017).

The original version of this chapter was revised: an error in the affiliation of a co-author was corrected. The correction to this chapter is available at
https://doi.org/10.1007/978-3-031-06516-3_37

While literature indicates the relevance of smart collaboration and has developed ideas on how to implement a smart collaboration strategy (Gardner and Matviak 2020a, b), it is rather silent on how to bring smart collaboration to the next level. By next level we refer to how to define smart collaboration including desirable behavior and how to make smart collaboration work within a firm that is already familiar with the concept of smart collaboration. Taking smart collaboration to the next level is different from initiating it because this requires a firm to make smart collaboration a top priority within the entire organization and set something in motion that ensures that employee behavior truly shift from good intentions to consistent practice. The following research question guides our design science research project: *how to make smart collaboration work effectively beyond its initiation?*

To develop design knowledge on how to make smart collaboration work in multidisciplinary teams, we engage in a design science field study. More specifically, we do a design science study with a European digital transformation firm (named The firm to assure anonymity). Using The firm as our case study we follow van Aken et al. (2012) design science methodology. We start by formulating the practical problem, which we subsequently analyze. Based on the analyses we develop a solution design for advancing smart collaboration at The firm. Finally, we evaluate the solution design, and infer design principles based on this case for a broader class of smart collaboration issues in multidisciplinary teams.

Our study contributes to the smart collaboration literature (Gardner 2017, Gardner and Matviak 2020a, b; Edmondson 1999, 2018) and has an immediate practical implication. First, our study makes a theoretical contribution to the body of design knowledge on smart collaboration. While previous studies have outlined artifacts on how to initiate smart collaboration (Gardner 2017), we complement this literature by suggesting a situated artefact on improving and advancing smart collaboration for multidisciplinary teams. Second, we make a theoretical contribution by inferring design principles (van Aken 2004; van Aken et al. 2012). These design principles may guide the improvement of smart collaboration for a broader class of smart collaboration issues in professional service firms and beyond. Third, this study has immediate practical implications. Providing guidance on how to improve smart collaboration in this case, may guide other firms by improving smart collaboration within their firms through analogical reasoning.

2 Problem Definition

Conceptually, we approached the problem definition using Minto's SCQ-framework (Minto 2009). The SCQ-framework describe a problem by outlining a current situation (S), a complication (C), and a resulting question (Q) (Minto 2009). We used the SCQ-framework because it is an established model to define practical problems (Minto 2009) and particularly improvement problems (Gregor and Hevner 2013).

Empirically, we approached the problem definition using semi-structured interviews. The base for these semi-structured interviews consisted of a careful selection of interviewees that represented different departments within the organization to obtain a comprehensive picture about the current state of smart collaboration. Semi-structured interviews are a type of interview in which the interviewer asks only a few predetermined questions while the rest of the questions are not planned upfront (van Aken et al. 2012).

Semi-structured interviews were conducted with several partners, directors, and senior managers throughout the firm to get a broad view on the current state of smart collaboration. The first round of semi-structured interviews helped us to explore the main issues with smart collaboration at The firm. The second round of semi-structured interviews did help us to check the validity of the problem statement, the causes, and its consequences (van Aken et al. 2012).

Situation. The situation for The firm can be described as follows: The firm started to grow rapidly in a few years' time as the company needed to transform from a pure strategy consultancy firm to a combined consultancy and technology firm to be able to offer digital transformation propositions to the market to meet its client needs. The firm did so with a combined consultancy and technology approach to offer a unique solution to their clients. The complexity of digital transformation can be described as a very complex problem with many interrelated questions considering technology, people, and content. This complexity can well be solved by having the best experts looking at the problem from different perspectives rather than tackling the problem one-dimensionally. Therefore, The firm needed to adopt a different collaboration strategy as consultants alone couldn't solve these complex digital transformation projects. They needed to reach out to other teams within the firm. This was the reason to start with smart collaboration within The firm. So, The firm had to collaborate across different competency and sector teams to drive digital transformation for its clients which was perceived to be challenging.

Complication. While smart collaboration was successfully initiated, the leadership team realized that there is still potential to improve smart collaboration. A partner at The firm expressed this as follows: 'Smart collaboration is overall a great approach, but we still have some issues in further realizing its full potential.' Similarly, the director operations at The Firm told us: 'Although we find Smart Collaboration important, we don't address each other when other teams are not involved in the deal process. We haven't been able to guide our colleagues into pragmatic readiness yet.'

3   Problem Analysis

In the problem analysis phase, we explored and validated the causes of the problem (see Fig. 1). The result is a problem-oriented theory on the analysis subject (van Aken et al. 2012). The analysis that has been executed consists of a combined empirical and theoretical analysis (van Aken et al. 2012). The empirical analysis consists of two rounds of interviews. In total, we held fifteen interviews of which five interviews in the first round and ten consecutive interviews in the second round. Each interview lasted for around thirty to forty-five minutes. The purpose of the first interview round was to explore the main causes holding back smart collaboration within The firm. The purpose of the second interview round was mainly to validate the causes (van Aken et al. 2012). The theoretical analysis was performed to strengthen our empirical analysis because it may provide additional and/or alternative explanations or causes (van Aken et al. 2012).

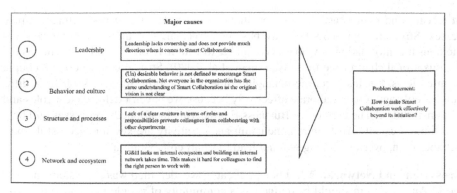

Fig. 1. Problem analysis

Leadership. A first potential cause we identified was a lack of adequate leadership behaviors. We adopted the definition of leadership by the firm which considers leadership to be taking ownership, show the right exemplary behavior and be able to connect the dots by understanding the potential of all departments, being vulnerable and acknowledge what you don't know when it comes to smart collaboration. Leadership came up in a couple of interviews. For instance, the founder of The firm said 'smart collaboration stands or falls with leadership behavior. Our leadership team doesn't automatically operate from a smart collaboration perspective.' And the director operations said: 'it is not clear what we can expect from our leaders and what we do and don't when it comes to smart collaboration.'

These empirical findings also seem partly supported by literature on smart collaboration. For example, Gardner and Matviak (2020a, b) point out that people at the top do face fewer collaboration obstacles. One reason is that leaders' views are biased, and few people say 'no' to a leader's request for help (Gardner and Matviak 2020a, b). Though incentives and KPIs are a barrier for collaboration from a leadership point of view as many partners report their firm's compensation and performance management structure as a barrier to collaboration.

Behavior. A second potential cause we identified was a lack of clarity on desirable and undesirable behaviors. Behavior can be described as an attempt on the part of an individual to bring about some state of affairs – either to effect a change from one state of affairs to another, or to maintain a currently existing one (Ossorio 2006). Employee behavior came up in a couple of interviews. For instance, a partner said; 'we have a tendency towards like-mined people and the overarching vision of The firm doesn't always correspond with the teams 'own people first' mindset.' The partner Platform Services expressed it this way: 'it is not always clear what is meant with smart collaboration because it is simply not explained very well from the start'.

These empirical findings also seem to be supported by literature on smart collaboration. For example, Gardner and Matviak (2020a, b) points out how behavior can be a barrier in implementing smart collaboration. When collaborating, one needs faith in others' professionalism, skill set and capabilities.

Structure and Processes. A third potential cause we identified was structure and processes. Structure represents the way business divisions and units are organized and includes the information of who is accountable to whom. In other words, structure is the organizational chart of the firm (Waterman et al. 1980). Structure came up in a couple of interviews. For instance, the managing director Platform Services said, 'it is difficult for colleagues to collaborate effectively because we haven't defined clear roles and responsibilities.' The partner for Business Engineering mentioned: 'processes will help to a limited extent. Trust, entrepreneurship and creativity are key for successful smart collaboration, over-organizing will not lead to smart collaboration.'

Ecosystem and Network. A last potential cause we identified was ecosystem and network. An ecosystem should be defined as a community of people in conjunction with the artifacts in their environment, interacting as a system. Several characteristics of an ecosystem are: each element has its role, it is interconnected, adaptive and self-sustaining (Feld and Hathaway 2020). Ecosystem and network issues came up in a couple of interviews. For instance, the managing director data and analytics said; 'the culture of asking for help needs to be developed. We need structural competence centers in the ecosystem, so all employees know who to contact for the development of a new solution for example'. Similarly, the director People & Culture mentioned: 'an ecosystem and a network are something you build and comes with experience'.

These empirical findings also seem to be supported by literature on smart collaboration. For example, Casciaro et al. (2020) point out that the struggle to relate to others is seen as a barrier for innovation and thus collaboration. The core challenge of operating effectively at interfaces are simple: learning about people on the other side and relating to them. Simply does not mean easy: human beings have always struggled to understand and relate to those who are different (Casciaro et al. 2020).

4   Solution Design

In the solution design phase, we developed a situated artifact in two main steps. First, we defined the design requirements for the solution design. Second, we elaborated the most promising solutions in a detailed solution design. The result includes organizational support for the solution and change plan (van Aken et al. 2012).

4.1   Design Requirements

First, we defined the design requirements. Design requirements are the criteria that should be met by the to be solution design (van Aken et al. 2012). We followed van Aken et al. (2012) in differentiating four types of design requirements: functional requirements, user requirements, boundary conditions and design restrictions (van Aken et al. 2012). To define the design requirements, we conducted an interview with the project sponsor at The Firm. The following design requirements were identified:

a)   **functional requirement.** Realization of the solution demonstrates more smart collaboration on a higher professional level, starting from the business development phase and being visible and present all the way up to the delivery phase of projects and programs within The firm.

b) **user requirement.** Adjustment of behavior is visible in the solution, i.e., behavior change in a sense that there is more collaboration happening between the different teams, and a mindset change is visible from doing it yourself to collaboration with other disciplines.

c) **boundary conditions.** the new smart collaboration approach should fit into the firm's culture of caring and daring and should support people from all backgrounds to embrace the new approach.

d) **design restriction.** within a period of 6 to 12 months the firm should be able to reach a breakthrough in the change of their collaborative behavior. Meaning that the firm should develop to the next level of smart collaboration and collaboration must be part of the 'new normal'.

4.2 Object Design

Based on the design requirements, we next started to develop a solution design (see Fig. 2). A solution design can be defined as 'the solution of the defined problem through a design of the system to be realized' (van Aken and Berends 2018). To develop a solution design, we conducted a solution design workshop. The solution design workshop consisted of a two-hour ideation session where several partners from The firm participated. The purpose of the solution workshop was to discuss the future state of smart collaboration and draft an initial solution design.

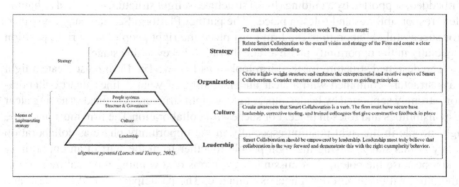

Fig. 2. Smart collaboration solution design

The Lorsch and Tierney (2002) alignment pyramid has been used as a scaffold to develop the solution design. The goal of this framework is to structure and sequence the various components of the solution design into: strategy, leadership, culture, and organization (Lorsch and Tierney 2002). The framework can be explained as follow: alignment is a consequence of two separate but interdependent phenomena: the choices the firm's leadership make over time on a handful of critical dimensions and the behaviors of the professionals who implement those choices day by day (Lorsch and Tierney 2002). Based on the framework an aligned strategy, organization, culture, and leadership were designed, which are further explained below.

Strategy. The first decision that The firm must take is about its strategy. Strategy is defined as a stream of decisions made over time, which reflects the goals of the firm and how the firm achieves those goals (Lorsch and Tierney 2002). The firm's strategy is to empower people, align business and technology to enable high speed digital transformation for their customers. To accomplish this strategy one of The firm's key differentiators is smart collaboration. This was also stressed by one partner who explained that 'We should start with creating clarity on The firm's overall vision and relate this to smart collaboration. We must explain the 'why' i.e., make the context clear and relate this to how smart collaboration fits in the bigger picture.'

The designed strategy looked as follows: The firm must relate Smart Collaboration to the overall vision and strategy and define a clear and common understanding of Smart Collaboration (that includes desired behavior). This will set the first cornerstone of the foundation to make Smart Collaboration work within The firm. The participants found this strategy a good solution primarily because they believe smart collaboration starts with desired behavior. Therefore, The firm must define this desired behavior first to be able to train and guide people in the desired direction.

Organization. The second critical choice The firm must take is about its organization. Organization encompasses a set of critical choices that every firm must make: about how it will attract, develop, evaluate, and reward its people. About its management structure and about its governance, including the form and distribution of its ownership for professional service firms (Lorsch and Tierney 2002). Its relevance was also outlined by the partner Retail who stated that: smart collaboration will work when it is naturally embedded, supported by a guiding (light) structure. A light structure is defined as having clear responsibilities and roles in place.' The partner Platform Services suggested that: 'for successful collaboration The firm must place the right people in the right position especially in the opportunity phase as collaboration is key at this stage.

The designed structure for the Firm looked as follow: The Firm must create a light way- structure combined with a clear understanding of what defines smart collaboration, strongly supported by leadership. A light-weight structure is defined as having clear responsibilities and roles in place. For successful collaboration The firm must place the right people in the right position especially in the opportunity phase as collaboration is key at this stage. Having the right people together from the start of an opportunity is key because the potential of missing out in terms of a winning proposal by not collaborating with different disciplines is immense. The participants found this designed structure the right solution to further improve smart collaboration as they believe structure should be more considered as guiding principles. The firm must embrace the creative and entrepreneurial aspect of smart collaboration. This lightweight structure needs to be combined with the support of leadership. This is the foundation to make smart collaboration work.

Culture. A third critical choice the firm must take is about its culture. Culture can be seen as a force for alignment. Next to that, culture is amorphous, it is intangible, and it directly affects the behavior of every single person in the organization. Culture is dynamic and something you manage daily. You shape the culture of your firm by the decisions you make or facilitate, which then affect behavior, which subsequently becomes part of 'how things are done here' (Lorsch and Tierney 2002). Culture was also seen to be very important by leaders of the firm. For instance, a partner said: 'as long as we do make progress on smart collaboration, and we do realize that smart collaboration is a verb and doesn't have an end-state this will give us some leeway moving to the desired behavior.' And the director Platform operations mentioned: 'we should have a foundation in place to help and guide colleagues do the right things. We must be able to refer to the right behavior and help and correct each other when necessary. Therefore, we must introduce guiding principles to support each other, and this requests more openness, transparency and vulnerability from people.'

To create a desired culture to make smart collaboration work The firm must create awareness that Smart Collaboration is a 'verb'. The firm must have secure base leadership, corrective tooling, and trained colleagues that give constructive feedback in place. The participants found this designed culture a good one because it is supported by the 'caring and daring' culture of The firm and they believe that this cultural design will help colleagues moving to the next phase of Smart Collaboration.

Leadership. The last critical choice the firm must take is about its leadership. Leadership within a professional service firm can be phrased as leading from within the organization As there are other stakeholders within the firm (partnership model) a leader should always take a joint decision. This can be seen as leadership without control and therefore a leader needs to be seeking agreement and building consensus which can be very difficult considering the many complex problems the firm faces today (Lorsch and Tierney 2002). The partner Platform Services underlined the relevance of leadership when stating that 'smart collaboration is about leadership: someone needs to grab the driver seat and start establishing this from the start.'

To make smart collaboration work successful leadership should reward learning from mistakes, introduce guiding principles, and empower role models to give guidance and support people and refer to the right behavior. The participants found this designed solution for leadership a good one as they believe that smart collaboration should be empowered by leadership to become successful and to make smart collaboration work effectively.

5   Evaluation

The solution design was also evaluated. An evaluation of design objects is important in design science (Venable et al. 2016). We performed a descriptive evaluation and an observational evaluation (Hevner et al. 2004). A descriptive evaluation is an informed argument for the artifact's utility (Hevner et al. 2004). An observational evaluation means that we observed the use of the artifact within the firm (Hevner et al. 2004). A broader evaluation testing the effectiveness of the solution design will be performed after one year of implementation.

Descriptive Evaluation. The solution design meets most of the outlined design requirements. The solution design will foster more smart collaboration on a higher professional level, starting from the business development phase and being visible and present all the way up to the delivery phase of projects within The firm. The solution design also meets the user requirement to make behavioral change visible in such a way that more collaboration is happening between the different teams. The design restriction that smart collaboration should reach a breakthrough within 6 to 12 months still needs to be evaluated in a couple of month time. Finally, the solution design also met the boundary condition that the new smart collaboration approach should fit into The firm's culture of 'caring and daring'.

Beyond this descriptive evaluation, the project was also evaluated to be very successful by the leadership team of the firm. One of the partners evaluated the solution design as follow: 'The research project on "how to make smart collaboration work at The firm" and accompanying solution design boosted our journey around this key value driver for our clients and company. Multiple improvement points were identified to take away existing barriers and facilitate further collaboration. In addition, tangible insights were created at strategic, organizational, cultural and leadership level on how to further improve. Now it comes to the execution and step by step progress in our collective behavior. This is a challenge. The direction is clear, next step is to grow from good to great.' (Partner, The firm).

Observational Evaluation. The first observation of the solution design took place during a workshop that we've organized in October 2021. The purpose of the workshop was to create awareness amongst all participants (partners and directors of The firm) about the importance of smart collaboration for The firm. Furthermore, we paid attention to creating a safe atmosphere to exchange experiences about both desirable behavior in favor of smart collaboration versus undesirable behavior that is preventing colleagues from collaborating.

After creating this open and transparent atmosphere the participants were asked to identify their own behavior and evaluate what is going well versus how they can improve. The workshop ended with a series of smart collaboration 'commitments' from all participants on what behavior to leverage to improve smart collaboration from good to great. A few of the guiding principles included: a) 'standard involvement of competency teams from the start in any service offering and ensure compliance'. b) 'Be bold and take the lead: be open-minded, practice it yourself and experience what Smart Collaboration can bring.' c) 'Don't talk about each other, speak with each other and address behavior that is not in line with Smart Collaboration (constructive feedback).'

6 Learnings

Based on this field study of smart collaboration, we inferred learnings that are applicable to a broader class of similar design problems (Gregor et al. 2020). The learnings are formulated as design principles. Design principles are 'chunks of general knowledge, linking an intervention, or artefact with a desired outcome or performance in a certain field of application' (van Aken 2004). Design principles are a form of design knowledge, 'that can be used in designing solutions to problems in the field of question' (van Aken 2004). Taken together, we propose the following two learnings:

Design Principle 1. To improve smart collaboration, a firm should relate smart collaboration to the overall vision and strategy of the firm and create a clear and common understanding of smart collaboration.

We inferred this design principle because a lack of direction and no common understanding of what defines smart collaboration lead to one of the main issues around smart collaboration that were mentioned amongst multiple interviewees during the problem analysis phase.

This design principle is related to a firm's strategy discussed in the smart collaboration literature (e.g., Gardner and Matviak 2020a, b). Gardner and Matviak (2020a, b) note that to implement a firm-wide smart collaboration strategy, it is essential to understand the organization's starting point; where is collaboration happing today; what are the barriers to increasing collaboration; and what are the bright-spot examples that can be held up to demonstrate the benefits of collaboration effectively.

Our insight is related to this idea in literature (Gardner and Matviak 2020a, b), yet goes beyond that. Whereas literature talks more about how to implement a smart collaboration strategy and advocates to start with a diagnostic analysis, our study addresses the importance of relating smart collaboration to the overall strategy of the firm and define a clear and common understanding of smart collaboration to set the first cornerstone of the foundation taking smart collaboration to the next level. Thus, this design principle represents an elaboration on the existing smart collaboration literature (van Aken et al. 2012).

Design Principle 2. To improve smart collaboration, desirable and undesirable behaviors should be defined explicitly.

We inferred this design principle based on the issues related to the lack of clarity related to appropriate behaviors. Without defining what behavior encourages smart collaboration and what behavior prevents colleagues from collaborating first it is not clear for colleagues within the firm what is expected from them, and this won't lead them into the right direction.

This design principle is related to understanding individual behavioral tendencies discussed in the smart collaboration literature (Gardner 2017; Gardner and Matviak 2020a, b). The smart collaboration literature suggests that hinges on behaviors within multidisciplinary teams. By making deliberate choices about how to behave in a team setting, people have the power to help the group collaborate more effectively (Gardner and Matviak 2020a, b).

Our design principle resonates with this conversation in the smart collaboration literature (Gardner 2017; Gardner and Matviak 2020a, b), yet it goes beyond it. Beyond making people aware of their behavior, it is important to provide employees with direction by defining what desirable behavior a firm wants to see when it comes to further improving smart collaboration. This gives people the opportunity to move to that desired behavior for collaboration.

Design Principle 3. To improve smart collaboration, it should be thought of as a process that needs to be worked on continuously.

We inferred this design principle because when it comes to culture a firm must realize that smart collaboration is a 'verb'. There is no such thing as an end-state of smart collaboration. This is something that a firm should be constantly working on. This insight gives The firm the leeway to move to the so-called desired behavior and collaboration culture. When creating a desired culture for smart collaboration a firm must have the following in place: a) secure based leadership where people feel secure to find help and be open to share ideas, b) corrective tooling to help and guide colleagues to do the right things c) trained colleagues that are able to give constructive feedback and know how to refer to the right behavior and correct old behavior attitudes.

This design principle is related to culture discussed in the smart collaboration literature. The smart collaboration literature suggests that culture can be seen as a force for alignment. Next to that, culture is amorphous, it is intangible, and it directly affects the behavior of every single person in the organization. Culture is dynamic and something you manage daily. The culture of a firm is shaped by the decisions that are made facilitated, which then affect behavior, which subsequently becomes part of 'how things are done here' (Lorsch and Tierney 2002).

Our learning represents an elaboration to existing literature on smart collaboration. It not only describes what to have in place to create a desired culture for smart collaboration (i.e., secure based leadership). Beyond that our study outlines that the realization of smart collaboration being a 'verb' and does not have an end-state should provide a firm an important insight that smart collaboration is something that a company should be constantly working on.

7 Conclusion

This study was motivated by a practical problem, as well as a design problem (Seckler et al. 2022). While previous smart collaboration literature provides insights into introducing smart collaboration to a firm, little is known about fully integrating smart collaboration into the firm's operations. In this design science project, we addressed this question. Taken together, the study contributes to the body of design knowledge in three ways. First, by developing an artifact for improving smart collaboration. Second, by outlining more general design principles on improving smart collaboration in professional service firms. Third, by providing initial empirical evidence for the quality of the proposed design object. We hope that scholars and other firms may benefit from these initial ideas on moving smart collaboration from good to great.

References

Burnes, B., Cooke, B.: Kurt Lewin's field theory: a review and re-evaluation. Br. Acad. Manag. **15**, 408–425 (2013)

Casciaro, T., Edmondson, A., Jang, S.: Cross-Silo leadersip: a powerful path to innovation. Rotman Management Fall (2020)

Edmondson, A.C.: Psychological safety and learning behavior in work teams. Adm. Sci. Q. **44**(2), 350–383 (1999)

Edmondson, A.: The fearless organization: creating psychological safety in the workplace for Learning, Innovation and Growh. Harvard Business School (2018)

Feld, B., Hathaway, I.: The Startup Community Way, Evolving an Entrepreneurial Ecosystem. Wiley (2020)

Gardner, H.: Smart Collaboration: How Professionals and Their Firms Succeed by Breaking Down Silos. Harvard Business Review Press (2017)

Gardner, H., Matviak, I.: Implementing a smart collaboration strategy, Part 1: building the case for change. Harvard Law School Center on Legal Profession (2020a)

Gardner, H., Matviak, I.: Implementing a smart collaboration strategy, Part 2: optimizing invididuals' and leaders' collaborative behaviors. Harvard Law School center on Legal Profession (2020b)

Gregor, S., Chandra Kruse, L., Seidel, S.: Research perspectives: the anatomy of a design principle. J. Assoc. Inf. Syst. **21**(6), 2 (2020)

Hevner, A.R., March, S.T., Park, J., Ram, S.: Design science in information systems research. MIS Q. **28**(1), 75–105 (2004)

Lorsch, J., Tierney, T.: Aligning the Stars: How to Succeed When Professionals Drive Results. Harvard Business School Press (2002)

Minto, B.: The Pyramid Principle: Logic in Writing and Thinking: Pearson Education (2009)

Ossorio, P.G.: The Behavior of Persons. Descriptive Psychology Press (2006)

Seckler, C., Mauer, R., vom Brocke, J.: Design science in entrepreneurship: conceptual foundations and guiding principles. J. Bus. Venturing Des. (2022, in press)

van Aken, J., Berends, H., Van der Bij, H.: Problem Solving in Organizations: A Methodological Handbook for Business and Management Students. Cambridge University Press (2012)

van Aken, J.E., Berends, H.: Problem Solving in Organizations. Cambridge University Press, Cambridge (2018)

van Aken, J.E.: Management research based on the paradigm of the design sciences: the quest for field-tested and grounded technological rules. J. Manag. Stud. **41**(2), 219–246 (2004)

Venable, J., Pries-Heje, J., Baskerville, R.: FEDS: a framework for evaluation in design science research. Eur. J. Inf. Syst. **25**(1), 77–89 (2016)

Waterman, R.H., Peters, T.J., Phillips, J.R.: Structure is not organization. Bus. Horiz. **23**(3), 14–26 (1980)

The Chimera of the Simple Organization: What is the Relevant Design Knowledge Needed to Guide Small Business Digital Transformation?

Sarah Hönigsberg[1]([envelope]) [iD], Malshika Dias[2] [iD], Barbara Dinter[1] [iD],
and Munir Mandviwalla[3] [iD]

[1] Chemnitz University of Technology, Chemnitz, Germany
{sarah.hoenigsberg,barbara.dinter}@wirtschaft.tu-chemnitz.de
[2] University of New South Wales, Sydney, Australia
m.dias@unsw.edu.au
[3] Temple University, Philadelphia, USA
munir.mandviwalla@temple.edu

Abstract. The digital transformation of small businesses is different from larger businesses. Applying large business management approaches on a smaller scale may lead to missed opportunities to achieve meaningful digital transformation. In this paper, we explore what is the relevant design knowledge needed to guide small business digital transformation. To answer this question, we systematically reviewed small business and IS literature to identify seven key characteristics relevant to digital transformation. Based on these characteristics, we propose 20 mechanisms for small business digital transformation that are justified and illustrated using retrospective analysis of nine different cases across three continents. While some of the mechanisms are well known and relate to larger organizations, we also identified mechanisms that are unique to the small business context. With that, our contributions are twofold. We contribute to theory by identifying relevant design knowledge for small business digital transformation, and to practice by proposing mechanisms and real-world examples, especially for the design of small business platform providers.

Keywords: Small business · Digital transformation · Design principle · Action design research

1 Introduction

Forty years ago, Welsh and White [44] argued that "a small business is not a little big business". According to the authors, small businesses are different from larger businesses; we cannot apply large business management approaches on a smaller scale. The management literature has made significant progress since then on identifying small business issues. However, there is very little accumulated information systems (IS) research on small businesses [12]. Further, recent nascent research on digital transformation suggests that extant theoretical assumptions are not fully transferable to the small business context [30, 40].

© Springer Nature Switzerland AG 2022
A. Drechsler et al. (Eds.): DESRIST 2022, LNCS 13229, pp. 274–285, 2022.
https://doi.org/10.1007/978-3-031-06516-3_21

The above issues are important because small businesses, often referred to as small and medium-sized enterprises (SMEs), represent more than 90% of all businesses, about 60–70% of employees, and 55% of GDP worldwide [6]. In the United States, there are 30.7 million small businesses compared to 19,699 big businesses [43], Australia has 2.35 million small businesses compared to 4,471 big businesses [39], and Germany has 2.5 million small businesses compared to 11,897 big businesses [36]. These figures underscore the importance of small businesses to the economy and thus the need to understand and serve their entrepreneurial unique needs.

These small businesses are now focusing on digital transformation to compete and survive in the global inter-connected economy. Modern platforms such as Shopify, Wix, WordPress, and others are accelerating the process by providing powerful low-cost capabilities. These platforms are often used by small businesses as a vehicle for digital transformation. Yet, it is unclear if the design of these platforms which tend to focus on generic scalable capabilities fully meet the needs of small business, and whether they bring new challenges [29]. Moreover, some businesses are so unique that they still may need to innovate by pursuing new digital solutions, and/or manage their dependency on prior investments. Yet, for all of these scenarios, theories to guide design and use are limited [30].

Over the past two decades, the digital transformation of businesses has been widely researched in the IS field. Existing literature has looked at the transformation of business processes, work, organizing, business models, organizational structures, value creation, strategies, capabilities, resources, and other related concepts [14, 17, 37]. While the contributions of such research have advanced our knowledge, the focus of those studies are larger businesses. Given the larger business context, participants, and associated data, we question whether the findings are applicable across all businesses, specifically design knowledge. For instance, an enterprise resource planning (ERP) system for a global retail firm with thousands of employees such as Walmart, requires capabilities such as COMMIT or ROLLBACK given the volume of transactions, likelihood of errors from many users, crashes, network issues, and so on. Are these capabilities relevant for a sole proprietor retail business? Such a business may need some ERP-like capabilities such as tracking inventory, but the context of use and needs will likely be very different. Therefore, the overall goal of this study is to ask, Welsh and White's forty-year-old question again in the context of design, i.e., go beyond the assumption that small business design knowledge is the same as "little big business" design knowledge [44].

Specifically, our research question is: What is the relevant design knowledge needed to guide small business digital transformation? To answer this question, we (a) systematically review the prior small business literature to identify characteristics relevant to digital transformation (b) review the IS literature on digital transformation and particularly as it relates to small businesses, and (c) derive theoretical design knowledge that can inform small business digital transformation. Our derived design knowledge provides a foundation for small businesses and entrepreneurs, as well as platform providers, to create innovative solutions to foster digital transformation.

In the next sections, we first systematically review literature to identify insights, next we derive theoretical design knowledge, and finally we illustrate the design concepts using retrospective analysis of action design research (ADR) studies in the US, Germany, and Australia.

2 Research Approach

Our research approach includes two parts, first, we conducted a literature review and then, we conducted a retrospective analysis of ADR studies in the US, Germany, and Australia based on the results of the literature review.

An important source for design knowledge is the extant business and IS literature on small businesses. Therefore, the objective of the literature review is to systematically identify characteristics of small businesses relevant to the context of digital transformation. For this study, we focused on articles published between 2000–2021 on (1) digital transformation relevant topics in small business specific journals, and (2) small business articles in IS basket-of-eight journals (see Table 1).

Table 1. Literature review corpus details

Selected Journals (Number of hits / numbers of relevance)	
Small Business Specific Journals	**IS Journals**
Family Business Review (2/1)	European Journal of Information Systems (3/2)
International Journal of Entrepreneurship and Small Business (23/3)	Information Systems Journal (4/1)
International Journal of Globalisation and Small Business (2/0)	Information Systems Research (4/0)
International Small Business Journal (2/0)	Journal of AIS (0/0)
International Small Business Journal: Researching Entrepreneurship (5/0)	Journal of Information Technology (3/1)
Journal of Family Business Management (2/2)	Journal of MIS (2/0)
Journal of Family Business Strategy (3/0)	Journal of Strategic Information Systems (2/1)
Journal of Small Business and Enterprise Development (17/7)	MIS Quarterly (3/0)
Journal of Small Business and Entrepreneurship (11/7)	
Journal of Small Business Management (8/5)	
Journal of Small Business Strategy (4/2)	
Small Business Economics (19/1)	
Small business journals (=12): 98 hits, 30 relevant after abstract check, 28 after full text check.	IS journals (=8): 21 hits, 5 relevant after abstract check, no change after full text check.

We searched in the titles, abstracts, and keywords using multiple spellings and with OR-operator. For the small business journals, the search terms were: computerization, process reengineering, automatization, transformation, and digitalization. For the AIS journals, we included: computerization, process reengineering, automatization, transformation, and digitalization, in combination with SME, small, family, and entrepr*.

We followed an abductive coding approach. First, a characteristic schema for small businesses was derived from selected key articles. Then, articles from the corpus were coded using the schema, newly identified categories and subcategories were included, and finally our coding schema was consolidated.

We integrated the literature review with the findings of nine separate cases conducted across three different continents of smaller businesses of less than 50 employees (cf. Table 2). We apply the design knowledge codification scheme of Gregor et al. [21] as a lens to analyze the cases. For each of the identified key characteristics relevant to digital transformation, we used our cases to examine the small business' goals in the specific context and identify the mechanisms employed to achieve the goals. The formulation of our findings as design principles captures the design knowledge in accessible form, providing mechanisms for digital transformation. All authors individually coded the cases from different regions using the schema before we brainstormed the mechanisms. Lastly, we followed an iterative process to improve the definitions of the mechanisms. The Gregor et al. [21] is relevant because it emphasizes goals in context (i.e., small businesses) and the mechanisms for achieving these goals. Next, we illustrate the results.

Table 2. Case details about ADR studies

Country	Short description	Case ID
Australia	3-year study in a retail network in the building and construction industry consisting of 25 specialized stores to develop a digital transformation roadmap. Individual stores had a store manager and a minimum of 5 to maximum of 45 employees to manage their suppliers and customers. IT systems are shared in the network	AUS (hardware)
Germany	3.5-year study in a textile production network involving three businesses. The companies collaborate in their daily business and have jointly embarked on a digital transformation project introducing a digital platform. They have 12, 18, and 24 employees	EU1 (textile)
	4-month study in a metal working network involving three businesses. The companies have a close collaboration in production and have jointly started a digital transformation project introducing a digital cross-company IT support. They have 3.5, 10, and 20 employees	EU2 (metal)
	8-month study in a retail network involving five businesses. The network consists of a clothing producer and four retail stores. Driven by the producer, they have jointly started a digital transformation project introducing an IoT platform. The producer has 20 employees and the retail stores around 5	EU3 (textile)

(continued)

3 Characteristics of Small Businesses

We identify seven relevant characteristics of small businesses based on our literature review (see Table 3). We found that most researchers (70%) describe small businesses

Table 2. (*continued*)

Country	Short description	Case ID
United States	1.5-year study digitally transforming 74 small businesses using 2-week agile sprints, primarily in retail or service industries, of which 52% are sole proprietors or have 1 full-time employee, and the remaining have less than 30 employees. We focus on 5 of these businesses to illustrate the retrospective analysis	US1 (cosmetics) US2 (discount store) US3 (stationery) US4 (hair salon) US5 (alcohol)

based on their limited resources and capabilities. Because of their lack of financial and human resources, small businesses allocate less resources for digital transformation [40] and often depend on the capabilities of individual employees compared to IT departments of larger companies [28]. In contrast, small businesses have strong networks and work collaboratively to overcome limitations [9, 16]. Some studies suggest incremental resource reconfiguration and reorganization might be an approach for small businesses rather than disruption [12, 13]. Strong networks and adaptability are therefore important for small business digital transformation.

The culture of small businesses is identified as either traditional or entrepreneurial, which is the focus for many of the studies (64%). Traditional small businesses, mostly family-owned, tend to be less innovative in digital transformation as personnel resistance impedes the ability to continuously renew the firm [34, 40]. Overall, our analysis shows that most small businesses have an entrepreneurial focus and try to develop a culture of risk taking. Some studies identify the role of their "owner-manager" in creating an entrepreneurial culture [9, 41].

The literature also considers organizational structure, business processes, and business models to analyze small businesses in the context of digital transformation. Small businesses are often controlled centrally by one person [28, 29], who is referred to as the owner-manager [41], compared to distributed and hierarchical structures of larger companies. In general, small business's operational processes are organic and informal, hence there is more flexibility to adapt [16]. In terms of strategy, small businesses tend have a long-term goal and dynamic planning [42] although digital strategy has become a recent consideration [40]. Some small businesses have even adopted new business models through digital transformation [3, 7]. These organizational factors and their variations also differentiate small businesses from larger companies.

Small businesses use intra- and inter-organizational approaches for digital transformation. Digital transformation of internal operations, both in entrepreneurial as well as traditional family-owned small businesses, has been studied as a topic of research in the past decade [35]. Such digital transformation initiatives have benefitted from dynamic resources and flexible processes of small businesses compared to more standardized and strategically planned approaches in larger companies [30, 40]. Moreover, small businesses develop strong inter-organizational networks and share resources and capabilities for digital transformation [2, 12]. In return, digital transformation also helps small businesses to overcome resource limitations and be more innovative [35] as well

Table 3. Literature review on small business characteristics

Reference	Resources & Capabilities			Culture		Processes		Firm Structure	Business Model	Digital Transformation		Location & Market
	Limited	*Specialized*	*Network*	*Traditional*	*Entrepreneurial*	*Strategic*	*Operational*			*Intra-Org*	*Inter-Org*	
Canhoto et al. [12]	X	X	X			X	X			X	X	
Mandviwalla & Flanagan [30]	X	X		X	X					X	X	
Soluk & Kammerlander [40]	X	X	X	X	X	X	X	X				X
Akpan & Ibidunni [1]	X				X				X			X
Akpan et al. [2]	X		X		X	X	X		X	X	X	X
Albats et al. [3]	X		X		X	X	X				X	
Ano & Bent [5]		X		X	X		X			X		
Beckmann et al. [9]	X	X	X	X	X	X	X	X				X
Cannas [13]	X		X									
Proksch et al. [33]	X				X					X	X	
Bollweg et al. [10]	X				X				X	X	X	X
Depaoli et al. [16]	X		X	X	X		X				X	
Fachrunnisa et al. [18]	X				X					X		X
Fauzi & Sheng [19]	X		X						X		X	X
Holopainen et al. [25]												
L'Écuyer & Raymond [27]	X						X			X		
Rashid & Ratten [34]			X	X	X				X	X	X	X
Rosin et al. [35]	X	X			X							
Baber et al. [7]					X				X			X
Pelletier & Cloutier [31]	X	X	X		X	X			X	X	X	
Li et al. [29]	X				X			X			X	
Gherhes et al. [20]	X					X						
Taiminen & Karjaluoto [41]	X					X		X			X	X
Hamilton [22]			X	X	X		X					X
Baumard [8]		X	X		X	X						X
Lee et al. [28]								X				
Pollard & Svarcova [32]							X					X
Butler & Murphy [11]		X	X		X							X
Hatum & Pettigrew [23]	X			X		X		X				X
Daniel [15]	X					X				X	X	
Tse & Soufani [42]	X		X	X	X				X			
Kickul [26]				X			X					
Anaya [4]	X			X	X	X						X

as bring in knowledge and resources using programmatic inter-organizational linkages [31]. Finally, external environmental conditions such as the location, market, industry, and competition have also influenced the digital transformation of small businesses.

In sum, our literature review revealed a number of small business characteristics that are relevant for digital transformation. We focus next on inferring design knowledge from the characteristics identified by the literature, and using retrospective analysis on the nine cases to illustrate the design knowledge.

4 Designing for Small Businesses

In this section, we present the derived small businesses design knowledge. Figure 1 summarizes the small business characteristics that impacted the design and use in our cases in the left column. Based on the characteristics, the second column infers digital requirements. The last column summarizes the requirements into a set of digital mechanisms. The design principles can be read from the figure as follows: In the context of small businesses characterized by [resource limitations]: To allow [low cost for non-essential components and low budget allocation on IT], implement the mechanism of [modularization].

Limited resources influence the case companies to focus on low digital costs using multiple mechanisms. In AUS and EU3 we see *Appropriation* where free and open-source software was customized and *Rental* where cloud services were subscribed instead of on-premise hosting and owning the infrastructure (e.g., IoT platform). In addition, *Modularization* of IT services in US1-5 and EU3 provides the opportunity to mix and match suitable solutions. Overall, these three mechanisms address the small businesses resource limitations.

Incremental digital transformation and IT adoption are desirable to overcome the limited capabilities that most small businesses face. Masking is a mechanism to intentionally shield the user from complex issues. In EU1 a neural network was implemented as a "black box" module for a retrieval system.

Capability limitations and the traditional culture of small businesses suggest IT adoption will be incremental, and traditional practices tend to persist. Therefore, in addition to modularization, *Guidance* was an important mechanism in the AUS case, where there was a focus on maintaining tradition. These mechanisms facilitate the gradual detachment or transformation of traditions. Similarly, in the US2 case, making users familiar with process changes associated with new technology was an important aim. The case company was uncomfortable with e-commerce because it is different from a physical cash register. *Skinning*, layering traditional ways of operating on the ecommerce engine can address this challenge. Even if embedding of traditional routines is inefficient, the comfortable symbiotic relationship that has grown between employees and customers of these small businesses is important.

The entrepreneurial culture shapes the value system of small businesses suggesting the need to support curiosity and the desire to innovate while exploring creative solutions. In the AUS case, we observed how the *Discovery* mechanism was leveraged to highlight new services and capabilities in the IT system to promote learning. Family members assumed central responsibilities and developed an interest in building up IT expertise

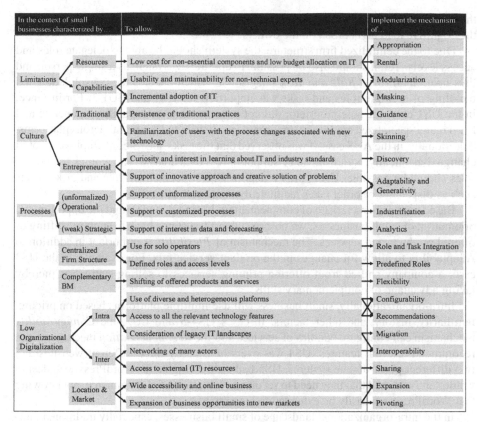

In the context of small businesses characterized by…	To allow…	Implement the mechanism of…
Limitations — Resources	Low cost for non-essential components and low budget allocation on IT	Appropriation / Rental
Limitations — Capabilities	Usability and maintainability for non-technical experts	Modularization
	Incremental adoption of IT	Masking
Culture — Traditional	Persistence of traditional practices	Guidance
	Familiarization of users with the process changes associated with new technology	Skinning
Culture — Entrepreneurial	Curiosity and interest in learning about IT and industry standards	Discovery
	Support of innovative approach and creative solution of problems	Adaptability and Generativity
Processes — (unformalized) Operational	Support of unformalized processes	
	Support of customized processes	Industrification
Processes — (weak) Strategic	Support of interest in data and forecasting	Analytics
Centralized Firm Structure	Use for solo operators	Role and Task Integration
	Defined roles and access levels	Predefined Roles
Complementary BM	Shifting of offered products and services	Flexibility
Low Organizational Digitalization — Intra	Use of diverse and heterogeneous platforms	Configurability
	Access to all the relevant technology features	Recommendations
	Consideration of legacy IT landscapes	Migration
Low Organizational Digitalization — Inter	Networking of many actors	Interoperability
	Access to external (IT) resources	Sharing
Location & Market	Wide accessibility and online business	Expansion
	Expansion of business opportunities into new markets	Pivoting

Fig. 1. Derived design knowledge

to support their business. *Adaptability* and *Generativity* are also important whereby the system can be modified to support unforeseen solutions. This was evident in the cases of EU1 and EU2, where workflow-defining wizards were reconfigurable via a management console, and interfaces for external services were provided.

Adaptability also plays a major role in non-formalized processes. Small businesses have a strong interest in avoiding rigid solutions. On the other hand, we also observed that IT-supported processes should be highly customized to the context. In almost all cases, the mechanism that improved the adoption of new IT systems was *Industrification*, where highly specific business processes and terms were layered on top of basic generic capabilities such as inventory management, e.g., for hair salons, technical textile development, or the construction industry.

Although, or maybe because, strategic processes tend to be weaker in small businesses, owners typically show a high interest in solutions that provide new insights into their operational data and forecasting. In the AUS and EU3 cases, managers of small businesses benefit greatly from business *Analytics* and reports to forecast the future. Especially in highly dynamic market environments, many decisions by the owners are based on ad-hoc reactions to keep the company on track. In the case of EU1, it was therefore shown that data analysis and reporting could play an essential role in reducing the cognitive load and burden on the owners.

Due to the centralized firm structure, the system should be able to delegate roles and access levels. Yet, it should also be possible to operate the system as a single person and thus take on all roles, *Role and Task Integration*, which enables the consolidation and bundling of multiple roles and tasks was important for US1 and EU1-3. For instance, in the US1 case, the sole proprietor did not have the time or capability to operate and learn many specialized application environments distributed across numerous platforms. Additionally, in the AUS case, it was observed that the tasks and roles of employees could change dynamically, e.g., from an IT supporter to a data analyst, and a quick transfer of roles should be possible. Using the *Predefined Roles* mechanism, role and task presets such as dispatcher or order taker facilitate dynamic role allocation.

Based on the characteristic of complementary business models and the opportunistic orientation of small businesses, we observed that IT systems have to support shifting of offered products and services. The mechanism of *Flexibility* is important in addition to Adaptability to allow for changes in the product-service mix. For example, in the US3 case, a company shifted from offering printing services to selling stationery, thereby taking advantage of complementary skills.

Intra-organizationally, small business will use multiple platforms based on pricing, familiarity, history, and other factors. In cases US4-5 and EU2, the *Configurability* mechanism can configure bundles of services and the *Recommendation* mechanism can recommend relevant features. US4 was overwhelmed by three different websites and two different point-of-sale systems. US5 had an existing static WordPress web design vendor and assumed that they need to set up a new platform for ecommerce, not knowing that WordPress can easily be extended to e-commerce.

In the intra-organizational landscape of small businesses, especially traditional family businesses, legacy systems have been in operation for a long time. The AUS case showed that *Migration* mechanisms (e.g., replacing proprietary file formats) are important to keep the IT systems usable and maintainable. In the cases of EU1-2, the mechanism *Interoperability* to share data between systems and modules was implemented. In the cases of AUS and EU1-3, the *Sharing* mechanism provides a shared infrastructure and efficient resource exchange. These shared platforms can help small businesses stay closely connected to their local communities. Finally, digital transformation can in most cases expand access to new customers, markets, and product mixes. In AUS and US1 as well as US5, we see that the mechanisms of *Expansion* and *Pivoting* are important for growth (e.g., integrating with eBay to expand to new markets).

5   Discussion and Conclusion

In this study, we ask if the design knowledge needed for small business digital transformation is different from what we know from larger businesses. To answer this question, we systematically reviewed small business and IS literature to identify seven key characteristics relevant to digital transformation (Table 3). These characteristics lead to 20 mechanisms (Fig. 1) that are justified and illustrated using retrospective analysis of nine different cases across three continents.

Our results show that there are similarities and differences. For example, in the context of larger firms, Yoo et al. [45] identify modularization and layering as important mechanisms appliable to all businesses, Silver [38] discusses guidance, while recommendation systems, analytics, flexibility, appropriation, and interoperability are well known concepts. We show that these issues are important for smaller businesses. However, we also identify mechanisms that are specific to smaller firms, such as rental, masking, skinning, discovery, industrification, task and role integration, and pivoting. Further, some concepts such as flexibility have a differential meaning; for larger businesses flexibility likely means relatively small changes to product details, while for smaller businesses, it means the capability to completely change the product mix.

One potential limitation of this study and most other related research is a definitional challenge. In the United States, small businesses are defined as having fewer than 500 employees, whereas in Australia and Germany, it is fewer than 200 and 250 employees respectively. These governmental definitions carry over to the research literature. This is problematic since our work shows that a business with one or two employees will likely face different environmental, strategic, and operational conditions, and consequently different digital transformation issues, compared to for example a business of 250 employees. To avoid such theoretical mix-ups, in this study we specifically focus on businesses of less than 50 employees, include a wide variety of business types in the analysis, and go across regions. These businesses constitute the vast majority of all small businesses (in the US about 75% of all firms have 1–9 employees Headd [24]). However, additional work is needed to fully delineate the boundary conditions. Overall, to our knowledge this is the first such study to focus on and identify relevant design knowledge for small businesses. The results also have important implications for practice, especially the design of small business platforms.

References

1. Akpan, I.J., Ibidunni, A.S.: Digitization and technological transformation of small business for sustainable development in the less developed and emerging economies: a research note and call for papers. J. Small Bus. Entrepreneurship 1–7 (2021)
2. Akpan, I.J., Soopramanien, D., Kwak, D.-H.: Cutting-edge technologies for small business and innovation in the era of covid-19 global health pandemic. J. Small Bus. Entrep. **33**(6), 607–617 (2021)
3. Albats, E., Podmetina, D., Vanhaverbeke, W.: Open innovation in SMEs: a process view towards business model innovation. J. Small Bus. Manag. 1–42 (2021)
4. Anaya, J.A.: The promotion of Hungarian small and medium-size enterprises in accordance with guidelines for European Union enlargement. J. Small Bus. Enterp. Dev. **7**(1), 18–26 (2000)
5. Ano, B., Bent, R.: Human determinants influencing the digital transformation strategy of multigenerational family businesses: a multiple-case study of five French growth-oriented family firms. J. Family Bus. Manag., 1–16 (2021)
6. Arnold, C.: The foundation for economies worldwide is small business. International Federation of Accountants, Issues and Insights (2019). https://www.ifac.org/knowledge-gateway/contributing-global-economy/discussion/foundation-economies-worldwide-small-business-0. Accessed 10 Jan 2022

7. Baber, W.W., Ojala, A., Martinez, R.: Effectuation logic in digital business model transformation. J. Small Bus. Enterp. Dev. **26**(6/7), 811–830 (2019)
8. Baumard, P.: An asymmetric perspective on coopetitive strategies. Int. J. Entrep. Small Bus. **8**(1), 6–22 (2009)
9. Beckmann, M., Garkisch, M., Zeyen, A.: Together we are strong? A systematic literature review on how SMEs use relation-based collaboration to operate in rural areas. J. Small Bus. Entrepreneurship 1–35 (2021)
10. Bollweg, L., et al.: Drivers and barriers of the digitalization of local owner operated retail outlets. J. Small Bus. Entrep. **32**(2), 173–201 (2020)
11. Butler, T., Murphy, C.: An exploratory study on IS capabilities and assets in a small-to-medium software enterprise. J. Inf. Technol. **23**(4), 330–344 (2008)
12. Canhoto, A.I., et al.: Digital strategy aligning in SMEs: a dynamic capabilities perspective. J. Strateg. Inf. Syst. **30**(3), 101682 (2021)
13. Cannas, R.: Exploring digital transformation and dynamic capabilities in agrifood SMEs. J. Small Bus. Manag. 1–27 (2021)
14. Chanias, S., Myers, M.D., Hess, T.: Digital transformation strategy making in pre-digital organizations: the case of a financial services provider. J. Strateg. Inf. Syst. **28**(1), 17–33 (2019)
15. Daniel, E.: An exploration of the inside-out model: E-commerce integration in UK SMEs. J. Small Bus. Enterp. Dev. **10**(3), 233–249 (2003)
16. Depaoli, P., Za, S., Scornavacca, E.: A model for digital development of SMEs: an interaction-based approach. J. Small Bus. Enterp. Dev. **27**(7), 1049–1068 (2020)
17. Dremel, C., et al.: How AUDI AG established big data analytics in its digital transformation. MIS Q. Exec. **16**(2), 81–100 (2017)
18. Fachrunnisa, O., et al.: Towards SMEs' digital transformation: the role of agile leadership and strategic flexibility. J. Small Bus. Strateg. **30**(3), 65–85 (2020)
19. Fauzi, A.A., Sheng, M.L.: The digitalization of micro, small, and medium-sized enterprises (MSMEs): an institutional theory perspective. J. Small Bus. Manag. 1–26 (2020)
20. Gherhes, C., et al.: Distinguishing micro-businesses from SMEs: a systematic review of growth constraints. J. Small Bus. Enterp. Dev. **23**(4), 939–963 (2016)
21. Gregor, S., Chandra Kruse, L., Seidel, S.: Research perspectives: the anatomy of a design principle. J. Assoc. Inf. Syst. **21**(6), 1622–1652 (2020)
22. Hamilton, E.: Entrepreneurial learning in family business. J. Small Bus. Enterp. Dev. **18**(1), 8–26 (2011)
23. Hatum, A., Pettigrew, A.: Adaptation under environmental turmoil: organizational flexibility in family-owned firms. Fam. Bus. Rev. **17**(3), 237–258 (2004)
24. Headd, B.: Small business facts: the role of microbusiness employers in the economy. U.S. Small Business Administration, Office of Advocacy (2017). https://advocacy.sba.gov/2017/08/01/the-role-of-microbusiness-employers-in-the-economy/
25. Holopainen, R., Niskanen, M., Rissanen, S.: The impact of internet and innovation on the profitability of private healthcare companies. J. Small Bus. Entrepreneurship 1–25 (2020)
26. Kickul, J.: Promises made, promises broken: an exploration of employee attraction and retention practices in small business. J. Small Bus. Manag. **39**(4), 320–335 (2001)
27. L'Écuyer, F., Raymond, L.: Enabling the HR function of industrial SMEs through the strategic alignment of e-HRM: a configurational analysis. J. Small Bus. Entrepreneurship 1–33 (2020)
28. Lee, S.M., et al.: Effects of IT knowledge and media selection on operational performance of small firms. Small Bus. Econ. **32**(3), 241–257 (2009)
29. Li, L., et al.: Digital transformation by SME entrepreneurs: a capability perspective. Inf. Syst. J. **28**(6), 1129–1157 (2018)
30. Mandviwalla, M., Flanagan, R.: Small business digital transformation in the context of the pandemic. Eur. J. Inf. Syst. **30**(4), 359–375 (2021)

31. Pelletier, C., Cloutier, L.M.: Conceptualising digital transformation in SMEs: an ecosystemic perspective. J. Small Bus. Enterp. Dev. **26**(6/7), 855–876 (2019)
32. Pollard, D., Svarcova, J.: Promoting knowledge transfer to Czech SMEs: the role of human resource development in increasing absorptive capacity. Int. J. Entrep. Small Bus. **8**(4), 499–515 (2009)
33. Proksch, D., et al.: The influence of a digital strategy on the digitalization of new ventures: the mediating effect of digital capabilities and a digital culture. J. Small Bus. Manag. 1–29 (2021)
34. Rashid, S., Ratten, V.: A dynamic capabilities approach for the survival of Pakistani family-owned business in the digital world. J. Family Bus. Manag. **10**(4), 373–387 (2020)
35. Rosin, A.F., et al.: Digital new ventures: assessing the benefits of digitalization in entrepreneurship. J. Small Bus. Strateg. **30**(2), 59–71 (2020)
36. SBA fact sheet, The European Commission Directorate-General for Internal Market, Industry, Entrepreneurship and SMEs (2019). https://ec.europa.eu/docsroom/documents/38662/attachments/12/translations/en/renditions/native. Accessed 15 Jan 2022
37. Sebastian, I., et al.: How big old companies navigate digital transformation. MIS Q. Exec. **16**(3), 197–213 (2017)
38. Silver, M.S.: Decisional guidance for computer-based decision support. MIS Q. **15**(1), 105–122 (1991)
39. Small Business Counts, Australian Small Business and Family Enterprise Ombudsman. https://www.asbfeo.gov.au/sites/default/files/2021-11/ASBFEO%20Small%20Business%20Counts%20Dec%202020%20v2_0.pdf. Accessed 15 Jan 2022
40. Soluk, J., Kammerlander, N.: Digital transformation in family-owned mittelstand firms: a dynamic capabilities perspective. Eur. J. Inf. Syst. **30**(6), 1–36 (2021)
41. Taiminen, H.M., Karjaluoto, H.: The usage of digital marketing channels in SMEs. J. Small Bus. Enterp. Dev. **22**(4), 633–651 (2015)
42. Tse, T., Soufani, K.: Business strategies for small firms in the new economy. J. Small Bus. Enterp. Dev. **10**(3), 306–320 (2003)
43. United States Small Business Administration, Office of Advocacy (2019). https://cdn.advocacy.sba.gov/wp-content/uploads/2019/09/24154243/Frequently-Asked-Questions-Small-Business-2019-12.pdf. Accessed 31 Jan 2022
44. Welsh, J.A., White, J.F.: A small business is not a little big business. Harvard Bus. Rev. 18–32 (1981)
45. Yoo, Y., Henfridsson, O., Lyytinen, K.: Research commentary—the new organizing logic of digital innovation: an agenda for information systems research. Inf. Syst. Res. **21**(4), 724–735 (2010)

Models of Impact: A Methodology and a Toolkit to Generate Sustainable Business Models

Matthew Manos[1] , Samir Chatterjee[2(✉)] , and Nagla Alnosayan[2]

[1] University of Southern California, Los Angeles, CA 90007, USA
manosm@usc.edu
[2] Claremont Graduate University, Claremont, CA 91711, USA
profsamir1@gmail.com

Abstract. In this paper, we address the challenge of how social entrepreneurs can create a business model that can generate revenue while at the same time have an impact on society. We describe a novel methodology that we call Models of Impact (MOI) along with a toolkit. MOI has been used by thousands of entrepreneurs worldwide who have found it to be extremely useful. We present its usefulness and efficacy through a variety of use case studies.

1 Introduction

Most technical entrepreneurs working in a startup environment focus hard on building an innovative product but forget that an elegant solution does not automatically translate into a successful business. Businesses must find an elegant business model, with the right price, messaging, and delivery channel to the right customers to have a sustainable and viable business.

The idea of "social entrepreneurship" has struck a responsive chord [1]. These entrepreneurs combine the passion of a social mission with a business-like determination. They want to have an impact on the community they serve. Social entrepreneurs like non-profits are focused on generating revenue but are driven by a desire to leave an impact on society and the world. Hence the problem we are dealing with here is *how can social entrepreneurs create a business model that can be financially fruitful (revenue generating) and yet have an impact?*

Revenue model typically refers to the method a business or organization uses to earn revenue from the target market. An *Impact model* refers to a method that allows for a non-profit organization, or for-profit businesses, to operate sustainably and effectively while simultaneously maximizing impact in the community they serve (see https://reginald.gumroad.com/l/moiv5). If one focusses only on the impact model, they will feel fulfilled, but that sense of purpose will not last long due to financial constraints. If you only have a revenue model, you might get wealthy, but ultimately you will feel a lack of motivation and purpose. The challenge is to find a business model that balances both the impact and revenue and helps to create a venture that can support and fulfill the social entrepreneur. This is a challenging problem being faced by social entrepreneurs worldwide.

Whenever a business enterprise is established, it either explicitly or implicitly employs a particular business model that describes the design or architecture of the value

© Springer Nature Switzerland AG 2022
A. Drechsler et al. (Eds.): DESRIST 2022, LNCS 13229, pp. 286–297, 2022.
https://doi.org/10.1007/978-3-031-06516-3_22

creation, delivery, and capture mechanisms it employs [2]. The essence of a business model is in defining how the enterprise delivers value to customers, entices customers to pay for value, and converts those payments to profit. It thus reflects management's hypothesis about what customers want, how they want it, and how the enterprise can organize to best meet those needs, get paid for doing so, and make a profit.

In this paper, we describe a novel methodology (called Models of Impact) and a toolkit for helping to create a business model that can balance revenue and impact aspects in an effective manner. This methodology has been used by thousands of entrepreneurs worldwide who have found it to be extremely useful. In the next section we discuss some related and background work. In Sect. 3, using the DSR methodology, we describe the design of the models of impact. In Sect. 4, we present evaluation of the methodology and the toolkit via three different user case studies. In Sect. 5, we provide some critical reflection of our work and discuss few limitations. Finally, in Sect. 6 we conclude with the main contribution of our research and discuss future possibilities.

2 Related Work and Literature Review

2.1 Business Models and Social Impact

According to Magretta [3], "a good business model answer's Peter Drucker's age-old questions: who is the customer? And what does the customer value? It also answers the fundamental questions every manager must ask: How do we make money in this business? What is the underlying economic logic that explains how we can deliver value to customers at an appropriate cost?" Studies have found that entrepreneurial and established organizations that innovate their business models experience improved performance [4, 5]. As a result, Business Models Innovation (BMI), which adds the "innovation" dimension to business models, has emerged as an area of interest for both practitioners and academics.

However, the process for generating a new business model is challenging. Therefore, there are several tools to guide companies through the process. For example, Osterwalder [6] established the Business Model Canvas (BMC), which is frequently used in practice. The BMC has nine building blocks that show how the company plans to deliver value. The building blocks are: key partnerships, key activities, key resources, value propositions, customer relationships, channels, customer segments, cost structure, and revenue stream.

For companies that aim to make a social impact, this impact must be incorporated in the business model. Social impact, as Stephan et al. [7] state, is the beneficial outcome resulting from positive social change; which is defined as "the process of transforming patterns of thought, behavior, social relationships, institutions, and social structure to generate beneficial outcomes for individuals, communities, organizations, society, and/or the environment beyond the benefits for the instigators of such transformations." According to [6], business models with a social mission have a "triple bottom line" accounting for environmental, social, and financial costs. Thus, the BMC contains extra Blocks for the social and environmental costs of a business model (negative impact) and the social and environmental benefits of a business model (positive impact). According to [6], "just as earnings are increased by minimizing financial costs and maximizing income, the triple bottom line model seeks to minimize negative social and environmental impacts and maximize the positive." Given the complexity and limited resources available for social entrepreneurs, education is key to enable them to generate sustainable business models.

2.2 Social Entrepreneurship Education

Various approaches have been adopted to teach social entrepreneurship such as the theory of change model [8, 9] and the social enterprise audit [10]. Fox et al. [11] also describe simulation in entrepreneurship education and explain that "in most cases, the games simulate decision, choice, and action frameworks well, and have a good level of fidelity for the chosen audience. Learners gain access to appropriate processes and have an opportunity to have fun and play "as if" they were the founder of a business." Despite the availability of these approaches, a review of the BMI literature highlights a gap in researching the role of learning and experimentation specifically for BMI [12].

2.3 Revenue and Impact Models

In the area of social entrepreneurship, the key challenge is to find the right balance between revenue and impact model(s) (see Fig. 1).

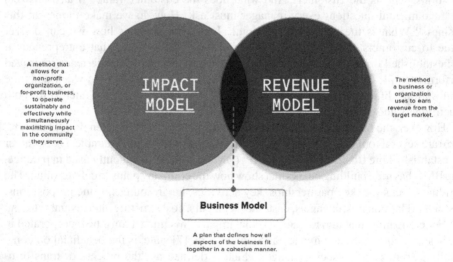

Fig. 1. Business model that balances the impact and revenue models

A revenue model is the strategy of managing a company's revenue streams and the resources required for each revenue stream. Over the years several different types of revenue models have emerged. We created a glossary of the most popular terms that are used in the context of revenue model. The glossary was created out of literature search as well as from our observations of how companies are creating revenue for their businesses. The complete list of revenue model is too big to describe here. Instead, we show below in Fig. 2 a sample of revenue model and provide few definitions of them so that the reader can understand the context. The full glossary can be accessed at https://reginald.gumroad.com/l/moiv5.

12 Impact Models	12 Revenue Models
1 Jobs for Transitional Communities	1 Hourly Rate
2 Product for Service/Access	2 Project/Flat Rate
3 Conditional Discounts	3 eCommerce
4 Sharing Economy	4 Pay-What-You-Want
5 One for One	5 Freemium
6 Cradle-to-Cradle Products	6 Donations
7 Crowdfunding	7 Membership/Subscription
8 Civic/Social Incubator or Accelerator	8 Advertisement/Advertising
9 Open Source	9 Sponsorship
10 Sliding Scale Rates	10 Free Sample
11 Access to Education	11 Cross-Subsidy
12 % of Profit or Revenue	12 Secondary Revenue

Fig. 2. Samples of revenue and impact model

Hourly Rate: A structure for paying for a service provider's work. Typically, when someone is working on an hourly rate, it is for a small job, or for maintenance, and an estimate of hours is provided prior to commencement.

Freemium: Originally known as "crippleware", the Freemium model offers users with multiple tiers of packages for a product, with one of those tiers always being free. Most commonly leveraged in the digital space, the free tier includes a limited number of features, while the paid tiers offer a substantially more robust experience/suite of features (e.g., *DropBox, LinkedIn*).

Cross-Subsidy: A revenue model/pricing structure in which the purchases of a consumer directly fund another product/initiative of the brand they are buying into without them realizing it. Put simply, a cross-subsidy is what happens when one thing pays for another thing (e.g., *Microsoft/XBOX, Sony/PlayStation, Gillette Razors*).

Figure 2 also shows a sample of impact models. An *Impact model* is a method for creating sustainable impact on people, community, and the planet. While the full exhaustive list is available in the glossary, below we provide a few examples and their definitions.

Sharing Economy: A collaborative economy that is built around the concept of sharing physical or intellectual resources between peers (e.g., *Burning Man, Task Rabbit, Uber, Lyft, Airbnb, Good Things Everywhere*).

One for One: A model that allows customers to purchase a product that additionally sponsors a product of equal or lesser value to be sent to individuals/communities/organizations in need (e.g., *TOMS, One Laptop Per Child, BOGO Bowl*).

Cradle-to-Cradle Products: Products designed such that once consumed they are easily collected, segregated and converted to new products (e.g., *Aluminum cans)*.

3 Research Methodology

The Models of Impact methodology was developed following the Design Science Research [13] method. First, we framed the problem as follows. We initially recognized that most entrepreneurs generate business models that focus on revenue instead of social impact and that there are limited resources that address the social impact while designing a business model. We validated this problem by speaking to several startup owners as well as emerging entrepreneurs. This was part of the relevant cycle. In the rigor cycle, we adapted concepts from the business canvas model BMC to further inform the design. We also noted down our own observations about how companies are using revenue models to generate revenue. A glossary was next created. We also aimed to make the process for generating a social impact model fun and engaging. Hence, we created a game that uses randomization for business model generation. The game can be played by entrepreneurs or for that matter anyone thinking of starting a business. The initial randomization method used a shuffled deck of cards. In later iterations, we used a 12-sided dice. The game is described in detail below. Finally, the design cycle combined the context requirements with outputs of the rigor cycle to build the toolkit called "Models of Impact". We evaluated its utility and usefulness through several case studies. In fact, to date the Models of Impact game have been played by over 50,000 people in nearly 150 countries.

3.1 Kernel Theory – Game-Based Learning

The theory of game-based learning [14] involves a new way of training the employees of companies. We are referring to the use of games for learning. Definitions of game-based learning mostly emphasize that it is a type of game play with defined learning outcomes [17]. Usually, it is assumed that the game is a digital game, but this is not always the case. A corollary to this definition is that the design process of games for learning involves balancing the need to cover the subject matter with the desire to prioritize game play [14].

Game-based learning is built upon a constructivist type of learning [15]. What does this mean? Constructivism posits the need to provide students with the necessary tools so they can build their own procedures in order to solve a problem. This implies a participatory process by students, who interact with their environment to solve the situation that is being set out to them. Safe practice, experiential learning and interaction are the pillars upon which the theory of game-based learning stands. Learning through games allows students to experiment in non-threatening scenarios and acquire knowledge through practice and social interaction both with the environment and their peers.

3.2   The Artifact Design: Models of Impact Game and Toolkit

"Models of Impact" is a role-playing and ideation game that simulates the process of generating innovative business models. It includes the collection of 200+ models (revenue and impact in a glossary) and instructions to guide players through a series of activities. There are four steps in the game: learn, invent, program, and report (see Fig. 3). Since randomization is central to the game's experience, players use a n-sided dice (like the dice used in Dungeons and Dragons; n can be 6, 12, or 20) to combine impact models, revenue models, and other factors that generate a new idea.

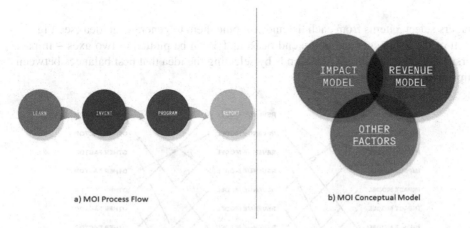

a) MOI Process Flow

b) MOI Conceptual Model

Fig. 3. MOI process flow and conceptual model

The game has the following steps.

Step 1: Learn
In the "learn" phase, players explore the collection of revenue models, impact models, and other factors. After that, players select 12 models of each to experiment with. The players all have access to the glossary and they learn from it and choose 12 revenue models, impact models and other factors. What is "other factors"? If the game is being played in a community room, it typically will include 12 emerging issues, or exciting trends, resources or interests that the people in the room have. If the game is being played inside a corporation, then it will include 12 different skill-sets and organizational competencies that the company has. At the end of learn phase, the players have a drawing board which would look something like Fig. 4 below.

Step 2: Invent
The invent phase consists of 3 rounds. We select a 12-sided dice to roll. In round 1, each player rolls the die 3 times. The first number the dice lands on dictates which *revenue model* should be selected. The second number the dice lands on would indicate which *impact model* to select. The third number would indicate which item on the list of *other factors* to select. In Round 2 each player will select 2 items from each list. In round 3, the

12 Impact Models

1 Jobs for Transitional Communities
2 Product for Service/Access
3 Conditional Discounts
4 Sharing Economy
5 One for One
6 Cradle-to-Cradle Products
7 Crowdfunding
8 Civic/Social Incubator or Accelerator
9 Open Source
10 Sliding Scale Rates
11 Access to Education
12 % of Profit or Revenue

12 Revenue Models

1 Hourly Rate
2 Project/Flat Rate
3 eCommerce
4 Pay-What-You-Want
5 Freemium
6 Donations
7 Membership/Subscription
8 Advertisement/Advertising
9 Sponsorship
10 Free Sample
11 Cross-Subsidy
12 Secondary Revenue

12 Other Factors

1 Walking the Dog
2 Public Transit
3 Social Media
4 Eating Food
5 Facilitating Workshops
6 Skateboarding
7 Drinking Coffee
8 Consulting Businesses
9 Going to Museums
10 Listening to Music
11 Writing
12 Traveling

Fig. 4. A 12-sided dice which would pick impact, revenue, and other factors

players select 3 items from each list and combine them to generate an idea (see Fig. 5). Each of the idea generated at the end of Round 3 can be plotted in two axes – impact versus revenue. The invent phase ends by selecting the idea that best balances between impact and revenue.

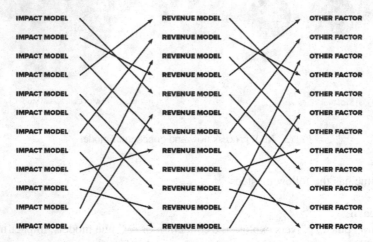

Fig. 5. Invent the best business model

Step 3: Program
In the program phase, players are asked to complete the "Models of Impact Canvas." The canvas template is shown below in Fig. 6. Each section of the template has 2 questions that the team is asked to fill. The questions are shown below.

Step 4: Report
Finally, the report phase is where players present the idea to a peer for feedback using a method called "TOAST" which stands for Transparency, Opportunity, Analysis, Strategy, and Transformation.

IMPACT MODEL(S)
What kind of impact do you want to make with this product/service/initiative/program? How do you measure your impact?

PRODUCTS/SERVICES	VALUE PROPOSITION
What are you creating? How do you ensure your product/service/initiative/program works well, and creates the impact you are hoping to achieve?	What makes this product/service/initiative/program unique? What other complementary or competing products/services/initiatives exist, and why are you better?
TALENT/OPERATIONS	CUSTOMERS/PARTNERS
What kind of talent and resources will you need to realize this impact? How will you find the talent and resources you need?	Who will you work with to create this impact? Who won't you work with? Who are your clients, funders, and networks?

REVENUE MODEL(S)
How does your product/service/initiative/program fund itself? How can you incorporate multiple revenue streams?

Fig. 6. The MOI Program Canvas and its associated Questions

4 Evaluation – User Case Studies

Models of Impact has been played by over 50000 people across 150 countries. Below we describe 3 different cases where the toolkit has been used and demonstrate its usefulness.

4.1 Use in Education

As of 2021, Models of Impact has been downloaded by faculty and students spanning 80+ colleges and universities. In addition, it is frequently used within incubator and accelerator programs to expand a participant's vocabulary for revenue models, while also introducing the concept of social enterprise. We have also heard of the tool's use in younger age groups, and the first author has personal experience leveraging this tool in the high school setting as well.

The MOI methodology and toolkit has been successfully used in a senior capstone course, which is known as "The Garage Experience" at the University of Southern California. The University's newly established Academy focuses on business innovation and entrepreneurship. The Academy seeks to empower the next generation of thought leaders, innovators and entrepreneurs through a unique educational experience focused at the intersection of four essential areas: the arts and design; technology; venture management; and communication. These new literacies for the 21st century combine to create a new disciplinary expertise that will prepare the graduates to adapt quickly to rapidly changing work landscapes, and to rethink, reimagine, and reapply.

The Garage Experience is a capstone course that undergraduate seniors experience, with innovative projects leading to operational prototypes and viable enterprises, mentored by faculty and industry experts. The Garage is a unique state-of-the-art facility with cutting-edge technology and mentored support. They have access to cutting edge hardware, software and mechanical tools for the production of prototypes, promotional materials and the development of professional presentations. Faculty from a variety of disciplines, industry experts and visionaries, and peer mentors work with students to help them conceptualize their ideas and test their work with authentic audiences and consumers. Students have an opportunity to "pitch" their ideas to potential employers, patrons, sponsors, and/or funding entities.

The first year the Garage Experience was offered, the most challenge and difficulty that students faced was to come up with a business idea that can generate revenue as well as have an impact. Many student ventures and projects had difficulty appropriately balancing impact and revenue. But in the following year, when the first author introduced the Models of Impact framework as a tool for helping the students see the potential for their ventures, the student teams generated several noteworthy business model concepts and many of the students even went on to garner venture funding. As a result, Models of Impact became a permanent fixture in the Garage Experience course at USC, as well as in the freshman year business courses, allowing the students to bookend their experience in the school with insights and deep reflection into social enterprise.

4.2 Use in a Large Non-profit Organization

The American Heart Association is a nonprofit organization in the United States that funds cardiovascular medical research, educates consumers on healthy living and fosters appropriate cardiac care in an effort to reduce disability and deaths caused by cardio-vascular disease and stroke [16]. They were looking for help to define the organization's strategic value proposition, including a range of new business opportunities, through the year 2030.

In 2016, verynice, a design strategy practice founded by our first author was selected by the American Heart Association to engage in a 10 month-long strategic initiative to help the organization. Models of Impact was leveraged as part of this initiative in order to engage a wide range of stakeholders in the ideation process regarding future lines of business the organization could head in. Specifically, the MOI toolkit was used to help AHA team of strategists imagine several revenue and impact model scenarios that the organization could further explore.

A Senior Strategist from AHA states "it's a challenge to get traditional thinkers out of their comfort zone and try new approaches. MOI is a great way to facilitate complex thinking in an approachable way that gives unexpected insights". In total, MOI was used to develop over 50 new business models for the organization, of which a portion entered a pilot phase, or a phase of further evaluation by the organization (Fig. 7).

Following the engagement, we learned that the Models of Impact tool was one of the drivers in deciding to hire verynice instead of some of the big-name consulting firms you might expect. This was due to the unconventional nature of the methodology, but also due to the fact that it was designed to encourage participation in the ideation process. This was in stark contrast to traditional methods for recommending lines of business, which are typically generate solely through desk research and market analysis. Therefore, Models of Impact offered a more "human-centered" take on business model development which was identified as innovative and unique.

Fig. 7. Models of Impact gameplay at American Heart Association strategic planning retreat

4.3 Use in Community Events

The most common audience of the Models of Impact experience has been conference attendees at events spanning the fields of design and social entrepreneurship. The Models of Impact game has its debut at a conference held in 2015 in Los Angeles called The Heart Series (https://www.theheartseries.com/).

Prior to this conference, Models of Impact existed solely as an online glossary, highlighting 100 different models of impact, which included revenue models and impact models.

Based on the success of this initial pilot, the first author began iterating upon the game mechanics of Models of Impact for use in future conferences and events. Specifically, the game was picked up by General Assembly for use within a series of courses.

Following the success of the game in General Assembly, a school in Moscow, the Strelka Institute, found out about the game online, and invited the first author to come to their school to put on an event while also developing an online course inspired by the game. In addition, courses on social entrepreneurship at the ArtCenter College of Design and the California College of the Arts were developed using the game.

It is interesting to note that, the majority of Models of Impact downloads actually come from outside the United States. This is in part due to the ambassador program our community events helped spark.

Something fascinating is the Models of Impact framework's ability to serve as an ethnographic tool; to highlight key issues within local communities. This is due to the framework's use of "other factors", which are lists of key topics of interest to the audience at-hand. Depending on where the game is played, the content is completely different as this is entirely driven by the audience. For example, in Mexico City, a business named Disruptivo has utilized the Models of Impact framework and methodology to introduce social entrepreneurship to over 10,000 students and professionals. In Russia, Models of Impact ambassadors, Ekaterina Zatuliveter and Grigory Martishin have traveled to many cities across the country to perform the game with hundreds of students and professionals.

The community events are of note as it indicates the Models of Impact process is not necessarily only valuable as a consultative or classroom tool, but also for bringing communities together to brainstorm, ideate, and problem solve the challenges their communities face.

5 Some Reflections and Limitations

The models of impact (MOI) presented here differs from BMC as it is meant for social entrepreneurs who want to find the right balance between revenue and impact. Our evaluation is more evidentiary, and we show mass adoption and usage of the methodology across a wide group of industries. We acknowledge a limitation that this MOI is best developed in a collaborative and community setting. Also, the glossary has many different revenue and impact models to consider that can be overwhelming.

6 Conclusions and Future Work

Business models are widely used but the process of generating a business model that balances revenue and social impact is often challenging and time-consuming for both social entrepreneurs and managers. In this paper, we describe a method to generate a Business Model that draws design principles from game-based learning and BMC. The method includes four steps: Learn, Invent, Program, and Report.

We believe that this method has implications for both practice and academia. For entrepreneurs and managers, the method provides an engaging step-by-step approach to developing an innovative business model. For academia, the method adds to the literature describing the process of generating a business model with a focus on social impact. It also contributes to the research on social entrepreneurship education.

From a DSR perspective, the utility and effectiveness are clearly demonstrated by the tremendous actual adoption of the methodology and toolkit by wide range of organizations worldwide. Over 50000 individuals have played the game in nearly 150+ countries.

Looking to the future, this method has the potential to be applied and evaluated in other contexts. In addition, more research is required to assess the social impact of the business models generated by the method and toolkit.

References

1. Dees, J.G.: The meaning of social entrepreneurship (1998). http://www.sogenc.org/dosyalar/6-TheMeaningofsocialEntrepreneurship.pdf
2. David, J.: Teece, business models, business strategy and innovation. Long Range Plan. **43**(2–3), 172–194 (2010). https://doi.org/10.1016/j.lrp.2009.07.003
3. Magretta, J.: Why business models matter. Harv. Bus. Rev. **80**(5), 86–92, 133 (2002). PMID: 12024761
4. Cucculelli, M., Bettinelli, C.: Business models, intangibles and firm performance: evidence on corporate entrepreneurship from Italian manufacturing SMEs. Small Bus. Econ. **45**(2), 329–350 (2015). https://doi.org/10.1007/s11187-015-9631-7

5. Zott, C., Amit, R.: Business model design and the performance of entrepreneurial firms. Organ. Sci. **18**, 181–199 (2007)
6. Osterwalder, A., Pigneur, Y., In Clark, T., Smith, A.: Business model generation: a handbook for visionaries, game changers, and challengers (2010)
7. Stephan, U., Patterson, M., Kelly, C., Mair, J.: Organizations driving positive social change: a review and an integrative framework of change processes. J. Manag. **42**(5), 1250–1281 (2016). https://doi.org/10.1177/0149206316633268
8. TOC - Theory of Change Model. https://www.theoryofchange.org/what-is-theory-of-change/. Accessed 1 July 2022
9. Bacq, S.: Social Entrepreneurship Exercise: Developing your "Theory of change". Entrepreneur & Innovation Exchange, 5 October 2017. https://eiexchange.com/content/289-social-entrepreneurship-exercise-developing-your. Accessed 11 Jan 2022
10. Fernhaber, S.A.: Actively engaging with social entrepreneurs: the social enterprise audit. Entrepreneurship Educ. Pedagogy (2021). https://doi.org/10.1177/25151274211047443
11. Fox, J., Pittaway, L., Uzuegbunam, I.: Simulations in entrepreneurship education: serious games and learning through play. Entrepreneurship Educ. Pedagogy **1**(1), 61–89 (2018). https://doi.org/10.1177/2515127417737285
12. Foss, N.J., Saebi, T.: Fifteen years of research on business model innovation: how far have we come, and where should we go? J. Manag. **43**(1), 200–227 (2017). https://doi.org/10.1177/0149206316675927
13. Hevner, A., Chatterjee, S.: Design Research in Information Systems: Theory and Practice. Springer, New York (2010). ISBN 9781441956538
14. Plass, J.L., Homer, B.D., Kinzer, C.K.: Foundations of game-based learning. Educ. Psychol. **50**(4), 258–283 (2015). https://doi.org/10.1080/00461520.2015.1122533
15. GBL – Theory of game-based learning. https://www.game-learn.com/en/resources/blog/the-theory-of-game-based-learning/. Accessed 1 July 2022
16. AHA American Heart Association. https://heart.org. Accessed 1 July 2022
17. Shaffer, D.W., Squire, K.R., Halverson, R., Gee, J.P.: Video games and the future of learning. Phi Delta Kappan. **87**(2), 105–111 (2005). https://doi.org/10.1177/003172170508700205

Sustainability and Responsible Design (Environmental Issues, Human Values and Ethical Design)

Introduction to the Sustainability and Responsible Design Track

Nigel P. Melville[1], Nicolas Prat[2], and Stefan Seidel[3]

[1] University of Michigan
npmelv@umich.edu
[2] ESSEC Business School
prat@essec.edu
[3] University of Liechtenstein
stefan.seidel@uni.li

Abstract. This track invites research that foregrounds practical impact aligned with environmental sustainability challenges (e.g., the 17 Sustainable Development Goals of the United Nations) and social and responsible design grounded in pertinent concepts and theories. Design science research has a major role to play through the development of artifacts that contribute to sustainability. It should also ensure that the processes to develop artifacts are sustainable, ethical, and in accordance with human values (e.g., sustainability and responsibility by design). We identify three key challenges of applying design science research to achieve the goals of sustainability and responsible design: early engagement, transdisciplinary involvement, and multidimensional evaluation criteria.

Keywords: Sustainability · Responsible design · Values

In the digital age, complex and interconnected technologies and systems enable myriad new business opportunities. From a sustainability perspective, examples include decarbonization, sustainable energy systems, and the circular economy. From a responsibility perspective, important characteristics include fairness, inclusiveness, transparency, explainability, accountability, security, safety, and robustness. While such opportunities to advance sustainable, responsible, and equitable societies abound, mere analysis of related problems is insufficient to drive change at the pace required. Moreover, practice is well ahead of research in these domains. Examples include the Artificial Intelligence Act proposed by the European Parliament targeting trustworthy AI and the Model AI Governance Framework developed by the Singapore government.

Design science research has the opportunity to develop artifacts that address the challenge of sustainability (e.g., through the application of artificial intelligence to regulate energy consumption or blockchain to implement circular supply chains). In addition to its potential contributions to sustainability through the development of artifacts, design science research should ensure that the design process is sustainable and responsible. This may be achieved, for example, through the development of design theories or principles.

The Sustainability and Responsible Design track of DESRIST is intended to address this research opportunity by advancing design science research that promotes and proposes artifacts that directly address these societal challenges. We adopted an inclusive approach to papers in the track and invited design science research that is either design-focused (i.e., focuses on designing, building, and testing socio-technical artifacts related to sustainability and responsible design) or design-oriented (i.e., involves observation or creation following behavioral sciences leading to descriptive statements that inform design, such as design principles). This allowed us to cast a wide net to achieve a set of academically rigorous and practically impactful submissions.

The accepted papers provide a sense of design science research's potential to significantly contribute to the achievement of the goals of sustainability and responsible design. However, it is also clear that significant challenges exist for applying design science research to achieve these goals, and we identify three such challenges: early engagement, transdisciplinary involvement, and multidimensional evaluation criteria.

First, engaging early in the development and implementation of emergent digital technologies bears the potential for design science research to actively contribute to this development, such as through participating in the formation of general design principles and technology frameworks, standards, or regulatory elements. This can help to both support sustainability and responsibility related to the technologies' design as well as to their application to implement sustainability and responsibility at individual, organizational, and societal levels. Key contemporary examples include emergent applications of artificial intelligence and Internet of Things technologies, as the papers in this track illustrate.

Second, for the design science research community to significantly contribute to the accomplishment of the Sustainable Development Goals of the United Nations, it will have to actively address these problems' complexity by engaging with various stakeholders and disciplines, consider their approaches to problem solving, and add value through our capabilities in rigorously developing justified sociotechnical solutions. This way, we can contribute to the requisite variety needed to address these problems. Example application fields from the papers accepted to this track include smart home technologies (requiring the engagement with, for instance, industrial engineering) and risk management under consideration of artificial intelligence.

Finally, value judgements about what constitutes "good" design need to consider multidimensional evaluation criteria—such as the aforementioned fairness, inclusiveness, transparency, explainability, accountability, security, safety, and robustness. These evaluation criteria need to be constantly questioned and adjusted to the evolving requirements of sustainability and responsibility under consideration of the wider institutional context at regional, governmental, and international levels. Beyond immediate utility, the long-term impact of artifacts needs to be evaluated. One paper in this track considers the emancipatory impact of information systems and highlights how design science research can help develop principles and artifacts for promoting emancipation.

In summary, the accepted papers demonstrate the significant potential of design science research to advance environmental sustainability and social and responsible principles as embodied in the Sustainable Development Goals of the United Nations, and suggest future research directions in this domain. In the digital age, sustainable and responsible design is coming to the forefront, which requires transdisciplinary approaches embodied in the general theme of DESRIST 2022 and reflected in all papers in the Sustainability and Responsible Design track.

Towards Designing Smart Home Energy Applications for Effective Use

Saskia Bluhm[1]($\boxtimes$) (iD), Philipp Staudt[2] (iD), and Christof Weinhardt[1]

[1] Institute of Information Systems and Marketing, Karlsruhe Institute of Technology, Karlsruhe, Germany
saskia.bluhm@kit.edu
[2] Energy Initiative, Massachusetts Institute of Technology (MIT), Cambridge, USA

Abstract. To reduce climate change, considerable behavioral changes are required from private households, who often have a low energy literacy and are therefore unaware of the necessary behavioral change.

We introduce a Design Science Research project with the aim to increase energy literacy. To this end, we contribute a theory-grounded design theory for a Smart Home Energy Application based on effective use.

In comparison to previous approaches for designing Smart Home Energy Applications, the design process is user-centered.

We combine semi-structured interviews with a structured survey and a literature review to derive meta requirements and deduct preliminary design principles mapping them to a prototype.

The intermediate results of this study inform research and practice by providing valuable insights on how users interact with a Smart Home Energy Application. The design principles enable the design of information systems allowing for effective use and contribute to a more sustainable energy behavior of households.

Keywords: Energy literacy · Design science · Effective use theory

1 Introduction

As households are accountable for a significant share of the final gross energy consumption (e.g., 28.9% in Germany in 2020 [32]), they are a relevant interest group that needs to be targeted regarding emission reduction to achieve the international climate goals. In the case of private households, the associated necessary Sustainable Energy Transition (SET) translates into a more sustainable energy consumption including heat, transportation and electricity consumption. However, energy is a product fulfilling only functional needs [28] and energy usage is an abstract process not providing any visible feedback [11]. Therefore, energy is considered a low-involvement good, meaning that it only gains relevance in case of shortage, which makes it harder to attain consumers' interest and motivation [28]. This is underlined by various studies stating that energy literacy, the conscious knowledge of energy consumption and consequences, is low [21]. However, the seemingly low energy literacy of citizens contrasts with the importance of

A. Drechsler et al. (Eds.): DESRIST 2022, LNCS 13229, pp. 303–314, 2022.
https://doi.org/10.1007/978-3-031-06516-3_23

citizens and the necessity to understand and address their needs in order to successfully achieve a SET (e.g., [31]). Therefore, it is necessary to sensitize citizens and encourage them to actively participate in the energy transition through an understanding and consequently an adaption of their behavior. With this study, we present the first results of a larger Design Science Research (DSR) project [18] aimed at identifying Design Principles (DP) for a Smart Home Energy Application (SHEA) based on smart meter data ensuring effective use by consumers. This study comprises a rigorous description of the problem space derived from interviews, a literature review in the next chapter and a large survey among owners of PV systems, the first derivation of Meta Requirements (MR) and DPs as well as the demonstration of the first prototype. We also provide an outlook on the setup of the DSR project, overall. In particular, this study answers the following research question:

What are the relevant design principles for the development of a SHEA that enables an effective use by users to increase energy literacy?

2 Related Work and Theoretical Foundations

In this chapter, we briefly outline previous studies and findings in the area of energy literacy and associated digital tools. Furthermore, we extensively describe our theoretical foundation within the theory of effective use.

Energy Literacy and IS. The broad term "energy literacy" covers both content knowledge on a cognitive level and citizens' understanding of energy including affective and behavioral aspects [21]. DeWaters et al. [6] define an energy literate person as someone, who is able to take informed actions and make sustainable energy decisions by using her or his understanding of the impacts of energy generation and consumption on the environment and global community. Over the last years, several studies have been published revealing the low level of energy literacy within the population all over the world [22] and the need to do more research on how to increase this level [33]. This is also affirmed by the authors of [36] stating that customers "lack information about the environmental consequences of their choices" [p. 12] preventing them from a more sustainable energy consumption behavior. The authors of [31], for example, investigate how to engage people to participate and change their energy behavior stating that many people are still unaware of the consequences of their current energy behavior. Promoting energy literacy can thus foster a shift in knowledge and perception of energy, thereby facilitating responsible, sustainable energy related decisions and behavior. Therefore, it is relevant to gain knowledge on how to engage the general public for a SET by helping them to become more energy literate.

Information Systems (IS) have been identified as key enablers in the transformation of organizations and the society towards more sustainable behavior as they provide information, which can then motivate behavioral and economic actions [8]. According to the authors of [36], an IS "can distribute information to consumers to influence the use of a physical flow system" [p. 9] enabling them to make informed decisions about their energy consumption patterns. This is consistent with the suggestions of the author of [23] to develop IS to influence individual consumption schemes. Various projects and tools that provide energy feedback to their users and influence consumption behavior are described in the literature (e.g., [5, 26]). While early studies in this research area have focused on dedicated in-home energy displays, recently, studies have concentrated on the use of simple and cheaper mobile SHEAs (e.g., [14, 24, 25, 27, 30]). Even though there are different projects implementing SHEAs to help people understand their energy behavior, they mostly focus on purely capturing and transmitting the data (e.g., [14]), and either face the issue of not being used or evaluated over a longer period of time (e.g., [30]), or they do not measure the actual effect they have on the users' knowledge and behavioral changes (e.g., [27]). While the use of user-engaging designs is already present on the research agenda in other research areas, like customer service (e.g., [15]) or crisis response (e.g., [29]), studies taking a user-centered, theory-based design approach within the household energy sector are lacking, but encouraged by different researchers (e.g., [10, 14]). To the best of our knowledge, there is no structured research on designing a SHEA user-centered with the aim of increasing users' energy literacy inducing more sustainable energy usage decisions. With our research, we contribute to the area of Green IS, which has been established to tackle the issues of environmental problems providing suitable information driven solutions [35]. We provide valuable insights on current user interaction with existing SHEAs and derive preliminary DPs.

Effective Use Theory. To maximize the benefits of IS, they must be used effectively [2]. A basic assumption behind effective use is related to the purpose and nature of an IS. It assumes that systems are not used just for the sake of using them, but to support other tasks and achieve some other goals [13]. For this matter, Burton-Jones et al. [2, p. 633] established the effective use theory defining "effective use as using a system in a way that helps attain the goals for using the system." Effective use is an objective concept, i.e., it focuses on observable behavior instead of what is perceived by the users (which would be perceived usefulness referring to a user's expectation or perception). One central challenge is the measurement of those objective qualities, which could be assessed in terms of performance. Effective use is constructed on three hierarchical dimensions stemming from representation theory [2, 3, 34]. Every lower level is necessary, but not sufficient for the next higher level. At the start, an (1) unimpeded, intuitive access to and interaction with the system's representations is necessary (*transparent interaction*) allowing the user to (2) obtain representations, which reflect the underlying represented domain faithfully (*representational fidelity*). Finally, the user is enabled to (3) act upon this faithful representation to improve his or her state (*informed action*). In our case, users need to be able to easily access and intuitively navigate through the SHEA (transparent interaction). Such a seamless interaction saves time and helps users to focus on the system's information, which is critical to an effective performance [9]. On the contrary, effectiveness is reduced if users are not able to find and appropriately use features needed to gain knowledge about their energy behavior. Representational fidelity then fosters the effectiveness by increasing the understanding and reducing uncertainties through an appropriate presentation of the relevant information. In our case, this means incorporating those features and their forms of representation that help users to understand their energy behavior. If representational fidelity is high, users do not need to spend time verifying the presented information. Finally, users reach an increased state within the energy domain, thereby reducing errors and increasing effectiveness if the level of informed action is high. In our case, this means that users are enabled to evaluate their energy behavior, being able to make sustainable energy decisions. For example, this could include increasing their share of renewable energy by using energy at the time that energy is generated (on a sunny day during the day instead of at night), or the decision to install own renewable energy generating capacities. On the contrary, an ill-informed action might lead to spending time on recovering from errors. In conclusion, transparent interaction activates the informing potential of an IS, representational fidelity then ensures this potential is positive, and informed action leverages it [20]. While existing research on SHEAs for increased energy literacy mainly focuses on the representational fidelity by just showing the data to the users (e.g., [14]), we propose to expand this focus to the level of informed action by measuring the effects of the SHEA usage on energy literacy and behavioral change. To address this, we propose to actively engage users in the design process and build an artifact based on the effective use theory. In general, the challenge when designing an effective use system is to learn what effective use involves and how this can be achieved and measured [7]. We describe our corresponding methodology in the next chapter.

3   Research Methodology

Figure 1 shows the used general DSR Methodology based on Kuechler and Vaishnavi [18] and the design cycles based on Hevner et al. [17]. In this paper, we summarize the findings of the first three steps of Design Cycle One, namely the awareness of the problem, the suggestion and the development of the prototype (boxes in grey). We argue that the DSR approach is well suited for our research question as it can seek a solution to a real-world problem, which is of practical interest [17]. Moreover, the DSR approach allows us to combine the existing knowledge within the areas of energy literacy and SHEA design with theoretical foundations of effective use. Also, this approach allows for an execution of build-and-evaluate-loops to test the effective use of our developed artifact and improve it, correspondingly [17]. This provides a rigorous grounding and enables us to make a contribution to the existing knowledge base. Our DSR project is set up over three design cycles. In the first design cycle, we test our artifact in a behavioral laboratory experiment. In the following two design cycles, we then test it in different field settings over an extended period of time. Overall, our research project aims to ultimately contribute a design theory, delivering prescriptive knowledge for designing SHEAs that increase users' energy literacy leading them to more sustainable energy decisions through effective use [16].

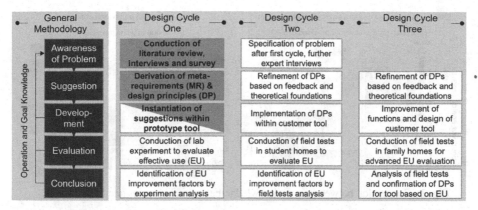

Fig. 1. Design science research methodology (based on Kuechler and Vaishnavi 2008).

4 Designing a Smart Home Energy Application

In this chapter, we report on the results from the first steps of the described DSR project. We begin by a detailed description of the awareness of the problem and then move on to the suggestion and development phases.

Problem Awareness Overview. To understand potential current issues, we firstly started our research with semi-structured interviews with participants of an existing field study on the helpfulness of a provided SHEA [27]. The participants were asked, for example, if the SHEA has helped them to understand their energy behavior better and if it had led to behavioral changes. Also, they were asked more explicitly about certain features within the SHEA, like those in Fig. 3, and their helpfulness. In addition, they were asked about the interaction with the SHEA, i.e., why they had (or not had) used the SHEA and whether it helped them. Second, to broaden the insights on energy behavior beyond that specific pilot project with few respondents to the general public, we conducted an online survey with home owners possessing Photovoltaics (PV) panels. We focus on this particular group (1) because they have invested in energy generation technology and are therefore more familiar with the subject overall and (2) because owners of PV panels are often provided with a SHEA by the vendor to track their energy generation and consumption. After screening out participants not fulfilling this criterion and participants not giving the right answer to an attention check within the survey, we received 408 valid completed surveys. Participants were asked whether they had access to a web-based or mobile SHEA to track their energy consumption and generation. Furthermore, we asked participants about a) the helpfulness of prevalent features, b) their perceived increase in energy knowledge and behavioral changes since owning a PV system, and c) whether those perceived changes were linked to using the SHEA. The presented survey results in this paper are based on participants, who affirmed that a corresponding SHEA was provided to them. Thirdly, we conducted a literature review in addition to the empirical research to ensure an inclusion of existing knowledge on SHEA solutions.

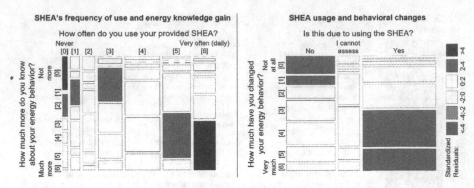

Fig. 2. Connection between energy knowledge/behavioral changes and SHEA usage.

Results: In regard to SHEA usage, the majority of the survey participants stated to use their SHEA frequently. However, more than 10% of the participants never or almost never use their provided SHEA. On the contrary, a majority of the interviewed field project participants stated that they rarely used the SHEA and rather relied on the accompanying weekly reports that summarized their weekly activities. With our user-centered design approach, we aim to address those participants that have not been using the SHEA. Given that a majority of users stated a regular interaction with the SHEA in the survey, we further investigated the perceived effect on their energy literacy. The two mosaic plots in Fig. 2 visualize our results of a statistically significant (0.000 significance level each) dependence between the gain in energy knowledge and the frequency of use of the SHEA (left), and between behavioral changes and the helpfulness of the provided SHEA (right). The shadings visualize patterns of deviation from independence. A blue tile shows that the number of participants within that group is higher than expected assuming independence of the features, while a red tile would mean that the group is smaller than expected. The results of the left plot show that the participants, who stated that they had gained much additional knowledge on their energy behavior since having a PV system installed have mostly used their SHEA on a daily basis (bottom right corner). This dependence can still be confirmed on the second level of the expressions with a lighter shading. In the right mosaic plot, it can be seen that participants stating they have changed their energy behavior very much mostly affiliate this with the use of their SHEA (bottom right corner). These findings indicate that a SHEA might lead to a higher (perceived) energy literacy and induce behavioral changes. However, the associated causality remains to be shown. On the contrary, there is a correlation between participants stating that they have not learned anything since owning a PV system and never having used their SHEA (upper left corner, left plot). In addition, most participants stating they had not changed their behavior do not refer this to using the SHEA (upper left corner, right plot) raising the question of why they do not use a SHEA, yet. In sum, these survey results point out existing issues, which we address with our DPs. To identify features, which are relevant to users and help them to increase their level of energy literacy, we provided the survey participants a list of prevalent features derived from the interviews, the literature and existing solutions, not claiming completeness. To take into account that the participating PV owners might have a range of SHEA of various development levels, we asked, whether participants had access to such features and whether they find or would (if they currently did not have access to that feature) find them helpful or not. With 88% of survey participants finding it helpful, energy consumption (and generation) history is the most important feature, and therefore needs to be included (see Fig. 3). This is followed by the current consumption and an overview of costs and revenues. For example, 80% of the participants have access to the consumption history in their currently used SHEA and find its usage helpful, 8% of the participants do not have access to that feature, but would find it helpful, 12% of the participants have access to that feature in their SHEA, but do not find it helpful, and only 1% of the participants do not have access to that feature and would not find it helpful. The results of Fig. 3 therefore deliver relevant insights for the derivation of DPs.

Feature	I use it and find it helpful.	Not available, but I would find it helpful.	Total: Found helpful	Available, but I do not find it helpful.	Not available, and I would not find it helpful.	Total: Not found helpful
Consumption History	80%	8%	88%	12%	1%	13%
Current Consumption	80%	5%	85%	13%	1%	15%
Costs and Revenues	43%	26%	70%	17%	13%	30%
Ad-hoc Notification	33%	33%	66%	21%	13%	34%
Reference Values	19%	38%	57%	22%	21%	43%
Action Recommendation	17%	40%	57%	22%	22%	43%
Goal Setting	20%	31%	51%	20%	29%	49%
Energy Mix	27%	23%	50%	20%	30%	50%
News Feed	17%	24%	41%	21%	38%	59%
Comparisons	16%	23%	39%	20%	41%	61%
Investment Recommendation	12%	23%	35%	23%	42%	65%

Fig. 3. Evaluation of features

Identified Issues and Meta-requirements. The following issues have been identified throughout the interviews, the survey and the literature review. The interviewees stated that the login burden was very high (**I1**), which already led to an early frustration when needing to find the right login information. In addition, the graphical user interface was perceived non-intuitive (**I2**) by the interviewees as some SHEA features were difficult to find, which led to decreasing interaction with the SHEA over time. The issue of complicated SHEA handling can also be found in literature [12] and was stated within the qualitative comment section of the online survey. These issues conflict with the first level of effective use as they do not grant unimpeded access. The SHEA needs to be designed in such a way that it has an intuitive GUI in order to be effectively used (**MR1**). The interviewees also stated that data was sometimes missing or faulty (**I3**), which is why they did not trust the data. Similar problems were faced in other studies, too [12, 26]. In the survey, some participants stated that they do not use a SHEA because the have privacy concerns (**I4**). Therefore, it needs to be ensured that the data is transmitted privately and correctly (**MR2**) to fulfill the second level of the effective use theory (representational fidelity). Furthermore, the interviewees stated that they did not actively use the SHEA due to boring or non-intuitive data representations (**I5**). Self-explaining data visualizations, with the most relevant information emphasized properly (**MR3**), are important within (energy) learning contexts [19] to prevent information overload and make the SHEA usage interesting and efficient for users. This is confirmed by the survey results. Another major issue identified in the interviews, the literature [1, 14, 26] and the survey is the inattention to users' characteristics and motivation (**I6**). Some of the latter stated that their provided SHEA would not give them any additional information, because they already feel energy literate enough. Others are only interested in cost reductions and can therefore gather the relevant information directly from their smart meter without the need for using a SHEA. Again, these issues impede representational fidelity as the users do not receive enough information relevant to them or the information is not presented in an intuitive way. Therefore, we derive the MR, that data visualizations need to be adjustable (**MR4**), so that users can decide on their own, which form of representation they want to use. Based on that, the SHEA should include user interaction elements (**MR5**) to actively engage them. It should also be possible for users to customize features by selecting them from a list of available features (**MR6**). As identified within the survey results (see Fig. 3), it is, for example, important to include an easy to understand and customizable time-series representation of the energy consumption and generation. Other features are only important to few users but still provide a benefit to some. Interviewees state that they missed actively being given feedback after they had made changes within the SHEA or changed their behavior (**I7**). This hinders the fulfillment of level three of the effective use theory (informed action). We therefore derive the MR of incorporating individualized feedback (**MR7**) and including information on consequences of behavior (**MR8**), which facilitates making informed decisions. Moreover, interviewees complained about non-transparent processes (**I8**) and the high complexity of additional explanations (**I9**), which can also be found in other cases in the literature [1, 12]. This lack of understanding leads to a decrease in SHEA interaction and consequently decreases the ability to take informed action. Therefore, low-complex mechanisms need to be incorporated (**MR9**), and understandable explanations shall be used (**MR10**). This in turn enables users to understand the underlying concepts and therefore, to take informed actions based on the provided information.

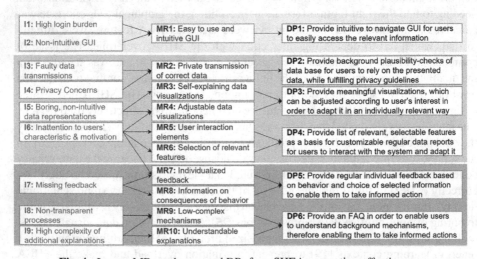

Fig. 4. Issues, MRs and proposed DPs for a SHEA promoting effective use.

Suggestion. To address the nine main issues identified, we derive ten preliminary MRs [17] based on our kernel theory, the effective use theory. From those MRs, we formulate a preliminary set of six DPs following the approach of Chandra [4] that suggests DPs should be action and materiality oriented and therefore "prescribe what an artifact should enable users to do and how it should be built in order to do so" [p. 4043], see Fig. 4 for an overview. The set of derived MRs addresses all three levels of effective use. MR1 addresses users' unimpeded access to the system and therefore, level 1 of the effective use theory. MR2 - MR6 call for data representations, which reflect the underlying represented domain faithfully and therefore, level 2 of the effective use theory. MR7 - MR10 address the ability of users to take informed action and therefore, level 3 of the effective use theory. Due to the fundamental importance of technical aspects, MR1 and MR2 are translated into one DP each (**DP1** and **DP2**). For the remaining four DPs, we can translate two MRs into one DP, respectively. MR3 and MR4 summarize findings about data visualizations and therefore, lead to **DP3**. MR5 and MR6 combine the need of user interaction elements with the concrete selection of features and are summarized in **DP4**. MR7 and MR8 specify the finding that feedback is desired by users, which is reflected in **DP5**. Finally, MR9 and MR10 summarize the insights on the importance to reduce the complexity of underlying processes. Therefore, they are translated into **DP6** to enable users to make informed decisions based on a deeper understanding of the energy domain.

Development. We argue that a SHEA instantiating our DPs increases energy literacy and sustainable behavior of its users because these DPs are formulated based on the rigorous analysis of current issues related to such SHEAs. In the development phase, those DPs have to be instantiated within the SHEA. In Fig. 5, the derived DPs are linked to representations from the first prototype version of the artifact. DP1 is instantiated as a menu tab, which allows for an easy navigation through the most important functions. For DP3, an exemplary data visualization graph of heat costs with highlighted additional performance indicators is depicted. DP4 is instantiated as a list of features, which can be activated via check boxes. For DP5, the prototype shows an example for a direct feedback stating that the user has accepted a certain recommendation that increases renewable energy consumption. DP6 is instantiated as an information icon on each page, which leads to further explanations. DP2 concerns background processes, which are not explicitly depicted.

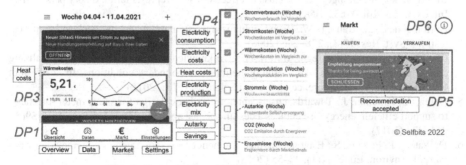

Fig. 5. Instantiation of DPs within SHEA prototype

5 Conclusion and Outlook on Expected Contribution

Improving energy literacy of private households is of central importance for the success of the energy transition. The IS domain can contribute to this task by developing design knowledge on SHEAs that help consumers to better understand their energy consumption and related consequences. Within the introduced DSR project, we aim to contribute a theory-grounded design theory for a SHEA that allows for effective use. This increases the users' energy literacy leading to a more sustainable energy behavior. Throughout the project, necessary features and data visualizations fostering energy literacy are identified and incorporated into the SHEA design. For a holistic view, we combine semi-structured interviews with a structured survey and a literature review to derive meta requirements and deduct a first set of corresponding design principles. Furthermore, we report on the corresponding prototype. The resulting DPs enable the design of a SHEA that empowers users to make more sustainable energy decisions based on their personal circumstances and current energy behavior. Our research provides insights on how users interact with existing SHEAs and which features and design elements are perceived positively by users. The results of this study already inform research and practice and provide valuable insights on how to design corresponding information systems that contribute to a more sustainable society. For future research, a focus needs to be set on actually measuring effective use of our SHEA and establishing a link to energy literacy, including the development of appropriate measurement scales. Another interesting discussion point for future work is to take the perspective of possible SHEA providers, such as municipal utilities, and examine how their goals align with the objective of increasing energy literacy through SHEAs.

Acknowledgements. This research is funded by the German Federal Ministry of Education and Research (BMBF) within the Innovations for Tomorrow's Production, Services and Work (funding number 02K18D000) and implemented by the Project Management Agency Karlsruhe (PTKA).

References

1. Buchanan, K., Russo, R., Anderson, B.: The question of energy reduction: the problem(s) with feedback. Energy Policy **77**, 89–96 (2015)
2. Burton-Jones, A., Grange, C.: From use to effective use: a representation theory perspective. Inf. Syst. Res. **24**(3), 632–658 (2013)
3. Burton-Jones, A., Straub, D.W.: Reconceptualizing system usage: an approach and empirical test. Inf. Syst. Res. **17**(3), 228–246 (2006)
4. Chandra, L., Seidel, S., Gregor, S.: Prescriptive knowledge in is research: conceptualizing design principles in terms of materiality, action, and boundary conditions. In: 2015 48th Hawaii International Conference on System Sciences. IEEE (2015)
5. Dalen, A., Kraemer, J.: Towards a user-centered feedback design for smart meter interfaces to support efficient energy-use choices a design science approach. Bus. Inf. Syst. Eng. **59**(5), 361–373 (2017)
6. DeWaters, J., Powers, S.: Establishing measurement criteria for an energy literacy questionnaire. J. Environ. Educ. **44**(1), 38–55 (2013)

7. Eden, R., Fielt, E., Murphy, G.: Advancing the theory of effective use through operationalization. In: ECIS 2020 Research Papers (2020)
8. Elliot, S.: Transdisciplinary perspectives on environmental sustainability: a resource base and framework for it-enabled business transformation. MIS Q. **35**(1), 197 (2011)
9. Eysenck, M.: Attention and Arousal: Cognition and Performance. Springer, Heidelberg (1982)
10. Fitzpatrick, G., Smith, G.: Technology-enabled feedback on domestic energy consumption: articulating a set of design concerns. IEEE Pervasive Comput. **8**(1), 37–44 (2009)
11. Fredericks, A.D., Fan, Z., Woolley, S.I.: Visualising the invisible: augmented reality and virtual reality as persuasive technologies for energy feedback. In: 2019 IEEE SmartWorld/SCALCOM/UIC/ATC/CBDCom/IOP/SCI, pp. 1209–1212 (2019)
12. Gamberini, L., et al.: Saving is fun: designing a persuasive game for power conservation. In: 8th International Conference on Advances in Computer Entertainment Technology, pp. 1–7 (2011)
13. Gasser, L.: The integration of computing and routine work. ACM Trans. Inf. Syst. **4**(3), 205–225 (1986)
14. Geelen, D., Mugge, R., Silvester, S., Bulters, A.: The use of apps to promote energy saving: a study of smart meter-related feedback in the netherlands. Energ. Effi. **12**(6), 1635–1660 (2019)
15. Gnewuch, U., Morana, S., Maedche, A.: Towards designing cooperative and social conversational agents for customer service. In: Proceedings of the International Conference on Information Systems (ICIS) (2017)
16. Gregor, S., Hevner, A.R.: Positioning and presenting design science research for maximum impact. MIS Q. **37**(2), 337–355 (2013)
17. Bichler, M.: Design science in information systems research. Wirtschaftsinformatik **48**(2), 133–135 (2006). https://doi.org/10.1007/s11576-006-0028-8
18. Kuechler, B., Vaishnavi, V.: On theory development in design science research: anatomy of a research project. Eur. J. Inf. Syst. **17**(5), 489–504 (2008)
19. Kukulska-Hulme, A., Traxler, J.: Design principles for learning with mobile devices. In: Rethinking Pedagogy for a Digital Age, pp. 181–196. Routledge, New York (2020)
20. Leonardi, P.M.: Activating the informational capabilities of information technology for organizational change. Organ. Sci. **18**(5), 813–831 (2007)
21. Martins, A., Madaleno, M., Dias, M.F.: Energy literacy: what is out there to know? Energy Rep. **6**, 454–459 (2020)
22. Martins, A., Madaleno, M., Dias, M.F.: Women vs men: who performs better on energy literacy? Int. J. Sustain. Energy Plan. Manag. **32**, 37–46 (2021)
23. Melville, N.P.: Information systems innovation for environmental sustainability. MIS Q. **34**(1), 1–21 (2010)
24. Mogles, N.: How smart do smart meters need to be? Build. Environ. **125**, 439–450 (2017)
25. Nuss, C.: Developing an environmental management information system to foster sustainable decision-making in the energy sector. In: ECIS 2015 Proceedings (2015)
26. Quintal, F., Jorge, C., Nisi, V., Nunes, N.: Watt-i-see. In: International Working Conference on Advanced Visual Interfaces, pp. 120–127. ACM (2016)
27. Richter, B., Golla, A., Welle, K., Staudt, P., Weinhardt, C.: Local energy markets - an it-architecture design. Energy Inform. **4**(S2), 1–21 (2021)
28. Rundle Thiele, S., Paladino, A., Apostol, S.A.G.: Lessons learned from renewable electricity marketing attempts. Bus. Horiz. **51**(3), 181–190 (2008)
29. Ruoff, M., Gnewuch, U.: Designing conversational dashboards for effective use in crisis response. In: ECIS 2021 Research-in-Progress Papers (2021)
30. Snow, S.: Where are they now? Revisiting energy use feedback a decade after deployment. In: PervasiveHealth: Pervasive Computing Technologies for Healthcare, pp. 397–401 (2019)

31. Steg, L., Shwom, R., Dietz, T.: What drives energy consumers?: engaging people in a sustainable energy transition. IEEE Power Energ. Mag. 16(1), 20–28 (2018)
32. Umweltbundesamt: Energieeffizienz in Zahlen: Entwicklungen und Trends in Deutschland (2021)
33. van den Broek, K.L.: Household energy literacy: a critical review and a conceptual typology. Energy Res. Soc. Sci. 57, 101256 (2019)
34. Wand, Y., Weber, R.: On the deep structure of information systems. Inf. Syst. J. 5(3), 203–223 (1995)
35. Watson, R.T., Boudreau, M.C., Chen, A.J.: Information systems and environmentally sustainable development: energy informatics and new directions for the is community. MIS Q. 34(1), 23 (2010)
36. Watson, R.T., Lind, M., Haraldson, S.: The emergence of sustainability as the new dominant logic: implications for information systems. In: ICIS Proceedings (2012)

Human Safety and Cybersecurity

Introduction to the Human Safety and Cybersecurity Track

Mohammadreza (Reza) Ebrahimi[1], Mala Kaul[2], and H. Raghav Rao[3]

[1] University of South Florida
ebrahimim@usf.edu
[2] University of Nevada, Reno
mkaul@unr.edu
[3] University of Texas, San Antonio
hr.rao@utsa.edu

Abstract. The human safety and cybersecurity track for DESRIST 2022 invites studies contributing to design knowledge at the intersection of information systems and security. Two accepted papers offer new solutions to cybersecurity problems from the perspectives of artificial intelligence and security culture. The third accepted paper uses design science research to develop a taxonomy for the emergent problem of malware-as-a-service. While the importance of technical factors in cybersecurity cannot be minimized, cybersecurity must be holistically examined to include human (both social and behavioral) factors, as well as other inter-disciplinary dimensions, such as culture, legal systems, business risk, and compliance. Consequently, we propose three areas that would benefit from, and contribute to, using design science research for future cybersecurity research.

Keywords: Design science research · Cybersecurity research

1 Purpose of the Cybersecurity Track

Rapid advancements in connectedness, computational power, and accessibility of cyberinfrastructures have introduced cybersecurity as a grand challenge in modern societies. Design Science Research (DSR) is a means of rigorously searching a solution space and providing artifacts that contribute to understanding and solving cybersecurity problems. It presents an approach to bolster cybersecurity infrastructures and increase human safety in society. Securing cyberspace against nation-state or individual adversaries is a multi-disciplinary research area spanning computational, design science, social, and behavioral sciences.

Design science scholars are uniquely positioned to contribute to this area of research by applying (design) knowledge to examine organizational, social, and behavioral cybersecurity challenges, as well as developing knowledge by designing and evaluating novel artifacts to address practical human safety and cybersecurity concerns. To this end, the "Human Safety and Cybersecurity" track aims to bring together researchers and practitioners to share, disseminate, and communicate their novel artifact designed through a DSR lens to improve safety and security in cyberspace. This track fosters studies that expand the design knowledge base at the intersection of information systems and security. Research in this area include a broad variety of studies that develop novel artifacts, methodological knowledge, and/or theoretical contributions for many topics of interest with high societal impacts.

2   Cybersecurity and DSR: The Future of the Field

From observing the emerging studies in the field and from monitoring promising future research directions, we anticipate the emergence of more cybersecurity research in, (but not limited to,) three broad categories. Each of these categories highlight several important security challenges that require interdisciplinary effort such as in information systems (IS), computer science/engineering (CS), social and behavioral sciences.

ML/AI-Enabled Cybersecurity

This category includes design artifacts that leverage machine learning and artificial intelligence (ML/AI) in important tasks such as cyberthreat hunting and risk mitigation, adversarial attack discovery against cyber defense infrastructures and their mitigation, automatic vulnerability detection and remediation, malware detection and analysis, phishing detection and prevention, botnet detection, and intrusion detection. Tackling research in this category requires contributions from computational fields, such as IS and CS, to create DSR-enabled artifacts. It also calls for contributions from behavioral and social fields to understand the motivation of attackers, insider threats, and human adversaries in conjunction with their utilized attack vectors to operationalize the attack. Given the rapid advances in this subfield, this category could include the design of artifacts using AI for core functionality (e.g., security chatbots). Future research in this area could seek to address the integration of ML/AI approaches with static rule-based approaches to cybersecurity detection tools from a design science theory perspective.

Unintended Consequences of Systems Design on Human Safety and Cybersecurity

This research category is mainly concerned with understanding the unintended effects of security systems on humans, both as operators of those systems and as the end users. With the increasing rate of adopting automated reasoning in cyber defense applications, and with the increasing complexity of security systems, important concerns are likely to emerge. These concerns include privacy attacks on ML/AI artifacts, such as data de-anonymization and differential privacy attacks that can reveal private user data or sensitive information about organizations or reveal their defense strategies to adversaries. Furthermore, investigating the presence of algorithmic biases within DSR-enabled defense solutions could be another fruitful interdisciplinary research direction.

Mediating the Relationship Between Human and Cybersecurity

This category involves interdisciplinary research that spans from Neuro-IS tools and methods to understand behavioral information security, to design theorizing for human and digitalized security. In this category, some promising research areas are around cybersecurity failures, systemic analyses of how humans are crucial to either the success or failure of cybersecurity systems, and design science approaches to security mitigation techniques. This category also includes UX-DSR aimed at making security tools and systems easy to use (as in the case of chatbots), both in small and large enterprises and for the general public. Finally, this category includes design science research on security training and education programs. Future research directions in this category could concern themselves with developing theories around the interface between humans and security systems.

Designing Information Security Culture Artifacts to Improve Security Behavior: An Evaluation in SMEs

Olfa Ismail[✉]

Institute of Technology, Nantes, France
`Olfa.Ismail@univ-nantes.fr`

Abstract. This article examines the relationship between the information system security culture and the security behaviors of users of the information system (IS). This research follows the design science in information systems research guidelines proposed by [43] to conceptualize the IS security culture in its context, where we propose a model based on Schein's three-level culture model (1985) [15], and evaluated at the level of our research context, which is SMEs, through a qualitative study conducted with twenty-two users belonging to eight French small and medium-sized enterprises (SMEs). The results of this study show that there is a strong relationship between IS security culture and user behaviors related to IS security, in the sense that a positive security culture is conducive to the creation of security behaviors.

Keywords: IS security culture · Security-related behaviors · Design science research

1 Introduction

On the one hand, organizations are investing in the security of their IT infrastructures, and implementing technical measures, and on the other hand a number of studies have applied various techniques to motivate employees to adopt secure intentions and behaviors. Despite these efforts, employees remain the "weak link" in organizational IT security [1]. So, we find that there are, first and foremost, human behavior issues, where people lack understanding of the threat and risks.

For [2] organizations face security risks related to their information assets, which can also come from their own employees. Organizations need to focus on employee behavior to limit security failures if they wanted to establish an effective security culture. IS security culture should be considered as part of the IS security program to guide employee behavior. Such a culture can help protect the IS and minimize the risk posed by employee behavior [3]. Security researchers have consistently argued that creating an IS security culture is essential to changing attitudes, perceptions, and instilling good security behaviors [3, 4]. For example, [5] show that there is a significant and positive relationship between decisions that concern information security and information security culture.

© Springer Nature Switzerland AG 2022
A. Drechsler et al. (Eds.): DESRIST 2022, LNCS 13229, pp. 319–332, 2022.
https://doi.org/10.1007/978-3-031-06516-3_24

Such that improving an organization's information security culture will have a positive influence on employee behaviors, which can mitigate information systems risks.

An interesting number of works address the relationship between IS security culture and security-related behaviors [5–8]. These studies were carried out in the context of large companies that have a better maturity in IS security compared to that of smaller ones. Small and medium-sized enterprises (SMEs) have neither the material and technical resources [9] nor the human and financial resources [10] to properly manage their IS security. Also, SMEs generally do not have procedural policies, nor do they define the responsibilities of users of their information systems [11]. According to [12] the IS security culture has serious problems concerning its implementation in SMEs. That's why SMEs have many theoretical interests: they have specific features, with regard to information and communication technologies (ICT) and ICT security, which justify a better understanding of security issues. Moreover, it seems to us that these issues are more interesting at the level of SMEs, which leads us to focus our research on this type of companies, especially with regard to our field.

We study in this paper, the relationship between culture and behavior, how a strong security culture can lead the IS user to adopt security behaviors such as using strong passwords that are difficult to retrieve and hard to guess, making regular backups, controlling the dissemination of personal information and company data etc. This leads us to ask the following questions: What constitutes a security culture? What is the relationship between IS culture and security-related behaviors of IS users in SME's? To answer these questions, we start with Designing Information Security Culture artifacts based on Design-Science Research (DSR) Guidelines, then we present the results of our qualitative study carried out within eight SMEs, which aims to enrich our conceptual model resulting from DSR.

2   Background

According to [13] IS security culture is often explained using a variety of established theories and principles from other research fields. Among these theories, we note the strong presence of theories related to organizational culture. We cite as an example the research of [14] which includes Schein's (1985) [15] cultural model and Hofstede's (1997) [16] national cultural framework; both of which come from organizational science.

2.1   Organizational Culture

Organizational culture is defined by [17] as *"a pattern of shared basic assumptions that the group has learned in solving its external and internal adaptation problems."* [15] made distinctions between three cultural layers, namely artifacts, shared beliefs and values, and basic assumptions which are presented in the following Fig. 1:

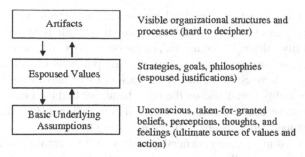

Fig. 1. Levels of culture (Schein, 1985)

These layers range from the very tangible manifestations that we can see and feel to the deeply embedded base, to the unconscious assumptions that Schein defines as the essence of culture. In between these layers are various beliefs, values, norms, and rules that members use as a way to represent the culture to themselves and to others. Organizational culture may have different subcultures based on sub-organizations or functions. For [18] IS security culture is a subculture with respect to the general functions of the company. It should support all activities in such a way that IS security becomes a natural aspect in the daily activities of every employee. Through two case studies [19], found that organizations with a consistent culture, characterized by employees who follow a code of practice or ethics, will be able to implement and adopt IS security policies more easily. Another study by [20] shows that security culture is influenced by organizational culture, through an in-depth case study within a large organization. And another more recent study by [21] shows that organizational culture has a strong causal influence on IS security culture.

2.2 IS Security Culture

Based on the elements that define what an information system is, what culture is and the definitions proposed in the literature on information security culture, we propose a definition of IS security culture which is as follows: "Information systems security culture is the set of visible and invisible manifestations shared by the members of an organization. These manifestations include assumptions, beliefs, values, artifacts, and formal and informal practices that influence the actions and behaviors of users regarding the protection of the organization's information system". This definition makes it possible to identify the elements that could be particularly important in describing the implementation of security practices by the users of an information system. This definition also provides a different perspective on the relationship between elements of culture and the security behaviors that are influenced by those elements.

[22] propose a holistic framework of IS security culture with a distinction between factors that constitute and factors that influence this security culture. This classification was previously proposed by [23]. They proposed a framework that considers the major key human factors associated with IS security culture suggested by previous frameworks

and adds new factors to see the potential link between these factors and IS security culture. According to these authors, this framework makes it possible both to improve and to evaluate the security culture. It is composed, on the one hand, of the factors that influence the IS security culture: management support, security policy, ethics, security education and training, and risk assessment, and of the factors of organizational behaviors (job satisfaction, personality traits), and on the other hand, we find the factors that make up the IS security culture: security awareness, security ownership and security compliance which we will explain more detailedly in the following lines:

Security ownership: Security ownership refers to how employees perceive their responsibilities, roles and willingness to act constructively to improve their security performance and that of the organization [23]. Security ownership means when the users show interest in IS security first, then if they admit that they have a share of responsibility in the security of their company's IS, starting with their workstation and the data concerning their scope of responsibility and moving on to a sense of responsibility for the security of their company's IS.

Security awareness: Security awareness is when users understand the potential problems related to IS and become aware of the importance of their role in security. This is what leads to their commitments on this topic [24]. In this research, we refer to security awareness as everything that is the knowledge of the security measures taken in the SME, that is, does the user know the security measures implemented in the company? Then, the knowledge of the threats which means if the user is aware of the possible threats that can put the company's information system in danger, and also, if the user is aware of how to protect himself or how to handle these security threats.

Security Compliance: According to [24] in an organization where there is a strong or healthy security culture, compliance would be expected to be a visible feature of the culture. Compliance is reflected in the staff's knowledge of security policies and procedures. The role of security awareness as an antecedent of compliance was identified by [25], who found that security awareness influences users' intentions to comply with security policies, and for [26] security awareness is associated with user perception of sanctions (through perceived certainty and perceived severity of sanctions), which in turn determines user compliance. For example, an employee who takes part in a security training, or if he has read a security charter or a security policy has complied with security. This compliance may be converted to a security behavior such as the application of security measures recommended during the training or written in the charter, for example the regular change of passwords, backups, protection of confidential data etc. But if an employee has complied with security, attended training or read a security policy and then failed to demonstrate any security behavior, then we are talking about compliance and not actual security behavior.

If we take Schein's theory of the three levels of culture (1985) [15], we see that each factor that constitutes the security culture corresponds to a level of culture proposed by Schein. Thus, security property corresponds to the basic assumptions, security awareness corresponds to the shared values and finally, security compliance corresponds to the artifacts as presented in Fig. 2:

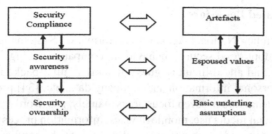

Fig. 2. Positioning of the factors that constitute the IS security culture on three levels of culture

Relationship Between Basic Assumptions and Security Ownership
For [15], culture as a set of basic assumptions defines for us what to pay attention to, what things mean, how to react emotionally to what is happening, and what actions to take in various types of situations. We believe that the security property can be placed on the first culture level 'Basic Assumptions', this security property refers to how employees perceive their responsibilities, roles and willingness to act in a constructive way to improve their own safety performance and that of the organization [23].

Relationship Between Shared Values and Security Awareness
Security awareness defines when users understand the potential problems related to the ISS and become aware of the importance of their role in terms of security. This is what leads to their commitments on this topic [24]. We have located this awareness at the second level of Shared Values Culture which is all group learning that reflects one's beliefs and values, one's sense of what should be [15].

Relationship Between Artifacts and Security Compliance
On the surface is the artifact level, which includes all the phenomena one sees, hears, and feels when encountering a new group with an unfamiliar culture. Artifacts also include the organizational processes by which behavior becomes routine, and structural elements such as charters, formal descriptions of organizational functioning, and organizational charts. If the observer lives long enough in the group, the meaning of the artifacts becomes increasingly clear, [15]. Within this level of culture, we located security compliance. According to [24] in an organization where there is a strong or healthy security culture, compliance would be expected to be a visible trait of culture. Compliance results in staff knowledge of security policy and procedures.

Research on IS Security Culture in SMEs: Some research has focused on the study of safety culture in SMEs [13, 27–33]. Take the example of the study by [29] which explores the subject of the development of an IS security culture in SMEs and the national context in which SMEs operate. These authors conducted an interpretative study based on a literature review, two focus groups, and three case studies in Australian SMEs. Then, they proposed a holistic framework to foster an IS security culture in SMEs within a national framework. The study showed that cooperation, collaboration, knowledge sharing and learning between employees of Australian SMEs is a potentially interesting activity.

2.3   Security-Related Behaviors

According to the French National Agency for Information Systems Security (ANSSI), it is important to adopt good security behavior in companies: using quality passwords that are difficult to find and difficult to guess, making regular backups, controlling the dissemination of personal information and company data, etc. [34] proposes a tool that measures security behaviors in seven focus areas, namely, password management, email use, internet use, social media use, mobile devices, information processing, and incident reporting. We are concerned here with actual behavior, not to be confused with behavioral intention, which is a measure of the strength of intention to perform a specific behavior depending on attitudes and subjective norms, as distinguished in [35] TRA (Theory of Reasoned Action) and [36] TBP (Theory of Planned Behavior). In the IS field, effective security-related behaviors can be, for example, choosing a strong password, regularly backing up information, regularly running updates and anti-virus software, or locking one's office.

Security Related Behaviors in SMEs: Among the works that have sought to under-stand the behaviors related to the security of actors in SMEs, we cite those of [37]. The main results of his study tell us that personal characteristics are the main driver of security-related behaviors in SMEs. The six most important factors were personal moti-vations, maintaining privacy, job motivations, business motivations, habit, and experi-ence. The limitations of employee security-related behaviors are mainly due to lack of time, in other words the balance between working time and the time that can be allo-cated to safety-related behaviors. The limitations are also linked to a lack of information, awareness, and training, likely caused by time availability issues, and more generally, a financial resource problem.

2.4   Relationship Between IS Security Culture and Security-Related Behavior

First, according to [38] security behavior refers to a set of basic security activities that end users must follow in order to maintain the security of the information system, as defined by the security policy. And according to [17] culture is "*a set of structures, routines, rules, and norms that guide and constrain behavior*". Several authors in the security field have suggested that creating a security culture will influence employee security behavior [39–41]. A study by [8] which examined the influence of security and work relationship factors on employees' security compliance decisions, showed that security culture, job satisfaction, and perceived organizational support positively affect employees' security compliance intentions. Another study by [5] presents three aspects of IS security decision making, namely, knowledge of policies and procedures, attitude toward policies and procedures, and self-reported behavior that were examined in conjunction with organizational factors that may increase human cyber vulnerabilities. Their results from a survey of 500 Australian employees revealed a significant positive relationship between IS security decision making and IS security culture. This suggests that improving an organization's security culture will positively influence employee behavior, which in turn should also improve compliance with security policies. This means that the risk to an organization's IS and data will be mitigated. And according to a more recent study conducted by [42] the concept of security culture has also been found to be significant in influencing security policy compliance behavior.

3 Methodology

We follow the seven guidelines proposed in [43] design science in information systems research: Design as an Artifact, Problem Relevance, Design Evaluation, Research Contributions, Research Rigor, Design as a research process, and Communication of Research. We will present each guideline and how we apply it to our research.

Guideline 1: Design as an Artifact

Perceptions and fit with an organization are critical to the successful development and implementation of an information system. Equally crucial are the capabilities of constructs, models, methods, and instantiations, as well as design science research efforts needed to create them. Artifacts constructed in design science research are rarely complete information systems that are used in practice. Instead, artifacts are innovations that define the ideas, practices, technical capabilities, and products through which the analysis, design, implementation, and use of information systems can be achieved effectively and efficiently [44, 45].

In our case, from the literature, previous research, and the link between Schein's model and the components of an IS security culture, we propose a model (Fig. 3) that conceptualizes the IS security culture and its three artifacts which are: security ownership, security awareness, and security compliance. The application of this model together with the understanding and analysis of its three artifacts making up the IS security culture allow the improvement of security-related behavior.

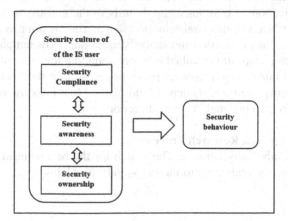

Fig. 3. Model of the IS security culture, its artifacts and its influence on security-related behavior.

Guideline 2: Problem Relevance
Behavioral science approaches this goal through the development and justification of theories explaining or predicting phenomena that occur. Design science approaches this goal through the construction of innovative artifacts aimed at changing the phenomena that occur. In our research, we have built a model composed of IS security culture artifacts aimed at modifying and improving behaviors towards security behaviors.

Guideline 3: Design Evaluation
Because design is inherently an iterative and incremental activity, the evaluation phase provides essential feedback to the construction phase as to the quality of the design process and the design product under development. A design artifact is complete and effective when it satisfies the requirements and constraints of the problem it was meant to solve [43]. The utility, quality, and efficacy of a design artifact must be rigorously demonstrated via well-executed evaluation methods. Design-science research efforts may begin with simplified conceptualizations and representations of problems. We have tried to be as rigorous as possible in the presentation and construction of our artifacts, which we believe simplify the representation of an IS security culture. The evaluation of designed artifacts typically uses methodologies available in the knowledge base, for example observational, analytical, and descriptive method etc. In our case we have carried out qualitative case studies to evaluate our artifacts and our designed model.

Guideline 4: Research Contributions
Effective design-science research must provide clear contributions in the areas of the design artifact, design construction knowledge (i.e., foundations), and/or design evaluation knowledge (i.e., methodologies). The ultimate assessment for any research is, "What are the new and interesting contributions?" We will detail our contributions and answer this question in the rest of this work and more precisely in the conclusion.

Guideline 5: Research Rigor
Rigor addresses the way in which research is conducted. Design-science research requires the application of rigorous methods in both the construction and evaluation of the designed artifact. In behavioral-science research, rigor is often assessed by adherence to appropriate data collection and analysis techniques. Overemphasis on rigor in behavioral IS research has often resulted in a corresponding lowering of relevance [46]. At first, we based our work on rigorous previous research in the field of information security, but secondly, we tried to adopt a field method that is as rigorous as possible, which will be presented in detail in the next section.

Guideline 6: Design as a Research Process
Design science is inherently iterative. The search for the best or most optimal design is often intractable for realistic information system problems. Our research presents

a model to follow which is composed of the artifacts of the IS security culture, and subsequently allows to improve security behaviors.

Guideline 7: Communication of Research

Design-science research must be presented both to technology-oriented as well as management-oriented audiences. Although the presentation of this research is intended for an audience of managers who can adapt the proposed model to improve IS security behaviors of users, the document also contains important and useful information for an audience familiar with IT security resources and security protocols.

4   Data Collection

Qualitative research is characterized by an in-depth evaluation of the motivations and obstacles to the development of an IS security culture. It helps to explain the psychological mechanisms that can form the security culture of the user's IS. Qualitative data thus highlights the importance of context, people and individual outcomes, and thus provides a deeper understanding of what is actually happening. This is what clarifies the interest of such an approach for this research, given that we are trying to understand reality in depth, as perceived by the actors. Generally, qualitative research is carried out with significantly smaller groups of respondents than in the case of quantitative research [47] in order to gather meaningful and in-depth information regarding the different aspects of the behavior of the interviewed. In addition, in this research, our first objective is to verify and test the quality of our model and its artifacts, as opposed to quantitatively testing and generalizing our model, which will happen at a later stage.

In order to confront our theoretical frame and our designed model with the field, we adopted a qualitative research method through semi-directive interviews with 22 IS users in 8 French SMEs. The interviews lasted on average 25 min per person. Each interview was recorded after obtaining permission from the interviewee. Then, each interview was transcribed in order to be able to draw a larger part of the "discussion". We used the Nvivo software to code and analyze our results, which will be presented in the following section.

5   Case Study: Evaluation in SMEs

In order to classify users and estimate their security culture levels, we have gone through the three topics that represent the factors making up security culture: security ownership, security awareness, and security compliance. Each theme is divided into several subtopics that will be presented below:

Security Ownership

For this theme, we used the following subtopics: interest in safety, responsibility for safety, and who is responsible for safety? Each sub-theme is composed of several questions from the interview guide. We present in Table 1 an example of a sub-theme which is the interest in security expressed by the respondents with the categories of answers,

Table 1. Interest expressed by users in IS security

Subtopic	Category	Number out of 22 users	Example of verbatims
Interest in security	Interested	13	*Yes, it's important to know how to pay attention to what we say, to know how to use our computer in a very controlled way" (Jennyfer)*
	Not interested	9	*"it's not a field that interests me" (Robin)*

the number of respondents in each category, and examples of verbatims expressed by the respondents.

Security Awareness

Security awareness is composed of the following sub-topics: knowledge of measures taken, knowledge of other types of threats and how to protect oneself against IS security risks and threats. Table 2 represents the sub-topic "knowledge of other types of threats".

Table 2. Knowledge of the types of threats and potential risks related to IS security

Subtopic	Category	Number out of 22 users	Example of verbatims
Knowledge of other types of threats	Knowledge	9	*"But it can come from within the company and not necessarily from an external threat! Afterwards, there are viruses, emails where you have to click on the file and then you will be infected by a virus" (Jennyfer)*
	No knowledge	13	*"No! I don't know!" (Danielle)*

Security Compliance

For the compliance sub-theme, we considered the aspect of training, whether the users had had ISS related training, or not. Among all the users, 3 of them belonging to company A (Jennyfer, Pierre, Catherine) have received security training. Only one user from company B (Marie-Laure) has received RGPD training that we consider related to information security.

Estimation of the Security Culture of Each User

We will estimate the level of security culture of the users through the matrices by referring to our interview guide and more precisely, the questions that concern the security culture consisting of: security ownership, awareness and compliance. After assessing the security culture of each participant, we classified these users into three levels: Level

1: Low level of security culture (5 users), Level 2: Medium level of security culture (10 users), Level 3: High level of security culture (7 users).

Security-Related Behaviors Performed by Users
In this element, we will estimate the level of security-related behaviors such as the frequency of password changes, the strength of the chosen passwords as well as the backup of data by the users. After evaluating the security behaviors of each user, we will classify them into three levels: Level 1: Low security behaviors (8 users), Level 2: Medium security behaviors (8 users), Level 3: Strong security behaviors (6 users). 17 users out of 22 (77%) keep the same level in security culture as in security behaviors, those who have a strong level in security culture (ownership, awareness and compliance) remain on level 3 (strong) in the classification of security behaviors (password policy, backups), those who have an average level in culture keep an average level in behaviors, and finally, those who are classified at a low level of security culture also have a low level of security behaviors. For other users who have a single level difference between their culture and their behavior, these changes in level may be due to other factors such as the age or position of the user.

6 Discussion

Our results are consistent with the study by [5] which shows that SSI culture has a significant influence on employees' attitudes toward security policy and procedures. The study by [48] which examines the relationship between CSSI and security behavior. Although they did not focus solely on the effect of the SSI culture construct on safety behavior, their findings provided more comprehensive results on the relationship between safety culture and employee safety behavior compared to other studies. Specifically, they found that security culture had a significant effect on attitude and normative belief in social engineering resistance. Another study by [49] shows the influence of organizational culture, countermeasures, and security procedures on employees' security behaviors. Their study shows that the deterrent effect of procedural security countermeasures increases ISS awareness. This awareness, in turn, tends to prevent malicious actions by employees and encourages secure behaviors. A more recent study by [21] show the significant influence of IS security culture on user security compliance behaviors. Our results add to these studies to show the importance of a security culture that results from several factors, including executive security awareness, training and awareness etc., in influencing security behaviors.

7 Conclusion and Further Work

This paper presents an application of design science in IS security research, following guidelines proposed by [43]. We conduct a qualitative study in the field of IS security carried out in eight French SMEs by integrating 22 IS end-users, with the following objective: Verifying our model and its artifacts in the context of SMEs which suffer the most from IS user security behavior problems. We designed this model to present the artifacts of an IS security culture and how it can improve security behaviors. The results of our study show that most of the users interviewed have the same level in security culture as in security behaviors. Those who have a strong level in security culture remain on level 3 (Strong) in the classification of security behaviors, and vice versa. This allows us to assert that a positive security culture of an IS user is favorable to create security-related behavior such as regular password change, backup, and regular updates. The great contribution of this research is that it proposes a model that simplifies the components of an IS security culture and its relationship with security behaviors. On the theoretical level, our research shows that SMEs, despite their modest means compared to large companies, can set up training and awareness-raising actions on IS security within the SME, intended for users of the company's IS. These actions must be adapted to the context of the SME, with a simple and inexpensive approach. Nevertheless, our research has its limits regarding the generalization of the data and the model that we have designed. This is why our next step is to test our model on a larger sample of SMEs, with more participants.

References

1. Silic, M., Lowry, P.B.: Using design-science based gamification to improve organizational security training and compliance. J. Manag. Inf. Syst. **37**(1), 129–161 (2020)
2. Tolah, A., Steven, M., Furnell, S., Papadaki, M.: Furnell, S., Papadaki, M.: An empirical analysis of the information security. Comput. Secur. **108**, 102354 (2021). ISSN 0167-4048
3. Martins, N., Da Veiga, A.: An information security culture model validated with structural equation modelling. In: Proceedings of the 9th International Symposium on Human Aspects of Information Security and Assurance, HAISA, pp. 11–21 (2015)
4. Wiley, A., McCormac, A., Calic, D.: More than the individual: examining the relationship between culture and information security awareness. Comput. Secur. **88**, 101640 (2020)
5. Parsons, K., Young, M., Butavicius, M.A., McCormac, A.: The influence of organizational information security culture on information security decision making. J. Cogn. Eng. Decis. Making **9**(2), 117–129 (2015)
6. D'Arcy, J., Greene, G.: The multifaceted nature of security culture and its influence on end user behavior. In: IFIP TC 8 International Workshop on Information Systems Security Research, pp. 145–157 (2009)
7. Alfawaz, S., Nelson, K., et Mohannak, K.: Information security culture : a behaviour compliance conceptual framework. In: Australasian Information Security Conference (AISC), Brisbane, Australia (2010)
8. D'Arcy, J., Greene, G.: Security culture and the employment relationship as drivers of employees' security compliance. Inf. Manag. Comput. Secur. **22**, 474–489 (2014)
9. Labodi, C., Michelberger, P.: Necessity or challenge-information security for small and medium enterprises. Ann. Univ. Petrosani Econ. **10**(3), 207–216 (2010)
10. Lee, Y., Larsen, K.R.: Threat or coping appraisal: determinants of SMB executives' decision to adopt anti-malware software. Eur. J. Inf. Syst. **18**(2), 177–187 (2009)
11. Helokunnas, T., Iivonen, L.: Information security culture in small and medium size enterprises. In: e-Business Research Forum. Tampere University of Technology, Tampere (2003)
12. Hutchinson, D., Armitt, C., Edwards-Lear, D.: The application of an agile approach to it security risk management for SMES. In: Proceedings of the 12th Australian Information Security Management Conference, Perth, Australia, 1–3 December 2014 (2014)
13. Ngo, L., Zhou W., Warren, M.: Understanding transition towards information security culture change. In: Proceeding of the 3rd Australian Computer, Network & Information Forensics

Conference. Edith Cowan University, School of Computer and Information Science, pp. 67–73 (2005)

14. Karlson, F., Astrom, J., Karlson, M.: Information security culture – state-of-the-art review between 2000 and 2013. Inf. Comput. Secur. **23**(3), 246–285 (2015)
15. Schein, E.H.: Organizational culture and leadership, 358 p. Jossey-Bass Publishers, San Francisco (1985)
16. Hofstede, G.H.: Cultures and Organizations: Software of the Mind. McGraw-Hill, New York (1997)
17. Schein, E.H.: Organizational Culture and Leadership, vol. 2. Wiley, Hoboken (2010)
18. Schlienger, T., Teufel, S.: Information security culture: the socio-cultural dimension in information security management, security in the information society: visions and perspectives. In: IFIP TC11 International Conference on Information Security (Sec2002). Kluwer Academic Publishers, Cairo (2002)
19. Kokolakis, S., Karyda, M., Kiountouzis, E.: The insider threat to information systems and the effectiveness of ISO17799. Comput. Secur. **24**(6), 472–484 (2005)
20. Tang, M., Li, M., Zhang, T.: The impacts of organizational culture on information security culture: a case study. Inf. Technol. Manage. **17**(2), 179–186 (2015). https://doi.org/10.1007/s10799-015-0252-2
21. Solomon, G., Brown, I.: The influence of organizational culture and information security culture on employee compliance behaviour. J. Enterp. Inf. Manag. **34**(4), 1203–1228 (2021)
22. Tolah, A., Furnell, S.M., Papadaki, M.: A comprehensive framework for cultivating and assessing information security culture. In: The Eleventh International Symposium on Human Aspects of Information Security & Assurance (HAISA), HAISA 2017, pp. 52–64 (2017)
23. Alnatheer, M., Chan, T., Nelson, K.: Understanding and measuring information security culture. In: Pacific Asia Conference on Information Systems, p.144 (2012)
24. Da Veiga, A., Martins, N.: Defining and identifying dominant information security cultures and subcultures. Comput. Secur. **70**, 72–94 (2017)
25. Haeussinger, F., Kranz, J.: Information security awareness: its antecedents and mediating effects on security compliant behavior. In: Proceedings of the International Conference on Information Systems ICIS 2013, Milan, Italy (2013)
26. D'Arcy, J., Hovav, A., Galletta, D.: User awareness of security countermeasures and its impact on information systems misuse. Inf. Syst. Res. **20**(1), 79–98 (2009)
27. Kuusisto, T., Ilvonen, I.: Information security culture in small and medium size entreprises. Frontiers of E-business research, Tampere University of Technology: University of Tampere, Finland (2003)
28. Dojkovski S., Warren, M., Lichtenstein, S. : Information security culture in small and medium sized enterprises: a socio-cultural framework. In: Proceedings of the 6th Australian Conference on Information Warfare and Security, 24–25 November 2005. Deakin University, Geelong (2005)
29. Dojkovski, S., Lichtenstein, S., Warren, M.: Fostering information security culture in small and medium size enterprises: an interpretive study in Australia. In: European Conference on Information Systems (ECIS) (2007)
30. Williams, P.A.: What does security culture look like for small organizations? In: Proceedings of the 7th Australian Information Security Management Conference (2009)
31. Kaur, J., Mustafa, N.: Examining the effects of knowledge, attitude and behaviour on information security awareness: a case on SME. In: 3rd International Conference on Research and Innovation in Information Systems (2013)
32. Lopes, I., Oliveira, P.: Understanding information security culture: a survey in small and medium sized enterprises. In: Rocha, Á., Correia, A.M., Tan, F.B., Stroetmann, K.A. (eds.) New Perspectives in Information Systems and Technologies, Volume 1. AISC, vol. 275, pp. 277–286. Springer, Cham (2014). https://doi.org/10.1007/978-3-319-05951-8_27

33. Santos-Olmo, A., Sánchez, L.E., Caballero, I., Camacho, S., Fernandez-Medina, E.: The importance of the security culture in SMEs as regards the correct management of the security of their assets. Future Internet **8**, 30 (2016)
34. Parsons, K., McCormac, A., Butavicius, M., Pattinson, M., Jerram, C.: Determining employee awareness using the human aspects of information security questionnaire (HAIS-Q). Comput. Secur. **42**, 165–176 (2014)
35. Davis, F.D., Bagozzi, R.P., Warshaw, P.R.: User acceptance of computer technology: a comparison of two theoretical models. Manage. Sci. **35**(8), 982–1002 (1989)
36. Ajzen, I.: The theory of planned behavior. Organ. Behav. Hum. Decis. Process. **50**(2), 179–211 (1991)
37. Barlette, Y.: Les comportements sécuritaires des acteurs dans les Systèmes d'Information des PME. Doctoral thesis in management sciences from the University of Montpelier I, 383 p. (2006)
38. Padayachee, K.: Taxonomy of compliant information security behavior. Comput. Secur. **31**(5), 673–680 (2012)
39. Alhogail, A., Mirza, A.: Information security culture: a definition and a literature review. In: Computer Applications and Information Systems, pp. 1–7 (2014)
40. Da Veiga, A., Eloff, J.H.P.: A framework and assessment instrument for information security culture. Comput. Secur. **29**, 196–207 (2010)
41. Van Niekerk, J.F., Von Solms, R.: Information security culture: a management perspective. Comput. Secur. **29**, 476–486 (2010)
42. Nasir, A., Arshah, R.A., Ab Hamid, M.R.: A dimension-based information security culture model and its relationship with employees' security behavior: a case study in Malaysian higher educational institutions. Inf. Secur. J.: Glob. Perspect. **28**(3), 55–80 (2019)
43. Hevner, A.R., March, S.T., Park, J., Ram, S.: Design science in information systems research. MIS Q. **28**(1), 75–105 (2004)
44. Denning, P.J.: A new social contract for research. Commun. ACM **40**(2), 132–134, (1997)
45. Tsichritzis, D.: The dynamics of innovation in beyond calculation: the next fifty years of computing. In: Denning, P.J., Metcalfe, R.M. (eds.) Copernicus Books, New York, pp. 259–265 (1998)
46. Lee, A.: Inaugural editor's comments. MIS Q. **23**(1), v–xi (1999)
47. Igalens, J., Roussel, O.: Méthodes de recherches en gestion des ressources humaines, Paris, Economica, Recherches en gestion (1998)
48. Flores, W.R., Ekstedt, M.: Shaping intention to resist social engineering through transformational leadership information security culture and awareness. Comput. Secur. **59**, 26–44 (2016). ISSN 0167-4048
49. Connolly, L.Y., Lang, M., Gathegi, J., Tygar D.J.: Organizational culture, procedural countermeasures, and employee security behaviour: a qualitative study. Inf. Comput. Secur. **25**, 118–136 (2017)

Emerging DSR Methods and Processes

Introduction to Emerging DSR Methods and Processes Track

Kieran Conboy[1], Hanlie Smuts[2], and John Venable[3]

[1] National University of Ireland Galway
Kieran.conboy@nuigalway.ie
[2] University of Pretoria
hanlie.smuts@up.ac.za
[3] Curtin University
j.venable@curtin.edu.au

Abstract. The environment in which Design Science Research (DSR) is conducted is constantly changing. Purposeful artifacts resulting from prior DSR that have been adopted into practice become part of the milieu and change the nature of the world. Research is becoming more interdisciplinary. Purposeful artifacts are becoming more complex. The research environment itself changes, with new emphases on different application areas, such as sustainability, or new technological developments, such as artificial intelligence. How to better accumulate design knowledge (especially across disciplines) has become more important. Papers in this track address current and future states of this ever-changing world. There are two main topic areas of papers in this track. One group of papers focuses on design knowledge itself and how it can better be developed. The other focuses on methods for more specialized domains.

Keywords: Design science research methodology · Design knowledge · Design knowledge accumulation · Transdisciplinary research

1 Introduction to the Track

Design Science Research (DSR) Methods and Processes (as well as Tools and Techniques) guide DSR researchers in planning and conducting DSR. The Emerging DSR Methods and Processes track seeks contributions that would stimulate scholars to critically reflect on the scholarship, paradigms, methods, and fundamental assumptions in DSR.

The focus on *emergence* is appropriate because the environment in which DSR is conducted is constantly changing. The world and consequently research about it (behavioral and organizational research) and creating new purposeful artifacts that impact on it (design science research) is becoming more and more interdisciplinary. Purposeful artifacts are becoming more complex and design science is becoming actively applied in more and more disciplines. The purposeful artifacts that have previously been designed, developed and adopted into practice become part of the milieu and change the nature of the world, with benefits and possibly causing new problems. Moreover, new problems inevitably come to the fore regardless of the success or failure of any particular designed artifact. The research environment itself changes, with increasing transdisciplinarity (the theme of this conference), new emphases on different areas, such as sustainability, new and emerging enabling technologies, such as blockchain and artificial intelligence, new explanatory knowledge that enables new purposeful artifacts, new forms of funding and collaborating on research, and new methodological tools and practices. Together, these all inspire the need and potential for improved DSR methods and processes.

Against this background, the track particularly seeks research on philosophy, methods, processes, tools, and techniques that address the theme of the conference – The Transdisciplinary Reach of Design Science Research. Because all applied disciplines undertake DSR in some form (although they may not use the term DSR), there are many ripe opportunities for considering how DSR in Information Systems and Technology fits and integrates with DSR in other disciplines, as well as how DSR practices in other applied disciplines (or Sciences of the Artificial) can contribute to methodological practices in DSR in IS and IT.

The track encourages both conceptual and empirical study submissions that advance our understanding and facilitate improvement of DSR methods and processes. Conceptual studies could concern foundations of DSR including paradigms, ontologies, epistemologies, ethics, the nature of artefacts and human purposes, etc., where such conceptualizations advance our knowledge about design science methods and practice. Empirical studies can contribute evidence concerning the strengths, weaknesses, requirements, efficacy, effectiveness, efficiency, and/or ethicality of existing and emerging DSR methods and processes, particularly in transdisciplinary contexts.

2 Main Directions of Track Papers

The track received a good number of submissions and accepted six papers. The papers in the track fall in two clusters. The first cluster concerns the nature and development of design knowledge as the outcome of DSR. This has long been an important topic in DSR and is particularly relevant with the relatively recent focus on Design Knowledge Accumulation [2]. The second cluster concerns DSR methods for particular purposes or contexts, building on the trend in more specialized DSR methodologies, e.g. [1].

References

1. Bilandzic, M., Venable, J.R.: Towards participatory action design research: adapting action research and design science research methods for urban informatics. J. Community Inform. **7**(3), (2011). http://ci-journal.net/index.php/ciej/article/view/786/804
2. vom Brocke, J., Winter, R., Hevner, A., Maedche, A.: Special issue editorial–accumulation and evolution of design knowledge in design science research: a journey through time and space. J. Assoc. Inform. Syst. **21**(3), 9 (2020). https://doi.org/10.17705/1jais.00611

Reviewers for the *Emerging DSR Methods and Processes* Track

Toward a Method for Reviewing Software Artifacts from Practice

Ulrich Gnewuch(✉) ⓘ and Alexander Maedche ⓘ

Institute of Information Systems and Marketing (IISM), Karlsruhe Institute of Technology (KIT), Karlsruhe, Germany
{ulrich.gnewuch,alexander.maedche}@kit.edu

Abstract. Solving real-world problems with innovative and novel artifacts is at the core of design science research (DSR). Given DSR's emphasis on a strong connection to the real-world, artifacts for solving a particular problem may not only be described in extant literature, but also exist in practice. This is particularly the case for software artifacts. Therefore, DSR scholars need to explore the state of the art and demonstrate the novelty of their software artifact relative to existing artifacts in research *and* practice. However, while methodological guidance for conducting literature reviews is abundant, there is little guidance on how to review *software artifacts from practice*. This paper takes a first step toward addressing this gap by proposing and illustrating a seven-step method for reviewing software artifacts from practice. Our research provides actionable guidance for DSR scholars on how to support the claim that their software artifact constitutes a substantial contribution to knowledge.

Keywords: Design science research · Software artifact · Practice · Review · Method

1 Introduction

Design science research (DSR) aims to solve real-world problems with innovative and novel artifacts [1]. Consequently, artifacts play a key role in conducting DSR in information systems (IS) and often the contribution of a DSR project is the artifact itself [1]. In order to claim a substantial contribution to knowledge, researchers need to demonstrate their artifact's novelty, generality, and significance [1, 2]. Novelty is particularly important because the "artifact must be innovative, solving a heretofore unsolved problem or solving a known problem in a more effective or efficient manner" [1, p. 82]. Therefore, novelty is often the key difference between artifacts developed in DSR and artifacts developed by professional designers who use established design knowledge (e.g., "best practice" artifacts) to solve familiar problems in a routine way [2].

Against this backdrop, a fundamental step in any DSR project is to survey prior literature to identify "any prior design theory/knowledge relating to the class of problems to be addressed, including artifacts that have already been developed to solve similar problems" [2, p. 349]. Gregor and Hevner [2] emphasize that "if this survey is not done

© Springer Nature Switzerland AG 2022
A. Drechsler et al. (Eds.): DESRIST 2022, LNCS 13229, pp. 337–350, 2022.
https://doi.org/10.1007/978-3-031-06516-3_25

carefully, the developed artifact risks not being really new and it will not be possible to demonstrate an unquestioned claim to a contribution to knowledge" (p. 349). Thankfully, there is extant methodological guidance [e.g., 3–5] and tool support [e.g., 6] that can assist scholars in conducting literature reviews to identify, analyze, and synthesize the content of the literature. Subsequently, the findings from the literature can be used to "provide a baseline of knowledge on which to evaluate the novelty of new artifacts and knowledge resulting from the research" [2, p. 343].

However, DSR's strong focus on solving real-world problems rather than problems without practical relevance suggests that practitioners themselves may also create artifacts to address those problems. This is particularly the case for instantiations in the form of software artifacts in areas in which the fast-moving tech industry is ahead of academia [7]. For example, due to the resources needed to train and deploy large-scale natural language models such as GPT-3, innovative software artifacts in this area are often developed by big tech companies [8]. Therefore, it is likely that not all innovative software artifacts can be found in a literature review. However, since they already exist in practice, it seems important to also include them in the baseline of knowledge on which to evaluate the novelty of a software artifact developed in a DSR project. Otherwise, the designed artifact may be able to successfully demonstrate its novelty relative to literature, but risks not being really new compared to the state of the art in practice.

While methodological guidance for conducting literature reviews is abundant, there is little guidance on how to review software artifacts from practice in a systematic way. Recently, Chandra Kruse et al. [9] proposed a novel approach for analyzing existing real-world artifacts based on archaeological approaches to identify specific design features and understand underlying design decisions. However, similar to how the literature review process includes not only the analysis of a particular study but also tasks such as searching the literature and screening potential studies [10], the process of reviewing software artifacts from practice should also extend beyond the analysis of a particular artifact and consider other important tasks related to the identification and selection of a set of relevant software artifacts. At the same time, there are excellent examples in the literature in which the authors conducted a review of software artifacts from practice as part of their work [e.g., 11, 12]. For instance, Spohrer et al. [11] systematically reviewed more than 100 mobile health apps in the context of their DSR project to show that few existing apps focus on alleviating stress with progressive muscle relaxation. However, since these examples are limited to a particular case, it might be difficult to generalize their approach to other classes of artifacts. Hence, there is a lack of methodological guidance on how to review software artifacts from practice in a systematic way.

Therefore, the objective of this paper is to take a first step toward a method for reviewing software artifacts that are not described in extant literature but exist in practice. Drawing on the framework of generic steps in the literature review process [10], we propose a seven-step method for conducting reviews of software artifacts from practice. Subsequently, we explain how we have applied it in our own review of public crisis response dashboards that initially motivated this research effort. In addition, we demonstrate its broader applicability with another illustrative case [11]. Finally, we also discuss the challenges that occur when reviewing software artifacts from practice. In sum, we believe that our method can assist other DSR scholars in overcoming key difficulties when reviewing software artifacts from practice.

2 Conceptual and Methodological Foundations

2.1 Software Artifacts in Research and Practice

Artifacts play a central role in DSR since the goal of any DSR project is to produce an artifact to solve a real-world problem [1]. DSR artifacts can be broadly distinguished into four categories with different levels of abstraction: constructs, models, methods, and instantiations [1, 2]. Instantiations in the form of IT artifacts can be understood as "bundles of material and cultural properties packaged in some socially recognizable form such as hardware and/or software" [13, p. 121]. In this paper, we focus on instantiations in the form of software that are often developed for a specific design problem at hand [2]. We refer to this category of DSR artifacts as "software artifacts".

With some exceptions [e.g., 14], software artifacts developed in DSR are rarely full-grown IS that are used in practice [1]. DSR scholars primarily seek to contribute new design knowledge to the knowledge base rather than applying existing knowledge to solve a familiar problem in a routine way [2]. However, many innovative software artifacts exist in practice, particularly in areas in which the fast-moving tech industry is ahead of academia [7]. In contrast to *research software artifacts* that are targeted for the scientific community and usually described in a research paper, *software artifacts from practice* are targeted for professionals and used in environments outside academia [1, 15]. Given that such software artifacts are usually not documented in the research literature and therefore more difficult to identify and review than research software artifacts, we specifically focus on the process of reviewing software artifacts from practice.

2.2 Literature Review Process

A review of prior, relevant literature is essential in any type of research to create a solid foundation for advancing knowledge [3]. Over the years, a set of established guidelines has been proposed on how to review the literature in a systematic and rigorous way [e.g., 3–5]. Moreover, tools can support the literature review process [e.g., 6]. While literature reviews may differ from one type to another (e.g., narrative review, meta-analysis), there is general agreement on the existence of six generic steps in the review process [10]. According to Templier and Paré [10], these steps are:

1. *Problem formulation*: Justifying the need for the review, identifying the review's main objectives, and articulating research questions; Defining the concepts or variables at the heart of the review.
2. *Literature search*: Searching the literature and making decisions about the suitability of material to be considered in the review.
3. *Screening for inclusion*: Evaluating the applicability of the identified material; Screening potential studies for relevance based on predetermined rules or criteria.
4. *Quality assessment*: Assessing the scientific quality of the selected studies in terms of the rigor of research design and methods.

5. *Data extraction*: Extracting applicable information from each primary study included in the sample and deciding what is relevant to the problem of interest.
6. *Data analysis and synthesis*: Collating, summarizing, aggregating, organizing, and comparing the evidence extracted from the studies; Presenting the findings.

Although these steps are in sequential order, a literature review is an iterative process and many activities can be initiated during the planning stage and refined later [10].

3   A Method for Reviewing Software Artifacts from Practice

This research effort was initially motivated by our own DSR project. In this project, we designed and evaluated a conversational dashboard for the COVID-19 pandemic to improve less tech-savvy user's interaction with the dashboard and enhance their effectiveness and efficiency in finding the information they need [16]. In the course of publishing our DSR project, we were asked by reviewers to not only demonstrate the novelty of our dashboard artifact relative to dashboards described in the literature, but also to show that its features are novel compared to existing public crisis response dashboards used in practice (e.g., the Johns Hopkins University COVID-19 dashboard [17]). While the first task was relatively straightforward due to the range of *established* literature review methods, *the second task turned out to be a challenge, particularly because there was no suitable method for reviewing* software artifacts from practice *in the extant literature. Although we found a useful approach for analyzing the design of a particular software artifact* [9] as well as several papers in which a review of a class of software artifacts *was conducted* [e.g., 11, 12], there was no end-to-end method that we could readily apply to systematically review existing public crisis response dashboards and demonstrate the novelty of our own dashboard.

Based on this observation, we started our research effort by exploring established methods for reviewing the literature with the aim of finding a set of steps that could also guide us in our review of software artifacts from practice. Although we did not find a method that perfectly fit our objective, the six generic steps of the review process proposed by Templier and Paré [10] offered a good starting point. These steps were synthesized from different types of literature reviews [10] and have been used as a foundation in the recent work of Wagner et al. [6] on the use of artificial intelligence in literature reviews. Therefore, in our review of public crisis response dashboards, our goal was to find a way to translate each of these steps to the review of software artifacts from practice by identifying similar or equivalent activities and criteria. Additionally, we assessed whether any additional steps were needed during our review. In Table 1, we present an overview of the seven steps we took. Although they are presented in sequential order, there is no expectation that researchers would always actually proceed in that order. Moreover, it should be noted that not every DSR project may require a review of software artifacts. While it could save DSR scholars from potential frustration down the road when they find out that an artifact—similar to the one that they are currently developing—already exists in practice, conducting the review also requires time and effort that could be spent on other important DSR activities (e.g., developing the artifact).

In the following, we describe each step of our method, highlight its similarities or differences with its corresponding step in the literature review process, and explain how we applied it in our own review of public crisis response dashboards.

Table 1. A method for reviewing software artifacts from practice and its application in our own work

	Step	General description	Application in our Review
1	Problem formulation	Determining the review's main objectives with respect to software artifacts in the problem or solution space [18]; Defining the artifact's characteristics, properties, or features at the heart of the review; Defining the scope or boundaries of the review	• Main objective: Demonstrate the novelty of our dashboard artifact relative to existing public crisis response dashboards in practice (=solution space) • Relevant artifact features: (1) supported interaction modalities (e.g., GUI) and (2) and learning or support features (e.g., help buttons, tooltips) • Further information on the provider of the dashboard, target users, and crisis context
2	Software artifact search	Searching for potentially relevant artifacts (e.g., via the Internet, in major app stores, or by contacting experts) and making decisions about their suitability to be considered in the review	• Two search strategies: (1) Extraction of links from reviews of COVID-19 dashboards in medicine journals and (2) Multiple keyword searches on Google and Bing combining the term "dashboard" with a term for a crisis (e.g., "wildfire", "flood") and screening the first ten pages of results • Links to 43 public crisis response dashboards were bookmarked
3	Screening for inclusion	Screening software artifacts based on predetermined rules or criteria to determine their relevance (e.g., include artifacts only when they focus on relevant stakeholders, needs, goals, and requirements [19])	• Two key inclusion criteria: (1) the dashboard should target the general public and (2) is designed to address the needs of average users who want to find real-time information in times of crisis • This stage of the review narrowed down the data set to 28 dashboards

(continued)

Table 1. (*continued*)

Step	General description	Application in our Review
4	Quality assessment	Assessing the quality of the selected artifacts, not in terms of scientific quality but rather in terms of practical relevance (e.g., development stage, user feedback, dissemination among users and developers)	• Quality assessment was conducted by analyzing the data visualizations of each dashboard, testing its main functionalities (e.g., filters, drill-downs), and checking the date of the last update of data in the dashboard. Dashboards were removed when they had not been updated for over a year and their main functionalities were not working properly • Five dashboards were removed, resulting in a final set of 23 dashboards
5	Data extraction	Extracting applicable information from each artifact (e.g., by engaging with and trying out the artifact) and deciding what is relevant to the problem of interest	• To extract general information (e.g., provider, type of crisis) and information about relevant design features, all 23 dashboards were carefully inspected, their websites were examined, and supporting documents were read • The extracted information was stored in a large spreadsheet
6	Documentation and archiving	Documenting, storing, and archiving the artifact itself (to the extent possible) and any related material that was used as a source of information in the review	• For each dashboard, interactive snapshots of its web pages were taken using the archiving site archive.today at the time of data extraction (for an example, see: https://archive.ph/UfssR) • Additional screenshots were taken for all relevant design features of the dashboard
7	Data analysis and synthesis	Collating, summarizing, aggregating, organizing, and comparing the evidence extracted from the included artifacts; Presenting the findings in a meaningful way	• The extracted information was coded and analyzed iteratively in order compare and aggregate design features identified in the dashboards • Results were compiled into a large table that lists all reviewed dashboards based on nine dimensions (e.g., provider, type of crisis, design features)

Step 1: Problem Formulation

Similar to a literature review, the first step in a review of software artifacts from practice is to determine its main objectives and define the artifact's characteristics, properties, or features at the heart of the review. Given that software artifacts contain design knowledge that links a certain solution space to a certain problem space [18], a review of software artifacts from practice can be motivated by one of at least two objectives corresponding to these components. First, software artifacts could be reviewed to better understand the space of all possible solutions to a particular problem (i.e., solution space). In many cases, software artifacts may exist in practice that could be considered the baseline for any new artifact. Second, software artifacts could be reviewed to better understand the problem space. Although there may be problems and problem classes that do not involve any existing artifacts, the centrality of information technology in IS research [13] makes it likely that many problems that DSR scholars aim to solve relate to software artifacts in some way. In such a case, reviewing existing software artifacts from practice may provide a valuable source of information to explore and define the problem space. Regardless of the objective, the second key activity is to define what characteristics, properties, or features are to be analyzed in the review. This could, for example, include implemented design features [cf. 9], success metrics (e.g., product revenue, app store rating), or target users of the artifact. Finally, due to the complexity and diversity of software artifacts in practice, DSR scholars should also define the scope and boundaries of the review by specifying the class of artifacts they are interested in.

As our review was motivated by the need to demonstrate the novelty of our dashboard artifact relative to existing public crisis response dashboards used in practice, its main objective was to better understand the solution space—that is, which public crisis response dashboards already exist and how are they designed. To avoid being too narrow-scoped, we not only considered COVID-19 dashboards, but also dashboards designed for other types of crises (e.g., wildfires, floods). To investigate the novelty of our dashboard's design features, we focused the review on similar or related design features: (1) supported interaction modalities (e.g., GUI, natural language) and (2) learning or support features (e.g., help buttons, tooltips). In addition, we were interested in the dashboard provider (e.g., government, health organization), its target users (e.g., general public, emergency response team), and its crisis context (e.g., pandemic, wildfire).

Step 2: Software Artifact Search

In this step, DSR scholars need to construct an initial sample of potentially relevant software artifacts from practice by applying different search methods. Similar to literature reviews, scholars can aim at a coverage that is comprehensive, representative, pivotal, or selective [20]. For literature reviews, Templier and Paré [10] recommend using multiple search strategies (e.g., academic database search, backward and forward searches) and multiple data sources (e.g., journal articles, conference proceedings). A similar broad approach should be taken to search for software artifacts that are used in practice, however with different search strategies and very different data sources. While there are widely-accepted databases for scientific publications (e.g., EBSCO-host, IEEE Xplore), this is arguably not the case for software artifacts used in practice, thus posing a challenge for replicability and transparency. However, for many classes of artifacts, valid alternatives are available that allow searching for mobile apps (e.g.,

Apple's App Store, Google Play Store), desktop software (e.g., Microsoft Store, Mac App Store), web applications (e.g., GetApp; https://www.getapp.com/), and open-source software projects (e.g., GitHub, Launchpad). Another alternative is to conduct a keyword search on search engines (e.g., Google, Bing, Yahoo) and platforms for business software reviews (e.g., Capterra, Software Advice). While this approach is somewhat similar to querying an academic database, it is important to note that search results can vary even when using the same exact keywords because search engines also take into account other information such as the type of device and the location. An important final step in a literature review is to conduct a forward and backward search [3]. Similarly, there are websites for finding alternatives to a particular software artifact (e.g., AlternativeTo; https://alternativeto.net/) and for competitor analysis (e.g., https://craft.co/). Additionally, contacting practitioners (e.g., industry experts, software developers) and joining online communities (e.g., on the Reddit platform) offer opportunities to get first-hand information on the relevant class of software artifacts. Finally, the software artifacts identified during the search need to be collected for the next step. Instead of downloading the paper, scholars need to install the software artifact itself (e.g., mobile or desktop app), if possible, or bookmark a link to each possibly relevant artifact (e.g., web app).

A major challenge in our review of existing public crisis response dashboards was that there was no central database or platform available to conduct the search. To construct our initial sample, we therefore used two search strategies. First, we identified several recently published standalone reviews of COVID-19 dashboards in medicine journals [e.g., 21], from which we extracted links to public COVID-19 dashboards. Additionally, to identify dashboards for other types of crises, we used a keyword search on Google and Bing. More specifically, we conducted multiple searches by combining the term "dashboard" with a term for a crisis (e.g., "wildfire", "flood") using a Boolean AND. We also experimented with synonyms for the term dashboard (e.g., "map"), but the resulting hits were either duplicates or irrelevant. Given that we aimed for a representative rather than comprehensive coverage of public crisis response dashboards, we decided to screen the first ten pages of results for each keyword search and clicked on links that appeared to lead to a dashboard. When we identified a relevant result, we bookmarked the dashboard website. This step led to the identification of 43 dashboards.

Step 3: Screening for Inclusion

After identifying a set of potentially relevant software artifacts from practice, DSR scholars need to screen them to determine their relevance. This step is similar to that of a literature review, in which a set of predetermined criteria is used as a basis for including or excluding studies [10]. Typical criteria in a literature review relate to a study's focus on a certain theory, domain, or level of analysis. A similar approach, albeit with different criteria, should be used to separate the relevant software artifacts from the irrelevant ones. One strategy is to adopt the criteria from Maedche et al.'s [19] conceptualization of the problem space to include software artifacts only when they focus on those stakeholders, needs, goals, and requirements that are relevant in the context of the current DSR project.

Following this approach, in our review of public crisis response dashboards, we adopted two key inclusion criteria. First, the dashboard should be designed for the general public (i.e., stakeholders). This allowed us to exclude dashboards that primarily targeted emergency response teams or domain experts (e.g., physicians). Second, the dashboard should be designed to address the needs of average users who want to find real-time information in times of crisis. This enabled us to exclude dashboards that were primarily designed to provide a historical overview of past crises. This stage of the review narrowed down the data set to 28 dashboards.

Step 4: Quality Assessment
The next step is to assess the quality of the selected software artifacts. The quality assessment in a review of software artifacts from practice differs considerably from that in a literature review. In a literature review, this step would focus on the scientific quality of the selected studies (e.g., rigor of research design and methods) [10]. However, scientific quality would not be an appropriate basis for judging the quality of a software artifact from practice. Most importantly, the main goal of practitioners is to solve a real-world problem using a software artifact, but not to rigorously apply research methods and reflect on the designed artifact from a theoretical perspective [2]. Therefore, different quality dimensions are needed to assess software artifacts from practice. Given the strong connection between rigor and relevance in DSR [1], one strategy is to focus on the artifact's practical relevance rather than its scientific rigor. Observable indicators of the practical relevance of a software artifact include its development stage (e.g., mockup vs. fully-functional application), user feedback (e.g., rating in the app store), and dissemination among users or developers (e.g., number of forks of a GitHub repository).

Since no such information was available in our review of public crisis response dashboards, we conducted the quality assessment by analyzing the data visualizations of each dashboard, testing its main functionalities (e.g., filters, drill-downs), and checking the date of the last update of data in the dashboard. Our reasoning was that a dashboard can have only limited practical relevance when it has not been updated for over a year and its main functionalities are not working properly. As a result, five dashboards were removed, which resulted in a final set of 23 dashboards.

Step 5: Data Extraction
After determining the final set of software artifacts included in the review, the next step is to extract applicable information from each artifact and collect this data in an organized way (e.g., in a spreadsheet). While the fundamental idea is similar to that of a literature review, the actual approach is rather different. In a literature review, researchers would primarily focus on identifying fragments of qualitative and quantitative data in the body of the paper [6]. While some software artifacts that are used in practice may come with a documentation in textual or graphical form (e.g., company presentations, product videos, online tutorials), the primary focus of the review should be the artifact itself. Therefore, an essential activity in this step is to actively engage with, try out, and scrutinize the software artifact to the extent possible. Additional information can then be extracted from publicly accessible secondary sources (e.g., user reviews, news articles) and by contacting practitioners that were or still are involved in the design of the artifact (e.g., software developers, product managers).

In our review of public crisis response dashboards, we carefully inspected each of the 23 dashboards, examined the websites on which they were deployed, and read supporting documents (e.g., newspaper articles). During this process, we extracted general information (e.g., dashboard provider, type of crisis) and information about the supported interaction modalities (e.g., GUI, natural language) and implemented design features related to learning or support (e.g., help buttons, tooltips). We then stored all in information in a large spreadsheet.

Step 6: Documentation and Archiving

A crucial step in the process of reviewing software artifacts from practice is to document, store, and archive the artifact itself (to the extent possible) and any related material that was used to extract information for the subsequent analysis. This is not a typical activity in the literature review process [10], simply because all studies included in the review will persist over time since they are published in a journal or in conference proceedings. Hence, any researcher who is interested in a particular study, may look up the paper to verify the results reported in the literature review. However, this is much more difficult when it comes to software artifacts from practice because (1) not all of them might be publicly accessible, (2) some may require up-front payments, and (3) they are likely to change over time or even disappear. Given the research transparency movement in IS and other fields of research [22], this step is becoming increasingly important in DSR as well [23]. One solution would be to follow Lukyanenko and Parsons' [23] recommendation of storing all relevant material in a repository (e.g., by the Open Science Framework) that can be accessed by reviewers and prospective readers of the DSR paper. Relevant material includes the artifact itself in the form of source code (if open source) or application files (e.g., apk-files of Android apps), links to the artifact, interactive snapshots of all web pages (e.g., using archive sites such as archive.today), screenshots of important features, and additional documents (e.g., manuals, news articles).

In our review of public crisis response dashboards, we were unable to download the software artifacts because they were web applications and the source code was not provided. Instead, we took interactive snapshots of the dashboard's web pages using the archiving site archive.today at the time of data extraction (for examples, see: https://archive.ph/UfssR or https://archive.ph/MnpqD). In addition, we took screenshots of all relevant design features of the dashboard.

Step 7: Data Analysis and Synthesis

The final step in the process of reviewing software artifacts from practice is similar to that of a literature review. In this step, researchers need to collate, summarise, aggregate, organize, and compare the evidence extracted from the artifacts and present their findings in a meaningful way (e.g., in tabular form) [10]. Depending on the review's main objective, this step can take various forms. If the objective is to better understand problems surrounding an existing class of software artifacts, researchers could follow the design archaeology approach proposed by Chandra Kruse et al. [9] by taking different viewpoints (e.g., designer vs. user), examining functional and symbolic properties of the artifact, and exploring both intended and unintended consequences. Researchers could also rely on established methods and techniques (e.g., Grounded Theory method) for the analysis of the extracted evidence. Finally, the findings should be presented in a meaningful way, for example using a matrix that aggregates and organizes artifact characteristics, properties, or features rather than concepts in the literature [3].

Since the objective of our review was to demonstrate the novelty of our dashboard relative to existing public crisis response dashboards, we focused our analysis on the design features that were at the core of the knowledge contribution in our DSR project. Therefore, we iteratively coded and analyzed the extracted information about the dashboards to compare our new features (i.e., natural language-based interaction, interactive guided tour) with similar features implemented in existing dashboards in practice. In addition, we analyzed general functional features (i.e., what actions were possible in a dashboard: selecting, filtering, drill-downs, etc.) and visual features (i.e., what kind of data visualizations were used: maps, KPIs, line charts, etc.). We then compiled the results into a large table that listed all reviewed dashboards and their features. Based on our results, we were able to show that existing public crisis response dashboards had focused on graphical rather than conversational user interfaces as their main interaction modality and that most learning and support features were simple help buttons or tool tips rather than an interactive guided tour, demonstrating the novelty of our artifact.

4   Demonstrating the Applicability of the Method

To demonstrate the broader applicability of our method for reviewing software artifacts from practice, we provide a proof-of-concept demonstration of its applicability with an illustrative case. The illustration is taken from a DSR project conducted by Spohrer et al. [11] that investigated how combinations of different behavior change techniques within one mobile health app influence users' app use. Drawing on theories of protection motivation and social upward comparison, the authors designed and evaluated four prototypes of a mobile health app for stress alleviation. Their findings show that while design features of protection motivation and social upward comparison theory in isolation have positive effects on use, their combination negatively impacts use. As part of their work, the authors conducted a review of existing mobile health apps for stress alleviation. Due to the great level of detail provided in the paper's appendix, we selected it as an example to instantiate our method within the context of their work (Table 2).

Table 2. Example of reviewing mobile health apps for stress alleviation

	Step	Extracted from Spohrer et al. [11, Appendix F]
1	Problem formulation	The paper does not explicitly mention the review's objective. However, based on the discussion in the paper (p. 528), the main objective seems to be to show that there are only very few mobile health apps that implement progressive muscle relaxation exercises for stress alleviation (i.e., better understanding the solution space). At the heart of the review were design features of protection motivation and social upward comparison theory (e.g., push messages, performance visibility page) and implemented methods of stress alleviation (e.g., breathing exercises, meditation)

(continued)

Table 2. (*continued*)

Step		Extracted from Spohrer et al. [11, Appendix F]
2	Software artifact search	The authors searched for mobile stress alleviation apps in both the Google Play Store and the Apple App store by conducting a keyword search for the term "stress"
3	Screening for inclusion	In the Google Play Store, apps identified by the keyword search were included if they belonged to the category "Health & Fitness", leading to a selection of 71 Android apps. In the Apple App store, apps identified by the keyword search were included if they belonged to the category "Health & Fitness" and were free. After removing duplicate apps, 56 additional iOS apps were selected
4	Quality assessment	The paper does not explicitly mention quality assessment activities or criteria
5	Data extraction	Android apps were installed on a OnePlus 3 smartphone, while iOS apps were installed on an iPad. If required, a registration for the app was done, but no premium services were purchased. Subsequently, the features of the apps and previews of premium content were manually examined to extract information. More specifically, the authors searched for functions of social comparison, available statistics of training sessions, and options for push messages. They also tested the implemented methods of stress alleviation for several minutes. Additionally, the apps remained installed on the test devices for a period of two weeks to record all incoming notifications. In addition, the authors collected the number of downloads, number of reviews, average rating, and publishing date for all apps
6	Documentation and archiving	For each app, the authors provide a link that directly leads to the page of the app in the Google Play Store or the Apple App store
7	Data analysis and synthesis	The results of the review are synthesized in the form of a comprehensive table that includes the extracted data for all 127 apps. For each app, the table provides key metrics (e.g., rating), lists implemented methods of stress alleviation, and indicates whether or not the app offers a particular feature (e.g., push messages)

5   Discussion and Outlook

Motivated by the lack of methodological guidance in our own DSR project [16], we took a first step toward a method for reviewing software artifacts from practice. Drawing on the generic steps of the literature review process [10], we proposed a seven-step method and applied it in our own review of public crisis response dashboards. In addition, we instantiated our method within the context of a recently published DSR project that included a review of mobile health apps [11] to demonstrate its broader applicability. Currently, we apply and evaluate our method in another DSR project that focuses on a different class of artifacts (i.e., prototyping tools).

The method described in this paper is not meant to be a final product, but rather a starting point for discussion and further investigation. We identified several open questions and challenges that arise when reviewing software artifacts from practice. First, the actual application of our method may vary considerably depending on the selected class of software artifacts. For example, a review of web applications requires a different set of search strategies than a review of business software. Second, identifying all potentially relevant software artefacts is difficult, if not impossible, because artifacts may still be under development, are not publicly available, or even disappear over time. Third, software artifacts in practice may be covered by copyright protection and access to them may be restricted due to the use of confidential or commercial information, which could make it difficult for researchers to extract, analyze, and share information about a particular artifact. Finally, there are also alternative methods for assessing the novelty of design knowledge. For example, Iivari et al. [7] propose a method that involves asking practitioners to assess the novelty of design principles. Our paper adds to this line of research by shifting the focus to the (software) artifact itself and providing a means to compare a software artifact developed in DSR against existing artifacts in practice.

In summary, we believe that our method for reviewing software artifacts from practice is a useful addition to the toolbox of methods that DSR scholars can use to explore the state of the art in practice and demonstrate the novelty of their artifacts.

References

1. Hevner, A.R., March, S.T., Park, J., Ram, S.: Design science in information systems research. MIS Q. **28**, 75–105 (2004)
2. Gregor, S., Hevner, A.R.: Positioning and presenting design science research for maximum impact. MIS Q. **37**, 337–355 (2013)
3. Webster, J., Watson, R.T.: Analyzing the past to prepare for the future: writing a literature review. MIS Q. **26**, xiii–xxiii (2002)
4. Kitchenham, B.: Procedures for performing systematic reviews. Keele Keele Univ (2004)
5. Templier, M., Paré, G.: A framework for guiding and evaluating literature reviews. Commun. Assoc. Inf. Syst. **37**, 112–137 (2015)
6. Wagner, G., Lukyanenko, R., Paré, G.: Artificial intelligence and the conduct of literature reviews. J. Inf. Technol. (2021, forthcoming)
7. Iivari, J., Rotvit Perlt Hansen, M., Haj-Bolouri, A.: A proposal for minimum reusability evaluation of design principles. Eur. J. Inf. Syst. **30**, 1–18 (2019)
8. Nature: The big question. Nat. Mach. Intell. **3**, 737–737 (2021)
9. Chandra Kruse, L., Seidel, S., vom Brocke, J.: Design archaeology: generating design knowledge from real-world artifact design. In: Tulu, B., Djamasbi, S., Leroy, G. (eds.) DESRIST 2019. LNCS, vol. 11491, pp. 32–45. Springer, Cham (2019). https://doi.org/10.1007/978-3-030-19504-5_3
10. Templier, M., Paré, G.: Transparency in literature reviews: an assessment of reporting practices across review types and genres in top IS journals. Eur. J. Inf. Syst. **27**, 503–550 (2018)
11. Spohrer, K., Fallon, M., Hoehle, H., Heinzl, A.: Designing effective mobile health apps: does combining behavior change techniques really create synergies? J. Manag. Inf. Syst. **38**, 517–545 (2021)
12. Gleasure, R.: Conceptual design science research? how and why untested meta-artifacts have a place in IS. In: Tremblay, M.C., VanderMeer, D., Rothenberger, M., Gupta, A., Yoon, V. (eds.) DESRIST 2014. LNCS, vol. 8463, pp. 99–114. Springer, Cham (2014). https://doi.org/10.1007/978-3-319-06701-8_7
13. Orlikowski, W.J., Iacono, C.S.: Research commentary: desperately seeking the "IT" in IT research—a call to theorizing the IT artifact. Inf. Syst. Res. **12**, 121–134 (2001)

14. Lukyanenko, R., Parsons, J.: Easier crowdsourcing is better: designing crowdsourcing systems to increase information quality and user participation. In: vom Brocke, J., Hevner, A., Maedche, A. (eds.) Design Science Research. Cases. PI, pp. 43–72. Springer, Cham (2020). https://doi.org/10.1007/978-3-030-46781-4_3
15. Gill, A.Q., Chew, E.: Configuration information system architecture: Insights from applied action design research. Inf. Manag. **56**, 507–525 (2019)
16. Ruoff, M., Gnewuch, U.: Designing conversational dashboards for effective use in crisis response. In: Proceedings of the 29th European Conference on Information Systems (2021)
17. Johns Hopkins University: COVID-19 Dashboard (2022). https://coronavirus.jhu.edu/map
18. vom Brocke, J., Winter, R., Hevner, A., Maedche, A.: Special issue editorial – accumulation and evolution of design knowledge in design science research: a journey through time and space. J. Assoc. Inf. Syst. **21**, 520–544 (2020)
19. Maedche, A., Gregor, S., Morana, S., Feine, J.: Conceptualization of the problem space in design science research. In: Tulu, B., Djamasbi, S., Leroy, G. (eds.) DESRIST 2019. LNCS, vol. 11491, pp. 18–31. Springer, Cham (2019). https://doi.org/10.1007/978-3-030-19504-5_2
20. Cooper, H.M.: Organizing knowledge syntheses: a taxonomy of literature reviews. Knowl. Soc. **1**, 104–126 (1988)
21. Ivanković, D., Barbazza, E., Bos, V., Brito Fernandes, Ó., Kringos, D.: Features constituting actionable COVID-19 dashboards: descriptive assessment and expert appraisal of 158 public web-based COVID-19 dashboards. J. Med. Internet Res. **23**, e25682 (2021)
22. Burton-Jones, A., Boh, W.F., Oborn, E., Padmanabhan, B.: Editor's comments: advancing research transparency at MIS quarterly: a pluralistic approach. MIS Q. **45**, iii–xviii (2021)
23. Lukyanenko, R., Parsons, J.: Design theory indeterminacy: what is it, how can it be reduced, and why did the polar bear drown? J. Assoc. Inf. Syst. **21**, 1343–1369 (2020)

SeniorDT: A Design Thinking-Based Approach to Requirements Engineering Involving Elderly Users

Alexandra Jussli[1]($\boxtimes$), Kathrin Kim[1], Heiko Gewald[1], and Jason Thatcher[2]

[1] University of Applied Sciences Neu-Ulm, Wileystraße 1, 89321 Neu-Ulm, Germany
alexandra.jussli@hnu.de
[2] Fox School of Business, Temple University, 1801 Liacouras Walk, Philadelphia, PA 19122, USA

Abstract. Organizations are challenged to design solutions that increase the quality of life and well-being of elderly people because they inadequately understand the needs of this specific target group. Design thinking (DT) is a promising methodological framework for understanding the wants and needs of users. However, DT's fast and highly interactive style is not fully inclusive, making it ill-suited for elderly participants. This research presents the SeniorDT framework, which affords opportunities for including elderly participants in a multi-stakeholder setting. Our framework is developed using the action design research methodology, which builds on field data gathered during a long-term DT project. On this basis, we derive theoretical and practical implications for conducting DT with older participants.

Keywords: Action design science research · Requirements engineering · Elderly users · Design thinking · SeniorDT

1 Introduction

Design thinking (DT) is "an approach to foster the process of designing through an iterative process of human-centered idea generation and evaluation in a team context" [1, p. 1]. Many organizations have utilized DT to gather deep user insights to inform the design of better products and services, applying different frameworks and process models to support this process [2]. As DT involves carefully assessing users' needs and developing ideas and solutions to meet those needs collaboratively, such frameworks and methods rely on a high level of empathy with users [3].

Since designers and engineers typically differ considerably from elderly end-users in terms of age, lifestyle, attitudes, and cognition, organizations face challenges in applying DT to design products and services for the elderly [4]. Overcoming such challenges is important because the elderly population is an increasingly important consumer segment, and demand for elderly-friendly products and services is expected to increase in the coming years [5]. In response, researchers and practitioners have called for adapted DT

A. Drechsler et al. (Eds.): DESRIST 2022, LNCS 13229, pp. 351–362, 2022.
https://doi.org/10.1007/978-3-031-06516-3_26

approaches that consider the specific characteristics of and foster collaboration with elderly people [6].

In this study, we refer to people broadly as 'elderly' who are in retirement, which happens around the age of 60 and heavily impacts living conditions and lifestyle choices [7]. However, evidence and practical experience show that elderly people have extremely heterogeneous desires, needs, health restrictions, physical and mental capabilities, and lifestyles [6]. Assessing how such heterogeneity should inform product and service design is challenging because our knowledge of the range of elderly people's perspectives on elderly-friendly technology is limited [8]. For example, elderly people with good vision might experience big buttons on mobile phones as stigmatizing.

However, adapting DT to designing for elderly people is difficult because 'elderly people' are by no means a homogeneous user group. Classical DT approaches were developed for the business context, where the limitations posed by involving elderly participants were less relevant [6]. Specifically, classical DT has well designed to collect data about the specific characteristics, knowledge, and experience of elderly people [9], failing to account for well-documented changes in physiological and psychological capabilities that people experience as they age and failing to address how to encourage elderly people to participate actively in DT activities [10]. To realize the potential of using DT with elderly participants, designers must consider how to incorporate their perspectives and "design for the other" [4].

This research contributes to the design science by developing a senior design thinking (SeniorDT) method and illustrating how to adjust the DT framework to better incorporate elderly users in the design thinking process. In order to develop a new DT-based approach, we follow the Action Design Science Research (ADR) approach developed by Sein, et al. [11]. Accordingly, we formulate the problem based on extant literature, then develop, refine, test and apply the artifact, SeniorDT, in practice. The empirical basis of this field study is a project, which applied SeniorDT with elderly participants in two design cycles. Throughout these cycles, we reflect on the experiences and formulate the learnings. To compare our SeniorDT with an application of classical DT, we conducted a baseline project with younger participants in a business setting. This study concludes with a discussion of our findings, their implications for DT frameworks, their limitations, and directions for further research.

2 Literature Review

Modern requirements engineering methods are user-centric, i.e., they position intended users in the middle of design processes. In user-centric design approaches, user groups who systematically differ from "average users" and, thus, require additional attention, are often referred to as "sensitive user groups" [12]. Some user-centric design approaches specifically address the inclusion of sensitive user groups. For example, Gregor, et al. [12] describe how to account for diversity in physical and cognitive abilities, such as hearing impairments, declining attention spans, which are common among sensitive user groups [6] and, in the context of the current study, among the sensitive user group of elderly people.

In addition to limited psychological, cognitive, and physical capabilities, elderly people also frequently demonstrate reduced levels of creative thinking [13]. Because people's tendency to align their thinking towards familiar patterns increases as they grow older, they may ignore novel or unfamiliar helpful ideas [6]. For example, studies demonstrate that elderly people less easily perceive the usefulness and value of techno-logical innovation [14]. This issue could result from the limited technology experiences of elderly users, who did not grow up using IT [15]. Hence, elderly people's interest in and ability to participate in design activities, could be limited by their capabilities and preferences, even though participation could increase their well-being and the quality of their social interactions [6].

The current state identifies the problems of older DT participants' participation and collaboration, which hampers designing products with and for this target group. To over-come such limitations, researchers suggest adapting design workshops to account for the potentially restricted physical and cognitive abilities and levels of creative thinking of elderly users [6]. Hakobyan, et al. [16] suggest eliminating tasks that require older participants to read and write on their own and actively soliciting elderly participants to participate in prototypes and reviewing material. Reflecting on the fast and iterative nature of classical DT, van der Westhuizen, et al. [17] report that elderly people strug-gle to collaborate and feel limited trust in the method. To overcome these challenges, evidence suggests emphasizing verbal explanations and one-to-one interactions [16]. To effectively conduct design workshops with elderly users, designers need to build trusting relationships with elderly people and educate them on the value of collaboration [16].

3 Methodological Approach

To ensure methodological rigor in our research project we chose to follow the Action Design Research Approach suggested by Sein, et al. [11]. ADR comprises four iterative stages: problem formulation (1), building, intervention, and evaluation (2), reflecting and learning (3), and formalization of learnings (4). Figure 1 illustrates how these stages are connected and shows the corresponding sections in this paper.

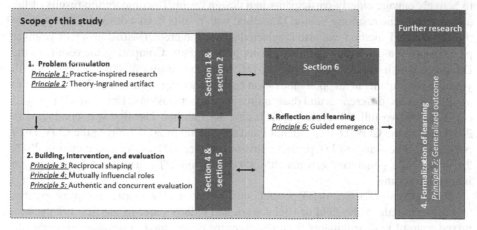

Fig. 1. Action design research approach (Sein et al. (2013))

Following the ADR method, our research adopted the recommended stages as follows: Stage 1 identifies the specific problems of seniors' participation and collaboration. We use the introduction and literature review to describe the details of this practical problem. The introduction reflects on the identified issues out of a theoretical perspective (stage 1). Section 5 demonstrates the reciprocal shaping of the SeniorDT method (stage 2) based on authentic insights, gathered during a real-life project describes in Sect. 4. The discussion functions as reflection and learning stage by reflecting the findings against the background of the practical issues and the theoretical state of science (stage 3). Formalization and learning (stage 4) – which is not part of this research yet – would consist of transforming the gained insights into concrete design principles for Design Thinking with older participants.

We chose ADR as guiding methodological framework for our research as it combines research, development and evaluation by generating authentic insights and continuous learning while developing/applying the artifact in practice [11]. This more iterative approach of research enriches design science by referring the design activity continuously back to the practitioners' perspective and the current state of theory, which contributes to solve the issue of balancing relevance and rigor [18]. This creates value by encouraging the ADR researcher to develop a rich, interpretative understanding the project and the social context, which differs from the positivist logic found in some classical design science approaches [19]. Hence, ADR is better suited to the Design Thinking context than other design science methodologies. ADR is particularly useful for building authentic understanding of the perspectives and attitudes of workshop participants. Prior research has applied the ADR approach in DT contexts and found it useful for understanding user participation and learning [20]. We therefore use the ADR approach for methodologically guiding our development of SeniorDT.

4   Project Background

This paper presents the results of a research program focusing on adapting DT methods to actively engage elderly participants in a design cycle. To compare the results of the application of the resulting SeniorDT method with results from a design cycle applying the classical DT method, we also conducted a baseline project with a group of younger participants, mainly with IT or engineering backgrounds. Comparing the results of the DT project with elderly people (SeniorDT) with the results of the DT project with younger participants in an open innovation business setting (classical DT) enabled us to identify specific differences and draw more specific conclusions. The SeniorDT project consisted of two full DT cycles, each lasting six months. The first was conducted in 2019 (before the COVID-19 pandemic) and the second in 2021 (during the COVID-19 pandemic). The standard DT project consisted of three DT cycles conducted in 2018, 2019, and 2021, generating new insights into conducting DT in a multi-stakeholder open innovation setting.

Participants in the SeniorDT project consisted of elderly people, company experts, and professionals in the field of social work and elderly care. In the first DT cycle, a mixed team of ten participants from these groups contributed to developing a mhealth application. The second DT cycle focused on fostering technology adoption among elderly people and included a mixed team of fifteen participants. The first cycle was then evaluated thoroughly based on insights from ethnographical observations, such as field notes taken during the project and collaborative real-time and retrospective reflection, and interviews with a focus group, refined with the help of DT experts, and discussed in informal interviews with the participants to create an optimized second DT cycle.

5   SeniorDT - Design and Development

During the literature review we formulated participation and collaboration as main problems we aim to target with developing SeniorDT. The initial development stage draws on insights from the baseline project, expert interviews, and the extant literature. Generated insights are used to adapt the DT process following the six-stage process developed by Plattner, et al. [21]: *understand* (1), *empathize* (2), *synthesize* (3), *ideate* (4), *prototype* (5), and *test* (6). In the following, we describe the adaptions:

1. We added a *'consolidation'* stage to the beginning of the DT process to clarify participants' expectations.
2. We spread out the workshop days over several weeks to give elderly participants sufficient regeneration time in between.
3. We added open coffee breaks after workshop sessions to give elderly participants who do not have the endurance for workshop collaboration, the opportunity to contribute.
4. We fostered team dynamics by holding team check-ins and check-outs, where participants could reflect on the goal of each session and collaboration, and by engaging a facilitator with practical experience working with elderly people to assess the mood of the participants.

Figure 2 illustrates the initial version of SeniorDT:

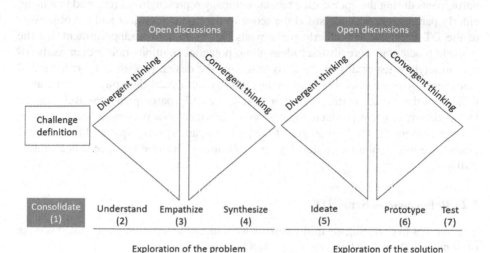

Fig. 2. Initial version of SeniorDT

The project began with a consolidation phase (1) consisting of two workshop sessions. In the first session, a pool of relevant topics was generated, which was translated into a concrete design challenge in the second session of the consolidation phase. The understanding phase (2) was performed by company experts' presentations and interviews with doctors. In the emphasizing phase (3), short observations in an elderly care home were organized. On this basis, the synthesis (4) and ideation (5) phases were conducted based on classic DT methods. Click dummies were utilized in the prototyping (6) and testing (7) phases at a residential complex for elderly adults. This shift in location enabled us to engage the facilities' tenants as end-users.

5.1 Demonstration and Evaluation of the Initial Version

We evaluated our initial version of SeniorDT based on focus group discussions, informal interviews with workshop participants, and interviews with DT experts, documenting our results as field notes. The findings were iteratively discussed among the researchers and the project participants. Benefits were noted in terms of team formation and insights into contextual factors. Based on our evaluation, we concluded that the initial version of SeniorDT required improvements in two main areas: participation and collaboration.

The issue of **participation** affected all stakeholders. Company experts were often interrupted by urgent phone calls and company representatives reported difficulties freeing themselves of their professional responsibilities for several hours at a time. The elderly participants attended the first two two-hour sessions and the first four hours of each of the remaining two eight-hour workshop days. The elderly participants reported difficulties keeping up with the speed of the exchanges, the frequency of topic changes, and the prevalence of English jargon. They reported feeling insecure about their role, confused about how they were expected or able to contribute to the design process, and embarrassed to ask questions because they did not want to be perceived as stupid.

The issue of **collaboration** also had many facets. Based on discussions with elderly participants during the open coffee breaks, company representatives reported that many elderly participants misunderstood the scope of the research project and the objectives of the DT activities. The elderly participants expressed their disappointment that the workshop outcome were abstract ideas about potential solutions rather than ready-to-use prototypes. Especially at the early stages of the design process, expert input and statements by other workshop participants heavily influenced the opinions and contributions of the elderly participants. For instance, elderly participants passively agreed to the already existent products the company representatives presented and has issues criticizing them. At the later stages of the process, participants expressed their lack of confidence in contributing to developing a mhealth application because it is a 'digital artifact.'

5.2 Refinement of SeniorDT

The findings from testing the initial version were incorporated to create a refined version of SeniorDT (Fig. 3). Measures were taken to improve:

Recruiting

1. The DT facilitator focused on building trusting relationships with the elderly participants before the project started, such as by calling them individually several times to discuss the location and time.
2. Company managers were given a gatekeeper role and asked to assign one subordinate each to guarantee the organization's commitment to the project.

Collaboration

1. A facilitator explicitly clarified the roles of the participants before each task and highlighted the contribution of the elderly participants.
2. The DT facilitation began with warmups requiring contributions from every participant.
3. DT facilitation utilizes check-ins and check-outs to describe the goals of each phase and progress toward reaching the project goals in detail.

Comprehension

1. The research team adapted classic DT materials and templates to meet the needs of the elderly participants, such as by avoiding English jargon, using larger fonts, larger paper, and materials familiar to elderly participants, such as napkins, for prototypes.
2. Workshop leaders provided ample seating so that elderly participants could sit down without having to ask.
3. Workshop leaders provided simple and clear handouts outlining the goals and structure of the phases and activities.
4. The workshop leaders simplified the workshop phases and activities by focusing on the key elements, thus shortening the workshops significantly.
5. The research team consolidated the potentially confusing six-stage iterative process developed by Plattner, et al. [21] into four clear phases: consolidate the challenge, investigate the problem, find an idea, and develop a solution (see Fig. 2 below).

Authenticity

1. In the consolidation phase, the elderly participants identified relevant topics in a first session, and then company experts formulated a design challenge based on interviews in a second session.
2. A DT facilitator specified the role of each participant to ensure that the elderly participants would share their perspectives and opinions and that company experts would listen.

3. The workshop leaders simplified the prototyping and testing sessions to make design
    activities more accessible to the elderly participants.

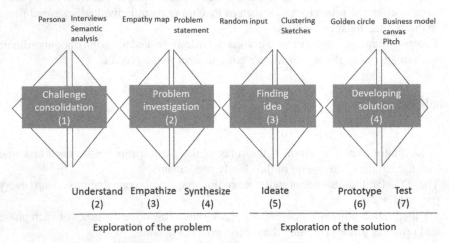

Fig. 3. Refined version of SeniorDT

During Phase 1 of SeniorDT, Challenge consolidation, a group of elderly people
discussed relevant topics from their perspectives based on the extreme-user method.
On this basis, company experts conduct interviews with elderly people to gain deeper
insights into their needs and perspectives and develop a design challenge in 'how might
we' form. A key method of Phase 2 is the development of a fictitious persona from
whose perspective a hypothetical point-of-view statement can be generated. In Phase
3, the participants generated ideas utilizing random-input and clustering techniques,
sketching the final idea on a napkin. In Phase 4, the participants developed the final idea
into a possible solution using business development methods such as the golden circle,
business model canvas, and preparing a pitch.

5.3   Evaluation of the Refined Version of SeniorDT

Compared to the design cycle in which we applied our initial version of SeniorDT, we
observed changes in each of the four categories outlined in Sect. 5.2 above:

Participation
The refined version of SeniorDT enabled elderly participants to participate significantly
more than previously. For example, five out of eight elderly participants engaged in more
than one event, three of whom participated throughout. Unfortunately, several participants dropped out due to health issues or because they had to care for a close relative, and
were thus unable to commit to participating in a series of events. To our disappointment,
participation among company representatives and social workers declined: only three

out of seven participated throughout. These dropout rates might be caused by the rinsing COVID cases in Germany.

Collaboration
Elderly participants highlighted the role of trust, suggesting that involving a "trustworthy" institution, such as the church, in the project would further increase their willingness to collaborate.

Comprehension
Elderly participants reported that they could follow the activities better in the design cycle using the refined version of SeniorDT than in the design cycle using the initial version of SeniorDT. It is noteworthy that, their feedback specifically addressed the facilitator's calm and patient attitude. We observed that facilitation using timeboxing was ineffective because the elderly participants have their own individual pace of working and often contribute by telling stories, from which other participants could generalize in the discussion. This demonstrates that the elderly participants depended on the support of their groupmates to clarify the tasks and empathetically "overlook" any difficulties they were having with the activities. Finally, we observed that elderly participants did not respond well to gamification approaches and were reluctant or unable to hypothetically imagine states, clinging instead to the notion that the prototypes (and organizations) developed would become real.

Authenticity
In both the initial and the refined versions of SeniorDT, company experts appreciated authentic user insights, acknowledging their value and relevance in their everyday business. Specifically, they singled out the value of collaborative activities that foster closeness to a target group, deepen their methodological knowledge, strengthen ties with other institutions, and challenge classical approaches followed in their companies. We observed that low-threshold workshop outcomes adapted to meet elderly users' needs and emotions facilitated authentic contribution.

6 Discussion: Reflection and Learning

The unique needs and limitations of elderly people often make it difficult for them to participate fully and authentically in traditional design theory (DT) approaches. This research presents a new SeniorDT approach, which includes modifications of the activities, methods, and structure of classical DT approaches that facilitate a greater willingness to participate, a higher level of collaboration, better comprehension, and more authentic contributions among elderly DT participants, yielding more valuable insights for designers of products and services for elderly users and consumers. The ADR method we present responds to calls in extant literature in terms of identifying four action fields for DT adaption when it comes to activities with elderly people, namely adaption of the DT process, facilitation, settings and material, and recruitment [22]. Hence, we like to reflect on our insights to deliver more general findings:

1. **Process**

    Our results demonstrate how adapting the DT process contributes to engaging elderly participants. This group requires a slow introduction to the process by starting with a consolidation phase and working with elderly participants and experts separately at the outset. In addition, fast and iteration as typical DT style [23] are not sufficient when it comes to workshop activities with elderly people. Grouping activities into logical phases helps elderly participants feel less overwhelmed by rapid topic changes.

2. **Facilitation**

    The facilitator is especially vital as we observe that elderly participants often relate their experience directly to the facilitator. Specific emphasis should be put on teambuilding and warm-up activities that enable participants to feel safe contributing. It is important to align all activities with elderly participants' physical and cognitive capabilities, such as by not requiring difficult movements or overly demanding abstract thinking.

3. **Settings and material**

    All materials and language used should be familiar to elderly participants. In order to support consistent participation, elderly participants must be able to access the workshop site easily and feel comfortable with the physical setting. To avoid exhaustion and stress, the sessions should be short but not feel rushed. Handing out a simple, large-print schedule of each session allows elderly participants to process the information at their own speed and refer to the schedule as often as they want to, building trust in the process.

4. **Recruitment**

    Achieving strong design cycle results applying SeniorDT principles rely on the active and committed participation of a range of stakeholders balanced between company representatives, social workers, and elderly participants. The gatekeeper approach, which involves managers in recruitment decisions, increases organizations' level of commitment to the project. Our findings indicate that additional resources and time are required to secure committed participation among elderly participants than among younger stakeholders in the business context.

Generally, our findings underscore the value of DT in generating valuable and authentic user insights and contributing to teambuilding [24]. However, effectively involving elderly participants in design cycles sheds light on potential limitations of core fields of actions for adapting DT to elderly participants. Since many elderly people lack the stamina to attend long and intense workshops and feel overwhelmed if they are overstimulated, involving elderly participants in design cycles using SeniorDT requires greater empathy and a sharper focus on those activities that best support the process.

6.1 Limitations and Further Research

As with any research, our study is limited in several ways. First, the elderly participants in this study are highly active in a single non-profit organization in Germany, which might bias the results in terms of the physical and cognitive characteristics and socio-economic status that affect activities in the late stage of life. Due to COVID-19 pandemic restrictions, we were severely limited in terms of workshop locations and participant recruitment. Future research should compare workshop results in more diverse settings, such as in different cultural settings, including a broader sample of the older generation, such as those living in elderly care homes, and welcome individuals only willing or able to attend parts of the workshop sessions.

Second, the majority of the participants in our study participated in both design cycles implementing the initial and the refined versions of SeniorDT. It can be assumed that participants learned from one iteration to the next. Future studies using SeniorDT should include "naive" participants.

Third, we undertook this study in the context of a research project. Future research is required applying SeniorDT in "real-life" circumstances, with an authentic design intention, to assess how stakeholders' and participants' levels of trust and motivation differ.

Fourth, researchers investigating the elderly population might benefit from applying an ADR or design science context. In this regard, studies utilizing these two approaches might reveal if the insights generated in this paper support a better inclusion of sensitive users into design activities, which would contribute to the development of design science approaches, making the best use of older participants.

Last, but not least, it is important to state that action design research contributes by deriving concrete design principles, aiming to support practice [11]. Therefore, we will build on the generated learnings of this study by formulating concrete principles, which DT facilitators can use for DT activities, aiming to design with and for the elderly.

Acknowledgments. We thank all participants in the workshops informing this research. This publication was funded by the German Ministry for Education and Research through the project Innovative Hochschule (IHS) project number 03IHS024C.

References

1. Dolak, F., et al.: Design thinking and design science research. presented at the DESRIST Positioning Paper (2013)
2. Waidelich, L., et al.: Design thinking process model review. In: 2018 IEEE International Conference on Engineering, Technology and Innovation (ICE/ITMC), pp. 1–9 (2018)
3. Dorst, K.: The core of 'design thinking'and its application. Des. Stud. **32**, 521–532 (2011)
4. Jussli, A., Gewald, H.: Senior DT-a design thinking method to improve requirements engineering for elderly citizens. In: 2021 IEEE 29th International Requirements Engineering Conference Workshops (REW), pp. 240–247 (2021)
5. Yang, D., et al.: Integrating cooperative design and innovative technology to create assistive products for older adults. In: Proceedings of the International Association of Societies of Design Research Conference (2019)
6. Sorgalla, J., et al.: Improving representativeness in participatory design processes with elderly. In: Proceedings of the 2017 CHI Conference Extended Abstracts on Human Factors in Computing Systems, pp. 2107–2114 (2017)
7. Jonsson, H.: The first steps into the third age: the retirement process from a Swedish perspective. Occup. Ther. Int. **18**, 32–38 (2011)
8. Meurer, J., et al.: Designing for way-finding as practices–a study of elderly people's mobility. Int. J. Hum Comput Stud. **115**, 40–51 (2018)

9. Dodge, R., et al.: The challenge of defining wellbeing. Int. J. Wellbeing **2**, 222–235 (2012)
10. Wildenbos, G.A., et al.: Mobile health for older adult patients: Using an aging barriers framework to classify usability problems. Int. J. Med. Inform. **124**, 68–77 (2019)
11. Sein, M.K., et al.: Action design research. MIS Q. 37–56 (2011)
12. Gregor, P., et al.: Designing for dynamic diversity: interfaces for older people. In: Proceedings of the Fifth International ACM Conference on Assistive Technologies, pp. 151–156 (2002)
13. Righi, V., et al.: When we talk about older people in HCI, who are we talking about? Towards a 'turn to community' in the design of technologies for a growing ageing population. Int. J. Hum. Comput. Stud. **108**, 15–31 (2017)
14. Goonetilleke, R.S., Au, E.Y.L.: Enhancing the life of the elderly–an application of design thinking. In: Goonetilleke, R., Karwowski, W. (eds.) Advances in Physical Ergonomics and Human Factors. AHFE 2019. AISC, vol. 967, pp. 388–396. Springer, Cham (2020). https://doi.org/10.1007/978-3-030-20142-5_39
15. Duque, E., et al.: A systematic literature review on user centered design and participatory design with older people. In: Proceedings of the 18th Brazilian Symposium on Human Factors in Computing Systems, 2019, pp. 1–11 (2019)
16. Hakobyan, L., et al.: Participatory design: how to engage older adults in participatory design activities. Int. J. Mob. Hum. Comput. Interact. (IJMHCI) **7**, 78–92 (2015)
17. van der Westhuizen, D., et al.: Engaging communities on health innovation: experiences in implementing design thinking. Int. Q. Community Health Educ. **41**, 101–114 (2020)
18. Susarapu, S., Lee, A.: Lessons that action research offers to design science in information systems. In: SAIS 2005 Proceedings (2005)
19. Maccani, G., et al.: Action design research: a comparison with canonical action research and design science. In: At the Vanguard of Design Science: First Impressions and Early Findings from Ongoing Research Research-in-Progress Papers and Poster Presentations from the 10th International Conference, DESRIST 2015. Dublin, Ireland, 20–22 May 2015, pp. 69–76 (2015)
20. Becker, F., et al.: Taking action: extending participatory action design research with design thinking (2019)
21. Plattner, H., et al.: Design-Thinking. Springer, Heidelberg (2009). https://doi.org/10.1007/978-3-642-13757-0
22. Hendricks, S., et al.: A modified stakeholder participation assessment framework for design thinking in health innovation. In: Healthcare, 2018, pp. 191–196 (2018)
23. Brenner, W., Uebernickel, F., Abrell, T.: Design thinking as mindset, process, and toolbox. In: Brenner, W., Uebernickel, F. (eds.) Design Thinking for Innovation, pp. 3–21. Springer, Cham (2016). https://doi.org/10.1007/978-3-319-26100-3_1
24. Black, S., et al.: Design thinking, organizational behavior (2019)

A Granular View of Knowledge Development in Design Science Research

Nicolas Prat[1]($\boxtimes$) (iD), Jacky Akoka[2,3] (iD), Isabelle Comyn-Wattiau[1] (iD), and Veda C. Storey[4] (iD)

[1] ESSEC Business School, Cergy-Pontoise, France
{prat,wattiau}@essec.edu
[2] CEDRIC-CNAM, Paris, France
jacky.akoka@lecnam.net
[3] IMT BS, Évry-Courcouronnes, France
[4] Georgia State University, Atlanta, GA, USA
vstorey@gsu.edu

Abstract. Design science research (DSR) should contribute to both the prescriptive and descriptive knowledge bases. Despite its maturity, a granular understanding of how DSR develops knowledge, while utilizing and contributing prescriptive and descriptive knowledge, remains incomplete. Creating such a granular understanding requires a detailed typology of design knowledge, a unifying vocabulary of operations, and an identification of which operations can be applied to produce different knowledge types. We propose that "triplets of dynamic knowledge", relating source and target knowledge types through operations, can be defined, and combined to develop design knowledge. We provide a vocabulary of operations on knowledge types and investigate the relationships between knowledge types and operations. We illustrate triplets that can improve fitness, projectability or confidence. The goals of the granular view of knowledge development are to guide researchers without constraining them, and to progress a finer-grained description and accumulation of knowledge development in DSR.

Keywords: Design science research · Design knowledge · Knowledge development · Knowledge type · Operation · Triplet of dynamic knowledge

1 Introduction

Design science research (DSR) has matured, both in the production of knowledge and in its evaluation [1–3]. DSR in information systems (IS) has positioned itself with respect to behavioral research [4, 5], which develops theories explaining or predicting IS-related phenomena. DSR focuses on how to solve problems by developing artifacts. Initially, behavioral research and DSR were considered distinct, contributing to the descriptive knowledge base (Ω-knowledge [6]) and prescriptive knowledge base (λ- knowledge [6]) respectively. However, it is now commonly accepted that DSR may contribute both types of knowledge [7, 8].

© Springer Nature Switzerland AG 2022
A. Drechsler et al. (Eds.): DESRIST 2022, LNCS 13229, pp. 363–375, 2022.
https://doi.org/10.1007/978-3-031-06516-3_27

Despite its maturity, a granular understanding of how DSR develops knowledge, utilizing and contributing λ-knowledge and Ω-knowledge, remains incomplete. We need fine-grained models of scientific inquiry [9] that represent how knowledge can be combined and developed in the λ-knowledge and Ω-knowledge bases. We concur with Lee et al. [10, p.5] that *"missing is a granular understanding of design theorizing process, i.e., what are specific elements and activities involved in the design theorizing process?"*: although detailed typologies of design knowledge have been proposed [8, 11], the activities to develop knowledge are either described incompletely, or at a level of detail too high to account for all types of prescriptive or descriptive knowledge. Developing design knowledge should improve fitness, projectability, or confidence [11]. To this end, in addition to being aware of the different design knowledge types, researchers need to know what operations to apply to what knowledge types to improve projectability, fitness, or confidence. This requires a detailed vocabulary to describe these operations, and an understating of how the operations may improve fitness, projectability, or confidence. A granular understanding of knowledge development will help researchers in advancing their research. This is necessary to address the wicked problems characteristic of DSR. At the same time, there is a need for knowledge accumulation. There are many DSR projects that researchers may reuse, replicate, or extend. A granular view of knowledge development in DSR will enable the formalization of knowledge development, and thus the accumulation of knowledge, at a detailed level.

The research question becomes: *How can we describe and understand the development of design knowledge at a granular level, recognizing that knowledge development in DSR should contribute to fitness, projectability, or confidence?* To answer this question, we make minor adaptations to the typology of design knowledge [8, 11] and propose a unifying vocabulary of operations consistent with the level of detail of this typology. We investigate the relationships between knowledge types and operations to identify which operations can be applied to different knowledge types to produce new ones. We propose and illustrate *triplets of dynamic knowledge*, relating source and target knowledge types through operations, and specify their effects (individually or in succession) on projectability, fitness, and confidence. We present the triplets as possible operationalizations of two archetypal movements of vom Brocke et al. [11], and identify a new movement. The objectives of our granular view of design knowledge development are to guide researchers by suggesting possible triplets (without constraining them) and to detail how knowledge is developed and accumulated in DSR.

This paper proceeds as follows. Section 2 reviews the literature on knowledge development in DSR, motivating a granular representation. Section 3 presents the typology of design knowledge, proposes a detailed and unifying vocabulary of operations, and investigates the relationships between knowledge types and operations. Section 4 presents examples of triplets, or successions of triplets, relating them to the dimensions of fitness, projectability, and confidence. Section 5 concludes the paper.

2 Literature Review

We distinguish five categories of research related to knowledge development in DSR:
(1) methodologies or high-level views of knowledge development, (2) theorizing, (3)
processes or frameworks for defining design principles or theories, (4) conceptualization
of knowledge development as knowledge moments, and (5) interplay between DSR
projects and human knowledge bases.

Several high-level views of the DSR process have been proposed. Peffers et al. [12]
define a DSR methodology. The methodology for action design research [13] includes
formalization of learning, generalizing outcomes. Kuechler and Vaishnavi [14] present a
cyclical DSR process. Vom Brocke et al. [11] represent the accumulation of DSR knowledge across projects as journeys along a tri-dimensional space: projectability, fitness,
and confidence. Four movements are identified: abstraction, generalization, amplification, and contextualization. The authors provide a high-level view: the DSR chunks
positioned along this space are typically at the granularity level of projects.

Multiple papers explore theorizing in IS. Lee and Baskerville [15] propose a generalizability framework which applies both to positivist and interpretive research. In DSR,
the concept of projectability [16] is preferred to generalizability. Lee et al. [10] consider
theorizing in DSR as operating in two domains: instance (problem and solution) and
abstract (problem and solution). They propose a framework with four activities: abstraction, de-abstraction, solution search, and registration. They do not rely on a detailed
typology of design knowledge. Their four activities are high-level, in that they are not
related to specific types of design knowledge.

Research on developing design principles includes a method for their development,
which is systematic, but rigid [17]. Mandviwalla [18] proposes a process based on
prototyping for design theory construction; a more focused framework [19] centers
around abstraction for two specific components of design theories.

According to the DSR genres framework [7], a study has successive knowledge
moments, characterized by a goal (design or science, i.e., prescriptive or descriptive)
and scope (idiographic or nomothetic). Building upon this framework, Akoka et al. [20]
define knowledge paths as sequences of knowledge nodes characterized by their goal
and scope. They do not specify the operations between nodes. Herwix and Rosenkranz
[9] distinguish knowledge production episodes (similar to knowledge moments), but not
their sequencing. Rothe et al. [21] characterize design knowledge by its scope and goal
and conceptualize DSR knowledge development as a knowledge creation process with
three mechanisms: injection, folding, and enhancement.

Drechsler and Hevner [8] distinguish project design knowledge from human knowl-
edge bases (with Ω- and λ-knowledge), identifying six modes of utilizing or contributing
knowledge, through high-level operations such as "informs" or "are reused".

Thus, there is a need for a granular view of knowledge development. Prior research:
(1) provides a high-level view; (2) focuses on a specific aspect of knowledge development
(e.g., abstraction into design theories); (3) uses a characterization of knowledge that lacks
detail; or (4) lacks a detailed, unifying vocabulary of operations.

3   Design Knowledge Types and Operations

Recognizing the dynamic and pluralistic nature of DSR [7], this research considers knowledge development at a granular level as operations between knowledge types. Similar to other work (e.g., [21]), we consider knowledge development as typically found in academic publications, which generally do not mention temporary design project knowledge. Thus, we focus on "human knowledge bases" [8]. We slightly adapt the typology of design knowledge, define a unifying vocabulary of operations, and investigate the relationships between knowledge types and operations.

3.1   Design Knowledge Types

Consistent with the term "design knowledge bases" [11], we refer to human knowledge bases as "design knowledge". This does not necessarily imply that any addition to these bases may be a DSR research contribution. Such a contribution requires some abstraction [22]. Moreover, knowledge development in DSR requires progression in projectability (in the problem space), fitness (in the solution space) or confidence (in evaluation) [11]. Figure 1 shows the typology of design knowledge used it this research, drawing heavily on the model of Drechsler and Hevner [8] and its adaptation [11].

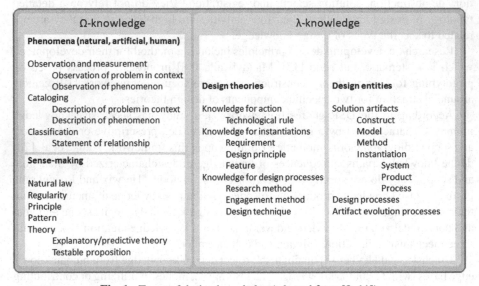

Fig. 1. Types of design knowledge (adapted from [8, 11]).

In Ω-knowledge, we understand "observation" broadly [23]. For example, participant observation, surveys, and measurement through sensors, are forms of observation. Following Seidel and Watson [23], we distinguish between the observation of a problem within its context and the observation of a phenomenon. Similarly, we distinguish two types of descriptions. Observation leads to description, which leads to conceptualization [23]. How conceptualization is performed depends on the paradigm (explanatory/predictive or prescriptive). In Ω-knowledge, we put description under the label "cataloging", according to the definition of the verb "catalog" ("*to list or describe (something) in an organized way*," https://www.learnersdictionary.com/definition/cat alog). We add statements of relationship under the label "classification". Similarly, we add "explanatory/predictive theory" and "testable proposition" under the label "theory". We make minimal changes to λ-knowledge, changing "principle" to "design principle" to avoid confusion with principles in Ω-knowledge. Solution artifacts are subdivided according to March and Smith [4]; instantiations are specialized [8].

3.2 Operations

The literature lacks a detailed, standardized vocabulary of operations on knowledge types. We thus need a vocabulary of operations for the representation of knowledge development at a granular level, with well-specified meaning. To define the vocabulary of operations, we used a conceptual approach, based on a review of the literature as well as on our own knowledge and experience. This iterative process included brainstorming on candidate terms, grouping similar terms into categories (e.g., operations related to abstraction or generalization), and identifying and resolving issues of synonymy, hyponymy, or hypernymy. The resulting vocabulary is provided, grouping the operations into four categories: bottom-up, top-down, solution search, and evaluation and inspection. This typology mirrors the four design theorizing activities of Lee et al. [10] (abstraction, de-abstraction, solution search, and registration). An operation has a source knowledge type (object of the operation) and a target knowledge type (result of the operation). The knowledge types are the final nodes in the typology of Fig. 1.

Bottom-Up Operations. *Strict abstraction* is as understood in the object-oriented approach [24], i.e., abstraction of an instance into a class, or abstraction of a class into a meta-class. The source and target knowledge types may be the same or different. *Loose abstraction* is abstraction broadly understood [25]. It refers to other types of abstraction than strict abstraction. In loose abstraction, the target knowledge type differs from the source knowledge type. *Strict generalization* is generalization as understood in the object-oriented approach, i.e., generalization of a class into a super-class. *Detail-preserving generalization* is generalization as understood by vom Brocke et al. [11]. Since the original level of detail is preserved, the generalized knowledge is not more difficult to operationalize than the original knowledge. In detail-preserving and strict generalization, the source and target knowledge types are the same.

Top-Down Operations. *Specialization* is the inverse of generalization. *Instantiation* is the inverse of strict abstraction. However, we reserve this term for instantiation from an abstract artifact to another abstract artifact (as opposed to a material artifact [22], i.e., as opposed to an instantiation), or from a system (e.g., a tool) to another system. *Application* relates an abstract artifact or a system (source knowledge type) to a product or process (target knowledge type). In *execution*, the source knowledge type is a system, and the target knowledge type is a product or process. *Implementation*, as commonly used, refers to the implementation of an abstract artifact into a system.

Solution Search Operations. *Derivation* builds a target knowledge type from a source knowledge type to progress towards the solution. For example, a system may be derived from requirements. In *augmentation*, an artifact is completed by another artifact, which enriches the solution without directly contributing to solving the problem. For example, a model may be completed with guidelines (a specific type of method) on how to use it. Combination, selection, transfer, and adaptation draw on vom Brocke [26]. *Combination* aggregates knowledge of a certain type to knowledge of the same or another type. Selection, transfer, and adaptation inject [21] knowledge from other knowledge bases into the current design knowledge base. In *selection*, the source knowledge is injected as is. In *transfer*, it is injected by analogy. In *adaptation*, it is injected after changes to adapt to the context of the current knowledge base.

Evaluation and Inspection Operations. *Revision* changes knowledge in the context of evaluation. The source and the target knowledge types are the same. *Corroboration* is the counterpart of revision, when evaluation reveals that no change to the evaluated knowledge is needed. *Observation* is the observation of a product or a process, typically in a context of evaluation (systems are not observed directly, but through the products or processes resulting from their application). *Examination* inspects abstract design knowledge, typically in evaluation (e.g., complexity of an algorithm).

3.3   From Knowledge Types to Knowledge Types Through Operations

This section examines the relationships between knowledge types and operations to explore which operations may be performed on which source knowledge types to produce which target knowledge types. From these operations, we will be able to define *triplets of dynamic knowledge* to progress projectability, fitness, or confidence.

We built a matrix with the knowledge types as rows and columns, with each cell containing the possible operations from the knowledge type in the row to the knowledge type in the column. The knowledge types are the final nodes in the typology of Fig. 1. However, we only consider the types in Ω-knowledge commonly referred to in DSR. The typology of λ-knowledge includes both the results and activities of DSR [8, 11]. We consider only design knowledge representing the results of DSR, leaving knowledge representing activities for future research. Thus, our matrix contains the knowledge types: observation of problem in context, observation of phenomenon, description of problem in context, description of phenomenon, statement of relationship, explanatory/predictive theory, testable proposition, technological rule, requirement, design principle, feature, construct, model, method, system, product, and process.

To populate the cells of the matrix (determine the operations that may operate on a source knowledge type to result in a target knowledge type), we combined a conceptual and an empirical approach. After filling and discussing the matrix collectively based on our knowledge of DSR, we proceeded to empirical evaluation, the purpose of which was to check if we had omitted operations from a target to a source knowledge type that appear in the literature. (Conversely, an operation from a source to a target knowledge type might be relevant even though it has not been reported in the literature.) The empirical evaluation was based on the 52 DSR papers published in MISQ from 2004 to 2020. These papers were selected by two of the authors by examining the abstracts, and full text as necessary. The selection criterion required that DSR be mentioned as the research method or that at least one DSR artifact be clearly articulated. From these 52 papers, a random sample of 22 papers was drawn. Two authors identified the operations from knowledge types to knowledge types used in all papers of this sample. This comprised several steps, including individual coding and discussion of disagreements. The empirical evaluation led to the addition of a few operations in the matrix. As expected, the resulting matrix is sparse, despite the many possible operations from knowledge types to knowledge types. Therefore, rather than a matrix, Table 1 shows the possible source and target knowledge types by operation.

Table 1. Source and target knowledge types by operation.

Operation	Source knowledge type	Target knowledge type
Strict abstraction	Model ∪ Method	Construct
	System	System
Loose abstraction	Observ. of prob. in context	Descript. of prob. in context
	Observ. of phenom	Descript. of phenom
	Observ. of phenom. ∪ Descript. of prob. in context ∪ Descript. of phenom	Statement of relationship
	Statement of relationship	Explan./predict. theory
	Observ. of phenom. ∪ Descript. of phenom. ∪ Statement of relationship ∪ Feature ∪ Method	Testable propos
	Construct ∪ Model ∪ Method ∪ System ∪ Product ∪ Process	Techno rule ∪ Design principle
	System	Model ∪ Method
Strict generalization, detail-preserving generalization, specialization	Descript. of prob. in context ∪ Descript. of phenom. ∪ Statement of relationship ∪ Explan./predict. theory ∪ Testable propos. ∪ Techno rule ∪ Requirement ∪ Design principle ∪ Feature ∪ Construct ∪ Model ∪ Method	Same as source knowledge type

(*continued*)

Table 1. (*continued*)

Operation	Source knowledge type	Target knowledge type
Instantiation	Construct	Model ∪ Method
	System	System
Application	Construct ∪ Model ∪ Method	Product
	Construct ∪ Method	Process
Execution	System	Product
Implementation	Construct ∪ Model ∪ Method	System
Derivation	Explan./predict. theory ∪ Requirement	Testable propos
	Descript. of prob. in context ∪ Explan./predict. theory ∪ Testable propos	Requirement
	Explan./predict. theory ∪ Testable propos. ∪ Requirement	Design principle
	Descript. of prob. in context ∪ Explan./predict. theory ∪ Testable propos. ∪ Requirement ∪ Design principle	Feature
	Testable propos	Method ∪ System
	Requirement ∪ Design Principle ∪ Feature	Construct ∪ Model ∪ Method ∪ System ∪ Product ∪ Process
	Descript. of prob. in context	System ∪ Product ∪ Process
Augmentation	Method	Model
	Construct ∪ Model	Method
Combination	Testable propos. ∪ Construct	Explan./predict. theory
	Construct	Statement of relationship
	Construct	Model
Selection, transfer, adaptation	Construct ∪ Model ∪ Method ∪ System ∪ Product ∪ Process	Same as source knowledge type
Revision, corroboration	Any knowledge type	Same as source knowledge type
Observation	Product ∪ Process	Observ. of phenom
Examination	Techno rule ∪ Requirement ∪ Design principle ∪ Feature ∪ Construct ∪ Model ∪ Method	Descript. of phenom

4 Triplets to Progress Projectability, Fitness, and Confidence

Based on Table 1, which shows which operations may be performed on which knowledge types to produce which knowledge types, Table 2 illustrate triplets of dynamic knowledge, with indication of changes to projectability, fitness, and confidence. These examples are taken from the literature or drawn from the authors' experiences.

Table 2. Triplets of dynamic knowledge for projectability, fitness, and confidence.

Movement	Triplets	Projecta-bility	Fit-ness	Con-fi-dence
Abstraction	Process ─ loose abstraction ─→ Design principle	↗	↘	↘
	System ─ strict abstraction ─→ System	↗	↘	↘
	System ─ loose abstraction ─→ Model	↗	↗	↘
Amplification	Descript. of prob. in context ─ derivation ─→ Requirement	=	↗	↘
	Requirement ─ derivation ─→ Model	=	↗	↘
	Construct ─ augmentation ─→ Method	=	↗	↘
Evaluation and demonstration	Model ─ implementation ─→ System	↘	↗	↗
	System ─ execution ─→ Product	↘	=	↗
	Model ─ corroboration ─→ Model	=	=	↗
	Product ─ observation ─→ Observ. of phenom.			

The triplets are classified by movement in the design knowledge space. Table 2 considers some movements and a few examples of triplets. In addition to the movements of abstraction and amplification [11], we add "evaluation and demonstration". The table illustrates how movements may be operationalized by operations on knowledge types. The triplets may be used for guidance (i.e., to develop knowledge by progressing fitness, projectability, or confidence) at the level of a single project, or between projects. Knowledge development in a project is represented as successions of triplets. In addition to guiding DSR researchers, this representation may be used to describe knowledge development and accumulation at a granular level. Even though for each triplet, the operation is performed on a single knowledge type (the object of the operation), the triplet may have secondary sources. A triplet results in a single knowledge type (the target). For example, a model may be revised or corroborated based on the qualitative or quantitative feedback of users (i.e., observation of phenomenon, according to the typology of design knowledge). The corresponding triplet has a primary source (the model revised or corroborated), a secondary source (the observation), and results in a revised or corroborated model, with improved confidence.

The movement of abstraction [11] is characterized by an increase in projectability and a decrease in fitness. At the granularity level of triplets, we observe that this is generally the case (and confidence decreases because the newly created knowledge is yet to be evaluated). For example, the triplet abstracting a system into another (strict abstraction) may represent the abstraction of a modeling tool into a metamodeling tool. We could also imagine a DSR project that starts by reverse-engineering a model from an existing system, this model being one of the artifacts produced in the project to solve the problem. In this specific case, the triplet (the last one represented in abstraction in Table 2) would result in both an increase in projectability and fitness.

Amplification (progressing fitness at the same level of projectability) may be achieved by different operations, e.g., derivation or augmentation. For example, a query language (construct) may be completed with guidelines (method).

In "evaluation and demonstration", the triplets are characterized by an increase in confidence. The implementation of a model into a system decreases projectability but increases fitness and improves confidence (proof of feasibility). Execution of a system, which results in a product (the data from execution) increases confidence by demonstration. As mentioned above, the two triplets in the last row of Table 2, taken together, improve confidence. Note that the last triplet, which observes a product (e.g., the result of execution of a system) does not increase confidence *per se*. To increase confidence, this observation should be used to revise or corroborate knowledge, e.g., a model.

To illustrate the triplets of dynamic knowledge on a specific DSR project, and how knowledge development improves projectability, fitness or confidence at a granular level, we consider a paper from our MISQ sample [27]. Based on the language-action perspective, used as kernel theory, the authors conjointly build a model and a method. They implement their approach and use the implemented system on an example to evaluate the approach. Beyond the system itself, the evaluation enables the corroboration of the model and method. Knowledge development for this example, represented as successions of triplets, is illustrated in Fig. 2. Due to space limitations, we do not illustrate the early phases of the DSR project. We use the same conventions as vom Brocke et al. [11] to illustrate progression in projectability, fitness, and confidence. Movements *between* cells in the grid of Fig. 2. materialize increase or decrease in fitness and projectability. However, *within* a cell, the relative placement of the knowledge types (e.g., "Model" and "Method") is not meant to represent their relative fitness or projectability. The letters before the operation names indicate their order of execution.

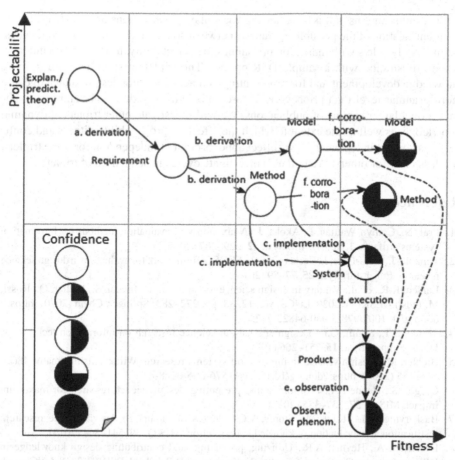

Fig. 2. Triplets of dynamic knowledge: knowledge development in Abbasi et al. [27].

5   Conclusion

To represent knowledge development at a granular level, we need a detailed typology of design knowledge, a detailed vocabulary of operations, and a representation of knowledge development that relates types of design knowledge to operations, with implications for projectability, fitness, and confidence. To this end, this paper proposes a granular view of knowledge development in DSR by introducing and illustrating *triplets of dynamic knowledge*. The triplets provide a way to capture and represent projectability, fitness, and confidence, serving as a common vocabulary for knowledge development in DSR. To define the triplets, we propose a detailed and unifying vocabulary of operations. The source and target knowledge types of the operations are the most detailed ones adapted from an extant typology of design knowledge. The possible operations from source to target knowledge types are systematically identified.

The contributions of this paper are the vocabulary of operations on knowledge types, the identification of the possible operations between source and target knowledge types, examples of triplets with indication of changes to projectability, fitness, and confidence, and an illustration with a sample DSR project. The triplets may be used for guiding knowledge development and for representing and accumulating design knowledge at a more granular level than prior work. Future work will include further empirical validation on a larger sample of publications. We will investigate other triplets of dynamic knowledge, as well as the extent to which the effect on projectability, fitness and confidence is context independent. This effect appears context independent for some triplets, and less clear for others. We will also investigate cycles in sequences of triplets.

References

1. Prat, N., Comyn-Wattiau, I., Akoka, J.: A taxonomy of evaluation methods for information systems artifacts. J. Manag. Inf. Syst. **32**, 229–267 (2015)
2. Venable, J., Pries-Heje, J., Baskerville, R.: FEDS: a framework for evaluation in design science research. Eur. J. Inf. Syst. **25**, 77–89 (2016)
3. Larsen, K.R., et al.: Validity in design science research. In: Hofmann, S., Müller, O., Rossi, M. (eds.) DESRIST 2020. LNCS, vol. 12388, pp. 272–282. Springer, Cham (2020). https://doi.org/10.1007/978-3-030-64823-7_25
4. March, S.T., Smith, G.F.: Design and natural science research on information technology. Decis. Support Syst. **15**, 251–266 (1995)
5. Bichler, M.: Design science in information systems research. Wirtschaftsinformatik **48**(2), 133–135 (2006). https://doi.org/10.1007/s11576-006-0028-8
6. Gregor, S., Hevner, A.: Positioning and presenting design science research for maximum impact. MIS Q. **37**, 337–355 (2013)
7. Baskerville, R.L., Kaul, M., Storey, V.C.: Genres of inquiry in design-science research: justification and evaluation of knowledge production. MIS Q. **39**, 541–564 (2015)
8. Drechsler, A., Hevner, A.R.: Utilizing, producing, and contributing design knowledge in DSR projects. In: Chatterjee, S., Dutta, K., Sundarraj, R.P. (eds.) DESRIST 2018. LNCS, vol. 10844, pp. 82–97. Springer, Cham (2018). https://doi.org/10.1007/978-3-319-91800-6_6
9. Herwix, A., Rosenkranz, C.: Making sense of design science in information systems research: insights from a systematic literature review. In: Chatterjee, S., Dutta, K., Sundarraj, R.P. (eds.) DESRIST 2018. LNCS, vol. 10844, pp. 51–66. Springer, Cham (2018). https://doi.org/10.1007/978-3-319-91800-6_4
10. Lee, J.S., Pries-Heje, J., Baskerville, R.: Theorizing in design science research. In: Jain, H., Sinha, A.P., Vitharana, P. (eds.) DESRIST 2011. LNCS, vol. 6629, pp. 1–16. Springer, Heidelberg (2011). https://doi.org/10.1007/978-3-642-20633-7_1
11. vom Brocke, J., Winter, R., Hevner, A., Maedche, A.: Special issue editorial–accumulation and evolution of design knowledge in design science research: a journey through time and space. J. Assoc. Inf. Syst. **21**, 520–544 (2020)
12. Peffers, K., Tuunanen, T., Rothenberger, M.A., Chatterjee, S.: A design science research methodology for information systems research. J. Manag. Inf. Syst. **24**, 45–77 (2007)
13. Sein, M.K., Henfridsson, O., Purao, S., Rossi, M., Lindgren, R.: Action design research. MIS Q. **35**, 37–56 (2011)
14. Kuechler, W., Vaishnavi, V.: A framework for theory development in design science research: multiple perspectives. J. Assoc. Inf. Syst. **13**, 395–423 (2012)
15. Lee, A.S., Baskerville, R.L.: Generalizing generalizability in information systems research. Inf. Syst. Res. **14**, 221–243 (2003)

16. Baskerville, R., Pries-Heje, J.: Projectability in design science research. J. Inf. Technol. Theory Appl. **20**, 53–76 (2019)
17. Möller, F., Guggenberger, T.M., Otto, B.: Towards a method for design principle development in information systems. In: Hofmann, S., Müller, O., Rossi, M. (eds.) DESRIST 2020. LNCS, vol. 12388, pp. 208–220. Springer, Cham (2020). https://doi.org/10.1007/978-3-030-64823-7_20
18. Mandviwalla, M.: Generating and justifying design theory. J. Assoc. Inf. Syst. **16**, 314–344 (2015)
19. Gregor, S., Müller, O., Seidel, S.: Reflection, abstraction and theorizing in design and development research. In: Proceedings of the ECIS, pp. 1–12. Association for Information Systems (2013)
20. Akoka, J., Comyn-Wattiau, I., Prat, N., Storey, V.C.: Evaluating knowledge types in design science research: an integrated framework. In: Maedche, A., vom Brocke, J., Hevner, A. (eds.) DESRIST 2017. LNCS, vol. 10243, pp. 201–217. Springer, Cham (2017). https://doi.org/10.1007/978-3-319-59144-5_12
21. Rothe, H., Wessel, L., Barquet, A.P.: Accumulating design knowledge: a mechanisms-based approach. J. Assoc. Inf. Syst. **21**, 771–810 (2020)
22. Gregor, S., Jones, D.: The anatomy of a design theory. J. Assoc. Inf. Syst. **8**, 312–335 (2007)
23. Seidel, S., Watson, R.T.: Integrating explanatory/predictive and prescriptive science in information systems research. Commun. Assoc. Inf. Syst. **47**, 284–314 (2020)
24. Jarke, M., Gallersdörfer, R., Jeusfeld, M.A., Staudt, M., Eherer, S.: ConceptBase—a deductive object base for meta data management. J. Intell. Inf. Syst. **4**, 167–192 (1995)
25. Schnizlein, D., Bowling, M., Szafron, D.: Probabilistic state translation in extensive games with large action sets. In: Proceedings of the IJCAI, pp. 278–284. Morgan Kaufmann (2009)
26. vom Brocke, J.: Design principles for reference modeling: reusing information models by means of aggregation, specialisation, instantiation, and analogy. In: Fettke, P., Loos, P. (eds.) Reference Modeling for Business Systems Analysis, pp. 47–76. IGI Global, Hershey, PA (2007)
27. Abbasi, A., Zhou, Y., Deng, S., Zhang, P.: Text analytics to support sense-making in social media: a language-action perspective. MIS Q. **42**, 427–464 (2018)

Towards a Scheme for Contribution in Action Design Research

Casper Solheim Bojer[✉] ⓘ and Charles Møller ⓘ

Department of Materials and Production, Aalborg University, 9220 Aalborg, Denmark
{csb,charles}@mp.aau.dk

Abstract. Researchers are increasingly asked to engage with industry in research projects and contribute to both practice and academia. Action Design Research (ADR) is gaining traction in IS due to its potential to achieve this dual goal. While the practical utility of ADR projects is obvious, the role of design science research (DSR) in knowledge abstraction and accumulation is still unclear and the subject of much discussion. Some scholars suggest DSR should build theory, some that it should test theory, while others suggest that its contributions lie elsewhere. While the elaborated ADR model of Mullarkey and Hevner (2019) clarified the potential for artefactual contributions at different abstraction levels throughout the research process, other types of contribution were left for further research. Drawing on reflections from an ongoing research project using ADR, as well as research on theorizing and DSR contributions, we present a tentative conceptual scheme that considers both empirical, artefactual, theory building, and theory testing opportunities in ADR. We discuss the benefits of the scheme in identifying contribution opportunities and reflect on its utility in research design for industrially engaged DSR.

Keywords: Design science research · Action design research · Theorizing · Theoretical contribution · Contribution

1 Introduction

Design Science Research has become an important research approach in IS due to its future-orientation and its potential to make knowledge contributions that are both rigorous and relevant (Hevner et al. 2004). It thus meets a need in a time where researchers are increasingly asked to engage in research projects with industrial partners that deliver both practical and academic contributions. As a result of this situation, several methods for conducting industrially engaged DSR research have been introduced in recent years. Action Design Research is one such method that focuses on real-world problem-solving at a client by the introduction of an ensemble artefact and subsequent abstraction of the knowledge obtained in the process (Sein et al. 2011). Intervention-based Research (IBR) (Oliva 2019), an Action Research-inspired method originating in Operations Management, also features real-world problem solving at a client, but focuses on the use of traditional theory building and testing for academic contributions. Industrially engaged

© Springer Nature Switzerland AG 2022
A. Drechsler et al. (Eds.): DESRIST 2022, LNCS 13229, pp. 376–387, 2022.
https://doi.org/10.1007/978-3-031-06516-3_28

DSR projects frequently span multiple years and it can therefore be necessary for institutional reasons to publish multiple contributions during the project, such as for doctoral students or early-career researchers. However, existing methodological work provides little guidance on how to transform an industrially engaged DSR project into multiple sequential knowledge contributions as the project unfolds. First steps towards providing such guidance are provided in the elaborated ADR model of Mullarkey and Hevner (2019) which lists potential artefactual contributions in each of their four ADR cycles (Diagnosis, Design, Implementation, and Evolution), however, they leave how ADR can make other contributions for further research. Recent research on contributions in DSR suggests that it has the potential to deliver many contributions in addition to artefacts and design principles, such as design theories (Gregor and Jones 2007; Iivari 2020), practical theories (Goldkuhl and Sjöström 2021), substantive technological theory (Iivari 2020), and empirical contributions (Goldkuhl and Sjöström 2021).

In this paper we attempt to advance the work initiated by Mullarkey and Hevner (2019) by synthesizing existing research on contributions in DSR with an emphasis on theorizing and relating it to the elaborated ADR process model. Drawing on reflections from applying ADR and attempting to plan a series of research contributions, we expand on the potential for contribution in the four ADR cycles. As our main contributions we: 1) provide a review of perspectives on contributions in DSR; and 2) develop a conceptual scheme for contributions in the four ADR cycles, which includes empirical, artefactual, theory building, and theory testing opportunities. We thus add to the discussion of knowledge contributions and accumulation in DSR. The overview provided by our conceptual scheme supports future ADR researchers in research design by providing guidance in terms of how to identify and publish valuable knowledge contributions, thereby making it easier to achieve the dual aims of contributions to practice and research.

In the next section, we cover extant literature on industrially engaged action-oriented DSR, theoretical contributions, and DSR contributions. We then present reflections from ongoing ADR research, before presenting our conceptual scheme for ADR research contributions and applying it to our research. Finally, we discuss implications for ADR research, compare our scheme to related work, and conclude on our contribution.

2 Background

2.1 Action-Oriented Design Science Research

As applied research fields are increasingly being asked to conduct industrially engaged research, they have developed action-oriented DSR methods that enable making both rigorous academic and practically relevant contributions. In IS, ADR is such a method aimed at inductively developing generalizable design knowledge by solving a specific problem through building and evaluating ensemble artifacts in an organizational setting (Sein et al. 2011). The main academic knowledge contributions in ADR are design principles that describe how to produce a (general) solution that addresses a class of problems. While theory-inspired design principles are formulated and refined throughout the process, the publishing of the design principles is presented as taking place at the end of the project in the Formalization stage, potentially with an additional contribution in the form of a theoretical refinement to the theories used (Sein et al. 2011, p. 44). Mullarkey and Hevner (2019) proposed the elaborated ADR process model, which consists of four iterative cycles each with a different purpose: 1) *Diagnosis*, 2) (conceptual) *Design*, 3) *Implementation*, and 4) *Evolution*. Each of these cycles consists of steps inspired by the original ADR model and produces different artefacts that has the potential to be formalized and published as an academic knowledge contribution. The potential for and importance of publishing the interim products of ADR is also acknowledged by Sein and Rossi (2019) in their response to the elaborated ADR model. However, Mullarkey and Hevner (2019) leave it for further research to integrate design theory development and do not address other forms of contributions.

In Operations Management (OM), IBR is gaining traction as an action-oriented DSR method. In IBR, theoretical frameworks are used to build interventions and make predictions of their results. Anomalies are considered as potentials for modifications to theory, while the organizational dynamics observed after intervening are framed as data that can be used for process theorizing (Oliva 2019). Top journals in OM have come to place less emphasis on the artefactual contribution, focusing instead on theory testing and theory building (Chandrasekan et al. 2020). This view on theory is thus much closer to that of Canonical Action Research (CAR) (Davison et al. 2012), with the addition of the potential for in/abductively generating process theory.

2.2 Theoretical Contribution

Theory is concerned with improving our ability to understand phenomena and is one of the main communication devices used to transfer knowledge in scientific discourse. Traditionally, theory has been conceptualized as being limited to conceptual abstractions consisting of constructs, relationships, and boundary conditions, with the aim of explanation and prediction of phenomena (Bacharach 1989). More recent discourse has broadened the scope to include theories with different purposes and formats. Gregor (2006) expanded the scope to include theories for analysis, theories for either predicting or explaining, and theories for design and action. It has likewise been recognized that theory can take different forms depending on the underlying meta-theoretical approach selected, which will in turn focus the inquiry on particular aspects of the phenomena (Burton-Jones et al. 2015).

While theories are generally highly regarded as a prime research outcome in IS, the focus on theory has recently come under critique. Avison and Malaurent (2014) suggests that we are facing a theory-fetish in IS, which prevents our field from making progress, while Alter (2017) states that the focus on theory limits the publication of a variety of other useful conceptual artefacts. In this paper we adopt an inclusive view of theory that contains all five theory types by Gregor (2006).

Individual publications rarely produce a complete theory. Most theoretical contributions either advance an existing theory slightly, or take the form of interim products of theorizing which can have an important role to play in advancing the academic discourse (Weick 1995). Examples of interim theorizing products include conceptual frameworks, models, and diagrams. Colquitt and Zapata-Phelan (2007) argues for distinguishing between building theory and testing theory and present a taxonomy for categorizing contributions based on the degree of theory building and testing present.

2.3 DSR Contributions

While the distinguishing feature of DSR lies in artefactual contributions (Hevner 2004), multiple authors have argued that empirical, and theoretical contributions are also possible (Ågerfalk 2021; Goldkuhl and Sjöström 2021). After artefactual contributions, theoretical contributions in the form of Type V (design) theories (Gregor and Jones 2007) have arguably received the most attention in the DSR community. While full design theories are not a necessary outcome of DSR, design theorizing and knowledge abstraction, makes up an important part of a DSR contribution (Baskerville et al. 2018). Gregor and Hevner (2013) argue for distinguishing DSR contributions based on the level of abstraction and maturity, which ranges from instantiations over nascent design theory to well-developed design theories. A popular (nascent) design theoretical contribution is design principles, which are prescriptive means-end statements. Synthesizing various formulations of prescriptive statements, Gregor et al. (2020) arrives at seven building blocks of design principles: implementers, aim, user, context, mechanisms, enactors, and rationale. Attempting to add clarity to the debate on design theories, Iivari (2020) propose to distinguish between three types of design theory: theory used to derive meta-requirements (Design Theory 1); theory used to explain why meta-requirements are satisfied by the meta-design (Design Theory 2); and theory used to explain the effects of the IT artefact (Design Theory 3).

In addition to design theory as contribution from DSR, several authors propose other types of theoretical contribution. Iivari (2020) propose that DSR can contribute by testing, refining, or proposing substantial technological theories (STT) from Bunge (1966). STT's are essentially applied versions of kernel theories that are close enough to the problem context to guide design and ground design theories. In his view, DSR can thus in addition to the artefact contribute with either 1) one or more types of design theory, or 2) STT. Goldkuhl and Sjöström (2021) argue that in addition to generating design theory, DSR has the potential to contribute with both building and testing of practical theory. Practical theory is theory that offers practical utility in the design inquiry process and can include traditional theories, e.g., for description and explanation, as well as other tools that are useful in problem diagnosis, planning & design, and evaluation (Goldkuhl and Sjöström 2021). Additionally, they suggest the potential for empirical contributions by reporting on the rich data collected and knowledge obtained as part of the design inquiry. The varied nature of DSR contributions is also acknowledged by Drechsler and Hevner (2018) that suggest the potential for theoretical contributions to both descriptive (type I-IV) and prescriptive knowledge (type V) of varying maturity, in addition to concrete instantiations. Table 1 summarizes the various viewpoints related to contributions from DSR.

Table 1. Viewpoints on potential contributions from DSR

Viewpoint	References	Description
Contribution as Artefact	Hevner et al. (2004)	DSR can contribute with artefacts in the form of constructs, models, methods, and instantiations
Contribution as Conceptual Abstractions	Mullarkey and Hevner (2019)	DSR can contribute with a variety of conceptual abstractions aimed at diagnosis, design, implementation, and evolution
Contribution as Empirical	Goldkuhl and Sjöström (2021); Ågerfalk (2021)	DSR can contribute with rich empirical descriptions based on close engagement with the problem & solution
Contribution as Theory Testing	Oliva (2019); Chandrasekan et al. (2020)	DSR can contribute with practical testing of type I-IV theories
Contribution as Inductive Process Theory-Building	Oliva (2019); Chandrasekan et al. (2020)	DSR can contribute with inductive building of process theories explaining the observed organizational transition from pre- to post-intervention
Contribution as Practical Theory	Goldkuhl and Sjöström (2021)	DSR can contribute with testing, refinement, and building of practical theories for diagnosis, design, and evaluation
Contribution as Substantive Technological Theory	Iivari (2020)	DSR can contribute with development of substantive technological theories inspired by the artefacts
Contribution as Design Theory	Gregor and Hevner (2013), Iivari (2020)	DSR can contribute with design theories that 1) theoretically ground meta-requirements, 2) explain why meta-design satisfies the requirements, 3) explain the effects of the artefact, or 4) all the above

3   Empirical Grounding: Reflections on Ongoing ADR Research

We reflect on ADR contributions by means of an ongoing three-year research project following the elaborated ADR model (Mullarkey and Hevner 2019), where the project is currently halfway. The goal of the project is to develop an approach that is both fast and scalable for development and real-life evaluation of machine learning (ML) based IS aimed at internal process innovation. The problem setting is a large Danish manufacturing company that is in the process of building big data and analytical capabilities, but currently finds the process of development and evaluation of ML-based systems too slow to enable rapid exploration. The research project thus sits at the intersection of IS and Operations Management. In addition to the approach and associated design knowledge, it was expected that the research project would deliver more traditional contributions to existing relevant academic knowledge bases. Three knowledge bases were identified in an initial research design phase and used to theoretically ground and frame the project: business process management, enterprise architecture, and dynamic capabilities. However, it was at this stage unclear what the nature of these contributions would be.

The main artefactual outcome of the research project is the approach, which includes a high-level design process, as well as design principles, suggested architectures for the different layers of the IS, and one or more instantiations of the approach presenting proof-by-construction. Following the conceptual artefacts presented by Mullarkey and Hevner (2019), this would amount to one or more systems (the ML-based IS), and one process (the approach), and several design and diagnosis artefacts. In addition, the combination of architectures, constructs, and design principles is a form of nascent design theory (Gregor and Hevner 2013). Table 2 showcases the expected outputs from the research project (in bold) mapped to the range of potential artefacts listed by Mullarkey and Hevner (2019).

Table 2. Potential contributions by ADR cycle according to Mullarkey and Hevner (2019) with the expected artefactual contributions of our research project in bold.

Stage	Diagnosis	Design	Implementation	Evolution
Contribution	**Conceptualization of Problem and/or Solution, Requirements Definition,** Technical Specification, **Assessment of Existing Tools,** Critical Success Factors **Nascent Design Theory**	**Design Features Design Principles Models Architectures Implementation Methods Constructs Nascent Design Theory**	**Systems** Algorithms Programs Databases **Processes Nascent Design Theory**	Modification to any of the previous artefacts Nascent Design Theory

Engaging with the literature in one of the iterations of the *Diagnosis* phase led to the research area of big data analytics (BDA) capabilities. While some progress was made on conceptualization of BDA capabilities, empirical research was scarce, and theory related to their evolution and value creation mechanisms was nascent. This led us to the realization that our close collaboration with our industrial partner and the embeddedness of the main author presented us with the opportunity to contribute to this debate through rich empirical descriptions or early theoretical contributions. Where and how these contribution opportunities fit with the ADR process was not evident, and thus following Sein et al. (2011), our early research designs envisaged them as taking place at the end of the project, after design, evaluation, and further data collection was finished.

4 A Conceptual Scheme for ADR Contributions

Our research design evolved as the *Diagnosis* and *Design* phases unfolded based on engagement with the problem context and DSR literature. Recent contributions on the role of theory in DSR made it evident that empirical and theoretical contributions do not have to be add-ons at the end of the research project. Instead, they can take place during the project, after one or more iterations of one of the four cycles. The iterative process of rethinking our research design led us to reflect on the learnings we achieved in the process. Figure 1 shows our updated conceptualization of the role of theory in ADR, where each iteration of an ADR cycle provides the opportunity to engage in both theory testing, as emphasized in IBR and CAR, and theory building, for a variety of theory types. In the *Problem Formulation/Planning* stage, the problem and solution are grounded in existing knowledge. Practical theories can aid understanding and assessment of the situation, and design theories can be deductively developed using kernel or substantive technological theories. These theories present the theoretical framework used in the design of artefacts, as per the *Theory-ingrained artefact* principle, and the design will thus contain theory-driven hypotheses. These hypotheses are tested through *Evaluation* where the designed artefacts are introduced into the existing situation, bringing about change, and a new situation. Depending on whether the new situation matches our expected situation, the hypotheses are corroborated or falsified. During both stages, practical theories can be used to inform or shape artefact creation and evaluation. In terms of inductive theorizing, rich data is collected on the existing situation in the *Problem Formulation/Planning stage*, on the development of the artefact in *Artifact Creation,* and on the performance of the artefact in *Evaluation,* using methods such as participative observation, interviews, process performance measurements, etc. As a result, once reaching the *Reflection* stage, the researchers(s) have the results of their hypotheses tests as well as a rich empirical database that can serve as the foundation for a theoretical contribution.

While there is potential for both empirical contributions, and inductive and deductive theoretical contributions in all the four cycles, the nature of the contributions will differ for each cycle due to differences in content, aim, methods, and the existing theories employed. Table 3 shows our conceptual scheme, which provides an overview of the roles of theory in each of the four stages and the potentials for contribution.

In the *Diagnosis* phase, rich empirical data on the problem situation and context is collected using, e.g., interviews, participative observation, document analysis, etc. This rich empirical data, if the context or problem is novel and interesting, can with good narrative be turned into an empirical contribution, which might inspire future type IV and type V theorizing. To structure the data collection and obtain understanding of the often-complex situation, existing practical theories and type I-IV theories can be used. By combining one or more theories, a theoretical or conceptual framework can be constructed, which can serve to produce artefacts in the form of conceptualizations of the problem and the solution space. Confronting the theoretical framework with the

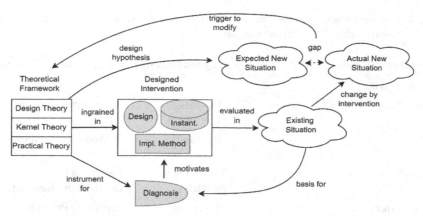

Fig. 1. Role of theoretical framework and artefacts (in blue) in ADR. Inspired by (Oliva 2019).

organizational situation allows for testing the practical validity of these theories in terms of their ability to understand and explain the problem and solution space, e.g., as assessed by practitioners. Adjustments to practical theories based on *Reflection* or development of novel ones can serve as potential contributions if formalized. Even if the practical theory proves useful without modification, reporting the test result can still make a theoretical contribution if the context of use extends the current boundaries of the theory. Kernel theory can also be used to generate theory-based *Requirements*, through the conversion to STT, thus constituting theorizing for a Design Theory 1 (Iivari 2020).

In the *Design* phase, rich empirical data on the conceptual design process, such as actions, events, and the evolving design is collected. While this data can serve as an important foundation for theorizing about the design process, it is perhaps less useful as an empirical contribution on its own, unless some aspect of the design process followed was particularly novel or surprising. In this phase, kernel theory can be used in theorizing for a Design Theory 2 (Iivari 2020), which explains why the design satisfies the requirements, and a Design Theory 3, which explains the effects that the introduction of the designed artefact into the problem context will produce. In both cases, the kernel theory will likely need to be translated to a STT to be concrete enough for design theory derivation. The design in this case can consists of all the six artefacts listed by Mullarkey and Hevner (2019). Practical theories might be used as a source of inspiration or for the generation of constructs, as well as serving as guidance in assessing the value of different design options (Goldkuhl and Sjöström 2021).

In the *Implementation* phase, an instantiation of the ensemble artifact is tested out in the organizational context thus providing the first in-situ evaluation of the instantiation, but also the problem framing, theoretical framework, and the conceptual design. Due to the emergent nature of the artefacts and the often-complex nature of the problem situation, it is likely that modifications are needed to one or more of the above elements. If detailed data is collected on the outcome of the implementation, this can serve as the foundation for Type I-IV theorizing. As an example, focusing data collection on the dynamics of the environment after introduction of the artefact can enable inductive process theorizing, as emphasized in IBR.

Table 3. Scheme for potential contributions in each of the four ADR cycles. Potential contributions are shown by either 'X' or elaborating text.

Potential contribution	Diagnosis	Design	Implementation	Evolution
Theory Building				
Design Theory	Hypothesis, Propositions		In-/Abductive Building	
STT	Hypothesis, Propositions		In-/Abductive Building	
Type I-IV	Theorizing Products		Theorizing Products, In-/Abductive Building	
Practical Theory	Theorizing Products, Theory Modifications		Theorizing Products, Theory Modifications, In-/Abductive Building	
Theory Testing				
Design Theory			X	X
STT			X	X
Type I-IV	X		X	X
Practical Theory	X	X	X	X
Non-theory				
Rich Empirical Descriptions	X	X	X	X
Artefacts (see Mullarkey and Hevner 2019)	X	X	X	X

In the *Evolution* phase, rich empirical data can be collected on the evolution of the artefact and its environment as the ensemble artefact emerges from continual interaction and redesign (Sein et al. 2011). This data can be used for inductively theorizing about the evolution of this class of solutions and its effects on the environment. Each evaluation in the *Evolution* phase is thus a repeated test of any unmodified ingrained theories and new tests of any changes to the theoretical framework and provides the opportunity for revision to any of the previous artefacts developed or theories used.

4.1 Application for Research Design

To demonstrate the utility of our conceptual scheme, we present the results of applying it in our project for research design. The theoretical framework we arrived at for our case through multiple iterations in *Diagnosis* and *Design* can be seen in Table 4.

Engaging with the conceptual scheme in our current iteration of research design, we identified five potential publications, with one of them optional (#4) pending results of testing the practical theories in the first three cycles. Our identified contributions range from practical theorizing, through conceptual design theorizing, to testing of practical and design theory, and finally a case study featuring a rich empirical description and nascent inductive theorizing for BDAC, see Table 5.

Table 4. Overview of the theoretical framework in our project, categorized by role.

Role of Theory	Theoretical Framework Components
Practical Theories	Business Process Management, Work Systems Theory, Enterprise Architecture
Kernel Theories	Dynamic capabilities, Digital Infrastructure, Process Innovation, Technology Innovation, Big Data Analytics capabilities (BDAC)
Design Knowledge	Architecture & Development Processes (Software Engineering & Machine Learning), Explorative Process Prototyping

Table 5. Application of the scheme for research & publication design in our case.

Cycle	Publication Number & Nature of Contribution
Diagnosis	#1: Type I Practical Theorizing + Design Theory 1 Theorizing
Design	#2: Models, Architectures + Design Theory 2 & 3 Theorizing
Implementation	#3: Instantiated Approach + Tested Design Principles *#4: BPM/EA Testing & Modification – if justified*
Evolution	#5: Case Study + Nascent Type IV Theorizing for BDAC

5 Discussion

Our conceptual scheme provides a synthesis of different opportunities for contribution in ADR and relate them to the elaborated ADR model and IBR. We see the conceptual scheme as a useful tool for research design, where it can be used as a basis for exploring potential publication strategies. This is particularly relevant for early-stage researchers, who often need to publish several contributions during a multi-year research project. From our conceptualization of contribution in Fig. 1 and as exemplified in our application of the scheme, the feasibility of making certain research contributions in ADR depend on 1) the results obtained by interaction with the context, and 2) the theoretical framework and methods employed. The research design and publication strategy will thus have to be revisited as the research process unfolds, but when this should happen is not addressed in the elaborated ADR model. We found that doctoral practicalities required us to make an initial design before starting ADR and revisiting it periodically.

Compared to previous work on conceptualization of contributions in DSR, we focus on the temporal aspect of the potential for contribution. Compared to the conceptualization of Dreschler and Hevner (2018), we expand on the potential for contribution to descriptive knowledge by distinguishing between practical theory, kernel theory, and substantive technological theories and emphasize the potential for empirical contributions. Compared to Maedche et al. (2021) our conceptualization suggests that it is possible for the research to be classified in different quadrants at different points of the research project, e.g., making observation-based descriptive statements in the *Diagnosis* stage, and in later stages contributing with creation-based prescriptive statements.

In line with Iivari (2020), we found that it was difficult to distinguish between artefactual and theoretical contributions, particularly when considering the abstraction principle of Mullarkey and Hevner (2019). This was the case for both practical theories and design theories. As examples, take the problem conceptualization artefact of Mullarkey and Hevner (2019) and a practical diagnostic theory as introduced in Goldkuhl and Sjöström (2021), or design principles vs. design theory. We thus believe that the DSR community stands to gain from further rigor in the discussion of contributions.

6   Conclusion

We present a conceptual scheme for potential research contributions in ADR based on a synthesis of extant literature on theorizing and contributions in DSR. We show that ADR projects have the potential to make empirical, theoretical, and artefactual contributions in each of the cycles of *Diagnosis, Design, Implementation*, and *Evolution*. We thus highlight the potential for mixed configurations of contributions throughout a DSR project. Our conceptual scheme supports industrially engaged DSR researchers in research design and publication planning, by providing an overview of the space of potential contributions. This should prove especially useful for early-stage researchers, who must deliver multiple publications during their industrially engaged research projects. The conceptual scheme we propose is only a first step towards a thorough understanding of the theorizing potential in ADR. Further research should identify exemplars of the contribution opportunities, although a challenge here is that not all ADR-based contributions are likely to be advertised as such. In addition, how to best integrate research design activities with the elaborated ADR model remains an open question.

References

Mullarkey, M.T., Hevner, A.R.: An elaborated action design research process model. Eur. J. Inf. Syst. **28**(1), 6–20 (2019)
Hevner, A.R., March, S.T., Park, J., Ram, S.: Design science in information systems research. MIS Q. **28**(1), 75–105 (2004)
Sein, M. K., Henfridsson, O., Purao, S., Rossi, M., Lindgren, R.: Action design research. MIS Q. **35**(1), 37–56 (2011)
Oliva, R.: Intervention as a research strategy. J. Oper. Manag. **65**(7), 710–724 (2019)
Gregor, S., Jones, D.: The anatomy of a design theory. Association for Information Systems (2007)
Iivari, J.: A critical look at theories in design science research. J. Assoc. Inf. Syst. **21**(3), 10 (2020)
Goldkuhl, G., Sjöström, J.: Design science theorizing: the contribution of practical theory. In: Hassan, N.R., Willcocks, L.P. (eds.) Advancing Information Systems Theories. TWG, pp. 239–273. Springer, Cham (2021). https://doi.org/10.1007/978-3-030-64884-8_7
Sein, M.K., Rossi, M.: Elaborating ADR while drifting away from its essence: a commentary on Mullarkey and Hevner. Eur. J. Inf. Syst. **28**(1), 21–25 (2019)
Chandrasekaran, A., de Treville, S., Browning, T.: Intervention-based research (IBR)—what, where, and how to use it in operations management. J. Oper. Manag. **66**(4), 370–378 (2020)
Davison, R.M., Martinsons, M.G., Ou, C.X.: The roles of theory in canonical action research. MIS Q. **36**(3), 763–786 (2012)
Bacharach, S.B.: Organizational theories: Some criteria for evaluation. Acad. Manag. Rev. **14**(4), 496–515 (1989)

Gregor, S.: The nature of theory in information systems. MIS Q. **30**(3), 611–642 (2006)

Burton-Jones, A., McLean, E.R., Monod, E.: Theoretical perspectives in IS research: from variance and process to conceptual latitude and conceptual fit. Eur. J. Inf. Syst. **24**(6), 664–679 (2015)

Avison, D., Malaurent, J.: Is theory king? Questioning the theory fetish in information systems. J. Inf. Technol. **29**(4), 327–336 (2014)

Alter, S.: Nothing is more practical than a good conceptual artifact... which may be a theory, framework, model, metaphor, paradigm or perhaps some other abstraction. Inf. Syst. J. **27**(5), 671–693 (2017)

Weick, K.E.: What theory is not, theorizing is. Adm. Sci. q. **40**(3), 385–390 (1995)

Colquitt, J.A., Zapata-Phelan, C.P.: Trends in theory building and theory testing: a five-decade study of the academy of management journal. Acad. Manag. J. **50**(6), 1281–1303 (2007)

Ågerfalk, P.J., Karlsson, F.: Theoretical, empirical, and artefactual contributions in information systems research: implications implied. In: Hassan, N.R., Willcocks, L.P. (eds.) Advancing Information Systems Theories, pp. 53–73. Technology, Work and Globalization. Palgrave Macmillan, Cham (2021). https://doi.org/10.1007/978-3-030-64884-8_2

Baskerville, R., Baiyere, A., Gregor, S., Hevner, A., Rossi, M.: Design science research contributions: finding a balance between artifact and theory. J. Assoc. Inf. Syst. **19**(5), 358–376 (2018). https://doi.org/10.17705/1jais.00495

Gregor, S., Hevner, A.R.: Positioning and presenting design science research for maximum impact. MIS Q. **37**(2), 337–355 (2013)

Gregor, S., Chandra Kruse, L., Seidel, S.: Research perspectives: the anatomy of a design principle. J. Assoc. Inf. Syst. **21**(6), 2 (2020)

Bunge, M.: Technology as applied science. In: Rapp, F. (eds.) Contributions to a Philosophy of Technology. Theory and Decision Library, vol. 5, pp. 19–39. Springer, Dordrecht (1966). https://doi.org/10.1007/978-94-010-2182-1_2

Drechsler, A., Hevner, A.R.: Utilizing, producing, and contributing design knowledge in DSR projects. In: Chatterjee, S., Dutta, K., Sundarraj, R. (eds.) Designing for a Digital and Globalized World. DESRIST 2018. LNCS, vol. 10844, pp. 82–97. Springer, Cham (2018). https://doi.org/10.1007/978-3-319-91800-6_6

Maedche, A., Gregor, S., Parsons, J.: Mapping design contributions in information systems research: the design research activity framework. Commun. Assoc. Inf. Syst. **49**(1), 12 (2021)

Designers and Collaborative DSR

Introduction to Designers and Collaborative DSR Track

Leona Chandra Kruse[1], Pascal LeMasson[2], and Rob Gleasure[3]

[1] University of Liechtenstein
Leona.chandra@uni.li
[2] MINES ParisTech
pascal.le_masson@mines-paristech.fr
[3] Copenhagen Business School
rg.digi@cbs.dk

Abstract. The increasing sophistication and interconnectivity of digital systems creates vast possibilities for designers and design teams, provided they have the necessary tools, structures, and knowledge. This means designers must develop collaborative processes and systems that allow them to harness insights from a range of actors, such as technology specialists, artists, managers, and of course, the intended users. These new possibilities enable and require strong interaction with transdisciplinary design research to better model how these new ways and means can relate to improved generativity and resilience of design - or understand the risk of impeding them. These new possibilities raise new questions for design methods, procedures, supporting tools, and design theory (e.g., C-K theory, axiomatic design, situational method, etc.). This track invites research on the designers and teams that can effectively navigate these challenges, as well as the processes and/or systems that they can use. It invites participants to link empirical works with theoretical approaches.

Keywords: Collaborative DSR · Designer behaviors

1 Designers Collaboration in Transdisciplinary Design

The increasing sophistication and interconnectivity of digital systems creates vast possibilities for designers and design teams, provided they have the necessary tools, structures, and knowledge. This means designers must develop collaborative processes and systems that allow them to harness insights from a range of actors, such as technology specialists, artists, managers, and of course, the intended users. Integrating insights from such a wide range of actors requires that designers can switch between communication and development modes, and find creative ways to balance contrasting design priorities.

For this reason, these new collaborative processes and systems are well suited to transdisciplinary design research approaches. These approaches encourage teams to explore emerging possibilities that may improve the generativity and resilience of their designs - or better understand the risks and impediments. It also encourages design teams to tackle larger issues that require multifaceted social and technical problematization and complex dynamic design solutions.

These new possibilities raise questions for established design methods, procedures, supporting tools, and design theory (e.g., C-K theory, axiomatic design, situational method, etc.). They challenge not only the disciplinary logics of these methods, procedures, tools, and theories; they also challenge their ability to rely on any one logic. Instead, they require an assemblage of logics to manage the assemblages of social and technical elements.

2 Bridging the Transdisciplinary Chasm

This track presents three papers that illustrate this combination of transdisciplinary approaches and dynamic design solutions. More importantly, they show how designers and teams can effectively navigate these challenges, as well as the processes and/or systems that they can use. The first paper, authored by Stefan Cronholm and Hannes Göbel, seeks to bridge the gap between academia and industry in pursuing a transdisciplinary Action Design Research (ADR). Their collaboration model addresses three challenges: researcher intervention in practitioner contexts, reciprocal shaping between artifacts and design principles emerged from theory and practice, and researcher and practitioner learning.

On the other hand, the other two papers highlight the importance of accumulating design knowledge through all phases of DSR. Any DSR projects, especially transdisciplinary ones, draw on domain-specific knowledge from multiple disciplines and sectors. Stakeholders must be able to absorb the knowledge, and future transdisciplinary projects should also benefit from the design knowledge. Ernestine Dickhaut, Andreas Janson, and Jan Marco Leimeister analyzed the ongoing practices within the DSR community in codifying and accumulating design knowledge. Based on their analysis, they derive five implications for future transdisciplinary DSR. Oscar Diaz, John Venable, and Xabier Garmendia put forward a model of design knowledge appropriation. In this model, design knowledge appropriation is viewed as a peer-to-peer journey.

All three papers address timely and relevant issues for promoting transdisciplinary DSR. They have their own unique contributions as single papers, but their combined contributions have even greater potential to pave the paths toward a knowledge view of transdisciplinary design collaboration. We thank our transdisciplinary reviewers for their critical and developmental comments. Their transdisciplinary knowledge has indeed helped to carve out the contributions of each paper.

Action Design Research – Models for Researcher-Practitioner Collaboration

Stefan Cronholm$^{(\boxtimes)}$ ⓘ and Hannes Göbel ⓘ

University of Borås, 501 90 Borås, Sweden
{stefan.cronholm,hannes.gobel}@hb.se

Abstract. One essential characteristic of the Action Design Research (ADR) method is researcher-practitioner collaboration (RPC). The purpose of this paper is to present theoretical models for RPC collaboration in ADR projects. The models involve conditions, actions, and consequences concerning RPC challenges. A grounded theory approach was applied to identify the RPC challenges. The challenges were identified in a collaborative ADR project consisting of four researchers and nine organizations from the industry sector. The identified main challenges are: researcher intervention in practitioner contexts, reciprocal shaping between artifacts and design principles emerged from theory and practice, and researcher and practitioner learning. The contribution to practice, which consists of future ADR projects involving collaboration between researchers and practitioners, involves specific actions to be taken.

Keywords: Action-design research · ADR · Researcher-practitioner collaboration · Collaboration · Design science research

1 Introduction

Design science research (DSR) is established as a widely accepted research approach in Information Systems (IS) (e.g., Gregor and Hevner 2013; Vaishnavi and Kuechler 2015). This fact has created a need for DSR methods (Cronholm and Göbel 2019). One well-cited research method within DSR is Action Design Research (ADR) (Sein et al. 2011). One main characteristic of the ADR method is to respond to the dual mission of making theoretical contributions and assisting in solving the problems of practitioners (e.g., Sein et al. 2011). Moreover, Sein et al. (2011, p. 43) emphasize that "researchers bring their knowledge of theory and technological advances, while the practitioners bring practical hypotheses and knowledge of organizational work practices". This collaborative aspect of the ADR method aims to increase the organizational relevance of the designed artifact and to encourage interaction between researchers and practitioners. The targeting of practitioners and the practitioners' organizations means that several scholars regard the ADR method as a collaborative researcher-practitioner approach (e.g., Petersson and Lundberg 2016; Haj-Bolouri et al. 2018; Göbel and Cronholm 2016; Henriques and O'Neill 2021).

As RPC is presented as a central dimension of the ADR method, it is surprising that the support for RPC only consists of a few sentences such as "Deciding the roles and scope

© Springer Nature Switzerland AG 2022
A. Drechsler et al. (Eds.): DESRIST 2022, LNCS 13229, pp. 393–404, 2022.
https://doi.org/10.1007/978-3-031-06516-3_29

for practitioner participation" and "A critical element is securing long-term commitment from the participating organization(s)" (Sein et al., p.40). The cooperative aspect of the ADR method requires guidance on researcher-practitioner collaboration (RPC) when it is used in research projects (Haj-Bolouri et al. 2018). Henriques and O'Neill (2021) state that RPC collaboration is paramount in design-oriented projects (such as research projects guided by the ADR method) in order to find the best solutions for socio-technical problems and that additional methods and approaches are required and welcome. In this paper, we refer to research projects guided by the ADR method as ADR projects. Based on our analysis of a collaborative ADR project, which we in this paper refer to as the ADR project, we argue that *the guidance concerning collaboration in the ADR method primarily responds to the question "why" and not "how" to collaborate* (see Sect. 5). This means that there is a lack of prescriptive guidance on RPC. Therefore, the aim of this study is to present theoretical models for RPC collaboration in ADR projects. These models correspond to the theoretical contribution, and they involve relationships between conditions for challenges, actions taken to address challenges, and consequences of actions taken. In this study, we define a challenge as something that is regarded, either by researchers or practitioners, as a threat to successful collaboration. The contribution to practice, which are future ADR projects involving collaboration between researchers and practitioners, consists of specific actions that can be taken. Our research question reads: what RPC challenges can be identified in ADR projects?

Understanding issues related to RPC is a critical aspect of project planning, artifact design and evaluation, and learning. Therefore, we have analyzed an empirical research project guided by the ADR method. In the following section, we will present a literature review concerning RPC. Next, we will briefly describe the ADR method and the ADR project. After that, the research design is presented. Then, we will present our findings and theoretical models. Finally, conclusions will be drawn.

2   Literature Review

In order to find existing knowledge on RPC within ADR projects, we searched the Scopus database, which is the largest within information systems (IS). The keywords used were "Action Design Research" and "Researcher-Practitioner Collaboration". The search returned only six articles. Out of these six articles, three neither discussed collaboration nor ADR-projects, one reflected upon researcher-industry collaboration but not in ADR projects, and two involved reflections on researcher-practitioner collaboration in ADR projects. Therefore, we expanded our literature search to include backward reference searching, which meant that we reviewed relevant articles cited in the returned articles (i.e., snowball sampling, e.g., Naderifar et al. 2017). This expansion resulted in one more relevant article. The three articles that present knowledge about RPC in ADR projects are presented below.

Matzner et al. (2018) have suggested a conceptual framework for joint research projects. The framework can be regarded as an extension of ADR, and it involves both researchers' and business partners' interests. Moreover, the framework consists of a straightforward process involving the following phases: formulation of research needs, societal goals, political goals; formulations of research and business goals, design; analysis; development; full launch; and formulation of research and business outcomes.

Haj-Bolouri et al. (2018, p.11) present findings concerning how scholars engage with and use the ADR method. They have specifically identified three fundamental challenges concerning researcher-practitioner collaboration: (1) how to balance the competing interests of the organizational stakeholders with the interests of a research community; (2) how to balance the situated implementation of the designed IT-artifact for the practitioner needs against the research need of produce generalizable knowledge; and (3) how to balance the findings between specific and generalizable research outcomes.

Otto and Österle (2012) have identified principles for knowledge creation in collaborative DSR projects. The principles are developed for DSR in general and not specifically for ADR projects. However, we regard the ADR method as a part of the superior DSR concept. Otto and Österle (2012) state that collaborative forms of DSR require that knowledge be created across the boundaries of the research community and the practitioners' community. The main findings are six principles for knowledge creation in collaborative DSR: formalize shared goals, conduct full learning cycles, allow trial and error, make significant commitments, and involve complementary roles.

Based on the literature review, we can conclude that only a few articles present findings from RPC in ADR projects. Consequently, there is limited knowledge. In order to synthesize the literature review, we can conclude that only one of the articles is based on primary data while the others have collected data from other ADR researchers by using interviews or surveys. Another insight is that all the articles have developed models, principles, or challenges concerning RPC. Furthermore, the type of knowledge developed in the articles varies between descriptive, normative, and prescriptive. Nevertheless, we considered the identified articles as valuable input to our study. Our literature review can be criticized for being too limited. The reason for not involving other DSR approaches/methods such as Hevner et al. (2004) and Peffers et al. (2007) is that they are not explicitly stating that DSR is a collaborative researcher-practitioner approach. We argue that RPC is an essential quality of the ADR method, which can be derived from its recommendation to intervene in organizational contexts.

3   The RPC Project and the ADR Project

The purpose of the analyzed ADR project was to develop design principles and tools supporting organizations in their utilization of data to improve digital services. The ADR project involved four researchers and nine organizations in Sweden. The project was conducted over a period of three years. The industry sectors that the organizations represented were the automobile industry, telecommunications, and IT. The researchers consisted of two professors and two PhD students from the field of IS. The touchpoints between researchers and practitioners consisted of: a) project meetings, b) workshops including all the researchers and practitioners, and c) individual meetings between researchers and organizations.

The ADR project was guided by the ADR method. One purpose of the ADR method is to provide guidance for the building of artifacts shaped by the organizational context during development and use. The ADR method consists of four stages which are: (a) Problem Formulation (identify and conceptualize research opportunities based on existing theories and technologies), (b) Building, Intervention, and Evaluation (design and evaluate the artifact and articulate the design principles; (c) Reflection and Learning (move conceptually from building a solution for a particular instance to applying that learning to a broader class of problems), and (d) Formalization of Learning (formulate general solution concepts). Due to lack of space, we refer to Sein et al. (2011) for a detailed description of the ADR method.

At the end of the ADR project when several RPC challenges were addressed, we realized that it provided an excellent opportunity to analyze RPC. This meant that we identified RPC challenges in parallel with the fulfillment of the objectives of the ADR project. The ADR reasons for selecting this ADR project for analyzing RPC were: a) it consisted of frequent interactions between researchers and practitioners, b) it provided access to organizational settings and c) it provided access to rich data from intervention in nine organizations. The RPC challenges were identified and analyzed by two researchers who also participated in the ADR project. In this paper, we focus on the RPC challenges and actions taken to address the challenges.

4   Research Method

We applied the Grounded Theory Method (GTM) in order to identify and analyze RPC challenges. GTM is a qualitative research method that seeks to develop a theory grounded in systematically gathered and analyzed data (Goldkuhl and Cronholm 2019). Urquhart et al. (2010) state that GTM "… has proved to be extremely useful in developing context-based, process-oriented descriptions and explanations of information systems phenomena" (p. 358).

Strauss and Corbin (1998) distinguish between three coding steps in the use of GTM: (1) open coding, which is aimed at formulating categories based on analysis of concepts and attributes (i.e., circumstances in ADR project and actions taken), (2) axial coding, which is aimed at identifying relationships between categories and sub-categories in order to provide more complete explanations (i.e., relating specific circumstances to specific actions), (3) selective coding, which is aimed at integrating categories and refining theory (i.e., identifying the overall theme of this study). These three coding steps overlap and should not be interpreted as strictly sequential. During the steps, we analyzed: (a) notes taken from discussions among the researchers and practitioners during project meetings and workshops, (b) collaborative actions taken, and (c) project documentation. According to Strauss and Corbin (1998), identified categories could be logically structured according to an action-oriented paradigm consisting of three inter-related meta-categories: conditions, actions, and consequences. A condition defines a specific circumstance (e.g., a condition for a challenge to appear), an action/interaction describes something that occurs under particular circumstances (e.g., an action taken to address the challenge), and a consequence is a result that is dependent on the conditions and actions/interactions (e.g., consequences of the action taken to address the challenge). The use of meta-categories resulted in relationships between the categories, which were utilized when creating theoretical models.

5 Main Challenges

We have identified three main challenges in the ADR Project: researcher intervention in practitioner contexts, reciprocal shaping between reciprocal shaping between artifacts and design principles emerged from theory and practice, and researcher and practitioner learning. The formulation of the three main challenges is a result of integrating smaller units (sub-categories) into larger units (main categories). The description of each main challenge follows the order of the meta-categories. Each main challenge commences with a description of the conditions for the challenge identified in the ADR project, statements identified in the ADR method that are supposed to support ADR projects to manage the challenge, and explanations for why the ADR project is considered the ADR statements to be insufficient. After that, we present the actions undertaken in the ADR project to address the challenge. These actions were based on creative problem-solving discussions among researchers and practitioners in the ADR project and, to some extent, on guidance from the ADR method. Finally, we present the consequences of the action taken.

5.1 Challenge 1: Researcher Intervention in Practitioner Contexts

Conditions: Intervention is a core concept in the ADR method. Sein ct al. (2011) state that learning from organizational contexts is imperative and requires comprehensive intervention in organizational settings. Moreover, Sein et al. (2011) argue that the ADR method simultaneously supports the building of innovative IT artifacts in an organizational context and learning from the intervention while addressing a problematic situation. These statements inform about, in an excellent way, *why* intervention is essential. Unfortunately, the ADR method does not inform about *how* intervention can be organized in ADR projects. In the ADR project, the intervention in organizational contexts consisted of evaluations of the tools for data utilization. Our analysis of the ADR project identified that the following actions were taken to support researcher intervention in practitioner contexts:

Action 1: Creation of a Researcher-practitioner Agreement. The ADR project formulated a researcher-practitioner agreement, which became the basis for a shared understanding of the purpose of the project. The agreement defined the roles and responsibilities of the researchers and the practitioners. Moreover, the agreement specified that evaluations of the tools for data utilization should be conducted in organizational contexts.

Action 2: Collaborative Planning of Intervention. In the ADR project, the researchers and practitioners planned all activities related to the intervention. This meant that project goals, activities, and schedules were jointly formulated. In order to fulfill the project goals, the ADR project was staffed by competencies of the researchers and the organizations that were of equal importance. The researchers contributed theoretical, methodical, and technical knowledge, while the practitioners contributed with organizational and technical knowledge.

Action 3: Viewing Intervention as a Tool for Moving from the Specific to the Generic. Sein et al. (2011) explicitly suggest a move from the specific-and-unique to generic-and-abstract. Moreover, they describe three levels for this conceptual move: 1) generalization of the problem instance, 2) generalization of the solution instance, and 3) derivation of design principles from the project results. This means that the generalization of knowledge is a crucial component of the ADR method. In the ADR project, the intervention activities were regarded as a critical part of the generalization process since the purpose was to collect contextual data used for generalization in the forthcoming ADR-stage "Reflection and learning".

Consequences: The consequences of the actions taken supported the engagement of the practitioners and their input throughout the ADR project. For example, the researcher-practitioner agreement, which explicitly defined the expectations of each project member, provided transparency and reduced vagueness. Moreover, the collaborative planning of intervention activities increased the incentives and motivation among the practitioners. It also strengthened the convergence of shared interests between the researcher and practitioners. Furthermore, the collection of contextual data was imperative in order to grasp each organization's contextual characteristics. The ADR project used these characteristics to generalize the solution instance (the tools for data utilization). The fact that intervention was regarded as an essential part of generalization created a better understanding of the ADR project as a research project.

Another identified consequence was that trust steadily increased between the researchers and practitioners due to the collaborative planning and their willingness to share valuable knowledge. We also identified that practitioners shared information between themselves and that this openness contributed to trust. A high level of trust was necessary since the researchers and the practitioners were dependent on each other's inputs and efforts. The fact that the ADR project jointly designed and conducted interventions resulted in the researchers and practitioners continuously investing resources in the ADR project.

Our findings are supported by two statements from the practitioners which supported the consequences of the actions taken: "The project plan that included a description of the responsibilities of both parties made the expectations of each other more transparent" and "We appreciated the opportunity to evaluate the tool in our organization since it meant that we had a real impact on the development".

5.2 Challenge 2: Reciprocal Shaping Between Artifacts and Design Principles Emerged from Theory and Practice

Conditions: The second main challenge concerned the reciprocal shaping between the tools for data utilization (the artifacts) and the design principles. Reciprocity can be understood as a relationship of mutual dependence, action, or influence, and a mutual or cooperative interchange of favors between two parts (Gouldner 1960). One fundamental advice of the ADR method is to respond to the dual mission of making theoretical contributions and assisting in solving the problems of practitioners (e.g., Sein et al. 2011). However, the ADR project found that the ADR method does not provide sufficient support concerning the dual mission. This was experienced as problematic since the primary interest of the researchers was to create general design knowledge about the development of tools for data utilization, while the primary interest of the practitioners was to develop tools that could help them exploit data to improve their services offered to customers. Inevitably, there were competing interests in the ADR project. Our analysis of the ADR project identified that the following action was taken to support the dual mission:

Action: Capitalizing on the Mutual Interests of Researchers and Practitioners. The ADR project discovered a *mutual dependency* between the development of the tools and design principles. The iterative development of the design principles followed the iterative development of the tools for data utilization. This meant that the feedback from evaluations conducted in the practitioners' organizations affected the design of the tools for data utilization and provided valuable knowledge to refine the design principles. The researchers and practitioners utilized this dependency for reciprocal shaping between the evolving tools and emerging design principles. Moreover, the evaluations also resulted in new needs for consulting theory, which the researchers did. This meant that both the formulation of the design principles and the development of the tools for data utilization were based on theoretical insights and empirical evidence. Our analysis of the reciprocal shaping is illustrated in Fig. 1.

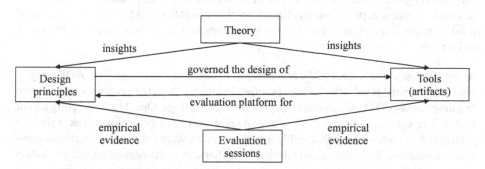

Fig. 1. Reciprocal shaping of design principles and the tools for data utilization.

The reciprocal shaping involved:

- The development of the tools was guided by the design principles that emerged during the iterations. This meant that the tools provided a platform for the evaluation of the design principles.
- The development of the design principles was guided by empirical feedback from the use of the tools. This meant that the advances of the design principles were used to shape the tools.

Consequences: The researchers and practitioners experienced an increased understanding of each other's interests. For example, shared insights were developed concerning the dependencies between the development of the design principles and the tools. These shared insights increased the acceptance towards solving both the scientific problem and the problem that existed in practice. A quote from one of the practitioners reads: "In the beginning of the project we were interested in tools for data utilization, but now we are equally interested in the design principles".

5.3   Challenge 3: Researcher and Practitioner Learning

Conditions: The third identified main challenge was how to enable learning for *both* researcher and practitioners. Sein et al. (2011, p. 44) state that "the reflection and learning stage moves conceptually from building a solution for a particular instance to applying that learning to a broader class of problems". Moreover, Sein et al. (2011, p. 44) state that "Conscious reflection on the problem framing, the theories chosen, and the emerging ensemble is critical to ensure that contributions to knowledge are identified". These statements are focusing on learning that concerns the researchers. The ADR project could not find much guidance in the ADR method that addresses learning for practitioners. In order to support commitment and motivation, the ADR project was organized to support learning for both researchers and practitioners.

Action 1: Joint Formulation of Individual and Shared Learning Outcomes. The ADR project recognized that there existed both individual and shared interests between the researchers and the practitioners. Based on this insight, the ADR project organized joint workshops that aimed to identify relationships between project goals and learning outcomes.

Action 2: Implementation of Mechanisms for Promoting Learning. The ADR project also implemented mechanisms for promoting learning. The ADR project organized two learning arenas: A) Dyadic researcher-practitioner meetings. One dyadic meeting meant that 1–2 researchers interacted with one organization (2–3 practitioners) at a time to jointly reflect on how the goals and learning outcomes were fulfilled in specific organizational contexts. B) Multi-organizational workshops. A multi-organizational workshop involved all the nine organizations and the researchers. The purpose was to implement a mechanism that promoted learning on a higher generalization level which involved the overall project goals and learning outcomes. Finally, the companies were invited to present learning outcomes at several occasions.

Action 3: Joint Formalization of Learning. This action aimed to enable the integration of both researcher and practitioner aspects in written and oral communication of project results. The formalization of learning involved a) joint publishing of scientific papers, b) joint publishing of technical papers addressing practitioner fora, and c) joint presentations of project results to the practitioners' organizations.

Consequences: One consequence of the dyadic researcher-practitioner meetings resulted in mutual learning among researchers and practitioners. The researchers learned from the practitioners' application of the tools in their organizational contexts, and the practitioners learned how the tools could support them to improve services offered to customers. However, the learning from the dyadic meetings was highly contextual.

Another consequence regarding the multi-organizational workshops was that they supported the generalization of contextual knowledge gained from the dyadic meetings. As mentioned above, contextual results were used as input to "move from the specific-and-unique to generic-and-abstract". The involvement of all the organizations in the multi-organizational workshops also meant that they learned from each other by sharing business knowledge. This learning included new knowledge on service strategies, processes based on data analysis, customer relationship management, and new ideas for services that could be offered. A quote from one of the practitioners reads: "One reason to participate in the project is to interact and learn from other organizations".

6   Theoretical Models

Glaser and Strauss (2017) state that a substantive theory emerges from the conceptual categories grounded in the data. A substantive theory is developed for a real empirical domain, which in our case is collaborative ADR projects. In order to present a substantive theory for RPC challenges in ADR projects, we have developed four theoretical models. As mentioned in Sect. 4, the structure of the theoretical models followed the action-oriented paradigm consisting of three meta-categories: conditions, actions, and consequences (see Fig. 2, 3, 4 and 5).

In order to explain how to interpret the models, we provide an example. The example is from Fig. 4 describing the challenge "Reciprocal shaping between artifacts and design principles emerged from theory and practice": a) the conditions inform about existing circumstances (e.g., competing interests), b) the actions taken inform about what arrangements can be made to address the challenges (e.g., creation of a research design that allowed for reciprocal shaping of the artifact and design principles), and c) the consequences inform about what happened when the actions were taken (e.g., researchers and practitioners experienced an increased understanding of each other's interests).

In the next step, we identified the overarching category that integrated the three challenges. The overarching category was formulated as follows: RPC challenges in ADR projects, which corresponds to the central theme of our study (see Fig. 5). Our analysis of the main challenges resulted in that the first one, "Researcher intervention in practitioner contexts", was regarded as a *condition* for the other two main challenges since it constitutes a crucial point of departure for RPC. The second main category, "Reciprocal shaping between artifacts and design principles emerged from theory and practice", is regarded as an *action/interaction* since it constitutes a primary concern for RPC and is affected by the main challenge "Researcher intervention in practitioner contexts". The third main challenge, "Researcher and practitioner learning", is considered a *consequence* since the likelihood of learning will increase if the first and second main challenges are addressed. Vice versa, learning will probably be obstructed if ADR projects fail to manage the first and second main challenges. Finally, we checked logical errors in order to ensure consistency and coherency within and between the models.

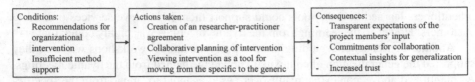

Fig. 2. Model for researcher intervention in practitioner contexts.

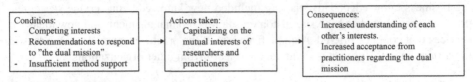

Fig. 3. Model for reciprocal shaping between artifacts and design principles emerged from theory and practice.

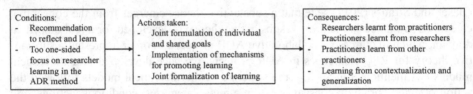

Fig. 4. Model for researcher and practitioner learning.

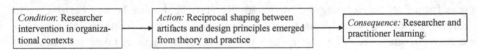

Fig. 5. The overarching theme: RPC challenges in ADR projects

7 Discussion

Based on an analysis of the empirical ADR project, we found that there initially was a rift between the interests of the researchers and practitioners, the collaboration was more difficult in practice than on the paper, and the ADR method primarily responded to the question "why to collaborate" and not "how to collaborate". These observations required extended support for RPC when using the ADR method. As mentioned in Sect. 1, the RPC support from the ADR method is limited. A comparison of our results with both the ADR method and the literature review reveals that our theoretical models extend prior knowledge about RPC in ADR projects by: a) presenting explicit categories regarded as either conditions, actions, or consequences, and b) explaining logical relationships between conditions, actions, and consequences.

Furthermore, it can be argued that the theoretical models are not specific to ADR projects but to RPC in general. However, we argue that these models are essential to managing ADR projects because they correspond to one primary characteristic: "The [ADR] method conceptualizes the research process as containing the inseparable and inherently interwoven activities of building the IT artifact, intervening in the organization, and evaluating it concurrently" (Sein et al. 2011, p. 37). This recommendation, as a whole, is not prominent in other DSR approaches/methods. However, we cannot foresee any barriers for them to be considered in future collaborative ADR projects, DSR projects, or general IS projects that are building artifacts.

8 Conclusion

In Sect. 1, we stated that support for collaboration in the ADR method primarily responds to the question "why" and not "how" to collaborate. Therefore, the aim of this study was to present theoretical models for RPC collaboration in ADR projects involving support for prescriptive actions. We have identified three main challenges concerning RPC: researcher intervention in practitioner contexts, reciprocal shaping between artifacts and design principles emerged from theory and practice, and researcher and practitioner learning. The knowledge contribution to practice consists of explicit actions that can be taken to address collaboration challenges experienced in ADR projects. In this case, the practice consists of ADR projects facing RPC challenges. We can conclude that the actions taken supported the ADR project to manage the identified challenges. The knowledge contribution to theory consists of theoretical models.

Our conclusions are based on findings from one empirical study. The problem of the generalization of findings in qualitative studies is a well-known challenge. In order to support the reuse of the findings in this study, we have provided transparent descriptions of the conditions, actions, and consequences. Therefore, we hope that our models will be considered in future ADR projects. However, we recognize that some adjustments may be needed due to the contextual characteristics of the ADR method. Therefore, to further evaluate the theoretical models created in this study, we suggest that they are evaluated in future projects concerning RPC.

References

Cronholm, S., Göbel, H.: Evaluation of action design research. Scand. J. Inf. Syst. 31(2), 35–82 (2019)

Glaser, B.G., Strauss, A.L.: Discovery of Grounded Theory: Strategies for Qualitative Research. Routledge, Abingdon-on-Thames (2017)

Göbel, H., Cronholm, S.: Nascent design principles enabling digital service platforms. In: Parsons, J., Tuunanen, T., Venable, J., Donnellan, B., Helfert, M., Kenneally, J. (eds.) Tackling Society's Grand Challenges with Design Science. DESRIST 2016. LNCS, vol. 9661, pp. 52–67. Springer, Cham (2016). https://doi.org/10.1007/978-3-319-39294-3_4

Goldkuhl, G., Cronholm, S.: Grounded theory in information systems research–from themes in IS discourse to possible developments (2019)

Gouldner, A.: The norm of reciprocity: a preliminary statement. Am. Sociol. Rev. 25, 161–178 (1960). https://doi.org/10.2307/2092623

Gregor, S., Hevner, A.: Positioning and presenting design science research for maximum impact. MIS Q. 37(2), 337–355 (2013)

Haj-Bolouri, A., Purao, S., Rossi, M., Bernhardsson, L.: Action design research in practice: lessons and concerns. In: Proceedings of the European Conference on Information Systems (ECIS) (2018). https://www.researchgate.net/profile/Amir_Haj-Bolouri/publication/326092 466_Action_Design_Research_in_Practice_Lessons_and_Concerns/links/5d14da8d458515c 11cfd6bdd/Action-Design-Research-in-Practice-Lessons-and-Concerns.pdf

Henriques, T.A., O'Neill, H.: Design science research with focus groups–a pragmatic meta-model. Int. J. Manag. Proj. Bus. (2021)

Hevner, A.R., March, S.T., Park, J.: Design research in information systems research. MIS Q. 28(1), 75–105 (2004)

Matzner, M., et al.: Digital transformation in service management. SMR-J. Ser. Manage. Res. 2(2), 3–21 (2018)

Naderifar, M., Goli, H., Ghaljaie, F.: Snowball sampling: a purposeful method of sampling in qualitative research. Strides Dev. Med. Educ. 14(3), 1–6 (2017)

Otto, B., Osterle, H.: Principles for knowledge creation in collaborative design science research. In: Proceedings of the International Conference on Information Systems (ICIS), Orlando, CA (2012). http://citeseerx.ist.psu.edu/viewdoc/download?doi=10.1.1.670.3393&rep=rep1& type=pdf

Peffers, K., Tuunanen, T., Rothenberger, M.A., Chatterjee, S.: A design science research methodology for information systems research. J. Manag. Inf. Syst. 24(3), 45–77 (2007)

Petersson, A.M., Lundberg, J.: Applying action design research (ADR) to develop concept generation and selection methods. Procedia Cirp 50, 222–227 (2016)

Sein, M.K., Henfridsson, O., Purao, S., Rossi, M., Lindgren, R.: Action design research. MIS q. 35(1), 37–56 (2011)

Strauss, A., Corbin, J.: Basics of Qualitative Research: Techniques and Procedures for Developing Grounded Theory. Sage, Thousand Oaks (1998)

Urquhart, C., Lehmann, H., Myers, M.: Putting the 'theory' back into grounded theory: guidelines for grounded theory studies in information systems. Inf. Syst. J. 20, 357–381 (2010)

Vaishnavi, V.K., Kuechler, W.: Design Science Research Methods and Patterns: Innovating Information and Communication Technology. CRC Press, Boca Raton (2015)

Are Journals and Repositories Enough? Design Knowledge Accumulation as a Diffusion of Innovation Practice

Oscar Díaz[1]([envelope])[iD], John R. Venable[2][iD], and Xabier Garmendia[1][iD]

[1] University of the Basque Country (UPV/EHU), San Sebastián, Spain
{oscar.diaz,xabier.garmendiad}@ehu.eus
[2] Curtin University, Perth, WA 6845, Australia
j.venable@curtin.edu.au

Abstract. The accumulation of the design knowledge (DK) resulting from Design Science Research (DSR) requires other DSR researchers to appropriate, use, evaluate, modify, and/or extend prior DSR artifacts. Unfortunately, much DK (especially software artifacts) is never appropriated by other researchers for further DSR activity. The lack of take-up of DSR outcomes by other researchers represents a significant waste of resources, reduces the contribution of a DSR project and, most significantly, is a major barrier to the accumulation of DSR knowledge. We believe this problem is mainly a social one. DK appropriation is a decision supported by a communication effort, which suggests relevance of Diffusion of Innovation (DoI) theory. While journals and repositories can make quality DK and IT artifacts find-able and available for reuse, supplementary and alternative communication channels may better enable and encourage DK appropriation decisions and thereby, DK accumulation longitudinally over multiple DSR projects. Based on this perspective, this paper explores a peer-to-peer decentralized communication pattern for DK dissemination and appropriation for further DSR projects and DK accumulation. Specifically, we propose (1) a model of DK accumulation as a DoI process (2) two new 'communication channels' (i.e., Appropriation Sessions and Marketplaces), and (3) questions (based on UTAUT) to (self-)assess the likelihood of new DK appropriation.

Keywords: Design Science Research · Design Knowledge · Design artifact · Appropriation · Knowledge accumulation

1 Introduction

Design Science Research (DSR) in the field of Information Systems (IS) has a problem; Design Knowledge (DK) Accumulation in DSR is considered to be weak or inadequate [16]. Vom Brocke et al. [16] characterise the current state of DSR DK accumulation as "monolithic" (single DSR project), with "scarce reuse" and without "DK accumulation and evolution across projects" [16, p. 521]. Given

© Springer Nature Switzerland AG 2022
A. Drechsler et al. (Eds.): DESRIST 2022, LNCS 13229, pp. 405–416, 2022.
https://doi.org/10.1007/978-3-031-06516-3_30

the poor state of DK accumulation, the current, conventional DSR practice of concluding a DSR project with the dissemination of DK at the end and relying on traditional publication through conferences and journals seems inadequate, i.e. continuing to do the same thing and expecting a different outcome is unlikely to work.

Effective approaches for DK accumulation are not only technical (e.g. curating and placing DK into repositories) but mainly social. For example, the findings of [6,11] on software reuse within organizations support the importance of social aspects of reuse. Similarly, Crowston et al. [3] noted that Open Source Software processes include social processes, such as Socialization, Decision making, Leadership, and Collaboration, and necessitate the emergence of certain states, including Trust, Level of commitment, and Shared mental models (among others). We note that enacting social processes and developing the desired emergent states all require communication beyond placing artifacts into repositories and relying on potential knowledge accumulators to find and fetch them. It is the vision of the authors that improving DK accumulation also requires improvements to the communication between DK producers and other design researchers as DK consumers. DK accumulation requires effective and efficient communication. This leads us to our research question: *RQ: How could the communication between DK producers and other design researchers as DK consumers be improved with the aim of furthering DK accumulation?*

The intent of this paper is to better conceptualize the process of DK dissemination, communication, transfer, and appropriation by other DSR researchers in order to progress DSR practice. Informed by Diffusion of Innovations (DoI) theory, we propose (1) a model of DK accumulation (2) recommendation for two 'communication channels' (i.e., Appropriation Sessions and Marketplaces), and (3) the use of the UTAUT model to characterize the peer profile insofar as appropriation is concerned. We start by introducing the problem.

2   DK Accumulation as a Problematic Phenomenon

In their editorial introduction to the *Journal of the Association for Information Systems* special issue on *DK accumulation in DSR*, Vom Brocke et al. assert that "To date, most studies focus on a single DSR project, aiming at deriving DK within a project, while DK accumulation and evolution across projects is rarely considered as an antecedent or contribution of the project. ... The limited DK accumulation in DSR is problematic because single contributions tend to remain isolated with little to no relation to other solutions. We refer to this as the *monolithic structure* of DK" [16, p. 521].

Consequences are many-fold. "First, current DSR projects miss the opportunity to reuse DK, which would increase both the efficiency and effectiveness of the research process. Second, DSR projects miss the opportunity to compose DK contributions toward building solutions to more complex real-world problems. Third, DSR projects (once they are published) lack validity checks of DK such as currency and timeliness, thus missing the opportunity to update DK as needed" [16, p. 521]. These are serious problems indeed for DK accumulation in DSR.

As for causes of this problem, Lukyanenko and Parsons [9] raise the issue of "Design Theory Indeterminacy" (DTI), i.e. incomprehensibility, ambiguity, and incompleteness of a design theory (one form of DK), which is problematic for deploying (instantiating) the DK outcomes of DSR (by practitioners, but also by researchers) and therefore DK accumulation. Accordingly, they call for research to improve the clarity of DK, increase DSR process transparency, and increase sharing DSR artifacts, especially instantiations, e.g. by placing instantiation artifacts into curated libraries, e.g. GitHub or WordPress. It should be mentioned, however, that curated libraries are not a panacea. Fichman and Kemerer [6] studied software reuse and concluded that the amount of software reuse was lower than hoped or expected. They found that the causes related more to organizational than to technical issues and suggest that incentive alignment is an issue (and potential solution). Similarly, Morisio et al. [11] studied success and failure factors in software reuse and found that social factors, including organization, processes, and human involvement, could be addressed to enhance software reuse.

Baskerville and Pries-Heje [1] state that "studies reveal that projection is often only achieved by incorporating one of the original contributors", suggesting that "one cannot easily make actual projections of DSR artifacts without deep knowledge about their projectability". While incorporating one of the original contributors into a subsequent DSR project (a social practice) is not a problem in and of itself, none of the original contributors may be available or willing to work on another DSR project [1].

We can consider this problem from a somewhat different perspective. That DSR projects do not build upon prior DK primarily means that DSR researchers do not appropriate potentially valuable prior DK. Presumably, DSR researchers do not appropriate prior DK because (1) they are unaware of the prior DK (2) they do not see the relevance of the prior DK (3) they do not understand and/or find it difficult to make use of the prior DK, or (4) they perceive problems and do not see the value in making use of the prior DK. These causes of the problem suggest a view of DK Accumulation as a communication endeavor.

3   DK Accumulation as a Communication Endeavor

DK Accumulation requires a 'message' to circulate from the sender (message composer) to the receiver (message interpreter). Differences can be found in the sort of message and the communication pattern.

The Message. Distinct proposals exist for what is to be communicated, namely:

- 'DK chunk' is the term introduced by Vom Brocke et al. to denote "a component, which has both process character (reproducible design activities) and outcome character (a justified claim that links a certain solution space to a certain problem space via evaluation" [16],

- Publication-related material is the proposal of journals such as *MIS Quarterly* [2]. Among other transparency practices, MISQ will support archiving of supplementary materials provided prior to, during, and after the review and publication process, but these will not undergo a review process; they will simply be available to reviewers and editors during review and to readers after publication,
- Research-related material is the strategy of Doyle and Luczak-Roesch [4,5]. The authors recommend the Open Science Framework (OSF) generally, and Registered Reports (RR) more specifically, as an alternative (or supplementary) means to disseminate DK at a more detailed, granular level and also to receive feedback on it during the DSR process, which is not possible in the traditional journal paper model.
- Software is a common instantiation artifact in DSR in IS, hence, the topic of software reuse is a closely related topic. A specific form of software reuse that is perhaps more relevant to DK accumulation is Open Source Software, where software is collaboratively developed and may be provided for reuse under various forms of licenses [7].

The Communication Pattern. We can envisage two patterns: centralized vs. peer-to-peer. In a centralized pattern, a repository sustains asynchronous communication between the agents. Most of the previous references resort to repositories (aka Knowledge Base or Body of Knowledge) for senders to leave 'the message' and receivers to collect 'the message', whether this is a 'DK chunk', publication-related material, or other sort of artifacts related to the DK. Alternatively, a peer-to-peer pattern does not rely (solely) on a central repository to govern the interaction but allows agents to share information and resources directly without relying on a dedicated central server. This model includes the possibility of synchronous as well as asynchronous communication and of research collaboration between different research projects (e.g., as suggested above by [1]). In a similar vein, Peffers et al. [12] highlighted that the entry point for a DSR project may take advantage of output generated by a previous researcher (e.g., a publication). Extending that idea, a DSR project may build upon prior DSR work and DSR projects can be conceptualized as collaborative endeavors where different research groups collaborate longitudinally. Unfortunately, such collaboration is outside the scope of Peffers et al. [12], and they do not describe how other partners can be involved.

This paper explores a peer-to-peer pattern with DK as 'the message' including IT artifacts themselves (i.e. instantiations, especially software). This vision further suggests viewing DK Accumulation as technology adoption. Accordingly, our approach is informed by Diffusion of Innovation theory.

4   Diffusion of Innovation

Diffusion of Innovation (DoI) is a social science theory that attempts to explain how new objects, ideas, and practices propagate. Specifically, its proponents

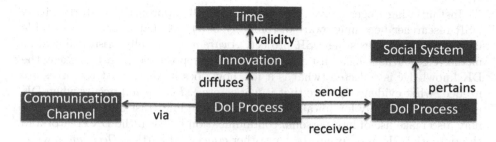

Fig. 1. DoI's main constructs

define DoI as "the process by which an innovation is communicated through certain channels over time among the members of a social system" [14]. Rogers identified five stages to the innovation-diffusion process: (1) Knowledge (2) Persuasion (3) Decision (4) Implementation, and (5) Confirmation. In addition, he introduces five main constructs (see Fig. 1):

- *an innovation* is any novel thing, idea, procedure, or system. In this paper, we consider DK as playing the role of the *innovations*.
- *communication channels* are the various ways that innovations are distributed from a source of origin to a recipient. Channels can be categorized as mass media or interpersonal and as localite (within the social system) and cosmopolite (outside the social system). Almost all mass media channels are cosmopolite.
- *a source* is an individual or an institution that originates a message.
- *time* captures the insight that innovations are not adopted instantly, but instead they are spread out and must remain relevant over time. This is particularly pertinent in DSR research due to 'the ephemeral nature of DK' where problem and solution spaces are in constant flux [16],
- *social system* reflects the fact that DoI is influenced by the social structure of the social system. A social system is a set of interrelated units that are engaged in joint problem solving to accomplish a common goal. In this paper, we consider the social system to be the DSR research community and its expanding collection of practices, members, and values, working towards the shared goal of DK Accumulation.

5   Instantiating DoI for DK Accumulation

This section places DK accumulation as an instantiation of Diffusion of Innovations (DoI); see Fig. 2. Importantly, the accumulation process does not rely exclusively on the existence of a Knowledge Base as illustrated in the DK accumulation models of [13,16]. As free agents in a socio-technical process, the DK sender and the DK receiver are free to employ (or not) whichever mechanisms they choose in a discourse leading to appropriation (or not), of course including (but not limited to) traditional publication and retrieval processes.

Instantiating Rogers's five stage DoI model, DK appropriation starts with a DSR researcher becoming aware of (possibly new) DK that might be a suitable basis for a new or existing DSR project. *Awareness* typically arises from mass media (e.g. journals, email list announcements or repositories). At this stage, the DK knowledge is collected (what is it for, how does it work, what resources are needed, what evidence is there that it works, etc.). *Persuasion* occurs when DK is examined carefully for suitability, including building trust and confidence. It may also make use of interpersonal communication between the DK creator and the potential DK appropriator(s) - or other concerned parties. *Decision* is when the potential DK appropriator(s) decide(s) whether (or not) to appropriate the DK for a particular DSR project (or projects). *Implementation* happens when the new DK is deployed into a DSR project. Sometimes, problems arise, which may lead to communication with the DK originator, other sources of information (e.g. trouble shooting guides or FAQs), or other people with expertise (e.g. other users). Finally, *Confirmation* occurs when the DSR project is in full swing making use of the DK. Note that the traditional publication process provides only limited support for building trust/confidence, and no direct support for persuasion/negotiation. Such activities would typically require alternative channels to the traditional publication process. This section elaborates on these alternative channels in the light of DoI.

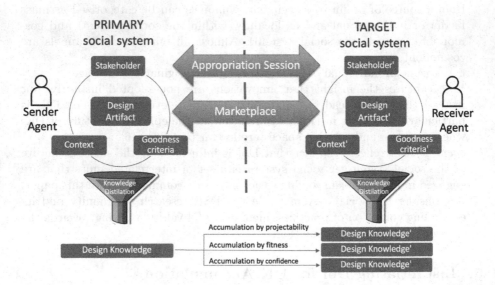

Fig. 2. DK accumulation as a DoI instance.

5.1 The Innovation

For our purpose, we regard DK as the innovation to be diffused. This includes five main components: (1) the problem to be solved (ideally grounded on empirical data) (2) the design-ingrained IT artifact itself (ideally grounded on Kernel Theory/Justificatory Knowledge) (3) the Measurement model used to assess its utility (4) the Setting (or Context) where this utility arises from artifact use, and (5) the resulting Design Theory [8,17] or Design Principles [10].

Note that DK is not limited to the design principles but includes IT artifacts themselves (i.e. instantiations, especially software). In line with the recommendations of Lukyanenko and Parsons [9], we believe the existence, availability, and quality of IT artifacts (e.g. source code for software artifacts) can play a major role in engaging research peers in appropriating and building on the underlying DK. This moves us to the next DoI constructs.

5.2 The Agents

For our purpose, agents are limited to research teams playing the role of 'the sender' and 'the receiver'. The sender and receiver are 'equal-footing peers', each with freedom to transfer or receive DSR outcomes and undertake collaborative action (or not). The model highlights opportunities for facilitating the receiver's self-interest to spur DK accumulation. Specifically, three main avenues are regarded to 'link' agents, in line with Vom Brocke et al.'s proposal [16]. Augmenting *projectability* (by generalizing or abstracting) can be accomplished by expanding upon the context, actors, and or behavior supported or expected from the designed artifact. Augmenting *fitness* (by amplification or contextualization) can be accomplished by modifying the designed artifact. Augmenting *confidence* can be accomplished by improving the quality and rigor of the evaluation or by replicating existing evaluations.

Assessing the potential for DK receiver agents' likely perceptions of the new DK's suitability for appropriation for further DSR might be useful. To this end, we adopt the Unified Theory of Acceptance and Use of Technology (UTAUT) model [15]. Specifically, we draw a parallel between intention and use of technology by users with intention and appropriation of DK by potential receiver DSR researchers. We make recommendations based on each of the four UTAUT independent variables: (1) performance expectancy (2) effort expectancy (3) social influence, and (4) facilitating conditions. For each variable, we rephrase its description for DK purposes. Mimicking the UTAUT model, we also provide a set of questions for senders to rate their agreement to self-assess whether the information that they provide is likely to be convincing and motivating for potential receivers.

Performance expectancy is defined as "the degree to which an individual believes that using the system will help him or her to attain gains in job performance" [15]. In the present context, we can rewrite this construct as the degree to which *a research group* (the receiver) believes that *appropriating* the *DK* could help realize its *vision for knowledge advancement*. A *vision for knowledge advancement* can be framed along the three dimensions proposed for DK accumulation as discussed above, namely, projectability, fitness, and confidence [16].

Increasing performance expectancy for future research building upon the senders' DK outcomes can be done in several ways. First and foremost is clearly communicating the suggested future research and how it builds on existing knowledge, as well as the potential significance of that research. Second, clearly communicating about the designed artifact, details of its design, how and why it works, etc., builds confidence in the receiver that the artifact could work in the generalized or abstracted contexts to enhance projectability or could be successfully enhanced to achieve the amplification or contextualization to improve fitness, as suggested for further research. Third, clearly communicating about the evaluation(s), how they were done, the rigor of the findings and their limitations further increases confidence that further research is likely to be fruitful.

Self-assessment questions:

- I find appropriating the DK could be useful to realize my vision for knowledge advancement.
- I envisage ways to contribute towards the projectability, fitness, and confidence of the DK.
- Appropriating the DK increases my productivity to realize my vision for knowledge advancement.
- Appropriating the DK increases my chances of getting proof-of-concept for my planned application context.
- Appropriating the DK increases my chances of getting proof-of-value for my research setting.

Effort expectancy is defined as "the degree of ease associated with the use of the system" [15]. In the present context, we can rewrite this construct as the degree of ease associated with the *appropriation* of the *DK*. What is key here is to reduce the perceived effort expectancy of potential receivers for appropriating the artifact/DK and research required, by clearly describing the potential/suggesting further research, the artifact and its DK, as well as its evaluation, and also explicitly communicating why the effort required to appropriate the artifact and conduct the further research is likely to be low.

As above for performance expectancy, in addition to clear and quality communication, various means can reduce perceived effort expectancy in potential receivers. First, suggesting how further evaluations or artifact improvements might be made reduces the effort required by potential receivers. Second, publication of supplemental materials to aid potential receivers (e.g. user guides, installation manuals, FAQs, or instructional videos) and providing clear references to what is available and how to access them reduces perceptions of how difficult it might be to appropriate the new designed artifact. Multiple channels can be used for such publishing, whether supported by publication outlets and repositories or not. Third, if the sender is interested, they may further publish suggestions that they are open for providing support, answering questions, or even collaborating on further suggested research. Such statements of openness need to be clear as to scope, clear as to how to make contact, and, preferably, enthusiastic in order to motivate the potential receivers. Provision of assistance and collaboration are clear ways to reduce the effort expectancy of eventual receivers.

Self-assessment questions:

- It is easy for me to understand the relevance of the contextual elements.
- It is easy for me to understand the rationales behind the Design Principles.
- It would be easy for me to install the artifact.
- It would be easy for me to use the artifact (e.g., the existence of documentation).
- I understand the vision provided for future research.
- It would be easy for me (or my research group) to conduct the proposed future research.
- The proposed future research is doable with the resources at hand.
- The proposed future research is significant enough to be worth my while.

Social influence is defined as "the degree to which an individual perceives that important others believe he or she should use the new system" [15]. In the present context, this refers to the extent that *appropriation* of existing *DSR knowledge* and *building on that knowledge* is considered valuable by 'important others' such as journal editors, editorial boards, conference committees, PhD committees, colleagues, or organizational superiors.

As every organization is different, encouraging and assessing whether other colleagues or organizational leaders would provide positive social influence is difficult. However, research streams that have a positive track record and established significance (and demand for publications) are likely to receive positive social encouragement. Highlighting the potential significance of proposed future research itself provides social influence and will encourage others to do the same. Further, pointing to other literature that suggests the importance of the proposed future research topic(s), e.g. editorials from journal editors or calls for papers of upcoming conferences, also points out that there is extant social influence supporting the appropriation and continued research on the DSR topic.

Self-assessment questions:

- I can identify journals and conferences that are open and supportive of publishing the future research that is suggested.
- The publications that are likely to accrue from further research would generally be adequate to support tenure or promotion.
- The research that is suggested would generally be considered to be a suitable, doable, and significant enough topic for an Honors/Masters/PhD degree.
- I would recommend undertaking the proposed future research to my colleagues.
- I would say positive things about this DSR and the resulting design knowledge insofar as appropriation is concerned.

Facilitating conditions are defined as "the degree to which an individual believes that organizational and technical infrastructure exist to support the use of the system" [15]. Now the goal is appropriation. We recommend that the resources required to appropriate and use the designed artifact need to be made clear and precise. The sender might also provide assistance, in the manner discussed earlier, which also reduces effort expectancy. As above, we again invite self-assessment or assessment by colleagues by rating agreement with the following statements:

- A typical university or research group would likely have the resources (time, space, skills) necessary to appropriate the DK.
- The offer of assistance from or collaboration with the original authors of the design knowledge during the appropriation activity and/or subsequent research is believable and helpful.

5.3   The Communication Channels

In addition to existing mass media channels (e.g. journals and repositories) and interpersonal communications (e.g. emails to/from DK originators/authors) we propose two new communication channels as potentially interesting for DK Accumulation: Appropriation Session and Marketplaces.

From Demo Sessions to Appropriation Sessions. We suggest the idea of 'Appropriation Sessions' as a means to promote DK appropriation. Appropriation Sessions move beyond Demo Sessions. An Appropriation Session would not be so much about the work's design, rigor or relevance, but more about the potential of the work to be appropriated and expanded upon, i.e., opportunities to advance knowledge. Such sessions might brainstorm about needed projections, fitness improvements from solutions, solution enhancements, or explore partnerships. Speakers could describe opportunities for support, assistance, and/or partnership in transitioning to new DK accumulation regions. Compared with manuscripts, Appropriation Sessions offer the opportunity to customize presentation for the audience. If a technical audience, focus on building fitness by describing technical challenges raised by your DK. If a domain audience, then focus on projectability by describing contextual limitations. If addressing practitioners, then focus on relevance by volunteering to replicate the evaluations within their own setting.

From Repositories to Marketplaces. A marketplace is a platform where vendors can come together to sell their products or services to a curated customer base. The role of a marketplace is to bring together the right vendors and the right customers, and the business model is to earn a commission from each sale. Marketplaces are essentially communication platforms. Unlike a repository-like online store, a marketplace does not have an inventory on its own. The added-value is in ensuring vendors are adhering to quality regulations and guidelines while accounting for content curation and trust. Think of *Airbnb*. It does not explicitly market products or services to individuals. Rather, it provides support for a peer-to-peer model whereby two individuals engage to buy and sell goods and services directly with one another. The value proposition of *Airbnb* is in building trust. Trust by Design is the main piece of *Airbnb* business model. Likewise, we believe there is room for a 'DK marketplace'. This goes beyond moving distinct assets to a central repository to provide 'DK curation' or 'trust building'. As travelers might be cautious about where they sleep, discerning DSR researchers may want to investigate which 'shoulders you climb onto'. Besides a searchable DK inventory, a robust system of credential verification and reviews for both the sender agent and the receiver agent might provide a better basis for a 'community of research practice'.

6   Conclusion

When it comes to DK accumulation, communication is key. As a supplement to central repositories, this work explores a peer-to-peer model by conceptualizing DK accumulation as a DoI practice. Rephrasing, Rogers' definition, DK accumulation becomes the process by which an innovation (i.e., new DK) is communicated through certain channels (e.g., a DK marketplace) over time (pressured by the DK ephemeral nature) among the members (i.e., the sender and the receiver) of a social system (i.e., the DSR community). This work further draws on UTAUT to suggest ways to increase receiver agents' trust and confidence in high-performance expectancy and low effort expectancy, as well as improving the potential for improved social conditions and facilitating conditions that increase the likelihood of new DK appropriation and thereby increase DK accumulation.

However, the proposed model and recommendations are new, have not been tried, and, consequently, the paper does not provide evidence of evaluation to support any conclusive claim of utility for purpose. The first stumbling block is to implement the two communication channels proposals, i.e., Appropriation Sessions and Marketplace. The former would involve a community effort, led by relevant conference organizers (e.g., DESRIST and HICSS). Marketplace websites are widely used in the so-called 'social economy' (e.g., Amazon, Fnac), yet their potential has been largely overlooked by the research community, which still, to a large degree, relies on traditional publication means. Open Science in general, and initiatives such as the Open Science Framework (OSF) [5] are a step in the right direction. However, the currently weak state of DK accumulation shows that it is more demanding, communication-wise, than supporting DK transparency or DK dissemination through repository-based approaches alone can accomplish effectively. Evaluating the conceptualization and practices recommended in this paper would allow the DSR community to assess the extent to which DK appropriation and accumulation follows a pattern similar to the Diffusion of Innovation.

References

1. Baskerville, R.L., Pries-Heje, J.: Projectability in design science research. J. Inf. Technol. Theory Appl. (JITTA), **20**(1), 3 (2019). https://aisel.aisnet.org/jitta/vol20/iss1/3

2. Burton-Jones, A., Boh, W.F., Oborn, E., Padmanabhan, B.: Editor's comments: advancing research transparency at mis quarterly: a pluralistic approach. Manag. Inf. Syst. Q. **45**(2), iii-xviii (2021)

3. Crowston, K., Wei, K., Howison, J., Wiggins, A.: Free/libre open-source software development: what we know and what we do not know. ACM Comput. Surv. **44**(2), 71–735 (2012)

4. Doyle, C., Luczak-Roesch, M., Mittal, A.: We need the open artefact: design science as a pathway to open science in information systems research. In: Tulu, B., Djamasbi, S., Leroy, G. (eds.) DESRIST 2019. LNCS, vol. 11491, pp. 46–60. Springer, Cham (2019). https://doi.org/10.1007/978-3-030-19504-5_4

5. Doyle, C., Luczak-Rösch, M.: This paper is an artefact: on open science practices in design science research using registered reports. In: 53rd Hawaii International Conference on System Sciences, HICSS 2020, Maui, Hawaii, 7–10 January 2020, pp. 1–10. ScholarSpace (2020). https://doi.org/10.24251/HICSS.2020.619

6. Fichman, R., Kemerer, C.: Object technology and reuse: lessons from early adopters. Computer **30**(10), 47–59 (1997). https://doi.org/10.1109/2.625304

7. Fitzgerald, B.: The transformation of open source software. MIS Q. **30**(3), 587–598 (2006). http://www.jstor.org/stable/25148740

8. Gregor, S., Jones, D.: The anatomy of a design theory. J. Assoc. Inf. Syst. **8**, 312–335 (2007). http://aisel.aisnet.org/jais/vol8/iss5/1

9. Lukyanenko, R., Parsons, J.: Research perspectives: design theory indeterminacy: what is it, how can it be reduced, and why did the polar bear drown?. J. Assoc. Inform. Syst. **21**(5), 1 (2020)

10. Meth, H., Mueller, B., Maedche, A.: Designing a requirement mining system. J. Assoc. Inform. Syst. **16**(9), 2 (2015)

11. Morisio, M., Ezran, M., Tully, C.: Success and failure factors in software reuse. IEEE Trans. Softw. Eng. **28**(4), 340–357 (2002). https://doi.org/10.1109/TSE.2002.995420

12. Peffers, K., Tuunanen, T., Rothenberger, M.A., Chatterjee, S.: A design science research methodology for information systems research. J. Manag. Inform. Syst. **24**(3), 45–77 (2007)

13. Reining, S., Ahlemann, F., Mueller, B., Thakurta, R.: Knowledge accumulation in design science research: ways to foster scientific progress. SIGMIS Database **53**(1), 10–24 (2022). https://doi.org/10.1145/3514097.3514100

14. Rogers, E.M., Singhal, A., Quinlan, M.M.: Diffusion of innovations. In: Stacks, D.W., Salwen, M.B., Eichhorn, K.C. (eds.) An Integrated Approach to Communication Theory and Research, 3rd edn. Routledge (2019)

15. Venkatesh, V., Morris, M.G., Davis, G.B., Davis, F.D.: User acceptance of information technology: toward a unified view. MIS Q. **27**(3), 425–478 (2003). https://doi.org/10.2307/30036540

16. Vom Brocke, J., Winter, R., Hevner, A., Maedche, A.: Special issue editorial-accumulation and evolution of design knowledge in design science research: a journey through time and space. J. Assoc. Inform. Syst. **21**(3), 9 (2020). https://doi.org/10.17705/1jais.00611

17. Walls, J.G., Widermeyer, G.R., El Sawy, O.A.: Assessing information system design theory in perspective: how useful was our 1992 initial rendition?. J. Inform. Technol. Theory Appl. (JITTA), **6**(2), 43–58 (2004). https://aisel.aisnet.org/jitta/vol6/iss2/6

Analyzing Design Knowledge Representation in Design Science Research and Deriving Recommendations to Support Design Knowledge Codification

Ernestine Dickhaut[1]([✉]) [ID], Andreas Janson[2] [ID], and Jan Marco Leimeister[1,2] [ID]

[1] University of Kassel, Kassel, Germany
{ernestine.dickhaut,leimeister}@uni-kassel.de
[2] University of St. Gallen, St. Gallen, Switzerland
{andreas.janson,janmarco.leimeister}@unisg.ch

Abstract. The goal of design science research is the generation of novel artifacts. Thereby DSR projects generate valuable design knowledge, thus, underscoring the importance to codify of design knowledge for achieving scientific progress. The research community observes that DSR projects generate a large amount of design knowledge, but the developed knowledge often ends as a single success story. To counter this situation, we analyze the variety of design knowledge representation forms that have been published in the AIS Senior Scholars' Basket in design science research papers. Based on our systematic literature review, we identify prevalent ways of design knowledge representations. We provide as a central contribution how to effectively communicate design knowledge through the derivation of recommendations that provides practical guidance to support researchers and practitioners in making design knowledge contributions reusable and applicable.

Keywords: Design knowledge · Codification · Design science research

1 Introduction

Design science research (DSR) offers an important paradigm for conducting applicable and rigorous research to real-world design problems [1]. Therefore, DSR aims to generate prescriptive knowledge about the design of information systems (IS) artifacts [2], oftentimes supported through well-cited DSR approaches for conducting DSR projects such as the three cycle view of Hevner [3] and the DSR process by Peffers et al. [1]. The overall *"goal of DSR is to generate knowledge on how to build effectively innovative solutions to important problems"* ([4], p.15) by finding solutions (solution-space) for design problems (problem-space) [4]. The generated design knowledge can be represented in different forms such as design patterns, design principles, design theories, and design artifacts [4, 5]. Typically, a design project has two outcomes – an artifact and a design theory [6], the latter summarizes knowledge on how to design the artifact [7].

A. Drechsler et al. (Eds.): DESRIST 2022, LNCS 13229, pp. 417–428, 2022.
https://doi.org/10.1007/978-3-031-06516-3_31

Although, the approaches by Peffers et al. [1] and Hevner [3] aim to provide guidance on how to conduct, evaluate, and present design science research, the DSR community observes that the projects neglect the transfer of generated design knowledge. DSR projects may produce artifacts and theories that are rarely reused [5, 6]. Thus, design knowledge is often lost at the end of the projects and buried in digital libraries of conference proceedings and journals [6]. The limited design knowledge reusability in the IS community is problematic, as single contributions tend to remain isolated with little to no relation to other solutions [5]. This is accompanied by the problem that valuable knowledge is lost, although it could be useful in new projects, thus, hindering the progress of science. The lack of reuse also brings with it that the generated design knowledge does not leap from research into practice [8].

An important reason that makes design knowledge difficult to share and accumulate is the fact that design knowledge has certain characteristics and abstraction levels, especially if it is not represented in a codified form [9, 10]. To counter this situation, we review the variety of design knowledge representation forms that have been published in the AIS Senior Scholars' Basket. With our paper, we aim to provide a holistic picture of different DSR codification forms. Therefore, we investigate how DSR papers share generated design knowledge in IS journals and draw conclusions on how to codify design knowledge by answering the following research question.

RQ: How is design knowledge represented in design science research papers in leading IS journals?

To answer our research question, we first conduct a systematic literature review following vom Brocke et al. [11] and Webster & Watson [12] to identify DSR papers that conduct DSR in IS journals. Second, we analyze how design knowledge is represented in extant literature. Afterwards, we draw conclusions regarding associations between knowledge generation, purpose, and representation forms to provide guidance on how to facilitate design knowledge accumulation for reuse by deriving recommendations based on our review.

2   Theoretical Background

2.1   Design Science Research and the Importance of Design Knowledge

We first want to go deeper into the design science research paradigm and analyze the meaning of accumulating and codifying design knowledge. In the last decades, design science research became an established and widely used research method in information systems research [13]. DSR provides a structure for constructing artifacts [10] and it oftentimes follows process methods [13, 24] to bring the practical development of artifacts into IS research. The outcome of DSR projects is typically two-fold: design artifacts and design theories [10, 14]. Thus, resulting in a large range of DSR projects with different design outcomes. Not only does the application field of DSR vary but also how authors apply and ultimately present DSR [13]. Conducting DSR oftentimes means solving design problems by developing and evaluating artifacts with the help of applying concepts, such as (design) theories and design principles, to map and support design processes [1].

One thing all DSR projects have in common is the generation of valuable and novel design knowledge [15]. As Peffers et al. [1] recommend in their DSR guidelines, the communication of the design outcomes is one important part of the overall project. DSR projects accumulate design knowledge through building, testing, and extending artifacts across projects and publications [10]. The accumulation and codification of knowledge is the essence of theories and knowledge sharing [5]. Gregor et al. [10] remark on the importance of design knowledge codification to make design science formalizable through design theories.

Design knowledge is one specialized part of knowledge, namely knowledge to design an artifact including used methods and constructs to design the artifact [10]. The knowledge literature contrasts different types of knowledge, such as tacit and explicit knowledge [16], which impact a person's ability to codify knowledge [17]. Design knowledge is a special form of knowledge, namely knowledge to design a system including methods and constructs [10]. While explicit knowledge can be easily transferred, other types of knowledge (such as tacit knowledge) are difficult to transfer [9]. Typically, knowledge is developed by an individual [16] through applying previous knowledge in new contexts. Van Aken defines design knowledge as *"[...] knowledge that can be used to produce designs. The general design knowledge in the repertoire of the senior designer is compiled by him/ her over the years through formal education and through learning on the job"* ([18], p. 9).

2.2 Design Knowledge Accumulation to Facilitate Reuse

As DSR establishes its position as an important part of IS research, more and more researchers are pointing out the importance of design knowledge accumulation and codification [4, 19]. Numerous scholars, such as vom Brocke et al. (2019) and Rai (2017), call for approaches that effectively deal with the accumulation and codification of design knowledge in DSR in high-caliber IS journals [5].

To counter the problem, recent literature, for example, by Chandra Kruse and Nickerson [5], analyzed the essence of design in-depth and derived key design elements to facilitate design knowledge accumulation. Vom Brocke et al. [4] provide a framework on how to position design knowledge contribution in problem and solution space by providing a set of principles that facilitate knowledge accumulation. Other research, such as the design knowledge typology by Müller and Thoring [9] or the design knowledge taxonomy by Dickhaut et al. [15] provide frameworks to conceptualize design knowledge and facilitate the understanding of design knowledge properties.

To understand how design knowledge is actually reused in practice, Chandra Kruse et al. [20] analyze the reuse of design principles with practitioners. Schoormann et al. [21] look at the reusability of design principles in the literature. However, the literature still lacks an analysis of the different ways in which design knowledge is represented to understand how design knowledge has been codified for dissemination in design science research so far. Thus, the goal of our paper is to analyze how previous design science projects codify their generated design knowledge through published papers.

3 Identifying and Classifying Design Knowledge Representation Forms

3.1 Systematic Literature Review

In the following, we describe our literature search process that provides the empirical basis for our analysis. Furthermore, we explain the data analysis techniques used in this paper to analyze how previous DSR journal papers codify design knowledge.

We conducted a systematic literature analysis according to vom Brocke et al. [11] and Webster & Watson [12] to identify the literature foundation of our paper. The goal of our systematic literature is to identify papers that conduct DSR methods and are published in the AIS Senior Scholars' Basket: Management Information Systems Quarterly (MISQ), Journal of Management Information Systems (JMIS), Journal of the Association for Information Systems (JAIS), Information Systems Research (ISR), European Journal of Information Systems (EJIS), Information Systems Journal (ISJ), Journal of Strategic Information Systems (JSIS), Journal of Information Technology (JIT). We focus on high published DSR papers because most conference papers examine a small part of big design science projects. In addition, we see the highest potential to learn how to codify design knowledge in a useful way from high published journal papers. Reasons such as long and hard review iterations force the author team to carefully make their acquired design knowledge available.

Table 1. Overview of searched journals.

Outlets	Total hits	Relevant hits
Management Information Systems Quarterly (MISQ)	121	18
Journal of Management Information Systems (JMIS)	85	26
Journal of the Association for Information Systems (JAIS)	114	34
Information Systems Research (ISR)	50	6
European Journal of Information Systems (EJIS)	115	24
Information Systems Journal (ISJ)	60	4
Journal of Strategic Information Systems (JSIS)	24	2
Journal of Information Technology (JIT)	52	1
Sum	**621**	**115**

To cover a broad set of publications, we use the keywords "design science" in the databases. Table 1 provides an overview of the results. The initial number of 621 papers was reduced by reading the papers' title, abstracts, and keywords. We reduced the literature by eliminating papers that are out of our scope such as papers that dealt with design science research from a conceptual or methodological viewpoint. Resulting in a selection of 115 papers, that are relevant for our following analysis.

The 115 relevant papers were analyzed following an iterative process aggregating the insights. The iterative process was started by two of the researchers who independently code a subset of 5 randomly chosen articles. Next, we re-examined the original subset and analyzed variations in coding. We proceeded iteratively with the coding until all 115 papers were independently coded.

3.2 Coding Frame

We use a theoretical frame to analyze the resulting 115 papers regarding design knowledge representation. The coding frame is based on literature on DSR and design knowledge generation or codification. In the following, we present the underlying theoretical understanding to be as transparent as possible during our analysis. In general, our coding frame is based on the essay by Gregor and Hevner to positioning and presenting design science research [22], Nonaka's knowledge creation theory [16], and vom Brocke et al.'s guidance on how to accumulate design knowledge [4].

The generation of design knowledge takes place in a variety of ways, which is an important characteristic to understand its nature. So design knowledge may be generated with the goal to develop *principles of form and function* [23], by developing an *instantiated implementation* [23], developing a *prototypical design* [24], through the development of a *method* [25], or by developing *models* [26, 27].

We describe below how we classify the design outcomes and give examples for each cluster. *Principles of form and function* describe the design of artifacts generally and provide instructions on how to design those elements. A lot of design science research papers develop design principles which we classify as one example of principles of form and function.

Papers that develop programs or high-fidelity systems are classified *as instantiated implementation* while mock-ups, prototypes, or low-fidelity programs are coded as *prototypical design*. We distinguish instantiated implementation from prototypes by the degree of completion. While prototypes are developed exemplarily for evaluation or demonstration, instantiated implementation can actually come to use.

DSR papers that provide step-by-step instructions and provide users concrete directions to do something are classified as *method* development. A more formal artifact output is the development of models to understand or explain occurrences. Thus, the design knowledge origin represents our first coding frame to understand design knowledge representation forms. We use the frame as a mapping to analyze differences between different design science research artifacts. Our second coding frame is related to the level of abstraction. Thus, knowledge may be context-specific, which is often the case if the knowledge is less abstracted and applied in one specific case [16]. If design knowledge is abstract and applicable in many cases, there are few in-depth details.

To go more in detail, our third coding frame focus on the knowledge expression level. We distinguish tacit, explicitly articulated, and explicitly codified design knowledge [16]. Tacit knowledge is not represented or hardly represented at all. This makes the knowledge hard to grasp. The codification of design knowledge may occur in different forms. Structured text-based codification approaches focus on codification in texts, mostly as highlighted key points of structured lists. Another clear presentation form are tables. Prototypes or screenshots are often used to provide graphic visual support.

DSR papers that use no structured codification form are summed up as unstructured. Our last coding frame focuses on the main formulation and distinguishes descriptive and prescriptive design knowledge which is often used as a key indicator to analyze the knowledge reuse potential [21, 28].

4   Results: Status Quo of Design Knowledge Representation in Design Science Research

While design science research has been around for 30 years, its application and the knowledge codification in the IS discipline are very different. Our literature analysis revealed several insights, which we present in the following. We use the insights to derive recommendations on how to get the maximum out of design science research and how to improve design knowledge re-use. The use of design science research differs regarding the research outcome within the outlets (see Table 2).

Table 2. Overview of artifact outcome.

	MISQ	JMIS	JAIS	ISR	EJIS	JIT	ISJ	JSIS	Sum
Principles of form and function	12	5	24	2	15	0	3	1	**62**
Instantiated implementation	9	2	6	0	1	0	0	0	**18**
Prototypical design	5	10	12	0	8	1	1	0	**37**
Methods	4	6	7	2	2	1	0	2	**24**
Model	4	9	2	2	1	0	1	0	**19**

Thus, a major part of the DSR papers develop principles of form and function, namely 62 papers. Some of these papers combine the development of an artifact such as an instantiated implementation together with a prototypical design. Here, the design object supports the practical evaluation of the principles. Most of the papers provide a general overview of knowledge from the solution-space, knowledge from the problem-space, process knowledge, and object knowledge. The principles of form and function papers focus on providing process knowledge and design knowledge from the problem-space (see Table 3). Most of the codified design knowledge is generally applicable resulting in more abstract knowledge. The principles of form and function papers in our analysis use primary text-based codification forms such as highlighting the knowledge through marking the knowledge bold to provide the information in a clear way.

We identified only 18 papers whose outcomes are instantiated implementations. Our analysis demonstrates that the papers differ in their way of presenting design knowledge, especially in the integration of visual representations and the inclusion of problem knowledge. Almost all papers present the knowledge behind the problem space and integrate screenshots or graphical representations. Only a few papers develop context-specific design knowledge and most of the papers integrate generally applicable knowledge by abstracting their key findings.

Table 3. Design knowledge representation.

	Principles of form and function	Instanti-ated imple-mentation	Proto-typical design	Methods	Model
Unit of design					
Object knowledge	◐	◐	◕	◐	◐
Process knowledge	◕	◕	◕	●	◕
Problem-space knowledge	◕	●	◕	●	●
Solution-space knowledge	◐	◐	◐	●	◐
Level of abstraction					
Context specific	◔	◔	◐	◔	●
Generally applicable	◕	◐	◐	◕	◔
Knowledge representation					
Tacit	○	○	○	○	○
Explicitly articulated	◐	◔	◐	◔	◐
Explicitly codified	◐	◐	◐	◕	◐
Codification format					
Structured text-based	●	●	●	●	●
Structured tabular	◔	○	◔	◔	◔
Graphic visual	◐	◕	◕	◐	◕
Unstructured	○	○	○	○	○
Main formulation					
Descriptive knowledge	◐	◐	◕	◔	◕
Prescriptive knowledge	◐	◐	◐	●	◔
Legend High ● Rather high ◕ Moderate ◐					
Rather low ◔ Low ○					

We classify 37 papers whose design outcomes are prototypical designs. The proto-typical design papers differ little from those that develop an instantiated implementation. As a rule, these papers clarify very well how the design process has proceeded and define the knowledge through process knowledge. Many of the papers combine descriptive and prescriptive knowledge which comes from describing the artifacts developed. In addition, another way to use DSR is the development of a method to provide step-by-step guidance. In our analysis, the development of a method is the goal of 24 papers in our analysis. The papers that develop methods clearly distinguish themselves from the other papers by providing detailed guidance. This is also shown by the fact that these papers primarily use prescriptive design knowledge and thus convey precise design information.

In our analysis, 19 papers' outcomes are models. In contrast to the primarily used, prescriptive design knowledge are the papers whose outcomes are models. Here, mainly descriptive design knowledge is presented. However, the papers rather use a visual representation to convey their artifact.

5   Critical Discussion of the Status Quo and Recommendations

In the following, we will discuss the status quo of design knowledge codification and provide recommendations for moving our field further in codifying and accumulating design knowledge. We illustrate our recommendations with examples from prior research, although we note that the selected papers are just examples.

As seen in our analysis (Sect. 4) principles of form and function are a common way to codify design knowledge. Principles of form and function can be represented in different ways. In addition to the visual highlighting – specially marked or listed in a table – the expression differs in the use of descriptive and prescriptive knowledge. Chandra Kruse et al. [29] propose a formulation approach of design principles that is clear and precise. We would like to highlight the paper from Recker [30] as one illustrative example to provide precise design knowledge and equally shows how the developed design principles are anchored in the solution-space and problem-space. In the paper, the author develops design principles to improve the state-tracking ability of covid-19 dashboards. Thereby the design principles are not only developed and presented but also related to the underlying "aim, mechanism, and rationale of the design principle" by providing a clearly arranged overview in which the developed design principles are set in relation to their design objective. Thus, the author provide knowledge on how the problem-space by presenting the theoretical foundation together with the application field (object knowledge) and the mechanisms to achieve the design, leading to the first recommendation:

Recommendation 1: *Include aim, mechanism, and rationale of the design knowledge.*

Papers that develop principles of form and function combine the text-based representation with graphic visual details. An illustrative example is Seidel et al. [31], who develop design principles for systems that support organizational sensemaking in environmental sustainability transformations. In their paper, the authors use a clearly arranged form to provide text-based design knowledge and demonstrate the design of their principles through various graphics and artifact screenshots. A combination of structured text-based knowledge and graphic-visual insights achieves a transfer to the practical implementation, which makes the knowledge very specific but still generally applicable through more abstract design principles.

Recommendation 2: *Support abstract principles of form and function by providing specific design applications through graphic-visual details.*

The report of an instantiated implementation is difficult because a running program must be described as comprehensibly as possible but mostly text based. Representations, such as the description of the system architecture or the interface challenge the authors. One paper that we would like to highlight here is the paper by Nguyen et al. [32] who develop a learning analytic system. In their paper, the authors derive design principles, which they then specify in more detail for the application field and develop a learning analytics system. To meet the challenge of providing insights into the developed technology the authors include a visual presentation of the underlying architecture. Thus, they communicate architectural design knowledge related to the actual implementation.

Recommendation 3: *Include detailed sketches of your system architecture to provide system insights.*

The papers that develop prototypes demonstrate process knowledge can be communicated in an application-oriented manner. We would like to reference the paper from Meth et. al [33] who propose a design theory for requirement mining systems. The authors solve the challenge that the prototype cannot be presented through text by integrating a screenshot and enriching it with further explanations. To demonstrate the functionalities and technology, the authors use a process-oriented figure. The figure visualizes how the individual stakeholders in the system interact with each other.

Recommendation 4: *Provide insights into the technology use through process-oriented figures.*

DSR projects are often conducted over a long period of time and include several crucial events that contain valuable knowledge. In most cases, project findings are less codified on an ongoing way but tend to be codified toward the end of the project. To get around this, design journeys or evolution graphics on how design knowledge unfolds through multiple revisions are helpful. They provide an overview of the course of the project and prevent design knowledge from being lost [8]. Design science tool support approaches can also provide valuable guidance as for example the "MyDesignProcess" tool [34]. A good example to demonstrate design evolutions is the paper from Widjaja et al. [35] who visualize their design evolution and go into detail about their individual five design artifacts and their progress. This makes it possible to see the entire development process and understand how individual components are interlocked with each other.

Recommendation 5: *Use design journeys or evolution figures to accumulate as much design knowledge as possible.*

6 Conclusion and Future Research Directions

The aim of our paper is to analyze design knowledge representation in design science research papers and to derive recommendations to codify developed design knowledge in a rich, reusable way. To answer our research question, we conducted a systematic literature review and analyzed all papers in the AIS basket of eight that perform DSR.

Our results show how different the design artifact is as a DSR project outcome, but also within the comparison of the artifacts the papers differ in their way of presentation. Our observations confirm the findings of previous literature. For example, the degree of abstraction of codification varies greatly by design outcome, which is consistent with the findings of Wache et al. [36].

Design principles papers often follow the formulation guidelines of Chandra Kruse et al. [19] and thus generate prescriptive design knowledge. With the derivation of our five recommendations, we provide researchers and practitioners with guidance on how to improve the codification of design knowledge. The recommendations are based on our literature review and offer scope for further research. For example, further research can address the evaluation of these recommendations or further elaborate them into a framework for codifying applicable reusable design knowledge.

Due to our search string "design science" we cover a large part of design papers but there are a vast of papers that design artifacts but use another term such as action design research [37]. Further research could use these search strings and extend the search to other design disciplines such as human-computer interaction, computer science or specific conferences such as DESRIST and analyze how they codify design knowledge. Our analysis focus on journal papers could lead to a possible bias of editorial policies in these journals which often forces design science researchers to submit their research to design-related journals or conferences [38]. Overall, we provide a foundation for the discussion on how to codify reusable and applicable design knowledge.

Acknowledgements. We would like to thank Antonia Tolzin for her support during the paper analysis. The second author acknowledges funding from the Basic Research Fund (GFF) of the University of St.Gallen.

References

1. Peffers, K., Tuunanen, T., Rothenberger, M.A., Chatterjee, S.: A design science research methodology for information systems research. J. Manag. Inf. Syst. **24**, 45–77 (2007)
2. Hevner, A.R., March, S.T., Park, J., Ram, S.: Design science in information systems research. MISQ **28**(1), 75–105 (2004)
3. Hevner, A.R.: A three cycle view of design science research. Scand. J. Inf. Syst. **19**(2), 4 (2007)
4. vom Brocke, J., Winter, R., Hevner, A., Maedche, A.: Accumulation and evolution of design knowledge in design science research – a journey through time and space. J. Assoc. Inf. Syst. (JAIS) **23**, 9–49 (2020)
5. Chandra Kruse, L., Nickerson, J.V.: Portraying design essence. In: HICSS, pp. 4433–4442 (2018)
6. Brendel, A.B., Lembcke, T.-B., Muntermann, J., Kolbe, L.M.: Toward replication study types for design science research. J. Inf. Technol. **36**(3), 198–215 (2021)
7. Gregor, S., Jones, D.: The anatomy of a design theory. Assoc. Inf. Syst. **8**(5), 1 (2007)
8. Reining, S., Ahlemann, F., Müller, B., Thakurta, R.: Knowledge accumulation in design science research: ways to foster scientific progress. Database Adv. Inf. Syst. **53**(1), 10–24 (2022)

9. Müller, R.M., Thoring, K.: A typology of design knowledge: a theoretical framework. In: 2010 Proceedings of the Americas Conference on Information Systems (AMCIS), pp. 300–310 (2010)
10. Gregor, S., Hevner, A.R.: Positioning and presenting design science research for maximum impact. MIS Q. **37**, 337–355 (2013)
11. Vom Brocke, J., Simons, A., Riemer, K., Niehaves, B., Plattfault, R., Cleven, A.: Standing on the shoulders of giants: challenges and recommendations of literature search in information systems research. Commun. Assoc. Inf. Syst. (CAIS) **37**(1), 9 (2015)
12. Webster, J., Watson, R.T.: Analyzing the past to prepare for the future: writing a literature review. MIS Q. **26**(2), 13–23 (2002)
13. Engel, C., Leicht, N., Ebel, P.: The imprint of design science in information systems research: an empirical analysis of the ais senior scholars' basket. In: Proceedings of the ICIS 2019 (2019)
14. Baskerville, R., Baiyere, A., Gergor, S., Hevner, A., Rossi, M.: Design science research contributions: finding a balance between artifact and theory. JAIS **19**, 358–376 (2018)
15. Dickhaut, E., Janson, A., Leimeister, J.M.: Conceptualizing design knowledge in is research – a review and taxonomy of design knowledge properties. In: HICSS 55 (2022)
16. Nonaka, I., Toyama, R.: The knowledge-creating theory revisited: knowledge creation as a synthesizing process. Knowl. Manag. Res. Pract. **1**, 2–10 (2003)
17. Polanyi, M.: Tacit knowing: its bearing on some problems of philosophy. Rev. Mod. Phys. **34**, 601–616 (1962)
18. van Aken, J.E.: Valid knowledge for the professional design of large and complex design processes. Des. Stud. **26**, 379–404 (2005)
19. Chandra Kruse, L., Seidel, S.: Tensions in design principle formulation and reuse. In: Designing the Digital Transformation DESRIST Research in Progress Proceedings of the 12th International Conference on Design Science Research in Information Systems and Technology, pp. 180–188 (2017)
20. Chandra Kruse, L., Purao, S., Seidel, S.: How designers use design principles: design behaviors and application modes. J. Assoc. Inf. Sys. (JAIS) (2022)
21. Schoormann, T., Möller, F., Hansen, M.R.P.: How do researchers (re-)use design principles: an inductive analysis of cumulative research. In: Chandra Kruse, L., Seidel, S., Hausvik, G.I. (eds.) DESRIST 2021. LNCS, vol. 12807, pp. 188–194. Springer, Cham (2021). https://doi.org/10.1007/978-3-030-82405-1_20
22. Gregor, S., Hevner, A.R.: Positioning and presenting design science research for maximum impact. MIS Q. **37**(2), 337–355 (2013)
23. Gregor, S.: The nature of theory in information systems. MIS Q. **30**(3), 611–642 (2006)
24. Lim, Y.-K., Stolterman, E., Tenenberg, J.: The anatomy of prototypes. ACM Trans. Comput. -Hum. Interact **15**, 1–27 (2008)
25. Peffers, K., Tuunanen, T., Rothenberger, M.A., Chatterjee, S.: A design science research methodology for information systems research. JMIS **24**(3), 45–77 (2007)
26. Recker, J., Lukyanenko, R., Jabbari, M., Samuel, B.M., Castellanos, A.: From representation to mediation: a new agenda for conceptual modeling research in a digital world. MIS Q. **45**, 269–300 (2021)
27. Li, M.M., Peters, C., Leimeister, J.M.: A hypergraph-based modeling approach for service systems. In: Yang, H., Qiu, R. (eds.) INFORMS-CSS 2018. SPBE, pp. 61–72. Springer, Cham (2019). https://doi.org/10.1007/978-3-030-04726-9_7
28. Im, I., Hars, A.: Knowledge reuse - insights from software reuse. In: 1998 Proceedings of the Americas Conference on Information Systems (AMCIS), pp. 601–603 (1998)
29. Chandra, L., Seidel, S., Gregor, S.: Prescriptive knowledge in is research: conceptualizing design principles in terms of materiality, action, and boundary conditions. In: HICSS, pp. 4039–4048 (2014)

30. Recker, J.: Improving the state-tracking ability of corona dashboards. Eur. J. Inf. Syst. **30**, 476–495 (2021)
31. Seidel, S., Chandra Kruse, L., Székely, N., Gau, M., Stieger, D.: Design principles for sense-making support systems in environmental sustainability transformations. Eur. J. Inf. Syst. **27**, 221–247 (2018)
32. Nguyen, A., Tuunanen, T., Gardner, L., Sheridan, D.: Design principles for learning analytics information systems in higher education. Eur. J. Inf. Syst. **30**(3), 1–28 (2020)
33. Meth, H., Mueller, B., Maedche, A.: Designing a requirement mining system. J. Assoc. Inf. Syst. (JAIS) **16**(9), 2 (2015)
34. Morana, S., et al.: Research prototype: the design canvas in mydesignprocess. In: Proceedings of the DESRIST 2018 Conference (2018)
35. Widjaja, T., Gregory, R.: Monitoring the complexity of it architectures: design principles and an it artifact. 1536–9323 21, 664–694 (2020)
36. Wache, H., Möller, F., Schoormann, T., Strobel, G.: Exploring the abstraction levels of design principles: the case of chatbots. In: Proceedings of the International Conference on Wirtschaftsinformatik (WI) (2022)
37. Sein, M.K., Henfridsson, O., Purao, S., Rossi, M., Lindgren, R.: Action design research. MIS Q. **35**(1), 37–56 (2011)
38. Österle, H., et al.: Memorandum on design-oriented information systems research. Eur. J. Inf. Syst. **20**(1), 7–10 (2011)

Education and DSR

Introduction to Education and Design Science Research Track

Asif Gill[iD], Lisa Seymour[iD], Robert Winter[iD]

[1] University of Technology Sydney
asif.gill@uts.edu.au
[2] University of Cape Town
lisa.seymour@uct.ac.za
[3] University of St.Gallen
robert.winter@unisg.ch

Abstract. The Education and DSR track is a premier forum for research, applications and experience reports on challenges and best practices in (a) teaching and learning DSR as well as (b) using DSR for teaching and learning. As curricula develop slowly, DSR is often underrepresented in curricula and courses on research design and methods, and we invite contributions that offer guidance on what and how to teach in a DSR course in a way that enables new and early career academics to conduct DSR according to high standards.

Keywords: DSR education

Design Science Research (DSR) focuses on the design, development and evaluation of novel artifacts or new knowledge. Purposefully designed artifacts are not only key to the design and management of effective information systems and technology, but also for teaching and learning. It comes therefore at no surprise that education is among the fields where (intervention) design-oriented scientific approaches have a long tradition [1]. Across academic disciplines, there is an increasing interest in DSR where it is being taught in research method courses and is also being used to address challenges in teaching and learning. Therefore, relation of DSR and education has at least two facets which we included in the DESRIST track on educational issues: (1) teaching and learning DSR as a methodology and (2) designing and evaluating teaching and learning approaches and systems.

As scientific curricula gradually develop, and in the face of the long-term dominance of descriptive social sciences in business schools, DSR is often underrepresented in programs and courses on research design and methods. We therefore invite contributions that offer guidance on what and how to teach DSR in a way that enables new and early career academics to conduct DSR according to high standards – not only on the Ph.D. but also at the Masters level [2]. Besides offering an alternative research paradigm to business school students and educating new generations of design researchers, this field also allows to create synergies with related fields like entrepreneurship [3] or organization sciences [4] whose methods education can benefit from the experience in IS DSR education, just to name a few. Besides analyzing specific DSR challenges and solutions in the context of research education, identifying potentials and limitations of mutual learning between DSR education in research and practice, reporting foundational research on DSR competencies and skills, developing methods of teaching DSR competencies and skills, evaluating teaching and assessment methods in DSR education, reporting empirical studies describing DSR education in different contexts, reporting pedagogical approaches for DSR education in distributed and remote digital environment, and analyzing educational technologies for DSR education, DSR lecturers and students can benefit from presenting and disseminating successful syllabi, teaching materials and experience reports.

Another aspect of the relation between education and DSR is that purposefully designed artifacts are useful in solving many challenges within the educational domain. The COVID-19 pandemic and resultant need for digital and remote education disrupted education systems globally, forcing rapid digital transformation in weeks. The challenges encountered include the lack of human capability, digital technology infrastructure and related artefacts needed to support and enable digitally connected and remote education. While being in the traditional academic settings, many educators did not have the experience or skills in creating and delivering online courses and assessments. This situation was further complicated due to the lack of readily available and transformable digital contents, appropriate digital technology and required remote connectivity. Following this disruption, new and promising artifacts have been designed and evaluated that enable digital and remote education. Regardless of whether traditional or novel forms of teaching and learning are concerned, the methodology of DSR provides an effective and efficient way to develop innovative approaches, systems and interventions. In particular, with the collaborative, participative and action-oriented potentials of DSR, educational solutions may be planned, developed and managed in a balanced, systematic, transparent and efficient way by referring to the vast design and evaluation experience in IT and IS fields.

Exemplary uses of DSR in the educational domain are included in this track: DSR is used to create a virtual toolbox to engage and guide teachers when creating their courses. DSR was used to design e-assessment moderation systems and co-innovation spaces. While applications of DSR seem promising, the DSR method is not yet well established in curricula and in courses on research design and methods. Novice to experienced researchers struggle with the many elements needed to convincingly conduct and present DSR and to choose between multiple study design alternatives. This can be assisted by uses of DSR in this track, including examples of research design checklists and a DSR taxonomy aiming to help researchers when embarking on DSR research. With this first DESRIST track on educational issues, we want to establish teaching and learning issues as a permanent concern in the DSR community.

References

1. Winter, R.: Design science research in business research – with special emphasis on infor mation systems. Zeitschrift für Berufs- und Wirtschaftspädagogik – Beihefte, 233–246 (2014)
2. Winter, R., vom Brocke, J.: Teaching design science research. In: 42th International Conference on Information Systems (ICIS 2021), Austin TX (2021)
3. Seckler, C., Mauer, R., Brocke, J.V.: Design Science in entrepreneurship: conceptual foundations and guiding principles. J. Bus. Ventur. Des. Forthcoming (2022)
4. Romme, A.G.L.: Making a difference: organization as design. Organ. Sci. **14**, 558–573 (2003)

Designing Virtual Toolboxes to Guide Educators in Creating Online Learning

Lea Blecher[1,2]([envelope])[iD], Lara Riefle[1][iD], and Tomi Kauppinen[2][iD]

[1] Karlsruhe Institute of Technology, Karlsruhe, Germany
lea.blecher@alumni.kit.edu, lara.riefle@kit.edu
[2] Aalto University, Espoo, Finland
{lea.blecher,tomi.kauppinen}@aalto.fi

Abstract. Online learning has gained an increasingly important role at universities, schools, and companies, which was boosted by the pandemic to yet another level. Given that online teaching requires different skills compared to traditional teaching, educators face challenges when creating online learning. Research is looking at these challenges from various perspectives to provide guidance. However, the guidance provided is often not interactive or engaging, and thus does not motivate to explore possibilities in online learning more widely. This paper explores how to design virtual toolboxes to engage and guide educators when creating online learning. Conducting a design science research project, we propose theory-grounded design principles and instantiate them in an interactive toolbox. Our artifact is evaluated with educators from seven European universities to iteratively improve the design foundation. We contribute valuable design knowledge that enables researchers and practitioners to develop tools in the field of online learning. In addition, we propose a novel toolbox that supports educators when creating online courses.

Keywords: Design science research · Online learning · Virtual toolbox

1 Introduction

Online learning has become increasingly relevant in many areas such as schools, universities and companies. The pandemic showed once again how important well-designed online courses are today. In particular, the field of higher education is transforming rapidly with emerging opportunities in online learning [12]. Educators want to keep their teaching at a high-quality level. However, compared to a traditional classroom setting, online teaching requires different competences and presents new pedagogical challenges [20]. The way students interact, and the way course content is delivered, changes radically with online learning [17]. As a result educators need guidance on how to best design and

The research is funded through Joint Programs: Embedding Virtual Exchange (JPROV) by the European Commission Erasmus+ Programme and Aalto Online Learning - Online Hybrid Lab.

© Springer Nature Switzerland AG 2022
A. Drechsler et al. (Eds.): DESRIST 2022, LNCS 13229, pp. 433–444, 2022.
https://doi.org/10.1007/978-3-031-06516-3_32

deliver online courses [24]. A number of studies aim to support educators in creating high-quality online courses. For example, research on online learning theories or pedagogical approaches provides a starting point for designing online courses that provide a good learning experience for students [2, 4, 26]. Other researchers examine general success factors such as an increased social presence for effective online teaching [30]. However, these studies do not provide actionable guidelines, recommendations and activities that educators can implement with reasonable effort in new or already existing courses. Research shows that the quality of online courses is particularly dependent on educators adopting practices appropriate for online teaching [6]. Therefore, other studies focus on what competences a successful educator should have and how to acquire those [28, 35]. While checklists or locally collected slide decks in departments may provide guidance on acquiring certain competences, these are rarely interactive or use visual elements - although interactivity can engage educators and support them in their learning process [25, 34]. In addition, there is no central repository for educators where all recommendations are gathered and presented in a meaningful, actionable way. Aiming to fill this gap, we explore the following research question: *How to design a virtual toolbox in order to support educators when creating online learning courses?*

We address this research question by conducting a design science research (DSR) project and develop an interactive and engaging, freely available toolbox that is accessible to all educators to support them in creating high-quality online courses. In three design cycles, design knowledge for virtual toolboxes for educators providing guidance on creating online learning is developed and evaluated. Based on a literature review and a requirements' elicitation workshop with educators, we propose four design requirements (DRs) and derive design principles (DPs). These principles are instantiated in an artifact and evaluated. Building on the evaluation results, the design knowledge is iteratively complemented and improved, yielding a set of six DPs.

2   Foundations and Related Work

Online learning removes temporal and spatial restrictions of traditional teaching and provides students with a good learning experience [29]. In online learning, educators and students are at a distance while students access learning materials and interact with fellow students through technology [26]. To ensure a reasonable learning outcome, online courses need to be well-designed [26]. The pandemic pushed the need for online settings to yet another level, resulting in many educators entering a virtual classroom for the first time. Given that online teaching requires different competences than traditional teaching [35], educators need guidance on what practices and tools to draw on when teaching online. There are several studies that address how to best design an online course. For example, studies on learning theories serve as a foundation for the development of appropriate online course materials [2]. In the wake of the Covid-19 pandemic, studies on pedagogical approaches in online learning revealed that previously used approaches no longer work in a changed learning environment. For example, as personal contact points in online environments are weakened, Itow [19] recommends practices such as fostering a relationship with students to improve the learning experience. Further research points to factors that make an online course a success. For example, Richardson and Swan [30] showed that an increased social presence in online teaching is an important factor for students being satisfied with their perceived learning performance. Educators themselves are crucial in improving the quality of online courses by applying practices that are suitable for online teaching [6]. Therefore, several studies focus on the role of educators [7]. Research suggests specific sets of competences that educators should require to successfully teach online [28]. Moreover, Taylor and McQuiggan [35] examine what support educators need to obtain these proposed competences. For example, they indicate that educators need flexibility in learning new skills. Otherwise, professional development doesn't fit into already busy schedules [35].

To provide guidance, standards and frameworks have been developed to enable educators to meet the current challenges. Baran and Correia [6] develop a conceptual framework, indicating how educational settings can motivate educators exploring online learning possibilities by offering workshops, a peer-group community or rewards and recognition. However, the study does not provide practices that educators can immediately adopt in their online courses. While handbooks [6] or checklists [5,31] provide more actionable guidelines, these textual descriptions of recommendations are not interactive or engaging and, thus, do not motivate educators to explore the topic more widely [25,34].

3 Overview of the Design Science Research Project

Design Science Cycle	Design Cycle 1	Design Cycle 2	Design Cycle 3	⊟ Performed steps ⊟ Planned steps
Awareness	Workshop with educators	Review of usability literature	Review of co-development literature	
Suggestion	Synthesis DRs, development of DP	Refinement of DPs	Refinement of DP	
Development	Instantiation of artifact	Instantiation of improved artifact	Instantiation of improved artifact	
Evaluation	Interviews with users	Focus group workshop	Field study	
Conclusion	Interview analysis	Focus group analysis	Evaluation analysis, further research	

Fig. 1. Overview of our iterative design cycles and their research activities

This research project follows the DSR approach by Kuechler and Vaishnavi [22] to investigate design knowledge for toolboxes that enable educators to create high-quality online learning. This approach is particularly suited to address our research problem as it allows to solve a real-world problem by iteratively designing, evaluating, and improving the artifact's usability and applicability [16]. We structured our research along the phases of awareness of the problem, suggestion, development, evaluation, and conclusion in three cycles. Figure 1 provides an overview of the actions performed in the respective phase of the DSR cycle.

The focus of the **first cycle** was to gain an understanding of the design requirements (DRs) and to translate those into theory-driven initial DPs. We started with a workshop and a literature review to grasp the challenges educators face in creating online courses and assess the support research offers for those challenges. In total, we purposefully sampled 38 educators, professors and other lecturers from seven European universities from Sweden, Finland, Germany, Portugal, France, Italy, and Spain, to elicit requirements for future guidance. Based on the derived DRs, we developed a set of theory-grounded DPs that describe the generic functions and capabilities of the artifact [8]. In particular, we built our DPs based on the interactivity effects model [34], the multimedia principle [25], and usability literature [27]. We instantiated the DPs in an initial artifact and subsequently evaluated the DPs in semi-structured interviews and user tests with four educators. The educators (avg. age = 31 years) were purposefully sampled and had, on average, two years of experience with teaching in general and 1.5 years with online teaching. This first evaluation episode focused on usability. For the interviews we followed the guidelines of Glaeser and Laudel [14] and, building on ISO 9241-110 on human-system interaction, we developed an interview guideline [18]. The ISO standard specifies principles to ensure the usability of a system, i.e., its effective, efficient and satisfying use [18], which is why we regarded it as a useful foundation for the evaluation interviews. The results confirmed the validity of the proposed requirements and revealed possibilities for further improvement - leading to the addition of DP5 (cf. Sects. 4 and 5).

The aim of the **second cycle** was to enrich the design's theoretical foundations with an expanded literature review and to improve the artifact. Building on the results of the first evaluation cycle and an in-depth literature review on usability, we refined and extended the DPs. Accordingly, a new and improved artifact was instantiated, which was evaluated using a focus group workshop. Six purposefully sampled educators from various disciplines from Sweden, Germany, Finland, and Portugal took part in the focus group workshop. These educators were more experienced in teaching in general (on avg. 10.7 years), yet were rather new to teaching online (on avg. 1.5 years). Hence, we considered them suitable to evaluate the artifact. We decided on a focus group workshop since it offers an opportunity for participants to discuss and build on each other's comments. The workshop structure was developed according to the recommendations of Gibson and Arnott [13]. Results of the evaluation episode (cf. Sect. 5) provided the starting point for the next cycle.

The **third cycle** focused on further refinements of the DPs and the artifact. Prompted by the results of the focus group workshop, a literature review on co-development approaches was conducted to further extend the DPs. Subsequently, a final quantitative evaluation of the enhanced artifact will be performed. The results of the three design cycles are described below.

4 Designing Virtual Toolboxes to Support Educators in Online Learning

Based on three successive design cycles, we identified four DRs and developed six associated DPs to contribute design knowledge for creating engaging virtual toolboxes. The DRs and DPs are described in the following.

4.1   Design Requirements for Virtual Toolboxes

We derive our first and second DR from a workshop with educators on the topic of challenges in online learning and how to overcome those. Insights of the workshop showed that educators are highly interested in new methods, activities and tools that enable high-quality online learning. Yet, educators also pointed out that they currently lack guidance in this area. Ideas such as the establishment of training for educators before launching an online course revealed the desire for a solution that allows learning about online course design. Thus, we formed our first requirement: *The toolbox should enable learning about how to improve online course design (DR1).*

In addition, workshop participants expressed the observation that existing information about online course design often covers only conceptual foundations. The educators stated that abstract information will not motivate them to work on the implementation of recommendations. Hence, our second requirement becomes: *The toolbox should provide actionable content to motivate the implementation of practices (DR2).*

Due to steadily enhancing possibilities of web applications, research indicates that it is not sufficient to merely make the application usable, but it is important to move beyond that [23]. One crucial aspect for the development of successful online applications is that they engage users [11]. User engagement is concerned with the quality of the user experience, highlighting the positive aspects of interacting with an online application and creating a desire to use it repeatedly [23]. Thus, to ensure that the artifact is used repeatedly, our third DR is: *The toolbox should engage users and inspire them to create high-quality online courses (DR3).*

To satisfy user needs, usability is a core aspect when developing an interactive system [21]. This includes, for example, that users can easily understand for which purpose they can utilize the system and how they interact with it. Further, an accessible and familiar interface can help the user to accomplish the tasks [27]. Thus, our fourth requirement becomes: *The toolbox should be easy to use and provide a well-structured interface to reduce the effort required to create online courses (DR4).*

4.2   Design Principles for Virtual Toolboxes

In three design cycles, based on the DRs and insights from theory, prior research, and two evaluation episodes, we propose six DPs that describe how to design virtual toolboxes to support educators in creating online learning.

Research provides considerable evidence on how appropriate content design can enhance users' learning process [25]. For example, in order to understand how a bicycle pump works, learners can read a text describing its functions. However, when in addition to words, graphics explain the process, learners can understand complex relationships more efficiently as both the visual and verbal channels of the brain are used for learning [25]. These findings are grounded in the multimedia principle, which states that humans tend to learn better from words and pictures combined than from words alone [25]. Thus, addressing DR1, to support educators in learning how to design high-quality online courses, the multimedia principle is incorporated in our first DP: *Provide the toolbox with a combination of textual and visual information to maximize the learning outcome (DP1).*

Interactivity has been identified as one of the main drivers of user engagement [33]. It can be defined as "the extent to which users can participate in modifying the form and content of a mediated environment in real time" [32, p.84]. An important observation regarding interactive systems is that users are active and capable of performing actions, merely being passive recipients [34]. Sundar's [33] interactivity effects model suggests that interactive elements in the form of modality and message interactivity promote user engagement. Modality interactivity focuses on the features that are available on the interface to offer users the ability to initiate interactions. Message interactivity implies that users receive responses from the system depending on their previous actions [34]. Therefore, to address DR3, we form our second DP: *Provide the toolbox with interactive elements to engage users (DP2).*

In addition to modality and message interactivity, Sundar [33] showed that source interactivity promotes user engagement. Source interactivity describes the degree to which the interface allows users to manipulate the displayed information from the system [34]. Thus, we propose: *Provide the toolbox with customizable elements that allow users to decide which details are important (DP3).*

Research has shown that time is one of the greatest barriers for educators to engage with materials or training for creating online learning [35]. Therefore, it is particularly important that the content of the toolbox comprises explicit guidelines that are easy to implement (cf. DR2). Thus, we form our fourth DP: *Provide the toolbox with specific implementation guidelines to ensure the adoption of recommendations is quick and easy (DP4).*

Results of our first evaluation episode revealed that functional as well as content-related explanations are important for users' understanding. In particular, usability literature provides guidance for the improvement of the artifact. Nielsen [27] suggests providing a short and precise documentation to help users understand how to complete their tasks. Especially, descriptions of how the toolbox can be used and explanations of educational concepts applied in the artifact should improve the usability [27] (cf. DR4). Thus, we enhance our design foundation with: *Provide the toolbox with a description of the content and the visualization to support understanding (DP5).*

During the second evaluation episode, participants of our focus group workshop expressed the need to foster a community around the toolbox. Research indicates that a co-development approach can lead to higher user engagement and an increased motivation to use the co-created toolbox [9, 15]. A possibility to add practices enables the user to continuously co-design the content of the toolbox. Hence, educators have the opportunity to share their knowledge with fellow educators. In addition, the toolbox is constantly updated with new recommendations and latest developments. Thus, we propose the sixth DP: *Provide the toolbox with elements that enable educators to complement the content (DP6)*.

4.3 Instantiation

Our proposed DPs were instantiated in a first artifact. The artifact was developed using the JavaScript library D3.js, which allows developing interactive visual elements using web standards. The toolbox is implemented as a website which is freely available to all educators. To generate an initial content basis, we invited educators from seven universities and seven European countries to share their practices for creating and enhancing online courses. From those we performed a data cleaning and derived generic recommendations and practices and used them in the first artifact. So far, 12 practices and 11 tools are included in the artifact. In the following, using an exemplary user story, we demonstrate how the toolbox can be used and how the DPs were instantiated.

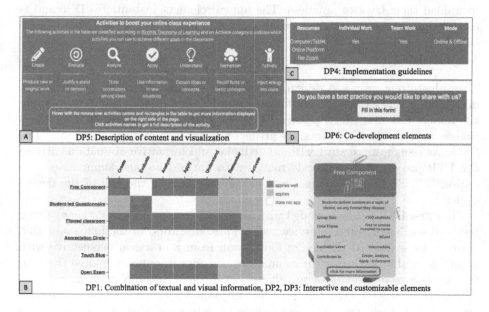

Fig. 2. Instantiation of the proposed DPs in a virtual toolbox

Imagine, an educator wants to design a new online course for the upcoming term. As she does not have much experience with online teaching, she is looking for guidance and visits the virtual toolbox. When opening the toolbox, she first finds a short description of how to use the toolbox (cf. DP5; Fig. 2; A). In addition, she is introduced to Bloom's taxonomy [1], which is used in the toolbox to structure the recommendations and practices. As the taxonomy categorizes learning objectives into different levels of complexity, from basic knowledge to advanced creation [1], we regarded it as a useful structuring approach for the toolbox (cf. DP5; Fig. 2; A). The instantiation of DP5 with a short description of how to use the toolbox as well as the explanation of the educational concepts applied in the toolbox ensure understanding and usability [27].

Next, a matrix visualization helps her grasp quickly which learning objectives the different practices pursue (Fig. 2; B). The combination of visual content and textual explanations enables a quick understanding of complex relationships and thus supports learning [25] (cf. DP1; Fig. 2; B). Also, by hovering over and clicking on different practices, she can interactively explore them. This interactivity is intended to support user engagement [34] (cf. DP2, DP3; Fig. 2; B).

Having found an interesting practice, she clicks on it to display specific implementation guidelines (cf. DP3, DP4; Fig. 2; B,C). This direct reaction of the toolbox promotes interactivity and, thus, facilitates user engagement [34].

After exploring the toolbox for some time, she feels better prepared to create the new online course. In order for more educators to benefit from it, she shares the virtual toolbox with some more experienced colleagues and asks them to upload their favorite practices. The upload element instantiates DP6 and is intended to promote user engagement (cf. DP6; Fig. 2; D).

5   Evaluation

To evaluate our proposed design, we refer to the framework for evaluation in design science (FEDS) [37]. We followed the FEDS's recommendation to apply the human risk and effectiveness strategy because a crucial goal of the evaluations was to consistently prove the artifact's benefits in real situations [37]. The framework suggests to start with an artificial and formative evaluation early in the DSR project and to quickly move on to naturalistic and summative evaluation [37]. So far, the artifact was evaluated twice at the end of the design cycles.

The first DSR cycle concluded with an evaluation episode consisting of a user test and semi-structured interviews with four educators. In the first evaluation episode, we evaluated the design foundation from a practical perspective with regard to usability. During the evaluation, the educators first explored the artifact at their own pace. Subsequently, we asked them to complete tasks with the assistance of the toolbox, e.g., selecting an online learning activity to energize students. The tasks were designed to help us determine possible comprehension or usability issues related to the artifact. Semi-structured interviews based on ISO standards enabled us to evaluate whether the artifact is easy to use and identify usability issues. In sum, we received positive feedback regarding the applicability and usability of the toolbox in creating online courses. In addition, we received valuable feedback on the importance of improving understanding for the use of the artifact. To enhance usability, we thus extended our design foundation and included DP5 specifying a short introductory description of the toolbox and the concepts used.

For the second evaluation episode, we conducted a focus group workshop to evaluate the artifact's applicability. Further, we evaluated whether the proposed

DPs and the resulting artifact meet educators' needs of getting guidance when creating online courses. Educators explored the artifact and answered a set of open-ended questions such as "How would you use the toolbox to assist you when creating online learning?". The questions initiated a discussion on improvement potential and further development ideas. The resulting rich data set provided a useful source for our evaluation phase [36]. This evaluation episode revealed the need to build a community around virtual toolboxes to continuously extend the content. As a result, we reviewed literature on co-development approaches and added an additional design principle, DP6. DP6 contains the possibility for educators to co-design the toolbox with the submission of own practices and, hence, addresses the evaluation results. Finally, the evaluation results indicated that the artifact motivates users to explore more, e.g., participants expressed that the hovering functionality makes them curious to get more specific instructions.

6   Discussion

6.1   Implications for Research and Practice

In this research paper, we propose and evaluate a design foundation that guides the development of a virtual toolbox to support educators when creating online learning. In particular, we propose six theory-grounded DPs, that we instantiate and evaluate in three design cycles. Overall, the results of our evaluation indicate that designing a toolbox based on our DPs can engage educators and guide them in creating online learning. We therefore contribute with valuable design knowledge that extends previous research [31,35] on guidance for creating online learning and serves as a starting point for future research. In the following, we want to point out the main contributions of this research paper.

Our design foundation was developed and evaluated in close collaboration with educators from various European universities. The DRs indicate which requirements tools should fulfill to support educators in creating online learning. Not only the toolbox's content is important, but also its representation. Further, the DPs build on insights from theory and prior research and, for example, seek to foster user engagement by providing interactive elements. Our results revealed that an interactive visualization as well as actionable guidelines reduce the effort and increase educators' motivation to learn about high-quality course design. Thus, our results open up future research opportunities for developing guidance for educators. Future research might draw on the presented design knowledge to explore how to develop support tools in adjacent areas. Studies in the field of lifelong learning indicate that besides university, learning continues in all areas of life [3]. Hence, the proposed generic DRs and DPs might be used to create interactive tools that engage users and promote learning, e.g., in the context of corporate knowledge transfer [38].

Furthermore, the introduced interactive freely available virtual toolbox provides educators with a novel tool to interactively learn about online course design. It not only provides suggestions for practices that have proven to be successful in online learning, but also actionable recommendation on their implementation. The toolbox visualizes the material in an interactive way to motivate educators to explore it and to improve their online courses. In addition, with the co-development approach, educators have the unique opportunity to actively share their experience and co-create online learning.

6.2   Limitations and Future Research

Although our research follows established guidelines for conducting DSR [22], there are some limitations that need to be discussed. So far, we conducted two evaluation episodes, including interviews and a focus group workshop. However, our evaluation remained formative, which is why our artifact will need to be evaluated in another summative evaluation [37]. Second, we note a limitation with regard to sampling the workshop participants in the second evaluation episode. The toolbox has been iteratively developed and tested in collaboration with educators that have already started exploring online teaching. This might indicate that they have an intrinsic interest to improve their online course design, which might bias their evaluation of the artifact. Therefore, future evaluation episodes should also consider educators that have no prior experience.

These limitations also point the way for future research activities in the third cycle of our DSR project. We will conclude the third design cycle with a summative evaluation, conducting a field study with a diverse set of educators. Following Checkland's [10] guidelines, this evaluation episode will focus on the impact the artifact has on efficacy, effectiveness, and efficiency. That is, we examine whether the artifact supports and improves the design process of online teaching (efficacy); whether the artifact can be used successfully for creating online courses (effectiveness); and whether the use of the artifact requires an inappropriate amount of time or any additional resources (efficiency).

7   Conclusion

Schools, organizations, and higher education are in a stage of transition towards online learning. Yet, designing online learning requires different skills and methods compared to traditional teaching. Hence, educators seek guidance on how to create online courses. This paper presents the findings of our DSR project on how to design a virtual toolbox that guides educators in creating high-quality online learning. We derive four DRs and six theory-grounded DPs, that are instantiated and evaluated with educators. The proposed design foundation may serve as a knowledge base to develop engaging online tools providing guidance with online learning. In addition, we present the virtual toolbox for creating online learning - a powerful tool that can interactively guide educators striving to create high-quality online learning. Our evaluation shows that the toolbox can increase educators' motivation to learn about high-quality online course design.

References

1. Anderson, L.W., Krathwohl, D.R., Bloom, B.S.: A Taxonomy for Learning, Teaching, and Assessing: a Revision of Bloom's Taxonomy of Educational Objectives. Longman, New York (2001)
2. Arghode, V., Brieger, E.W., Mclean, G.N.: Adult learning theories: implications for online instruction. Eur. J. Training Dev. **41**(7), 593–609 (2017)
3. Aspin, D.N., Chapman, J.D.: Lifelong learning: concepts and conceptions. Int. J. Lifelong Educ. **19**(1), 2–19 (2000)
4. Bailey, C.J., Card, K.A.: Effective pedagogical practices for online teaching: perception of experienced instructors. Internet High. Educ. **12**(3–4), 152–155 (2009)
5. Baldwin, S.J., Ching, Y.-H.: An online course design checklist: development and users' perceptions. J. Comput. High. Educ. **31**(1), 156–172 (2019). https://doi.org/10.1007/s12528-018-9199-8
6. Baran, E., Correia, A.P.: A professional development framework for online teaching. TechTrends **58**(5), 96–102 (2014). https://doi.org/10.1007/s11528-014-0791-0
7. Baran, E., Correia, A.P., Thompson, A.: Transforming online teaching practice: critical analysis of the literature on the roles and competencies of online teachers. Distance Educ. **32**(3), 421–439 (2011)
8. Baskerville, R., Pries-Heje, J.: Explanatory design theory. Bus. Inf. Syst. Eng. **2**(5), 271–282 (2010). https://doi.org/10.1007/s12599-010-0118-4
9. Benz, C.: Is it more than allocating funds? exploring the effect of enterprise crowdfunding on employee engagement. In: Proceedings of the 55th Hawaii International Conference on System Sciences, pp. 6984–6993 (2022)
10. Checkland, P.: Soft systems methodology: a thirty year retrospective. Syst. Res. Behav. Sci. **17**(suppl.), 11–58 (2000)
11. Doherty, K., Doherty, G.: Engagement in HCI: conception, theory and measurement. ACM Comput. Surv. **51**(5), 1–39 (2019)
12. Dwivedi, Y.K., et al.: Impact of COVID-19 pandemic on information management research and practice. Int. J. Inf. Manag. **55**, 1–20 (2020)
13. Gibson, M., Arnott, D.: The use of focus groups in design science research. In: 18th Australasian Conference on Information Systems, vol. 26, pp. 327–337 (2007)
14. Gläser, J., Laudel, G.: Experteninterviews und Qualitative Inhaltsanalyse. Verlag für Sozialwissenschaften, Wiesbaden (2010)
15. Guzel, M., Sezen, B., Alniacik, U.: Drivers and consequences of customer participation into value co-creation: a field experiment. J. Prod. Brand Manag. **30**(7), 1047–1061 (2020)
16. Hevner, A., Chatterjee, S.: Design Science Research in Information Systems, vol. 22, pp. 9–22. Springer, Boston (2010). https://doi.org/10.1007/978-1-4419-5653-8_2
17. Huett, J., Moller, L., Foshay, W.R., Coleman, C.: The evolution of distance education: implications for instructional design on the potential of the web. TechTrends **52**(5), 63–67 (2008)
18. ISO 9241-110: Ergonomics of human-system interaction - Part 110: interaction principles. International Organization for Standardization (ISO), Geneva (2020)
19. Itow, R.C.: Fostering valuable learning experiences by transforming current teaching practices: practical pedagogical approaches from online practitioners. Inf. Learn. Sci. **121**(5–6), 433–442 (2020)

20. Jiménez-Zarco, A., Békés, V., Khalili, H., García-Morales, V.J., Garrido-Moreno, A., Martín-Rojas, R.: The transformation of higher education after the COVID disruption: emerging challenges in an online learning scenario. Front. Psychol. **12**, 1–6 (2021)

21. Kim, J., Han, S.H.: A methodology for developing a usability index of consumer electronic products. Int. J. Ind. Ergon. **38**(3–4), 333–345 (2008)

22. Kuechler, B., Vaishnavi, V.: On theory development in design science research: anatomy of a research project. Eur. J. Inf. Syst. **17**(5), 489–504 (2008)

23. Lalmas, M., O'Brien, H., Yom-Tov, E.: Measuring user engagement, **6** (2014)

24. Martin, F., Ritzhaupt, A., Kumar, S., Budhrani, K.: Award-winning faculty online teaching practices: course design, assessment and evaluation, and facilitation. Internet High. Educ. **42**, 34–43 (2019)

25. Mayer, R.E.: Introduction to multimedia learning. In: The Cambridge Handbook of Multimedia Learning, New York, Second Edition, pp. 1–24. Cambridge University Press (2014)

26. Mohamed, A.: Foundations of educational theory for online learning. In: Theory and Practice of Online Learning, vol. 2, pp. 3–32. Athabasca University Press, Athabasca (2004)

27. Nielsen, J.: Enhancing the explanatory power of usability heuristics. In: Conference on Human Factors in Computing Systems - Proceedings, pp. 152–158 (1994)

28. Oliver, K., Osborne, J., Brady, K.: What are secondary students' expectations for teachers in virtual school environments? Distance Educ. **30**(1), 23–45 (2009)

29. Panigrahi, R., Srivastava, P.R., Sharma, D.: Online learning: adoption, continuance, and learning outcome-a review of literature. Int. J. Inf. Manag. **43**, 1–14 (2018)

30. Richardson, J.C., Swan, K.: Examining social presence in online courses in relation to students' perceived learning and satisfaction. J. Asynchronous Learn. Netw. **7**(1) (2003)

31. Smith, T.: Fifty-one competencies for online instruction. J. Educators Online **2**(2), 1–18 (2005)

32. Steuer, J.: Defining virtual reality: dimensions determining telepresence. J. Commun. **42**(4), 73–93 (1992)

33. Sundar, S.S.: Social psychology of interactivity in human-website interaction. In: Oxford Handbook of Internet Psychology, pp. 1–18. Oxford University Press (2012)

34. Sundar, S.S., Jia, H., Waddell, T.F., Huang, Y.: Toward a theory of interactive media effects (TIME) four models for explaining how interface features affect user psychology. In: The Handbook of the Psychology of Communication Technology, pp. 47–86. Wiley Blackwell, Chichester (2015)

35. Taylor, A., McQuiggan, C.: Faculty development programming: if we build it, will they come? Educause Q. **31**(3), 28–37 (2008)

36. Tremblay, M.C., Hevner, A.R., Berndt, D.J.: The use of focus groups in design science research. In: Design research in information systems, Boston, pp. 121–143. Springer (2010). https://doi.org/10.1007/978-1-4419-5653-8_10

37. Venable, J., Pries-Heje, J., Baskerville, R.: FEDS: a Framework for Evaluation in Design Science research. Eur. J. Inf. Syst. **25**(1), 77–89 (2016). https://doi.org/10.1057/ejis.2014.36

38. Von Krogh, G., Ichijo, K., Nonaka, I.: Enabling Knowledge Creation: How to Unlock the Mystery of Tacit Knowledge and Release the Power of Innovation. Oxford University Press, New York (2011)

DSR Teaching Support: A Checklist for Better DSR Research Design Presentations

Marcel Cahenzli[✉]

University of St.Gallen, Müller-Friedbergstrasse 8, 9000 St. Gallen, Switzerland
`marcel.cahenzli@unisg.ch`

Abstract. Students that first learn about and wish to apply Design Science Research (DSR) perceive difficulties in communicating DSR research designs. This, however, is an important communication use case, since more senior design researchers need to gain a good understanding of the DSR research design propositions in order to provide adequate feedback and thus, support the new generation of design researchers. This study features an artefact that fills junior design researchers' unsatisfied need for support in presenting DSR research designs. The artefact was built based on knowledge from the problem environment (i.e., a research methods course) and the emerging body of literature on DSR communication. It is evaluated in a natural field experiment, and the results indicate that the artefact is useful. A contribution of this article is the artefact itself, which is presented explicitly and can be re-used freely by DSR instructors.

Keywords: Design Science Research · DSR communication · Teaching support

1 Introduction

In a feedback session about research design proposals, a student who pitched a Design Science Research (DSR) research design came up to the teaching staff—including the author of this article. He asked: "How am I supposed to present a convincing DSR research design if I have not conducted the study yet? Unlike in descriptive research, I can hardly predict the iterations, the requirements for a solution, or even the outcomes." With that question, this student is not alone. Across various DSR courses and eight semesters of a research methods course (including both descriptive and design research), the author observed that presentations of DSR research designs are often ill-structured, unclear, and considered by students as being more complicated than presentations of descriptive research designs. While most students understand the underlying principles of DSR, their difficulties in communicating a study design make evaluating their course performance, their research designs, and ultimately the course itself difficult for DSR instructors. Having identified this issue as a problem class, the author has conducted a DSR study to create a communication support artefact that instructors can provide to their students, as outlined in this article.

A. Drechsler et al. (Eds.): DESRIST 2022, LNCS 13229, pp. 445–457, 2022.
https://doi.org/10.1007/978-3-031-06516-3_33

In a broader context, presenting and interpreting Design Science Research (DSR) work has been found to be challenging for design researchers, reviewers, and editors alike [1]. This is not just an issue that concerns junior design researchers and students but also more experienced researchers seeking to express their design research projects and outcomes in an acceptable form [2]. Thereby, "given the complexity of DSR projects and the various ways a DSR project might contribute to (design knowledge), how comprehensively and effectively a DSR project is planned and communicated can effect its likelihood of success" [3]. The DSR community has recognized the importance of communication [4] and brought forth support for various specific communication situations [e.g., 1, 3, 5, 6]. While this support tends to focus on article-writing, many other communication situations exist (e.g., grant proposal writing, project pitch meetings, or student presentations [7]). This article contributes to this growing DSR communication literature by adding DSR students' use case of communicating DSR research designs. This is a relevant use case because better communication of research plans by junior design researchers allows instructors to provide them with better feedback and to help them create better DSR studies, contributing to their professional evolution into effective design researchers. That the educational context for DSR is a current and high-relevance issue for the IS community can be evidenced, for example, by the fact that there was a professional development workshop at ICIS 2021 entitled "Teaching Design Science Research" [8], or that there is an "Education and DSR (EDSR)" track at DESRIST 2022.

In this study, the DSR methodology by Peffers et al. [9] is used as a reference approach. After presenting the knowledge base and how this reference approach was implemented, the emerging artefact is presented in its entirety. It is a checklist artefact that DSR instructors can provide to their students. It informs students about what to present, in which order, and, to some degree, at what level of abstraction. The article ends with the evaluation of the artefact. A natural field experiment was used to evaluate its effectiveness in the real-world context.

2 Background Knowledge

This background knowledge section provides pointers to literature that support the relevance of the research problem and the need for an artefact, as well as relevant knowledge for the artefact creation.

2.1 Context of the Research Problem and Need for a Solution

Already in their seminal article about the DSR methodology, Peffers et al. [9] have identified "communication" as a relevant topic for design researchers. While the communication of DSR projects was not focal in their article, it has two main appearances. First, it is the sixth phase of a DSR project (i.e., the summative communication of a DSR study): "Communicate the problem and its importance, the artefact, its utility and novelty, the rigor of its design, and its effectiveness to researchers and other relevant audiences" [9]. Second, Peffers et al. [9] suggest that design researchers may use the

DSR methodology as a guiding framework for communicating their research projects ("This effort contributes to IS research by providing a commonly accepted framework for successfully carrying out DS research and a mental model for its presentation", [9]). In the subsequent years, a stream of DSR Communication literature has slowly started to manifest itself. It contains analyses about publication-related problems [e.g., 4], as well as support for effectively communicating research projects. These discussions are mostly concerned with summative, academia-facing article-writing [1, 9, 10], but there is also guidance on how to communicate aspects of design research projects (e.g., the problem space [5]; design theory [2]; design principles [2]), or how to present projects to non-academic audiences [e.g., 3, 6].

Especially junior design researchers seem to seek and be grateful for explicit guidance on how to present their design research projects (e.g., as cited in [4]: "Thanks to the DSR giants for publishing guidelines on DSR. This was very helpful in knowing how to present our work."). While there is a further need to develop support for communicating DSR projects in general, one particular research gap is that there is a lack of support for presenting DSR projects at earlier (non-complete) project stages [3], including project plans [7]. The latter is an important communication use case for junior design researchers and students. After all, more experienced design researchers can provide useful feedback only if the project plans are communicated effectively. In the design research study presented in this article, this use case provides the research problem (i.e., lack of guidance on how to present DSR research designs in the context of teaching DSR). The research question is: How can students present their DSR research designs in the context of a research methods course?

2.2 Knowledge that Informs the Artefact Design

The knowledge that informs the artefact design includes two conceptually different parts: knowledge from and about the problem environment and knowledge from past research [11, 12].

Knowledge about the Problem Environment and Design Requirements.
Because the design requirements for a solution are based on the problem environment, the problematic communication use case is presented before the design requirements.

The communication use case is the presentation of a DSR research design in the context of a research methods course. The specific course used for implementing and evaluating the artefact is a master course at a Swiss university in a business innovation program. The students learn about descriptive and prescriptive research during this course. They construct research designs in small groups as part of their graded assignments. After two intermediary presentations of their research designs, the students record a voice-over-PowerPoint presentation. That presentation can be up to fifteen minutes long, and it is the primary constituent of their examination. For this reason, the students' motivation to perform well (i.e., to convince the professors of their understanding of the course contents and their ability to apply this knowledge) is high. The students are free to choose with whom they wish to form a group and for what research problem they wish to create a research design. They can create a research design for a descriptive or for a prescriptive research project. However, the interest for this article lies in the prescriptive research projects.

In an initial, pragmatic design iteration, the instructors have created a general checklist about what students ought to present in the final presentation to satisfy the informational needs that underlie the grading. This has proven helpful for students that presented descriptive research project designs. However, the groups that opted for DSR research designs were unsure about what aspects of their research designs to present, in what order to present them and how to explicate iterations. With this starting point, the research problem for this design research study was identified. To further clarify the problem and specify the design requirements, the author has elicited the needs of the instructors and created a set of design requirements based on discussions with the instructors and the course materials. The following tables present the informational needs and the design requirements for an artefact that emerged from this process.

Table 1. Informational needs to be satisfied by student presentations

Informational Aspect: Questions to be answered
Research Problem: What is it, how does it materialize, why does it not disappear?
Research Question: What is it, how does it specify the problem, why is this sensible?
Research Gap: What is the gap, and how was that gap identified/investigated?
Knowledgebase: What is it in this study, how is it used, and why?
Methodology: Which reference approach is used, how was it chosen and applied?
Design Requirements: What are the requirements, how are they elicited and why so?
Procedures: Why are which procedures used for artefact design and evaluation?
Target Outcomes: What is it, and why is the proposed approach suitable to reach it?

Table 2. Requirements (R1–4) of instructors and students toward a supporting artefact

R1: The artefact must specifically support students in presenting DSR research designs in the context of a research methods course
R2: The artefact must support the students in creating presentations that satisfy the central stakeholder needs
R3: The artefact must support students in the explication of their research design presentations
R4: The artefact must integrate well into a research methods course environment

Knowledge Based on Past Research. This study is informed by research about general DSR communication (in particular, a general framework for DSR communication, see: [7]) and existing approaches for addressing related communication issues.

General DSR Communication. According to the framework of DSR communication in [7], effective communication of DSR projects relies on characteristics of a specific communication situation and a communication design process (Fig. 1). The characteristics inform the process, and these include the role of the audience, the means and format of communication or the project stage. According to the explanations in their article, characteristics of a communication situation have consistent effects on how the communication is designed. For example, the role of the audience is the main determinant of the purpose of communication, and the stage of a project affects the selection of contents and how these content elements are presented. The communication design process consists of five steps, during which knowledge about the communication situation is accounted for.

This framework is use case agnostic and should therefore also be applicable to the use case of student presentations. "Applying" it can mean one of two things in this context: Either the framework is used to communicate a DSR project (including the last step of explicating the communication story), or the framework is contextualized by adding information about a use case to generate more specific guidance [7]. The latter is the approach chosen for answering the research question and, thus, the need for guidance in the use case of student presentations of DSR research designs.

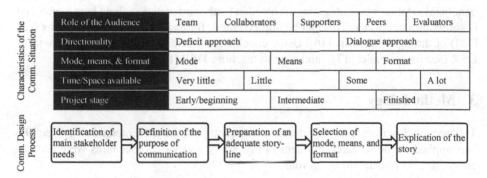

Fig. 1. Framework of DSR communication, [7]

Using One-Page Overview Artefacts. One approach to shaping such guidance is based on the idea of a single-page portrayal tool. Succinct overviews tools that help capture complex information are also referred to as visual inquiry tools [13]. Such tools are gaining traction as solutions to help navigate complexity. A famous example of such a tool is the Business Model Canvas [14]. There are two recent IS contributions in the context of communicating DSR projects that use the underlying principle of creating an overview of essential aspects that should be accounted for [i.e., 3, 15]. Fundamentally, these contributions present a sheet with pre-defined boxes into which a user can insert information. The usefulness of these artefacts lies in the purposeful selection of adequate dimensions (boxes) to fulfil the purpose of the tool [13]. The DSR grid [3] consists of six dimensions deemed essential to describe a DSR project comprehensively and effectively (problem description, input knowledge, research process, key concepts, solution description, output knowledge). While these dimensions are described further in the manuscript, the 'DSR grid' itself is visualized with white boxes (i.e., without trigger statements that clarify further what information should be added to each box). In contrast, the Portrait of Design Essence [15] consists of nine dimensions, each of which is described with a triggering statement (i.e., an instruction on what to insert into the boxes). Both help identify what is essential to be communicated about a design research project and both simplify the communication task by focusing on core dimensions. This general idea is also used for the artefact that is created in this study. After all, the dimensions that are essential can be specified (based on the informational needs of the audience of the use case, see Table 1). Based on the problem description, merely providing general statements about necessary contents (similar to the dimensions without further prompts in [3]) is ineffective for the focal use case here. However, adding specific prompts might be useful (as in [15]).

Using Lists of Ordered Items to Ensure Completeness. In DSR methodology literature, the provision of general dimensions to consider or core guidelines to follow have gained acceptance while raising requests for more specific instructions (e.g., in the case of the seven guidelines in Hevner et al., 2004; see: [16]). Hence, while it is perceived as beneficial to know what categories to consider, further information about how to proceed is sometimes necessary. This can be implemented, for example, by using prompts (see [15]) or through checklists [16]. Using checklists as guiding artefacts is not new to IS DSR (see for example: [17]), and even to teaching DSR [8].

3   Methodology

This section describes how the reference approach (i.e., the DSR methodology, see [9]) was applied to the research problem in this study and what procedures were used to ensure that the evaluation is rigorous.

3.1   Reference Approach

This study relies on the DSR methodology [9] and considers both the relevance and the rigor cycle in the sense of the three-cycle view of DSR [11]. This implies that (1) the research is informed by the problem environment and the existing knowledge base, (2) that the research contributes to the problem environment and the knowledge base, and (3) that the problem environment is used for evaluating the artefact to ensure its usefulness. The coupling of the DSR methodology and the three-cycle view of DSR is illustrated in Fig. 2, where the reference approach (DSR methodology, gray) indicates the general research process. The rigor cycle (ensuring that the study is conducted rigorously and that it builds upon and contributes to existing literature) and the relevance cycle (ensuring that the research addresses a relevant problem and that the solution is useful) indicate how this process is informed and how it contributes to the knowledge base and the stakeholders. These two cycles are presented in black. The third cycle is the design cycle, which is depicted in the original DSR methodology (gray). Figure 2 also indicates the section numbers in which at least some of the respective processes or results are described.

3.2 Procedures

Not all steps and certainly not all aspects of each step of a DSR project can be presented in a single research article [1]. For this reason, the contents that are outlined explicitly need to be selected [3]. Regarding the operationalization of the research design (i.e., the procedures used), two central processes are presented here: The demonstration of the artefact (i.e., its implementation in a research methods course) and the evaluation of the artefact (i.e., a natural field experiment).

Demonstration. The artefact was created in collaboration with two lecturers of a research methods course. The final version of the artefact (see Sect. 4) was approved by these lecturers. They confirmed that they believe that student groups would be able to convince them more effectively of their understanding of the DSR methodology and of the suitability of their DSR research designs if they use the artefact as compared to the status quo without it. The author has thereafter implemented the artefact in the course material of this research methods course to demonstrate that it can be used in its intended environment. Specifically, the artefact consists of four parts (see Sect. 4), each of which was placed on an individual page of the slide deck that is presented to the students. The artefact was placed in the course presentation along with the instructors' general checklist (see Sect. 2.2). With that, the conceptual and operational feasibility of the artefact (i.e., the demonstration) is fulfilled [9].

Evaluation. The demonstration merely provides evidence that the artefact should work and that it can be implemented or used in its intended environment. It is the task of a more formal evaluation to provide evidence of how well the artefact performs in practice [9]. The identification of observable effects in a natural environment is a research goal that requests for high external validity (hypothesized effects can be observed in the natural environment) rather than internal validity (hypothesized effects between constructs can be observed in a controlled environment [18]). While experiments are generally suitable to test hypotheses, it is the natural field experiment that is best for testing external validity [18, 19]. For this reason and given the research question and the access to a research methods class, the author opted for conducting a natural field experiment to evaluate the artefact.

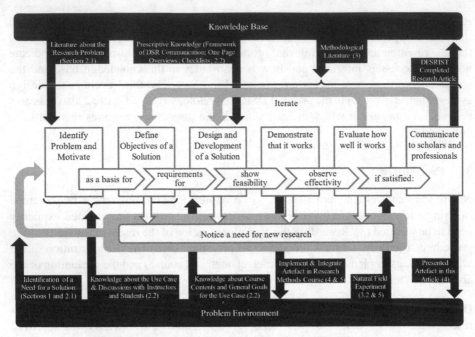

Fig. 2. Implementation of the DSR methodology in this study [9, 11]

The field experiment is natural in the sense that it is conducted in the natural environment, within which the effect of the manipulation should become observable (i.e., an improvement of student presentations), and the participants remained unaware of their participation in the experiment. To operationalize this experimental setting, two conditions were used. The first condition is a control group. For this group, the presentations from spring of 2019 were used. Because the subsequent year would have been the spring semester of 2020, an extraordinary semester in many respects during which a pandemic disturbed both teaching activities, and student collaboration patterns, the presentations of 2021 were used for the manipulated condition. The manipulated condition is characterized by the provision and in-class presentation of the artefact, whereas all other teaching material, modalities, and task descriptions remained exactly the same.

To evaluate the effects of the artefact, the recorded voice-over-PowerPoint presentations of both conditions (n = 18, with 9 presentations per condition) were assessed by independent design researchers. A total of 21 evaluators sequentially watched and evaluated one of sub-set of four presentations, yielding a total of 84 observations (42 evaluations of the manipulated and 42 of the control group). The sub-sets given to the evaluators collectively covered all eighteen presentations. The evaluators are themselves design researchers, and they were acquired by using the personal network of the author. After a short briefing about the task, the participants took, on average, 72 min. The study was conducted as a double-blind design, where neither the instructor nor the evaluators themselves were aware of the condition of each presentation. Unbeknown to the evaluators, they each evaluated two presentations of manipulated and two presentations of un-manipulated groups. The selection and order of the presentation were randomized but with two presentations of each group in a set of four presentations.

The survey that the evaluators were requested to fill in consists of seven-point Likert scale questions (1 = full disagreement, 4 = neutral, 7 = full agreement) about the informational needs that students ought to fulfil (see Table 1). For example: "Research Problem: It is clear to me what the proposed research problem is, how it materializes, and why it does not disappear." In addition, the evaluators were asked whether they think that the students have understood well how to create a DSR research design (i.e., the goal of the course).

4 Artefact Presentation

The design of the artefact itself is inspired by the ideas outlined in Sect. 2.2. Thereby, the artefact design process was based on the framework of DSR communication (Fig. 1). Hence, knowledge from the problem environment was used to contextualize this framework. The design of the artefact was based on the idea of using one-page overview artefacts, such as the boxes for various dimensions that need to be addressed by the communication as presented in vom Brocke and Maedche [3], combined with triggering statements as presented in Chandra Kruse and Nickerson [15]. However, to provide enough granularity (and thus, make the artefact more applicable), many more statements are used in this artefact than in [15]. The final artefact features four dimensions ('boxes' in the sense of the DSR Grid [3]) and 29 triggering statements. The artefact can be freely re-used by instructors of DSR and is therefore presented in full here (Table 3). (While the artefact can be presented on one page, it was presented to the students of the natural field experiment split into one dimension per presentation slide).

Table 3. Presentation of the artefact

Research Problem, Research Question, and Reference Approach
1. The design problem is: _____ (neutral description of the situation)
2. This is a problem for: _____ (which stakeholder group(s)?)
   i. ... whose goal it is to: _____ (focal goals that are not reached)
   ii. ... whose challenges include: _____ (problem-focused challenges)
   iii. ... in the context of: _____ (which context factors accentuate or perpetuate the problem?)
3. This is a relevant problem, because: _____ (provide evidence, e.g., scope * scale, hence, number of stakeholders affected * effect size)
4. We focus on the specific aspect outlined in this research question: _____
5. The research objective is: _____ (what should be designed?)
6. To achieve this, we proceed as follows: __ (summarizing statement indicating the research approach, e.g., the reference approach of Peffers et al., 2007)

Design Methodology and the Knowledgebase
7. We use the following design methodology: __ (presentation of the operationalization of the approach, optional: references to, e.g., Peffers et al., 2007)
8. We justify the choices for our approach as follows: _____
9. We research existing solutions as follows: _____
   i. Existing solutions (from research and practice) are inadequate, because: ___
   ii. However, the following general explanations or solution approaches are promising as a basis for this project: _____
   iii. Based on this foundation, our contribution consists of: _____ (name a specific artefact type and use this type consistently)

Requirements, Construction, and Validation
10. We gather, analyze, and prioritize the design requirements as follows: _____
11. During the artefact construction, we proceed as follows: _____
12. We validate our design as follows: _____
    i. We iterate the design activity until the following conditions are met: __
    ii. We show that the artefact is useable in practice by: _____
    iii. We prove the usefulness of the artefact as follows: _____
13. (For each empirical study: Adequate description of data, namely:
    i. What data is gathered? (quant/qual, content, volume)
    ii. Why and to what end (in the construction process) are these specific data gathered?
    iii. How exactly are these data gathered? Why is this a suitable approach?
    iv. How are these data analyzed? Why is this a suitable approach?

Discussion and Implications
14. Our research design is based on the following assumptions/comes with the following limitations: _____
15. Our research contribution (design knowledge) is: _____
16. Our results enable the following future research: _____
17. This is how our results provide usefulness to practitioners: _____

5   Evaluation Results

The evaluation results can be seen in Table 4, with the averages for the non-manipulated (0) and the manipulated (1) groups and the p-value of a one-tail t-Test.

Table 4. Results and t-test from the evaluation of presentations

Item group:	0 (n = 42)	1 (n = 42)	diff.	t-Test
Clarity about the research problem	5.262	5.548	5.4%	0.160
Clarity about the focus of study (RQ)	4.976	5.190	4.3%	0.210
Clarity about the research gap	4.595	4.548	−1.0%	0.449
Clarity about the knowledge base	4.548	4.548	0.0%	0.500
Clarity about the general approach	4.619	5.238	13.4%	0.047
Clarity about the requirements	4.548	4.595	1.0%	0.444
Clarity about the design process	4.619	4.667	1.0%	0.440
Clarity about the artefact	4.786	4.714	−1.5%	0.409
Goal of the course achieved?	4.619	5.143	11.3%	0.036
Average across all items	4.730	4.910	3.80%	0.182

The average evaluation across all items is 3.8% higher in the manipulated groups than in unmanipulated groups. However, this overall average effect is not significant (p = 0.182). Indeed, many of the informational needs are neither negatively nor positively affected by the manipulation. However, four items have received higher scores (clarity about the research problem, the focus of the study, the general approach, and the achievement of the goal of the course). Two of these items are statistically significant (general approach: p = 0.047; goal of the course: p = 0.036). Hence, all else being equal, the effect of using the artefact leads to better clarity about the research approach and allows students to more clearly express their understanding of DSR (i.e., reach the goal of a DSR methodology class). In natural field experiments, significance values tend to be weaker than in controlled environments because of confounding variables. For this reason, the non-significant but perceptible differences might indicate that the artefact may still affect these variables (i.e., the clarity of the research problem and of the focus of study).

Therewith, the main takeaway of the field experiment is that using the artefact (1) has no negative effect on student presentations; (2) significantly improves the clarity about the approach ("I understand which research approach was chosen, how it is applied, and why this is a suitable approach for addressing the research problem"); (3) significantly improves the users' ability to convince the instructors that they have understood how to create a good research design; (4) may improve the clarity about the research problem and the focus of the study. Beyond these insights, the artefact furthermore satisfies the requirements for a solution as outlined in Table 5.

Table 5. Evaluation of the requirements against the artefact

Table 2	Commentary on requirement satisfaction
R1	The checklist was created for this use case and tested within the use case of presenting a DSR research design in a research methods course, and students are highly supported by the triggering statements
R2	Whereas only some of the informational needs are better satisfied with the artefact, there were no adverse effects. Hence, there may be room for further improvement, but the artefact has a positive average effect
R3	The prompts for each of the four dimensions of the artefact clarify what should be presented and in which order
R4	The artefact integrated well into the course material in the course used for the evaluation. However, the one-page format is generally suitable for distribution in a DSR course setting (e.g., on slides or a PDF)

6   Conclusion

This study addresses the need of students of DSR for support in presenting DSR research designs by considering both knowledge from the problem environment (i.e., research methods courses) and existing literature (e.g., about communicating DSR in general [7], presenting complex information [3, 13, 15], use of checklists [8, 16, 17]). By contextualizing the DSR communication framework [7], an artefact emerged that significantly positively affects the perceived student understanding and the clarity of their DSR research design presentations. It can be easily re-used by DSR instructors, who can thus provide better feedback and help students become better design researchers.

Because the communication of DSR in general (not only research designs and for students) is a pertaining issue, future research could produce further artefacts that apply to other situations, such as conference presentations, article writing, or practice-facing communication—extending the emerging body of DSR communication literature.

References

1. Gregor, S., Hevner, A.R.: Positioning and presenting design science research for maximum impact. MIS Q. **37**(2), 337–355 (2013)
2. Gregor, S., Jones, D.: The anatomy of a design theory. J. Assoc. Inf. Syst. **8**(5), 313–335 (2007)
3. vom Brocke, J., Maedche, A.: The DSR grid: six core dimensions for effective capturing of DSR projects. Electron. Mark. **29**, 379–385 (2019)
4. Tremblay, M.C., VanderMeer, D., Beck, R.: The effects of the quantification of faculty productivity: perspectives from the design science research community. Commun. Assoc. Inf. Syst. **43**(1), 34 (2018)
5. Maedche, A., Gregor, S., Morana, S., Feine, J.: Conceptualization of the problem space in design science research. In: Tulu, B., Djamasbi, S., Leroy, G. (eds.) Extending the Boundaries of Design Science Theory and Practice. Lecture Notes in Computer Science, vol. 11491, pp. 18–31. Springer, Cham (2019). https://doi.org/10.1007/978-3-030-19504-5_2

6. Mirkovski, K., Doyle, C., Liu, L.I.: Use of video narratives to increase relevance in design science research. In: ECIs 2020 Research-in-Progress Papers 18 (2020)

7. Cahenzli, M., Beese, J., Winter, R.: Communication of design research: a use-case agnostic framework and its application. In: Chandra Kruse, L., Seidel, S., Hausvik, G.I. (eds.) The Next Wave of Sociotechnical Design. Lecture Notes in Computer Science, vol. 12807, pp. 162–173. Springer, Cham (2021). https://doi.org/10.1007/978-3-030-82405-1_18

8. Winter, R., vom Brocke, J.: Teaching design science research. In: 42th International Conference on Information Systems (ICIS 2021), Austin TX (2021)

9. Peffers, K., Tuunanen, T., Rothenberger, M., Chatterjee, S.: A design science research methodology for information systems research. J. Manag. Inf. Syst. **24**(3), 45–77 (2007)

10. vom Brocke, J., Winter, R., Hevner, A.R., Maedche, A.: Accumulation and evolution of design knowledge in design science research – a journey through time and space. J. Assoc. Inf. Syst. **21**(3), 520–544 (2020)

11. Hevner, A.R.: A three cycle view of design science research. Scand. J. Inf. Syst. **19**(2), 87–92 (2007)

12. Hevner, A.R., March, S.T., Park, J., Ram, S.: Design science in information systems research. MIS Q. **28**(1), 75–105 (2004)

13. Avdiji, H., Elikan, D., Missonier, S., Pigneur, Y.: A design theory for visual inquiry tools. J. Assoc. Inf. Syst. **21**(3), 695–734 (2020)

14. Osterwalder, A., Pigneur, Y.: Business Model Generation: A Handbook for Visionaries, Game Changers, and Challengers. John Wiley & Sons, New York (2010)

15. Kruse, L.C., Nickerson, J.V.: Portraying design essence. SSRN Electron. J. (2018)

16. Hevner, A., Chatterjee, S.: Design Science Research in Information Systems, pp. 9–22. Springer, Boston (2010). https://doi.org/10.1007/978-1-4419-5653-8_2

17. vom Brocke, J., Simons, A., Riemer, K., Niehaves, B., Plattfaut, R., Cleven, A.: Standing on the shoulders of giants: challenges and recommendations of literature search in information systems research. Commun. Assoc. Inf. Syst. **37**(1), 9 (2015)

18. Cahenzli, M., Aier, S., Haki, K.: Design decisions in behavioral experiments: a review of information systems research. In: Proceedings of the 42th International Conference on Information Systems (ICIS 2021), Austin, TX, p. 17 (2021)

19. Gupta, A., Kannan, K., Sanyal, P.: Economic experiments in information systems. MIS Q. **42**(2), 595–606 (2018)

System Design Principles for Intergenerational Knowledge Sharing

Irawan Nurhas[1,2](✉) ⓘ, Xelia Mattick[1] ⓘ, Stefan Geisler[1] ⓘ, and Jan Pawlowski[1,2] ⓘ

[1] Hochschule Ruhr West University of Applied Sciences, Bottrop, Germany
irawan.nurhas@hs-ruhrwest.de
[2] University of Jyväskylä, Jyväskylä, Finland

Abstract. Up to four generations are potentially involved in education and workspaces. This means that people of different generations can increasingly learn together and share knowledge virtually in the digital age. Nevertheless, the principles for designing systems to support intergenerational knowledge sharing (IKS) are inconclusive. Our results demonstrate the value of applying design science research methodology to capture design principles for IKS systems. We articulate what design goals should be considered and bring more conceptual clarity to this phenomenon by presenting five design principles: a) positive personalization, b) progressive design ecosystem, c) effectual system design, d) iterative goal reflection, e) coopetitive intergenerational tasks. By reflecting on the design process and formalizing a class of design principles, we contribute to design-oriented IKS systems in the digital age.

Keywords: Intergenerational knowledge sharing · Intergenerational innovation · Design principles · Design science research

1 Introduction and Problem Awareness

This study explores the design principles (DPs) underlying digital technology to facilitate intergenerational knowledge sharing (IKS). IKS in this study is defined as knowledge sharing between younger adults and older adults with an age difference of at least 20 years who interact with each other via digital technology [17]. The content of knowledge sharing in this study relates to startup development, thus involving actors between older (experienced) adults and young (potential startup) innovators. Given the current state of the knowledge economy and the digital age, leveraging technology to facilitate such collaboration is becoming increasingly crucial for organizations, including startups [1, 11, 20, 21]. For example, video calls can be used to hold meetings, real-time collaborative ideation using digital whiteboards [3, 11, 21], and physical objects and digital spaces can be mixed to accommodate people with different technology backgrounds [7, 11].

On the one hand, research on IKS emphasizes the importance of identifying barriers to digital media use for both generations, such as technology selection, complexity, and user background [17, 21]. On the other hand, various strategies to facilitate digital knowledge sharing between generations, such as different forms of gamification and

© Springer Nature Switzerland AG 2022
A. Drechsler et al. (Eds.): DESRIST 2022, LNCS 13229, pp. 458–469, 2022.
https://doi.org/10.1007/978-3-031-06516-3_34

competency-based learning, have been vigorously promoted to provide meaningful positive experiences [1, 3, 13]. However, there is limited research on the phenomenon of digital platforms for IKS in the context of startup innovation [17, 20]. Existing IKS systems that could assist practitioners in designing IKS systems focus primarily on older adults and grandchildren [3, 13, 21] and do not consider the principle of meaningful experiences (and gamification) for diverse generations of adults or the principles of IKS about startup innovation in the digital space [17, 20]. As a result, there is a scarcity of consolidated normative theories on building an IKS system for learning startup development. This is a problem because it prevents the design inclusiveness of different actors [11, 21] in the startup ecosystem from combining and improving their knowledge. Therefore, we address the lack of general knowledge for digital systems that facilitate knowledge sharing in startup development between generations.

Outlining generic DPs as a set of proposed solutions to solve a (class of) problem is a widely endorsed and favored strategy for informing practitioners and researchers about technological meta-artifacts [10, 18]. In this regard, we contend that purpose-driven normative DPs for IKS systems could promote more vital co-innovation [13, 14], strengthen design for social inclusion [13, 17, 23], and assist practitioners and researchers in understanding and improving universal technology design for knowledge sharing. Hence, we formulate the following research question (RQ): How should knowledge-sharing systems be designed to support startup innovation learning in intergenerational ecosystems?

By proposing a set of design principles as meta-artifacts of study [8, 10, 16, 19], this study leverages Design Science Research (DSR) to improve the status quo in research and practice [19]. Meta-artifacts are human-made solutions to system design problem(s) and can be products or processes for the (class of) problem(s) [8, 10]. As a formalization for reflection(s) on the entire DSR, five principles are proposed in this study: positive personalization that goes beyond individualization; a progressive ecosystem for flow experiences; an effectual strategy in system design by optimizing the fit between available design resources and the competencies of different generations, iterative reflection on goals; and finally, coopetitive intergenerational tasks, or orchestrating the power of collaboration and competition. Five DPs are provided at a higher level of abstraction to assist practitioners and researchers in comprehending the means to build IKS systems for learning startup development. The following section describes the methodology in detail.

2 Research Methodology

The Design Science Research (DSR) methodology [19] was chosen for this study because it provides an iterative process for improving knowledge and meta-artifacts [10, 16, 19]. In DSR, the proposed meta-artifact is based on both scientific literature and expert/user studies, with a series of assessments, performed to ensure rigor. DSR allows different evaluations, both qualitative and quantitative methods [8, 16, 19] The results of each process in DSR can be cross-referenced with the previous procedure so that knowledge grows and is systematically refined in each cycle [19]. Moreover, the systematic approach facilitates validating and generating valid DPs as produced meta-artifacts [10,

18, 19]. Overall, DSR meets our requirements for a flexible and high-quality research methodology designed to deliver design-oriented knowledge.

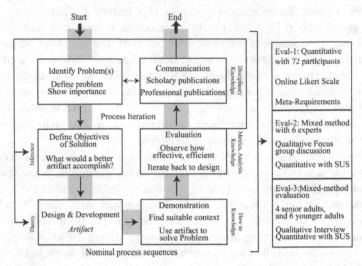

Fig. 1. Process-oriented design science research was applied in this study. Adopted from Peffers et al. [19]

Based on the DSR process, the initial problem for this study was identified and presented in the previous section. The class of problems and design solutions was elaborated through the reflection of a systematic literature review [22] in the objective definition. In previous studies [17], the systematic literature review process of 75 pieces of literature is explained in greater detail. The method was then combined with creative and abductive thinking (or the selection of the best possible solution(s) to solve the problem based on available information from literature and experience) during the design and development process. Overall, three validation processes were conducted. Eval-1 validated the class of problems quantitatively as meta-requirements based on the feedback of 72 participants (male: 48; female: 24; age range from 18 to >65 years). The number is based on feedback returned after the questionnaire is openly visible to an online crowd-working platform's targeted audience. The Eval-1 is a Likert-scale on importance (1–5: strongly agree) online questionnaire. The problem and positive expectations and various IKS design interventions were gathered from the literature [17]. Design and development were conducted based on identified relevant literature in the solution definition process and followed by the artifact's demonstration. The first demonstration of meta-design was a paper prototype. The initial paper prototype was evaluated with the help of three user experience experts, and the pre-evaluation results were used to develop a web-based app as a high-fidelity prototype. The derived meta-requirements and the gained design knowledge were compared with existing literature for the high-fidelity prototype.

The high-fidelity prototype was developed and evaluated. A two-stage process was used to support the previous assessment results for the evaluation. The first stage, known as Eval-2, consisted of an expert group discussion (N: 6; male: 3; female: 3;

expertise: digital learning, digital collaboration, intergenerational collaboration, global innovation, startup entrepreneurship). The number of participants was based on the available members of the invited group to participate in the study. This was followed by a quantitative survey using the System Usability Scale (SUS) [2]. For the second stage, called Eval-3, a set of questions based on the meta-requirements of the first iteration was created to help guide the interview. These questions were used to find out what users liked and didn't like.

Eval-3 included ten participants, five of whom were German and five Indonesian. The group was divided into younger and older adults. The number of participants is relatively small, but a good number [15] for a qualitative study that provides an almost perfect balance between younger and older adults and different cultural backgrounds. The younger ones were under 35 years old, and the older ones were over 55 years old. For the German group, two older and three younger participants were interviewed (three women and two men). The Indonesian group consisted of two older and three younger individuals (two women and three men). The evaluation took about 60–80 min per person and could be conducted face-to-face or via videoconference. Participants first rated the meta-requirements and meta-design to determine which requirements and design features were most or least important. Participants then chose the order in which they thought the meta-requirements and meta-design should be ranked.

Moreover, ten questions from the SUS [2] were asked of participants in Eval-2 and Eval-3. SUS scores were calculated to identify which usability aspects can be improved, combined with observations made during the demonstration, to identify further which design features need to be refined and support reflection on proposed DPs. The following section will present the meta-artifact of the study.

3   Result

Through the DSR process, this study generates prescriptive knowledge in the form of artifacts [8, 10, 18, 19]. Artifacts can be software, frameworks, and guidelines [18] representing DPs for developing research-based technologies and improving the status quo. The artifacts of the study can be summarized in Fig. 2. Figure 2 shows the DPs derived from meta-requirements appraisals and demonstrated meta-designs. Figure 2 depicts three rows of blocks related to different concepts: meta-requirements as a set of goals, meta-design as interventions to address or achieve the meta-requirements [10, 16], and the proposed DPs based on iterative reflection. The top block is the meta-requirements block, the middle block is the meta-design block, and the bottom shows the DPs. The arrows connecting the blocks illustrate how the DPs are derived from the meta-requirements.

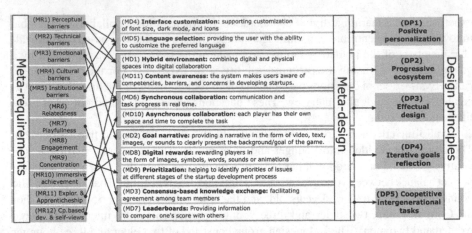

Fig. 2. Overview of design principles for IKS systems.

3.1 Elaboration on Meta-requirement

The meta-requirements derived from the design science research process are goals that encompass both the expectations of the different generations for the IKS system and the removal of barriers that (may) be encountered in IKS on specific topics (related to global startup innovation). The identified meta-requirements include twelve elements. The meta-requirements are higher-level abstractions of barrier dimensions that include perceptual barriers (MR1): different perceptions due to possible cognitive or physical limitations of particular generations [5, 7, 17]. The challenges of different styles and preferences in (digital) communication [11, 17] (Source: Eval-1: *"a different perspective on technology"*). (MR2) operational or technical challenges (Source: Eval-1: *"older people find it challenging to understand newer technology"*), (MR3) emotional barriers (MR4), cultural barriers (Source: Eval-1: *"cultural decisions are difficult"*), and (MR5) institutional barriers [1, 14, 17] (Source: Eval-3: *"it can be misunderstood as not to work by other colleges in the workplace if the knowledge exchange platform is not yet known and particularly conducted in a playful environment"*).

Meta-requirements also include positive expectations of well-being and the development of human potential as a goal of IKS [5, 6, 13, 17] These meta-requirements are as follows: (MR6) connectedness with others (MR7) and playfulness [5, 6, 13, 17] Motivation and engagement, and concentration (MR9). There is also a need for immersion (MR10) and achievement. Finally, (MR11) social interaction for apprenticeship and exploration (MR12), competency development, and self-assessment [3, 5, 7, 17, 20].

In Eval-1, although meta-requirements related to barriers on IKS had mean values of importance of 2.87–3.06, more than 90% of participants agreed with the presence of meta-requirements related to barriers. In addition, some comments on the comprehensiveness of barriers were as follows: *"I think most are included," "all are listed above," "there may be different approaches, but I think everything is included,"* and *"the list is comprehensive."* Participants in Eval-2 and Eval-3 commented on a variety of goals and barriers, which provided insight into specific meta-requirements and how to fine-tune them. In Eval-2, expert panels agreed that several meta-requirements were critical, including the gamification component [4, 6, 13], technical and operational barriers, perceptual barriers, knowledge sharing and improvement, and social interaction [7, 14, 14, 17]. Some comments on specific meta-requirements are as follows: Technical-operational: *"can be overcome with a little practice,"* Knowledge sharing and improvement: *"I think this should be the main goal of collaboration in general," "this requirement can help improve and enhance skills."* In Eval-3, we discovered how important the game aspect is for knowledge sharing: *"it is crucial that people have fun with the system and experience positive emotions,"* and the usefulness of a consensus process for knowledge sharing: *"If you have a game, you can discuss it and learn from each other, which I think is beneficial."* Unlike the experts on the panel, technical barriers seem to be an essential factor in Eval-3 for both generations: *"technical and operational barriers are critical if you do not know how to play,"* and *"understanding how to operate the system is critical."* The meta-requirements and associated evaluation criteria inform the importance of playfulness, positive emotions, and technical and operational barriers that should be prioritized for implementation.

3.2 Demonstration of Meta-design

The meta-design was developed by combining creativity with proposed interventions from the literature while thinking about meta-requirements. Creativity is essential in the design process that drives innovation to achieve meta-requirements [8, 10, 18]. Thus, design science research enables researchers to embrace creative risks and reflect knowledge through practical instantiation [9, 10, 19]. Based on the reflection on meta-requirements, the initial concept, which was based on previous studies [3–5, 7, 13], was to make a digital board game that could be played in the same room and allow for remote collaboration.

The board game was chosen because it can facilitate entertaining knowledge sharing, promotes playfulness (MR7), interaction, and social relationships (MR6, MR11), and more importantly, is accessible to a variety of age groups [3–5, 7, 13, 21]. A hybrid system was developed that incorporates digital and physical space into knowledge-sharing activities. A hybrid system was chosen to take advantage of physical objects in terms of control interaction from non-digital experiences, with the goal of overcoming technological and perceptual limitations and enabling immersive experiences [3, 7, 11]. Moreover, a hybrid system was used to combine the strengths of the tangible and intangible interface. The system provides a target narrative in the form of video, text, graphics, or audio to effectively communicate the story and purpose of the system to MR2 and MR1. Consensus-based knowledge sharing [12] is used to overcome perceptual and emotional barriers through customization of the user interface and language to overcome cultural, perceptual, and institutional barriers [4, 5, 17, 21].

The system incorporates game aspects such as leaderboards and digital incentives to further encourage playfulness and concentration [3–6, 13]. In addition, synchronous and asynchronous collaboration are used to facilitate communication and autonomous work between generations [14, 17]. The meta-design was demonstrated in two design cycles. A low-fidelity and a high-fidelity prototype demonstrate the meta-design to satisfy the meta-requirements. Figure 3 shows a low-fidelity prototype created by applying the meta-design to a paper prototype.

The content of the game relates to the competencies, obstacles, and challenges of entrepreneurship in digital startups to reflect the increase in topics related to entrepreneurial universities [12, 17, 20]. A collaboration narrative was developed in which each team had to collect one hundred points based on team members' consensus on the importance of a discussion topic related to competencies, obstacles, and challenges in specific innovation processes (four innovation processes: ideation, matching, design and development, and commercialization) [17]. This cumulative score is divided into four sections, each representing the four innovation activities. Consensus can be reached when the team draws an action card that presents three topics for discussion (each member gives a score, and after everyone is done scoring, the game displays all the answers and compares whether there is consensus or not). The more consensus is reached, the fewer action cards are removed, and the faster a team finishes the game, the fewer action cards determine the best team to finish the game.

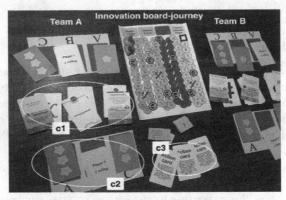

Fig. 3. Paper prototype meta-design for IKS system. C1: topic cards to achieve consensus; C2: rating cards by the player; C3: action-cards instruction for the player to pick a topic for discussion.

Based on an initial test of the paper prototype with three user experience experts, several improvements were suggested related to minimizing the process (or points to be collected) to complete the game (Fig. 3, Innovation Board Journey), providing a brief explanation of the topic of each discussion, and providing a visual overview of the points collected by the group. Overall, the consensus mechanism can stimulate discussion (on essential topics such as barriers, competencies, and competing interests of startups). The paper prototype was transformed into a web-based application as a high-fidelity prototype. The Meteorjs framework[1] was used to create a real-time application. A hybrid environment was created using webNFC[2]. Action cards (Fig. 3, C1) and rating cards (Fig. 3, C2) can be replaced with printed near field communication (NFC) cards. Figure 4 shows a general view of the high-fidelity prototype, with a description of meta-design written next to the picture. Each team has its own URL in the web app as a high-fidelity prototype. Each player registers their NFC card via a browser on a smartphone or can

---

[1] https://www.meteor.com/ (last access: 18.01.2022).
[2] https://w3c.github.io/web-nfc/ (last access: 18.01.2022).

play without an NFC card. Each player receives a short 3-min video that can be skipped. This video explains the purpose and process of the game. After logging in to the main dashboard, the consensus game scans the NFC action card. Communication is done via video chat through JITSI[3]. In the case of consensus, there is feedback on the accumulated points and animation in the form of a sound and fireworks celebrating the event. The number of action cards in each activity of the innovation process is played out at the end of the game as a reflection on which topics of discussion still have differences in perception and which the team has the same perception of an issue. A leaderboard shows the team's position and which team completed the game with the fewest action cards.

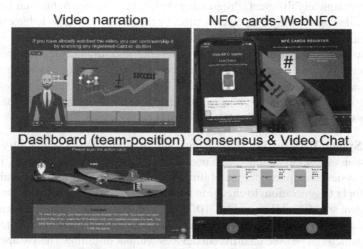

Fig. 4. Web-based prototype for an IKS system.

3.3 Reflection and Formalization of Proposed Design Principles

Based on the series of evaluation processes in design research, five DPs were identified as suggested system design interventions to support knowledge sharing in intergenerational contexts. Comments from study participants were also used to support the analysis. The suggested DPs, based on the overall process of DSR, are:

Positive Personalization: The IKS system should provide beyond customization and a more personal approach to software and hardware design to support positive emotions and wellbeing enhancement for a different generation. It personalizes the IKS system design to enhance positive emotions such as joy, exploration, empathy, and compassion, supporting embedded human potential and well-being. The meta-designs to fulfill this DP are MD1, MD4, MD5, and MD7. There is a need for personalization for digital safety, dialog, accessibility, language, visualization, appearance, and localization to support cultural differences between users and generations. Some of the competing

---

[3] https://jitsi.org/ (last access: 18.01.2022).

comments that go beyond customization and more about positive personalization are in Eval-2: "Customizing is a "nice to have featured," it does not impact the game's results." Furthermore, from Eval-3: *"I could not play this game in another language at all," "It is essential that people have fun with the game and have positive emotions. Otherwise, there is no motivation for future games."*

Progressive Ecosystem: The IKS systems should enable environmental adaptation gradually. The content, learning and adaptation process, challenges, and knowledge for exchange improved gradually for the quality and quantity of the content. Progressiveness aims Where the changes go unnoticed by the user until the content and process are finished or completely different. Progressive design in an intergenerational ecosystem can be provided by showing the position, time, or progress of the knowledge exchanged and the phase currently relevant to the knowledge exchange. Thus, the aim is to provide system feedback that is transparent, measurable, and (digitally) rewarding. Eval-2 contains some pertinent comments to the second DPs: *"...it is vital to understand the intention and phases of the game."* also due to time constrain in Eval-1:*" Time involved in learning about new strategies and redesigning courses."* Examples of meta-designs to fulfill this DP are MD1, MD5, MD8, and MD11.

Effectual System Design: The IKS systems should optimize the availability of technology resources, user experience, and user skills to interact with the system. Effectual interactive systems support interoperability and leverage current tools, available time, and space for both generations to engage in knowledge sharing. Examples of applied DPs for this system are MD3, MD6, and MD10. In meta-design, some features have also been applied to support the implementation of these DPs, such as web-based applications and WebNFC, which can be used on different devices without installing a native application. Some comments on these DPs are Eval-3: *"I think it will be difficult for older people to routinely use newer technologies," "..When something is so complicated, especially when you are older, it can really be a problem.."* and *"I think Synchronous collaboration is very important and the dial-in video option is also good."*

Iterative Goals Reflection: The IKS system should help both generations identify, evaluate, and re-evaluate common goals. The system should help manage shared goals that are transparent, iterative, and based on the common interests of both generations. The system should be developed based on reflections and goal narratives that are adaptable and clear through various forms of communication, such as text, images, and videos. Some meta-designs applied to support this DP are MD2, MD7, MD8, MD9, and MD11. Some comments that are relevant to this DP are Eval-2: *"The continues discussion supports the agreement between the team members," "the game was really fun and a new approach consensus about competencies, barriers and other aspects,"* and from the Eval-3: *"I think it is more important to find a consensus with your team to learn about each other..."*.

Coopetitive Intergenerational Tasks: The IKS system should engage both generations with simultaneous collaborative and competitive tasks. Developing design strategies that combine collaboration and competition in a playful environment can promote knowledge sharing. Game elements such as earning points and the leaderboard are two examples that can be used simultaneously to provide coopetitive activities for both generations. Some comments supporting the need for this DP come from Eval-3: *"It was fun to play together, but it was also motivating to do well because you can compare your results to the other teams," "Motivation to finish well/fast because there is a leaderboard, so you seriously want to make it to the end," "It is super handy to see where you agree. That also promotes the whole idea of the game"*. Some applied mate-designs for these DPs are MD3, MD7, MD8, and MD11.

While the SUS score for the web-based application with 16 participants from Eval-2 and Eval-3 was still not optimal at 46.7 (SUS-Eval-2 = 60.0; SUS-Eval-3 = 38.8), the goal of the apparent prototype in this study was to demonstrate the applicability of the DPs through meta-design and reflect user preferences to refine and gain a better understanding of the DPs [8–10, 19]. According to observations made during Eval-2 and Eval-3, one of the main problems was the implementation of webNFC for hybrid environments, where users spent most of their time trying to get the NFC card to work through the web browser. The complexity of setting and activating the webNFC function in the browser and the inconsistency of the content was the main technical challenges. Users can use the system without webNFC, but the inconsistent visual design instructions and clear instructions on how knowledge sharing works are also problematic. Overall, the initial high-fidelity prototype still has room for improvement, particularly concerning the SBS questions about usability (mean = 2.4 out of 5, the higher the better), instructions, i.e., whether users need help using the system (mean = 3.6 out of 5, the lower the better), and whether they need to learn a lot before they can get started with the system (mean = 3.3 out of 5, the lower the better). Therefore, basic usability features such as precise tasks or goals and ease of use are always important when designing IKS systems.

4 Discussion

In this study, five DPs were identified as salient design-oriented knowledge contributions in terms of theoretical contributions. These DPs were derived from meta-requirements and meta-design. Unlike previous studies [13, 14], this study diversified the content of the IKS system in startup development and context for IKS, which could help practitioners design IKS systems that focus on younger and older adults. Consistent with previous research [3, 5, 13], gamification strategies positively influence both generations. Compared to previous studies, this study adds to the system requirements for IKS in startup development [1, 13, 20, 21], which can be adopted in further studies on skill development in academic and entrepreneurial settings.

In general, the results of the mixed-methods evaluation in DSR show that the identified meta-artifact is a promising approach to help IKS understand startup development processes. Based on different contexts and design goals, some DPs should be prioritized for further study. There is room for improvement in meta-design, narrative content of questions, and selection of a more user-friendly hybrid technology. We demonstrated the meta-design as part of the DSR artifact for practical implementation. We evaluated the implementation of webNFC as a potential tool that can facilitate a hybrid environment for IKS. The high-fidelity prototype demonstrates the applicability of the proposed DPs.

On the one hand, the implementation of the meta-design serves to validate the relevance of the meta-design as a practical intervention of the DPs. On the other hand, it aims at a reflection process to better understand the relevance of the DPs to IKS. The use of webNFC also allows the user to interact directly with the NFC card through the web browser without installing a dedicated app (other technologies that could be used for hybrid environments in the future include web-based augmented reality). As far as we know, this study is one of the first studies to report on the use of webNFC.

Overall, some meta-design improvements are still needed to demonstrate the proposed DPs better. However, some features and analyses can provide a solid foundation for the further development of IKS systems. This research developed a more abstract level of DP capable of covering all meta-requirements and meta-design. Qualitative content analyses of experts, user preferences, and SUS also reflect the applicability and relevance of meta-requirements to the study context. The results of this study contribute to the provision of prescriptive knowledge based on problem-oriented research [19]. Implementing a hybrid environment using WebNFC leads to the application of new solution(s) to new problems [8, 9]. The study's domain-specific knowledge gained and demonstrated was shared with the scientific community, startup entrepreneurs, and students. As DSR emphasizes, effective research should consider applicable design [8–10, 19]. This study demonstrated that the DVs were appropriate for the study setting. The iterative evaluation process led to a deeper understanding of the IKS system design. To sum up, DSR was applied in this study to propose five DPs for the IKS system through a serial evaluation process. The DPs were fine-tuned based on the meta-requirements and meta-design.

References

1. Becker, K.L., et al.: Better together? examining benefits and tensions of generational diversity and team performance. J. Intergener. Relat., 1–21 (2020)
2. Brooke, J.: SUS: A "Quick and Dirty" usability Scale. In: Usability Evaluation in Industry. CRC Press, Boca Raton (1996)
3. Costa, L., Veloso, A.: Being (Grand) players: review of digital games and their potential to enhance intergenerational interactions. J. Intergener. Relat. 14(1), 43–59 (2016). https://doi.org/10.1080/15350770.2016.1138273
4. De la Hera, T., et al.: Benefits and factors influencing the design of intergenerational digital games: a systematic literature review. Societies 7(3), 18 (2017)
5. Derboven, J., et al.: Designing for collaboration: a study in intergenerational social game design. Univ Access Inf Soc. 11(1), 57–65 (2012)
6. Fu, F.-L., et al.: EGameFlow: a scale to measure learners' enjoyment of e-learning games. Comput. Educ. 52(1), 101–112 (2009)
7. Furr, N.R., Snow, D.C.: Intergenerational hybrids: spillbacks, spillforwards, and adapting to technology discontinuities. Organ. Sci. 26(2), 475–493 (2015)
8. Gregor, S., et al.: Research perspectives: the anatomy of a design principle. J. Assoc. Inf. Syst. 21(6), 2 (2020)
9. Gregor, S., Hevner, A.R.: Positioning and presenting design science research for maximum impact. MIS Q. 37(2), 337–356 (2013)
10. Iivari, J.: The IS Core - VII: towards information systems as a science of meta-artifacts. Commun. Assoc. Inf. Syst. 12(1), 37 (2003)

11. Li, C., et al.: Supporting intergenerational memento storytelling for older adults through a tangible display: a case study. Pers. Ubiquit. Comput. (2020)

12. Lieberman, H., et al.: Common consensus: a web-based game for collecting commonsense goals. In: Presented at the ACM Workshop on Common Sense for Intelligent Interfaces January (2007)

13. Loos, E., de la Hera, T., Simons, M., Gevers, D.: Setting up and conducting the co-design of an intergenerational digital game: a state-of-the-art literature review. In: Zhou, J., Salvendy, G. (eds.) Human Aspects of IT for the Aged Population. Design for the Elderly and Technology Acceptance. LNCS, vol. 11592, pp. 56–69. Springer, Cham (2019). https://doi.org/10.1007/978-3-030-22012-9_5

14. Lyashenko, M.S., Frolova, N.H.: LMS projects: a platform for intergenerational e-learning collaboration. Educ. Inf. Technol. **19**(3), 495–513 (2014). https://doi.org/10.1007/s10639-014-9333-9

15. Molich, R.: A critique of "how to specify the participant group size for usability studies: a practitioner's guide" by Macefield. J. Usabil. Stud. **5**(3), 124–128 (2010)

16. Möller, F., Guggenberger, T.M., Otto, B.: Towards a method for design principle development in information systems. In: Hofmann, S., Müller, O., Rossi, M. (eds.) Designing for Digital Transformation. Co-Creating Services with Citizens and Industry. LNCS, vol. 12388, pp. 208–220. Springer, Cham (2020). https://doi.org/10.1007/978-3-030-64823-7_20

17. Nurhas, I., et al.: Barriers and wellbeing-oriented enablers of intergenerational innovation in the digital age. Univ. Access Inf. Soc. (2021)

18. Offermann, P., Blom, S., Schönherr, M., Bub, U.: Artifact types in information systems design science – a literature review. In: Winter, R., Zhao, J.L., Aier, S. (eds.) Global Perspectives on Design Science Research. LNCS, vol. 6105, pp. 77–92. Springer, Heidelberg (2010). https://doi.org/10.1007/978-3-642-13335-0_6

19. Peffers, K., et al.: A design science research methodology for information systems research. J. Manag. Inf. Syst. **24**(3), 45–77 (2007)

20. Perez-Encinas, A., et al.: Intergenerational entrepreneurship to foster sustainable development: a methodological training proposal. Sustainability **13**(17), 9654 (2021)

21. Reis, L., et al.: Technologies for fostering intergenerational connectivity and relationships: scoping review and emergent concepts. Technol. Soc. **64**, 101494 (2021)

22. Webster, J., Watson, R.T.: Analyzing the past to prepare for the future: writing a literature review. MIS Q. **26**(2), xiii–xxiii (2002)

23. Yip, J.C., et al.: How to survive creating an intergenerational co-design group. Interactions **23**(4), 65–67 (2016). https://doi.org/10.1145/2933395

User Experience Requirements of Digital Moderation Systems in South Africa: Using Participatory Design Within Design Science Research

V. Rajamany$^{(\boxtimes)}$ ⓘ, J. A. van Biljon ⓘ, and C. J. van Staden ⓘ

School of Computing, UNISA, Pretoria, South Africa
7232969@mylife.unisa.ac.za, {vbiljja,vstadcj1}@unisa.ac.za

Abstract. The digital transformation within the global educational environment led to a transformation in assessment strategies and the increased use of ICTs in assessments. Digitization offers innovative teaching and learning opportunities. But it also introduces new challenges to current quality assurance processes. A narrative literature review revealed a scarcity of empirical evidence on dedicated digital moderation systems and no representation of teachers' views could be found. The purpose of this paper is to report on an investigation into the requirements for a digital moderation (eModeration) system to enhance teachers' user experience (UX) of moderation practices in the school environment. Design science research (DSR) is the paradigm applied to guide the alignment of the findings from a literature review on eModeration requirements with the findings from a Participatory Design (PD) intervention for eliciting UX requirements for an eModeration system. The context is school teachers in South Africa. The methodological contribution of this paper is the transdisciplinary approach of using DSR to guide both the literature review and the PD interaction towards a synthesis of the requirements and the implementation in a prototype eModeration system. The theoretical contribution is the evidence based UX design requirements of an eModeration system.

Keywords: User experience · eModeration · Participatory design

1 Introduction

The increasing adoption of digital technologies in the education landscape has led to a global transformation in assessment strategies [1]. While digitization presents innovative opportunities in the teaching and learning environment, new challenges are introduced to moderation processes. Moderation is an aspect of quality assurance conducted at various stages in the assessment process and refers to procedures used to establish confidence in the outcomes of assessment decisions made by teachers [2, 3]. A narrative literature review revealed a scarcity of empirical evidence on ICT-mediated moderation practices [4] and no evidence of teachers' requirements for a digital moderation system could be found. This provides the rationale for our investigation into the requirements for a digital

A. Drechsler et al. (Eds.): DESRIST 2022, LNCS 13229, pp. 470–482, 2022.
https://doi.org/10.1007/978-3-031-06516-3_35

moderation system to enhance teachers' user experience (UX) of moderation practices in the school environment.

Moderation is a core requirement in ensuring the integrity of assessments and the credibility of the educational system [5]. The transformation to eAssessment processes [6] requires a corresponding shift from a paper-based to digital moderation (eModeration) processes. Despite evidence of an emerging trend in eModeration research [4], there is very little evidence of research into the UX of eModeration. Of the 37 papers reviewed, 7 identify eModeration requirements, and of these, 3 investigated the teachers' perspective. Educational institutions are encouraged to shift as many activities as possible to the "digital work-zone" [7, p. 369]. Thus, to ensure successful digitization, educational institutions need evidence-based strategies.

Hevner et al. [8] propose DSR as an inclusive approach where technology and their utility are evaluated in terms of the practical implications. March and Smith [9, p. 251] emphasize that "Real problems must be properly conceptualized and represented, appropriate techniques for their solution must be constructed, and solutions must be implemented and evaluated using appropriate criteria." Therefore, we select DSR as the paradigm to guide this transdisciplinary study into how teachers can participate in refining the UX requirements for a digital moderation system.

This article argues for actively involving teachers and moderators in refining the UX requirements extracted from literature to obtain context-specific requirements for an eModeration system. The research design involves a literature review and PD as data capturing strategies. Despite the similarity in the goals of designing effective artifacts in response to real-world problems, the intersection of DSR and PD is largely unexplored and thus this study makes a novel methodological contribution.

2 Literature Review

A narrative literature review [10] was used to synthesize the requirements of an eModeration system from the existing literature. A narrative review aims to consolidate previous work to identify gaps in existing knowledge [11]. In selecting relevant literature, conference proceedings and journal articles written in English with moderation as the focus were included. Publications in domains other than education and eLearning systems were excluded. Searches were conducted using specific IT database vendors like Web of Science, INSPEC and Scopus [12]. This literature review into eModeration systems draws largely from research by Berger [13], Rajamany et al. [14] and Van Staden [15]. Berger [13] and Van Staden [15] identify success features of information systems albeit from different viewpoints. While Van Staden [15] discusses the use of an eModeration system in the SA tertiary environment, Berger [13] discusses an eAssessment system in tertiary education which, for the purposes of this research, has been adapted for the digital moderation of assessments (cf. Table 1).

Rajamany et al. [16] identify eModeration UX requirements based on a triangulation of data from a literature review, a survey of 64 moderators and teachers and a focus group interview. Based on the literature, the general system features of an eModeration system depicted in Table 1, were further refined to extract more specific eModeration UX requirements. These UX eModeration requirements are depicted in Table 2.

Table 1. Features of an information system

Requirement	Explanation	Reference
Reusability	Ability to reuse content on different platforms	[13, 14]
Manageability	Ability of the system to track moderation processes	[13]
Accessibility	Access to and delivery of content irrespective of time or place	[13, 14]
Durability	Unnecessary to redesign content when the system is updated	[13]
Scalability	Marginal effort is utilized to expand the system	[13]
Affordability	The system must be cost effective for principal users	[13, 14]
Security and reliability	Each user should be authenticated	[13, 15]
Usabality	The system should be user friendly and intuitive	[13]
Portability	The system should be easily hosted on another server	[13]
Infrastructure	Access to adequate applications and internet infrastructure	[13, 15]
Bandwidth	Adequate bandwidth to increase system efficiency	[13, 15]

Table 2. UX requirements identified from literature

UX requirement	Reference	UX requirement	Reference
Annotation tools	[13, 17]	Legibility	[17]
Audit Trail	[16, 17]	Multi-user technology	[16]
Availability	[14, 18]	Notifications	[19]
Capability	[20]	Output quality	[20]
Compatibility	[19]	Productivity	[[17, 19]
Completeness	[20]	Reliability	[13]
Complexity	[13]	Reporting	[19]
Confidence	[19]	Satisfaction with functions	[20]
Cost saving	[13, 17, 19, 21]	Security	[13, 19]
Cross platform	[13]	Self-efficacy	[20]
Data Currency	[20]	Task performance	[19]
Ease of use	[16]	Technical support	[18]
Efficiency	[18]	Time saving	[19]
External communication	[16]	Timeliness	[19]
Flexibility	[13]	Training and Experience	[16]
Format	[13, 18]	Usefulness	[16]
Infrastructure and Resources	[19]	Voice over button	[16]

3   Methodology

3.1   Introduction

The research design is guided by the DSR paradigm with PD as the data capturing strategy. DSR research uses design as the primary method to produce knowledge that is new and interesting to a community [22, 23]. The fundamental principle of DSR as a research method within IS, is the development of knowledge to either create new products or propose enhancements to current artifacts [24]. Given DSR's commitment to change and impact, the users' input and perceptions are imperative in ensuring the relevance of the artifact for the target community [25]. Design artifacts can contribute to the scientific body of knowledge, at the same time, these artifacts are expected to provide solutions to practical problems. Considering this "duality", DSR endeavors require the collaboration of researchers and users [26, p. 2].

PD is a methodology that places "human beings at the center of the design process" of technology solutions [27, 28]. PD uses the actions of "explore, approximate, then refine" [29, p. 168] to describe the way in which stakeholders cooperatively design systems to suit the needs of users [27, 28].

Having considered DSR and PD individually, we will now outline the points of intersection and alignment between these methods.

- Design as a research technique: DSR makes use of design as a research technique and its focus on human creativity provides a point of intersection with PD [27, 29]. Interestingly, this nexus has not been explored in any depth towards purposely aligning these methodologies.
- Context as imperative: The objective of DSR projects is usually motivated by circumstances in the external domain within which designed artifacts are to be integrated [25]. This objective resonates with PD's emphasis on user participation in the co-design of products [30].
- Involving stakeholders: The objective of a DSR project to provide broader impacts to stakeholders rather than merely developing and evaluating artifacts further aligns with the objectives of PD [25]. Thus, participants' interpretations contribute different layers of expertise to the final outcome [31]. Indeed, Robertson and Simonsen [30, p. 6] argue that results are more likely to be flexible, accessible, adaptable, and robust when "different voices are heard, understood and heeded" during the design process.
- Inter-disciplinary application: PD is a research method used in the interdisciplinary field of Human-Computer Interaction whereas DSR is used in Information Systems. Therefore, a research design aligning these approaches towards solving a real-world problem can be considered transdisciplinary. Transdisciplinary research is characterized by an interpenetration of epistemologies as the dissolution of disciplinary boundaries is a precondition for the construction of novel methodologies tailored to the problem and its context [32]. The variability of criteria and indicators resulting from the dissolution of disciplinary boundaries has the potential to create tensions between disciplines, as practices for ensuring validity and reliability are dependent on these criteria. This is managed by confining PD to the data capturing strategy so that the interaction is limited to the transfer of requirements as explained in the next section.

Based on Drechsler and Hevner's [25] four-cycle view of DSR consisting of the iterative Change and Impact, Relevance, Design and Rigor cycles, this study considers PD as a component of DSR. Thus, the cyclical process of continual reflection and iterative development characteristic of PD supported the DSR approach taken in this study (cf. Fig. 1). The following section describes the stages in PD and then the fit between PD and DSR is described based on the DSR process depicted in Fig. 1. The three stages in PD research, as identified by Spinuzzi [29] are:

- Stage 1: Initial exploration of work - during this stage, designers familiarize themselves with all aspects of how users of the system being developed work including the technologies used.
- Stage 2: Discovery processes - the discovery processes allow designers and users to clarify the users' goals and to agree on the desired outcome of the project.
- Stage 3: Prototyping - during this stage, designers and users iteratively shape technological artifacts to fit into the envisioned work environment of Stage 2. Working prototypes using the inputs of one or more users may be conducted in situ.

Stages 1 and 2 of the PD process occur within the Change and Impact and Relevance cycles of the DSR process where the emphasis is on a general understanding of user needs and the environment in which the artifact will be deployed [25]. During this stage, user needs were elicited from the literature review. Stages 2 and 3 overlap with the Relevance, Design and Rigor cycles of DSR where designers seek to understand the work environment and artifacts are iteratively designed for the specific context in which the artifact will be implemented [33]. On the Relevance side, the need for a new artifact was articulated as eModeration requirements based on the literature review and participant comments. On the Rigor side, applicable knowledge was obtained from the literature and triangulated with the empirical data (teachers/moderators input in PD design). Thus, the collection of data relating to UX requirements of an eModeration system during the PD workshops occurred within the Relevance and Design cycles of the DSR process. The stages are repeatedly revisited in the PD methodology thus facilitating information flow between stages 1 and 2 and stages 2 and 3 within the iterative processes of DSR.

3.2 Data Collection

This study required the collection of opinions from stakeholders who have experience in the moderation process. A purposive sampling technique was used to select domain experts based on their proficiency and experience of moderation processes. Thus, data was collected from a sample of teachers and moderators with the ability to communicate their experiences and opinions in an articulate, expressive, and reflective manner as recommended by Etikan et al. [34]. Data was collected from 15 national, regional and cluster moderator and teachers during two PD workshops in November 2021. All participants were double experts, i.e., experienced IT teachers as well as experienced moderators having more than 5 years of experience in their positions as IT teachers and/or moderators.

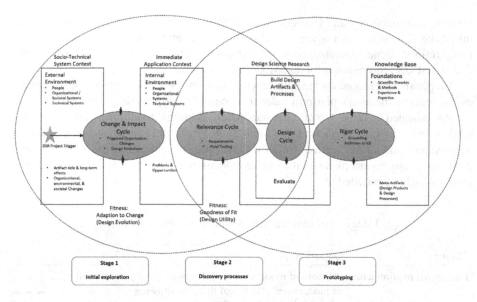

Fig. 1. Mapping of participatory design to DSR (based on Drechsler and Hevner's [25])

Participants firstly worked individually to answer five pre-defined questions ranging from determining the need for an eModeration system to detailing the functionality to include in such a system. Participants thereafter worked in groups of between three and four to brainstorm ideas for the most important functionality required. Each group created idea webs (cf. Fig. 2) based on a standard outline detailing the stakeholders of an eModeration system, the requirements of an eModeration system, the constraints/challenges to the use of such a system and the important functions that the system should have [14]. Considering the stakeholders, two of the four groups identified assessment and verification bodies as additional stakeholders. Regarding the constraints, load shedding, bandwidth and connectivity were issues that all groups identified as of concern. All groups identified alerts and notification of progress as important features of an eModeration system which supports findings from the literature (cf. Table 2).

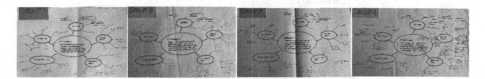

Fig. 2. Idea webs

3.3 Results

The requirements and functions that participants indicated on their idea webs and brainstorming posters formed the basis for eliciting teacher requirements for an eModeration system. The functional and UX requirements from the PD interactions were imported into Atlas.ti version 9 to analyze the data. The themes and codes were thereafter iteratively refined. Table 3 indicates participant responses and the coding specifically for the functional UX requirements for an eModeration system.

Emphasis was placed on the help functionality, the need for a quick response time, customized notifications, platform independence and multiple subject integration.

As indicated in Table 3, participants included additional requirements that were not evident in the literature reviewed (cf. Table 2). For instance, a progress bar, a ticketing help system, and a FAQ section. Notably, these requirements contribute to aspects that domain experts regard as integral to an eModeration system thus adding value to the existing body of knowledge.

Table 3. UX requirements identified from PD workshops

Theme	Quotation	Code
Functional requirements	"History of moderation"; "History of proof of moderation"; "A visual timeline showing who did what and when"	Audit trail
	"Ensure security; "Some other people could see my work or students work"; "Login with secure email and password"	Security
	"Ability to cross-reference and synch with all documents or items moderated"	Synchronization
	"Stage by stage analysis of content/completion; "Show development of moderation"	Progress bar
	"Work on latest version-so no version errors"	Versioning
	"Ability to have predefined comments; Database of comments which are customizable. "The ability to easily comment; Maybe by saving a voice note or mark easily"	Pre-defined comments
	"Perhaps if it is collaborative it would help - maybe work on MS Teams together- moderator and examiner"	Collaboration
	"A centralised location like Microsoft Teams for live collaboration and chat"	Centralization
	"Tracked deadlines"	Tracking

(*continued*)

Table 3. (*continued*)

Theme	Quotation	Code
	"Structured system → allows for stages in moderation process; "Upgrade IEB Postbox to include facilities where teachers can upload SBA and PAT in predefined organized folders"	Organized structure
	"Ticket/Help system", "FAQ"	Support
	"Platform independent, Mobile application easy to scan and be alerted"	Platform
	"Report generation"	Reporting
	"Notification errors if things are missing, or requirement not met"; "A notification when things are uploaded, edited and/or deleted. "A central team with high response times e.g. upload and receive notification when feedback is ready"	Notifications
UX requirements	"Intuitive design"; "Intuitive Interface"	User friendly
	"Flexibility in uploading and editing or correcting submissions"	Flexibility

The specific UX variables contributing to the benefits of using an eModeration system were: customized notifications, an intuitive interface, a database of customizable comments and the facility for a live video chat. The provision of annotation tools is indicated in the literature as an important requirement for an eModeration system (cf. Table 2). During group design discussions, two groups indicated the need for the moderator to "comment on the document". While participants discussed including a function to edit documents online and adding a plugin to enable them to do so, the functionality of annotation tools was omitted in the final design. The literature provides a convincing argument for the inclusion of annotation tools. Annotation tools were thus included as a task requirement for an eModeration system [16, 35, 36]. Various statements made by participants indicate the significance of the need to "track changes", "track documents", "track deadlines" and to "generate a history of the proof of moderation" which are context specific requirements for incorporation in an eModeration system.

4 Findings

During the second PD workshop, each group produced illustrations of their design ideas (cf. Fig. 3). The other participants placed pink stickers on these posters to indicate the ideas they liked the most. The frequency of likes for each design item was calculated as depicted in Table 4.

Table 1 illustrates the general features of an information system applicable to eModeration but does not consider context specific eModeration UX requirements. Based on

Fig. 3. Design ideas

Table 4. Popularity of design ideas[1]

Ideas I Like	Group 1			Group 2			Group 3			Group 4		
	Item	No	%	Item	No	%	Item	No	%	Item	No	%
	Calendar	3	20	Moderation Progress	1	6.7	History of proof of moderation	3	20	FAQ	1	6.7
	Week ahead	1	6.7	Customised notifications	3	20	Live chat with moderator	6	40	Timeline	1	6.7
	Templates	1	6.7	Voice notes	4	26.7	Comments	1	6.7	Automatic updates	2	13.3
	Chats	1	6.7	Proof of moderation	1	6.7	Voice notes	1	6.7	OCR	1	6.7

the broad features outlined in Table 1 and a review of literature specifically on eModeration systems [16]. UX requirements were listed in Table 2. UX requirements identified from literature were compared to those identified from PD workshops (Table 5).

Table 5. Comparison of requirements[2]

Variables	Literature review	PD workshops	Variables	Literature review	PD workshops
Annotation tools	✓		Reminders of deadlines		✓
Audit Trail	✓	✓	Reporting	✓	✓
Availability	✓		Security of information	✓	✓
Calendar		✓	Timeliness	✓	✓

---

[1] Partial table illustrated. The complete table can be accessed at: https://rb.gy/hye2tj.

[2] Partial table illustrated. The complete table can be accessed at: https://fliplink.io/VX6IV.

The requirements that were identified in the literature review as well as the PD workshops were included in the final refined requirements (cf. Table 6). Additionally, context specific requirements identified from PD workshops (cf. Table 3) together with the popular design ideas (cf. Table 4) were included based on stakeholder relevance.

Adopting Hassenzahl and Tractinsky's [37, p. 95] definition of UX as a "consequence of a user's internal state (expectations, needs, etc.), the characteristics of the designed system (e.g. usability, functionality, etc.) and the context within which the interaction occurs", the refined requirements were further categorized as user requirements, task requirements and system requirements to provide UX design requirements for eModeration as depicted in Table 6. Notably, UX requirements like digital literacy etc. depend on the intersection of these lower-level requirements.

Table 6. UX design requirements for eModeration

User requirements	Task requirements		System requirements	
• Digital literacy • Self-efficacy • Training and experience	• Annotation Tools • Audit trail • Automatic updates • Built in templates • Calendar • Checklist • Customizable comments • Customized notifications • Multi-user technology • Progress bar • Shared folders • Voice over button	• Choose moderator • Functional help • Instant feedback • Live video chat • Online editing • Reminders of deadlines • Reporting • Technical support • Tracking	• Accuracy • Availability • Capability • Centralized data storage • Compatibility • Completeness • Complexity • Cross platform • Data Currency • Dependability • External Communication • Flexibility • Legibility	• Infrastructure and Resources • Multi-user authentication Web-based • Organized file structure • Output Quality • Quick response • Reliability • Response time • Robust hardware • Security • Synchronization

The design requirements extracted during the first three cycles of DSR together with the most popular design ideas (cf. Table 4) informed the development of a prototype during the fourth cycle of the DSR process (cf. Fig. 4).

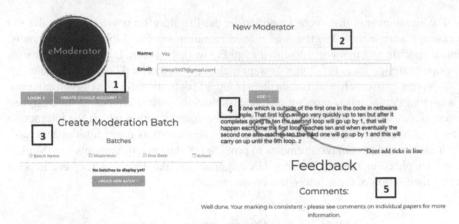

Fig. 4. Screenshots of core functionality

5 Conclusion

This paper reports on the use of PD as a data capturing strategy within a DSR study on designing an eModeration system for schools. Knowledge sharing during the design process fostered an in-depth understanding of future users and their needs. The main theoretical contribution is the empirically based domain specific design requirements for an eModeration system. Methodologically, the inclusion of a PD data capturing strategy within DSR was valuable in demonstrating the alignment between DSR and PD in terms of using design as research technique, the imperative of context and involving stakeholders, i.e. ensuring the relevance of the research to the educator community. Future research is necessary to evaluate the prototype developed and to engage additional stakeholders identified in the participants' idea webs. These include involving assessment bodies and school management in designing an eModeration system that is more flexible in serving the needs of all stakeholders.

Acknowledgement. This paper is based on the research supported by the South African Research Chairs Initiative of the Department of Science and Technology and National Research Foundation of South Africa (Grant No. 98564).

References

1. Bausili, A.V.: From piloting e-submission to electronic management of assessment (EMA): mapping grading journeys. Br. J. Educ. Technol. **49**(3), 463–478 (2018). https://doi.org/10.1111/bjet.12547
2. Parbhoo, J.: The implementation of moderation of assessment policy at a school and district: A case study. University of Cape Town (2011)
3. Colbert, P., Wyatt-Smith, C., Klenowski, V.: A systems-level approach to building sustainable assessment cultures: moderation, quality task design and dependability of judgement. Policy Futur. Educ. **10**(4), 386–401 (2012). https://doi.org/10.2304/pfie.2012.10.4.386

4. Van Staden, C., Kroeze, J., Van Biljon, J.: Digital Transformation for a Sustainable Society in the 21st Century, vol. 11701. Springer, Cham (2019). https://doi.org/10.1007/978-3-030-29374-1
5. SAQA. National Policy and Criteria for Designing and Implementing. Saqa 1, 26 (2015)
6. Ivanova, M., Durcheva, M., Baneres, D., Rodriguez, M.E.: eAssessment by using a trustworthy system in blended and online institutions. In: 2018 17th International Conference on Information Technology Based Higher Education and Training, ITHET 2018, pp. 1–7 (2018). https://doi.org/10.1109/ITHET.2018.8424805
7. Bejinaru, R.: Impact of digitalization on education in the knowledge economy. Manag. Dyn. Knowl. Econ. 7(3), 367–380 (2019). https://doi.org/10.25019/MDKE/7.3.06
8. Hevner, A., March, S.T., Park, J., Ram, S.: Design science in information systems research. MIS Q. 28(1), 75–105 (2004). https://doi.org/10.2307/25148625
9. March, S., Smith, G.: Design and natural science research on information technology. Decis. Support Syst. 15, 251–266 (1995)
10. Davies, I., Green, P., Rosemann, M., Indulska, M., Gallo, S.: How do practitioners use conceptual modeling in practice? Data Knowl. Eng. 58(3), 358–380 (2006). https://doi.org/10.1016/j.datak.2005.07.007
11. Grant, M.J., Booth, A.: A typology of reviews: an analysis of 14 review types and associated methodologies. Health Info. Libr. J. 26(2), 91–108 (2009). https://doi.org/10.1111/j.1471-1842.2009.00848.x
12. Cavacini, A.: What is the best database for computer science journal articles? Scientometrics 102(3), 2059–2071 (2014). https://doi.org/10.1007/s11192-014-1506-1
13. Berger, D.: Supporting Tool for Moderation in the Grading Process of Summative Assessments. Graz University of Technology Masters Thesis (2011)
14. Rajamany, V., Van Biljon, J., Van Staden, C.: eModeration adoption requirements for secondary school education: a critical literature review. IEEE 10(1109), 1–6 (2020). https://doi.org/10.1109/ictas47918.2020.233979
15. Van Staden, C.: User experience evaluation of electronic moderation systems: a case study at a private higher education institution in South Africa. Doctoral Dissertation, School of Computing, University of South Africa (2017)
16. Rajamany, V., Van Staden, C.J., van Biljon, J.: Requirements for an eModeration system in private schools in South Africa. In: Hattingh, M., Matthee, M., Smuts, H., Pappas, I., Dwivedi, Y.K., Mäntymäki, M. (eds.) I3E 2020. LNCS, vol. 12066, pp. 557–568. Springer, Cham (2020). https://doi.org/10.1007/978-3-030-44999-5_46
17. Johnson, M., Greatorex, J.: Judging text presented on screen: implications for validity. e-Learning 5(1), 40–50 (2008). https://doi.org/10.2304/elea.2008.5.1.40
18. ABC-Awards. eModeration Guide (2014). http://www.abcawards.co.uk/wp-content/uploads/2014/09/eModeration-Guide.pdf, Accessed 22 Mar 2018
19. New-Zealand-Qualifications-Authority, Digital Moderation Consultation Outcomes (2016). http://www.nzqa.govt.nz/assets/About-us/Future-State/Digital-Moderation-Consultation-Outcomes.pdf, Accessed 28 Apr 2018
20. Rajamany, V.: eModeration Requirements: A Case Study in Private Secondary Schools in South Africa. Masters Dissertation, School of Computing, University of South Africa (2020)
21. Newhouse, C.: Digital portfolios for summative assessment. In: ACEC2014 Now It's Personal, pp. 1–8 (2014)
22. Hevner, A., Chatterjee, S.: Design science research in information systems, pp. 9–22 (2010). https://doi.org/10.1007/978-1-4419-5653-8_2
23. Vaishnavi, V., Kuechler, W., Petter, S.: Design science research in information systems. In: DESRIST, vol. 39, no. 3, pp. 1–9 (2017). http://www.desrist.org/design-research-in-information-systems/

24. Goldkuhl, G., Ågerfalk, P., Sjostrom, J.: A design science approach to information systems education. In: Maedche, A., vom Brocke, J., Hevner, A. (eds.) DESRIST 2017, LNCS, vol. 10243, pp. 383–397. Springer, Cham (2017). https://doi.org/10.1007/978-3-319-59144-5

25. Drechsler, A., Hevner, A.: A four-cycle model of IS design science research: capturing the dynamic nature of IS artifact design. In: Breakthroughs and Emerging Insights from Ongoing Design Science Projects: Research-in-progress papers and poster presentations from the 11th International Conference on Design Science Research in Information Systems and Technology, pp. 1–8 (2016). https://cora.ucc.ie/handle/10468/2560

26. Otto, B., Oesterle, H.: Principles for knowledge creation in collaborative design science research. In: Thirty Third International Conference on Information Systems, pp. 1–17 (2012)

27. Clemensen, J., Rothmann, M.J., Smith, A.C., Caffery, L.J., Danbjorg, D.B.: Participatory design methods in telemedicine research. J. Telemed. Telecare 23(9), 780–785 (2017). https://doi.org/10.1177/1357633X16686747

28. Kopeć, W., Skorupska, K., Jaskulska, A., Abramczuk, K., Nielek, R., Wierzbicki, A.: LivingLab PJAIT: towards better urban participation of seniors. In: Proceedings - 2017 IEEE/WIC/ACM International Conference on Web Intelligence, WI 2017, pp. 1085–1092 (2017). https://doi.org/10.1145/3106426.3109040

29. Spinuzzi, C.: The methodology of participatory design. Tech. Commmun. 52(2), 163–174 (2005). https://doi.org/10.1353/csd.2015.0028

30. Robertson, T., Simonsen, J.: Challenges and opportunities in contemporary participatory design. Des. Issues 28(3), 3–9 (2012)

31. Wanick, V., Bitelo, C.: Exploring the use of participatory design in game design: a Brazilian perspective. Int. J. Serious Games 7(3), 3–20 (2020)

32. Wickson, F., Carew, A.L., Russell, A.W.: Transdisciplinary research: characteristics, quandaries and quality. Futures 38, 1046–1059 (2006). https://doi.org/10.1016/j.futures.2006.02.011

33. Van der Merwe, A., Gerber, A., Smuts, H.: Guidelines for conducting design science research in information systems. SACLA 5(4), 1–17 (2019). https://doi.org/10.17150/2308-6203.2016.5(4).689-697

34. Etikan, I., Musa, S., Alkassim, R.: Comparison of convenience sampling and purposive sampling. Am. J. Theor. Appl. Stat. 5(1), 1–4 (2016). https://doi.org/10.11648/j.ajtas.20160501.11

35. Greatorex, J.: Moderated e-portfolio project evaluation. Cambridge (2004)

36. Adie, L.: An investigation into online moderation. Assess. Matters 3, 5–27 (2011). http://search.informit.com.au/documentSummary;dn=515662774994571;res=IELHSS

37. Hassenzahl, M., Tractinsky, N.: User experience - a research agenda. Behav. Inf. Technol. 25(2), 91–97 (2006). https://doi.org/10.1080/01449290500330331

"Designing" Design Science Research – A Taxonomy for Supporting Study Design Decisions

Hanlie Smuts[1](✉) ⓘ, Robert Winter[2] ⓘ, Aurona Gerber[1,3] ⓘ, and Alta van der Merwe[1] ⓘ

[1] Department of Informatics, University of Pretoria, Hatfield, Pretoria, South Africa
hanlie.smuts@up.ac.za
[2] Institute of Information Management, University of St. Gallen, St. Gallen, Switzerland
[3] CAIR, Centre for AI Research, Pretoria, South Africa

Abstract. The Design Science Research (DSR) paradigm is highly relevant to the Information Systems (IS) discipline because DSR aims to improve the state of practice and contribute design knowledge through the systematic construction of useful artefacts. Since study designs can be understood as useful artefacts, DSR can also contribute to improving conceptualizing a research project. This study developed a taxonomy with relevant dimensions and characteristics for DSR research. Such a taxonomy is useful for analyzing existing DSR study designs and successful DSR study design patterns. In addition, the taxonomy is valuable for identifying DSR study design principles (dependencies among characteristics) and subsequently for systematically designing DSR studies. We constructed the DSR study taxonomy through a classification process following the taxonomy development approach of Nickerson et al.

Keywords: DSR · Design science research · DSR study taxonomy · Research study design

1 Introduction

Even though the Design Science Research (DSR) paradigm is still relatively young within Information Systems (IS), it is highly relevant to the Information Systems (IS) discipline [1]. For the last two decades there has been an interest to establish DSR within IS as a way of creating different forms of knowledge and improve the state of practice through the systematic construction of useful artefacts. In this way DSR aims to contribute to both theory-building and having value for practitioners [2]. Peffers et al. [3] emphasized that DSR scholars often find themselves confronted with an excess of advice, options, and different expectations and opinions on how to execute a DSR study.

It is a challenge for any researcher to understand the different options available during the design of a research project, especially for those researchers that are involved in supervision and the design of postgraduate studies. In descriptive IS research the study design usually follows guidelines of authors such as Orlikowski & Baroudi [4] to

© Springer Nature Switzerland AG 2022
A. Drechsler et al. (Eds.): DESRIST 2022, LNCS 13229, pp. 483–495, 2022.
https://doi.org/10.1007/978-3-031-06516-3_36

assist with choosing between study design alternatives. For example, a researcher might decide to do an empirical research study with qualitative data, the research strategy would typically be case study research with the data collection being done using interviews. Several choices among different alternatives must be made by researchers during the design of any research study.

DSR research studies are no exception, and there are several choices that a scholar is confronted with when designing a DSR study. However, there is a lack of published guidelines with regards to all the alternatives that the researcher could consider. Existing guidelines often only identify a set of important design characteristics (e.g. the DSR grid [5]) or suggest very general principles (e.g. consider a DSR project as a generic staged process, or choose among a small number of very generic artifact types). While some suggestions provide a basis for certain combination alternatives (e.g. Engel et al. [6]), they do only present a few or very basic choices.

To assist with choosing between alternatives, we constructed a taxonomy that organizes the alternatives for the study design of DSR into dimensions with characteristics. This taxonomy can be used to design or analyze DSR studies, and even identify design patterns (such as dominant combinations of certain characteristics in different dimensions). The taxonomy may also be used as a basis to ultimately propose design principles for DSR studies. These patterns and principles would be useful for designing a feasible DSR research study, i.e. for avoiding incoherent choices and for choosing a study design that matches certain research objectives or a certain research context. This research therefore seeks to answer the following research question: What are the dimensions and characteristics of a taxonomy that a researcher should consider in order to design DSR studies and identify DSR study design patterns? To answer the research question, we did a review of the literature focusing on DSR studies and used Nickerson et al.'s classification method for developing a taxonomy [7].

In this paper we first introduce DSR briefly in Sect. 2 followed by a summary of Nickerson's method in Sect. 3. Section 4 provides an overview of the research method followed by our taxonomy construction, while Sect. 5 presents the resulting taxonomy. We conclude the paper in Sect. 6.

2 Design Science Research

Simon's Sciences of the Artificial [8] is widely accepted as the fundamental basis for DSR. Although there were many publications related to the value of the design of artefacts in the 90s and design-oriented research was well established in some research communities [9], the MISQ publication by Hevner et al. [10] had a big impact on legitimizing DSR as a research approach within the global Information Systems (IS) research community. Based on earlier work such as Nunamaker et al. [11], Walls et al. [12] and March and Smith [13], Hevner et al. [10] provided a conceptual framework for understanding, executing, and evaluating IS DSR research that emphasized the value of relevance and rigor during the design cycle. More or less in the same timeframe, Vaishnavi & Keuchler [14] started a web site focusing on DSR in IS. According to them, "DSR uses a set of synthetic and analytical techniques and perspectives for performing research in IS". They define "DSR as being involved in the creation of new knowledge, firstly through the development of artefacts and secondly through the study of the use of the artefact afterwards".

Within literature several studies concerned with the execution of DSR exist. The framework for understanding, executing and evaluating DSR provided by Hevner et al. [10] does not elaborate on the phases for executing a DSR project, but distinguishes between development and evaluation as two distinct phases. Vaishnavi et al. [14] provide a DSR process model for DSR project execution that is based on work from Takeda et al. [15]. Perhaps the mostly referenced approach is the DSR process model published by Peffers et al. [16] that consolidates various process model proposals. For the evaluation of the artefact, the pioneers working in this field were Pries-Heje, Baskerville & Venable [17], who published a number of articles building up to a framework for evaluation in design science (FEDS) [17]. FEDS is intended to assist DSR researchers in better understanding evaluation options in DSR, suggesting evaluation as a sequence of episodes rather than a design afterthought, but does not provide (yet) concrete guidance how to design study-specific "evaluation journeys".

Van der Merwe et al. [18] presented a set of guidelines for conducting DSR in IS [18]. The six guidelines included the contextualization of DSR in the IS field, as well as understanding the philosophical underpinning of research and the discourse on the nature of DSR. Other guidelines included the consideration of the role of the artefact in DSR, the selection of an appropriate DSR method for execution of the research study and ultimately strategizing on how research done in DSR should be communicated in a report [18].

Any scholar that needs to design a DSR study is therefore confronted with several perspectives and choices. The alternatives and subsequent consequences are however not always apparent [19]. In descriptive IS research, a researcher usually reflects on the philosophical underpinning of the research, the research strategy, data collection and data analysis. Several publications that guide the design of a descriptive research study exist, for example, the work by Saunders et al. [20] where they prescribe the research design to include the philosophy, approach, strategy, choices, time horizon and techniques and procedures (data collection and data analysis). However, guidance for designing descriptive IS research is only partially, if at all, applicable to DSR. Fundamental conceptual differences include the relevance and rigor cycles, the necessity of artefact construction, research contributions that include design knowledge, established evaluation practices etc. To address this lack of guidance in the design of DSR studies, this paper reports on a project that developed a taxonomy of DSR studies. The taxonomy with its dimensions and characteristics could be used to understand which alternatives are available as well as their implications when designing a DSR study.

3 Taxonomy Development Approach

Nickerson et al. studied classification in IS [4] and as main contribution of their work, they defined a taxonomy, as well as proposed a classification method for a taxonomy [4]. They formally define a taxonomy T as a set of n dimensions D_i ($i = 1, ..., n$), each consisting of k_i ($k_i \geq 2$) mutually exclusive and collectively exhaustive characteristics C_{ij} ($j = 1, ..., k_i$) such that each object under consideration has one and only one C_{ij}

for each Di, or T = {Di, i = 1,..., n | Di = {Cij, j = 1,..., ki; ki ≥ 2}}. They specified additional characteristics of taxonomies that need to be adhered to, including that taxonomies should be mutually exclusive (no object can have two different characteristics in a dimension) and collectively exhaustive (each object must have one of the characteristics in a dimension). Together these conditions imply that each object has exactly one of the characteristics in a dimension.

The classification approach of Nickerson et al. [7] is iterative and commences with determining the meta-characteristics and the ending conditions of the taxonomy. The meta-characteristics should be determined by the overall purpose of the taxonomy, while the ending conditions are both objective and subjective. For the purpose of this paper we summarize the ending conditions in Table 1.

Table 1. Ending conditions for taxonomy development [7]

	Condition	Description
Objective	Comprehensive object sampling and identification	A representative sample of objects has been examined, and no object was merged or split in the last iteration of the taxonomy development approach
Objective	Completion: taxonomy dimensions with characteristics	No new dimensions or characteristics were added in the last iteration of the taxonomy development approach, and no dimensions or characteristics were merged or split. Furthermore, at least one object is classified under every characteristic of every dimension (no 'null' characteristics)
Objective	Uniqueness: Dimension, Characteristic and Cell	Every dimension is unique and not repeated, and every characteristic is unique within its dimension (i.e., there is no dimension duplication). Each cell (combination of characteristics) is unique and is not repeated (i.e., there is no cell duplication). (This condition follows from mutual exclusivity of characteristics)
Subjective	Conciseness	The number of dimensions allow the taxonomy to be meaningful without being unwieldy or overwhelming
Subjective	Robustness	The dimensions and characteristics provide for differentiation among objects and allow for a description of sample objects

(continued)

Table 1. (*continued*)

	Condition	Description
Subjective	Comprehensiveness	All objects under consideration can be classified
Subjective	Extendible	A new dimension or a new characteristic of an existing dimension can be easily added
Subjective	Explanatory	The dimensions and characteristics can explain aspects of an object

After the execution of the first two steps, a choice must be made on whether the iteration is empirical-to-conceptual (bottom-up) or conceptual-to-empirical (top-down). In a bottom-up iteration, the researcher identifies a subset of objects that should be classified, and from an investigation of the objects, characteristics are identified. These characteristics are then refined into the taxonomy dimensions. In a top-down iteration, the dimensions of the taxonomy are conceptualized in a deductive and often intuitive way that is based on the researcher's knowledge. These dimensions are then refined by adding characteristics that allow for the classification of objects. For the development of a taxonomy, both types of iterations may be adopted, for instance, the first iteration might be conceptual-to-empirical, and a next iteration that refines the taxonomy could be empirical-to-conceptual. The iterations are performed until the specified ending conditions as specified in Table 1 are met.

4   Research Method

The aim of this study is to develop a taxonomy of DSR studies with its associated dimensions and characteristics. While every single study would represent a distinct instantiation of that taxonomy, a set of studies would allow to identify patterns, i.e. recurring instantiations that constitute frequently chosen study designs [21]. If the dependencies between specific choices within the taxonomy are well understood, such patterns could be the basis for formulating study design principles. For example, the recurring combination of a certain evaluation technique choice with a certain artefact type choice could indicate that, for that artefact type, a particular evaluation technique is recommended.

To develop the taxonomy we collected relevant articles using a keyword search with different combinations of the terms "design-oriented research" and "information system" and ("practical" or "applied"). The keyword search was executed in common databases such as SpringerLink, ACM, AIS, EBSCO Host and Google Scholar. We selected 461 peer-reviewed journal and conference papers. Secondly, we screened the identified set of papers and extracted 72 papers that used DSR as a research method and that provide data necessary for the taxonomy. We excluded non-English papers, duplicates, and papers that did not contribute any DSR study design considerations. We concluded a detailed screening of abstracts and analysis of the full text of the prospective papers and created a dataset (Appendix 1 [22]) that was utilized for the systematic development of a taxonomy of DSR dimensions and characteristics based on Nickerson et al.'s [7] method. The taxonomy development process [23, 24] was executed through several steps as described in Sect. 3. Firstly, we defined the meta-characteristics as the dimensions of design-oriented research with the assumption that all dimensions must describe the structural differences of design-oriented research. We adopted Hevner and Chatterjee's [19] fundamental dimensions of design-orientated research i.e. contribution, artefact type, and type of validation and framed our meta-characteristic within it. We proceeded through 4 iterations until all the extracted papers in our dataset were classified and the ending conditions were fulfilled as specified by Nickerson et al. [7].

In terms of the iterations, we initially adopted a conceptual-to-empirical iteration and integrated taxonomy dimensions identified in the literature review. During this iteration, we added one dimension scientific contribution [10]. The second, third and fourth iterations were empirical-to-conceptual and led to the classification of all the extracted papers in our dataset guided by the set of guidelines for conducting DSR in IS (refer Sect. 2) [18]. In these iterations, additional dimensions were identified namely construction mode [25, 26], procedure [27], data collection technique [28, 29] and evaluation technique [30].

Lastly, we performed a thematic analysis for each dimension from the taxonomy to identify, analyze and report patterns or characteristics within the data [31]. The purpose of a thematic analysis is to interpret and make sense of data in order to identify patterns or themes, emphasizing both organization and rich description of the data set and theoretically inform interpretation of meaning [32, 33]. Towards this purpose we followed an iterative approach identifying patterns of themes until all characteristics in a particular taxonomy dimension were classified (Appendix 2 [22]).

5 Results: Taxonomy for Design Science Research Studies

The taxonomy resulting from analyzing 72 DSR studies is shown in Fig. 1. It consists of seven dimensions, each with two to seven distinct characteristics.

In the context of IS research, the purpose of DSR is to study and find innovative solutions to problems and phenomena relevant to the domain. The aim of DSR studies is to inspect what is known and not known about the problem and solution set in order to find answers [19].

An outcome of DSR is an artefact that solves a domain problem which must be assessed against criteria of value or utility. The artefact type dimension of the taxonomy considers: what artefact type will be the outcome of the DSR research study? DSR artefact outputs are concerned both with utility [13] and theory [34]. For the artefact type dimension we adopted the existing topologies defined by March and Smith [13]. However, the existing classification of artefact types is quite coarse, and characteristics are not well-defined yet e.g. what type of model, design theory or design principle, characteristics overlap i.e. a model is an instance of a meta model, etc.

IS construction is the process of creating meaningful, working software-reliant work systems through a combination of design, validation and testing [35]. The question that the construction mode dimension of the taxonomy addresses is: what drives design-evaluate iterations? The main driver may either be the (theory-agnostic) search for sufficiently useful designs based on solution creation, solution evaluation and backtracking

Dimensions	Characteristics				
Artefact Type	Construct	Model	Method	Instantiation	Design Theory
Construction Mode	Build and evaluate			Theory-led construction	
Validation / Evaluation approach	Parallel with design		Only at the end		
Procedure	Specialize general solutions		Generalize specific solutions	Combine existing solution components in a novel way	
Contribution	Improvement	Invention	Exaptation		Routine design
Data collection techniques	Scientific procedure	Observation	Facilitated discussion	Survey	Secondary sources
Validation / valuation techniques	Experiment	Simulation	Prototype	Active participation	Formal proof	Case study	Empirical validation

Fig. 1. DSR design decision taxonomy

[8] - or the translation of descriptive knowledge and design theories into solution candidates and their subsequent iterative modification until a satisfactory solution is found [36].

Evaluation is the process of determining how well the designed artefact performs and the execution must be rigorously demonstrated via well-executed evaluation methods. The validation/evaluation approach dimension of the taxonomy aims to address the following question: when, during the DSR process, will the artefact be validated and/or evaluated? Due to the impact of evaluations on designer thinking, evaluation may be conducted parallel with design and thus inform design ("formative" or "concurrent" evaluation [37]). Evaluation may also only be conducted as an ex-post assessment of the value of the artefact ("summative" evaluation [38]).

The procedure dimension of the DSR taxonomy refers to the way the research outcomes were accomplished by following a series of ordered steps. These steps are typically concerned with answering the question: what specific steps guide the DSR process towards deriving a solution? A set of known, general solutions to the particular research problem may be considered as a starting point to derive a specific solution for the phenomenon under study. When the procedure of generalization of a specific solution is followed, the DSR study draws broad inferences from particular observations and applies them to the phenomenon under study. Alternatively, existing solutions may be applied in a novel manner to the phenomenon under study based on the characteristics and demands of the problem or the optimization the DSR study is attempting to deliver.

In DSR, knowledge is developed that enable the design of solutions for a particular problem domain. The contribution dimension intends to address the question: how does the DSR artefact contribute to the body of knowledge? The focus of DSR with an improvement contribution is to create better solutions by way of more efficient and effective products, processes, services, technologies, or ideas [39]. Invention points to radical breakthrough and entails research in new applications where little current understanding of the problem context exists and where no effective artefacts are available as solutions. DSR with an exaptation aim applies effective artefacts in a related problem area research situation to a field where effective artefacts are not available or are suboptimal. Design knowledge that already exists in one field is extended or refined so that it can be used in some new application area. Routine design ensues when existing knowledge for the problem area is well understood and when existing artefacts are used to address the opportunity or question – a characteristic that should usually not apply to design research [40].

Data-collection techniques allow us to systematically collect information about objects of study and about the settings in which they occur. The data collection technique dimension addresses the question: how will data be collected for the DSR study? Specific characteristics were classified in this instance namely scientific procedure, observation, facilitated discussion, survey and secondary sources. Scientific procedure uses the manipulation and controlled testing to understand causal processes e.g. an experiment in a lab, while observation refers to a technique involves systematically selecting, watching and recording behavior and characteristics of objects or phenomena. Facilitated discussion collects target audience opinions and attitudes about certain products, services or phenomena such as focus group discussion, and structured- and semi-structured interviews. The survey characteristic describes the opinion collection from a large population and includes hand-delivering questionnaires to respondents or using a web-based application to collect respondent opinion. Secondary sources refer to data that is collected by someone other than the user such as organizational records and data, manuals, and product specifications. Our characteristic classification set in this instance was based on the analysis of the papers extracted for the purpose of this study. It must be noted that, as many research studies use more than one of these techniques, a more comprehensive characteristics-set of data collection techniques will also include behavioral science data collection techniques such as one-on-one cognitive testing, debriefings, expert reviews, behavior coding, etc. [41, 42].

Evaluation in DSR is concerned with the evaluation of DSR outputs, such as theory and artefacts, and the validation/evaluation technique dimension answers the question: how (and not when) will the DSR artefact be evaluated/validated? In our classification we identified particular characteristics namely experiment (e.g. laboratory or field experiment), simulation (imitation of a situation or process e.g. computer simulation), prototype (preliminary version of application), active participation (e.g. action research), formal proof (using known facts and deduction rules of logic to reach conclusions), case study (investigates phenomenon within its real-life context), and empirical validation (e.g. statistical analysis) [38]. Similar to the data collection characteristic, many research studies use multiple data analysis techniques. Prat et al. [43] developed a taxonomy of evaluation methods for IS artefacts. They identified seven typical evaluation patterns of which experiment, simulation, empirical validation and formal proof were also identified in this study. In addition, they reported additional patterns such as demonstration, practice-based evaluation of usefulness (in this study we defined it as case study), laboratory, and algorithmic complexity analysis.

6 Using the Proposed Taxonomy to Identify Patterns of DSR Studies

The aim of this study was to develop a taxonomy of DSR studies with its associated dimensions and characteristics. The taxonomy could be used to design and analyze DSR projects, and subsequently identify DSR research patterns. Figure 2 shows how two exemplary DSR studies can be interpreted as "instantiations" of the general study design implied by the proposed taxonomy.

6.1 Example Studies

Example 1 (the solid line in Fig. 2) presents new organizational and technological options of process management and illustrated the concept by a prototype platform for process management and real-world application scenarios in the construction industry [26]. The paper finally presents an evaluation of the design-oriented research approach.

The authors highlighted that the dynamic nature of an organization is observable based on the dynamics of corporate systems and the impact of new conditions on process management. They identified the applicability of Web 2.0 applications such as wikis, social networks, social bookmarks, RSS feeds etc., a key feature as it enables high speed reaction to events and spontaneously support actions adequately to ensure their success. However, Web 2.0 applications have primarily been designed for private and not for business users. Therefore, the problem that they wanted to resolve with their research was to establish whether the design principles of Web 2.0 can be efficiently deployed in the business environment, particularly for the control of dynamics in process management. In terms of the artefact type, they created a real instance to develop a clear picture of actual deficits and to define possible options for action. Their chosen construction mode was therefore to "build and evaluate". Evaluation was done at the end of the project after they concluded steps such as exploration, participation, iteration and evolution. They produced a prototype-oriented system development with the intention to improve process design and execution. Upon conclusion of their DSR process, the authors identified essential and encouraging options for process management organization and for the development of new tools for process management.

In example 2 (the dotted line in Fig. 2), the paper describes the design process toward a functional reference model for business rules management for practitioners evaluating software solutions [44]. From a scientific perspective, the model represents a theory for designing and developing information systems with the objective of managing business rules. The model was evaluated in a company (real-world scenario) by using a survey. At the end of their DSR process, the authors established that the functional reference model for business rule management was beneficial regarding the advancement of the state of the art both in practice and in science.

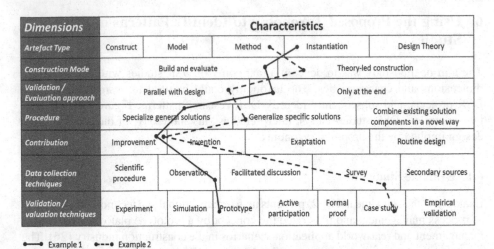

Fig. 2. Exemplary DSR studies as "instantiations" of the proposed taxonomy

6.2 DSR Research Patterns

The two studies shown in Fig. 2 illustrate how the taxonomy may support identifying DSR research patterns in future research. If a large number of studies can be "classified" we expect that statistical analysis would yield clusters of dominant "paths" across the taxonomy, i.e. typical forms how study design decisions across different dimensions are linked in published studies. We assume that certain "paths" are dominant, and that not all combinations of characteristics may be observed, because not every characteristic can be combined with every other characteristic. For example, it apparently makes not much sense to use simulation as an evaluation technique for constructs. The consideration of research patterns references similar studies such as Houy, Fettke [21] aiming to identify "compositional styles" or "stylized facts" for a large set of study designs.

7 Conclusion

The DSR paradigm in IS is fundamentally a problem-solving paradigm and aims to provide solutions to important and relevant business problems. Research design decisions span the choices from broad assumptions to detailed methods of data collection and analysis. In this study we classified the dimensions and characteristics of DSR studies and presented a DSR taxonomy. The DSR taxonomy was developed through the application of Nickerson et al's taxonomy development method [7]. The DSR taxonomy consists of seven dimensions, each with two to seven distinct characteristics. The DSR taxonomy should guide researchers with DSR choices when designing a DSR study by presenting available options. As a limitation, we acknowledge that researcher bias may be present in the dimensions and characteristics of the taxonomy, however, most classification artifacts include some form of bias, which is mediated by establishing consensus. Future research will aim to establish consensus in the IS DSR community for the taxonomy.

Future research will also aim to identify possible DSR research patterns (or "dominant study designs") using the taxonomy that could constitute a foundation to derive design principle candidates. In the domain of research study design, design principles would link research objectives (i.e., design requirements for research studies) to research features (i.e., characteristics of research study designs) on a generic level [45] and thus provide useful guidance for designing concrete and feasible DSR studies. Ultimately, the nature of DSR for IS research and IS practice may be considered in future research, as DSR in essence supports IS practice through the development of relevant and useful artifacts.

References

1. Goldkuhl, G.: Design research in search for a paradigm: pragmatism is the answer. In: Helfert, M., Donnellan, B. (eds.) EDSS 2011. CCIS, vol. 286, pp. 84–95. Springer, Heidelberg (2012). https://doi.org/10.1007/978-3-642-33681-2_8
2. Baskerville, R., et al.: Design science research contributions: finding a balance between artifact and theory. J. Assoc. Inf. Syst. **19**(5), 358–376 (2018)
3. Peffers, K., Tuunanen, T., Niehaves, B.: Design science research genres: introduction to the special issue on exemplars and criteria for applicable de-sign science research. Eur. J. Inf. Syst. **27**(2), 129–139 (2018)
4. Olikowski, W., Baroudi, J.: Studying information technology in organizations: research approaches and assumptions. Inf. Syst. Res. **2**(1), 1–28 (1991)
5. vom Brocke, J., Maedche, A.: The DSR grid: six core dimensions for effectively planning and communicating design science research projects. Electron. Mark. **29**(3), 379–385 (2019). https://doi.org/10.1007/s12525-019-00358-7
6. Engel, C., Leicht, N., Ebel, P.: The imprint of design science in information systems research: an empirical analysis of the ais senior scholar's basket. In: International Conference on Information Systems (ICIS), Munich, Germany (2019)
7. Nickerson, R., Varshney, U., Muntermann, J.: A method for taxonomy development and its application in IS. Eur. J. Inf. Syst. **22**, 336–359 (2013)
8. Simon, H.A.: The Sciences of the Artificial, 1st edn. MIT Press, Cambridge (1969)
9. Winter, R.: Design science research in Europe. Eur. J. Inf. Syst. **17**(5), 470–475 (2008)
10. Hevner, A., et al.: Design science in information systems research. MIS Q. **28**(1), 75–105 (2004)
11. Nunamaker, J., Chen, M., Purdin, T.: Systems development in information systems research. J. Manag. Inf. Syst. **7**(3), 89–106 (1991)
12. Walls, J.G., Widmeyer, G.R., Sawy, O.A.: Building an information system design theory for vigilant EIS. J. Inf. Syst. Res. **3**(1), 36–59 (1992)
13. March, S.T., Smith, G.F.: Design and natural science research on information technology. Decis. Support Syst. **15**, 251–266 (1995)
14. Vaishnavi, V., Kuechler, B.: Design Research in Information Systems. DSR in IS (2004). http://desrist.org/design-research-in-information-systems/
15. Takeda, H., et al.: Modeling design processes. AI Mag **11**(4), 12 (1990)
16. Peffers, K., et al.: The design science research process: a model for producing and presenting information systems research. In: DESRIST 2006, Claremont, CA (2006)
17. Pries-Heje, J., Baskerville, R., Venable, J.: Strategies for design science research evaluation. In: 16th European Conference on Information Systems (ECIS), Galway, Ireland (2008)

18. van der Merwe, A., Gerber, A., Smuts, H.: Guidelines for conducting design science research in information systems. In: Tait, B., Kroeze, J., Gruner, S. (eds.) SACLA 2019. CCIS, vol. 1136, pp. 163–178. Springer, Cham (2020). https://doi.org/10.1007/978-3-030-35629-3_11
19. Hevner, A., Chatterjee, S.: Design Research in Information Systems. Springer, Boston (2010)
20. Saunders, M.N.K., Lewis, P., Thornhill, A.: Research Methods for Business Students, 5th edn. Prentice Hall, New York (2009)
21. Houy, C., Fettke, P., Loos, P.: Stylized facts as an instrument for literature review and cumulative information systems research. Commun. Assoc. Inf. Syst. **37**, 10 (2015). https://doi.org/10.17705/1CAIS.03710
22. Appendices (2021). https://www.researchgate.net/publication/358316570_Appendix_1_-Dataset_created_from_papers_identified_extract
23. Remane, G., et al.: The business model pattern database: a tool for systematic business model innovation. Int. J. Innov. Manag. **21**(1), 1–61 (2017)
24. Nakatsu, R.T., Grossman, E.B., Iacovou, C.L.: A taxonomy of crowdsourcing based on task complexity. J. Inf. Sci. **40**(6), 823–834 (2014)
25. Mettler, T., Rohner, P.: Situational maturity models as instrumental artifacts for organizational design. In: Proceedings of the 4th International Conference on Design Science Research in Information Systems and Technology (2009)
26. Vanderhaeghen, D., Fettke, P., Loos, P.: Organizational and technological options for business process management from the perspective of web 2.0. Bus. Inf. Syst. Eng. **2**, 15–28 (2010). https://doi.org/10.1007/s12599-009-0087-7
27. Kiesow, A., et al.: Managing internal control: designing a wiki based information system for continuous process assurance. In: Thirty Sixth International Conference on Information Systems, Fort Worth (2015)
28. Österle, H., Otto, B.: A method for researcher-practitioner collaboration in design-oriented IS research. Bus. Inf. Syst. Eng. **2010**(5), 283–293 (2010)
29. Heger, O.: Value sensitive design in design science research projects: the cases of affective technology and healthcare technology. In: 14th International Conference on Wirtschaftsinformatik, Siegen, Germany (2009)
30. Vogel, J., et al.: Design and development of a process modelling environment for business process utilization within smart glasses. In: 9th International Workshop on Enterprise Modeling and Information Systems Architectures, Rostock (2018)
31. Vaismoradi, M., Turunen, H., Bondas, T.: Content analysis and thematic analysis: implications for conducting a qualitative descriptive study. Nurs. Health Sci. **15**(3), 398–405 (2013)
32. Alhojailan, M.I.: Thematic analysis: a critical review of its process and evaluation. West East J. Social Sci. **1**(1), 39–47 (2012)
33. Leedy, P.D., Ormrod, J.E.: Practical Research: Planning and Design, 12th edn. Pearson, Boston (2018)
34. Gregor, S., Jones, D.: The anatomy of a design theory. J. Assoc. Inf. Syst. **8**(5), 312–335 (2007)
35. Bollinger, T., Gabrini, P., Martin, L.: Software construction, p. 4-1–4-15. IEEE (2002)
36. Gregor, S.: Design theory in information systems. Aust. J. Inf. Syst. **10**, 14–22 (2002)
37. Sonnenberg, C., vom Brocke, J.: Evaluations in the science of the artificial – reconsidering the build-evaluate pattern in design science research. In: Peffers, Ken, Rothenberger, Marcus, Kuechler, Bill (eds.) DESRIST 2012. LNCS, vol. 7286, pp. 381–397. Springer, Heidelberg (2012). https://doi.org/10.1007/978-3-642-29863-9_28
38. Venable, J., Pries-Heje, J., Baskerville, R.: FEDS: a framework for evaluation in design science research. Eur. J. Inf. Syst. **25**, 77–89 (2016)
39. vom Brocke, J., Winter, R., Hevner, A., Maedche, A.: Special issue editorial –accumulation and evolution of design knowledge in design science research: a journey through time and space. J. Assoc. Inf. Syst. **21**(3), 520–544 (2020). https://doi.org/10.17705/1jais.00611

40. Gregor, S., Hevner, A.: Positioning and presenting design science research for maximum impact. MIS Q. **37**(2), 337–355 (2013)
41. Onwuegbuzie, A.J., Leech, N.L.: On becoming a pragmatic researcher: the importance of combining quantitative and qualitative research methodologies. Int. J. Social Res. Methodol. **8**(5), 375–387 (2005)
42. Isaac, S., Michael, W.B.: Handbook in Research and Evaluation: A Collection of Principles, Methods, and Strategies Useful in the Planning, Design, and Evaluation of Studies in Education and the Behavioral Sciences, 3rd edn. EdITS Publishers, Boston (1995)
43. Prat, N., Comyn-Wattiau, I., Akoka, J.: A Taxonomy of evaluation methods for information systems artifacts. J. Manag. Inf. Syst. **32**(3), 229–267 (2015)
44. Schlosser, S., et al.: Toward a functional reference model for business rules management. In: 47th Hawaii International Conference on System Science, pp. 3837–3846. IEEE (2014)
45. Meth, H., Mueller, B., Maedche, A.: Designing a requirement mining system. J. Assoc. Inf. Syst. **16**(9), 799–837 (2015)

Correction to: The Transdisciplinary Reach of Design Science Research

Andreas Drechsler, Aurona Gerber, and Alan Hevner

Correction to:
A. Drechsler et al. (Eds.): *The Transdisciplinary Reach of Design Science Research*, **LNCS 13229,**
https://doi.org/10.1007/978-3-031-06516-3

In an older version of chapter 10, there was an orthographical error in name of an author. "Dominic Siemon" was corrected to "Dominik Siemon".

In an older version of chapter 20, there was an error in the affiliation of a co-author. This has been corrected to "IG&H".

The updated original version of these chapters can be found at
https://doi.org/10.1007/978-3-031-06516-3_10
https://doi.org/10.1007/978-3-031-06516-3_20

Correction to: Guiding Refugees Through European Bureaucracy: Designing a Trustworthy Mobile App for Document Management

Alexandre Amard, Alexandra Hoess, Tamara Roth, Gilbert Fridgen, and Alexander Rieger

Correction to:
Chapter 13 in: A. Drechsler et al. (Eds.): *The Transdisciplinary Reach of Design Science Research*, LNCS 13229, https://doi.org/10.1007/978-3-031-06516-3_13

The updated version of this chapter can be found at
https://doi.org/10.1007/978-3-031-06516-3_13

© The Author(s) 2024
A. Drechsler et al. (Eds.): DESRIST 2022, LNCS 13229, pp. C2–C3, 2024.
https://doi.org/10.1007/978-3-031-06516-3_38

Author Index

Printed in the United States
by Baker & Taylor Publisher Services

Printed in the United States
by Baker & Taylor Publisher Services